MULTILINGUAL MATTERS 116
Series Editor: John Edwards

ɔLLEGE
ᴛᴇR

Can Threatened Languages Be Saved?

Reversing Language Shift, Revisited: A 21st Century Perspective

Edited by
Joshua A. Fishman

MULTILINGUAL MA
Clevedon • Buffa

D1375638

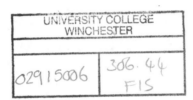
Library of Congress Cataloging in Publication Data
Can Threatened Languages Be Saved? Reversing Language Shift Revisited: A 21st
Century Perspective/Edited by Joshua A. Fishman.
Multilingual Matters: 116
Includes bibliographical references and index.
1. Language attrition. I. Fishman, Joshua A. II. Multilingual Matters (Series): 116
P40.5.L28 C36 2000
306.4′4–dc21   00-024283

British Library Cataloguing in Publication Data
A CIP catalogue record for this book is available from the British Library.

ISBN 1-85359-493-8 (hbk)
ISBN 1-85359-492-X (pbk)

Multilingual Matters Ltd
UK: Frankfurt Lodge, Clevedon Hall, Victoria Road, Clevedon BS21 7HH.
USA: UTP, 2250 Military Road, Tonawanda, NY 14150, USA.
Canada: UTP, 5201 Dufferin Street, North York, Ontario M3H 5T8, Canada.
Australia: P.O. Box 586, Artarmon, NSW, Australia.

Index compiled by Meg Davies (Society of Indexers).
Typeset by Archetype-IT Ltd (http://www.archetype-it.com).
Printed and bound in Great Britain by Biddles Ltd.

In memory of
Charles A. Ferguson
1921–1998
thanks to whom sociolinguistics became
both an intellectual and a moral quest

Contents

The Contributors

Professor **Efurosibina Adegbija** teaches at the Department of Modern European Languages, University of Ilorin, Nigeria. His major interests are sociolinguistics, pragmatics and applied linguistics, especially in a natural ESL context. His current research interest is language attidudes. He is the author of *Language Attitudes in Sub-Saharan Africa: A Sociolinguistic Overview* (Multilingual Matters) and he has published several journal articles on that topic. His present focus is on language and attitude change.

E. Annamalai, Director Emeritus, Central Institute of Indian Languages, works in the areas of language planning, language education, language contact and grammar. He has designed and guided research on the indigenous languages of India for their codification and use in education. He has been a Visiting Professor in Tokyo, Leiden and Melbourne. His recent publications include *Adjectival Clauses in Tamil* (Tokyo, 1996) and *Managing Multilingualism: Languages Planning and Use in India* (New Delhi, 2000).

Maria-Josi Azurmendi is Professor in the Department of Social Psychology, University of the Basque Country (Donostia/San Sebastian, in Spain). She is a specialist in sociolinguistics, psycholinguistic and social psychology and language, applied mainy to the Basque language. Her most recent book is *Psicosociolingüistica* (Bilbao, 1999).

Erramun Bachoc has been Associate Professor in the Department of Psychopedagogy of Language, Univerity of the Basque Country (Donostia/San Sebastian, in Spain). Currently, he is the president of the Basque Cultural Institute, for promoting the revival of the Basque language in Iparralde (Baiona/Bayonne, in France.

Nena Eslao Benton has been resident in New Zealand since 1971, after starting her research career as an urban anthropologist in the Philippines, specializing in family and kinship networks. She was involved in the planning and execution of the sociolinguistic survey of Maori language use carried out by the New Zealand Council for Educational Research in the 1970s, and directed an internship programme to train Maori students in all aspects of research, from planning and field work to publication. This led on to pioneering research on the recognition of prior learning in higher education. Her involvement in Maori language revitalization efforts has continued, most recently as a consultant to the NZ Government's Maori Development Education Commission.

Richard Benton is currently Director of the James Henare Maori Research Centre at the University of Auckland, New Zealand, and Associate Director of Te Matahauariki Institute at the School of Law of the University of Waikato. He first became involved in efforts to secure an acceptance of the Maori language as an essential part of New Zealand's national life as a student in the late 1950s. Since then he has studied, written about and lectured on language policy, revitalization of minority languages and related subjects in the Pacific, Southeast Asia, Europe and North America.

Professor **Richard Y. Bourhis** was educated in French and English schools in Montreal and then obtained a BSc in Psychology at McGill University and a PhD in social psychology at the University of Bristol, England. He taught social psychology at McMaster University in Ontario and then at the University of Quebec, Montreal where he is now full Professor. He has published extensively in English and French on topics such as cross-cultural communication, discrimination and intergroup relations, acculturation and language planning.

Michael Clyne, who holds a PhD from Monash University, is currently Professorial Fellow in Linguistics at the University of Melbourne and was previously Professor of Linguistics and Director of the Language and Society Centre at that university. His research interests are multilingualism/language contact, sociolinguistics, inter-cultural communication, and second language acquisition.

Joshua A. Fishman, PhD (Columbia University, 1953: Social Psychology); Ped.D. (Hon.) (Yeshiva University, 1978); D. Litt. (Hon.) (Vrije Universiteit Brussel, 1986). Distinguished University Research Professor, Social Sciences, Yeshiva University. 1966–, Emeritus, 1988, and Visiting Professor, Linguistics and Education, Stanford University, 1992–; Visiting Professor of Education, New York University, 1999–; Long Island University 2000–. Fellow at Centers for Advanced Study: Center for Advanced Study in the Behavioral Sciences, Stanford, California (1963–1964), Institute for Advanced Projects, East–West Center, Honolulu, Hawaii (1969–1969), Institute for Advanced Study, Princeton, N.J. (1975–1976), Netherlands Institute for Advanced Study, Wasenaar, Netherlands (1982–1983), Israel Institute for Advanced Study, Jerusalem (1983). Specialises in the sociolinguistics of minority languages, small languages and small language communities, particularly in connection with their language planning processes and reversing language shift.

Ofelia García is Dean of the School of Education at the Brooklyn Campus of Long Island University. She has published extensively on bilingual education, the education of language minorities, especially Latinos, bilingualism, sociology of language and US Spanish. A Fulbright Scholar and Spencer Fellow, she is the editor of *Educators for Urban Minorities*. In 1997 she co-edited, with Joshua A. Fishman, *The Multilingual Apple: Languages in New York City* (Mouton de Gruyter).

V. Gnanasundaram is Deputy Director of the Central Institute of Indian Languages. He has prepared learning/teaching materials and trained teachers for the minority languages of India. He coordinated the Institute's project to record India's endangered languages.

Durk Gorter studied sociology and sociolinguistics in Groningen, Amsterdam and Santa Barbara (USA). Since 1979 he has been a researcher in the sociology of language at the Fryske Akademy in Ljouwert/Leeuwarden, and a part-time Professor of Frisian at the University of Amsterdam. He has been involved in studies of the Frisian language situation and European minority languages on which he has published a number of books and articles. He is currently working on a book about language surveys in Friesland and he also does comparative work on the education of European minority languages in the framework of the Mercator-Education Network.

Nancy H. Hornberger is Professor of Education and Director of Educational Linguistics at the University of Pennsylvania Graduate School of Education. She specializes in sociolinguistics, educational anthropology, language planning and biliteracy. Recent publications include *Indigenous Literacies in the Americas* (Mouton, 1996).

Kendall A. King is Assistant Professor of Multilingual Multicultural Studies at New York University where she teaches courses in sociolinguistics and bilingual education. Her recent publications include *Language Revitalization Processes and Prospects* (Multilingual Matters, 2001).

Yolanda Lastra is Professor and Researcher at the Instituto de Investigaciones Antropológicas of the Universidad Nacional Autónoma de México. She has written on Nahuatl and Otomí dialectology and is author of *Sociolingüística para hispanoamericanos: una introducción* and *El otomí de*

Ixtenco. She is currently engaged in ethnohistorical and linguistic research on the Otomí.

Tiffany S. Lee holds a PhD in Sociology of Education, Stanford University. Dr Lee has research and professional interests involving the educational issues of Native Americans related to language, culture and community. She currently teaches in the Community-based Education Program at Santa Fe Indian School. Her goals are to continue research and service in academic programs serving Native American students.

Joseph Lo Bianco is the author of Australia's first National Policy on Languages and Director and Founder of Language Australia: The National Languages and Literacy Institute of Australia. He is Professor of Education at the University of Melbourne. Recent publications include: *Australian Literacies* (with P. Freebody, 1997) and *Striving for the Third Place: Intercultural Competence Through Language Education* (with C. Crozet and T. Liddicoat).

Daniel McLaughlin has worked for twenty-three years in American Indian education as a teacher, principal, program director, university professor, researcher and teacher educator. He received a PhD in Education and Anthropology from the University of New Mexico in 1987. He is the author of *When Literacy Empowers: Navajo Language in Print* (1992, University of New Mexico Press) and co-editor of *Naming Silenced Lives: Personal Narratives and Processes of School Change* (1993, Routledge). For the past six years, he has been a Program Specialist for Dini College's Dini Teacher Education Program.

John Maher is Professor of Linguistics at the International Christian University, Tokyo. He is author/editor of several books in English and Japanese: *Linguistic Theory for Language Teaching* (1993), *Diversity in Japanese Culture and Language* (1994), *Multilingual Japan* (1995), *Introducing Chomsky* (1996). He served as interpreter for the Ainu delegation to the UN, Geneva. A forthcoming work is *Ainu: A Grammatical Sketch* (Lincom Europa). His research interests include the languages of Japan, politics and language, Chomsky's philosophy of language, Freud and linguistic theory.

José Luís Morín is Assistant Professor at John Jay College of Criminal Justice in the Puerto Rican Studies Department. He has published on issues involving international law, indigenous peoples' rights, human rights and civil rights law, Latin America and Latino communities in the United States.

Pádraig Ó Riagáin is Research Professor at the Linguistics Institute of Ireland. His research interests are in sociology of language and language planning, particularly with regard to Irish and minority languages in Europe. He has been a consultant advisor in these fields to the Irish Government, the Council of Europe and the European Union. Recent publications include *Language Policy and Social Reproduction: Ireland 1893–1993* (Oxford Univerity Press, 1997).

Mari Rhydwen is a freelance writer and researcher. She did her doctoral research on Kriol literacy, subsequently worked on language loss and has taught at several Australian universities. She is the listowner for the endangered-languages list and was one of the founders of *Terralingua*. She is now sailing the world on her yacht (White Cloud) still teaching, researching and writing wherever she goes.

Klaudia M. Rivera is Associate Professor at the Brooklyn Campus of Long Island University. Dr Rivera's work addresses issues of literacy, language, gender and culture and their relationship to power and equality. Her most recent publication, entitled *Popular Research and Social Transformation: A Community-based Approach to Critical Pedagogy*, appeared in *Tesol Quarterly*.

Elana Shohamy is Directory of the Program in Language Education at Tel Aviv University. She is currently conducting research on the academic achievement of immigrant pupils and on the language of signs. Co-author of the 1999 *Languages of Israel*, her *Power of Tests: A Critical Perspective on the Use and Consequences of Language Tests* will appear in 2001.

Bernard Spolsky has been Professor in the Department of English at Bar-Ilan University since 1980. His most recent books are *Sociolinguistics* (1999), *The Languages of Israel: Policy, Ideology and Practice* (1999; with Elana Shohamy) and *Concise Encyclopedia of Educational Linguistics* (edited, 1999).

Miquel Strubell read Psychology and Physiology at the University of Oxford, and holds an MSc in the Psychology of Education from the University of London. He worked for the Government of Catalonia in the Language Policy directorate (1980–1999) and is now Deputy Director of the Department of the Humanities and Philology of the Open University of Catalonia, Europe's first fully telematic university.

Francisca Zabaleta has been director of sociolinguistic research on the Basque language in the Autonomous Government of Navarre (in Spain). Currently she is Associate Professor in the Department of Social Psychology, Public University of Navarre (Iruqa/Pamplona, in Spain).

Preface

Reversing Language Shift: The Best of Times, The Worst of Times

JOSHUA A. FISHMAN

I am acutely aware of how different the 'spirit of the times' is today, insofar as Reversing Language Shift (RSL) is concerned, in comparison to a decade ago when my first volume on this topic was completed and appeared (1990–1991). At that time it was an unformulated and an unnamed field on the one hand, and one that corresponded to the major interests of very few academics, notwithstanding its centrality for minority language advocates worldwide. Indeed, one reviewer laughed at the very thought that threatened languages could be saved from extinction. Today, efforts along such lines not only constitute a frequent topic of interest in the mainstream lay media but it is also no longer unusual to see sessions devoted to such efforts at academic conferences on all continents,[1] to receive organisational updates, e-mail postings and press releases on various aspects of this topic[2] and to hear of governmental, inter-governmental and international agency efforts in connection with it.[3] Books by several different authors are now beginning to be published focusing entirely on threatened languages[4] and newsletters as well as websites devoted to language-threats and their amelioration[5] are not only no longer an oddity but a full enumeration of those now available is urgently needed since no individual is able to keep tabs on them all.

As one of the pioneers in this area of study and endeavour, it is extremely gratifying to me to feel that I may have contributed to the development of this field, both practically and theoretically, and, even more so, to be able to revisit it a decade later and to discover how it is faring and how my original ideas have held up or need to be scrapped, revised or supplemented. I can remember when my course in sociolinguistics/sociology of language (University of Pennsylvania, spring 1960) was the only such course in the USA. My courses on reversing language shift (Stanford University, winters 1995–1999) may also have had that distinction. May they bear as much fruit as did their precursor in 1960, and do so in the short run too, rather than only in the long.

Notwithstanding all of the above welcome expressions of international and interdisciplinary concern, interest and involvement in the fate of threatened languages, a noticeably under-represented focus is that of applied directions, priorities and emphases. Actually, what seems to be most needed is a theoretically grounded thrust, derived from familiarity with a large number of cases of efforts on behalf of threatened languages in all parts of the world (therefore including experiences of developed, now developing and still little developed contexts) that can distill-out and propose generally applicable ameliorative principles which will, of course, still require local fine-tuning in light of particularly unique experiences, beliefs and circumstances. It has been my hope during the past decade that I may have proposed some constituents of such a theory-based applied thrust. The present volume represents an attempt to see whether and to what extent that is so in the eyes of other scholars as well.

Such a volume is both an opportunity to test consensus as well as an opportunity to air dissent. Just as any single-authored volume inevitably overestimates the degree of coherence and confirmation *vis-à-vis* the author's views, any multi-authored volume is likely to reveal a reverse imbalance, over-representing differences and disconfirmations relative to the views of that same particular author's approach. Both types of volumes are sorely needed if this area of specialisation is to continue to grow productively, as has happened with other areas that I have contributed to or even initiated during the past four decades, e.g. language maintenance and language shift, language and ethnic identity, language and nationalism, language planning and the sociology of bilingual education. These several fields represent a true reflection of my life rather than just of my professional interests. Accordingly, attention to reversing language shift among threatened languages is not only a logical but a personally fulfilling addition to and summation of the original quintet.

But, as my mother (a devoted and successful language activist in her own right) was fond of saying 'Ven s'iz shoyn gut, iz den gut?' (Even when things are going well, are they *really* going well?) New dangers have increasingly appeared on the horizons of threatened languages. Whereas heretofore their dangers derived from the superior armed might, wealth and numbers of their immediate neighbours or specific conquerors from afar, today's dangers are more ubiquitous. Today, the worldwide process of globalisation of the economy, communication and entertainment media, not to mention modernisation-based consumerism as a way of life have threatened to sweep away everything locally authentic and different that may stand in their way. As a result, even former 'RLS success stories' have encountered new and increased threats (often coupled with the post-nationalist fatigue that comes after winning endless battles without ever winning the war), and even hitherto unthreatened languages have begun to realise that they too are not really masters of their own homes and futures. Thus, all in all, RLS is still very far from entering a messianic age and must often run faster and faster if it is even to end up relatively in the same place as before. Nevertheless, the reader will find a few modest successes in the pages that follow as well as several more sophisticated empirical analyses, more advanced theoretical perspectives and more elegant practical suggestions. As in many other areas of modern life, RLS progress is revealed as taking three steps forward and two steps back; and while its progress is slow its woes and fears are numerous and it can hardly be said to be 'out of the woods' by any stretch of the imagination. But, like the war against cancer, the struggle against language-in-culture decimation still goes on with little likelihood of early and clear triumph. Indeed, it constitutes a veritable ode to the human spirit and to its endlessly fascinating capacity for creating working solutions out of complex ethnolinguistic repertoires (combining the old with the new, the authentic with the imported, and one language with another for function- ally distinct purposes).

As always, my wife Gella has contributed in very major ways to my thought and productivity via endless technical assistance and constant discussion of 'what works and what doesn't'. My gratitude to her knows no bounds for she has also provided me with whatever semblance of after- work 'normality' an academic can hope to attain. I am also thankful and indebted to research librarians (particularly John Rawlings), the interli- brary loan division (particularly Sonia Moss) and colleagues in linguistics and applied linguistics (particularly John Baugh, Kenji Hakuta, Amado Padilla, John Rickford and Guadalupe Valdes), all at Stanford University, where this work was begun, stimulated through teaching and helped along in various ways both large and small by superb secretarial/technical support (particularly Gina Wein, Michelle Murray and Elayne Weissler).

In addition, I am truly grateful to two colleagues at Yeshiva University (with which I have been associated in various capacities since 1960), Charles Swencionis, Chair of the Health Psychology Program, and Lawrence Siegel, Dean of the Ferkauf Graduate School of Psychology, for accommodating my bi-coastal schedule, thereby enabling me to continue teaching Test Construction and Medical Anthropology at that school on the Albert Einstein College of Medicine Campus in the Bronx. These courses provide me with two perspectives that have both methodologically and theoretically supplied me with novel and, therefore, all the more valuable perspectives on my sociolinguistic preoccupations. Finally, I am extremely grateful to Mark Alter, Chair of the Department of Teaching and Learning, and Miriam Eisenstein Ebsworth, Director of Doctoral Programs in Multilingual Multicultural Studies, both at New York University; Ofelia Garcia, Dean of the School of Education at Long Island University; and Ricardo Otheguy of the Linguistics Department at the CUNY Graduate Center for attaching me to their respective sociolinguistic programmes so that my contact with the field could continue to be nourished during those parts of the year that I spend in New York.

Although he departed this world for a better one in 1998, it is mostly of my friend and colleague Charles A. Ferguson that I will always be reminded, whether in connection with Stanford or with matters sociolinguistic more generally, equally so insofar as his intellect, his kindness and his spiritual sensitivity are concerned, and to whose blessed memory this volume is affectionately dedicated.

January 2000
Ferkauf Graduate School of Psychology,
Albert Einstein College of Medicine Campus,
Yeshiva University, Bronx, NY 10461

Notes

1. A few recent examples, of the dozens that could be listed here, are: Congreso Nacional de Linguistica (Monterey, Mexico), October 1999; International Conference on Minority Languages (Bilbao, Spain), December 1999; Second International Conference on Language Policy (Ramat Gan, Israel), December 1999.
2. Some examples of this kind are the *SSILA Bulletin* of the Society for the Study of the Indigenous Languages of the Americas <ssila@oregon.uoregon.edu>; the *Nat-Lang* list at <NAT-LANG@tamvm1.tamu.ed> focusing on aboriginal peoples; *Ogmios*, the publication of the Foundation for Endangered Languages (UK; also see its website, listed below); *Langscapes*, the newsletter of Terralingua: Partnership for Linguistic and Biological Diversity (contact <afallenb@wvi.com> and see website listing below); *El Pregonero*, the newsletter of the Asosiasion para la Konservasion i Promosion de la Kultura Djudeo-espanyola.
3. See, e.g. *Contact Bulletin* of the European Bureau for Lesser Used Languages (also note its website, below); *Euskararen Berripapera* of the Department of Culture of the Basque Government (e-mail contact <M-Meaurio@ej-gv.es>); the newsletter of the Frisian Academy (in Frisian), *Ut de Smidte*, obtainable by contacting <fa@fa.knaw.nl>, etc.
4. For starters, see, e.g. Maffi, Luisa (ed.) 1999 *Language, Knowledge and the Environment: The Interdependence of Cultural and Biological Diversity.* Washington, DC, Smithsonian Institute Press; Hertzfeld, Anita and Yolanda Lastra (eds) 1999 *Las causas sociales de la desaparicio'n y del mantenimento de las lenguas en las naciones de América.* Hermosilla (Sonora), Unison; an entire issue of *Practicing Anthropology* (1999, 21, No. 2) devoted explicitly to Reversing Language Shift; Nettle, Daniel

and Suzzanne Romaine, 2000 *Vanishing Voices: The Extinction of the World's Languages*, New York, Oxford University Press; Grenoble, Lenore and Lindsay J. Whaley, 1998. *Endangered Languages: Language Loss and Community Response. Cambridge, Cambridge University Press*. Two older publications, one contemporary with and the other slightly after my own 1991 volume (*Reversing Language Shift: Theoretical and Empirical Foundations of Assistance to Threatened Languages*, Clevedon, Multilingual Matters), that contributed in major ways to attracting linguistic attention to threatened languages were: Robins, Robert H. and Eugenius Uhlenbeck, 1991 *Endangered Languages*, New York, Oxford University Press, and Michael Krauss (1992) The world's languages in crisis, *Language* 68, 4–10. Since 1992 additional titles have appeared with increased frequency, both as books and as articles in linguistic and in sociolinguistic book-series and journals.

5.   For example, note Merkblatt: Documentation of Endangered Languages at http://www.volkswagen-stiftung.de/merkblat/merkdocu.html; the Linguistic Society of America's Committee on Endangered Languages and their Protection (LSA/CELP) sponsors the site http://www.ipola.org/endangered/index.html; Terralingua's website is http://www.terralingua.org; Asturian, an Iberian too often overlooked, can be accessed at http://www.asturies.com/asturiana; The (British) Foundation for Endangered Languages sponsors www.ogmios.org; The European Bureau for Lesser Used Languages' website is http://www.eblul.org. Even an almost extinct language, Livonian, has a website: geocities.com/tuksnesis/livonia/livonia.html, not to mention several of the languages reviewed in this volume, e.g. Yiddish: http://www2.trincoll.edu/~mendele/ and Aboriginal languages of Australia: http://www.dnathan.com/VL/austlang.htm. The number of websites devoted to this general area of interest is growing very rapidly.

Chapter 1

Why is it so Hard to Save a Threatened Language?
(A Perspective on the Cases that Follow)

J.A. FISHMAN

The recent well-justified alarm that many thousands of languages (a very high proportion indeed of all those now in existence) are dying and that thousands more are destined to die out during the first half of this century, important though it is, is not the immediate issue which this book seeks to address. Prognostications foretelling disaster are not enough. What the smaller and weaker languages (and peoples and cultures) of the world need are not generalised predictions of dire and even terminal illnesses but, rather, the development of therapeutic undertandings and approaches that can be adjusted so as to tackle essentially the same illness in patient after patient. However, just as the illnesses that have infected so many of the world's languages constitute a very recognisable syndrome that yet varies in kind and in degree from one infected language to another, so the diagnoses and cures that are required, fundamentally related though they may well be, must also vary, depending on the facts in each case. Fortunately, a start was made in that very direction as the previous century drew to a close. Fittingly, that start did not call itself a 'theory of the life and death of languages,' nor an account of 'why all languages – even English itself – must die sooner or later.' Instead, it called itself *Reversing Language Shift: Theoretical and Empirical Foundations of Assistance to Threatened Languages* (Fishman, 1991).

The approach, which this volume attempts to re-examine, refine, and revise, considers language illnesses and even language death *per se*, as just examples of varying degrees of severity of hitherto uncontrolled (largely because misunderstood) changes in the number and kinds of social functions for which particular languages are utilised at particular historical junctures. Such functional changes come as a result of contacts with neighbouring languages (including the cultures and resources of the neighbours that utilise these languages and that advocate, foster and even require them

1

for specific functions). Thus, any theory and practice of assistance to threatened languages – whether the threat be a threat to their very lives, on the
one hand, or a much less serious functional threat, on the other hand – must
begin with a model of the functional diversification of languages. If
analysts can appropriately identify the functions that are endangered as a
result of the impact of stronger languages and cultures on weaker ones,
then it may become easier to recommend which therapeutic steps must be
undertaken in order to counteract any injurious impact that occurs. The
purpose of our analyses must be to understand, limit and rectify the societal loss of functionality in the weaker language when two languages
interact and compete for the same functions within the same ethnocultural
community and to differentiate between life-threatening and non-life-
threatening losses. The study and practice of 'reversing language shift'
(RLS) is thus not only descriptive but also prescriptive in functional terms.
It does not merely use language-related adjectives ('prestigious', 'standardised', 'positively viewed'), which are of course, almost endless in
number, in conjunction with the health of languages, but it uses substantive
functional designations and seeks to determine whether the number or
power of the community members discharging these functions in a particular language is rising or falling. The analysis of languages in competition,
in terms of the societal functions that are involved, contested, lost or gained
in such interlanguage competition and the degree of 'cruciality' of these
functions for the future longevity of given languages, is what the study of
'reversing language shift' seeks to become, in both theoretical and practical
terms.

A Specific Culturally Related Language is not the same as Language in General

The Western world has had a love affair with its own languages for over
two centuries. Because of this love affair (the seeds of which the power and
prestige of the West has also sown throughout much, if not most, of the
world), it is easy to overstate the importance of language in human social
and cultural affairs. Language is not the only important consideration in
connection with the lives of peoples and nations, communities and regions.
There are also demographic, economic, geographic and yet other essentially co-occurring sociolinguistic factors that must be considered in the
study of the determinants and consequences of the sociocultural priorities,
values and behaviours of human collectivities. But because language is
such a central ingredient in most of the foregoing, and because of the love
affair with language mentioned earlier, language (specifically, a society's

perceived 'own' language) has been elevated to the stature of a prime consideration in the life of most human collectivities. In other words, we have made language into something even more important than it might otherwise have been in any case. Having done so, we are now doubly obliged to consider sympathetically what many human collectivities do when they perceive their own language to be threatened and why some protective and restorative actions are more successful than others. It does not help for doctors to tell depressed patients that they have no reason to be depressed. Similarly, it is not helpful for social scientists to tell a sociocultural collectivity that there are more important things to worry about than the maintenance of their own seemingly ailing language. The concern for certain ailments may appear to outsiders to be overblown, but they are usually by no means groundless or specious or inconsequential. This is so not only because social problems believed to be true tend to generate real social consequences, but because the true involvement of language in human culture and cultural identity is, when all is said and done, quite amazing. Collective worry about such an important factor in all human cultures and cultural identities must be taken seriously, because not to do so would have very serious and deleterious social consequences, both objectively and perspectively speaking.

Specific languages are related to specific cultures and to their attendant cultural identities at the level of doing, at the level of knowing and at the level of being.

Such a huge part of every ethnoculture is linguistically expressed that it is not wrong to say that most ethnocultural behaviours would be impossible without their expression via the particular language with which these behaviours have been traditionally associated. Education (in content and in practice), the legal system (its abstract prohibitions and concrete enforcements), the religious beliefs and observances, the self-governmental operations, the literature (spoken and / or written), the folklore, the philosophy of morals and ethics, the medical code of illnesses and diseases, not to mention the total round of interpersonal interactions (childhood socialisation, establishment of friendship and kinship ties, greetings, jokes, songs, benedictions, maladictions, etc.) are not only linguistically expressed but they are normally enacted, at any given time, via the specific language with which these activities grew up, have been identified and have been intergenerationally associated. It is the specificity of the linguistic bond of most cultural doings that makes the very notion of a 'translated culture' so inauthentic and even abhorrent to most ethnocultural aggregates. The fact that some few ethnocultures and cultural identities *have* been able to 'survive' translation is neither here nor

there. In translation they are *not* the same as they wère in their original (i.e. most of the associated features itemised above have changed and some have been literally 'lost in translation'). Every sociocultural collectivity interested in doing so has the right to strive for its own perceived authenticity via the language of its own preference. To claim that social meanings can remain the same when a different language, coming from a different ethnocultural point of origin, is employed, is to misinterpret the dynamics and symbols of 'insiders' to any culture. Translations may do for 'outsiders'. We all read translations of Hebrew, Greek and Latin, not to mention Sanskrit and other classical texts, but we cannot pretend, thereby, to be enacting the very same culture and cultural identity of the original authors and audiences of those texts. 'Insiders', in particular, may well want more than a translated culture and identity, particularly if what they conceive of as the 'real thing' can still be protected and intergenerationally transmitted.

But note how many of the overt 'doings' of ethnocultural membership are related to specific ethnocultural 'knowings'. Ethnocognitions go beyond the usual general association between language and cognition. The cultural colour system, the illness terminology, the kinship terminology, the body-part terminology, the very number system that is employed, the pronoun system (are there or aren't there formal and informal pronouns and if so, how many levels of different degrees of formality are required by the traditionally associated language?), whether verbs and adjectives recognise gender or whether such recognition can be avoided or obscured; these all represent specific ethnolinguistic interpretations of reality. As such, they are at any period in cultural time an indication of what particular cultures know only through their specific and traditionally associated languages. Through social change and social learning experiences these 'knowings' can be overridden or overturned, supplemented or modified, discarded or forgotten, but it is certainly not justified to say that the resulting 'remainder' is 'the same culture' as that which existed 'originally'. Cultural knowings constitute a huge portion of the sum total of cultural identity and human collectivities may well be justified in seeking to maintain and strengthen the very 'knowings' in terms of which they recognise themselves, the uniqueness of their culture and their intergenerational identification with one another.

Just as 'knowings' are somewhat more linguistically abstract than 'doings', so the 'being' aspect of the link between a specific language and ethnocultural identity/membership is more abstract (some might say 'mystic') than is the 'knowing' link thereto. 'Being' is the very intergenerational link itself, the corporeal link between generations via which a particular 'essence' is believed to be passed on. Ethnocultures consist, perspectivally, of genetically continuous human populations, and just as such populations are phenotypically defined (they often believe they can recognise each other on sight, even when others cannot do so), so, too, they often believe that their specific languages are part and parcel of this 'essential' bodily inheritance that one generation passes on to the next. Child development research has revealed that children begin to learn the phonology and the syntax of their prospective 'mother tongue' when they are still in the womb. Many ethnocultures have always supposed that this was so and since the culturally specific language issues forth from what is perceived as a culturally specific body-type and genetic pool, it is not uncommon to view the language as being yet another tangible contributor to authentic ethnocultural membership. To abandon the language may be viewed as an abandonment not only of the traditional doings and knowings, but as an abandonment of personal ancestral kin and cultural ancestral heroes *per se*. Similarly, guaranteeing or fostering the specific language's acquisition and use is often viewed as fostering one's own personal (in addition to the culture's) triumph over death and obliteration via living on in one's own children and grandchildren. Life and death imagery is pervasive in ethnolinguistic consciousness the world over (Fishman, 1997).

This is a mystic belief to which many are attracted on occasion. We all want to believe in life everlasting. The culturally specific language is often the vehicle and the beneficiary of such mystic beliefs. Wherever they are emphasised to the exclusion of the other two (more open-ended) dimensions mentioned above, they can come to be racist beliefs (and, therefore, harmful to those defined as 'outsiders'). However, more usually, the 'being' aspect involves nothing more than a further strong link between the culturally traditional specific language and personal responsibility (as well as personal reward) for the continuity of the language and ethnicity link. Ethnicity itself is a kinship-based myth (a myth because it is more important to believe it than that it be literally true) and the language of the intergenerational ethnolinguistic continuity experience is, therefore, likely to share in this kinship-based assumption (which is, fundamentally, a 'being' assumption).

From all of the above, it should be clear that a traditionally associated language is more than just a tool of communication for its culture. Such a language can mean much more to its ethnoculture than just languages in general or than the language capacity with which all humans are endowed. Such a language is often viewed as a very specific gift, a marker of identity and a specific responsibility *vis-à-vis* future generations.

Why Organising on Behalf of Reversing Language Shift is not Anti-modern

'Globalisation is the wave of the future', more than one recent news-paper headline (not to mention the received popular wisdom) has announced, and, to some extent, this is so. But globalisation is both a constructive and a destructive phenomenon, both a unifying and a divisive one, and it is definitely not a culturally neutral or impartial one. In our day and age, it is definitely the globalisation of pan-Western culture (and pop-consumer culture in particular) that is the motor of language shift. And since America-dominated globalisation has become the major economic, technological and cultural thrust of worldwide modernisation and Wester-nisation, efforts to safeguard threatened languages (and, therefore, inevi-tably, contextually weaker languages) must oppose the very strongest processes and powers that the world knows today. That, in a word, is exactly why it is so hard to save threatened languages.

But it is even harder than that. The necessarily unequal competition between the weak and the strong, the few and the many, the poor and the rich, would be bad enough. The case of threatened languages (which is just our short-cut way of referring to threatened cultures and cultural identi-ties) is rendered even more difficult by the fact that not only is the 'enemy' not recognised, but he / she is even *persona grata* within the very gates of the beleagureed defenders ('We have met the enemy, and he is us!', as the cartoon character Pogo pointed out more than a generation ago). As the 18 cases that constitute the bulk of this book amply indicate, most RLSers are not by any means aiming at a 'return to the golden past', when the interac-tion between peoples was minimal and, therefore, when local differences could be easily maintained. On the contrary; they generally aim at nothing more than to achieve greater self-regulation over the processes of sociocultural change which globalisation fosters. They want to be able to tame globalisation somewhat, to counterbalance it with more of their own language-and-culture institutions, processes and outcomes. They would like to 'call more of their own cultural shots', so to speak, and to make sure that globalisation's unification of the market (both in production and in consumption) is counterbalanced to a larger extent by an even greater emphasis on differential cultural values, skills, attitudes and beliefs that stem from and reinforce their own identity. Indeed, most RLSers do not even 'go the whole way' and do not aspire to independent statehood (the usual modern mechanism of establishing, maintaining and regulating cultural boundaries). They are committed to pursuing the goals of strengthening their own particular threatened language, culture and identity via peaceful political persuasion, advocacy of democratic cultural autonomy and self-initiated efforts to foster their own intergenerational continuity.

This is a difficult position to take and even a more difficult position to defend. In a sense, most RLSers are determined not only to fight an unequal struggle (even an unequal two-front struggle, if we count the struggle against the contextually stronger immediate neighbour as a separate struggle than the one against globalisation more generally), but to do so with one hand tied behind their backs. That is to say, not only is globalisation/modernisation as a whole not rejected, but an internal societal re-allocation of languages to functions is pursued that will also be partially acceptive of the culturally stronger Big Brother language. Though being themselves dominated, RLSers nevertheless do not generally strive at being hegemonic dominators. What most RLSers in this day and age seek is a reasonable compromise with respect to both struggles, so that they can gain the autonomy they need with respect to fostering their own language-imbedded cultural identities, while engaging in the worldwide encounter with modernisation via controlled interaction with neighbours both near and far. The charges of provincialism, intrapunitivism and Luddism that are sometimes hurled at RLSers by their opponents are totally unjustified. Not only that, but these very same opponents of RLS make sure that *their* own language *is* recognised and protected by the EU and by international trade, mass-media and fiscal conventions. Furthermore, the opponents of RLS, within their very own political borders, also face many of the same cultural identity dangers that so alarm RLSers, and, in partnership with RLSers, could perhaps mitigate those dangers better than they now do. Unfortunately, such partnerships of the strong with the weak, amounting as they do to power-sharing with the hitherto dominated, are generally few and far between. The absence of such partnerships is an indication of the provincialism of the strong, a 'dog in the manger' type of phenomenon that is much more dangerous than the self-protection of the weak.

Even were such power-sharing to be attained more commonly, the implicit 'open sesame' for co-admission to mainstream language and identity that such partnerships imply, would still continue to make it exceedingly hard to strengthen functionally threatened languages with any degree of success. This is due to the fact that a peaceful partnership with stronger neighbours also inevitably increases interaction with them and runs the risk of fostering dependency based interaction for the weaker party. The intrusion of outside authorities into the implementation of intimate, spontaneous, everyday life (an intrusion which strikes – as we will soon see – at the very heart of RLS) is a great danger for RLS. Indeed, it is as much a risk as is the more general intrusion of globalisation (masked Americanisation) into local/regional economic, educational and recreational pursuits as an outcome of large-scale 'partnerships' of any kind. All in all, therefore, RLS is a difficult and risky operation and requires a very fine sense of balance, an extremely delicate sense of boundary definition, of functional analysis (as to shared functions and exclusively dominated functions) and a constant recognition of priorities, such that the right thing to do is the right thing only if it is done at the right time and in the right sequence with other things. Such a combination of delicacy and stubbornness, of sensitivity and of priorities, is extremely difficult to achieve. This is why it is so hard to strengthen threatened languages. It is hard precisely because most advocates of RLS are not really adamantly against globalisation and national integration of any and all kinds. Furthermore, being against globalisation wouldn't make it any easier for their cause either, as is amply witnessed by the difficulties that even many major powers have with respect to holding globalisation at bay in their own larger and stronger language-and-culture arenas.

Most RLSers are not primordialists. They generally don't believe, as did Herder and other romantics of the 18th and 19th centuries, that their language is God-given and that it would be both futile and immoral to abandon that which is fated and eternal. They are constructivists through and through. They believe that the fate of their beloved language depends on the success of efforts that came before them as well as on the efforts that they themselves undertake on its behalf. In this respect they are rational and modern beings. Although their regard for and their stewardship of their cultural patrimony may strike others as 'romantic' or as suprarational, RLSers are far from being fuzzy-minded fanatics. They do have ideals and strong convictions, like many of the 'mainliners', which define and delimit their goals and their devotions, sacrifices and efforts. Moreover, they are men and women who undertake to alter reality by dint of their own efforts and not by virtue of relying on their faith alone. People who feel strongly, protectively, responsibly about their cultural identity, can be as constructivist and as rational as are the other constructivists with whom they differ! Indeed, RLSers may be said to be activated by such totally modern convictions as cultural democracy, the rights of populations to define their own identities and priorities, and the rights of minorities to march to a different drummer in an increasingly connected, materialistic and power-centred world that often appears to be willing to put globalisation above all else. RLSers believe that globalisation has undoubted benefits, but that when these benefits are pursued at the expense of their own cultural identity (at the same time that the mainstream is strong enough not to lose its identity to the same degree or at the same rate), this expense is then an altogether unjustified and uncalled-for sacrifice and comes at a cost that they will not agree to (Fishman, 1999). However, it is very difficult to resist selectively and partially both state and global integration, which is exactly what is called for, and that, again, is why it is ultimately so hard to strengthen a weaker language on a permanent basis.

How can Functions be both Differentiated and Shared in Furtherance of RLS Purposes?

A recurring cultural reality of all RLS efforts is the ethnolinguistic omnipresence of a Big Brother. He is either literally co-present in the living-space of the threatened language (as when two culturally different populations, also differing markedly in power, live intermixed one with the other), or when RLSers and their ethnolinguistically mainstreamed kin (whose greater power derives from their mainstream connections and support) live residentially intermixed one with the other, or when both of the above scenarios obtain. It is also a recurring ethnolinguistic reality that the speakers of the threatened language are mostly bilingual, almost always speaking (and often also reading and writing) the mainstream language as well as (or even better than and in preference to) 'their own'. Finally, it is also clear that this co-territoriality and the primarily uni-directional bilingualism that it fosters is likely to persist indefinitely into the future. The mainstream language yields too many advantages for RLSers and their supporters for them ever to give it up entirely, no matter how much danger it portends for their own threatened language. Indeed, they must learn to use it skilfully – as well as the media and other tools linked to it – and to do so to their own advantage rather than disadvantage.

While RSL-efforts may be focused on those co-ethnics ('kinfolk') who have partially or completely given up the threatened language, RLSers believe that it is the threatened language that those 'kinsmen' must (re)acquire, rather than that the mainstream language must be suppressed, whether among themselves, among their 'kinfolk' or among 'non-kinfolk'. Finally, it is commonly understood that the threatened language yields too few material or other-than-kinship advantages (in comparison to those yielded by the the mainstream language) for any significant number of mainstream individuals to acquire anything more than a smattering of convivial pleasantries or 'emergency phrases' in the threatened language. Threatened languages are destined to live with this problem (either forever or for a long, long time to come). The only way to escape from this problem of sharing language functions with another language (indeed, with the very language or languages that are causing the threatened status to begin with) is to establish fairly complete interactional or political boundaries *vis-à-vis* Big Brother. If the latter is not an available option (it is certainly not an immediately available option for the overwhelming majority of all threatened languages), and even the bulk of those ethnopolitical communities that have established such 'independence' still commonly indicate that they too experience many of the same threats that threatened languages experience, then another more symbiotic arrangement (a manageable arrangement, not a completely triumphant solution) must be sought.

There are many societal functions of language, but, to make things simpler for purposes of initial discussion, let us first divide them into two clusters, P and n-P. P functions are those that are more powerful (employment, higher education, mass media, government, etc.). If the threatened language[1] aspires to discharge these functions, we will write its abbreviation (Th) above a line intended to differentiate them from the n-P functions (family, friendship neighbourhood, community and, possibly, some type of community-controlled pre-school or elementary education). The notation

$$\frac{P}{n\text{-}P} : \frac{Th}{Th},$$

therefore implies that both power and non-power functions are discharged in the threatened language. Many threatened languages aspire to this ultimate state of affairs, distant though it may be from their current functional situation. Currently, their situation may be more like the following:

$$\frac{P}{n\text{-}P} : \frac{n\text{-}Th}{Th},$$

where n-Th stands for the constantly present non-threatened (mainstream) language. RLSers rarely aspire to remove completely n-Th from all of its P functions. A more realistic and, certainly initially, more feasible goal would be to try to share some of the P functions, e.g. secondary education or local employment with n-Th. That would be represented as follows:

$$\frac{P}{n\text{-}P} : \frac{n\text{-}Th/Th}{Th}.$$

More complicated situations are not uncommon, e.g. when both the P and the n-P functions have to be shared with Big Brother, either because so few members of the threatened ethnocultural group still really master their Th language, or, alternatively, because so much of their n-P interaction is with members of the n-Th ethnocultural group and the latter very uncommonly speak Th.

A common formulation of the reversing language shift task is to set as a goal the *elevation of Th from n-P to P functions*. The other problem, that of more exclusive Th control of the n-P functions, is less commonly recognised. The two problems are, as we will soon see, intimately linked, however. If Th is not successfully (intergenerationally) maintained at the n-P level (and mother tongue transmission is an informal, spontaneous, intimate n-P function), it will then have no mother tongue speakers within one generation who can use it for n-P functions. In that case, it can *still* discharge certain P functions, but they will have to be acquired anew generation after generation via exposure to a P institution that is under Th-control. Such institutions, like all P institutions, are typically under great n-Th influence, pressure or regulation. Thus, the loss of crucial intergenerational Th-related n-P functions and the difficulty of substituting for them a few institutionally based (rather than intergenerationally transmitted) Th-related P functions, is another reason why it is so difficult to save a threatened language.

Yet a further reason has to do with the functional compartmentalisation (i.e. the functional non-generalisability) of P vs n-P languages. A glance at the formulas above reveals two kinds of lines: the horizontal ones and the slanted ones. These lines pertain to the extent to which languages can be functionally compartmentalised (i.e. restricted to their established functions) as distinct from the extent to which they tend dynamically to overflow their functional boundaries. From the perspective of RLS, Th languages tend, at best, to become compartmentalised (i.e. functionally fixed), whereas n-Th languages tend to break out of any pre-existing functional compartmentalisation and to spread into new functions, both above and below the horizontal power divider. P languages are more commonly n-Th than Th and, because of their lesser compartmentalisability, they tend to threaten the n-P languages with which they are contextually associated. Thus, any complementary allocation of languages to functions tends to become unstable if this allocation runs counter to the major power differentials between the languages involved.

It is not enough, therefore, for a speech community to collectively decide on distinctive and complementary functions for the Th and n-Th languages which it utilises (hoping thereby to give the Th language a secure functional niche). Any such division is the easy part of RLS efforts. The hard part is making the division 'stick'. RLS requires making constant and repeated efforts not only to elevate the power-status of the Th language, but also making concerted efforts – efforts of will and efforts in terms of allocated resources – to reinforce recurringly the compartmentalisation of the n-Th language, so as to keep the latter from constantly generalising to new functions, whether above or below the horizontal power divide. The constant vigilance and insistence required by the n-P community of Th language users in order to compartmentalise continually and successfully the n-Th language of the P community is so substantial and unattainable that it also constitutes a reason why it is so difficult to strengthen threatened languages. Successful RLS requires those language communities who have less resources to do more in many respects than those language communities who have more resources. This represents a tremendous effort of will (conviction, commitment, dedication and ever-readiness to innovate and to find and commit new resources). RLS is hard and often discouraging work and we must not wonder that it so rarely succeeds quickly or sufficiently. But RLSers are a hardy breed and they do not take 'no' for an answer (certainly not for a definitive answer).

The surrounding larger context of social change must always be examined and exploited by RLSers in order to find possible new resources and opportunities. n-Th languages also develop problems: they can come to be viewed as bullies; they can come to be identified as politically incorrect and even 'gross'. Anti-'Ugly American'-sentiments, and growing opposition to 'Coca-Colonisation' and 'MacDonaldisation' on the one hand, and the renewed attractiveness of 'environmental protection and diversification', 'smaller is better' and the growth of 'Gemeinschaft over Gesellschaft' ethnic revival sentiments, on the other hand, are all relatively new changes in the ethnolinguistic climate of modern, interactive societies. These latter developments have tended to give RLSers new arguments and tactics. The adoption of international conventions on behalf of 'lesser used languages' and the need to pass scrutiny *vis-à-vis* 'linguistic human rights' for all states that wish to join the European Union, Nato or the European Commission, have also introduced a new 'atmosphere affect' *vis-à-vis* RLS. While it should be noted that none of the above extra-local developments can substitute for astute 'on the ground' functional allocations and prioritisations, nor for constantly sensitive and disciplined local control of compartmentalisation, taken together they do imply that a new spirit of the times may be taking shape. This spirit may not only encourage threatened languages to fend for themselves more successfully, but it may even encourage the non-threatened languages to help them do so.

So, how can functions both be separated and shared in furtherance of RLS purposes? The answer is 'with difficulty'. Nevertheless, there have been a few successes along these lines, not to mention a few lessons to be learned from these successes as well as from the failures that recent history has so amply recorded.

Principles and Stages of RLS

It is relatively easy to reconstruct historically, describe and analyse cases of RLS, one at a time. It is also easy to prescribe 'fixes' that cannot really be undertaken. It is relatively vacuous to suggest that the speakers of threatened languages should be 'larger in number', should establish 'more and stronger language supporting institutions' or should 'provide their language with more status'. It is of no help to tell a patient that he should attain health by getting better, or that he should get better by being healthier. These are redundant and non-operational bits of advice. If such advice could be followed, the patient would not be sick to begin with and the languages to which the advice is addressed would not be threatened. But it is not merely the case that such advice is impractical or non-operational. It is also non-theoretical insofar as it posits no priorities, establishes no sequences or linkages between events and provides no differential weights to the factors being highlighted, nor any explanation why other factors are being ignored (e.g. geographic, economic, linguistic, political, and so on).

It is one of the 'sad but true' facts of life that the resources available to threatened languages are often quite meagre and constantly fewer than those available to their Big Brother rivals and competitors. As a result, not only must resources be used sparingly but they must be used tellingly, i.e. in connection with gaining or securing functions that are both crucial and defendable. Threatened languages often have no *outside support of any operational significance* to fall back upon. Even if there are promises of assistance from outside the ranks of their own community of speakers and activists, these promises necessarily come at a price. If they are withdrawn, at the decision of the outside supporters, they can leave behind a void and a sense of defeat and betrayal which is worse than the initial threat that such assistance had initially promised to assuage. Thus, an initial policy decision that may be warranted is not to accept (or, at least, not to depend upon) outside support and to undertake only the most crucial efforts that can be independently conducted and maintained.

There are two key words in the above formulation: 'independent' and 'crucial'. 'Independent' has already been discussed. 'Crucial' implies an ability to identify the function(s) that can be regained at any particular time (something that the 'demography-institutions-status' blunderbuss does not do), as well as to link any other functions that are already operative to the crucial one(s) by means of a feedback system. The purpose of the feed-back system is to overcome the tendency of Th language functions to become compartmentalised. Home-neighborhood-community intimacy functions in threatened languages are not necessarily assisted via mass-media programmes in such languages. Not only are mass-media efforts in threatened languages few and far between (and infinitely weaker than those associated with the Big Brother rival), but even the few that do obtain are often not consciously and conscientiously linked to reinforcing home or school language functions. Similarly, school language efforts are often not linked to home-family-neighbourhood-community functions. Threatened languages cannot afford functionally diffuse or free-floating efforts. Or, to put it another way, threatened languages must establish both (1) *a priority of functions*, and (2) *a priority of linkages between functions* in order to derive the maximal benefit from their relatively weak resource base and unfavour-able resource competitive setting.

A very commonly adopted functional goal of threatened languages is to offer education in which those languages can operate as sole or, at least, as co-media. If the same threatened languages are not first acquired as ethnic mother tongues at home, before children arrive at school, and if, in addi-tion, they are not used out of school, after school and even after schooling as a whole is over, then the school has a much more difficult task on its hands. Its pupils always arrive already speaking another mother tongue rather than the threatened language on behalf of which the school has ostensibly been established. If the school cannot influence the parent body (actual or potential) also to learn and constantly to activate intimately the threatened language, then the school itself becomes one link in an established intergenerational sequence of teaching the threatened language as a second language (ThLSL) and on keeping it as a second language at least for another generation. Furthermore, if there are no efforts undertaken to teach adults of child-bearing age the threatened language as an active ThLSL, then parents whose period of compulsory schooling is far behind them (far enough behind them so that they may well have forgotten the ThLSL lessons that they themselves may have received in school during there own childhood days) will not be able to transmit that language as a mother tongue to their children so that these children, in turn, can bring it with them to school as a *first* language.

Clearly, therefore, if the school is not to become merely a ThLSL institu-tion, it must be preceded by (or at least accompanied by) adult language learning of the threatened language as a second language, by instruction in parenting via ThLSL, and then by substantial child acquisition of it as a first language (ThLFiL) *even before the pupils-to-be show up at school*. If the latter scenario is really to obtain, then a revitalised home-family-neighbourhood-community function must become rewarding and satisfying, even before parents have children and much before those children are sent off to school. But, at the same time, post- and out-of-school functions for the threatened language must also be increasingly assured for adolescents and young adults (e.g. clubs, sports teams, study groups, hobby groups, etc.), otherwise these young post-schoolers will have no further use for their threatened language until their own pre-parental period, by which time they may well have to relearn it. It is infinitely easier to socialise children into an environmentally utilised language (no matter how small that environment may be in relative terms) than into one that remains unutilised outside of the easily compartmentalised school-experience.

Thus, optimally, even efforts to achieve school functions for a threatened language need to be conceptualised and activated or implemented in a linkage system that starts with those adult functions and institutions that are *prior to and preparatory for* schooling for children. This linkage system must be one that *continues on to* adolescent and young adult functions *after and following upon* schooling for children. The functions (1) 'ThLSL for adults of child-bearing-age'; (2) 'erstwhile ThLSL becoming ThLFiL of family-home-neighborhood-community life'; (3) 'schooling in a ThLFiL'; and, finally (4) 'post-school adolescent and young adult activities in ThLFiL' are thus logically, naturally and functionally linked. It is the linkage that enables the threatened language to become a first language of a new generation and that enables the school for children to be more than constantly (intergenerationally) a second language teaching institution. Were this linkage to come apart, then the school would again lapse into being only a SL institution and the threatened language would become compartmentalised there, having neither backward nor forward linkages. The latter, indeed, is exactly what has occurred in many threatened language schooling efforts and has resulted in disappointment and disillusionment, with schools and with RLS efforts as a whole. Note, that the above scenario is not merely one which claims the importance of certain institutions, but one which links them sequentially, some efforts coming slightly beyond the stage of schooling and some coming slightly before the stage of socialisation into intimacy and informality for a new generation. In the same fashion, RLS-dedicated teachers must be linked to each other (for sharing teaching materials, curricular ideas and for desktop publishing) via the most modern media that can be under their own regulatory management (e.g. e-mail, websites) and they must become skilled at using such media for RLS purposes, both in connection with in-school and out-of-school Xish language exposure and activities.

A similar scenario would obtain if schooling in the threatened language is not considered to be the crucial initial target-function (some cultures do not consider their traditionally associated ethnic mother tongue to be suitable for formal literacy based education, but, prefer a classical language or a lingua franca for that function or functional cluster). But intergenerational mother-tongue transmission is still considered crucial in many of these very same cases. Accordingly, every functional goal must also be tackled in terms of the functions that precede it ('it' being the target function *per se*) and in terms of the subsequent functions that can reward and reinforce it. In each instance, however, the issues of sufficiency of resources, of independent self-reliance, of priorities and of forward and backward (feedback) sequencing must be carefully worked through. RLSers are initially relatively few in number and poor in means. But they are the hard-core of the self-sacrificing activists on behalf of the threatened language. They will be the first to re-acquire it in early adulthood as a fluent second language (by means of establishing adult learning centres, both for language fluency and for adult socialisation, activisation and outreach or community building purposes), they will be the first to establish informal home-family-neighbourhood communities, and they will found schools for their children whom they will raise as the first ThLFiL speakers in infancy and childhood. If their resources are not enough for full dayschools in lieu of compulsory education, they will found pre-school-schools, after-school-schools and, possibly, even other literacy related socialising institutions that are not under the direct control of the Big Brother authorities and that can, therefore, enable activists to concentrate their efforts exactly as RLSers determine and prefer.

The theory adumbrated here will be spelled out with local examples in several of the chapters that follow, and will be ignored, criticised and substituted for in other chapters. This volume constitutes an unforced attempt to compare the above general RLS theory with others, as well as with local descriptivisms and with *ad hoc*isms that masquerade as theories. RLS theory does not posit any evolutionary, inescapable or obligatory sequence of functional stages: it merely posits that there must be strategic support or linkage stages, both anticipatory to and subsequent to any crucial target function. These strategic support functions must be part of the RLS plan and must be sequenced in terms of their priorities, their preparatory and reinforcing capacities, the abilities and resources needed in order to initiate, attain or salvage these goals when and if outside support is not forthcoming or is forthcoming at too great a price *vis-à-vis* the convictions and the independent action prerogatives of the RLS movement. At all times the RLS plan keeps in mind the cost of aiming too high (at power functions), when such functions are the hardest to seize and to retain. To attempt to do so when the supporting prior intimacy functions have not yet been attained and solidified, is to build institutions without foundations, as well as institutions that must constantly be revitalised anew (and as SL institutions to boot) from the ground up, generation after generation, rather than instituting any self-priming intergenerational momentum.

Furthermore, RLS movements must realise from the very outset of their ideological clarification that ethnolinguistic authenticity and identity must be associated not only with Xish versions of modern Yish-dominated pop-culture and consumerism (which can be pursued in any language, including both the local Big Brother and English) but, even more importantly, with a continuing ethnohumanistic, ethnoreligious and ethnocultural constellation of beliefs, behaviours and attitudes. Only such a constellation will ultimately provide a rationale going beyond the economies of scale inherent in the materialist view of those who have essentially concluded that 'if you can't beat them, join them'. It is only the conviction that one's own-language-in-culture is crucially different and, therefore, worth sacrificing for ('vive la difference!') that makes RLS worthwhile, even though in the great majority of cases it means embarking on a carefully multilingual and multicultural existence for the foreseeable future. Although this may be considered a defeat by some RLSers, there is also good reason to consider it an honourable, enriching and constructive solution to the multiple ethnocultural identities which most modern human societies and individuals are increasingly destined to enact as an inevitible consequence of the complexity of ongoing globalisation.

Nevertheless, even this is a compromise position and a difficult goal to reach. It is beset by many differences of opinion, both among activists and academic specialists, and in conjunction with the negotiation of priorities and of linkages (forward and backward) between the crucial target functions and the functions that come before and afterwards. These analytic, theoretical and practical differences of opinion underline once more why it is so hard to save a threatened language, even for those who agree that saving such a language is both desirable and possible.

RLS and Civil Nationalism

The RLS ethos is still very much a child of the age of ethnonationalism. Although this age has not yet played itself out (not even in Europe, not to mention in the infinitely more diverse regions of Africa and Asia), it has pretty much run its course in the view of influential intellectuals in most European polities (Fishman, 1972). In those settings gravitating toward post-national EU-EC-Nato-OSCE membership, there is often a distinct weariness with the incessant efforts of ethnolinguistic minorities to preserve their own identities, regardless of whether such efforts are accompanied by the aspiration for independent statehood. RLS efforts that were once met with encouragement, being viewed as expressions of further democratisation (i.e. the spread of democracy from the political to the cultural or intercultural arena), are now more often met by disenchantment and opposition. Indeed, such efforts are often criticised as being 'too little and too late' by some, and as being 'disturbers of the peace' and 'expressions of provincialism and contraproductive balkanisation' by others.

In truth, movements for ethnolinguistic liberation, reunification and democracy have faced both types of opposition since the very beginning of the 19th century. However, both the criticism of disenchantment and the criticism of opposition have taken on a number of somewhat new surface manifestations since the ethnic revivals of the mid-1960s. The criticism of disenchantment, a type of criticism coming from individuals and groups that might have been counted upon to support the RLS efforts of the ethnolinguistic groups to which they themselves admittedly belong, stems from disappointment with the purportedly minimalist settlements that have been attained and accepted by groups that once advocated maximalist or apparently more extreme solutions. 'We thought the struggle for the language was part of a struggle for political independence, rather than just an amicable detente with the state' is a complaint that is often heard from many of those who are no longer as active for RLS as they once were. This disenchantment frequently sees the accommodations that have been reached or that are still being pursued with the Big Brother as a trap, or as a cul-de-sac from which the RLS movement cannot emerge whole, much less victorious.

Those who subscribe to this disenchantment are possessed by a malaise, if not a sense of doom or foreboding, believing that the cultural democracy or even cultural autonomy concessions that have been attained (and, purportedly, prematurely settled for) will ultimately (if not sooner) either be withdrawn outright by the Big Brother, or that they will inevitably simply be attrited by the silent weight of the preponderant numbers, resources and dynamism associated with the less compartmentalisable language of greater power. The disenchantment of maximalists robs many RLS movements of much of the valuable intellectual and motivational leadership that they once enjoyed and that they so obviously still need. In some cases, the maximalists form splinter groups of their own and in other cases they merely remain passively separated from the main body of the RLS effort. In either case they represent a loss to what might otherwise be a more united and, therefore, more successful joint effort.

Are they right? In some cases they may be, if the main movement has really seriously miscalculated how much further (toward how many additional concessions) the Big Brother might have been pushed, if pushing had continued longer and less agreeably. In other cases they are wrong, but their very existence serves as a warning to the Big Brother that a more troublesome and less easily appeasable opposition is in the offing and that if working arrangements are not arrived at and maintained with the 'Good Cop', then a less tractable 'Bad Cop' will have to be faced. I have yet to meet a threatened language community that does not evince differences of opinion, of tactics and of ultimately underlying objectives along such lines. Nevertheless, the so called 'extremists' or 'maximalists' who believe that possibilities for the crystallisation of new nation-states are definitely not over and done with in the post-nationalist world (at least not for *their* ethnolinguistic aggregate) and, indeed, that the 'RLS bandwagon' will 'go further if it is pushed harder and less accommodatingly', are markedly fewer and weaker in most parts of the globe as the 21st century begins, than they were during many other recent periods of history. The belated dismantling of the Soviet Union may tend to mask this phenomenon, but neither the pent-up grievances nor the long- and short-term deprivations that marked that setting and its underlying Herderian ethos and administrative framework, are readily encountered elsewhere. This does not mean that current ethnocultural grievances are weaker or that those who aspire to redress them are fewer. Rather, it means that those who are disenchanted with the readiness of RLS movements to compromise in multilingual–multicultural directions are generally outnumbered by those who view independent statist solutions to their ethnolinguistic grievances as no longer providing either the guarantees or the gratifications that were formerly attributed to such solutions.

At the other end of the oppositional continuum are the often far more numerous non-believers in RLS efforts as a whole (and most particularly when these movements are in their own backyards). These may be either right-wing defenders of the state or intellectual defenders of post-state regionalism or internationalism. Frequently, some of the former will masquerade as subscribing to the latter view, recognising its greater fashionability (particularly in many university circles). To the long-established charges of 'disturbers of the peace', 'destroyers of civility' and 'defenders of parochialism ('archaic tribalism', 'outdated separatism', etc.), they now point to the increased promise of supra-state entities such as the European Union. If currently well-established states are increasingly anomalous in the face of the growing internationalism of commerce, governmental practices, technology, fashions and tastes, what reasonable defence can there be, anti-RLSers ask, for the recrudescence of substate provincialism, isolationism and ethnocentrism?

The worldwide growth in the migrations of peoples out of their coun- tries and regions of origin and into countries and regions of greater afflu- ence and better-established democratic traditions has also provided anti- RLSers with a new bow to their quiver. Many formerly prototypic nation- states (e.g. Germany, Sweden, Spain, Netherlands, etc.) are now well along on the path to becoming state-nations, as a result of their vastly greater numbers of immigrants, migrants and refugees from afar, differing widely in race, ethnicity and religion from those of the mainstream. These newcomers, like immigrants almost everywhere, have only a very tenuous claim on (or expectation of) long-term ethnocultural and ethnolinguistic self-maintenance, whether with or without mainstream support. They will almost inevitably become incorporated into the mainstream, given suffi- cient socioeconomic mobility and ethnocultural permeability, within roughly two or three generations. At that point, German writers of Turkish extractions will be no greater oddity than are American writers of Hispanic extraction. Thus, instead of forming new pockets of parochialism, immi- grant-identities will more readily flow – by dint of mutual acceptance – in the direction of the greater advantages associated with mainstream ethnolinguistic identity. That being the case, the mainstreamers argue, there is no good reason why locally indigenous ethnocultural groups should do otherwise and not join the inevitable wave of the supra-ethnic future.

Obviously, RLSers are under attack from both defenders of the existing states (and their languages and ethnic identities) and defenders of the increasingly growing supra-states (and their growing supra-state languages and identities). In both cases, however, the existing states have managed to safeguard their own prerogatives (the EU now has 11 official languages, all of them being state languages, and may well yet have more – if only as a means of assuring France that French will always be protected against a confrontation with English and English alone). And in both cases the true complexities – and complexity accommodating potentials – of human identities are being seriously underestimated and reduced to the level of pauperisation. There will always be sub-state ethnocultural identi- ties within the identity repertoires of humankind, along with gender, religious, occupational, political, recreational and yet more and more special-interest and special-experience identities. The human capacity to juggle, combine and implement these identities should not be underestimated, for to do so is to impoverish the human experience itself. There will be no post-ethnic humanity, any more than there will be a post-religious one, or a post-gender one, or a post-language one, although local-language-and-local-ethnic-identity may well have to take its place in a much larger total repertoire of identities (given the new large scale identities that are becoming more pervasive) than was the case before. Clearly, until the genuine complexity potential of humankind is better understood and appreciated, there may be additional difficulties in providing assistance to threatened languages. The growing threat to the world's smaller languages is real, therefore, and has already been clarified, bemoaned and regretted, all to very limited effect. The criticism from below and the criticism from above directed at RLS make the provision of real assistance to threatened languages all the harder.

Summary

Why is it so hard to strengthen threatened languages? Because (1) the loss of a traditionally associated ethnocultural language is commonly the result of many long-ongoing departures from the traditional culture, thereby robbing that culture of most of its erstwhile and potential defenders and establishing a rival identity that does not require (although it may still claim to admire) the traditionally associated language; (2) organising on behalf of a traditionally associated but weakened language is competitively depicted and regarded as social mobility contraindicated, parochial and anti-modern; (3) in order to defend a threatened language some of its functions must be both differentiated from and shared with its stronger competitor – a tactically difficult allocation to arrive at and to maintain; (4) any functions to be regained by the threatened language must be simultaneously reinforced both from 'below' and from 'above' in terms of power considerations; and (5) the opposition to RLS is both statist and supra-statist, thereby labelling RLS efforts as simultaneously disruptive of local civility and of higher-order international advantage. Nevertheless, RLS can attain strategic functional allocations without descending into either sedition or parochialism, neither of which is in its own best interests. Only RLS efforts give voice to intimate lower-order identities that, albeit hard to defend from the biased point of view of incorporative modernity, are also harmful (both to the individual and to society) to deny.

We now turn to a dozen and a half cases of efforts on all continents to attain a variety of RLS goals. These cases deserve special attention because they provide clues and lessons for all RLS-efforts, operating under a variety of circumstances, on how to attain greater and more certain (even if usually only partial) successes, as well as on how best to avoid the partial failures that most of these efforts only incompletely escape. The examination and confrontation of a wide variety of separate cases is the basis upon which more effective theory and practice of RLS must ultimately be based.

Notes

1. The notational system X and Y (used since 1991 and now quite widely adopted) to designate diads of co-territorial threatened (X) and contextually unthreatened or less threatened (Y) languages, will be re-introduced in the chapters that follow, depending on the extent to which individual authors find them useful. The final (summary) chapter uses this older notational system entirely.

References

Fishman, Joshua A. (1972) *Language and Nationalism; Two Integrative Essays.* Rowley: Newbury House; also, reprinted in its entirety in his (1989) *Language and Ethnicity in Minority Sociolinguistic Perspective.* Clevedon: Multilingual Matters.

Fishman, Joshua A. (1991) *Reversing Language Shift; Theoretical and Empirical Foundations of Assistance to Threatened Languages.* Clevedon: Multilingual Matters.

Fishman, Joshua A. (1997) *In Praise of the Beloved Language: A Comparative View of Positive Ethnolinguistic Consciousness.* Berlin, Mouton de Gruyter.

Fishman, Joshua A. (1999) *Handbook of Language and Ethnic Identity.* New York, Oxford University Press.

Haugen, Einar (1953) *The Norwegian Language in America,* 2 vols. Philadelphia: University of Pennsylvania Press. Reprinted as one volume: 1969. Bloomington: Indiana University Press.

Chapter 2
Reversing Navajo Language Shift, Revisited

T. LEE and D. McLAUGHLIN

> When the words of all people become one, then the world will come to an end. Our language is holy, and when it is gone, the good in life will be gone with it. When the old ones said that the world would end with the disappearance of our language, they meant that the young people could not hear, understand, and heed the teachings, words of encouragement, expressions of love, scoldings, and corrections that were offered by the parents and elder relatives; nor would they be able to pray. Without prayers, our lives cannot be good, for without words there can be no prayers. (F. Alts'iisi, as quoted in Parsons-Yazzie, 1996: 52)

Introduction

We suspect that the elderly individual quoted above sounds all too familiar to those who, in this age of rapid economic expansion and technological change, struggle to ensure the survival of the planet's less prestigious, less powerful languages and cultures. For, in the past half-century, we have begun to become in some meaningful respects one world. Information to, from, and about almost anything, from anywhere, is available to many of us instantly. We readily communicate across daunting distances and complex cultural and linguistic boundaries.

At the same time, there is no question that the possibilities of our age come at a steep cost, and that we live in very dangerous times. Our era is one in which market forces are stronger now than they have ever been; in the last 20 years, the gaps between the wealthy and the poor have widened exponentially within the US and across the globe. 'We have become objects of a thrilling self-indulgence that has spawned an ecocidal desire endlessly to consume,' to quote Peter McLaren (1993: 201). In the process, individuals' cultural-identities and senses of agency have been spread out across the various landscapes that we inhabit with no common understanding of the myriad forms of economic, political, cultural, and linguistic oppression that we experience, no common vocabulary for naming these forms, and few collective strategies to contest and transform them (McLaren, 1993).

Of the world's 3000 to 8000 distinct languages, depending upon how one counts, only 300 might be considered 'power languages' and thus assured, amazingly, of surviving into the 22nd century. All of the other languages and peoples rest squarely in the pathway of modes of production that, in acting on behalf of the most privileged groups, produce widespread exploitation, marginalisation, urban and industrial pollution, and cultural and linguistic demise.

One need look no further than to the situation of American Indian groups to witness the extent of the chaos. Of some 500 aboriginal North American languages and cultures, fewer than 20 are characterised today by anything less than impending doom. In Alaska, where two generations ago there were some 23 native languages, only three are expected to survive the next decade, and only one is predicted to survive into the next generation (Krauss, 1992). As for Navajo, which is one of the healthier American indigenous languages and cultures by most measures, Diné language and ways of life are deeply imperiled. The shift from Navajo to English, rationalised in some quarters by the devil's own survival-of-the-fittest cultural Darwinism, as we will explain, is taking place with extraordinary speed.

What we will do in this chapter is describe some of the important contours of the shift from Navajo to English. Where we appear pessimistic, perhaps even fatalistic, about the shift, our aim is to bring attention of the dire threat to Navajo language and culture to the most important audience for this chapter and indeed for our life-work – Navajo activists, policy-makers, educators, and community leaders. Where we highlight important developments that Navajo family members, educators, linguists, and policy-makers have heroically enacted, our aim is to support such efforts. All along, we will validate the model for conceptualising language shift, and for outlining the work that is needed to reverse it, as established by Joshua Fishman in *Reversing Language Shift* (1991). From our own experiences in Navajo work and life contexts, specifically, we will validate Fishman's Graded Intergenerational Disruption Scale (the GIDS), and reaffirm his vital contention that the key to successful language revitalisation efforts is to focus on the intergenerational transmission of Xish (the imperilled language) within family, neighbourhood, and community contexts.

Three sections constitute the heart of our chapter. First, we present snapshot analyses of social, economic, political, religious and educational conditions that shape, and are shaped by, all aspects of language and culture shift, and efforts to reverse it, within the Navajo Nation as a whole.

Next, we explain in more detail the present status of Navajo language in relation to each of the eight stages of the GIDS. We then comment on the appropriateness of Fishman's model for conceptualising and working to effect the reversal of language shift.

Conditions that Undergird the Present Status of Navajo Language

As recently as a generation ago, nearly all Navajo people spoke Navajo. Navajo was the unmarked language of oral communication between Navajos at social gatherings, ceremonies, trading posts, chapter meetings, and work; in fields, canyons, and school hallways; on playgrounds and trips to town; and across the generations within nearly all family contexts (Spolsky & Irvine, 1982). The Navajo language today, however, faces an uncertain future. The Navajo Nation still has a great number of Navajo speakers, but it also has a large and growing number of non-Navajo-speaking tribal members. More than half of the tribe is under the age of 24; fewer and fewer children grow up as native speakers of their ancestral language. This section describes present-day conditions that frame the shifting dynamics of Navajo people's language use.

Land base

The Navajo Nation has the largest land base of any Native American tribe in the United States. It consists of some 25,000 square miles that span three western US states: Arizona, New Mexico and Utah. According to the 1990 United States census figures, the total number of Navajos living in the US was 219,198. The number of Navajos living within the Navajo Nation was 148,983. In 1993, it was estimated that the population within the Navajo Nation had grown to 154,962. While the Navajos' landmass is vast, the population density is small. The number of persons per square mile is only six (Rodgers, 1993).

Travel from one end of the Navajo Nation to the other requires an eight-hour drive. Across this distance exist hundreds of small reservation communities, which in turn fit within a matrix of chapters (110 local political units in number) that make up the Navajo Nation as a whole. Every four years, the members of each chapter elect a local president, vice-president, secretary, treasurer, manager, and grazing committee chair. Similarly, each chapter elects a representative that sits on the Navajo Nation tribal council in the nation's capital at Window Rock. All 110 chapters are organised by the Bureau of Indian Affairs into five administrative agencies. Within each agency are one or two towns, at which are clustered tribal and federal governmental offices, BIA boarding schools, public school districts that serve from three to 5000 students. In addition, the towns have super-markets and mini-mall shopping facilities, Indian Health Service hospitals, and housing compounds that are connected to the schools and medical facilities, or managed by the tribe and funded by federal low-income housing programmes.

Most houses on the reservation resemble mainstream dwellings, although they tend to be small and clustered at family camps, which in turn are widely separated from one another, sometimes by distances of many miles. Families have hooghans (traditional Navajo homes) for ceremonial purposes or as second dwellings. People in isolated areas also have main-stream houses, but many live in hooghans. Most housing units lack plumbing and kitchen facilities and are heated by wood. Many families haul water from the local chapter or community school and chop wood to heat their homes. In the past 20 years, there has been a slow but steady increase of housing developments built by the federal government's Department of Housing and Urban Development. These developments often include 30 or more single family units situated in rows of quarter-acre lots. The housing units relocate Navajo families into homes with electricity and running water, and thus make readily available satellite and cable tele-vision, within an island-like context very different from the widely sepa-rated family camps of rural reservation areas.

Subsistence

Forty-nine percent of all Navajo income derives from wages and sala-ries, 23% from general assistance, and 14% from social security. The proportion of unemployed persons nationwide is 28%; the percentage of unemployed and under- or temporarily employed individuals in many Navajo communities is much higher, sometimes as high as 85% (McLaughlin, 1992). Average wage and salary income was $19,720 in 1990; there were significantly lower averages for general assistance and social security: $3,543 and $4,831, respectively. The proportion of the total popu-lation that lives below the federal government's poverty line is 56%; many of these persons are elderly (Rodgers, 1993).

Given limited wealth and job opportunities, a primary focus for many Navajo families is simply to subsist. At the same time, subsistence occupa-tions that were once prevalent and distant from mainstream influence, such as sheep-herding, livestock-raising, and farming, are rapidly dimin-ishing. With population growth and depletion of the land through over-grazing, subsistence occupations no longer support Navajo families as widely as they did as recently as one generation ago. Based on recent census data, jobs that most Navajo people hold today are wage-earning and are located both in the fast-growing towns within each of the reservation agencies and in urban areas off the reservation.

Religious beliefs

Navajo people engage widely in traditional Navajo religious practices, as well as in Mormonism, the Native American Church, and the many varieties of Christianity. Many Navajos participate in two or more religions, usually a combination of traditional Navajo religion and the Native American Church, or traditional Navajo religion and a local Christian church. Navajo is spoken more in traditional Navajo ceremonies and in Native American Church meetings than it is in Christian affiliated services, although some Christian churches incorporate Navajo through Bible reading or in sermons.

Traditional religious practices are contexts where Navajo language has high status relative to English in that prayers and songs, and the powers that they invoke, must be called forth entirely in Navajo. Non-Navajo speaking patients and participants are told by Navajo-speaking relatives what to do. If a non-speaker is the patient and is required to pray in Navajo, a Navajo-speaking relative may 'sit-in' on the patient's behalf to pray in Navajo. At Native American Church prayer meetings, many of the songs and prayers are in Navajo; functional talk, however, tends to take place in Navajo and English, depending on the language abilities of the participants (Holm, 1995). For many Navajos, traditional religious practices constitute settings where Navajo speakers continue to use their ancestral language. The proportion of youth that participate in traditional religious activities, however, is unknown. Observations of and conversations with youth lead one to believe that they participate less in traditional religious activities than the generation that preceded them.

Education

According to the most recent available statistics, 24% of the Navajo population have graduated from high school, 10% have attended some college courses, and only 2% have earned a bachelor's degree. Despite these relatively low figures, Navajo children's attendance at school is now nearly universal. Approximately 60,000 Navajo children attend some 240 K-12 schools both on and adjacent to the Navajo Nation. Four thousand preschoolers attend approximately 160 Head Start programmes. Moreover, the numbers of young persons in schools are growing: indeed, the median age for members of the Navajo tribe is presently 22 (Rodgers, 1993).

According to 1990 US census figures, the Navajo Nation is the fastest-growing language minority group in the country.

Language demographics

In the 1990 census, most Navajo families reported that an 'American Indian language' was used in the home (107,665 of 130,520). However, many families also indicated that English was the only language spoken (22,855). By all accounts, the number of households where English is the only language spoken is growing. Still, Navajos are better off in comparison to other Native groups when it comes to use of a Native language in the home. For Navajos, 78% of children ages 5 to 17 speak both English and 'another language', presumably Navajo, in their homes (Reddy, 1993). One major problem with this data, though, is that proficiency levels of either languages spoken in the home are not reported.

Cause for alarm

The above socioeconomic and cultural-political conditions are cause for alarm insofar as the stability of the Navajo language is concerned. In the course of surveying the language abilities of Navajo children in the late 1960s, a study determined that families' access to paved roads, which at that time were far fewer in number than they are today, correlated directly to the young persons' speaking abilities. That is, the more access that the child and the family had to paved roads and all that they led to, the more apt the child and family were to speak English. Conversely, the more remote and isolated the family was from the many influences of the English-speaking world, the more apt the family members were to speak only Navajo (Spolsky, 1970).

The Navajo Nation today is a fundamentally different place from what it was 30 years ago. Only the most isolated and remote communities remain unconnected to the reservation highway system. Telephones, cell phones, electricity, cable and satellite television, and solar-powered 12-volt electricity systems that support radio, television, VCRs, the internet, and the like, are all widely available. Trading posts, which used to serve as information hubs in the communicative economies of reservation communities, have been replaced by 7–11 convenience stores owned by off-reservation, non-Navajo, English-dominant interests. Navajos' intermarriage with non-Navajos has increased dramatically.

Simply put, the Navajo Nation is no longer isolated from the rest of the world. There is little question in the minds of many Navajo language activists that these aspects of modern living, while representative of progress and helpful in many other respects, are intimately and cumulatively connected to the social fact of less and less Navajo. This is especially the case among Navajo youth and all of which renders the fine-grained analysis of the Navajo situation *vis-à-vis* Fishman's Graded Intergenerational Disruption Scale so vital.

Navajo Language in Terms of the GIDS

The present section analyses the vitality of the Navajo language specifically in terms of each of the eight stages of Fishman's Graded Intergenerational Disruption Scale (GIDS). As is described in each of the chapters of this book, the GIDS posits a stage-by-stage continuum of disruptions to a language's existence and continuity. The further the stage number from Stage 1, the greater the disruption and threat to the prospects for the language being passed on from one generation to the next. Fishman reported that Stage 6 on the GIDS, involving the intergenerational transmission of the heritage language from adult to child within home, neighbourhood, and community contexts, is an especially crucial period for reversing language shift. As we describe below, the Navajo Nation is experiencing significant change regarding language use in these critical contexts.

Stage 8: Reassembling the languages and/or acquiring them on an individual basis during adulthood

Fishman reported in *Reversing Language Shift* that the Navajo language is not 'so far gone' that it needs to be reassembled as a linguistic system. This characterisation is still accurate. There are a great number of Navajo speakers, even if the majority of speakers are adults and smaller percentages of children acquire Navajo as their first language. A standardised, widely accepted orthography developed by Robert Young and William Morgan has been in place since the 1930s (Young, 1992). Dictionaries and numerous learning materials document oral and written Navajo and promote its acquisition. Schools and curriculum centres have developed materials for teaching Navajo language at elementary and secondary levels. Since the mid-1980s, Diné College, the institution of higher education of the Navajo Nation, has had in place eight 300- and 400-level courses in Navajo language and linguistics; more than 600 Navajos have taken all eight courses (Slate, forthcoming). Navajo language is nowhere near GIDS Stage 8 some 10 years after Fishman first described the scale. Yet, given the sharp decrease in Navajo youths' abilities to speak Navajo, the language is decidedly more imperiled than it was a decade ago.

Stage 7: The maintenance of a vibrant and natural adult Xish-speaking society

Fishman wrote in 1991 that interactions in adult community life among Navajos take place primarily in Navajo, especially with neighbours and in local community activities. This characterisation is still true. Since most Navajo adults are bilingual, social context for the most part determines the choice of language. The majority of Navajo speakers today who choose to speak Navajo language most or all of the time are adults who are 30 years of age and older.

Traditional Navajo religious ceremonies and local chapter meetings are contexts in which Navajo language is still widely used among adults. Although the Native American Church is largely a pan-Indian religion, as we have described, on the Navajo reservation it is also a context where Navajo language is widely used. However, English is becoming more predominant among bilingual Navajos in other contexts. In Navajo tribal governance activities, other than at local chapter meetings, there is notice-ably more English spoken among adults both in addition to and in lieu of Navajo (Holm, 1995). English is predominant in tribal committee meetings, judiciary proceedings, tribal council meetings, and everyday activities of tribal employees.

An important factor that is operative in the choice of language involves the boarding school experiences of older adults, now in their fifties and sixties, who were removed from their homes and sent to school hundreds of miles away in the 1950s. Their experiences in English-only submersion were formative. Many individuals came back home determined to raise their children as English speakers so that they would not endure the hard-ships that the Navajo speakers encountered (Batchelder & Markel, 1997). Others were determined to regain and retain the language and culture that the boarding schools had aimed to erase (Sells-Dick & McCarty, 1997).

Ten years ago, Fishman stated that the most crucial Navajo-RLS efforts were not at the Stage 7 level because many Navajos are still speakers of their native language. However, as fluent Navajo monolingual adults and bilin-gual adults get older and English monolingual Navajos reach adulthood, the Navajo language may well move closer to this stage. Consequently, the utili-sation of Navajo for RLS purposes will become more important.

Stage 6: Creating the intergenerationally continuous Xish-speaking community via providing and stressing the link to family life, residential concentration and neighbourhood institutions

Weakening intergenerational transmission of the native language repre-sents the biggest change to Navajo over the last 10 years. Linkages between adults and youths in home, family, and community contexts through oral Navajo are increasingly diminishing. As we explain in the next section, it is at this stage that revitalisation efforts need to be concentrated, and to which all subsequent stages must also contribute, to prevent further erosion of the Navajo language.

Several recent studies have examined the level of Navajo spoken among Navajo people: all indicate a trend toward the rapidly decreasing use of Navajo among young children (Holm, 1993; Parsons-Yazzie, 1996; and Platero, 1992). The shift away from Navajo has been both decisive and swift. In the late 1960s, Bernard Spolsky (1969) surveyed the language abilities of Navajo six-year-olds and found 95% to be speakers of Navajo. In addition, 73% were determined to speak Navajo as well as or better than English. Twenty-three years later, Paul Platero (1992) evaluated Navajo-speaking abilities among children at Head Start centres. He found that over half of 682 Navajo children were monolingual speakers of English. More recently, Wayne Holm (1993) conducted a survey of kindergartners in all the elementary schools both on and off the reservation with a majority of Navajos and with some 3300 students in the sample. Less than one-third were rated by teachers as fluent in Navajo. Half (52%) had limited Navajo-speaking ability, most (87%) had at least passive knowledge of the language, and a few (13%) had no knowledge, not even passive knowledge, of Navajo.

In a qualitative study of Navajo language attrition, Evangeline Parsons-Yazzie (1995 and 1996) identified six reasons invoked by the adult Navajo speakers to explain why Navajo children do not acquire Navajo:

- English has become the common language among family and friends, especially when the child is away from the immediate and extended family.

- Children often spend a great deal of time away from immediate families in off-reservation settings where English greatly outweighs Navajo both in terms of usage and prestige.

- Many Navajo children are culturally ambivalent about Navajo. Internalising the lack of cultural identification of their parents, these young persons harbour shame for their own culture and hostility toward the language. Parsons-Yazzie described how this ambivalence produces language shift at the level of dyad: a monolingual Navajo-speaking grandmother talks to her grandchild in Navajo, the child answers in English. Parents of other children in Parsons-Yazzie's study explained that their children were ashamed of the Navajo language because they were afraid that their friends would laugh at them for attempting to speak it.

- While they can speak Navajo, some parents prefer to speak only English in the home to ensure their child's academic success in school.
- Some parents do not speak Navajo to children simply because they did not think that Navajo speaking abilities are important to later success in life.
- Finally, parents explained the lack of their children's and grandchildren's speaking abilities in Navajo as a function of English-only, or English-primarily, instruction at school. In nearly all cases, academic success is predicated on skills in speaking, reading, and writing English. Moreover, the majority of Navajo-speaking employees with whom many Navajo children have daily contact are bus drivers, teacher aides, and janitors, whose language skills become associated in children's eyes to the lower socioeconomic stations that these Navajo adults occupy in school hierarchies.

A more recent study sheds light on Navajo language use and attitudes among Navajo teenagers (Lee, 1999). In a sample of some 200 Navajo adolescents from five reservation secondary schools, students rated Navajo and English usage in five contexts which included: (1) how much students heard adults in their family speak Navajo and English among other adults; (2) how much adults spoke Navajo and English to the students; (3) how much the students spoke Navajo and English to adults; (4) how much students spoke Navajo and English with siblings; and (5) how much students heard Navajo and English in their community. The students rated Navajo language use in the five contexts according to a scale that read: 'only Navajo', 'mostly Navajo/some English', 'half and half Navajo and English', 'mostly English/some Navajo', and 'only English'. In the first context, the students reported to hear adults in their family speak mostly Navajo and some English. In the other four contexts, the students reported that equal proportions of Navajo and English were used. The teenagers still hear and speak much Navajo, but except for language spoken between adults only, English is equivalent to the amount of Navajo heard and spoken in their families and communities.

A comparison between the students early and then later in life showed differences in some of the categories. There was no change in how often adult family members spoke Navajo and English over the years, but students reported to hear increasingly more English than Navajo in community settings. The students also reported to speak more Navajo to their siblings and adult family members as they got older. That the teenagers in this sample spoke more Navajo as they got older, and in the process became more conscious of the imperilled status of the language, could reflect an important emerging trend.

Traditional religious contexts represent the strongest areas of Navajo reinforcement between adults and youth, precisely because they are where Navajo has higher status and utility than English. On average, approximately half of the students surveyed in Lee's study (1999) reported to participate in traditional or NAC ceremonies (111 out of 215). Slightly more than half participated in these religious ceremonies when they were under age 13 (125 out of 215). There was a slight reduction in how many participated over time. The students reported to hear either only Navajo or mostly Navajo in both traditional ceremonies and NAC meetings. The figures give some indication that Navajo is still widely used in traditional and NAC religious settings and that a fairly large number of Navajo youth participate in these ceremonies. The students were at least hearing Navajo language; we do not know how much they were speaking the language during ceremonies.

There was a significant difference, however, between the amount of Navajo and English heard during these ceremonies from the time the student was under age 13 to their present age (16 and above). The students heard less Navajo and more English at their present age than when they were several years younger. This suggests religious contexts that have been the strongest in Navajo language use are slowly but increasingly being influenced by the English dominant world.

Stage 5: Literacy via community schools that do not aim at meeting the compulsory education requirements

Schools utilise four approaches with regard to Navajo language and literacy instruction: (1) no Navajo; (2) Navajo as a means to learn English; (3) Navajo-as-supplemental; and (4) Navajo-as-integral (Holm & Holm, 1995). No matter the differences in Navajo language and literacy instructional approaches, all schools attempt to meet compulsory education requirements. In other words, there are no 'literacy via community schools' that do not aim to meet compulsory education requirements.

Stage 4a: Schools that are under Xish control and that can be attended in lieu of compulsory education

Of the total number of schools serving Navajo students, fewer than 10% are under the control of local reservation communities and the Navajo Nation as a whole. Of this total, only a handful of schools have implemented Navajo-as-integral programmes over the past 30 years. These schools include: Rough Rock, Ramah, Borrego Pass, Black Mesa, Little

Singer, Navajo Prep, and most successfully, Rock Point (Holm & Holm, 1990; McLaughlin, 1989 and 1992; Rosier & Holm, 1980). Students have been taught to read and write in Navajo before English at these schools. They have been expected to develop Navajo language abilities in every grade until graduation. In high school, Navajo is the medium of instruction for many courses, and the co-medium of instruction for all courses. Students are also expected to take Navajo content courses such as Navajo government, history, economics, and sociology all taught in Navajo. Holm and Holm (1995) reported that despite favourable data showing the effectiveness of these schools in student achievement and Navajo literacy, these programmes have not been widely replicated in other schools.

The funding situation of these schools has not changed: they are still dependent on the federal government, state government, or a combination of the two. One high school that established itself with the intention of making Navajo integral to its curriculum chose to seek state funding because of continual under-funding by the federal government. This institution's Navajo language programme is now a supplemental programme because of the concerns to meet state accreditation requirements and of concerns to continue receiving state funding (Lee, 1997).

Stage 4b: Schools for Xish pupils but under Yish control

Most of the schools on the reservation fall under GIDS category 4b. Nearly 9 of every 10 Navajo students attend public schools that are regulated by state departments of education in Arizona, New Mexico or Utah. The staffing in some cases may be largely Navajo, but the curriculum, operations, and personnel are governed by non-Navajo entities. School board positions in many instances are held by local Navajos, but the positions are constrained by state laws and policies when it comes to implementing elaborate Navajo language programmes, assuming that the schools are interested in implementing such programmes.

Several public schools have more serious school-wide Navajo language programmes than there were 10 years ago: at Fort Defiance, Window Rock, Chinle, Tuba City, Kayenta, and Monument Valley, Utah. All 11 Navajo majority public school districts in Arizona teach Navajo to meet the state's mandate to teach a native or foreign language. In addition, San Juan School District in southeastern Utah has begun to implement school-wide Navajo language and literacy programmes in each of the schools in the Utah strip of the Navajo Nation (Holm, 1999).

At the same time, only 10% of all K-12 Navajo students receive instruction in or about Navajo language and culture. Compounding the problem from language revitalisation perspectives, most school-based Navajo language and literacy programmes treat Navajo as supplemental education, thereby reinforcing English as the 'real' language of the school. The few monolingual Navajo-speaking children in elementary schools are linguistically isolated. They quickly learn that English is more valued than Navajo because it is the language of instruction, the language of their peers, the language of the tribe and community, and the language of the mainstream society. For young Navajos who are monolingual English speakers, the section of the day that is slated for Navajo language may be the only time these students interact with the language.

By high school, Navajo language programmes lessen dramatically. Most are the equivalent to a foreign language class. Lee found that in a sample of five school-based bilingual programmes, bilingual staff persons tended to speak English predominantly outside of the classroom. The teachers of Navajo language courses are also isolated and unsure how to teach a group of students that have a wide range in Navajo speaking and comprehension abilities. Most often, the teacher utilises the more fluent students as tutors for more limited students, thereby limiting the more fluent students' progress and development in Navajo. Many high school teachers of Navajo also complain of the limited resources available for secondary teaching. They state that the school's administration is unaware or unable to help locate more resources or provide more support. Consequently, students receive very basic instruction with modest to low expectations regardless of their speaking ability (Lee, 1999).

A successful Navajo immersion programme at Fort Defiance has provided precedence for programmes that can aid at reversing language shift in a type 4b school (Arviso & Holm, 1990). The goal of the K-5 programme has been to promote children's acquisition of oral and written Navajo. Kindergarteners and first graders spend the school day with communication and instruction almost entirely in Navajo language. Second and third graders spend half the day in Navajo and half in English. Evaluations of third and fourth graders have indicated that the immersion programme students do as well as monolingual English students in tests on English language ability, and the immersion students have done considerably better on tests of Navajo language ability. The majority of monolingual English students have actually tested worse in Navajo language ability than they did as kindergartners. The immersion students have benefited from this programme in a type 4b school with regard to their Navajo language abilities without falling behind, and even surpassing in some subject areas, their classmates in traditional monolingual English classrooms.

Stages 3, 2, and 1: Work sphere, mass media, higher education and government

At the risk of overgeneralising, it is safe to say that the use of Navajo has become concentrated among Navajo adults, and that Navajo language use is decreasing among children and youth and being replaced by English. In governance activities, which also make up a large portion of the work sphere, Navajo is used regularly in local chapter meetings. At tribal council meetings, Navajo is spoken. However, records are kept in English, so all Navajo is translated into English. English is seldom translated into Navajo. Committee meetings, which council delegates attend, tend to have more English than in whole council sessions. The President and Vice-President of the Navajo Nation are required to be fluent in Navajo. Council delegates are not. There are a few council delegates today who have limited or no speaking abilities in Navajo.

The Navajo tribe and businesses on the reservation require Navajo preference in hiring. Navajo language ability is not always considered a factor but is usually a hiring preference. Few high level tribal positions require Navajo language ability. Written Navajo is rarely used in tribal government operations. English is the written language and language of control for state and federal offices serving Navajo populations as well.

The Navajo court systems utilise Navajo and English. When all participants speak English, the court proceedings most often utilise English. All court documents are in English. State and federal courts serving Navajo populations make interpreters available when requested

Radio and newspaper media are largely English dominant. Radio stations on the borders of the reservation broadcast some Navajo news, music, advertising, and public service announcements. In addition to these Navajo programmes, the Navajo tribal station, KTNN, broadcasts Navajo Presidential reports, special events, sporting events, obituaries, and announcements about traditional events all in the Navajo language. All the same, the majority of the radio broadcasting across the reservation is in English. Moreover, younger Navajos are more likely to listen only to music or programming in English.

Newspapers that reach communities on the reservation are written almost entirely in English. The tribal newspaper, the *Navajo Times,* produces one page devoted to Navajo language, with puzzles, short stories, and vocabulary games for readers to complete. Most road signs are in English. Some advertisements, billboards, and brochures use some written Navajo, such as phrases or words, and often poorly spelled. One community school prints a newspaper and runs a local television station with Navajo language and content.

Affirmation of the GIDS – and What that Means in the Navajo Situation

In this section we measure our analysis of the health of the Navajo language in terms of the Graded Intergenerational Disruption Scale (GIDS). Before doing so directly, we want to point out that good things are taking place regarding the continuity of oral and written Navajo. In the past several years, the Diné Language Teachers Association has grown impressively from a very small group of dedicated activists to a much larger group of dedicated activists; more than 200 have attended each of its quarterly meetings in the previous year. The Diné Teacher Education Program at Diné College has produced its first group of Navajo language teachers with bachelor's degrees; interest in the programme is growing. Most significantly, the tribe has ordered that Navajo be the language of instruction in each of the Head Start centres, more than 160 strong, that it manages. Head Start personnel are presently piloting the development of Navajo immersion programmes, utilising the Maori model, in 12 centres in locations within each of the nation's five bureau agencies. More individuals from ever diverse walks of life and persuasion are recognising the imperilled state of the Navajo language and beginning to act to reverse the slide.

That's the good news. The bad news is that GIDS makes imminent sense in the Navajo context. The eight stages of the scale force us to analyse in fine-grained detail what is happening, and why we are losing the language. The scale forces us to acknowledge that the intergenerational transmission of Navajo is under ever-increasing assault, and that English is taking over. The central tenet of the GIDS, that successful RLS efforts must key in on the transmission of the language from one generation to the next inside family, neighbourhood, and community contexts, is borne out in our situation.

Facets of the problem are many. Critical linkages across generations inside the family, that once ensured that youngsters would acquire Navajo as their native language, are breaking down. The status and attraction of

Table 2.1 What one person can do

1	If you are a speaker of the native language, take and encourage others to take the initiative to help latent- and non-speakers learn. They must also not make fun of people struggling to learn.
2	Use existing language learning materials to teach and learn the native language.
3	Utilise taped stories to teach and learn the native language.
4	Create your own teaching and learning tapes, dialogues, and materials with the help of native speakers.

Table 2.2 What pairs of persons can do

1	Utilise immersion language teaching and learning techniques, i.e. the native speaker provides understandable input, the learner uses whatever native language he or she can, as well as English if necessary.
2	Develop a 'contract' between speaker and non-speaker that stipulates where and when to use the native language.
3	Utilise one-on-one researching and interviewing techniques to generate teaching and learning materials.
4	Use exchanges of letters, tapes, and other learning materials to learn and teach the native language.

Table 2.3 What families can do

1	Help individuals and families resolve the 'shame issue', i.e. the shaming of non-speakers and limited speakers who must struggle to learn the native language.
2	Develop a 'contract' among family-based speakers and non-speakers that stipulates where and when to use the native language and how to help non-speakers acquire it.
3	Encourage family gatherings that focus on language teaching and learning activities.
4	Organise family-based summertime language immersion activities.
5	Organise family-based weekend language immersion activities.
6	Encourage families to limit the intrusion of English-language media (i.e. television and videos) and to insert native language teaching and learning in that vacuum.
7	Organise parental support groups that focus on native language teaching and learning.
8	Encourage families of speakers in culturally appropriate ways to help families of non-speakers learn the native language.

non-native cultural elements to native youths and their families are pushing out opportunities for native language acquisition. The consciousness levels of families about the threat of language loss tend to be low. Many times, native speakers are critical and insensitive to the needs of non-, latent-, and less-proficient speakers, and thus inhibit the development and stabilisation of the language. Youth have reported on their unwillingness to develop their skills in Navajo because of the ridicule or reprimands they have experienced when speaking the language. Native language is inseparable from cultural identity and spirituality. In some cases, where schools in native communities are teaching native language and literacy, clarity about language, identity, culture, and spirituality is

Table 2.4 What communities can do

1	Encourage elders at senior citizens centres and other similar organisations to interact with and promote native language teaching and learning for younger groups of non-speakers.
2	Develop language nests at local preschools and Head Start Centres utilising the Maori model.
3	Organise fine-arts and dramatic productions that utilise and promote the native language.
4	Put up signs in the native language in different community settings (make sure they are written in standard form).
5	Organise community seminars that utilise the native language to focus on and solve other issues and problems.
6	Develop language institutes (for families and communities) that provide opportunities for non- and latent-speakers to learn the native language through intensive teaching and learning techniques.
7	Develop programmes for parents of children in bilingual programs; they, too, need to learn and utilise the native language.
8	Create 'banks' of language learning materials for individuals, families, and native organisations.
9	Organise community-focused meetings and conferences about native language loss and revitalisation issues.
10	Organise conferences and symposia in the native language on native plants and other culturally relevant topics.
11	Adapt 'Natural Way', 'Community Language Learning', and other appropriate teaching methods to teach and develop the native language.
12	Encourage individuals and organisations to explore teaching methods that will work in their communities.

lost. Many parents, grandparents, and educators ask, 'Whose business is it to teach native language?' 'It's the family's business', many educators say. 'It's the school's business', many families respond. New strategies must be designed and implemented in social engineering ways. However, many times the design and use of such strategies are consciously imposed. For this reason, there is often reluctance to use them. The GIDS helps us identify many of these painful issues.

More importantly, in forcing us to sift through the myriad complexities of the phenomenon, the GIDS facilitates individual agency. It enables individuals and groups of individuals to visualise what can and ought to be done. At a gathering of language activists several years ago (in which Daniel McLaughlin participated), lists of activities were developed that could be engaged at the levels of individual, pair of individuals, family, and community (CIWG, 1994). We have updated those lists, and recount them here. These activities provide operative links that are necessary for intergenerational transmission between family and community as discussed in Stage 6 of the GIDS. The activities encourage both Navajo speakers and non-speakers to engage themselves in learning and helping others to learn Navajo language. Table 4, in particular, lists activities that promote transmission of Navajo language at the community level. These activities address the community involvement that is necessary for reversing language shift.

Beyond actions that must be done in order to facilitate the intergenerational transmission of Navajo, there are overtly political and ideological actions that help to create conditions for language revitalisation:

- Air radio announcements that encourage individuals to learn the native language and not shame non-speakers.
- Air speakers' testimonials in support of the native language.
- Inform the general public about the virtues of bilingualism.
- Encourage speakers of the native language to use it at conferences about language use.
- Create 'If You Care About The Native Language, Use It' and 'I Speak the Native Language to My Child' posters, bumper-stickers, radio ads, buttons, T-shirts – in the native language.
- Publicise as widely and as much as possible information on the threat of native language loss.
- Encourage parents and grandparents to use and teach the native language.
- Document the success, or lack thereof, of different reversing-language-shift efforts.
- Explain as widely as possible that western-based institutions like schools cannot rescue the native language; parents, families, and native communities must deal directly with the issue of language loss.

Conclusion

What we have attempted to do in this chapter is provide an update on the Navajo situation that would serve readers of *Reversing Language Shift* (1991) and of this book as well. Our chapter also provides an update that would clarify the utility of Joshua Fishman's work insofar as Navajo language revitalisation is concerned, and that would support language activists within the Navajo Nation. The true measure of our effectiveness in addressing these purposes, of course, is not limited to the confines of these pages. In this regard, we are reminded of the wise words of Paulo Freire and Myles Horton, who in their book, *We Make the Road by Walking* (Freire & Horton, 1990), indicate what *must* come next. 'Without practice there is no knowledge', they explain. 'We have to have a certain theoretical kind of practice in order to know also' (pp. 97–8).

By this, we take Freire and Horton to mean that what comes next must centre around a commitment to the radical democratic belief in the inherent right of all peoples to self-determination and self-emancipation; a commitment to translating what we may understand about the knowledge/power axis to praxis; a dedication not merely to the development of more authentic descriptions of what is going on, i.e. how language shifts, but also to connecting those descriptions to processes of authentic social change. Our work must not only serve as an incitement to discourse but also as an incitement to action. We hope to have contributed to this end.

References

Arviso, M. and Holm, W. (1990) Native American language immersion programs: Can there be bilingual education when the language is going (or gone) as a child language? *Journal of Navajo Education* VIII(1), 39–47.

Batchelder, A. and Markel, S. (1997) An initial exploration of the Navajo Nation's language and culture initiative. In J. Reyhner (ed.) *Teaching Indigenous Languages* (pp. 239–47). Flagstaff, AZ: Northern Arizona University.

Community Issues Working Group (CIWG) (1994) Handouts on strategies for promoting Native languages in home, family, and community contexts. Developed at the Roundtable on Stabilizing Indigenous Languages: Creating an Agenda for Reversing Language Shift. Northern Arizona University, Flagstaff, AZ, 16–18 November.

Fishman, J. (1991) *Reversing Language Shift*. Clevedon: Multilingual Matters.

Freire, P. and Horton, M. (1990) *We Make the Road by Walking: Conversations on Education and Social Change*. B. Bell, J. Gaventa and J. Peters (eds). Philadelphia, PA: Temple University Press.

Holm, A. & Holm, W. (1995) Navajo language education: Retrospect and prospect. *Bilingual Research Journal* 19, 141–67.

Holm W. (1993) A very preliminary analysis of Navajo kindergartners' language abilities. Unpublished manuscript. Window Rock, Navajo Nation, AZ: Division of Diné Education.

Holm, W. (1994) Current status of Navajo language. Office of Dine Culture, Language, and Community Services. Unpublished manuscript. Window Rock, Navajo Nation, AZ: Office of Diné Language, Culture, and Community Services.

Holm, W. (1995) Navajo language use today by domain. Proposal for Native

American Language Act funding. Unpublished manuscript. Window Rock, Navajo Nation, AZ: Office of Diné Language, Culture, and Community Services.

Holm, W. (1997) Current status of Navajo language – update. Proposal for Native American Language Act funding. Window Rock, Navajo Nation, AZ: Office of Diné Language, Culture, and Community Services.

Holm, W. (1999) Navajo Nation language project: current status of Navajo language. Proposal for Native American Language Act funding. Window Rock, Navajo Nation, AZ: Office of Diné Language, Culture, and Community Services.

Holm, W. and Holm, A. (1990) Rock Point, A Navajo Way to Go to School: A Valediction. _Annals, AASSP_ 508, 170–84.

Krauss, M. (1992) The worlds' languages in crises. _Language_ 68, 6–10.

Lee, T. (1999) Sources of influence over Navajo adolescent language attitudes and behavior. Unpublished dissertation. Stanford, CA: Stanford University.

Lee, T. (1997) Navajo language programs in sixteen Navajo high schools. Unpublished dissertation proposal. Stanford, CA: Stanford University.

McLaren, P. (1993) Narrative structure, colonial amnesia, and decentered subjects: Towards a critical pedagogy of postmodern identity formation. In D. McLaughlin and W. Tierney (eds) _Naming Silenced Lives: Personal Narratives for Change in Educational Setting_ (pp. 201–35. New York: Routledge.

McLaughlin, D. (1992) _When Literacy Empowers: Navajo Language in Print_. Albuquerque, NM: University of New Mexico Press.

McLaughlin, D. (1989) The sociolinguistics of Navajo literacy. _Anthropology and Education Quarterly_ 20(4), 275–90.

Parsons-Yazzie, E. (1995) A study of reasons for Navajo language attrition as perceived by Navajo-speaking parents. Unpublished dissertation. Flagstaff, AZ: Northern Arizona University.

Parsons-Yazzie, E. (1996) Perceptions of selected Navajo elders regarding Navajo language attrition. _Journal of Navajo Education_ XII(2), 51–7.

Platero, P. (1992) Navajo Head Start language study. Window Rock, Navajo Nation, AZ: Division of Diné Education.

Reddy, M.A. (1993) Statistical record of Native North America. Detroit, MI: Gale Research, Inc.

Rodgers, L. (1993) _Chapter Images_, 1992 Edition. Window Rock, Navajo Nation, AZ: Division of Community Development.

Rosier, P. and Holm, W. (1980) _The Rock Point Experience: A Longitudinal Study of a Navajo School Program (Saad Naaki Bee Na'nitin)_. Washington, DC: Center for Applied Linguistics.

Sells-Dick, G. and McCarty, T. (1997) Reclaiming Navajo: Language renewal in an American Indian community school. In N. Hornberger (ed.) _Indigenous Literacies in the Americas: Language Planning from the Bottom Up_ (pp. 69–94). The Hague: Mouton.

Slate, C. (forthcoming) _Promoting Advanced Navajo Language Scholarship_. Tsaile, AZ: Diné Teacher Education Program, Diné College.

Spolsky, B. (1969) _The Navajo Reading Study_. Albuquerque, NM: Linguistics Department, University of New Mexico.

Spolsky, B. (1970) _The Navajo Reading Study_. Navajo Language Maintenance: Six-

Year-Olds in 1969. Progress Report #5. Albuquerque, NM: University of New Mexico.

Spolsky, B. and Irvine, P. (1982) Sociolinguistic aspects of the acceptance of literacy in the vernacular. In F. Barkin, E. Brandt and J. Ornstein-Galicia (eds) *Bilingualism and Language Contact: Spanish, English, and Native American Language* (pp. 73–9). New York: Teachers College Press.

Young, R. (1992) The evolution of written Navajo: an historical sketch. *Journal of Navajo Education* Vol. X(3), 46–55.

Chapter 3

How Threatened is the Spanish of New York Puerto Ricans?
Language Shift with vaivén

O. GARCÍA, J.L. MORÍN and K. RIVERA

Introduction

TV viewers nationwide have been fascinated by the New York life portrayed in 'Seinfeld'. Unlike the violence or the glamour usually associated with New York in the media, 'Seinfeld' put us in contact with daily life in New York among white, middle class New Yorkers. But when the penultimate episode portrayed Kramer accidentally setting fire to the Puerto Rican flag and stomping on it to put it out, the Puerto Rican community in New York, joined by many other New Yorkers, demonstrated and picketed.

The protest was important not only because of the message it sent to the media and the public at large about Puerto Rican pride and presence in New York, but also because it tells us something about where the New York Puerto Rican community is in relation to the rest of the New York community in terms of social power and prestige, identity, and especially language.

In the last two decades, many Puerto Ricans in New York have become regular viewers of English language TV shows like Seinfeld. Rarely do they need the Spanish language TV of *Univisión*, *Telemundo*, and *Galavisión*, although they´re still avid viewers of Spanish TV *novelas* [soap operas]. The bilingualism of Puerto Ricans, and even the shift to English of some, especially when compared to more recently arrived immigrant Latino groups, is pervasive. Yet, although they are increasingly English speaking, as we will see, they continue to self-categorise as Puerto Ricans, Hispanics or Latinos, using features of culture and language to do so. The Anglo majority also categorises them socially as Hispanics, using race, poverty, and colonial status to do so.

New York Puerto Ricans' use of the media and the way they´re there

44

portrayed is indicative in this regard. Culturally, although many watch English language television, many Puerto Ricans continue to enjoy the *novelas* which some TV stations are now transmitting with English subtitles, and TV Spanish music shows which do not demand full competence in Spanish. Socially, the media continues to portray New York Puerto Ricans negatively, much like the angry mob of New York Puerto Rican parade-goers who overturned Jerry´s car in the Seinfeld episode. It is the different direction that language takes from that of culture on the one hand and social prestige and power on the other that distinguishes the New York Puerto Rican community from other US ethnolinguistic groups in the study of language maintenance and shift.

Whereas many other US ethnolinguistic groups have achieved social and cultural integration as a result of their linguistic assimilation, the same has not happened with Puerto Ricans (see especially Urciuoli, 1997, Zentella, 1997a). Although increasingly English speaking, Puerto Ricans remain culturally and socially as separate from a US Anglo mainland identity, as the island, with its commonwealth colonial status, does from the United States. As a result of Puerto Rico's continuing colonial relationship to the United States, Puerto Ricans in the United States resemble, as Ogbu (1988) explains, a 'caste group', more similar to African Americans than to other immigrant groups.

Whether one categorises Puerto Ricans in the United States as a caste group or a 'colonised group' (Blauner, 1972), Puerto Ricans, along with Native Americans and African Americans, were forced into minority status through conquest and domination and face harsher and more persistent forms of discrimination than other racial and ethnic groups in the United States. Consequently, Puerto Ricans occupy a place in society from which social integration and assimilation becomes more difficult than for other immigrant groups such as European immigrants. These European immigrants are racially and culturally more similar to the dominant society and, to a larger extent, voluntarily come to the United States. Indeed, colonialism permeates the Puerto Rican experience. The colonial status of the island follows Puerto Ricans to the United States, where persistent discrimination and inequality are expressions of this status.

Yet, it is also the process of language shift itself that has distinguishing characteristics in the case of Puerto Ricans. As Puerto Ricans in the United States become bilingual and even English monolingual speakers, they hold on to selective features and signs of Spanish in different forms of discourse at different times, refusing to yield totally in semiotic character to English, the language of the coloniser. Although as we will see, shift to English is proceeding at the normal historical pace of three generations (see Fishman

1970, 1991; Fishman *et al.*, 1971), and Spanish language maintenance is not more than an ideal, the colonial status of the island is reflected in the linguistic *vaivén* (literally, coming and going, to-and-fro motion) of Spanish signs that continue to crop up in the English of New York Puerto Ricans who have shifted to English. The colonial status resonates in the effort English monolingual Puerto Ricans make to give linguistic expression to the *commmonwealth*, finding a *common way* of communicating, if only partially, with Spanish monolingual Puerto Ricans, and marking their distance from an Anglo identity.

Unlike ethnolinguistic groups who have completely relinguified, New York Puerto Ricans use this linguistic *vaivén* not only to mark their identity, but also to connect with the political reality of the island. This *vaivén* is also a product of the colonial stigmatisation to which New York Puerto Ricans have been subjected by the Anglo majority. Yet, like the steps of the *chá-chá-chá* of the 1950s which the word *vaivén* connotes ('*Cógele bien el compás, cógele bien el compás, cógele el vaivén, cógele el vaivén, de ese ritmo que se llama cha-cha-chá*' ['Get the beat right, get the beat right, get the coming and going, get the coming and going, of that rhythm that is called cha-cha-chá']), the linguistic *vaivén* neither brings about movement to a new space, nor harps back to an old space. The linguistic space of New York Puerto Ricans, even as English shift has occurred, continues to be marked by speaking English with Spanish linguistic and extra-linguistic signs.

This linguistic *vaivén* has little to do with the metaphorical code-switching of other US ethnolinguistic groups (see Gumperz, 1982), for besides acting as a cultural marker of identity, it acts as a societal and polit-ical marker, enabling New York Puerto Ricans to capture the physical world of their colonised island, while suggesting the distance kept by the Anglo majority. While metaphorical code-switching is usually associated with intracultural features of bicultural identity within a micro sociolinguistic framework, the concept of linguistic *vaivén* suggests intercultural sociopolitical shifts possible within a macro sociology of language framework especially as globalisation affects society in the new millennium and as oppression of ethnolinguistic minorities is increasingly recognised.

This paper contextualises the two related characteristics which define and distinguish the language space of New York Puerto Ricans from that of other US ethnolinguistic groups:

- The continued divergence between language on the one hand, and culture and social stigmatisation on the other; that is, language shift has not been always accompanied by cultural assimilation or structural incorporation.

- The continued *vaivén* of Spanish features after language shift, that is, the language shift of New York Puerto Ricans, recovers some common territory when in the presence of speakers of the ancestral language.

The question this paper then sets out to explore is whether this qualitative difference, created by a unique context in which colonised Spanish-speakers migrate back and forth, to-and-fro (both physically and emotionally), between their Spanish-speaking colony and one of the greatest English-speaking metropolises in the world, has any effect on the concept of language shift and of reversing language shift as proposed by Fishman in 1991. We turn first to an in-depth analysis of the colonial status of Puerto Rico.

Puerto Rico: 500 years of Colonialism – and Counting

A brief examination of the historical and present-day relationship between the United States and Puerto Rico provides insights into the many ways in which Puerto Rico's colonial status shapes the cultural and linguistic traditions of Puerto Ricans on the island and in the United States.

In 1493, on his second voyage to what is now known as the Americas, Columbus claimed the island of Borinquén, as it was known to the Taíno people, for the Spanish (Figueroa, 1977). Colonialism has persisted in Puerto Rico ever since. By the 1800s, Puerto Ricans, having developed their own cultural identity derived from native, European and African roots, sought to pursue their own political destiny separate and apart from Spain. But the island's autonomy from Spain achieved in 1897 through the Autonomic Charter was short-lived (Trías Monge 1977).

The United States, which had longed to possess Puerto Rico to gain military and economic advantage as part of its global expansionist strategy, took Puerto Rico as 'war booty' as a result of its war with Spain in 1898. Without consultation, Puerto Rico and Puerto Ricans were passed on from one owner to another (Maldonado-Denis, 1972). General Nelson Miles, who gained considerable notoriety in his military campaigns against Native Americans, was placed in charge of establishing the US authority over Puerto Rico in 1898. According to Fernandez (1994), contrary to Miles' assertions that the US military had come to impart the benefits of the 'liberal institutions' of the US government, military rule and occupation replaced the political autonomy obtained under the 1897 Autonomous Charter and the island's name was immediately changed to 'Porto Rico' to suit North American pronunciation. The Treaty of Paris, which ended the Spanish–American War, granted the United Stated Congress complete authority to decide the political status and civil rights of the inhabitants of the island – plenary power that many in the US Congress argue still resides with the United States (Trías Monge, 1997).

As with Native Americans, indigenous Hawaiians and Filipinos, the conquest of Puerto Rico by the United States included the forced assimilation and imposition of the English language. From 1898 to 1948 without consent of the Puerto Rican people, English became the official language of the public schools of Puerto Rico (Hernandez-Chávez, 1994; Karnow, 1989; Language Policy Task Force, 1992; Trask, 1993). Strong resistance to the English-only policy on the island and the decrease in literacy levels (Walsh, 1991) eventually led to the restoration of Spanish language instruction in the public school. The struggle to return to the use of Spanish language is indicative of the deep reluctance of Puerto Ricans to give up their linguistic and cultural identity. This strong cultural affinity continues to be reflected among Puerto Ricans in New York (as described in more depth later in this article) in their struggle for bilingual education, the establishment of cultural institutions, such as the Museo del Barrio and New York's Puerto Rican Day Parade, a parade which has grown to become the city's largest display of ethnic pride.

The island's political status as a colony inexorably results in a Puerto Rican population in the United States which has not necessarily made a clean break with the island, its people and its culture. The Jones Act which made Puerto Rican citizens of the United States in 1917, not only did not confer full civil and political rights to Puerto Ricans under the US Constitution, but it imposed citizenship on Puerto Ricans in spite of a unanimous vote by the Puerto Rican legislature to retain Puerto Rican citizenship (Fernandez, 1994). US citizenship – along with Puerto Rico's proximity to New York, as a major port of entry into the United States, the advent of air travel, and the availability of relatively low airfares – has permitted Puerto Ricans to travel to the United States with greater ease than those coming from other countries, connecting Puerto Ricans to their homeland in a manner that is unique to any other group that has come to the United States from any other land.

Commonwealth, the term used to describe the status of Puerto Rico since the early 1950s, did not substantively change the colonial nature of the relationship between the United States and the island. In considering the commonwealth designation, the US Congressional record is clear that the Congress' passage of a bill to allow Puerto Rico to adopt a constitution would not fundamentally change the political, economic and social relationship between the island and the United States (Fernandez, 1994, Trías Mónge, 1997). Even after a constitutional convention, ostensibly an exercise in self-government, the US Congress retained the power to amend unilaterally Puerto Rico's constitution and eliminated a section of the constitution modelled after rights conferred under the Universal Declaration of Human Rights (Trías Monge, 1997).

The US asserts its sovereignty over the island and its people, including the power to legislate and exercise control over the most important decisions governing the lives of the people of Puerto Rico (Fernandez, 1994; Lewis, 1974; Maldonado-Denis, 1972; Trías Monge, 1997). Although the United States succeeded in having the United Nations approve the removal of Puerto Rico from the List of Non-Self-Governing Territories in 1953, the United Nations has since reopened the case of Puerto Rico. The United Nations Decolonisation Committee has repeatedly reaffirmed since 1973 'the inalienable right of the people of Puerto Rico to self-determination and independence' (Trías Monge, 1997: 138).

Puerto Rico's colonial status is a fact to which all political parties on the island generally agree (Trías Monge, 1997: 140). Hence, Puerto Ricans living in the United States not only parallel a colonial group experience similar to Native Americans and African Americans, they are intrinsically linked to an ongoing colonial reality in their homeland.

All political parties on the island presently call for the decolonisation of Puerto Rico, with options varying from independence, statehood, or some form of 'enhanced' commonwealth. Those on the island who assert statehood as the means of resolving Puerto Rico's colonial dilemma premise their argument fundamentally on the notion that Puerto Rico's culture can be preserved even as a state of the United States, an assertion that is fervently contested by the other political factions on the island. With respect to language, even the most ardent pro-statehooders want Spanish to remain the language of the people of Puerto Rico, much to the chagrin of certain US Congresspersons. Ironically, those most willing to submit to US sovereignty are adamant in maintaining Spanish as the language of Puerto Rico. Language and the ability to maintain Spanish in Puerto Rico is undoubtedly a critical issue in the debate about Puerto Rico's future political status, with no one on the island willing to concede its demise.

Colonialism has shaped the destiny of Puerto Ricans and has in large part been responsible for the large migration of Puerto Ricans to the United States. US supported economic development schemes such as 'Operation Bootstrap' and 'Fomento' relied on widespread migration of Puerto Ricans to the United States, and to New York in particular, as a form of 'escape valve' for the many rendered unemployed in the major economic transition of the 1940s and 1950s (Maldonado-Denis, 1972: 312). Puerto Ricans have thus brought, and continue to bring with them, to New York and other parts of the United States the legacy and reality of Puerto Rico's colonial situation. Reflected in their experience is the ever-present sense of identity and culture integrally tied to language.

Studies of the Language Use by Puerto Ricans of New York

The language use of the Puerto Rican community in New York, especially that in East Harlem, has been carefully studied since the Language Task Force of the Center for Puerto Rican Studies was set up in the 1970s. In 1971, Fishman *et al.* published their pioneer work on bilingualism among Puerto Ricans in Jersey City. The study examined how Puerto Ricans used code-switching to mark their identity. Based on Fishman´s use of diglossia (1970), the study predicted the complete shift to English of the Puerto Rican community studied, as it documented the lack of functional compartmentalisation of Spanish and English in that community.

The work of the Language Policy Task Force of the Center for Puerto Rican Studies 1980; Pedraza *et al.*, 1980; Pedraza, 1985 as well as the early work of Zentella (1982), challenged the concept of diglossia for Puerto Ricans of East Harlem as proposed by Fishman. It suggested instead that Spanish and English did not exist in separate domains in the East Harlem Puerto Rican community, and that code-switching was a stable mode of expression that did not signal language shift.

In 1980 and 1981 Poplack studied the code-switching of the East Harlem Puerto Rican community, focusing on its syntactic structure. At the end of the 1980s, Poplack (1988), comparing the East Harlem Puerto Rican community to that of Ottawa, argued that the frequent intrasentential switching of New York Puerto Ricans had less rhetorical importance than in Canada, and that it was an established permanent discourse mode in the community.

But in the 1990s, as the New York Puerto Rican community in East Harlem changed radically, follow-up studies indicated that language shift had indeed taken place as the speakers moved away, and as other Spanish speaking groups and African Americans moved into barrios that were once predominantly Puerto Rican. Most important in this regard is the work of Ana Celia Zentella. Her recent book *Growing Up Bilingual. Puerto Rican Children in New York* (1997a) reviews, extends and revises her previous work in the community. Zentella refers to the 'bilingual/multidialectal repertoire' that distinguishes the New York Puerto Rican community

(1997: 41). She identifies three Spanish dialects spoken by the New York Puerto Ricans she studied in East Harlem:

- Standard PR Spanish.
- Popular PR Spanish.
- English-dominant Spanish.

But it is the range of English dialects identified by Zentella that distinguishes the sociolinguistic context of Puerto Rican New Yorkers from other US ethnolinguistic groups:

- Standard NYC English.
- Puerto Rican English.
- African American Vernacular English.
- Hispanised English.

In the case of Puerto Ricans in New York, English is not only the language of power and of the coloniser; it is also the language of African Americans, equally poor and powerless, with whom they increasingly share their lives and their communities. This double identification of English, not only with power, but also with poverty and racial stigmatisation, is also responsible, as we will see, for the linguistic *vaivén* of the shift. The *vaivén* greatly distinguishes Puerto Ricans in New York not only from African Americans but also from other US ethnolinguistic groups who live in less intimacy with African Americans and for whom English is only identified with groups that hold power.

Zentella (1997a) places the East Harlem Puerto Rican community of the 1980s between Stages 5 and 6 on Fishman's Graded Intergenerational Disruption Scale, blaming the greater language shift on 'the reluctance of parents to insist that they be addressed in Spanish, and the widespread use of English in all children's activities' (p.77). Based on the work she conducted in one block (*el bloque*) in the New York Puerto Rican community of East Harlem, and after following for 10 years four of the children of *el bloque* who had become mothers, she is surprised to find 'the shift of child rearing language to English primarily' (p. 240). According to Zentella (1997b), in 13 years *el bloque's* children 'moved conclusively toward the English end of the language proficiency spectrum' (p. 187). But Zentella (1997a) also concludes that 'they [the toddlers observed] seemed to acquire the bilingual skills that would identify them as members of their community' (p. 241). Zentella cautions that one cannot study the parental language behaviour of the New York Puerto Rican community without understanding fears about racial, ethnolinguistic and economic subordination.

She concludes 'parental behaviors change as they pursue a better life for their children, but usually at the expense of Spanish' (p. 243).

An explanation of this phenomenon is given in Bonnie Urciuoli's *Exposing Prejudice: Puerto Rican Experiences of Language, Race, and Class* (1997). Urciuoli's revealing book explains the linguistic behaviour of Puerto Ricans with the concept of 'racialisation'. She claims that Puerto Ricans are seen in racial terms, and that therefore their use of Spanish becomes ideologically problematic in a white Anglo English-speaking world.

The shift to English of the New York Puerto Rican community, coupled with their maintenance of a separate identity and of features of the ancestral language and culture even after shift, is also confirmed in Lourdes Torres (1997) recent study of the Puerto Rican community of Brentwood (a suburb of New York City). Reporting results of a survey, Torres concludes 'across generations, Spanish is used less than English. At the same time, in most cases Puerto Ricans report using both languages rather than either Spanish or English exclusively' (p. 17).

As we approach the new millennium, scholars studying the New York Puerto Rican community continue to confirm the maintenance of their separate identity, a product of their colonial relationship with the United States and the 'racialisation' to which they have been subjected.

At the same time, scholars have been documenting the rapid language shift that is taking place in the community, although the *vaivén* of linguistic features continues, for many, to accompany their separate identity. For New York Puerto Ricans, however, the struggle between succumbing to total shift to English or maintaining Spanish features as a symbol of cultural affiliation and social resistance or even the product of stigmatisation, is an important one. If the language trend of shift continues and if the community gave up its linguistic *vaivén*, barring any change in the political status of the island, the New York Puerto Rican community could become more similar, linguistically and socially, to the African American community, with little promise of equality. The continued use of Spanish linguistic features, even after language shift has taken place among Puerto Ricans, leaves open the possibility of their *vaivén* to the island where they can experience to a large extent being like others, being a majority, being just Puerto Ricans.

We now turn to analysing aspects of the sociolinguistic context of New York Puerto Ricans in the last two decades.

The Early Spanish Language Context of the New York Puerto Rican Community

The early history of the New York Puerto Rican community has been well documented in *Memorias de Bernardo Vega* (see Andreu Iglesias, 1984) as well as in Sánchez-Korrol ([1983], 1994). By the 1920s the 100,000 Puerto Ricans in New York lived predominantly in East Harlem, the Lower East Side (Loisaida) and the Greenpoint section of Brooklyn, around the Navy Yard.

There were many Puerto Rican clubs and associations in East Harlem and the Navy Yard (see Sánchez-Korrol [1983], 1994). By 1940 approximately 70% of the 61,000 Puerto Ricans in New York City lived in Manhattan, mainly in *El Barrio* as East Harlem became known (Zentella 1997a).

The Puerto Rican community in New York grew steadily in the 1940s and 1950s, at a time when there was little foreign immigration into the city as a result of the discriminatory Johnson-Reed Act of 1924, as well as the ensuing depression. In 1940, 88% and in 1950, 83% of Puerto Ricans in the United States were living in New York City (García, 1997). In 1950 there were 246,000 Puerto Ricans in New York City. By then, Puerto Ricans resided mostly in the South Bronx as a result of urban relocation policies (Zentella 1997b). Residential segregation kept the New York Puerto Rican community tightly organised around family and traditions.

It was in public schools where the two cultures and two languages came sharply into contact. In 1949 there were 30,000 Puerto Rican students in New York City schools. In 1956, Puerto Rican students represented one-eighth of the student population, and by 1965 that ratio had increased to one-fifth (*El Diario*, 1993). By the 1970s one-fourth of school children in New York were Puerto Rican, and their dropout rate was an alarming 60% (*El Diario*, 1974). At this time, there were very few Spanish-speaking teachers, and although special classes were formed for Puerto Rican children, many students continued to fail. In 1972 the Puerto Rican Legal Defense and Education Fund filed a lawsuit against the Board of Education of the City of New York on behalf of 15 Puerto Rican schoolchildren and their parents. The suit resulted in court-mandated bilingual education programmes through the Aspira Consent Decree.

Puerto Rican Spanish was brought to the public sphere through bilingual education in an effort to teach children English and educate them bilingually. But as Puerto Rican Spanish made its entrance into the classroom, the Spanish of the schoolchildren themselves was beginning to change, as more and more children started coming from other Latin American countries.

The Immigration Act of 1965 abolished the national origin system, and an influx of other Spanish speakers, as well as immigrants from Asia and Africa, changed, as we will see, the New York City sociolinguistic landscape (García, 1997). In 1970, Puerto Ricans made up 66% of all New York Latinos. By 1980 that figure had decreased to 61%, and 10 years later Puerto Ricans accounted for only 50% of New York Latinos, a proportion likely to be even less because of the large number of undocumented immigrants among other Latinos.

The Influx of Other Spanishes as Puerto Rican Spanish Undergoes Shift

In 1990 Spanish was spoken by one-and-a-half million New Yorkers at home, representing 20% of New Yorkers. In fact, there are more Spanish speakers in New York than in 13 Latin American capitals (García, 1997). Twenty-seven percent of those aged five and over who spoke Spanish at home (397,380 speakers) are Spanish monolingual speakers (García, 1997). This creates the Spanish language surround in which New York Puerto Ricans live and that Zentella so well documents in her study (1997a). When speaking about the homes in *el Barrio*, Zentella says that Spanish was always 'in the background' (1997a: 50). And she reports that children had at least receptive ability in Spanish because otherwise they missed out on what was happening in the home and in the community.

Besides being used extensively in homes and Latino neighbourhoods, Spanish is much used in public. There are four full-time Spanish language AM radio stations: WSKQ, WKDM; WADO and WJIT. A Spanish language radio show, *'El vacilón de la mañana'* on 97.9 FM, is the second ranking radio talk show in New York City. Full Spanish language television programming is provided by WXTV (Univisión), WNJU (Telemundo), and a cable channel, *Galavisión*. There are two Spanish language dailies in New York City, one of which *El Diario La Prensa*, published since 1913, calls itself '*El Campeón de los Hispanos*' ['The Champion of Hispanics']. Spanish is so prevalent in New York City that New Yorkers can do business in Spanish with Con Edison, the utility company, and NYNEX, the telephone company. And New Yorkers can find Spanish language services in most governmental agencies and the court system.

The vitality of Spanish in New York and its effect on its use by Puerto Ricans is most evident in the rich and dynamic music that is part of the New York Puerto Rican community. Puerto Rican music, and what is commonly referred as *Salsa*, has been a focal point for Puerto Rican cultural identity. For decades, New York City has been a breeding ground for the development of *Salsa*, a sound heavily influenced by the Puerto Rican experience in New York. Tito Puente, Ray Barretto and Eddie Palmieri are among the artists who have played a role in the development of the Puerto Rican

Table 3.1 Puerto Ricans and other Latinos in New York: 1980 and 1990

	Total population	Latinos	% Latinos	Puerto Ricans	% Puerto Ricans	Other Latinos	% Other Latinos
1980	7,071,639	1,406,389	19.9	852,833	12.1	553,556	7.8
1990	7,322,564	1,783,511	24.4	896,763	12.2	886,748	12.1

Source: Demographic Profiles. A Portrait of New York City's Community Districts from the 1980 and 1990 Censuses of Population and Housing. Department of City Planning, August 1992

musical scene. But it is a tribute to the strength of Spanish in New York that New York Puerto Rican singers such as Mark Anthony, La India, and Brenda K. Starr who started out singing in English have only become popular when they began singing songs in Spanish. Despite frequent attempts to popularise English lyrics with *Salsa* rhythms, *Salsa* primarily remains a linguistic and cultural domain where Spanish is most vibrant among New York Puerto Ricans.

Presently, Spanish in New York reflects the diversity of Latin American varieties, as migration from Puerto Rico has levelled off, while immigration from all Latin America has sharply increased. Besides Puerto Ricans, there are five other New York Latino groups with over 50,000 people. They are, in order of size: Dominicans, Colombians, Ecuadorians, Mexicans and Cubans. (For a complete breakdown of all New York Latino groups, see Zentella 1997b.)

Table 3.1 displays the demographic data for Latinos and Puerto Rican in the city in the last two decades, confirming both the vitality of Spanish speakers, as well as its increasing dialectal variation.

In the city as a whole, although the number of Puerto Ricans has remained fairly constant, it is the number of other Latinos that has grown by leaps and bounds. Whereas the number of Puerto Ricans has only increased by 5.2%, the number of other Latinos has increased by 60.2%, making Puerto Ricans barely half of the New York Latino population. It is also important to note that Puerto Ricans are increasingly native born. Whereas in 1970 almost 60% of the US Puerto Rican population had been born in Puerto Rico, in 1990 only 40% remained island born (US Census, 1970 and 1990).

Because most of the other Latino groups are more recent arrivals, they are generally Spanish speakers, helping to pull the Spanish of Puerto Ricans as they communicate with each other. In fact, Zentella (1990) has pointed to the lexical levelling that is occurring as Puerto Ricans, Dominicans, Colombians and Cubans try to communicate with each other. At the same time, English-speaking ability, or the inclusion of English features in their discourse, gives Puerto Ricans added status among other Latinos in poor Bronx and Brooklyn neighbourhoods, marking them as more knowledgeable of the ways of New York. So English-speaking ability and bilingualism act as status characteristics, pushing New York Puerto Ricans towards the English end of the continuum. It is this pull and push, this *vaivén*, pulled by the need to communicate with other Spanish speakers, pushed by the need to be a legitimate part of an Anglo world, that gives the shift to English of Puerto Rican New Yorkers unique characteristics.

Puerto Rican Neighbourhoods. Dislocation and Reshuffling as Spanish and English Invert Status

That Puerto Rican poverty can also be lived out in English is masterfully portrayed by Zentella (1997a) in her description of the dislocation of *El Barrio*. In the section meaningfully titled, 'The End of *el Bloque*: "Ahora la gente no se conocen"' ['Now people don't know each other'] Zentella explains:

> Between 1981–91, a series of events removed most of *el bloque's* families. Suspicious fires accelerated the deterioration of two of the tenements and the city condemned them as uninhabitable . . . By the end of the decade only six of the 20 families with children remained . . . Most families were as poor as, or poorer than, they had been in 1979, and many had been devastated by divorce, disease, and drugs. Staying in *El Barrio* or in poverty did not guarantee their maintenance of Spanish, and some lost out on both economic and linguistic fronts . . . The breakup of *el bloque* dislodged the children from networks that had fostered bilingualism, and took each child down distinct paths of language development. (Zentella: 137–39)

The dislocation of East Harlem described by Zentella was repeated throughout many other Puerto Rican neighbourhoods in New York. For this paper, we conducted a series of interviews among Puerto Rican residents of Bushwick, Brooklyn, in a local Pentecostal church. The comments that follow are typical as they reminisce about what Bushwick was like and what happened:

> On Bushwick Avenue there were five-story tenements with four apartments on the floor. There were no elevators and everyone who lived there was Puerto Rican. The row houses across the street were all Italian. But then gangs came in. Heroine was on the rise . . . At the same time, Reingold wanted to take over the whole vicinity to build a loading dock for the trucks. They destroyed the buildings, but there's

nothing to this day. Everybody moved in different directions. (M, 2nd gen., 37 years of age)

Los Puertorriqueños se fueron. Los dominicanos se están quedando con Brooklyn. Las bodegas de puertorriqueños son casuales. Hay una nada mas. (F, 1st gen., 56 years of age)

[Puertoricans left. Dominicans are taking over Brooklyn. The Puertorican *bodegas* are unusual. There's only one.]

En Grajam oía música típica [In Graham I listened to typical music] all over the place. En la Marqueta había *pasteles, alcapurria*. [In the Market there were *pasteles*, alcapurria.] Now it's the Market of Moore. I don't see pasteles, don't see music resound, don't see Puerto Rican flags . . . There were a lot of *cuchifritos*, a. . . lot. (M, 2nd gen., 28 years of age)

Just as the integrity of the traditional Puerto Rican neighbourhood has disappeared, so has the Spanish language for this last second generation male, except for his distinct switch to Spanish when he talks about music and food.

The cultural and linguistic dislocation is felt not only physically, but also spiritually and emotionally. One of the young men we interviewed explains it thus:

Now nobody cares about anybody. It's like gang rivalry, but without colors. Before was more, '*Si come uno, comen todos*'. (M, 2nd gen., 35 years of age)
[Before it was more, 'If one eats, all eat']

Significantly, this second generation young man switches to Spanish to repeat probably what his mother used to say to communicate the collaborative spirit of a poor but united community that characterised the early days of the New York Puerto Rican community.

The question remains, however, of where Puerto Ricans went. They left as one of the men told me, 'buscando algo mejor' [looking for something better], but his words are instructive of the different futures that awaited Puerto Ricans once they left Bushwick as well as the different linguistic features of second generation New York Puerto Rican discourse:

They left *buscando algo mejor*. They gave up on the neighbourhood and decided to relocate. Our restaurants used to be Spanish. The *bodegas* sold out. *Los puertorriqueños se metieron a ser maestros* [Puerto Ricans went into teaching], *en* Auto Repair Shops, Liquor Stores. But the majority went independent. *Compran ropa y venden* house to house *por*

la calle [They buy clothes and sell house to house on the street.] . . . The
crime rates dropped. Everybody is in jail. A lot of people went back to
Puerto Rico. The rest moved to Queens, Jersey. (M, 2nd gen., 37 years of
age)

Although some were able to escape the poverty of Bushwick to find better
things in Queens or Jersey, others ended up in other dark spaces, including
jail.

In 1990 the Latino poverty rate in New York City was 43% compared to
33% for African Americans, and 12% for whites (Institute for Puerto Rican
Policy 1996). And poor Puerto Ricans feel their separation from the rest of
majority society. A 74-year-old woman we interviewed in Bushwick
expresses it so:

Uno es pobre, vive de ayuda pública. Para la sociedad no somos nadie.
Somos insolventes. Se vive con esa mancha.
[You're poor, you live on public assistance. For society, we´re no one.
We´re insolvent. You live with that stain.]

Scarce economic resources is also the reason given for the decrease in
Puerto Rican migration to New York. One informant explains:

There are very few kids coming from Puerto Rico. They come, and then
go back. There are no resources to help them. No language help. The
government grants ran out. (M, 2nd gen., 34 years of age)

Yet another one explains:

Los puertorriqueños siguen viniendo porque hay mas oportunidades.
Pero ahora vienen a Atlantic City, a los campos también.
[Puerto Ricans keep on coming because there are more opportunities.
But now they come to Atlantic City, to the countryside also.]

But many younger English-speaking Puerto Ricans feel differently, and
talk about how they have been able to escape their parents´poverty. Indicative of this is the following comments from two young former Bushwick
residents: 'Puerto Ricans are up and coming. Everybody I know is a school
teacher or cop. Not too many are on welfare.' And when questioned about
the continuous poverty statistics on Puerto Ricans, they point to the aging
generation of their parents as the culprits: 'The old Puerto community is
older now and is on welfare and disability. But the young ones are up and
rising politically and socially.'

Nevertheless, Urciuoli (1997: 58) has concluded that Puerto Ricans have
the least contact with white New Yorkers, and the most contact with

African Americans and other Spanish speaking groups. But proximity and contact does not necessarily lead to good relations. Commenting on the tension between Puerto Ricans and African American males in the Bedford Stuyvesant neighbourhood to which the family moved from Bushwick, one of the second generation male informants recalls:

> We found a cheap apartment on top a Pentecostal Church in Bedford Stuyvesant. Inside the building everything was fine. But everyone else was African American. They used to call us the *miras*. There was a fight every day. At the junior high school, I started to get together with other Hispanics and started picking on the *morenos*.
> Then they used to call us, the crazy *miras*.

African Americans used the Spanish word 'mira' [Look], used to call attention and repeated frequently in public especially by mothers, to make fun of their Puerto Rican neighbours.

An analysis of where Puerto Ricans are living today can shed further light on how both Spanish and English have reversed roles in the Puerto Rican community, with Spanish, most often associated with poverty, being now linked also to middle-class status, and English, most often associated with prestige, being also linked to poverty.

Table 3.2 shows the residential pattern of Puerto Ricans and other Latinos in the five boroughs of New York in 1980 and 1990. Table 3.3 offers a summary of the percentage of change from 1980 to 1990 of Puerto Ricans and other Latino groups.

An analysis of Tables 3.2 and 3.3 reveals that the growth of the other Latino population has been most dramatic in the Bronx, a borough of traditional Puerto Rican settlement. In the Bronx, although the Puerto Rican population has also increased by 9.7%, other Latinos have grown by a dramatic 126.6%. Thus, although almost a half of Bronx residents are Latinos (44%) and although slightly over a fourth (29%) are Puerto Ricans, other Latinos, especially Dominicans, and more recently Mexicans and Central Americans, are rapidly making inroads.

Also significant is the fact that as Brooklyn, and especially Manhattan, lose Puerto Rican population, Queens and Staten Island continue to gain Puerto Ricans. This shift in Puerto Rican population suggests the attainment of more middle-class status, as the traditional *barrios* are abandoned. For example, the per capita income of Latinos in Jackson Heights and Elmhurst, the two Queens neighbourhoods where Latinos are concentrated, is $9,513, as compared to $5,943 in East Harlem, $5,457 in Williamsburgh (Brooklyn), and $4,696 in the Mott Haven section of the

Table 3.2 Puerto Ricans and other Latinos in the five boroughs: 1980 and 1990

	Bronx		Brooklyn		Manhattan		Queens		Staten Island	
	1980	1990	1980	1990	1980	1990	1980	1990	1980	1990
Total	1,168,972	1,203,789	2,230,936	2,300,664	1,428,285	1,487,536	1,183,038	1,951,598	352,121	303,081
Latino	395,138	523,111	393,103	462,411	335,247	386,630	263,548	381,120	19,353	30,239
% Latino	33.8	43.5	17.6	20.1	23.5	26.0	13.9	19.5	5.5	8.0
Puerto Ricans	318,138	349,115	275,758	274,530	166,302	154,978	80,909	100,410	11,499	17,730
% Puerto Ricans	27.2	29.05	12.4	11.9	11.6	10.4	4.3	5.1	3.3	4.7
Other Latinos	76,773	173,996	117,345	187,881	168,945	231,652	182,639	280,710	7,854	12,509
% Other Latinos	6.6	14.5	5.3	8.2	11.8	15.6	9.7	14.4	2.2	3.3

Source: Demographic Profiles. A portrait of New York City's Community Districts from the 1980 and 1990 Censuses of Population and Housing, Department of City Planning, August 1992

Table 3.3 1980–90 change of Puerto Ricans and other Latinos in New York City and the five boroughs

	% Change Latinos	% Change Puerto Ricans	% Change Other Latinos
New York City	26.8	5.2	60.2
Bronx	32.4	9.7	126.6
Brooklyn	17.6	–0.4	60.1
Manhattan	15.3	–16.8	37.1
Queens	44.6	24.1	53.7
Staten Island	56.2	54.2	59.3

Source: Demographic Profiles. A Portrait of New York City's Community Districts from the 1980 and 1990 Censuses of Population and Housing. Department of City Planning, August 1992.

Bronx, all three neighbourhoods of traditional original Puerto Rican settlement (Institute for Puerto Rican Policy, 1996).

But it is important to note again that income and language shift does not always correlate positively for Puerto Ricans and other Latinos. For example, in Mott Haven, the south Bronx neighbourhood with the highest poverty index in the city and with the lowest Latino per capita income, 27% of Latinos are monolingual Spanish speakers. Yet, in the more middle-class Jackson Heights and Elmhurst, 36% of Latinos are monolingual Spanish speakers.

This again is uncharacteristic of other US ethnolinguistic groups, although these figures mask differences between ways of language groups and ways of national groups. That is, although all Latinos have been 'racialised' by the majority, the experience of other immigrant minorities is clearly different from that of Puerto Ricans as 'caste' or 'colonised' groups.

Jackson Heights and Elmhurst have three times the number of other Latinos than Puerto Ricans. These other Latinos, although more recent and more Spanish monolingual, many times come with skills that help them achieve middle class status. They also have not suffered for long the inequities of living in a country that considers them a colonised inferior people and that subjects them to a marginal public education.

Puerto Ricans with middle-class status tend to move to more middle-class communities, sometimes white English-speaking communities, but mostly Latino middle class communities. The two Latino neighbourhoods in the Bronx with the highest per capita income among Latinos, West Farms and Soundview-Castle Hill ($9,739 and $10,121 respectively), also have the lowest percentage of Spanish monolingual speakers (19% and 16% of the Latino population respectively, with 59% of the population in both neighbourhoods being Latino). These middle-class neighbourhoods, mostly Puerto Rican, pull toward English. But as in Jackson Heights and Elmhurst, there are also Puerto Ricans who choose to join other Latino middle-class immigrants. Those are constantly pulled toward Spanish.

The Puerto Rican community in New York thus finds itself in three different patterns of language use and proficiency and neighbourhood income:

(1) Those who live in middle-class Latino neighbourhoods with high community bilingual proficiency (that is, only one of approximately six speakers are monolingual speakers of Spanish).

In West Farms and Soundview-Castle Hill

(2) Those who live in poor Latino neighbourhoods with mid- community bilingual proficiency (that is, only one of approximately four speakers are monolingual speakers of Spanish).

Neighbourhoods are listed here beginning with those with the lowest per capita income: *In Mott Haven, Hunts Point, Morris Heights-Mt. Hope, Belmont, Crotona Park East-East Tremont, University Heights-Fordham, Williamsburgh, Highbridge-West Concourse, Lower East Side, East Harlem.*

(3) Those who live in middle-class Latino neighbourhoods with low community bilingual proficiency (that is, approximately one of two speakers are Spanish monolinguals).

Jackson Heights, Elmhurst

For Puerto Rican New Yorkers, both English language shift and Spanish language maintenance are associated with middle-class status.

Although as with other US ethnolinguistic groups, middle class status often brings Puerto Ricans into more contact with English, it can also bring them into more contact with Spanish. And although poverty is associated with many of the neighbourhoods in which Puerto Ricans live, Puerto Rican poverty, as we saw earlier, is also lived out in English.

Puerto Ricans with Spanish in the Heart and Dominicans with Spanish in the Mouth

A comparison of Puerto Ricans with Dominicans, the fastest-growing Latino New York group, allows us to analyse further the role of Puerto

Ricans as language agents in the New York scene. From 1980 to 1990 while the Puerto Rican community grew only 5.2%, the Dominican community grew by 165%. Yet, Dominicans officially account for only 19% of the city Latinos (332,713), as compared to the half of Puerto Rican ethnicity (896,763). So despite the fact that 96% of Dominicans claimed to speak Spanish at home in 1990, as compared to 87% of Puerto Ricans, there are many more Spanish-speaking Puerto Ricans in New York (780,129), than Spanish-speaking Dominicans (319,392). However, this fact, derived from the 1990 census figures, masks ability in Spanish or degree of use, directing us to recognise that the presence of Spanish in New York homes is still in the hearts of Puerto Ricans, although perhaps Spanish may be used there seldomly or haltingly.

Although census figures do not reveal information about Spanish-speaking ability, English-speaking ability is accounted for. We know that 71% of Puerto Ricans in 1990 spoke English very well (636,657), whereas only 38% of Dominicans claimed to do so (126,426). The numbers of those Spanish-speakers from both groups who do not speak English well then comes surprisingly close, with 260,106 Puerto Ricans and 206,287 Dominicans claiming not to speak English well. Yet, Spanish speaking Puerto Ricans who need to speak Spanish because of limited English proficiency are certainly not the majority of New York Latinos, especially when we take into account the entire Latino universe in New York. Although Puerto Rican New Yorkers continue to identify with the Spanish language and continue to hold on to aspects of it in a linguistic *vaivén*, other New Yorkers increasingly see them as English speaking, with Dominicans having taken their place as 'the Spanish speakers' of New York.

That Spanish is in the hearts, although not always in the mouths of Puerto Rican, also has to do with the outstanding growth of the native-born Puerto Rican population, a factor which also greatly contributes to the pull towards English language shift. In 1970 60% of Puerto Ricans in the United States had been born in Puerto Rico. That figure decreased to 42% in the 1990 census.

Spanish for New York Puerto Ricans, like the Puerto Rican flag, has taken on American ways. Commenting on the way in which he displays the Puerto Rican flag today, one of the second generation males we interviewed in Bushwick told us:

I put my Puerto Rican flag on the rear view mirror. I never put it out the window, otherwise people say: 'Mira ese jíbaro con la bandera por la ventana.'
['Look at that hillbilly with the flag out the window'.]

Like the flag on the rear view mirror, the Spanish language is displayed only within American norms by second generation Puerto Ricans, with restraint and moderation, and communicating moving forward, although looking backwards. That is, like the discourse of this second generation speaker, Spanish is used within the context of English, reflecting, like the rear view mirror, an island reality that is always in the background and that is contained in the New York foreground.

Puerto Rican Identity and Language. 'Everybody I Know is like Spanglish'

The increased immigration from other Latin American countries clearly has diffused the original link that had existed between Puerto Rican identity and the Spanish language. One of the second generation men we interviewed complained about the lack of presence of Puerto Rican culture and speech in New York, as other Latinos took over the media and the schools.

> We're not exposed to Puerto Rican culture and of Puerto Rican language as we used to, even on TV. There are more transHispanic things on TV.

But in reality, the language-identity link between Puertoricanness and Spanish has been absent from the New York Puerto Rican community for a long time, as supported in studies by Attinasi (1979) and Zentella (1990c). In her recent book (1997a), Zentella explains how Puerto Rican identity was redefined in *el bloque* without a Spanish requirement in order to accommodate monolingual English youngsters. A second generation Puerto Rican we interviewed, working as a special education teacher in a school with a majority of Spanish speakers, had this to say when asked 'What makes a Puerto Rican in New York?'

> The music, the food, the way we talk, sometimes 'Mira Papi', like talking *con cariño*, sweet tone of voice. Traditions, *música típica*, you know, *lelolai, salsa, pernil, pastel, arroz con gandules*.

It is clear that the Spanish language is not listed as one of the components of Puerto Rican identity; although it is used intuitively, it is embedded in cultural expressions such as music, relationships, food, and ways of life. In the school in which this young man works, the majority of students are still of Puerto Rican descent, but Spanish is to them a second language. The Spanish speakers are now Hondurans and Mexicans. It is this young man whose words tell us a lot about how both Spanish and English and the mix between them is what defines a Puerto Rican New Yorker: 'Everybody I know *is* like Spanglish. *Un poquito español, un poquito inglés.'* ['A little bit Spanish, a little bit English.'] What makes this quote interesting is that this young man does not refer to the linguistic *vaivén* as something spoken, but as something lived, a Puerto Rican identity itself.

Asked if she thought that it was important to teach Spanish to her grand-daughter who accompanied her, a 74-year-old woman who had lived in Bushwick since 1950 told us:

> A los muchachos les enseñamos nuestra cultura, nuestra bandera y Dios. Los llevamos a la Parada para que se sientan puertorriqueños. Y les hablamos de Dios porque Dios no tiene raza.
>
> [To the children we teach our culture, our flag and God. We take them to the Parade so that they feel Puerto Rican. And we talk to them about God because God doesn't have any race.]

This grandmother cannot consciously distinguish between the Spanish that she speaks, her flag, and God. But although she consciously takes her granddaughter to the Pentecostal church where she learns about God, and takes her to the Puerto Rican parade, she cannot externalise the language she speaks as an object that could be taught, she merely speaks it, it is part of her, her culture, and her beliefs, and that is the way she transmits it to her granddaughter, who, of course, speaks English to her.

This idea that Spanish is part of the Puerto Rican being, although it´s not always in the mouth, is clearly expressed by the young Bushwick male who says:

> Spanish is always part of us. It´s innate. When you´re in New York, you don´t even think Spanish. When you get off the plane, you don´t speak English.

Some proficiency in Spanish is necessary for New York Puerto Ricans to continue the link to their island identity. One of the young males we inter-viewed put it this way:

> In Puerto Rico everybody is Puertorican. There´s more warmth. El calor. [The heat.] I can communicate better with my own. There I speak Spanish to older family members, but I speak English to the younger ones because most have learned it some in school.

The above quote communicates the changing language situation in Puerto Rico, for although Puerto Rico is fiercely Spanish speaking, more and more of the younger generation are learning English at school. So although in the past, the emotional and real link to the island had to be done in Spanish, it is becoming possible to a certain extent to speak English to island Puerto Ricans and to continue being 'Spanglish' even in the island.

This change in language situation in the island has major connotations for New York Puerto Ricans, for those who still come have much more familiarity with the English language than those who came before, and certainly more than other Latin American immigrant groups.

Spanish literacy and New York Puerto Ricans

The colonial status of Puerto Rico has greatly affected Puerto Ricans' ability to maintain Spanish or reverse their language shift. The past Puerto Rican migration to New York had low literacy rates in Spanish, a product of a colonised school system with a misguided policy of English language education for people who spoke Spanish only. This aging population remains trapped in poverty, unable to benefit from many adult English as a Second Language programmes or to connect with the Spanish language print that is now evident in billboards, and that appears as translations to the many governmental forms in an increasingly bureaucratic world.

Again, the degree of literacy in Spanish of the New York Puerto Rican population is also responsible for its differing linguistic *vaivén*. Spanish, in those homes, has always been the language of the heart and the home, whereas English (in the long-gone Puerto Rico they remember) was supposed to be the language of school and certainly of the literacy of the powerful United States (Walsh, 1991).

Although maintenance bilingual education in New York was the struggle of second generation Puerto Rican young adults in the early 70s, two factors weakened the effort:

(1) *'La lucha continúa'* ['The struggle continues'] most often referred to sociopolitical rights, rather than to language rights.
(2) They themselves many times lacked Spanish literacy, a product of going to school in English only and having lived in homes where Spanish was spoken, but neither read nor written.

Today, the use of Spanish print in Puerto Rican homes is scarce. The readership of *El Diario La Prensa* has shifted from being mostly Puerto Rican to mostly Dominican. Zentella (1997a: 214) confirms the predominance of English print in the homes of the former residents of *el bloque*.

Spanish in Schools for Puerto Ricans: From Schools for Shift and Maintenance to Schools to Reverse Language Shift

Nowhere is the shift of Puerto Ricans as Spanish speakers to Puerto

Ricans as English speakers with *vaivén* more evident than in the New York City public schools. In 1992–93, 355,889 Latino students were enrolled in New York City public schools, accounting for 36% of the total public school enrolment. Of these, 101,383 (28%) were identified as English language learners (Latino Commission on Educational Reform 1994).

As with the census, no quantitative data is available for the number who are Spanish speakers. But even more disturbing is the fact that the New York City Board of Education does not keep separate figures on Puerto Ricans, making it difficult to substantiate with quantitative data the change that has taken place.

Although bilingual education came into existence for Puerto Ricans as a result of the Aspira Consent Decree, few Puerto Rican children remain today in the transitional bilingual education classrooms, agents of language shift, where Spanish monolingual students acquire English. Transitional bilingual education classrooms today hold mostly Dominican and Mexican students.

In the 1970s maintenance bilingual-bicultural education programmes where Puerto Rican children were taught in both English and Spanish and where Puerto Rican culture and history were also taught were developed throughout the city. These programmes, staffed mostly by Puerto Rican teachers, and supported by the post-Civil Rights climate of the nation at large, had biculturism and bilingualism as goals. District 4 in East Harlem, for example, supported and developed a strong maintenance bilingual-bicultural education model. But as the political climate changed, as the Puerto Rican population became more dispersed, and more English speaking, and as other Latino groups, immigrants with a different sociohistorical connection to the United States, started to come into the city, maintenance bilingual education programmes started to take a turn.

Today, maintenance bilingual-bicultural education programmes have been mostly substituted by Dual Language Programmes where students who are fluent in English are taught with Spanish speakers who are not. The classic dual language model calls for half the students to be English-speaking and half not, with its primary goal being the full English language acquisition of those who have limited English proficiency, as well as their cultural assimilation. A secondary goal is to develop the second language of the English speakers. But a closer look inside those classrooms reveals a lot about the language shift that has taken place among Puerto Ricans in New York. Increasingly, the students who make up the English-speaking and non-Spanish-speaking population of the Dual Language Programmes are second and third generation Puerto Ricans, now lacking full fluency in Spanish. So, although on paper dual language programmes are integrated, they mostly remain ethnically segregated, with Latino students of differing language ability making up the student body. For the most part, Puerto Ricans make up the English-ability half, and Dominicans, Mexicans, and Central and South Americans make up the other Spanish-ability half. Dual language programmes for New York Puerto Ricans are clearly agents of reversing language shift.

The shift in the goals of bilingual education in New York City, however, are indicative not only of a changing political climate, but also of the changing population. Today, for the first time, there is a lack of cultural congruence between the bilingual teachers, now mostly Puerto Ricans, and the students. In the 1970s and early 1980s bilingual teachers were recruited from Puerto Rico and from the *barrios*, where programmes to educate para-professionals from the community cropped up.

But as the student-body in those programmes became less and less Puerto Rican, the viability of developing biculturism became more diffi-cult, on the one hand because of the cultural diversity of the Latino students themselves, on the other because although these teachers knew a lot about Puerto Rican culture and history, they seldom were knowledgeable of the Latin American world at large, having been mostly products of a US educa-tion. The parents have also changed, with immigrant Spanish-speaking parents who increasingly travel back and forth and who have not yet devel-oped a sense of being an ethnolinguistic US group, showing less commit-ment to bilingual education than Puerto Ricans. In the 1990s, the goals of bilingual education programmes in New York have increasingly narrowed to include only English language acquisition, with English as a Second Language programmes increasingly taking over Bilingual Education programmes.

Only dual language programmes, possible mechanisms of reversing language shift for Puerto Ricans, give a glimmer of hope. But in the difficult sociopolitical climate that ushers in the new millennium, even dual language programmes are being questioned, and the enthusiasm of the Puerto Rican community for them is at best mild.

New York Puerto Rican Institutional Changes

The Puerto Rican institutions that were created as a result of the Civil Rights struggles of the 1960s and 1970s have been under political, social and economic pressures that have resulted in their change or disappear-ance.

Academic departments of Puerto Rican studies have been closed or are experiencing serious cutbacks. For example, in the early 1990s, City College of New York changed the name of the Puerto Rican Studies Department to that of Latin American and Caribbean Studies. But this did not save it from losing departmental status and becoming just an academic programme.

Budgetary constraints have also been experienced in the Puerto Rican Legal Defense and Education Fund and the Institute for Puerto Rican Policy. This has led these two organisations to merge in order to survive. As we said earlier, few maintenance bilingual education programmes, responding to community life, exist. A noted exception is the educational programmes in El Puente, a community-based group in Williamsburg, Brooklyn. But even its alternative High School for Social Justice has shifted from having a mostly Puerto Rican population to one that is mostly Dominican.

The move to new standards in education can be particularly destructive of Spanish language efforts supported by school and society. As of this year, all high school graduates will have to pass an English Language Regents Exam, effectively eliminating the possibility that anyone without near-native English skills will be able to have a high school diploma. This, coupled with the rippling and continuing effects of Proposition 227 in California, has seriously eliminated the possibility of developmental maintenance bilingual education programmes, where Latino students could develop their Spanish language skills.

Nowhere has this shift been more evident than in the attacks experienced by the bilingual community college of City University of New York's Hostos Community College. Increasingly, the population there has also shifted from a Puerto Rican one to a mostly Dominican one. But increasingly, academic courses are taught in English only, closing the possibility of an Associate's degree to those who do not have full English proficiency.

As Spanish recedes from academic settings organised and run by the majority, it has taken refuge in the Pentecostal churches that have continued to crop up in Latino communities. Urciuoli points out:

> The Spanish-speaking Pentecostal churches stand out as a strikingly grass-roots phenomenon, a place in which Spanish is performed with authority, ceding no ground to English or Americans. (Urciuoli, 1997: 95)

The Pentecostal church in which we conducted our Bushwick interviews certainly gave us a glimmer of that reality, with Spanish being the unifying factor among the old and the young, the first and second/third generations. And although English was heard often in informal association, Spanish was the language not only of the heart and interior prayer, but also of proclamations of faith, of the reading of the Bible, and of religious instruction. In fact, the children, most in monolingual English classrooms, had learned to read and write Spanish during Bible study.

Conclusion: Shifting the Focus of Sociology of Language. From Language Shift/Language Maintenance to Reversing Language Shift

In 1991 Fishman's *Reversing Language Shift* turned the focus of language shift/language maintenance studies from mere descriptions of socio-linguistic situations to steps that can be taken by ethnolinguistic communities to do something about their weak sociolinguistic status. RLS, Fishman states, 'is an attempt . . . to adopt policies and to engage in efforts calculated to reverse the cumulative processes of attrition that would otherwise lead to the contextually weak language-in-culture becoming even weaker' (p. 81). Then, speaking of the New York Puerto Rican community, Fishman had warned that despite the large number of recently arrived monolingual Spanish speakers, one was left with 'the impression of a major language shift tidal wave underway under the surface' (p. 192).

Referring to Fishman's Graded Intergenerational Disruption Scale, Zentella 1997a placed the New York Puerto Rican community of the early 1980s between Stages 6 (Intergenerational informal oralcy and its demographic concentration and institutional reinforcement) and Stage 5 (Spanish literacy in home, community, and schools, especially in own instructional arrangements). But the previous analysis leads us to believe that in the last decade, the New York Puerto Rican community not only may have abandoned efforts of Spanish language maintenance but may have slipped from being between Stages 6 and 5 to being between Stages 7 and 6, having given up on almost all efforts of Spanish literacy and moving toward Stage 7 where Spanish is used for cultural interaction with the community based older generation.

It is clear that the New York Puerto Rican community has experienced great physical and demographic dislocation, severe social dislocation, and harsh cultural dislocation, all identified by Fishman (1991: 57–65) as leading to language shift. The New York Puerto Rican community has lost its demographic concentration, weakening its language network. It has had no increase in the use of Spanish in any domain, not in the family, nor work, nor education, nor religion, nor entertainment and mass media, nor in any political party or governmental function. There has been little effort to foster intergenerational Spanish language maintenance, although there has been limited interest in dual language programmes where New York

Puerto Rican children have the potential to acquire at least oralcy in Spanish.

Yet, it is unlikely that the New York Puerto Rican community will completely face language death or slip toward Stage 8 where Spanish would be spoken only by socially isolated old folks. But the mechanism by which this is so has little to do with organised efforts of a US ethnolinguistic group moving towards their ancestral language, and more to do with a colonised situation that keeps a linguistic *vaivén* going. This linguistic *vaivén* not only enables speakers to connect with their two sociopolitical realities, but is spurred by the discrimination and inferior education to which colonised minorities are subjected. New York Puerto Ricans continue to use Spanish signs when speaking among themselves and other Spanish speakers, even while speaking English. Urciuoli, defending the idea that the language of racialised bilinguals does not equal culture expressed a similar idea:

> When bilingual siblings gossip or tease in English and Spanish, the pragmatics of English is much more like the pragmatics of Spanish than it is like the pragmatics of English spoken with an Anglo doctor. (Urciuoli, 1997: 6).

It is clear that the English of New York Puerto Ricans has been infused with the colonised meanings of Puerto Rican Spanish and the meanings of the Spanish of other New York Latinos. The New York Puerto Rican community is often comfortable with its linguistic *vaivén*, showing bilingual ability over other monolingual Spanish speakers, but also over Anglo monolinguals. Thus, its comfort makes prospects of reversing language shift uninteresting, since there's little attachment to Spanish as a symbol of identity or as an instrument of greater social benefit. Yet, when the New York Puerto Rican community interacts in public forums, especially in public schools and in written form, English monolinguals and Spanish monolinguals evaluate the *vaivén* negatively, promoting linguistic insecurity. This clash moves the New York Puerto Rican community along the language shift axis, while the stigmatisation of the majority prevents it from completely undergoing shift. It is this distinct sociolinguistic pattern, reserved for colonised groups, that distinguishes the models of language shift/maintenance/language shift reversal for New York Puerto Ricans, who, like the steps of the cha-cha-chá, continue to mark their own linguistic space, both mainland and island, both Latino and Anglo, and reflecting, in language use, the invented and unique status of the political *commonwealth*.

Note

*   The term New York Puerto Ricans is used throughout this paper to avoid the negative connotations that have been associated with the term Nuyoricans. The authors wish especially to thank Juan Rodriguez from Long Island University who introduced us to the Bushwick Puerto Rican community. We're also grateful to Ana Celia Zentella for her reading of a previous version of this paper. Special thanks go to Nélida Pérez and Jorge Matos of the Library of the Center for Puerto Rican Studies for their helpful suggestions.

References

Andreu Iglesias, C. (ed.) (1977) *Memorias de Bernardo Vega*. Río Piedras, Puerto Rico: Ediciones Huracán.
Attinasi, J. (1979) Language attitudes in a New York Puerto Rican community. In R. Padilla (ed.) *Bilingual Education and Public Policy in the United States* (pp. 408–61). Ypsilanti, MI: Eastern Michigan University.
Blauner, R. (1972) *Racial Oppression in America*. New York: Harper & Row.
El Diario (1993) 80 años de historia: 1913–1993. La lucha por la educación, pp. 9–20.
El Diario (1974) Editorial. Victoria para la educación bilingüe, 4 de septiembre de 1974, p. 17.
Fernandez, R. (1994) *Prisoners of Colonialism: The Struggle for Justice in Puerto Rico*. Monroe, ME: Common Courage Press.
Figueroa, L. (1977) *History of Puerto Rico*. New York: L.A. Publishing Company.
Fishman, J.A. (1970) *Sociolinguistics: A Brief Introduction*. Rowley, MA: Newbury House.
Fishman, J.A. (1991) *Reversing Language Shift*. Clevedon: Multilingual Matters.
Fishman, J.A., Cooper, R.L. and Ma, R. (1971) *Bilingualism in the Barrio*. Bloomington: Indiana University Press.
García, O. (1997) World languages and their role in a US city. In O. García and J.A. Fishman (eds) *The Multilingual Apple. Languages in New York City*. Berlin/New York: Mouton de Gruyter.
Gumperz, J.J. (1982) *Discourse Strategies*. Cambridgeshire: Cambridge University Press.
Hernández-Chávez, E. (1994) Language policy in the United States: A history of cultural genocide. In T. Skutnabb-Kangas and R. Phillipson (eds) *Linguistic Human Rights: Overcoming Linguistic Discrimination* (pp. 141–158). Berlin/New York: Mouton de Gruyen.
Institute for Puerto Rican Policy (1996) *New York City Latino Neighbourhoods Data Book*. New York City: Institute for Puerto Rican Policy.
Karnow, S. (1989) *In our Image: America's Empire in the Philippines*. New York: Ballantine.
Language Policy Task Force (1992) English and Colonialism in Puerto Rico. In J. Crawford (ed.) *Language Loyalties* (pp. 63–71). Chicago: University of Chicago Press.
Language Policy Task Force (1988) *Speech and Ways of Speaking in a Bilingual Puerto Rican Community*. New York: Centro de Estudios Puertorriqueños.
Latino Commission on Educational Reform (1994) *Making the Vision a Reality: A Latino Action Agenda for Educational Reform*. New York City Board of Education.
Lewis, G.K. (1974) *Notes on the Puerto Rican Revolution*. New York: Monthly Review.

Maldonado-Denis, M. (1972) *Puerto Rico: A Socio-historic Interpretation.* New York: Vintage Books.
Ogbu, J.U. (1988) Cultural diversity and human development. In D.T. Slaughter (ed.) *Black Children and Poverty: A Developmental Perspective* (pp. 11–28). San Francisco: Jossey-Bass.
Pedraza, P. (1985) Language maintenance among New York Puerto Ricans. In L. Elías-Olivares, E. Leone, R. Cisneros and J. Gutiérrez (eds) *Spanish Language Use and Public Life in the United States* (pp. 59–72).
Pedraza, P., Attinasi, J. and Hoffman, G. (1980) *Rethinking Diglossia* (Language Policy Task Force Working Paper No. 9). New York: Centro de Estudios Puertorriqueños.
Poplack, S. (1980) Sometimes I'll start a sentence in Spanish y termino en español: Toward a typology of code-switching. *Linguistics* 18, 581–616.
Poplack, S. (1981) Quantitative analysis of a functional and formal constraint on code-swithcing (Centro de Estudios Puertorriqueños Working Paper No. 2). New York: Centro de Estudios Puertorriqueños.
Poplack, S. (1988) Language status and language accommodation along a linguistic border. In P. Lowenberg (ed.) *Language Spread and Language Policy: Issues, Implications and Case Studies* (pp. 90–118). Washington, DC: Georgetown University Press.
Sánchez-Korrol, V. 1983 [1994]. *From Colonia to Community* (updated edn). CA: University of California Press.
Torres, L. (1997) *Puerto Rican Discourse. A Sociolinguistic Study of a New York Suburb.* Mahwah, NJ: Lawrence Erlbaum.
Trask, H.K. (1993) *From a Native Daughter: Colonialism and Sovereignty in Hawai'i.* Monroe, ME: Common Courage Press.
Trías Monge, J. (1997). *Puerto Rico: The Trials of the Oldest Colony in the World.* New Haven, CT: Yale University Press.
Urciuoli, B. (1997). *Exposing Prejudice. Puerto Rican Experiences of Language, Race, and Class.* Boulder, CO: Westview Press.
Walsh, C.E. (1991) *Pedagogy and the Struggle for Voice: Issues of Language, Power, and Schooling for Puerto Ricans.* New York: Bergin & Garvey.
Zentella, A.C. (1982) Code switching and interactions among Puerto Rican children. In J. Amastae and L. Elías-Olivares (eds). *Spanish in the United States: Sociolinguistic Aspects* (pp. 386–412). Cambridge: Cambridge University Press.
Zentella, A.C. (1990) Lexical leveling in four New York City Spanish dialects: Linguistic and social factors. *Hispania* 73, 1094–2015.
Zentella, A.C. (1997a) *Growing Up Bilingual. Puerto Rican Children in New York.* New York: Blackwell.
Zentella, A.C. (1997b) Spanish in New York. In O. García and J.A.Fishman (eds) *The Multilingual Apple. Languages in New York* (pp. 167–201). Berlin / New York: Mouton de Gruyter.

Chapter 4

A Decade in the Life of a Two-in-One Language
Yiddish in New York City (Secular and Ultra-Orthodox)

J.A. FISHMAN

I remember the first time I realised that Jews as a whole were an item of considerable curiosity for many Christian Americans. I was then a freshman at the University of Pennsylvania, in Philadelphia, the city in which I was born and had grown up in predominantly Jewish neighbourhoods. The classmate in the seat next to me volunteered the information that I was the first Jew he had ever 'actually met, face to face'. He was surprised to find that I appeared 'to be just like anyone else'! The reason I mention this here is because many people, even sociolinguists among them, Jews and non-Jews, have equally uninformed and totally unrealistic images about Yiddish, images associated with its distant past: in the pogrom-ridden 'Old Country', or in turn-of-the-century immigrant pushcart America, or during the Holocaust, or in scenes of mourning mountains of dead bodies. How strange, it has seemed to them, to find that in many ways it is a language like any other, that it is 'still around', obeying the same laws of language-in-society life-and-death that apply to any and all languages, and that reversing language shift (RLS) efforts are underway in conjunction with it. However, just as it has been said about Jews that 'they are just like all other people, only a little more so', so Yiddish, without a country or a government to fend for it, is like all other threatened languages, 'only a little more so'. As the chasm within its ranks, between its secular Yiddishist and ultra-Orthodox advocates, i.e. between its most visible defenders and its most constant speakers, both deepens and widens, its situation provides us with many unusually striking opportunities to ponder RLS concerns, processes and outcomes as a whole.

74

In the Year 2050: 'Yiddish still Dying'

In mid-20th century, the *Jerusalem Post* tried humorously to anticipate headlines of the year 2000 and one of those that it felt reasonably sure about was 'Yiddish still dying.' However, while threatened languages generally are reacted to by a peculiarly affective mixture of sadness, tenderness and mirth, Yiddish is the proverbial and archetypical 'dying language'. For some reason it is also widely considered to be funny (naturally so, since it has ['had', for those who always refer to it in the past tense (such as Harshav 1990]), 'a terrific Yiddish sense of humour'. 'Hillary, Bubele', the *New York Post* intoned on 6 August 1999, when Hillary Clinton's senatorial campaign revealed that she had had a Jewish (and Yiddish-speaking!) step-grandfather. It is exceedingly rare for an article about Yiddish in the American press not to be 'played for laughs' via a sprinkling of Yinglishisms (yenta, shiksa, oy-vey, kvelling, gevald, meshuggah, shabbos, tuchis, tsuris, mohel, were all included in this one brief 'entre nous' put-down column), calculated to amuse or to titillate trendy English-speaking New Yorkers who generally consider Yiddish to be a fully owned subsidiary of English anyway). Yiddish is funny, but, of course it is also dying, already dead, or at the very least 'archaic', while at the very same time it is tender, expressive and folksy. Many of these contradictory views have been advanced by Jews themselves and 'they should know', because their own 'great-grandmother was Yiddish-speaking'. How to break out of this swirling mass of misinformation, wishful thinking and love–hate that has hung on for well over a century? With some resignation about my chances of making facts triumph over fiction, I set out to try to do so once again (for my previous attempts, see Fishman 1965, 1966, 1981, 1985, 1989).

The Current Overall Scene of Yiddish in New York City

What Paris is to French and French literature and culture, New York and Tel-Aviv/Jerusalem are to Yiddish, whether in secular or in ultra-Orthodox contexts. For secular Yiddishists in the USA, New York City (and, to some extent even its total greater metropolitan area) is the language's undisputed capital-cum-Mecca. Yiddish was already being spoken in New York City even before the American Revolution (the patriot Hyman Solomon wrote many Yiddish letters to family and business associates back 'home' (in Germany) and Yiddish letters from New York describing the first fourth of July and the adoption of the Constitution are well known to historians adept at using archival sources). But Yiddish became a truly major language in New York only when the mass immigration of Eastern European Jews began in the early 1880s. The city that had already become a prototypic 'primary settlement area' for various groups of immigrants and their children well before the beginning of the 20th century, and that has retained much of that very same flavour for the grandchildren and great-grandchildren of immigrants to this very day, is even more than that in the case of Yiddish. For Yiddish, New York is not only the great American metropolis, not only the great American immigrant city, but the American city on which Yiddish has left a permanent mark, not only in diet and in interactional style (referred to as 'argumentation and rudeness as a means of simple communication and human sociability'), but in accent, prosodics and lexicon as well. New York may well be the only city in which middle-aged Black and Hispanic residents who grew up in formerly Jewish neighbourhoods, now bemoan the fact that their own children don't even know the difference between a 'shmendrik[1] and a shabes-goy',[2] even as a mass of more common Yiddishisms (both lexical and grammatical) are fully in the popular domain and require no translation at all to 'native New Yorkers' of whatever background, even if they *are* often 'translated for those who may be from out of town'.

It is here, in New York, that Yiddish events, activities and artifacts that have disappeared (or never even had established themselves at all) almost everywhere else in the USA, can still be readily encountered rather than only sought out by the well informed. Neighbourhoods where Yiddish is the normal vernacular of young and old still exist; all-day-schools in which Yiddish is the normal language of instruction for Judaic subjects still function and even regularly increase in number; Yiddish religious lectures/courses and Yiddish literary events still regularly occur; Yiddish periodical publications are still issued and displayed on newsstands; an active youth group (*Yugntruf*) functions for those whose Jewish life-style is completely or, at least substantially, secular; Yiddish theatrical and choral performances are regularly listed even in the English dailies for the general public (not to mention the Anglo-Jewish weeklies); first-rate public library and university library collections are open to the public and to scholars alike; hundreds of old and new Yiddish books, musical records and tapes are available for purchase at several convenient locations; Yiddish courses for adults – both for college credit and for adult education – are available at schools, colleges, synagogues and community centres throughout the year; a resident Yiddish theatre still performs and provides special English-buffeted matinee performances for children; a handful of secular Yiddish supplementary schools for children still function, as do both a secular and an ultra-Orthodox publishing house; the headquarters of the Workman's Circle (the oldest and largest fraternal Yiddish secular organisation), the YIVO Institute for Jewish Research, the activist League for Yiddish and several other Yiddish-involved and Yiddish-promoting organisations quietly toil year-round. All in all, the above constitute an amazingly active scene for a purportedly dead language.

Although several of the above efforts (but by no means all of them) are functioning at a far lower level of intensity than was the case a decade or two ago, the very presence and persistence of those that are fading is noteworthy, particularly if one realises that sometimes no more than a few hundred individuals constitute their local activist core and a few thousand their total periphery. When the strikingly modernist Yiddish poet Moyshe Leyb Halpern (1886–1932) proclaimed New York to be 'our garden' (1919), he had no idea that more than three-quarters of a century after he boldly staked out this claim there would still be stalwarts, such as these activists, working tirelessly in what remains of that garden. Any twilight as prolonged as this one – not to mention that it is still high noon on much of the ultra-Orthodox side of the Yiddish street – may justifiably claim to have achieved stabilisation of one kind or another, if only to confound the detractors and the doubters that have long tried to hurry Yiddish along into the night.

The Secular Side of 'the Yiddish Street'

To fully realise the above, one must also comprehend that the course of New York's secular Yiddish efforts is not *only* down hill either, even though it has more often than not been moving in that direction for the past half century. During the course of the decade under review, the Yiddish Forward (*Forverts*), that celebrated its 100th anniversary in 1996, acquired a young (under 50 is young in the world of secular Yiddish involvement) Soviet trained and thoroughly professional editor who has transformed the paper into a lively and colourful weekly, has attracted a score of young writers and co-workers and now also publishes an Israeli edition as well. The YIVO's Uriel Weinreich Summer Program (initiated in 1968 and co-sponsored since then with Columbia University, where the noted linguist Uriel Weinreich himself had held the USA's first endowed chair in Yiddish)[3] – the premier Yiddish summer programme in the world (several other Yiddish summer programmes have since opened, e.g. in Oxford, London, Paris, Vilnius (Vilne), Kiev and Jerusalem / Tel-Aviv) – now regularly provides intensive courses at all levels to 50 or more students, most of them enrolled in masters and doctoral programmes at universities around the country and, indeed, around the globe. The last regularly performing Yiddish theatre, the *Folksbine*, founded c. 1915, has been reinvigorated by the appointment of two very young ('forty-something') directors, both

American born, native Yiddish speaking, and successful stage and musical stage personalities in English as well. A distinguished (but moribund) choral group has recently appointed an American born director of very similar youth, linguistic background and professional experience to be at its helm. An internecine 'orthographic war' that erupted during the prior decade quietly ended during the 1990s with a decisive defeat of the Young Turks. The latter had actually advocated a return to an earlier convention (after having previously erratically advocated an ultra-radical ortho-graphic system that attracted even less support), but failed to wean away any but a few members of that same group's associated writers from the YIVO's 'Unified Yiddish Spelling' (adopted in 1937).[4] Among the most adamant defenders of the 'Unified Yiddish Spelling' were a cadre of young university professors of Yiddish in New York, throughout the USA and worldwide. *Yugntruf* has established its own computer bulletin board/ chat group in Yiddish, to join three others that are Yiddish-focused but that are not, generally, conducted in Yiddish.[5] Perhaps even more unusual in the annals of threatened immigrant languages, *Yugntruf* also sponsors a 'writing circle', most of whose members are American born and in their 40's or younger, and a Sunday youth-group (*Pripitshik*) for elementary school-aged children that have at least one Yiddish-speaking parent.

The number of Yiddish 'vinklekh' (once or twice a month clubs, largely English speaking and Yiddish 'appreciating', for adults and senior citizens) continues to expand throughout the country (some 400 such clubs existing at this time), with the Greater New York Metropolitan area represented (although quite 'underwhelmingly' so) among its constituents. A nation-wide federation of all such 'vinklekh' has recently come into being for the purpose of sharing information, programmes and the convening of an annual conference. The Greater New York Metropolitan Area also boasts a small number of active 'zamlers' (collectors) for the National Yiddish Book Center in Massachusetts, making sure that the immigrant generation's Yiddish books are recycled (at quite elegant prices) to individual special-ists, libraries and university collections worldwide. The million-plus copies that the Center has amassed now contain by far the lion's share of all Yiddish books ever published and efforts to digitalise these texts (so as to preserve them permanently from the ravages of time) are now underway. As of this date some 100 Yiddish books are published annually in New York, mostly of ultra-Orthodox content, out of roughly 220–230 published annually worldwide (mostly in Israel where publishing costs are far lower but the majority of titles are still ultra-Orthodox in nature). Nevertheless, unfazed by the competition, secular Yiddish New York is looking forward to the technical compatibility of the internet and of the Web with Yiddish fonts, on-line Yiddish–English and English–Yiddish dictionaries (in the proper spelling, of course) and other such marvels of the 21st century.

All in all, although the secularist scene certainly has no reason to be self-satisfied or smug about its prospects, it can be pardoned for smiling more often than it used to. What a difference a decade can make, on the one hand, and on the other, 'the more things change the more they stay the same': neither the secular Yiddishist[6] *practical* prospects nor the *ideological* under-pinnings to the still substantial and varied efforts of this 'wing' of the Yiddish world are such as to currently engage either the attention or the adherence of the vast majority of American Jews, whether old or young, native or foreign born.

The Flavour of Secular Yiddish Efforts

What are some concrete examples of the enterprises, acts of devotion and sources of knowledge and inspiration that constitute the sinews of community-at-a-distance for secular Yiddishists in New York today? During the spring and summer of 1999, when this chapter was being written, my log of events showed the following items (among others):

February 1999: Under the large heading 'Summer's Yiddish Renaissance', the weekly English *Forward* (a fully independent spin-off of the Yiddish *Forverts*) started of an entire page devoted to events all over the country, three-quarters of which were in 'Metropolitan New York'. Of the more than two-dozen events enumerated and described, one is to be conducted entirely in Yiddish (the YIVO/Columbia summer session), one partially in Yiddish (the Workman's Circle annual 'Mame-Loshen' (mother tongue) weekend of 'seminars [in English], workshops [mostly in English] and entertainment [mostly in Yiddish]. A children's programme will be conducted in English and Yiddish, and the event includes outdoor activities and kosher meals.' All remaining listings refer to events – many explicitly related to Yiddish – conducted entirely in English.

February 1999: The weekly quarter-page advertisement of the Workman's Circle (founded in 1900, its first afternoon supplementary schools were opened in 1919, over socialist opposition that these schools would estrange Jewish children from the international proletariat) regularly placed in the (English) *Forward* is headed 'Where We Stand: Jewish Children, Their Families and the Jewish People'. Yiddish is mentioned in connection with the fraternal order's I.L. Peretz supplementary schools focus on '*familiarity with* Jewish history, Jewish holidays, Jewish rites of passage, and Jewish culture, particularly Yiddish literature, music and art'. Though 'the fundamental importance of Jewish education to the well-being of Jews and the Jewish people is universally recognised', no claim is made that the 1–2 brief sessions per week of the fraternal order's mere handful of remaining schools (out of what were well over a hundred in the early 1930s [Gelibter, 1935]) actually go beyond 'Yiddish appreciation' of one kind or another. 'Familiarity with' does not mean speaking, reading, writing or understanding the language by students for whom it is almost never the mother tongue.[7]

March 1999: The 'Friends of the Secular Yiddish Schools in America Archival Collection' appeal for support for their efforts to reconstruct the entire history of secular Yiddish schooling in the USA. The Collection, housed at Stanford University Libraries (Special Collections Division) includes all pedagogic materials and publications, memorabilia, minutes of School Board Meetings, note books, report cards and photographs pertaining to the four major networks of secular Yiddish schools (Zionist, Socialist, Communist and Non-political, each sponsoring its own schools, from pre-kindergartens to post-high school courses and teachers' seminaries), from before World War I to recent days, scattered throughout the length and breadth of the USA and numbering at their apex in the many hundreds. The work of the 'Friends' is conscientiously bilingual (in minutes, correspondence, newsletter and website), in Yiddish and in English, while the Archival holdings themselves are, by and large, in Yiddish.

May 1999: A cause-sensationelle was the 'desertion' of Janet Hadda, a well known and highly regarded Yiddish professor (at UCLA), writer, translator and literary critic. She published her doubts about the future of Yiddish in America (and her psychoanalytic interpretation of the unwillingness of admirers of the language to accept the death thereof) in *JQ* (*Jewish Quarterly*, one of the very best Anglo-Jewish literary and cultural journals today). Her article was then carried in toto in *Mendele*, the main Yiddish-interest e-mail bulletin board, together with the moderator's rejection of Hadda's theses, and then Hadda's response to that rejection. Thereafter, for many days, *Mendele* was practically monopolised by reader critiques of (and far more rarely, agreements with) Hadda's point of view, methodology and data. What made the situation even more poignant was the fact that similar noteworthy desertions had occurred in previous years (most visibly, that of Professor Ruth Wisse, at Harvard). Several of New York's most visible 'Mendelyaner'. participated in the e-mail storm.

June 1999: The annual Manger Prize for Yiddish Literature (Israel's top prize for literary or scholarly creativity in the world of Yiddish) was announced. Of the three prize recipients, two are professors (one, American-born and a Yiddish activist as well as researcher) most of whose major work is either in English or in Hebrew. Their biographies and parts of their bibliographies were reported in the Yiddish and Anglo-Jewish press, as well as in *Mendele*.

July 1999. The weekly homily on the Torah portion (*parshe fun der vokh*), prepared in Yiddish over the past several years and distributed via e-mail by a member of *Yugntruf*, announced that it was time for the 'summer break'. Its recipients (approximately 100 in all) are varied, but it tends to appeal primarily to secular Yiddishists with a more traditional (neo-religious) inclination and meagre exposure to the traditional sources. Sign of the times? Since the summer break this weekly e-mail 'newsletter' initially appeared only intermittently and currently seems to have lapsed entirely .

August 1999: A Yiddish terminology for computer topics, initially prepared a few years ago, is now being updated. The e-mail bulletin-board for Yiddish computer-matters constantly reports (almost exclusively in English) on new commercially issued programmes that can handle Yiddish and do so with all the letters and diacritics required by the YIVO's Unified Yiddish Orthography. The chat-group is committed to following the standardised 'Unicode' format so that Yiddish encrypted-diskettes or attachments prepared in accord with one programme will be readable by others. As compared to just a few years ago, there are now many Yiddish programmes that follow such a standard format.

30 August–6 September 1999: A biennial Toronto 'event', Ashkenaz, attracts many New York area visitors. Its website describes it as follows: 'A festival of New Yiddish Culture, . . . both richly traditional and thrillingly innovative. The largest festival of its kind in the world . . . eight extravagant days and nights of soul-searching, performance, provocative exhibition, celebrity, public spectacle . . . features klezmer ensembles, jazz musicians, poets, singers, painters, sculptors, actors, dancers, storytellers. Around the world, Yiddish culture is being reborn as artists and art-seekers of all kinds turn toward their roots.' Conspicuous by their absence: opportunities to learn, improve and actually to use Yiddish, although many many participants could 'sing along' when Yiddish songs were being presented.

September 1999: *Yiddishvokh*, a rare 'completely in Yiddish' week for the entire family (but with the accent on Yiddish-speaking singles and young folks, particularly those with Yiddish-speaking children) attracts well over 100 participants to its 24th annual 'happening'. 'You don't need to be able to read or write Yiddish. You don't even need to be a fluent Yiddish speaker. This is an all-too-rare real life Yiddish immersion situation, where you can eat, drink, laugh, joke, twist and shout, all in Yiddish!' The 'happening' is sympathetically reviewed in the *New York Times* (without any attempt at the usual low-brow humour) as being particularly unusual, because its participants are modern in every way, rather than ultra-Orthodox or even necessarily religious. In the last few years, some traditional religious ceremonies have been added to *Yiddishvokh*'s roster of events (e.g. a Friday night 'welcoming of the sabbath' and Saturday morning 'egalitarian' [i.e. men and women sitting together and participating equally] services [in Hebrew] with a Yiddish sermon on both occasions. Sign of the times?

September 1999: The YIVO announces the formation of a new 'Seminar in Yiddish' that will meet every other Friday from noon to 2.00 pm. Such a seminar had been lacking for many years during which practically all of the YIVO's efforts were in English only. The speakers at the Seminar will be 'scholars, doctoral candidates and personalities in the field of Yiddish studies'. It is expected that graduate students at universities throughout the Greater New York Metropolitan Area, working on topics that require a knowledge of Yiddish for access to primary source materials and references, will attend. The YIVO'S library and archives will be open on seminar days exclusively for those participating in the new seminar. The YIVO itself is now part of the Center for Jewish History and no 'tell-tale' Yiddish signs or sounds are in evidence in its new joint-quarters. Sanitised, 'de-ethnicised ethnic organisations' (Fishman, 1966) are still very much a reality on the American scene.

February–September 1999: During this same period there were six all-Yiddish centre-city 'evenings', on literary and other 'current' topics, sponsored and co-sponsored by 'Main line' Yiddish secular cultural organisations and oriented primarily to the 70+ generation (almost all of whom are of Yiddish mother-tongue). These events typically attract audiences of about 150 people. The largest of these is the Workman's Circle annual Passover meal and pageant (previously known as 'the third seyder' and now designated as a 'cultural seyder', to differentiate it from the traditional religious original), much of which consists of songs and poems in Yiddish interspersed with English connective remarks. A somewhat larger number of local 'evenings', convened in various boroughs outside of Manhattan, were also organised during this same period for the same age-group and generally attracted audiences that were from much to somewhat smaller.[8]

The Dimensions of Secular Yiddishist Identity and Behaviour

Secular Yiddishism was never a fully formed or definitively defined ideology. In pre-World War II Eastern Europe it fostered a non-religious (even an anti-religious) Jewish 'peoplehood' identity (just as did secular and generally Hebrew-oriented Zionism), but one which was Yiddish speaking. In addition, it often advocated non-immigration (whether to Palestine or to the Americas or other centres of resettlement outside of Eastern Europe) and generally adhered to one or another left-wing political preference. Although Yiddishism was generally secular in orientation, not unlike most other modern co-territorial Eastern European nationalist movements, it remained in close daily interactional proximity with the mass of religious and traditional Jews there, all of them living in settings in which language, ethnicity and religion were the normal triangualations for most Catholic, Uniate and Eastern Orthodox peoples as well. Yiddishism in pre-World War II Eastern Europe did not advocate political independence, as had most of the region's other minority nationalist movements since the very turn of the century. It frequently viewed some mixture of socialism and cultural autonomy as the desired bulwarks that would protect modern Jews against assimilation or relinguification within the local polity's majority population, even after the bonds of religion had ceased to serve them.

If secular Yiddishism was never fully defined in pre-World War II Eastern Europe, it was even less so in the USA, where no triangulation of ethnicity-religion-language existed and where Jews were viewed as religiously defined and increasingly became self-defined mainly (or even only) along such lines. Judging by the statements and behaviours of the majority of secular Yiddishist spokespersons and organisational members and sympathisers in the New York City area today, the primary dimensions of current 'Yiddishism in action' are implemented as follows:

(1)   Occasional spoken and even more rarely written or read use of the language. Even passive understanding is sometimes also slight, particularly so insofar as traditional Yiddish or modern 'learned' usage are concerned. Residential propinquity with ultra-Orthodox speakers is almost non-existent. Among young secularists, Yiddish is most often acquired as a second language rather than as a mother tongue.

(2)   Yiddish is most frequently a vehicle of spectator enjoyment and print and non-print media entertainment (via klezmer troupes [ensembles, bands, orchestras], choruses, theatre groups, festivals, musical tapes, mulitmedia extravaganzas, comedy sessions, and translated or even transliterated literary texts), rather than a vehicle of everyday face-to-face interaction.

(3)   Even home-based Yiddish involvement is very often via transliterated print and modern *virtual* technologies (e-mail, web pages, audio- and

video-cassettes), rather than via *actual* face-to-face interaction. Yiddish via secondary community (organisational and media programmes) institutions vastly predominates over Yiddish via primary community contacts in family and neighbourhood interactional settings.

(4) For the most part, non-religious Jewish identity and liberal left of centre political preferences. Lack of knowledge and lack of contact *vis-à-vis* religious speakers and their culture or communities is the rule. Lack of own residential concentration is sometimes portrayed as 'futuristic', but it essentially rules out forming a speech community in the usual sociolinguistic sense.

Secular Yiddishism is often at odds with – at least not linked into – such major modern Jewish-American developments as Zionist, 'religionist' (synagogue membership) or traditionalist (holiday and dietary observances) efforts and involvements. As a result, and because of the concomitant disappearance of most mainstream Yiddish fluency and daily use (outside of ultra-Orthodox circles, to which we will turn, below), Yiddishism has become largely peripheral and even exotic *vis-à-vis* the mainstream of New York City Jewish life. It is typified by several unusual and less than optimal developments relative to RLS efforts more generally: (a) a penchant for 'Yiddish entertainment and spectator sports'; (b) an organisational venue and organisational longevity skills (notwithstanding many admittedly serious losses in this connection over the years), rather than vernacular spontaneity. However, the future independent existence of such a former bastion of the secular Yiddish scene as the YIVO appears to many to be endangered by its current incorporation within a newly established, multi-organisational framework favoured by its newfound major contributors (none of whom are Yiddish speaking or Yiddish committed); and (c) a 'theoretical' preference for Yiddish Literary ('high') Culture ('theoretical' because precious little Yiddish literature in Yiddish is now generally read in these circles, even though an admiration for the literary culture continues to be avowed in the abstract) rather than the daily realm that is the expected functional realm of vernaculars. These three emphases are its major underlying claims to recognition today. Few would maintain that these claims come anywhere near to making up for the lack of daily language use, or of demographic centres of informal speech-network concentration, or of explicit ideological self-definition, or of practical RLS prioritisation within its own shrinking orbit.

Secular Yiddishism from an RLS Perspective

In terms of the GIDS stages, most secular Yiddishist RL clearly at either Stage 7 (for seniors well beyond their child-be at Stages 3 and 2 (local and supra-local media, performance ai ment events), often utilising the most modern technologi ... purposes. Such an allocation of functions also clearly leaves a yawning gap in connection with daily vernacular implementation in home-family-neighbourhood-community settings or in the intensive and prolonged school contexts closely linked to the former. The inevitable byproduct of the foregoing, particularly given the Yiddishist disarray insofar as prior ideological clarification is concerned, is that every successive generation of secularist Yiddishists must acquire Yiddish as a second language, ultimately acquiring it imperfectly from a prior generation that had also acquired it imperfectly. Clearly, the prominent spectator sport status of Yiddish in these circles is a direct consequence of the lack of facility *vis-à-vis* the normal speech-community life patterns of vernaculars everywhere.

Rather than belabouring the obviously unenviable position of Yiddish under secular auspices, it is actually rather remarkable to note what the remaining devotion to and fondness for the language have nevertheless accomplished. It is also remarkable that three generations after the Holocaust had annihilated the major reserve of its mother-tongue speakers, on the one hand, and after the major premises of the initial secularist ideological manifesto (most usually cultural autonomy, secular peoplehood and socialism) have become largely inoperative in today's American environment, on the other hand, secular Yiddishism continues to exist at all, given its heavy interaction with the general, non-Jewish environment of New York. Clearly, the dangers that secular Yiddishism faces are of two kinds: those that derive from its external close relationships with the modern secular world at large, and those that derive from its own internal ideological dynamics. Both of these dangers are to some extent modifiable and, in the present case, they are both also highly interrelated.

Is there a Future for Secular Yiddishism?

The answer to this question depends on whether stateless and residentially unconcentrated languages can maintain a completely 'secular existence (culture and identity) of their own' and, through that separateness, a language of their own in which their culture and identity can be best expressed? Our answer to the immediately above question must influence our answer to the question put by the section heading. If France is nervous about the ability of its culture and identity to withstand the onslaught of

..modern, English dominated, globalisation propelled secular modernism and consumer pop-culture, and if smaller state-forming ethnolinguistic groups the world over are complaining bitterly about the inroads of English dominated globalisation, secular modernism and consumer pop-culture into their local contexts, then what hope can there be for minority languages in contexts like those of secular Yiddishism in New York that veritably live within the lion's den *per se*? The power of RLS analysis is that it both points to what not to do (essentially more of the same 'buckshot' efforts that are labelled 'cultural work' [kultur-arbet] in Yiddish secular circles) and what would make most sense at the particular juncture at which it now finds itself. Of course, practical sense and ideological inertia may cancel each other out at any particular time and place.

In the very midst of a generational whirlwind of 'return to English speaking but tradition venerating Orthodoxy (and even ultra-Orthodoxy)', a return which has effectively robbed secular Yiddishism of any but the most minimal role in the consciousness of the last two younger generations, the time may have come to admit that progressive and secular Yiddish culture *per se* is also a great handicap for RLS and, therefore, a decided minus for the future of secular Yiddishism. Partaking of, participating in, and contributing to every aspect of English dominated secular modernism and consumer pop-culture as it does, secular Yiddishism's high-tech, spectator-sport and minimalist 'now and then' Yiddish (or, even just 'about Yiddish' or 'Yiddish appreciation', rather than intimate daily home–family use of Yiddish *per se*) lacks the separation and the insistence on difference that are needed in order to maintain its own beloved language as an actively functioning and intergenerationally transmissible vehicle within its very own ranks. That is not to say that its end is near. Asymptotic curves constantly approximate but never quite hit the baseline; nevertheless the area remaining under the curve may not be enough to enable a first language (mother tongue) generation to once more come into being.

With modern Yiddish literature and literary creativity as its optimal functional goal and icon, secular Yiddishism could benefit immensely from implementing the Maori-derived kehanga-reo model as long as a few natively Yiddish-speaking grandmothers and grandfathers (mostly foreign born) are still around. Judging by the Maori successes at a juncture when Maori was in worse straits than secularist Yiddishism is today, it would take but a few years before such childcare 'language nests' for toddlers and even pre-toddlers would produce a crop of Yiddish-speaking nursery school and pre-kindergartners, just at the time that their parents, who would simultaneously be studying 'Yiddish for home-family-neighbourhood-community life' (during evenings and weekends) would have learned enough Yiddish as a Second Language to more fully implement the language themselves at home. Such a two-front approach, involving grandparents, parents still of child-bearing age and newly-borns, would link Stages 7 and 6 and point the way to Stage 5 as the next step to take (assuming 4 was out of the question, due to resource limitations and continuing ideological opposition to weakening the public schools). The numbers involved in such a stage-linking venture would initially be small, but even the addition of a dozen Yiddish mother tongue tots living in a three-generational context would be a revolutionary accomplishment for secular Yiddishism.

At the ideological level, more of a 'plus' (additive) rather than an 'instead of' (subtractive) approach is clearly needed. Secular Yiddishism needs to be recast from its original 'nationalism, anti-clericalism, socialism plus literature' model to a model that stresses 'Jewish tradition-friendly Yiddish secularism' or 'Judaism plus' as an add-on modification to any other model of traditional Jewish life. Most religious Jews do not aspire to a 'Jewish secularism' of their own. Yiddishists might proudly claim *that* as a goal (via Yiddish theatre, choruses, media, scouting and camping, etc.) in addition to the usual range and variety of traditional observances that define traditional American Jewish communities. Cast in this light, 'Yiddish secularism plus Jewish traditions' might be viewed as an enrichment, whereas 'secular Yiddishism' is now often seen as an impoverishment of a thousand-year-old Great Tradition. Modern Israeli Hebrew, of course, could also possibly fill this same role (as the language of a separate Jewish secular life in the USA) for some, but Hebrew is largely identified in the USA with Israeli anti-clerical 'yordim' (those who have left the State of Israel) or with Israel *per se*. Fifty years of experience has proven that most traditional American Jews do not identify with Hebrew as a vernacular for themselves – however much they admire and respect it – whereas Yiddish was at least until recently the vernacular of their very own parents and / or grandparents – as much as they consider it lacking in chic, power or modernity and, therefore, 'not for them'. Once again we find the pattern which admires but does not implement what is viewed as the 'high language' from the Holy Land, and simultaneously rejects the possibility of re-adopting the personal-memories-suffused 'folk-language' of one's one posterity, even though some still have a passive command of it.

The 'folk language' (still referred to as a dialect or zhargon by some in the younger generation) might have more personal relevance, particularly if viewed as an 'extra plus' in connection with the secular lives that most of them also lead. The 'availability' of Hebrew is least attractive to those for whom RLS *vis-à-vis* Yiddish is on the agenda. A shift from secular

Yiddishism to 'Yiddish secularism plus' might provide entre into the larger world of moderately traditional young folks that now stand aside from Yiddish because for them it is 'too frum' (too religious, i.e. ultra-Orthodox in their personal experience), whereas once upon a time, for their grandparents, it was often associated with being too secular, 'left-wing' or even atheistic.

A conscientious shift from (a) secular Yiddishism to 'Yiddish secularism plus', and (b) from 'Yiddish appreciation' to 'active Yiddish use' via emphasising the first language acquisition locale of home-family-neighbourhood-community functioning, is obviously not for everyone. It may not appeal to many secular Yiddishists at first. But it is a beginning to the search for an answer to the dilemmas of 'being neither fully alive nor fully dead'. These are the dilemmas that typify Yiddish in secularist circles in New York as the 21st century opens. There are more young people who are professionally involved with Yiddish today than there were a generation ago (professors and teachers, translators and musicians, group leaders and entertainers, researchers and students), and there is a much more frequent acknowledgment of regret among many others that one's parents did not pass the language along to them (or that they were not interested as children in acquiring it). But it is not at all clear what can be done about these regrets, who should do it (e.g. who should try to draw those hundred or so college student studying Yiddish in New York at any one time into secular Yiddish society?), and, above all, how can a young secularist couple that decides to start a family and raise their children in Yiddish 'connect' with a corresponding speech community 'out there'? Unanswered basic questions such as these – much more than any lack of writers, readers or even speakers – reveal the great uncertainty and even the fundamental dangers that are ahead for secular Yiddishism in the city that is still its unofficial New World capital.

The Current Ultra-Orthodox Scene of Yiddish in New York

The ultra-Orthodox Yiddish scene in New York is almost the diametric opposite of the secularist scene that we have just reviewed. However, in addition to each 'scene' having strengths exactly where the other has weaknesses, they also interact with each other hardly at all and are, in fact, two soliloquies; each of them speaks but hears not the other. When Janet Hadda and other heretofore Yiddish speaking and Yiddish involved secular intellectuals decide to leave the fold, they often reveal that they know that an ultra-Orthodox Yiddish world exists and flourishes. On the other hand, they do not analyse its dynamics nor seek to understand the lessons to be learned from that world. All that secular Yiddishists see in the ultra-Orthodox is neanderthal-like religious fanaticism that does not create (nor even know about, much less read) world-class Yiddish literature. Nor does it even aspire to modern concepts of social justice and egalitarian gender roles. These 'fanatics' and their children may speak Yiddish at home, at work, at the house of worship and in school, but their Yiddish is replete with anglicisms and Germanisms and follows medieval orthographic conventions. Thus, secular Yiddishists curiously reject that which lives and is growing while they cleave to that which is admittedly wilting before their very eyes and is patently beyond their ability to revernacularise. Again we see a pattern which had typified all of the 20th century (first mentioned by Nathan Birnbaum at the very beginning of the 20th century [1906]) among huge blocks of Westernised Jews: not accepting the language and culture which lives and breaths, on the one hand, and not implementing the 'preferred but totally ethereal language and culture', which has little chance of being put into active use in their own midst. German, Polish and Russian Zionists, like the mainstream of American Jewry and even the secular Yiddishists in New York today were/are all trapped in a sociolinguistic cycle of rejecting that language which exists within reach and not implementing that language which they purport(ed) to prefer. The ultra-Orthodox sector alone seems to have implemented complementary (and, therefore, non-conflictual) functions for all of the languages to which they are exposed.

Although participants in the Mendele e-mail bulletin board discussion of Janet Hadda's resignation from the secular Yiddishist struggle almost unanimously rejected her point of view, they differed with respect to her dismissal of the ultra-Orthodox users of the language. Most agreed with her, however, that the ultra-Orthodox disinterest in the best of modern Yiddish literature and in modern secular progressive movements made them unworthy partners on behalf of the Yiddish 'cause'. However, only a minority of 'mendeliyaner' took sharp exception to the chorus of anti-Haredi views that nevertheless unite Wisse, Hadda and most of their sharpest critics.

I can only express my total dismay that a self-professed academic can call a language spoken by at least 200,000 Americans (1990 US Census figures, not emotional dismay, prejudice, politics) 'dead'. Facing the fact that Yiddish is spoken by an ever-growing, extremely traditional Jewish population (haredim) is sound scholarship. Systematically dismissing this group simply because one does not like haredim is not sound scholarship and borders on a blatant misrepresentation of reality, a 'crime' for academics who are committed to educating others. For those academics who believe that haredim are not interested in Yiddish literature, I suggest they start reading Haredi Yiddish publications where they will find pious poetry and various forms of Yiddish narrative. (xi/19/98, Bruce Mitchell)

Another defender of the ultra-Orthodox is also concerned about their literary reputation (and in the process of so doing, confirms the secular style of 'Yiddish as a sometime thing'):

Regardless of your personal opinion of these people . . . they are linguistically living what most of us only discuss on the internet or do as a hobby or nostalgic whim. If Yiddish is to survive into the 21st century, it is people like the readers of this paper [*Der yid*, the major ultra-Orthodox weekly in New York, see below] and many other papers like it that quietly publish on a regular basis, who will keep it alive . . . Yiddish . . . is their medium of communication, not a cause or a subject for study. However, by virtue of the fact that it has served for so long as the language of the Jewish people and as a medium for Torah [study of holy texts] they [also] consider it a holy language (according to one well known torah personality . . .). (xi/10/98, Hershl Goodman)

Suffice it to say, that the secular Yiddishist and the ultra-Orthodox Yiddish worlds are both intellectually and physically distant from each other, not knowledgeable about each other and in no way helpful to one other. To make matters worse, the latter has overtaken the former as the major force on behalf of the continuity of the language and that rankles the one and delights the other, thereby further distancing them from one another, not only intellectually, but emotionally as well.

Some Ultra-Orthodox Facts of Life

The best estimates (at which several investigators have independently arrived) put the number of ultra-Orthodox speakers of Yiddish in the USA at about 300,000. Almost all of the foregoing live in the Greater New York Metropolitan Area or in the counties immediately adjacent to it. As such, they are at least a hundred fold more numerous than are the secular Yiddishists, on the one hand, and they are daily speakers – most of them young and at or before child-bearing age, on the other hand. Their rate of demographic growth is extremely high and, as the total Jewish population in the USA (and in the Greater New York Metropolitan Area as well) steadily grows older and decreases in numbers, due both to age and to intermarriage, the ultra-Orthodox will become proportionately ever more prominent among its numbers. *Vis-à-vis* all other Yiddish speakers in the USA and in the GNYMA (including the unorganised and non-ideological 'middle range' speakers, situated between the Ultra-Orthodox and the secular Yiddishists), the former may already (or soon will) constitute the majority. They maintain over 1200 synagogues and smaller houses of worship and conduct a constantly growing number of Yiddish-using all-day-schools (108 in the early 1980s and approximately 150 today, i.e. roughly a third of the total number of Jewish all-day-schools in the USA today). They live in compact neighbourhoods where the bulk of their total vernacular activity is in Yiddish. The magnitude of their book and periodical production is hard to pin-point, since it does not reach or concern the secularist record keepers:

> When I inquired at the National Yiddish Book Center and YIVO not too long ago, I was told that they didn't know of anyone attempting to comprehensively collect and preserve 'that type' of Yiddish material. 'That type' . . . consists of many original books [as well as a large number of republished books that first appeared in ultra-Orthodox strongholds in Eastern Europe-JAF], poetry, journals and a myriad of audio tapes . . . , almost all of it being put out by small, independent publishers in Brooklyn and other centers . . . far surpass[ing] in output and consumption anything produced by the secular camp. (xi/10/98 Hershl Goodman; see also the comments by Aaron Nadler on the same date re new scholarly genres in Ultra-Orthodox literary production).

Interestingly enough, it is only at the YIVO, the erstwhile intellectual headquarters of secular Yiddishism, that young researchers from the two worlds of Yiddish see each other and spend many hours of many days 'virtually' together. In the YIVO's new and quite lavish reading room, these two worlds sit separately, reading quite different books and periodicals, and interacting with one another little if at all. The members of one world converse quietly, in English, and are fully familiar with the etiquette of the 'library and archives culture'. The others, in ankle-length kaftans and with earlocks swaying, converse less quietly, in Yiddish, and are intermittently scolded by the librarians (in English) for their infractions of that culture. ('Items should be returned to the shelves in exactly the same locations from which they were removed! Please return the material you have borrowed before requesting anything further!') Daily scenes of this kind tell us more about the secular and the ultra-Orthodox worlds of Yiddish in New York than either group of researchers may realise. Once again, Eastern Europeans are being 'civilised' by Westernised Jews. Once again, Yiddish is associated with a less polished but a more intergenerationally continuous tradition of language-in-culture and a tradition that is becoming increasingly literate in the process of contact.

Ultra-Orthodox Yiddish in Print: Insight into the Language's Communal Role

If substantiated (and I fully expect that it will be), the above-mentioned claims of Goodman and Nadler would constitute a particularly cruel irony, since the literary uses of Yiddish are so strongly entrenched in the secularist claim to fame and of such minor significance in the total ultra-Orthodox life-style. The literary uses of a language must inevitably reflect or complement the roles assigned to it in the total 'linguistic space', and even in the total 'cultural space', of its speech community. Among the ultra-Orthodox, Yiddish in print is still very often an *aide-memoire*, an auxiliary translation and commentary accompanying classical or rabbinic texts that simultaneously appear in Hebrew/Judeo-Aramaic. Accordingly, a special pre-holiday sale of a new edition of the Book of Psalms is advertised as 'the Book of Psalms that translates for you as you recite them, the translation being under every word, in a very clear Yiddish that is interspersed with and connects the verses themselves and provides you with a clear understanding of each and every prayer' (Translated from *Dos yidishe vort*, ix/1999, p. 26).

The major ultra-Orthodox Yiddish weekly, *Der Yid* (established in 1950) constantly reveals another facet of Yiddish in the community, namely, its role as the language of popular adult education. *Advice for a Good Life* (in two volumes) is advertised as 'written in easy and very readable Yiddish, beautifully laid out and a pleasure to look at, divided into topics and paragraphs, and brought to you with the approval of the most famous and dependable rabbis. Useful in every Jewish home! With the help of God, all will benefit from it!' (Translated from *Der Yid*. 15 October 1999, p. 49.)

Finally, also relevant to the often overlooked role of Yiddish in print among the ultra-Orthodox, it should be mentioned that every issue of *Der Yid* contains a 2–3 page section entitled 'For the entire family'. This section includes Judaism-centred games, riddles, jokes, puzzles (including crossword puzzles) as well as a separate sub-section 'For younger children'. Each issue closes with a reminder that 'the names of children who send in correct answers will be published and will be entered in a give-away of worthwhile books'. (The *Forverts* too introduced (1999) a very attractive but generally shorter and quite different monthly section of this kind.) There is also a publishing house entirely devoted to Yiddish (including Yiddish and

Hebrew) textbooks for ultra-Orthodox schools. Hundreds of such texts – almost entirely devoted to the Judaica curriculum – have now been published, given that all of the schools cover grades k through 8 and, in addition, there are also a smaller number of Yiddish-medium high schools for Grades 9 through 12. In addition, individual educators are constantly preparing and self-publishing story books for children (and for adults too), as well as story-tapes, song-tapes and Judaica review-tapes. Clearly, in parts of the ultra-Orthodox world there is a vibrant child market for suitable Yiddish material, something the secular Yiddish world has not had for more than 50 years. Finally, the circulations and numbers of pages per issue of the two major weeklies (the secular one and the ultra-Orthodox one) are also similarly discrepant. *Der Yid* has a certified circulation of over 50,000 and its issues are normally 72 tabloid-sized pages long, always accompanied by a supplement of another 40–44 pages. In comparison, the *Forvert*'s usual 24 pages tabloid sized [but two-coloured] pages are subscribed to by under 10,000.[9]

The Nature of Ultra-Orthodox Yiddish

Perhaps a few words should be said here about the 'quality' of Ultra-Orthodox Yiddish. This quality (often negatively commented upon in the secular Yiddish press) varies from very poor to very good, the former being noted for its high rate of quite unnecessary English borrowings (lexically and even grammatically) and the latter, by its infusion of learned Hebraisms. As is the case throughout the world, different varieties of the same language have come to typify speech networks that interact little with one another. This was true of Christian and non-Christian Latin in ancient Rome. But it was also true as late as mid-20th century with respect to the Arabic of Baghdadi Jews, Moslems and Christians (Blanc 1964), on the one hand, as well as of Bengali (Bengladeshi) among Moslems and Hindus in what was then East Pakistan (Dil, 1991), on the other hand. It would be a comparatively easy task to demonstrate that it is also true of secular and ultra-Orthodox Yiddish in New York. In matters orthographic the difference is even bolder, the YIVO's 'unified Yiddish spelling' having only the slimmest of slim footholds in the ultra-Orthodox world as a whole and particularly so, in New York.

Nevertheless, the distances between all of the ultra-Orthodox and secularist varieties (each group having more than one) are rather minor and the two communities *can* fully understand one another rather easily, whether in face-to-face or in written functions. Probably the greatest difference lies in the fact that the secularists have adopted (and probably even overstress, to compensate for their rather meagre daily use of the language) the modern Eastern European normifying tradition and recognise (or give lip service to) both norm-setting individuals and norm-setting institutions for this very purpose. Both normifying individuals and institutions for Yiddish are still lacking in the ultra-Orthodox world, probably because their most vital and prestigious publication and writing is in Hebrew/Judeo-Aramaic. For the language of some half million or more ultra-Orthodox daily speakers of Yiddish (combing their numbers in the USA, Israel, Montreal and Antwerp) to be declared 'deficient' by a few thousand secular devotees, most of whom rarely utilise the language that they love so much and that frequently cannot do so correctly themselves, is not only another instance of the 'Birnbaumian paradox' referred to several times above, but a total misplacement of secular Yiddishist emphases.

Yiddish Advocacy in Ultra-Orthodox New York

Two types of Yiddish advocacy are present in ultra-Orthodox New York. The first is oriented toward the more interactive and 'out-reach' involved segments of the Khasidic community itself. These segments have slowly lost Yiddish as their intergenerational vernacular and in this way they have been influenced – by virtue of their more frequent contacts and interactions – by the very Jews whom they themselves have sought to lead toward ultra-Orthodoxy. Foremost among the 'interactionist' ultra-Orthodox are the Lubavitcher, whose late (and perhaps last) Rabbi invariably preached, lectured, wrote and broadcast worldwide in impeccable and very learned Yiddish, even to audiences to whom his every word had to be translated. Since 'the Rebbe's' demise (in 1994), no substitute speaker of Yiddish of the 'very highest authority' has made an appearance in Lubavitsher circles. This may serve to further erode Yiddish there, notwithstanding the semi-official role that the weekly *Algemeyner Zhurnal* plays in this community. Some notable resistance to any such erosion has also appeared. Thus, in the February 1999 issue of their publication for women, *N'shei Chabad Newsletter*, Rabbi Reuven Wittkes writes (under the heading 'The Case for Total Immersion':

> I don't think there is any doubt in our minds that Yiddish is and should be an important part of our children's lives and their education. It is also apparent from the various *Sichos* [Talks] and *Igros* [Letters] of the Rebbe that the children should indeed be learning Yiddish. It is not the aim of this article to debate this issue, as it has been discussed at length many times in this and other fine publications. Within the context of this article, the need for Yiddish is accepted as a given. . . . But that

doesn't mean it comes easy. [However,] . . . I have found, after nearly two decades of teaching young children, that when Yiddish is the only language they hear in class, it quickly becomes familiar enough to them and [thereafter] learning in Yiddish is as simple for them as learning in English . . . [So] let's give them . . . the language that united the Jews through the generations, the language of the Rebbeyim [khasidic rabbis], the language of Moshiach [the Messiah]. (p. 59)

The above article was followed-up a month later by congratulatory letters from parents and students, including a call for more attention to Yiddish grammar and syntax, not only for the sake of the pupils but for that of the teachers themselves. In addition, one letter called for the constant (in school and out of school) use of Yiddish among the pupils themselves, rather than merely its use between them and their teachers. It was claimed that only such constant use would be fully in accord with the late Rebbe's wishes. Such intra-Khasidic advocacy (as well as similar advocacy of Yiddish within ultra-Orthodox but non-Khasidic circles) is probably both a good sign and a bad sign. On the one hand, the struggle for 'Yiddishising' the younger ultra-Orthodox generation is still ongoing and new and better efforts in that connection are underway. On the other hand, this implies that Yiddish has already generally been lost among many of the younger members of the most interactive ultra-Orthodox groups, where the parental and, particularly, the grandparental generations are still thoroughly Yiddish speaking.

In addition to the foregoing, Yiddish advocacy is also underway within ultra-Orthodox circles that are still fully Yiddish speaking intergenerationally but whose insistence or requirements in that connection sometimes seem to be wavering. Thus, a letter to the editor of *Der Yid* (13 August 1999, p. 6) complains about the increase in English advertising carried by the weekly:

Now I ask you: Is that proper? What would our late rebbe, of blessed memory, say about such goings on in the very paper that he established with so much of his own sweat and effort, . . . so that his followers could find a quiet corner in which to slake their thirst for knowledge without looking at journals and newspapers that are chock full of material that can harm one's own soul and the souls of one's posterity? This matter of Yiddish pertains to one of the three main separators between Jews and gentiles: names, clothing and language. (translated from Yiddish: JAF)

In a prior issue (10 April 1992), the wife of a rebbe warned and motivated the weekly's female readership as follow:

> All students carry a great responsibility to take an uncompromising position not to drown in the American sea. Let us turn back and reconnect with the lively and holy generations before us. Through Yiddish, the mother tongue, each Jew will feel the spark of his or her mother's heart and the fire of sanctity will light up and the presence of God will be felt in all of our homes. (p. 42, translated from Yiddish: JAF)

Summary: The Two Worlds of Yiddish in New York

The world – including most of the Jewish world – has long regarded Yiddish as dead or dying, because it could not imagine (and didn't really desire or aspire to) the continuity of a separate Yiddish culture and identity into and throughout the modern period. Many American Jews not only adopted this dubious stance *vis-à-vis* themselves, and joined the 'Yiddish is dead or dying chorus', but became its first and chief heralders. Furthermore, we have noted that within the very two-in-one worlds of Yiddish itself the doubt as to the survival (nay, the very existence) of 'the other wing' has become paramount. Neither wing has any sympathy nor sense of fraternity with the other. Each freely and fully foregoes the assests that the other could bring to a combined RLS struggle. Perhaps this is how other weakened groups fractionate. Each sees in the other only the most complete denial and rejection of its own existence and *raison d'etre*.

The two sundered worlds of Yiddish in New York can also be found, equally sundered, in Israel, in Antwerp, in Melbourne, in Montreal, i.e. wherever larger ultra-Orthodox and secular Yiddish speakers live side by side as non-interacting soliloquies. The secularists are concerned with Yiddish theatre, Yiddish song concerts, Yiddish literary awards and Yiddish lectures on intellectual topics and on current affairs. The ultra-Orthodox are concerned with Yiddish both as an auxiliary vehicle of co-sanctity as well as as the intra-communal vehicle of all vernacular pursuits, among adults and children alike. The old-world-like ultra-Orthodox, with their beards, side curls and black kaftans for men and with their kerchiefs, wigs and long black stockings for women, are all American born by now, but they are carefully more *in* America than *of* it. Their main concern is upholding the very compartmentalisation of Jewish vs non-Jewish traditions, customs and lifestyles into which the secularists seek to integrate in all but language.

Ultra-Orthodox Yiddish is firmly anchored in the home-family-neigh-bourhood and community nexus (Stage 6), with strong links to stages 5 and/or 4a (i.e. their very own schools that are fully under community auspices and control) and even reaching out to many businesses fully staffed by its own members (Stage 3). Secularist Yiddish has no such concentration at the real home-family-neighbourhood-community level. It uses the Internet for *virtual* community purposes and meets face-to-face for large group events, both of which are by and large unrelated to intergenerational mother-tongue transition. The ultra-Orthodox are growing by leaps and bounds, but are confronting and resisting some attri-tion 'at the edges', where its 'outreach activity' has brought it into intimate interaction with the less observant or completely non-observant American Jewish community as a whole, or where its economic pursuits have led it into interdependence with the mainstream of American life. On the whole however, the Ultra-Orthodox are maintaining (and even improving) their intergenerational mother-tongue continuity by expanding their institu-tional community feedback opportunities via schools, summer camps, family vacation settlements, neighbourhood study groups for adults and their own market for books, periodicals, tapes, newspapers and even local theatre performances.

In contrast with their status 10 years ago, the ultra-Orthodox would seem to be stronger now then they were then, although by no means totally problem-free, even in their own eyes, particularly with respect to the Stage 6 level and the subsequent institutional stages that must be carefully coordinated with and related to it. It is particularly in the work-sphere (Stage 3) that the ultra-Orthodox need to acquire additional economic opportunities via Yiddish for the younger generations down the pike. The secularists are weaker than they were a decade ago. They have lost a number of their most central and beloved institutions at Stages 2 and 3 and are about to lose the last octogenarians who are a direct link to the vibrant, natively Yiddish-speaking Eastern European culture that produced them originally. As their numbers decrease, they increasingly become a group of American born 'Yiddish as a second language' hobbyists for whom intergenerational mother tongue continuity is, generally speaking, neither intended nor possible. Its future in these networks is the same as the future of intergenerational hobby networks with respect to their special interests in a variety of pastimes or artistic and intellectual pursuits. From time to time, Secular Yiddishism may yet create some new great works of culture or scholarship, but, generally speaking, it revisits the past and, above all, it is not a real speech community, i.e. one that can foster the intergenerational childhood language acquisition and enculturation of its own offspring. The children and grandchildren of stamp collectors and history buffs do not form a community of interest, much less a speech community. They are not expected to become (nor do they by and large become) stamp collectors or history buffs themselves.

Conclusions

There is a century's worth of upheaval, heartache and renewal in the story of Yiddish in New York. A century ago it seemed that 'progress' would clearly triumph and that the secularist dream of a thoroughly modernised and socially 'progressive' Jewish people would fully displace the strictures and orthodoxies of the past. Both the Holocaust and the collapse of the left, on the one hand, and the incorporative triumph of the culturally and economically more open and advanced capitalist democracies, on the other hand, have resulted in the collapse of the progressive dream and a turn toward a more traditional and family oriented Judaism for many younger Jews. Some have even embraced ultra-Orthodoxy again, based on the implicit faith of their grandparents and the scrupulous implementation of God's commandments. This same turn (or turn-over) has characterised large populations the world over. The certainties of fundamentalism have proved to be much more comforting than the uncertainties of modernism. Fundamentalism erects barriers against the confusing and morally conflicted world of compromise, relativism, self-gratification and innovation. Accordingly, its barriers may also provide a much clearer boundary maintenance pattern for RLS than modernisation ever does or could do, particularly in the face of American controlled globalisation, consumerism and mass pop-culture.[10] The triumph of the ultra-Orthodox 'ugly duckling' is a Cinderella story seemingly made to order for RLS efforts on behalf of threatened languages.

Threatened languages can survive their contact with the modern world only to the extent that they can maintain strong communities and viable cultural boundaries within the lion's cave itself. If they oppose religious fundamentalism, as they mostly do, then it is up to them to devise equally sheltering boundaries of a secular nature. Where political boundaries are impossible or no longer serve as bulwarks against modern Big Brother's language-in-culture, then threatened languages must answer the dilemma of what other bulwarks they can propose, erect and successfully defend. Language itself is not enough of a bulwark to defend threatened cultures and identities. Certainly when the underlying cultures are practically identical, the Big Brother's language must displace the smaller one. Language cannot be the ultimate defence for threatened cultures and identities, because threatened languages themselves need defences: the distinctive values, cultural practices and beliefs (including uncompromising identity-beliefs) that make a distinctive language necessary and even possible. Yiddish *is* just like all other threatened languages in this connection – particularly like all other immigrant languages without any political boundaries at all (or anywhere) to fall back on – indeed, just like all the others 'but even more so'.

Notes

1. Lout, oaf, nincompoop.
2. A gentile employed to perform various tasks, such as lighting the stove or turning the electricity on/off, on Saturdays, when such activities are culturally defined as work and, therefore, prohibited by Orthodox strictures.
3. Earlier college level Yiddish courses had been given by A.A. Roback (Harvard), Nathan Suskind (CCNY and Yeshiva College), Judah Yaffe (at a World War II precursor of the New School for Social Research) and Max Weinreich (CCNY). Uriel Weinreich's programme at Columbia University's Department of Linguistics was the first (and remained the only one in the USA) to encompass a graduate course of Yiddish specialisation culminating in the award of the PhD.
4. It is this orthographic convention that is now recognised by almost all of the major secular literary journals and academic teaching centres throughout the world. This is a rare instance of largely successful, even if long delayed, corpus planning for a minority language that is totally without any official (state-related) enforcement apparatus.
5. At this writing the advent of Yiddish character e-mail and website capability that is compliant with all Unicode requirements is being eagerly awaited and frequently discussed by an e-mail chat group that focuses on the technical problems of Yiddish and cyberspace activity.
6. The term 'Yiddishist' has semantically metamorphosed during the past quarter century. From its original meaning of denoting those for whom Yiddish concerns constituted the very core of their Jewish identity, it has now come to denote anyone who is not ultra-Orthodox who is judged to have either full fluency or even just an active interest in Yiddish. The increasing rarity of the language outside of ultra-Orthodox circles doubtlessly underlies the semantic shift and the semantic blurring that has occurred. I will continue to use the term here as close to its original meaning as I can.
7. The new introductory textbook, issued for these schools in 1999, puts this somewhat more poetically: 'The goal for this curriculum is to make available to all, the beauty, the melody, the rhythm of Yiddish and the educational support for Yiddish holiday lore and pageantry' Borodulin, 1999: 1).
8. A few additional 1999 New York events that were sponsored by the secularist Yiddish sector can be found in the Congress for Jewish Culture's bilingual *In the World of Yiddish/In der velt fun yidish*, planned as an annual publication. On the other hand, my own records itemise many more New York events than does the Congress' publication, primarily because the latter attempts to give a positive worldwide picture, whereas my focus is entirely on the Greater New York City Metropolitan Area and does not attempt to screen out problematic material.

9. Another fervently Orthodox weekly, *Der Algemeyner Zhurnal*, is a full-sized (rather than tabloid sized) paper. It regularly has a 4–6 page English supplement and lists a registered circulation of *c*. 60,000. In addition, there are three other Ultra-Orthodox weeklies today, all of them entirely in Yiddish: *Der Blat*, Di *Tsaytung* un *Di Vokh*. Their circulations are uncertified but minimal estimates would put the total weekly ultra-Orthodox circulation at between 150,000 and 200,000.

10. By the time advanced English language skills may become important to many members of the male ultra-Orthodox community, English can be no more than a third language for them (after Yiddish and classical/rabbinic Hebrew). A Yiddish display ad in the *Algemeyner Zhurnal* of vi/25/99 [p. 3] reads: 'A Good Opportunity for Observant Young Men: Learn How to Read, Write and Speak English. This will help you earn a living, and also in daily life, e.g., in filling out important applications. You will also be able to become familiar with computer science, which has become an important key to the business world. Don't miss this rare chance!' It is from just such ultra-Orthodox circles that the heavily Yiddish impacted variety of English often called 'Yeshivish' initially stems. Although some Yiddish borrowings in English date back much earlier, Yeshivish has by now attained considerable currency among both Jews and non-Jews far removed from contact with the Ultra-Orthodox (Gold, 1981, Fishman, 1985). The precise reach of Yeshivish and other Yiddish borrowings in English is now being studied (Benor, MS).

References

Benor, S. (MS) What is 'Yeshivish', Who Knows it and How Much?

Birnbaum, N. (1906) Die todte Sprache; die lebende Nichtsprache. *Neue Zeitung*. 1(2) 14 September.

Blanc, H. (1964) *Communal Dialects in Baghdad*. Cambridge: Harvard University Press.

Borodulin, N. (1999) *Yidish oyf a gants yor/Yiddish Year Round*. New York: Workman's Circle.

Dil, A. (1991) *Two Traditions of the Bengali Language*. Cambridge: Islamic Academy.

Gelibter, F. (ed.) (1935) Di arbeter-ring shuln: ufkum un antviklung. In his *Shul almanakh: di yidishe moderne shul af der velt*. Philadelphia: Central Committee of the Workman's Circle Schools.

Gold, D. (1981) Jewish English. In C.A. Ferguson and S.B. Heath (eds) *Language in the USA*. Cambridge: Cambridge University Press.

Halpern, M-L. (1919) Undzer gortn. *In nyu-york*. New York: Vinkl .

Harshav, B. (1990) *The Meaning of Yiddish*. Berkeley: University of California Press.

Fishman, J.A. (1965) Yiddish in America. *International Journal of American Linguistics* 31(2) (entire issue). (Also published separately by Mouton, The Hague).

Fishman, J.A. (1966) *Language Loyalty in the United States*. The Hague: Mouton.

Fishman, J.A. (1981) *Never Say Die! A Thousand Years of Yiddish in Jewish Life and Letters*. The Hague: Mouton.

Fishman, J.A. (1985) *The Rise and Fall of the Ethnic Revival*. Berlin: Mouton.

Fishman, J.A. (1985) *Readings in the Sociology of Jewish Languages*. Leiden: E.J. Brill.

Fishman, J.A. (1989) *Yiddish: Returning to Life*. Amsterdam: Benjamins.

Chapter 5

Reversing Language Shift in Quebec[1]

R.Y. BOURHIS[2]

In his now classic framework, Joshua Fishman portrayed French Quebec as one of the three 'success stories' of 'Reversing Language Shift' (Fishman, 1991). French Quebec has emerged as a symbolic case for the 'Xish' language minorities of the world, for it shows that sustained language planning can reverse language shift even relative to the most powerful language of this millennium: English. The main goal of this chapter is to provide an analytic update of the Quebec sociolinguistic situation following the adoption of language laws designed to increase the status of French relative to English in the Province. Combining both the group vitality analysis and the reversing language shift framework, the first part of the chapter will analyse the circumstances which led successive Quebec governments to adopt language laws in favour of French during the last three decades. The second part of the chapter will provide an update of the French–English demolinguistic situation following 20 years of RLS efforts for the French language in Quebec. As inhabitants of a province of Canada or as members of a newly proclaimed independent state, the chapter will conclude with thoughts on how RLS policies have changed the vitality position of Francophones and Anglophones in the only French majority jurisdiction in North America.

Group Vitality and Language Shift and Quebec

In this section we propose that the ethnolinguistic vitality framework (Bourhis, 1979) can be seen as a necessary tool of analysis complementing the reversing language shift model proposed by Fishman (1991). We will seek to illustrate this point by providing an analysis of the vitality position of the Francophone and Anglophone communities of Quebec in the years leading up to the adoption of the *Charter of the French language* in 1977 (Bourhis, 1984a).

Given the rise of ethnic revival movements across the world in the latter part of the 20th century (Fishman, 1999), the group vitality framework was developed to analyse more systematically the relative sociostructural position of language groups in contact. As pointed out by Harwood *et al.*, (1994):

> It became clear that processes such as language shift, language atti-
> tudes, interethnic communication and ethnic conflict could no longer
> be studied in a sociostructural vacuum ... As pointed out by Johnson *et*
> *al.*, 1983, the concept of vitality emerged out of the critical need for situ-
> ating the sociolinguistic and social psychological processes underlying
> interethnic behaviour within their proper sociostructural contexts. (p.
> 172)

As it happens, the group vitality framework was originally conceived with the Quebec context in mind at a time when sociolinguistic research was being conducted to construct different components of Quebec's Charter of the French language (Giles *et al.*, 1977). Thus the group vitality concept was first proposed as an analytic tool designed to better assess the demographic, institutional support and prestige position of Quebec's French language majority relative to the English speaking elite of the day . The vitality of an ethnolinguistic group was defined as 'that which makes a group likely to behave as a distinctive and collective entity within the intergroup setting' (Giles *et al.* 1977: 308). The more vitality an ethnolinguistic group was assessed to have, the more likely that it was expected to survive collectively as a distinctive linguistic community within its bilingual or multilingual context. Conversely, ethnolinguistic groups that were assessed to have little vitality would be expected to eventually disappear as distinctive linguistic communities within the intergroup setting. Figure 5.1 shows the three broad dimensions of structural variables most likely to influence the vitality of ethnolinguistic groups: these are namely, demographic, institutional support and status factors. The elements comprising these factors will be briefly presented as they pertain to the sociostructural position of the Francophone and Anglophone communities during the decade leading up to the adoption of Bill 101.

Demographic variables are those related to the number of members comprising the ethnolinguistic group and their distribution throughout a particular urban, regional or national territory. Distribution factors refer to the numeric concentration of group members in various parts of the 'territory', their proportion relative to outgroup members, and whether or not the group still occupies its 'traditional' or 'national' territory. Number factors refer to the community's absolute group numbers, their birth rate, exogamy/endogamy, and their patterns of immigration and emigration.

Without using the vitality framework as such, Canadian social scientists

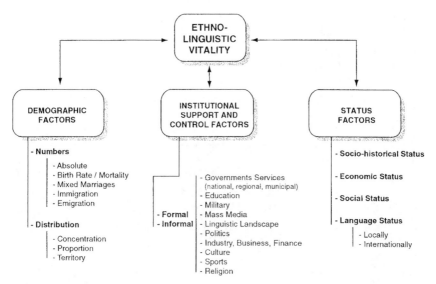

Figure 5.1 A taxonomy of the structural variables affecting ethnolinguistic vitality (adapted from Bourhis *et al.*, 1981)

from many disciplines were able to draw an accurate portrait of the demo-graphic vitality of Francophones and Anglophones during the 1970s. Most of this research was conducted for two important government enquiries: one commissioned by the Canadian Federal Government monitoring French–English issues across Canada (Royal Commission on Bilingualism and Biculturalism, B&B report; Canada, 1969) and the Quebec Government 'Gendron Commission' which focused on French sociolinguistic trends in the Province (Quebec, 1972).

The demolinguistic analyses provided in the B&B report (Canada, 1969) confirmed perceptions in Quebec that Francophones outside the Province were undergoing a severe and sustained rate of assimilation which endan-gered the long-term survival of Francophone minorities across most of Anglo-Canada (Castonguay, 1998; de Vries, 1994). Factors such as the isola-tion of small Francophone communities across the country, declining birthrate, French–English exogamy, lack of French language primary and secondary schooling, the legacy of anti-French laws and the dearth of provincial and federal government services offered in French, combined to erode the number of French mother-tongue speakers outside of Quebec (Bourhis, 1994a). For many Québécois francophones, the adoption of the Canadian Official Languages Act in 1969 providing federal services in

A quoi bon le Congrès de la langue française si John
Bull veut nous noyer par l'immigration intensive.

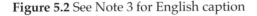

Figure 5.2 See Note 3 for English caption

French or English 'where numbers warrant' (Fortier, 1994) was seen as too little too late. Taking stock of these trends, Québécois nationalists adopted the slogan *'hors du Québec point de salut'* (beyond Quebec no survival) and revived older nationalist representations (Figure 5.2) of the shrinking territorial base of French speakers not just within Canada but also within North America. As a linguistic minority within Canada (28% in 1961) and North America as a whole (less than 2%), Quebec was portrayed by committed 'Xmen' as the last territorial enclave in which a 'normal' fully developed French society could survive within the New World.

On the demographic front during this period, more than 80% of the Quebec population spoke French as a mother-tongue, of whom more than three-quarters were *unilingual* French and used *only* French as their home language. With strong intergenerational transmission of French as the mother-tongue, Quebec language planners could intervene in favour of French with a 'full deck of cards' on the demolinguistic front. In terms of distribution, Francophones constituted the overwhelming majority in all the regions of the Province except in the West Island of Montreal where Anglophones were in the majority and predominantly unilingual English (70%). Francophones and Anglophones were more equally distributed in central areas of Montreal as well as in western parts of the Province adjoining the Ontario border and in the eastern townships. Though constituting the majority of the population in areas such as the West Island of Montreal, the English mother-tongue population (Anglophones) made up less than 15% of the overall provincial population. However, the intergenerational transmission of English was assured within the Anglophone minority, also bolstered by the language shift of many immigrants and Allophones who adopted English as their home language. The term *Allophone* is used to describe individuals who have neither French nor English as a mother-tongue regardless of whether such individuals are first or second generation immigrants. By the early 1970s, Allophones and immigrants made up 8% of the Quebec population, most of whom had settled in the Montreal region (88%) and tended to adopt English as the language of integration with the Anglophone host community.

At the same time, Gendron Commission studies documented trends which were not so favourable for French language maintenance in the Province (Quebec, 1972). Demographers confirmed the decline in the Quebec birthrate from one of the highest to one of the lowest in the Western world (Lachapelle & Henripin, 1980). This decline to well below the replacement value of 2.1 offsprings per woman meant that Francophones could no longer rely on the so-called 'revanche des berceaux' (revenge of the cradle) to maintain their demographic strength within Quebec

(Caldwell & Fournier, 1987). Without a sustained Francophone birthrate, reliance on immigration and the integration of immigrants to the Francophone linguistic community rather than to the Anglophone one became strategically important as a means of stemming the long-term decline of the Francophone population in the Province (Termote & Gauvreau, 1988). For the same strategic reasons, the Anglophone minority, whose fertility was every bit as low as that of the French majority, was also dependent on the immigrant population to sustain the demographic vitality of the English minority in the Province.

With the freedom to choose between the French or English educational system (from pre-school to university), the majority of immigrants sent their children to the English system as a way of maximising the economic and linguistic mobility of their progeny within North America. Furthermore, the Catholic school system of the day (both French and English at the primary and secondary level) did not accept immigrant background pupils whose religion was other than Catholic. However, the Protestant school system (mostly English) accepted pupils from all denominational backgrounds (d'Anglejan, 1984). Thus, over the years, a majority of first and second generation immigrant pupils integrated within the English (Catholic and Protestant) rather than the French linguistic milieu of the Province (McAndrew, 1996). For many Francophones, freedom of language choice in schools meant that the projected long-term demographic growth in Quebec favoured the Anglophone rather than the Francophone linguistic community. Furthermore, Francophone Xmen pointed out that without control over immigration, the Quebec Government could not readily portray Quebec as a French majority Province, making it difficult to attract immigrants from French-speaking regions of the world. Of more symbolic than demolinguistic significance, studies showed that while a small number of French mother-tongue speakers shifted to English as the language of the home, an even smaller number among the English mother-tongue minority adopted French as their home language.

Taking these factors into consideration, Quebec analysts provided optimistic, neutral and pessimistic scenarios regarding the future number of French speakers in the Province. Ideologically, while Francophone federalists favoured the optimistic projections, Quebec nationalists focused on the sombre scenarios thus fuelling existing insecurities about the survival of the 'French fact' in Quebec. Demolinguistic trends where the object of close scrutiny in the mass media along with debates about power sharing of state jurisdictions between the Canadian Federal Government and the Quebec Government. Thus, issues concerning the demographic vitality of the Francophone and Anglophone communities in the Province were used selectively by rival political parties proposing contrasting options for the future of the Province: independent Quebec vs Canadian federalism.

Within democracies, demolinguistic vitality represent 'strength in numbers' and can be used as a legitimising tool to empower majorities (and sometimes minorities) with the 'institutional completeness' (Breton, 1971) they need to shape their own collective destiny within the intergroup structure. Within the vitality framework, *Institutional Control* factors refer to the extent to which an ethnolinguistic group has gained formal and informal representations in the various institutions of a community, region or state (Figure 5.1). Informal support refers to the degree to which a linguistic group has organised itself as a pressure group to represent and safeguard its own ethnolinguistic interests in various state and private activities including: private primary and secondary education, mass media, business, finance, sports, culture and religion. Formal support refers to the degree to which members of an ethnolinguistic group have gained positions of control at decision-making levels in business, industry, mass media, cultural production, sports, religious institutions and within the government apparatus in education, the police, the judiciary and the civil administration. Ethnolinguistic groups who enjoy strong institutional control within the state and private institutions are in a better position to safeguard and enhance their vitality as a distinctive collective entity than ethnolinguistic groups that lack institutional control in these domains of activity.

Also contributing to the institutional control of language groups is the presence and quality of leaders who can head the informal and formal institutions representing their ethnolinguistic group. Gains on the institutional control front can depend on the emergence of Xmen activists and charismatic leaders who succeed in mobilising ethnolinguistic groups to fight in favour of their own language and cultural survival within multilingual settings. The absence of quality leadership can undermine gains achieved by previous generations of group members on the institutional control front and can mortgage future gains needed for the survival of the next generation of ethnolinguistic group members.

By the early 1970s both Quebec and Canadian nationalists had exceptional political leadership: Réne Levesque for the Québécois sovereignists and Pierre-Elliot Trudeau for the Canadian federalists. Charismatic in their respective political constituencies, the epic rivalries of these two politicians came to symbolise the growing clash between Canada's two solitudes. Early in their political careers the two leaders, along with Canadian and Québécois citizens, were confronted with the inescapable results of the Royal Commission on Bilingualism and Biculturalism (Canada, 1969). The study not only showed that Francophones were under-represented in the Canadian Federal Administration with English as the dominant language of work, but that with equal qualifications and experience Francophones had systematically lower wages than Anglophones across Canada. Even in Quebec, this wage gap held for bilingual francophones relative to unilingual anglophones in the workforce. English–Canadian control of the economy and financial institutions was documented and shown to account for the generally low position of Francophone employees within businesses and corporations across the Province. Results of the Gendron Commission (Quebec, 1972) confirmed these trends and showed that English, not French, was the language of business and upward mobility in Quebec. With the growing integration of a modernising Quebec within the Canadian and USA economy, the Gendron Commission concluded that without government intervention, the diglossic position of French as a low status language would worsen relative to the prestige position of English in the work world.

However, the position of the French majority was favourable on most of the other institutional support factors within the vitality framework. Francophones controlled most of the provincial and municipal civil administrations, managed their own French health care and educational system (from pre-school to university), owned and managed their own French mass-media (radio, TV, newspapers, book publishing), controlled the majority French Catholic religious system, created and consumed French language cultural products (music, literature, theatre) and participated in the provincial and federal political systems. Though lacking control of the major business, financial and banking institutions of the Province, Francophones took pride in their own network of French language financial co-operatives supporting local entrepreneurship and business.

By virtue of their historically dominant elite position, the Anglophone minority also enjoyed considerable institutional control in the Province. In addition to heading major business and financial institutions, Anglophones controlled their own English medium health care (hospitals, clinics) and educational system (from pre-school to university), led their own Catholic and Protestant English language religious institutions, owned and managed their own English language mass-media (radio, TV stations and newspapers), were involved in Quebec, Canadian and Anglo-American cultural and sport activities, and participated in municipal, provincial and federal politics.

Ethnolinguistic groups that have gained a measure of ascendancy on institutional support factors are also likely to enjoy *social status* relative to less dominant groups within the social structure. The status variables are those related to a speech community's social prestige, its sociohistorical status and the prestige of its language and culture both within its own territory and internationally (Figure 5.1). The more status a linguistic community is ascribed to have, the more vitality it could be said to possess as a collectivity. Though not as readily quantifiable as demographic and institutional factors, social psychological evidence shows that high status group position can contribute to a more positive social identity which in turn affects the will to mobilise in favour of enhancing the vitality of the ingroup language (Sachdev & Bourhis, 1991). Even with effective leadership, being a member of a disparaged low status language group can take its toll on the collective will to mobilise for the survival of the ingroup language and culture. The reality of a high or low status position is more vivid to the degree that status differentials between ethnolinguistic groups are perpetuated through language stereotyping (Genesee & Bourhis, 1988, Ryan & Giles, 1982), internalised through diglossic language norms and enshrined through language laws establishing the relative status of rival language groups (Wardhaugh, 1987).

The enduring international interest in the 'Quebec case' stems from the fact that at stake in this region is the ascendancy of two historically and culturally important languages in the Western world. Though a minority language in North America, French benefits from more vitality on the 'status front' than if the Quebec case involved a minority language of lesser historical or cultural influence in the West. Within Quebec, the diglossic situation in favour of English relative to French was felt mostly in the work world of bilingual contact zones in Montreal, western regions along the Ontario border, and in the eastern townships along the USA border. A rich tradition of research on the social psychology of language attitudes and bilingual communication convincingly documented the diglossic situation favouring English rather than French as the language of social prestige in these contact zones (Bourhis, 1994b; Bourhis & Lepicq, 1993; Genesee & Holobow, 1989; Hamers & Hummel, 1994; Lambert *et al.* 1960). To this day, studies show that Anglophone students tested in their English high schools within French majority regions such as Quebec city are likely to use as much English in their everyday lives as Anglophones tested in the West Island of Montreal where they are in the majority (Landry *et al.*, 1997). The same study with French high school students showed that Francophone students tested in the English majority West Island of Montreal were less likely to use French in their everyday life than Francophones tested in majority French settings such as Quebec city. Results point to the continuing appeal and prestige of the English language for Francophones and to the capacity of Quebec Anglophones to behave as majority group speakers regardless of their demographic density across the province (Landry *et al.* 1997).

Giles *et al.* (1977) proposed that demographic, institutional control and status factors combine to affect in one direction or the other the overall strength of ethnolinguistic groups. An ethnolinguistic group may be weak on demographic variables such as the case of Quebec Anglophones, but enjoy strong institutional control in the mass media and considerable status as speakers of English, the most powerful language in North America. In the Quebec context of the 1970s, Quebec Anglophones could be assessed as enjoying medium-high overall vitality relative to lower vitality groups such as Allophone immigrant communities and American Indian (First Nation) language minorities dispersed across the Province (Drapeau, 1998; Hamers & Hummel, 1998; Maurais, 1997). While enjoying strong vitality on the demographic front within Quebec, Francophones felt threatened as a language minority at the continental level (Figure 5.2) and had become quite sensitive to the lack of status accorded to French as a language of work and advancement in the business and financial world. As the higher vitality group within Quebec, a majority of Francophones elected the pro-independence Parti Québécois in 1976 whose first legislative act was to adopt the *Charter of the French Language* (Bill 101).

The need for considering the vitality position of language minorities within complex multilingual settings was also acknowledged by Joshua Fishman (1991) within his reversing language shift framework:

> In some respects, the GIDS (Graded Intergenerational Disruption Scale) may be thought of as a sociocultural reverse analog to the sociopsychological language vitality measures that several investigators have recently proposed; the higher the GIDS rating the lower the intergenerational continuity and maintenance prospects of a language network or community. The major difference between the two, in addition to their different substantive foci, is that the GIDS is at least a quasi-implicational scale, i.e. higher (more disrupted) scores imply all or of the lesser degrees of disruption as well. (p. 87)

The GIDS framework focuses on two central markers of language shift; intergenerational transmission of the Xish mother-tongue and the presence of a diglossic norm governing the use of the Xish vs Yish language in high vs low language functions of society. These two crucial indicators of language shift were not given central billing in the original vitality framework simply because the model was a more general one not specifically designed to guide when and where language planning efforts should be launched by Xmen. Diglossia was implied in the vitality framework dealing with both institutional support and the status factor of the model. The degree of control achieved by Xmen in the informal and formal functions of the state are central to the vitality framework (Figure 5.1). In turn, the position achieved by Xmen in the social structure has a cumulative impact on the role ascribed to the X language for high vs low functions uses within the society in question, the 'language status' factor included in the vitality model (Figure 5.1).

In the vitality framework, intergenerational transmission was implied within the demographic factors as part of the absolute number of speakers still using the Xish language. Contributing to the rise and fall of Xish language speakers within the vitality framework were the other important factors including birth rate, mixed marriages, immigration and emigration. It is clear that intergenerational transmission should be included as a distinct factor contributing to the demographic strength of Xish and Yish ethnolinguistic groups within the vitality framework.

Just as the objective vitality framework can be improved by the RLS model, the converse is also true. The RLS model can also be enriched by including in its analysis the full range of factors used to assess the relative vitality of language groups. It is clear from our Quebec example that the vitality framework can provide a more systematic tool of analysis for guiding RLS efforts than what remains implied in the RLS framework proposed by Fishman (1991). For instance, it is not evident that a strictly RLS analysis of the position of French in Quebec in the 1970s would have led to the conclusion that language planning in favour of French was in fact desirable or necessary. As we have seen, intergenerational transmission of the French language within the Francophone majority was virtually intact at this epoch. However, it is the Xmen analysis of the weak position of French on other vitality factors such as institutional control (the language of work) and demography (declining fertility, immigrant Anglicisation) which provided the ideological mobilising tool (threat to French survival) that convinced the Francophone majority that RLS was vital for the survival of their language. Thus it may be more useful to consider the vitality framework as a necessary *complementary* component of Fishman's (1991) graded intergenerational disruption scale rather than just the reverse analogue of the GIDS scale.

The ethnolinguistic vitality approach also offers another dimension likely to contribute to the RLS framework. Bourhis *et al.*, (1981) raised the issue of whether ethnolinguistic group members perceived 'subjectively' their sociostructural position in much the same way as suggested by 'objective' accounts provided by expert analysts and language planners. The subjective vitality questionnaire (SVQ) was proposed as a way of measuring group members' assessments of Xish and Yish vitality on each item constituting the demographic, institutional control and status dimensions of the 'objective' vitality framework (Bourhis *et al.*, 1981). A number of studies conducted with the SVQ showed that in many circumstances ethnolinguistic group members did perceive their vitality position along the same lines suggested by 'objective' assessments of the situation (Bourhis & Sachdev, 1984; Allard & Landry, 1994). In other circumstances, studies have shown that perceivers can be systematically biased in their assessment of ingroup and outgroup vitality. Harwood *et al.* (1994) have shown that these 'perceptual distortions' can favour ingroup or outgroup vitality depending on the social context but that such biases do not emerge on more obvious differentials between Xish and Yish vitality items. These perceptual distortions manifest themselves on items in which the degree of difference is objectively marginal. Sachdev and Bourhis (1993) have shown how both cognitive and motivational factors can help account for the accentuation or attenuation of ingroup and outgroup vitality differentials.

Furthermore, Allard and Landry (1986) proposed that subjective vitality perceptions could be more predictive of language behaviour by taking into consideration not only general beliefs about group vitality (SVQ, Bourhis *et al.* 1981) but also goal beliefs about respondents' own desire to behave in certain ways regarding key aspects of their owngroup vitality (goal beliefs: BEVQ). Thus Xmen may acknowledge that their owngroup vitality is weak and declining (SVQ) but have goal beliefs (BEVQ) reflecting an absence of motivation to reverse the situation through individual or collective action: some Xmen simply do not care about the decline of their owngroup ethnolinguistic vitality. Allard and Landry (1994) showed that a combination of both general beliefs (SVQ) and goal beliefs (BEVQ) could better predict key aspects of language behaviours, including intergenerational transmission of the Xish language, than only objective assessments of Xish and Yish vitality.

Do Xmen perceive the graded intergenerational disruption scale (GIDS) in the same way as expert language planners do? It is proposed that a subjective GIDS scale could be constructed to assess how militant and rank and file members of the Xish group perceive the severity of the intergenerational dislocation affecting their owngroup. Group members' subjective assessments of both their group vitality (SVQ & BEVQ) and the GIDS may be as important in predicting language behaviour and the success of RLS as the group's 'objectively' assessed vitality and GIDS. Subjective assessments of both the vitality and GIDS could be monitored with both lay and expert subsamples of the Xish population before RLS interventions and then again following sustained implementation of the

RLS programme. Combined with demolinguistic census data and socio-linguistic surveys, subjective perceptions of vitality and GIDS could help fine-tune future phases of the RLS intervention. Thus a combination of objective and subjective vitality and GIDS information is proposed as a more sensitive method of planning and implementing successful RLS interventions in the context of Fishman's (1991) GIDS.

Assessing 20 Years of Language Planning in Quebec

The social changes brought about by the 'Quiet Revolution' of the 1960s made francophones especially aware of the diglossic 'threat' posed to French through its co-existence with English as the prestige language of business and upward mobility (Rocher, 1992). As vividly argued in *Nègres blancs d'amérique* (White Niggers of America; Vallière, 1969), it was urgent for the working-class Francophone majority to challenge the Anglo-domination of the Quebec economy and the indolence of the French Canadian 'petite bourgeoisie'. Relative to its fading rural and religious past, the modernisation of Quebec society also meant that the French language had perhaps become the last symbol of Québécois identity in an increasingly materialistic and consumer-oriented society (Sachdev & Bourhis, 1990). With the French language emerging as the last bastion of Québécois distinctiveness it was perhaps inevitable that successive Quebec governments should find it necessary to legislate on language matters (Bourhis & Lepicq, 1993).

In the Quebec of the 1970s, Francophones were generally well endowed on the demographic and institutional control fronts while French language transmission was relatively free of intergenerational dislocation (Fishman, 1991). Nevertheless, Québécois intellectuals and activists (Xmen) were successful in focusing the attention of Francophones on the more problematic aspects of their fate as a French minority in North America. Factors identified as undermining the future of French in Quebec were: (1) the decline of Francophones in Anglo-Canada; (2) the drop in the birthrate of the Francophone population; (3) immigrant choice of the English rather than French school system for their children; and (4) Anglo-domination of the Quebec economy (d'Anglejan 1984; Laporte 1984). Between 1969 and 1996 successive Quebec governments promulgated a number of language laws designed to address each of the above factors undermining the long-term prospects of the French language in the Province (Bill 63, 1969; Bill 22, 1974; Bill 101, 1976; Bill 178, 1988; Bill 86, 1993; Bill 40, 1996). To this day, the Charter of the French Language (Bill 101) remains the most important of these laws (see Bourhis, 1984a for the text of Bill 101). For the architect of Bill

101, the late Camille Laurin, the goal of the law was not only to address current challenges to the maintenance of the French language but also to: 'redress past injustices and humiliations suffered by my people in my village and everywhere in Quebec' (Camille Laurin's last public speech, 11 December 1998, author's translation).

Bill 101 guaranteed the rights of every Quebecer to receive communications in French when dealing with the civil administration, semi-public agencies and business firms, including the right by all customers to be informed and served in French. The law also ensured the right of all workers to work in French and not to be dismissed or demoted for the sole reason that they were monolingual in French. As regards the language of work, Bill 101 essentially applied measures already in place since Bill 22. Business firms with more than 50 employees were required to apply for and obtain a Francisation certificate which attested that they had the necessary infrastructure to use French as the language of work within their organisation (Daoust, 1984; Bouchard, 1991). From 1996 onwards, the Francisation certificate was necessary for business firms wishing to tender their services or goods to the provincial government.

Bill 101 also guaranteed English schooling to all present and future Quebec Anglophone pupils. All immigrant children already in English schools by the time the Bill was passed along with all their current and future siblings were also guaranteed access to English schooling. However, the law made it clear that all subsequent immigrants to Quebec were obliged to send their children to French primary and secondary public schools. Nevertheless, the law did not affect freedom of language choice at the primary and secondary school levels for parents wishing to enrol their children in full fee-paying private schools. Furthermore, freedom of language choice was guaranteed to all post-secondary students who could choose to attend either French or English medium colleges (CEGEPS) and universities in Quebec. Finally Bill 101 contained a controversial clause which banned languages other than French from the 'linguistic landscape' including road signs, government signs and commercial store signs.

Though Bill 101 contained some measures related to corpus language planning, the major aim of the law was designed to improve the status of French relative to English in Quebec society (Bourhis & Lepicq, 1993). Cause and effect relationships are difficult to establish when evaluating the impact of language policies on language behaviour and language shift. The Quebec case is no exception and the above caveat must be taken into consideration when assessing the evidence presented in the remaining parts of this chapter.

Bill 101 and demolinguistic trends

The immediate reactions of many Francophones to Bill 101 were quite positive, since the law was seen as being effective in securing the linguistic future of the French majority in the Province (Bourhis, 1984b; Levine, 1990; Maurais 1987). On the demographic front, the proportion of French mother-tongue speakers increased slightly from 80.7% of the Quebec population in 1971 (4,866,410) to 81.5% (5,741,438) in 1996. French language use at home increased from 80.8% (4,870,100) in 1971 to 82,8% (5,830,082) in 1996. Taken together these trends in mother-tongue and home language use suggest an increasing intergenerational transmission of French from 1971 to 1996. Thus the 1996 census results suggest a language shift in *favour* of French as evidenced by the higher score in French home language use relative to the number of French mother-tongue speakers in the census. Though this shift is partially accounted for by changes in recent census methodology, the change is largely attributed to Allophones rather than Anglophones who have adopted French as the language of the home (Castonguay, 1998). This favourable trend for French is perhaps neutralised by the continuing weak fertility of the Quebec Francophone population: while the fertility rate in 1961 was 4.2 children per woman, this rate had dropped to only 1.6 by 1996. On this point Castonguay (1998) concludes: 'Over twenty years of insufficient fertility spells a coming decline in absolute numbers for the francophone population in Quebec – a fortiori in Canada as a whole – beginning early in the next century.' (p. 44).

The growing integration of Quebec Francophones within the North American economic and cultural mainstream is implied by the increase of French–English bilingualism among Francophones. Whereas only 26% of French mother-tongue speakers reported being French–English bilinguals in 1971, this proportion had increased to 34% in 1996. This rise in the number of Francophone bilinguals is especially evident in Montreal where French–English bilingualism remains advantageous for economic and cultural exchanges with local, Canadian and international partners.

Anglophone reactions to Bill 101 were largely negative because the law was seen as an attack on the traditional elite status of the English minority in the Province (Legault, 1992; Scowen, 1991; Stevenson, 1999). Bill 101 forced many Anglophones to see themselves as a minority group rather than as individual members of a dominant elite (Caldwell 1984, 1994, 1998). Following the election of the pro-sovereignty Parti Québécois in 1976, many Anglophones dissatisfied with Quebec's language and fiscal policies emigrated to Ontario and other provinces of Canada. As it turns out, emigration from the province and low fertility rate were key factors contributing to the erosion of the demographic vitality of Quebec Anglophone (Castonguay, 1998, 1999). Census results showed a decline of 12% in Quebec's English mother-tongue population between 1971 and 1981 (Caldwell, 1984). This net loss of 158,000 English mother-tongue speakers occurred among the more economically mobile elements of the Anglophone community, a good number of whom were unilingual English of British descent, in their twenties and more likely to be university degree holders. By the 1990s these out-migration trends took their toll on the proportion of Anglophones in Quebec: while English mother-tongue speakers made up 13% of the population in 1971 (789,000), this proportion dropped to only 8.8% by 1996 (622,000), a net drop of 167,000 English mother-tongue speakers in the Province. English language use at home dropped from 14.7% in 1971 (887,875) to 10.8% in 1996 (762,457). The difference in favour of English between home language use (10.8%) and English mother-tongue speakers (8.8%) testifies to the remarkable 'drawing power' of English in Quebec even after 20 years of Bill 101 implementation (Castonguay, 1997, 1999). Analyses of census results from 1971 to 1996 have shown that Allophones have been the source of this language shift in favour of English not only in Quebec but also across Canada (Castonguay, 1999).

Despite an optimal rate of intergenerational transmission, it is clear that the Quebec Anglophone minority is experiencing a sharp decline on more fundamental indicators of demographic vitality such as absolute and relative group numbers, out-migration and fertility rates. With a declining fertility rate from 3.3 children per woman in 1961 to only 1.6 in 1996 and few prospects for a substantial immigration from Anglo-Canada, Quebec Anglophones have recognised their growing dependence on the linguistic integration strategies of Allophones and international immigrants who settle in the Province.

In Canada the term 'Heritage languages' is used to denote languages other than the country's two official languages, English and French. In Quebec, the gradual equalisation of the drawing power of French and English as a result of Bill 101 has made the option of maintaining the Heritage language and culture more attractive for Allophone and immigrant communities in the Province (Bourhis, 1994b). The 1996 census results showed that Allophones made up 9.3% of the total Quebec population. Out of these 681,790 Allophones, the most important mother-tongue groups are the following: Italian (20%), Spanish (10%), Arabic (8.8%), Greek (6.5%), Chinese (6.2%) and Portuguese (5%). Analyses of the 1986 census data had shown that Heritage language maintenance was much stronger among Quebec Allophones than it is among Allophones who settled in Anglo-

Canada (Pendakur, 1990). For instance, whereas 68% of first generation immigrants who settled in Quebec reported they still used their Heritage tongue as their only language of communication at home (and 63% in 1991), only 48% of such groups outside Quebec still reported using their Heritage tongue as their home language. This difference in Heritage language maintenance was even more pronounced in the case of second generation Allophone groups in Quebec (63%) relative to their counterpart elsewhere in Canada (34%). Evidence from the 1996 census suggests that Allophones in Quebec remain more likely to retain their Heritage language use at home than Allophones in the rest of Canada.

Following power sharing deals reached with the Canadian Immigration Department from 1978 to 1991, the Quebec Government gained a measure of control in the selection of immigrants based on the specific employment and linguistic needs of the Province. In the last two decades the Quebec Ministry of Civic Affairs and Immigration has had some success in attracting immigrants with a knowledge of French, others from former French colonies and immigrants whose knowledge of a Romance language (e.g. Spanish) facilitated the learning of French. Indeed, studies have shown that immigrants with some knowledge of French are more likely to integrate within the Francophone host society while immigrants with a knowledge of English are more likely to integrate within the Anglophone host minority (Veltman, 1998). Clearly, the Quebec Government is committed to using the institutional control at its disposal for selecting and facilitating the integration of Allophones and immigrants to the Franco-phone host majority rather than to the Anglophone minority.

Growing linguistic tensions between the Francophone and Anglophone host communities put added pressure on Allophone minorities to openly 'take sides' in the Quebec linguistic debate (Bourhis, 1994b). One response for Allophones was to learn both French and English, a bilingualism trend which increased from 33% in 1971 to as much as 48% in 1996. Combining Allophones who know only French or both French and English, census results show that the proportion of Allophones who declared a knowledge of French increased from 47% in 1971 to 70% in 1996. Conversely, the proportion of Allophones declaring knowledge of English dropped from 70% in 1971 to 66% in 1996. Finally, Bill 101, along with immigration from Romance language countries, had an impact on the language shift patterns of recently arrived Allophone immigrants. Of the Allophones who settled in the Province before 1976, only 34% had adopted French as the language of the home, while for Allophones who arrived after Bill 101 (between 1976 and 1991), as many as 67% used French as *one* of their language at home (Quebec, 1996a).

Bill 101 and Montreal

Up to the beginning of the 20th century, Montreal was the financial capital of Canada and was a city whose population was predominantly English mother-tongue. The urbanisation and proletarisation of Quebec Francophones changed the demographic make-up of the city and by the 1950s Montreal had become a bilingual city with a predominantly French-speaking population. Today, the Montreal metropolitan region is the major urban centre of Quebec with a population of 3.3 million relative to the total Quebec population of 7 million. The proportion of French mother-tongue speakers in the Montreal region increased from 65% in 1951 to 70% in 1986 while it dropped slightly to 67% in 1996. Conversely, the proportion of English mother-tongue speakers in the Montreal region dropped from 26% in 1951 to 17% in 1986 and to only 13% in 1996. Since the 1950s, it is the arrival of Allophone immigrants which has had the greatest impact in changing the demolinguistic profile of the city. The proportion of Allophones increased from 8.6% in 1951 to 13% in 1986 and to 20% in 1996. While increasingly mixed today, it remains true that the West Island part of Montreal is predominantly Anglophone while Francophones form the majority in eastern regions of the island with considerable mixing of all ethnolinguistic groups occurring in the central regions of the Metropolis. Accounting for almost half the population of Quebec, multilingual Montreal remains quite distinct from other regions of the Province. Other urban centres are linguistically quite homogeneous with the French mother-tongue concentration ranging from more than 90% of the population (Québec city, Trois-Rivières, Sherbrooke) to 80% (Hull city region). The less urbanised regions of the Province are also predominantly Francophone, with 92% of the population declaring French as their mother-tongue.

When considering the dispersion of immigrants and Allophones settled in Quebec, one notes that the vast majority (88%) inhabit the Montreal region, thus constituting 16% of the total Metropolitan population. Allophone and immigrant communities concentrate in Montreal mainly because the city offers better economic opportunities and allows such groups to maintain the ingroup networks which provide the cultural and economic support needed to adjust more readily within the host society. The concentration of ethnolinguistic communities within the metropole has meant that it is the Montreal rather than the Quebec population as a whole that has had to adjust to the realities of multilingualism and ethnic pluralism in the Province.

Given the key role of Montreal in the Quebec economy, Francophone

Xmen consider that it is in this city that the fate of the French language will be determined in North America. It is the necessity of using French to communicate with the Francophone unilingual majority which has legitimised the quest for increasing the institutional status of French relative to English in Quebec. It is argued that if the majority of Montreal Francophones and Allophones become bilingual, then the rationale for using French will give way to the advantage of using English as the sole language of business and upward mobility within the city. Among French mother-tongue speakers in Montreal, the proportion of bilinguals increased from 38% in 1971 to 44% in 1986 and 47% in 1996. Likewise, English mother-tongue speakers who declared they were bilingual increased from 35% in 1971 to 54% in 1986 and to 62% in 1996. The proportion of Montreal Allophones who declared knowledge of both French and English increased from 35% in 1971 to 50% in 1986 while decreasing slightly to 49% in 1996.

Though militant Francophone Xmen view individual bilingualism as a potential threat to the status of French as the majority language of Montreal, others see the rise of bilingualism as an asset contributing to the cultural and economic dynamism of the city. Young adult bilinguals of Francophone, Anglophone and Allophone background share the common experience of having been educated at a time when Bill 101 was more or less accepted as a *fait accompli*. With college or university degrees, these young bilinguals often mix at work and play and develop intercultural communication strategies which include more balanced French–English language switching as part of their normal communicative repertoire (mutual language convergence, Amiot & Bourhis, 1999; Moise & Bourhis, 1994). While remaining attached to their respective ethnocultural community, these Montreal 'linguistic chameleons' are developing bicultural/multicultural identities which are called upon to suit the immediate needs of the cross-cultural encounter they happen to be in. Though not likely to generalise to the whole population of Montreal bilinguals, it remains true that younger subgroups of bilinguals are re-defining French–English–Allophone relations in a post-modern, less confrontational style than the older generation of Montrealers who actually fought the battles over language laws such as Bill 101.

In a 1997 telephone survey, the Conseil de la Langue française (CLF) sought to assess the impact of Bill 101 on the use of French and English as the language of 'public life' in settings such as shopping malls, local shops, banks, hospitals, and with civil servants at the provincial and local school levels (Béland, 1999). A large representative sample of Francophones, Anglophones and Allophones were surveyed across the Province including the greater Montreal region. Combining the language use situations into a single 'public language' measure, results showed a sustained use of French among both Francophones and Allophones but less so among Anglophones (cf. Moise & Bourhis, 1994). In greater Montreal, results showed that 97% of Francophones reported using exclusively or mostly French in these public settings, while only 3% reported using mostly English. The majority of Allophones (54%) reported using exclusively or mostly French in public settings, while 39% reported using mostly English and only 8% reporting using mainly their Heritage language. Taken together, these results suggest that French has achieved the status of the normal 'public language' for Montreal Francophones while for Allophones, French is gaining ground relative to English. In contrast, only 23% of Anglophones reported using mostly French in these public settings while 77% reported using exclusively or mostly English. Clearly, Quebec Anglophones, regardless of their bilingual skills, can still afford to use mostly English as their 'public language' in greater Montreal, a trend also obtained for Anglophones in regions of the Province other than the Montreal area.

Bill 101 and education

Unlike most other language minorities in North America, Quebec Anglophones benefit from the provision of a state funded English medium educational system starting from pre-kindergarten schooling up to collegiate and university level including graduate and post-doctoral studies (there are three publicly funded English universities in Quebec). The majority of Anglophones enrol their children in the English primary and secondary school board system. However, within the English system, Anglophone parents have been keen to enrol their children in French immersion programmes: the proportion of Anglophone pupils in French immersion classes increased from 24% in 1981 to 32% in 1998. Furthermore, a growing number of English mother-tongue pupils (Anglophones and immigrants) attend the French school system: from 10% in 1972 to 17% in 1995 (Quebec, 1996).

In the immediate aftermath of Bill 101, Anglophones were most concerned about the erosion of their demographic base resulting from the fact that most new immigrants to Quebec would have to send their children to French rather than English primary and secondary schools (Mallea, 1984). Bill 101 has had its intended impact on enrolments within the English primary and secondary school system in the Province. Allophone enrolment in the English school system dropped from 85% in 1972 to only 21% in 1995, while their enrolment in the French primary and secondary school system increased from only 15% in 1972 to 79% in 1995. Thus,

Anglophones can no longer count on immigrants to maintain the demographic base of their school system in the Province which dropped from 256,251 pupils in 1976 to only 111,466 in 1995. Studies suggest that this drop in the number of pupils attending the English school system is largely due to the application of Bill 101 (immigrants must enrol in French schools) while the low fertility of Anglophones also account for the decline (Quebec, 1996a). The out-migration of many unilingual Anglophones along with enrolment in French schools and the enduring popularity of French immersion classes contributed to the increase of French–English bilingualism among Quebec Anglophones from 37% in 1971 to as much as 62% in 1996.

As in the past, the 1996 census shows that the proportion of Quebec Anglophones with a university degree is greater (21%) than for Quebec Francophones (14%) and for the Canadian population as a whole (16%). Of those enrolled in post-secondary education, more than 92% of Quebec Anglophones chose English medium colleges and Universities, a trend which remained stable in the 1980s and 1990s. Anglophone enrolment in French at the collegiate level has increased marginally from 5% in 1980 to 6.6% in 1990, while enrolment in French universities has remained stable at around 7% up to the 1990s. A brain drain of English-speaking university graduates has also occurred since the adoption of Bill 101. From 1976 to 1986 the net out-migration of English-speaking university degree holders has been as high as 40% (26,550 graduates). Studies suggest that factors accounting for this exodus were: insufficient French language skills, political uncertainty in the Province and better job prospects in Anglo-Canada. However, a small proportion of those who left during this period were in fact Anglo-Canadians returning to their Province of origin after completing their university studies in Quebec. The out-migration to English Canada was less sustained in the decade from 1986 to 1996 (28% net loss, 21,688 graduates) and was more likely due to poor job prospects in a declining Quebec economy. Overall, during this 20- year period, English-speaking university degree holders were 12 times as likely to leave the Province as Francophone degree holders. The exodus of young university trained Anglophones is not only having a negative impact on the development of Quebec society as a whole but also undermines the capacity of the Anglophone minority to maintain its vitality in the Province.

Bill 101 is having much of its intended effect of not only increasing the proportion of Allophone groups enrolled in the French primary and secondary school system but has also had an impact on the use of French by Allophone pupils on school grounds and at home. A survey of Allophone pupils enrolled in Montreal French high schools showed that on school grounds (outside the classroom) Allophones reported using French 57% of the time, followed by English at 25% and Heritage languages at 18% (Giroux, 1992). In the family setting with their siblings the Allophone pupils reported using as much French (40%) as their own Heritage language (40%) while English use was at 20%. Another revealing measure of Allophone linguistic preferences can be obtained by considering enrolment in collegiate schooling and university where freedom of language choice remains in effect for all citisens of the Province. Allophone enrolment in French colleges increased from 18% in 1980 to as much as 40% in 1989 and to 46% in 1994. The 1989 collegiate entry figures are important because this age cohort represents the first group of Allophone students whose Grade 1 entry into the primary school system coincided with the first year of application of Bill 101 in 1978. The post-1989 figures reflect the fact that many Allophones schooled in the French secondary school system did decide to remain in the French system at the collegiate level. Indeed of those Allophones who were schooled in French secondary schools, as many as 64% enrolled in a French college in 1994. However, the 36% of Allophones schooled in the French system who switched to English colleges did so despite the academic risks involved in pursuing collegiate studies in a language other than the one used for studies at the secondary school level. Of the Allophones schooled in the English secondary school system very few are known to switch to French for their collegiate studies (less than 1%). Finally, the proportion of Allophone undergraduates who choose to attend French language universities increased from 42% in 1986 to 47% in 1994, while the majority still chose to attend English language universities.

Basically, many Allophones and immigrants settled in Quebec have opted for *trilingualism* as a cultural integration strategy for dealing with the presence of two rival host communities in their country of adoption. Allophones and their children maintain knowledge of their Heritage language because it is the mother-tongue of their parents, learn French because of the educational obligations of Bill 101 within a French majority Province, and adopt English because it remains the lingua franca of economic and social mobility in North America (Bourhis, 1994b). Bill 101 measures were designed to ensure that Allophones and immigrants have the opportunity to learn French through the school system. The law does not oblige Allophones to assimilate linguistically to the Francophone majority. However, many Francophone Xmen counted on Bill 101 to create a 'carry-over' effect promoting language shift to French and identification to the French rather than the Allophone or Anglophone cultural milieu. Such expectations, when not fully met, have made militant Xmen impatient if not intolerant towards Allophones who identify mainly with their owngroup, maintain Heritage language use at home or prefer integration within the Anglophone rather than the Francophone host community. Others argue that Allophones and immigrants do not need to identify *only* as Francophones or *only* as Anglophones when multiple group identification including the Heritage one remains a viable option especially in multicultural Montreal.

Given that Bill 101 obliged Francophone parents to enrol their children in the French public school system *only*, percentage enrolment of French mother-tongue students in French primary and secondary schools have remained stable in the last 20 years: 98% in 1972, 99% in 1995. However, the demographic decline of the Francophone population has meant that enrolment in the French school system dropped 25% in absolute terms during the period from 1971 (1,378,788 pupils) to 1995 (1,036,202 pupils). At the collegiate and university level, Quebec students have the choice to attend French or English language institutions. At both the college and university level, government data of the last 15 years shows that a steady 95% of Francophones choose to pursue post-secondary studies in French institutions, with just 5% choosing to attend English language institutions. Taken together, these patterns show that Bill 101 measures to restrict the language choice of Francophones at the primary and secondary school level are having their desired effect in maintaining Francophones within the French educational system at the collegiate and university level. These self-imposed restrictions on individual 'freedom of choice' also help consolidate the *collective* status of French as a language of higher education in the scientific, economic and cultural spheres, thus reducing the diglossic pressures on French relative to English in the Province.

Bill 101 and the language of work

The use of the French language and the proportion of Francophones within the Provincial Civil Administration has long been quite substantial to the point that the Provincial Government has had to announce hiring programmes to represent more fairly the proportion of Anglophones and Allophones (18%) in the general population. However, to this day, the Provincial Government has been slow in recruiting Anglophones and Allophones within its Civil Administration (3.5%), a failure noted in the 1998 annual *Report of the Quebec Human Rights Commission* (CDP, 1998)

Bill 101 was designed to improve the use of French as the language of work in privately owned industries, businesses, and financial institutions across Quebec. The most important measure to improve the use of French in the private work world was the mandatory 'Francisation certificates' which could only be delivered to businesses following linguistic analyses proving that French use was generalised within organisations of more than 50 employees. Most business firms did comply with the Francisation requirements and the proportion of Quebec businesses who received their French certification increased from 7.7% in 1980 to 71.6% in 1999 (Daoust 1984; Maurais, 1987; OLF, 1998). A study conducted by the Office de la langue française (OLF) showed that French was more likely to be used as the language of work (written and spoken) in business firms that obtained their Francisation certificate (more than 80% French use) than in those that did not (65% or less; Bouchard, 1998).

During the first decade of application of the Francisation law, a number of large Anglophone businesses covertly or overtly moved their base of operation from Quebec to other regions of Canada (Miller, 1984). Analysis of the Francisation certificate records compiled by the OLF showed that businesses whose ownership was Anglophone were the slowest in obtaining their Francisation certificates relative to businesses owned by Francophones and Allophones interests (Bouchard, 1991). The plateau reached in the early 1990s in the percentage of firms which obtained their Francisation certificate is explained by industry and organisational factors beyond the reach of the OLF. Companies whose Francisation remain problematic have the following profile: multinationals with head offices elsewhere in the world and whose organisational culture and software technology is mainly English, local firms using high technology and whose market is mainly international rather than local (e.g. aeronautic, software and bio-technology; Bouchard, 1998). Given the high 'value added' profile of these mobile job creating industries, the OLF has been patient in its drive to implement Francisation programmes in these firms.

The election of pro-independence governments, two referendums on Quebec separation, fiscal policies and the Francisation of the Quebec workplace contributed to the departure of many Anglo-Canadian business firms. The resulting out-migration of Anglophone employees and administrators had an impact on the position of Francophones and Anglophones in the work world. For instance in the Montreal region the proportion of Francophone administrators and professionals within the workforce increased from 55% in 1971 to 68% in 1991, while the proportion of Anglophones dropped from 34% in 1971 to just 18% in 1991. Also, the proportion of Francophones holding senior administrative positions increased from 41% in 1971 to 67% in 1991, while the proportion of Anglophones holding such positions dropped from 47% in 1971 to 20% in 1991. However, the linguistic networks of Quebec's two solitudes remain a reality within the Quebec corporate world. Studies showed that Francophone CEOs remained concentrated in French-owned large industries (91% in 1976; 87% in 1993) compared to their presence in industries owned by Anglophones (9% in 1976, 15% in 1993; Quebec, 1996a).

The modernisation of Quebec society and the cumulative effect of Bill 101 can also be credited for improving the income position of Franco-phones relative to Anglophones in the Province. Controlling for education, experience and age, studies showed that in 1970 Anglophone unilinguals or bilinguals earned 8% more in annual salary than bilingual Francophones and 16% more than unilingual Francophones. By 1990 the income gap between Francophones and Anglophones was considerably reduced or reversed in some cases. Carefully controlled studies showed that Anglo-phone unilinguals and bilinguals earned only 3% more than unilingual Francophone by 1990, while Francophone bilinguals earned 4% *more* than Anglophone unilinguals or bilinguals (Quebec, 1996a). In 1970, studies had shown that the 'income premium' for knowing English in Montreal was 16%. By 1980 this income premium decreased to 6% and was further eroded to only 3% in 1990.

Taking stock of these improvements in favour of Francophones in the work world, the Quebec Government task force evaluating the position of the French language since Bill 101 arrived at the following conclusion:

> The goals of francisation put forward by the Gendron commission have been reached to a substantial degree, gains are especially obvious in the network of businesses owned by Quebec Francophones. These fundamental changes have benefited Francophones whose income profiles have been largely redressed. The historical link between Francophone worker and low income is a thing of the past. (Quebec, 1996a: 68; author's translation.)

Research conducted by the CLF also showed that Bill 101 did improve the status and use of French as the language of work in Quebec business firms (Béland, 1991). In the Montreal region, self-report studies showed that the proportion of Francophone workers who declared working mostly in French (90% or more of the time) increased from 52% in 1971 to 63% in 1989, while among Allophones the increase was more modest, from 17% in 1971 to 24% in 1989 (Quebec, 1996a). Anglophone workers were least affected by language of work provisions since the use of mostly French ranged from only 2% in 1971 to 8% in 1989. However a drop in the use of mainly English at work (51% or more English use at work) was evident for the three groups of workers following Bill 101: for Francophones the drop in English use was from 12% in 1971 to only 6% in 1989, while for Allophones the drop was from 58% in 1971 to 37% in 1989. However, Anglophone workers still worked mostly in English with a drop from 86% in 1971 to 55% in 1989. Thus the Francisation features of Bill 101 had the intended effect of increasing the use of French at work especially for Francophone employees. After 20 years of Bill 101 application, the Quebec Government task force on the position of French concluded the following:

> French mother-tongue workers have gained their rightful position in the Quebec labour market. Gone are the days when French was predominant at the bottom of the labour market, bilingualism was necessary in the middle and English dominated at the top of the market'. (Quebec, 1996a: 71; author's translation.)

Given the Francisation goals of Bill 101, Francophone Xmen nevertheless bemoan the slow progress of French as the language of work for Allophone workers and remain sceptical of the gains in the use of French reported by Anglophone employees. Militant Xmen also lobby to expand the requirement of Francisation certificates to businesses of less than 50 employees. In effect, Bill 101 measures to improve the status of French at work have made it possible for Francophone employees to remain unilingual without being overly penalised on the income and job promotion front. However, with the growing integration of the Quebec economy within the continental market following the implementation of the North American Free Trade Agreement (NAFTA, 1991), it remains the case that Francophone business leaders, professionals and skilled technicians are increasingly bilingual, using English as the lingua franca of international trade, science, technology and communication (e-mail, electronic media).

Bill 101 and the Quebec linguistic landscape

> Slaves who become cruel masters themselves do great damage to the cause of abolition; previously disadvantaged RLSers who become cultural imperialists themselves, within their newly dominated network, do great damage to the RLS cause, not only locally or regionally but internationally as well. Francophone Quebec's restriction of the public use of English on store and street signs, now that French has unmistakenly come to the fore there, has harmed the moral and political position of francophone minorities outside of Quebec as well as the position of a variety of RLS efforts far outside the borders of Canada. (Fishman, 1991: 84)

Though most crucial for reversing language shift, the Bill 101 measures to enshrine French as the language of schooling for immigrants and to normalise French as the language of work were unlikely to produce immediate improvements in the status and use of French in Quebec. However, as the first legislative act of the Parti Québécois Government, Bill 101 had to be seen as having an immediate positive impact on the status of French, especially in Montreal. The architect of Bill 101, Dr Camille Laurin, understood the need for the Charter to: (1) make Francophones feel more secure about the place of French in Quebec; (2) send a clear message to Anglophones and Allophones that the status of French relative to English was changing in the Province. The Francisation of the Quebec 'linguistic landscape' was chosen as the highly visible domain in which the new power relationship between French and English would be symbolised in an immediately tangible way (Landry & Bourhis, 1997). In addition to changing road signs and government signs to 'French only' and replacing many English place names by French ones, Bill 101 stipulated that commercial store signs had to be in French only, except those dealing with religious, humanitarian or cultural products which could remain in any language. Enforced by the *'Commission de la protection de la langue francaise'* (CPLF), these linguistic landscape requirements had the advantage of producing highly visible changes in favour of French within a year of the adoption of Bill 101, thus comforting Francophones that Bill 101 was achieving its immediate goals set by the Parti Québécois Government.

Though some Francophones felt uneasy about effectively banning English from commercial signs, Xmen cited the Quebec Prime Minister, René Lévesque, who remarked that when immigrants saw a bilingual store sign in Montreal, the message they understood was that though French and English were present in the Province, knowledge of English was quite enough to 'get by' in Quebec. While Bill 101 was essentially aimed at enshrining French as one of the most valued dimensions of Québécois French identity, the demotion of English implied in the law also served to raise language as a more highly prized symbol of Quebec Anglophone identity (Sachdev & Bourhis, 1990). Thus the presence of French vs English within the Quebec linguistic landscape came to have much symbolic significance for members of each linguistic community (Landry & Bourhis, 1997).

Of the Quebec Anglophones who stayed after Bill 101, many mobilised as group members to defend their status as the English minority of the Province (Levine, 1990; Scowen, 1991). By 1982 this mobilisation culminated in the creation of an Anglophone pressure group, known as *Alliance Quebec*, whose aim was to safeguard and promote the linguistic interests of English Quebec (Caldwell, 1998, Legault, 1992; Stevenson, 1999). Subsidised by the Canadian Federal Government ($1.2 million/year) pro-English lobby groups such as 'Alliance Quebec' mobilised against key features of Bill 101 such as French only commercial signs and the education provisions forcing international immigrants to send their children to French schools. The intensity of Anglophone sentiments against the French-only commercial sign law is conveyed in the caricature published in the major English language newspaper of the Province (Figure 5.3).

By 1988, following Anglophone challenges of Bill 101, the Canadian Supreme Court ruled that French-only commercial signs contravened both the Quebec and Canadian Charter of Rights and Freedoms. While Quebec's right to require the predominant display of French as one of the languages on commercial signs was justified, requiring the exclusive use of French was not. The Canadian Court declared that individual rights to freedom of expression included the right to display commercial signs in the language of one's choice. In response to the Canadian Supreme Court ruling and in the midst of a heated linguistic debate, the Quebec Liberal Government adopted Bill 178, which stipulated that bilingual signs be allowed inside commercial stores with less than 50 employees but that only French would be allowed on outside commercial signs. Bill 178 was passed by invoking a Canadian Constitution 'override' clause exempting provinces from individual rights enshrined within the 'Canadian Charter of Rights and Freedoms' for renewable period of five years. The Canadian Charter of Rights was adopted by the nine Anglophone majority Provinces in 1982 but was never ratified by Quebec though the Province remains subject to its provisions. The Quebec Liberal Government had come to power in 1985 with a programme that favoured allowing languages other than French on commercial signs. Anglophone frustration with Bill 178 led to the formation of the 'Equality Party' calling for the repeal of Bill 178 and a return to full bilingualism in Quebec.

The Canadian Constitution 'override' clause stipulates that provincial laws that infringe individual rights either become nullified after five years or must be renewed or changed by the Provincial Government in question. With five years elapsed the Quebec Liberal Government decided to replace Bill 178 by a new commercial sign law that respected individual rights enshrined in the Canadian charter. Bill 86 allowed languages other than French on commercial signs as long as French was *twice as predominant* visually than the combined presence of other languages. Polls used to plan the law showed that over 64% of Francophones across the Province favoured bilingual commercial signs as long as French was twice as predominant, an option also endorsed by 60% of rank and file Parti Québécois sympathisers (Gauthier & Bourhis, 1993). Another 14% of Parti Québécois sympathisers preferred total 'freedom of choice' for the language of signs, while 28% favoured a return to the original Bill 101 measure of allowing only French unilingualism on commercial signs. A majority of Anglophones and

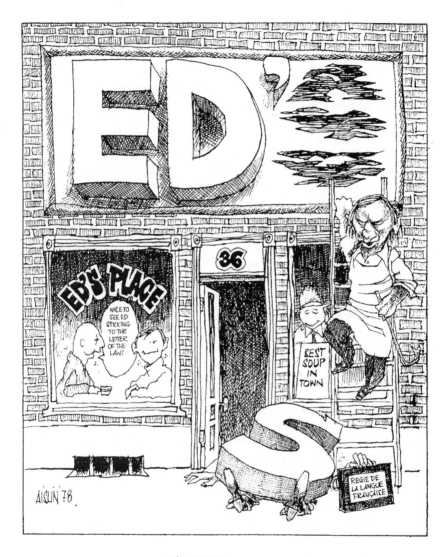

"HOW'S THAT, TURKEY?"

English possessive forms are illegal for a time
under Quebec's new language regulations

Figure 5.3

Allophones (54%) also endorsed the French predominance option though 40% still preferred the 'freedom of choice' option allowing store owners to decide which languages to use on their store signs. Taken together, the French predominance option rallied the majority of support across the three linguistic communities and given the degree of endorsement obtained even among Parti Québécois sympathisers, the Liberal Government quickly passed the new sign law in 1993. Support for the Bill 86 sign law increased by 1996, with Quebec-wide polls showing that 87% of Quebecers wanted to maintain the predominance of French on commercial signs. However, as in previous polls, results showed that 80% of Quebecers felt that despite the protection offered by laws such as Bill 101 and Bill 86, French was perceived to be 'very' or 'somewhat threatened' in Quebec.

To conform to Bill 86, stores could display only in French, or display twice as many messages in French than in other languages or display signs with French characters twice as predominant as those of all other languages combined. Importantly, a store was deemed as not abiding by the law if one message in a store was not translated in French even if all other messages were unilingual French. At conventions, trade fairs and international exhibitions and in stores selling cultural products in languages other than French such as bookshops, cinemas and video clubs, signs could be displayed in other languages without the presence of French. Non-commercial messages could also be displayed in other languages when such messages dealt with humanitarian, religious, political, ideological or strictly personal messages. Equal French–English bilingualism is authorised for public signs about health or public safety and for international events and in museums, cultural or scientific exhibitions and tourist information. However, advertising must be in French only on billboards, large-scale signs and advertising on public transportation vehicles.

After only two years of application, the OLF and CLF conducted three major studies on the Francisation of Montreal Island commercial signs (Quebec, 1997). The language of signs was studied by independent observers in 2008 Montreal stores in 1995, 2040 stores in 1996 and in 2016 stores in 1997. The proportion of these Montreal stores containing at least one message in French increased from 94% in 1995 to 97% in 1997 while the proportion of stores containing at least one message in English increased from 45% in 1995 to 50% in 1997. Across the island the proportion of stores displaying commercial signs only in English declined from 2.5% in 1995 to less than 1% in 1997, while in the West Island of Montreal where Anglophones are in the majority, this proportion declined from 3.8% in 1995 to 1.5% in 1997. The proportion of stores across Montreal displaying commercial signs only in French ranged from 46% to 49% during the study period. Thus after only four years of application, Bill 86 consolidated the Francisation of the Montreal linguistic landscape while respecting the rights of linguistic minorities to also use their own language on commercial signs.

However, after 15 years of French unilingualism on commercial signs resulting from Bill 101 and Bill 178, small and large stores in the West Island of Montreal were slow to introduce English bilingualism on their store signs as permitted within Bill 86. By 1996 militant Xmen within the Anglophone community began a campaign to boycott department stores which did not include the proper share of English on their store signs. The boycott campaign was successful and many department stores on the West Island changed from unilingual French signs to French–English bilingual ones. However, the 1998 Alliance Quebec campaign to change French unilingual signs in downtown Montreal through another boycott met the opposition of French trade unions who threatened a French majority boycott of downtown department stores if they shifted from unilingual French signs to bilingual ones. Caught in the cross-fire, downtown department store owners revealed that a 1993 secret deal with the Liberal Government had established a 'linguistic equilibrium' in which commercial signs would remain unilingual French for the sake of maintaining the linguistic landscape mainly French in downtown Montreal. Discussions with the Prime Minister in 1998 made it clear that the Parti Québécois Government also wanted to maintain the 'linguistic equilibrium' even if this meant that downtown store owners would forgo their right to post bilingual sign as allowed in Bill 86. The ensuing status quo on French unilingual signs in downtown Montreal divided the Alliance Quebec leadership. The older guard of the Alliance formed a rival association focused on improving the position of English through continuing dialogue with the Quebec Government. Other Anglophone Xmen stayed within the more militant 'Alliance Quebec' vowing to pursue their struggle for bilingual commercial signs, freedom of choice for the language of education of immigrant pupils, and preparing the pro-partition strategy for the next referendum on Quebec independence.

The application of the commercial sign law by the OLF and its enforcement by the CPLF gave rise to other highly publicised controversies which cumulatively deepened the linguistic insecurity felt by language minorities in the Province. For example in 1996, on the eve of Passover, the OLF notified Montreal grocery stores that they did not comply with the law because kosher products on their shelves were labelled in English, Hebrew or Yiddish only. As a result, a number of food chains removed kosher products from their shelves during Passover. Despite representations by the

Montreal Jewish community, the OLF had refused to exempt imported New York kosher products from the French labelling rule, though the law did provide exceptions for specialised items with no equivalent replacement product labelled in French within the Quebec market. In 1997 a long-established Jewish business selling tombstones was singled out by the CPLF because the old commercial sign was written with Hebrew lettering more predominant than French. Both these cases were eventually settled through special agreement with the Ministry in charge of Bill 101. In 1998, CPLF civil servants requested that most of the commercial signs in Montreal's China Town be replaced because Chinese lettering was more predominant than French ones. The Chinese Chamber of Commerce vehemently opposed these requirements claiming that French was less threatened by the presence of Chinese on commercial signs than by the influence of English in Quebec and North America as a whole. At the time of writing this case was still under review by the Conseil de la langue française.

Overall, militant Xmen agreed with CPLF vigilance in applying the French sign law, while other Francophones saw these interventions as too harsh given the progress already achieved for French in the linguistic landscape. However, the above language of signs controversies received much negative publicity in the Anglophone press not only in Quebec and Canada but also across the USA and Europe. In 1999, the Quebec government commissioned a Montreal polling firm to conduct focus group studies on Quebec language laws with influential Americans in New York, Boston, Atlanta and Chicago. The focus group study undertaken with respondents in the business, academic, tourist and journalism world showed that these well-informed Americans had a negative impression of Quebec's linguistic laws. When asked to think about Quebec in general the respondents mentioned the French language, the separatist movement and the determination of its population to conserve its language and culture. Themes emerging from the focus group discussions included negative and often inaccurate perceptions of the linguistic situation in the Province including the following statements.

> Public schools are all in French, and English-speaking students only have access to private or bilingual institutions. English is not permitted on signs and breaking sign laws merits a prison sentence. Quebec's language laws are discriminatory and restrictive. Half the respondents said they would rather work in Toronto than Montreal and business people would prefer to set up in Toronto to avoid having French imposed on

them. Those who had visited Quebec expressed an irritation with French-only signs and bilingual people who refused to speak English.

When asked to comment on the research, the President of the American Council for Quebec Studies stated that the study provided a fairly accurate account of what even educated Americans think of Quebec (*Montreal Gazette*, 8 May 1999). He noted that extreme cases of language issues are what usually made it into American newspapers, like the instance involving Hebrew lettering on signs and packaging. The President of the Council for Quebec studies concluded that: 'the more extreme cases are the ones that make it into public consciousness, and those are the ones that are retained'.

Whatever counter-publicity the Parti Québécois Government may intend to purchase in the mass media is likely to be quite expensive and not as influential in changing negative perceptions of Quebec language laws as stories filed by independent or syndicated journalists. Ministers and civil servants involved in the controversial applications of the sign law have not only undermined perceptions of the legitimacy of the law dealing with the linguistic landscape but also tarnished the reputation of other Bill 101 measures designed to maintain French in Quebec. Furthermore, it is the case that controversial applications of Quebec sign laws have been turned against the legitimate goals of language minorities seeking to 'reverse language shift' in other parts of Canada and in the world: the most immediate case in point being the 'English only movement' in the USA which regularly uses controversial features of Quebec language laws reported in the Anglo-American media to justify its campaigns against minority language maintenance in the US (Bourhis & Marshall, 1999).

Conclusion: RLS in an Intergroup Perspective

Remarkable gains for the French language have been achieved in Quebec through language laws such as the *Charter of the French Language*. As such, even with the advantage of a low intergenerational dislocation score to start with, Quebec remains a 'success story' of language planning for reversing language shift (RLS, Fishman, 1991). However, many Francophones still feel threatened demographically as a minority in North America while Anglophones feel threatened as a declining minority in Quebec.

For many Francophone analysts, Bill 101 was salutary, as it did defuse a potentially explosive clash between a Francophone majority at the bottom of the labour market and a dominant Anglophone elite at the top (Rocher, 1992). The 1970 October crisis, which brought the Canadian army on Quebec soil to 'neutralise' the activities of the guerilla 'Front de Libération du Québec' (FLQ), demonstrated the divisiveness of the class and ethnolinguistic cleavage existing within Quebec society at that time. Language policies such as Bill 101 could be seen as *one* of the democratically adopted measures which contributed to the institutionalised management of a class and ethnic conflict threatening to destabilise Quebec society (Esman, 1987). Thus RLS measures within language laws can be necessary tools allowing multilingual states to modernise more harmoniously.

For more militant Quebec nationalists, Bill 101 was perhaps too successful in reversing language shift, thus reducing the feeling of linguistic threat fuelling the drive for Quebec independence. Francophone Xmen also point out the numerous features of the original Bill 101 which were annulled or neutralised by Canadian Supreme Court rulings based on the 1982 Constitution and the Charter of Rights and Freedoms (Bourhis, 1994a). Xmen also point out weaknesses in the application of Bill 101 in the work world and education (Veltman, 1998) while bemoaning the enduring drawing power of English in the electronic and mass-media, not just in Montreal but across the Province (Barbeau, 1998). For many Francophone Xmen, total independence is offered as the ultimate solution which will allow a future Quebec state to adopt the full range of language laws deemed necessary to enshrine the status of French, free from Canadian Government interference with its constitutional protection of individual rights, the Official Languages Act (Fortier, 1994) and the 1988 Multiculturalism law (Fleras & Elliot, 1992).

Combined with an already declining birthrate, language policies such as Bill 101 had a dramatic impact on the group vitality of Quebec Anglophones. To survive as a minority, Anglophones had to transform themselves by becoming a bilingual and multicultural community sharing English as its lingua franca with Allophone and immigrants communities. However, it is not clear that the strong institutional control presently enjoyed by Anglophones will be sufficient to compensate for its eroding demographic base. Quebec Anglophones remain more mobile economically than Francophones and continue to leave the Province when seeking better employment within the Anglo-Canadian mainstream. Recent survey studies also suggest that close to half a million Anglophones would leave Quebec following a majority YES vote in the next referendum on Quebec independence.

In contrast, Quebec Allophones are less likely to leave the Province than Anglophones under such circumstances. With the drawing power of the two rival host languages neutralising each other, it is in Quebec that one finds Allophones with the highest intergenerational transmission rate of Heritage languages in Canada. It is especially in Montreal that Allophone and immigrant background individuals can most readily construct multiple group identities incorporating their own Heritage culture with two important cultures in the Western world, the English and the French.

Neither Francophones nor Anglophones can count on increased birthrate to improve their respective demographic position in the Province. Likewise, given the difficult economic situation in Quebec, neither Francophones nor Anglophones can count on attracting immigration from other Canadian provinces to improve the strength of their respective linguistic communities. By default, Allophones and international immigrants remain the most promising solution for improving the linguistic position of the two host communities. Both Francophones and Anglophones depend on the linguistic integration of immigrants to boost their respective linguistic position within the Province. However, Quebec's average share of international immigrants to Canada has dropped to only 16% of the total immigrant intake in the last decade, despite the fact that Quebec accounts for 23% of the Canadian population. Without a substantial increase in immigration or fertility rate, demographers expect the Quebec population to begin its decline within the next two decades (Castonguay, 1998, 1999).

Traditionally, 'Québécois' identity has been synonymous with French mother-tongue background, French ancestry and identification with French Canadian culture. However, especially in Montreal, the Francisation of immigrant background pupils through Bill 101 educational requirements implies that *knowing French* may be a sufficient condition for becoming a true 'Québécois' (Breton, 1988). Tensions arising from this redefinition of who *should be* and who *can be* a true 'Québécois' have been at the core of a growing debate on 'citizenship' in Quebec society (Gagnon *et al.*, 1996; Labelle, 1990; Taylor, 1992). At one pole of the ideological continuum (Bourhis *et al.*, 1997), the pluralist and civic orientations uphold that Allophones and immigrant background individuals can be considered 'Québécois' as long as they learn and use French as the language of 'public life' (e.g. at work, in shops, in hospitals) and participate in their civic duties and responsibilities (e.g. pay taxes, obey civil and criminal laws). Under this definition, Allophone and immigrant background citizens have no obligation to identify or participate in Québécois 'mainstream' cultural and political aspirations nor adopt French as the language of the home, as these are matters of private individual choice beyond the reach of the state as stipulated in the Quebec Charter of Human Rights. On the language front, this civic position is the one adopted by the Quebec Government in its official position on French as the language of 'public life' (Quebec, 1996b). Moreover, for those espousing the pluralists' position, Heritage language maintenance by Allophones is considered a 'linguistic capital' worth supporting financially by the state and likely to enrich the cultural and economic dynamism of Quebec society (Fleras & Elliot, 1992).

Towards the other end of the continuum are assimilationists who, in the Francophone camp, expect Allophones and immigrants to not only learn French and attend to their civic duties as Quebec citizens but also expect such individuals to espouse as 'their own' the cultural and political aspirations of the 'Québécois' mainstream (e.g. adoption of French as the language of the home, defence of the French language and culture against English, voting in favour of Quebec sovereignty). In turn, Anglophone assimilationists expect Allophones also to learn English, identify first as Canadian federalists and rally with older stock Anglophones in defence of the English fact in Quebec. Finally, at the extreme end of this continuum, Francophone 'exclusionists' are those who would find it difficult to accept as a true 'Québécois', immigrant background individuals who do not have French as a mother-tongue, have no Québécois French ancestry and lack identification with 'genuine Québécois' cultural and political aspirations. Among Anglophones, 'exclusionists' are most readily found among right-wing 'Reform party' supporters in Ontario and western Canada whose views tends to be anti-bilingualism, anti-immigration and anti-multiculturalism. In Quebec, the Reform Party commands no support as Anglophones can ill afford to exclude Allophone and immigrant background individuals likely to join their ranks for the cause of 'the English' in the Province. However, as endorsed in the Reform Party platform, there is strong Anglophone support for the *partition of Quebec* in the event of a majority YES vote for Quebec separation from Canada in the next referendum. Given that most Anglophones are against Quebec separation, a 1996 poll showed that over 80% of Quebec non-Francophones favour the partition of Quebec allowing English majority regions of the Province to remain within Canada following a majority YES vote for separation. In contrast, three-quarters of Francophones oppose the partition of Quebec following a YES vote for independence. In retrospect, RLS measures such as Bill 101 can be credited for having brought to the fore these competing definitions of 'Québécois' and 'Canadian' identity in an uncertain federation that may not survive the next century but may give birth to a number of new states in North America. Whatever the outcome of the Quebec independence debate, it remains true that laws such as the Charter of the French language will continue to be vital for the long-term survival of the only French majority society in North America.

Notes

1. Comments and suggestions concerning this chapter would be much appreciated and should be addressed to: Richard Bourhis, Département de psychologie, Université du Québec à Montréal, CP 8888, Succ. Centre-Ville, Montréal, Québec, Canada, H3C 3P8. Tel: (514) 987-3000 ext. 4852; Fax: (514) 987-7953; e-mail: bourhis.richard@uqam.ca
2. The author wishes to thank l'*Office de la langue française* and the *Conseil de la langue française* for their generous help in providing documents and research reports needed to write this chapter. The author would also like to thank the following individuals for their very helpful comments and suggestions on earlier versions of this chapter: Catherine Amiot, Geneviève Barrette, Pierre Bouchard, Charles Castonguay, Martine Cournoyer, Guy Dumas, André Gagnon, Denyse Lemay, Dominique Lepicq, Marie Mc Andrew and Morton Weinfeld.
3. English caption for Figure 5.2: This is the front page of a right-wing nationalist weekly magazine entitled *La Nation* published in 1937. The large headline announces the creation of a new Quebec autonomist party. The author's translation of the caption at the top of the picture is: 'The great threat'. The English translation of the caption at the bottom of the picture is: 'What is the use of a Congress on the French Language if John Bull (the British) seeks to drown us in a sea of immigration'. Francophones can be seen swimming to reach the precarious raft on which they huddle for survival. In the 1930s the majority of immigrants settling in Quebec came from the British Isles.

References

Allard, R. and Landry, R. (1986) Subjective ethnolinguistic vitality viewed as a belief system. *Journal of Multilingual and Multicultural Development* 7, 1–12.

Allard, R. and Landry, R. (1994) Subjective ethnolinguistic vitality: A comparison of two measures. *International Journal of the Sociology of Language* 108, 117–44.

Amiot, C. and Bourhis, R.Y. (1999) Ethnicity and French-English communication in Montreal. Poster presented at the *60th Convention of the Canadian Psychological Association*, Halifax, Nova Scotia.

d'Anglejan, A. (1984) Language planning in Quebec: An historical overview and future trends. In R. Bourhis (ed.) *Conflict and Language Planning in Quebec* (pp. 29–52) Clevedon: Multilingual Matters.

Barbeau, P. (1998) French in Quebec. In J. Edwards (ed.) *Languages in Canada*. New York: Cambridge University Press.

Béland, P. (1991) *L'usage du français au travail: situation et tendances*. Québec: Conseil de la Langue francaise. Montréal: Office de la langue française.

Béland, P. (1999) *Le français, langue d'usage public au Québec en 1997*. Québec: Conseil de la langue française.

Bouchard, P. (1991) *Les enjeux de la francisation des entreprises au Québec 1977–1984*. Montréal: Office de la langue française.

Bouchard, P. (1998) La francisation des entreprises au Québec: De la difficulté relative d'hier à la complexité de demain. *Colloque du Comité scientifique du réseau Sociolinguistique et dynamique des langues de l'Agence universitaire de la Francophonie.* Rabat: Maroc.

Bourhis, R.Y. (1979) Language and ethnic interaction: A social psychological approach. In H. Giles and B. Saint-Jacques (eds) *Language and Ethnic Relations.* Oxford: Pergamon Press.

Bourhis, R. (1982) Language policies and language attitudes: Le monde de la Francophonie. In E.B. Ryan and H. Giles (eds) *Attitudes Towards Language Variation* (pp. 34–62) London: Edward Arnold.

Bourhis, R. (1984a) Language policies in multilingual settings. In R. Bourhis (ed) *Conflict and Language Planning in Quebec* (pp. 1–28). Clevedon: Multilingual Matters.

Bourhis, R.Y. (1984b) Cross-cultural communication in Montreal: Two field studies since Bill 101. *International Journal of the Sociology of Language* 46, 33–47.

Bourhis, R.Y. (1994a) Introduction and overview of language events in Canada. *International Journal of the Sociology of Language* 105–106, 5–36.

Bourhis, R.Y. (1994b) Ethnic and language attitudes in Quebec. In J. Berry and J. Laponce (eds) *Ethnicity and Culture in Canada: The Research Landscape* (pp. 322–360). Toronto: University of Toronto Press.

Bourhis, R.Y., Giles, H. and Rosenthal, D. (1981) Notes on the construction of a 'Subjective vitality questionnaire' for ethnolinguistic groups. *Journal of Multilingual and Multicultural Development* 2, 145–55.

Bourhis, R.Y. and Lepicq, D. (1993) Québécois French and language issues in Quebec. In R. Posner and J.N. Green (eds) *Trends in Romance Linguistics and Philology, Volume 5: Bilingualism and Linguistic Conflict in Romance* (pp. 345–381). The Hague and Berlin: Mouton de Gruyter.

Bourhis, R.Y. and Marshall, D. (1999) The United States and Canada. In J. Fishman (ed.) *Handbook of Language and Ethnic Identity* (pp. 244–64). Oxford: Oxford University Press.

Bourhis, R.Y., Moise, C., Perreault, S. and Senécal, S. (1997) Towards an interactive acculturation model: A social psychological approach. *International Journal of Psychology* 32, 369–86.

Bourhis, R.Y. and Sachdev, I. (1984) Vitality perceptions and language attitudes. *Journal of Language and Social Psychology* 3, 97–126.

Breton, R. (1971) Institutional completeness of ethnic communities and personal relations of immigrants. In B.R. Blishen, F.E. Jones, K.D. Naegels and J. Porter (eds) *Canadian Society: Sociological Perspectives.* Toronto: Macmillan.

Breton, R. (1988) From ethnic to civic nationalism: English Canada and Quebec. *Ethnic and Racial Studies* 11, 85–102.

Caldwell, G. (1984) Anglo-Quebec: Demographic realities and options for the future. In R.Y. Bourhis (ed.) *Conflict and Language Planning in Quebec* (pp. 205–21). Clevedon: Multilingual Matters.

Caldwell, G. (1994) English Quebec: Demographic and cultural reproduction. In R.Y. Bourhis (ed) French-English language issues in Canada. *International Journal of the Sociology of Language 105–106,* 153–79.

Caldwell, G. (1998) English Quebec. In J. Edwards (ed.) *Language in Canada* (pp. 177–201). New York: Cambridge University Press.

Caldwell, G. and Fournier, D. (1987) The Quebec question: A matter of population. *Canadian Journal of Sociology* 12, 16–41.

Canada, (1969) *Royal Commission on Bilingualism and Biculturalism, Book III: The Work World*. Ottawa: The Queen's Printer.

Castonguay, C. (1997) Évolution de l'assimilation linguistique au Québec et au Canada entre 1971 et 1991. *Recherches sociographiques* 38, 469–90.

Castonguay, C. (1998) The fading Canadian duality. In J. Edwards (ed.) *Language in Canada* (pp. 36–60). New York: Cambridge University Press.

Castonguay, C. (1999) Getting the facts straight on French: Reflections following the 1996 Census. *Inroads: A Journal of Opinion* 8, 57–76.

CDP (1998) *Les programmes d'accès à l'égalité au Québec: Bilan et perspectives*. Québec: Commission des droits de la personne et des droits de la jeunesse.

Daoust, D. (1984) Francization and terminology change in Quebec business firms. In R.Y. Bourhis (ed.) *Conflict and Language Planning in Quebec* (pp. 81–113). Clevedon, England: Multilingual Matters.

Drapeau, L. (1998) Aboriginal languages: Current status. In J. Edwards (ed.). *Language in Canada* (pp. 144–59). New York: Cambridge University Press.

Esman, M.J. (1987) Ethnic politics and economic power. *Comparative Politics* 19, 395–418.

Fishman, J. (1991) *Reversing Language Shift*. Clevedon: Multilingual Matters.

Fishman, J. (1999) (ed.) *Handbook of Language and Ethnic Identity*. Oxford: Oxford University Press.

Fleras, A. and Elliot, J.L. (1992) *The Challenge of Diversity: Multiculturalism in Canada*. Scarborough, Ontario: Nelson Canada.

Fortier, I. (1994) Official language policies in Canada: A quiet revolution. *International Journal of the Sociology of Language* 105–106, 69–97.

Gagnon, F., McAndrew, M. and Pagé, M. (1996) Introduction. *Pluralisme, citoyenneté et éducation* (pp. 13–21). Paris, Montréal: L'Harmattan.

Gauthier, C. and Bourhis, R.Y. (1993) *Les québécois et la question linguistique et plus particulièrement la langue d'affichage commercial: Sondage d'opinion auprès des québécois*. Montréal: Crop inc. et Département de psychologie, UQAM.

Genesee, F. and Bourhis, R.Y. (1988) Evaluative reactions to language choice strategies: The role of sociostructural factors. *Language and Communication* 8, 229–50.

Genesee, F. and Holobow, N. (1989) Change and stability in intergroup perceptions. *Journal of Language and Social Psychology* 8, 17–38.

Giles, H., Bourhis, R.Y. and Taylor, D. (1977) Towards a theory of language in ethnic group relations. In H. Giles (ed.) *Language, Ethnicity and Intergroup Relations*. London: Academic Press.

Giroux, L. (1992) *Les adolescents montréalais et la télévision de langue francaise*. Montréal: Université de Montréal.

Hamers, J. and Hummel, K. (1994) The francophones of Quebec: Language policies and language use. *International Journal of the Sociology of Language* 105–106, 127–52.

Hamers, J. and Hummel, K. (1998) Language in Quebec: Aboriginal and Heritage varieties. In J. Edwards (ed.) *Language in Canada* (pp. 384–99). New York: Cambridge University Press.

Harwood, J., Giles, H. and Bourhis, R.Y. (1994) The genesis of vitality theory: Historical patterns and discoursal dimensions. *International Journal of the Sociology of Language* 108, 167–206.

Johnson, P., Giles, H. and Bourhis, R.Y. (1983) The viability of ethnolinguistic vitality: A reply. *Journal of Multilingual and Multicultural Development* 4, 255–69.

Labelle, M. (1990) Immigration, culture et question nationale. *Cahiers de Recherche sociologique* 4, 143–51.

Lachapelle, A. and Henripin, J. (1980) *La Situation Démolinguistique au Canada.* Montréal: Institut de Recherches Politiques.

Lambert, W.E., Hodgson, J., Gardner, R. and Fillenbaum, S. (1960) Evaluational reactions to spoken languages. *Journal of Abnormal and Social Psychology* 60, 44–51.

Landry, R., Allard, R. and Bourhis, R.Y. (1997) Profil sociolanguagiers de jeunes Francophones et Anglophones du Québec en fonction de la vitalité des communautés linguistiques. In G. Budach and J. Erfurt (eds) *Identité franco-canadienne et société civile québécoise* (pp. 123–50). Leipig: Leipziger Universitatsverlag.

Landry, R. and Bourhis, R.Y. (1997) Linguistic landscape and ethnolinguistic vitality: An empirical study. *Journal of Language and Social Psychology* 16, 23–49.

Laporte, P. (1984) Status of language planning in Quebec: An evaluation. In R.Y. Bourhis (ed.) *Conflict and Language Planning in Quebec* (pp. 53–80). Clevedon: Multilingual Matters.

Legault, J. (1992) *L'invention d'une minorité: Les anglo-Québécois.* Montréal: Boréal.

Levine, M. (1990) *The Reconquest of Montreal: Language Policy and Social Change in a Bilingual City.* Philadelphia: Temple University Press.

Mallea, J. (1984) Minority language education in Quebec and Anglophone Canada. In R.Y. Bourhis (ed.) *Conflict and Language Planning in Quebec* (pp. 222–60). Clevedon: Multilingual Matters.

Maurais, J. (1987) L'expérience québécoise d'aménagement linguistique. In J. Maurais (ed.) *Politique et aménagement linguistique* (pp. 359–416). Québec and Paris: Conseil de la Langue francaise, Le Robert.

Maurais, J. (1997) (ed.) *The Indigenous Languages of Québec.* Clevedon: Multilingual Matters.

McAndrew, M. (1996) Ethnicity in Quebec schools. *Pluralism and Education: Proceedings of the Conference on Pluralism and Cultural Enrichment in Education* (pp. 65–84). Dublin, Ireland: University of Ulster.

Miller, R. (1984) The response of business firms to the Francization Process. In R.Y. Bourhis (ed.) *Conflict and Language Planning in Quebec* (pp. 114–29). Clevedon: Multilingual Matters.

Moise, L.C. and Bourhis, R.Y. (1994) Langage et ethnicité: Communication interculturelle èa Montréal, 1977–1991. *Canadian Ethnic Studies* 26, 86–107.

OLF (1998) *Office de la langue française: Rapport annuel 1997–1998.* Montréal: Les publications du Québec.

Pendakur, R. (1990) *Speaking in Tongues: Heritage Language Maintenance and Transfer in Canada.* Ottawa: Department of Multiculturalism and Citizenship.

Quebec (1972) (Gendron Commission). *Report of the Commission of Enquiry on the Position of the French Language and on Language Rights in Quebec.* Québec: Editeur Officiel du Québec.

Quebec (1996a) *Le français langue commune. Rapport du comité interministériel sur la situation de la langue française*. Québec: Direction des communications, ministèere de la Culture et des communications (319 pp).

Quebec (1996b) *Le français langue commune: Proposition de politique linguistique*. Québec: Direction des communications, ministère de la Culture et des Communications (77 pp).

Quebec (1997) *L'évolution de la situation de l'affichage à Montréal de 1995 à 1997*. Québec; Conseil de la langue francaise. (http//www.clf.gouv.qc.ca).

Rocher, G. (1992) Autour de la langue: crises et débats, espoir et tremblement. In G. Daigle and G. Rocher (eds) *Le Québec en Jeu: Comprendre les grands défis* (pp. 423–50). Montréal: Les Presses de l'Université de Montéal.

Ryan, E.B. and Giles, H. (eds) (1982) *Attitudes Towards Language Variation*. London: Edward Arnold.

Sachdev, I. and Bourhis, R.Y. (1990) Language and social identification. In D. Abrams and M. Hogg (eds) *Social Identity Theory: Constructive and Critical Advances*. New York: Harvester/Wheatsheaf.

Sachdev, I. and Bourhis, R.Y. (1991) Power and status differentials in minority and majority group relations. *European Journal of Social Psychology* 21, 1–24.

Sachdev, I. and Bourhis, R.Y. (1993) Ethnolinguistic vitality: Some motivational and cognitive considerations. In M. Hogg and D. Abrams (eds) *Group Motivation: A Social Psychological Perspective* (pp. 33–52). New York: Harvester-Wheatsheaf.

Scowen, R. (1991) *A Different Vision: The English in Quebec in the 1990s*. Don Mills, Ontario: Maxwell Macmillan Canada.

Stevenson, G. (1999) *Community Besieged: The Anglophone Minority and the Politics of Quebec*. Montreal: McGill-Queen's University Press.

Taylor, C. (1992) The politics of recognition. In A. Gutmann (ed.) *Multiculturalism and the Politics of Recognition* (pp. 25–73). Princeton, NJ: Princeton University Press.

Termote, P. and Gauvreau, D. (1988) *La Situation Démolinguistique au Québec*. Québec: Conseil de la Langue Française.

Vallière, P. (1969) *Nègres blancs d'amérique*. Paris: Maspéro.

Veltman, C. (1998) Quebec, Canada and the United States: Social reality and language rights. In T. Ricento and B. Burnaby (eds) *Language and Politics in the United States and Canada: Myths and Realities* (pp. 301–15). Mahwah, NJ: Lawrence Erlbaum Publishers.

de Vries, J. (1994) Canada's official language communities: An overview of the current demolinguistic situation. *International Journal of the Sociology of Language* 105–106, 37–68.

Wardhaugh, R. (1987) *Languages in Competition*. Oxford: Blackwell.

Chapter 6
Otomí Language Shift and Some Recent Efforts to Reverse It

Y. LASTRA

The purpose of this chapter is to report on the language shift of Otomí, which started a long time ago, and some recent local efforts to reverse the trend. Otomí is spoken in central Mexico. It belongs to the Oto-Pamean family which includes three branches, Pame-Chichimeco, Otomí-Mazahua and Matlatzinca-Ocuilteco. The family belongs to the Oto-Manguean stock which consists of 10 families. Among its better-known languages are Zapotec and Mixtec. Most of the languages, except the Oto-Pamean ones, are located in the state of Oaxaca. Mangue, now extinct, was spoken in Nicaragua. The stock does not extend to the north as does the Yuto-Aztecan one; the northernmost Oto-Manguean language is Pame. An interesting fact about these languages is that Pame and Chichimec are located outside of Mesoamerica while the rest have belonged to the culture area for a long time.

Historical Background

The Otomí have lived in central Mexico for many centuries. We will refer to their ancient history, which may help explain what the situation was like at the time of the Spanish Conquest. That period, in turn, has had an influence upon the present-day situation. The Otomí were agriculturists and were probably one of the various ethnic groups present in Teotihuacan,[1] the largest and most important ancient city of Mexico, which flourished for several centuries from around 200 to 800 AD. They were certainly present in Tula, another important city, which goes back to the 8th century of our era and flourished from 950–1150/1200. After the fall of Tula the Otomí are mentioned explicitly in historical documents. The legendary king Xólotl gave an extensive territory to an Otomí leader and the kingdom of Xaltocan[2] was established in the early 13th century.

When the Mexica (later known as Aztecs) were on their pilgrimage to found Mexico they lived several years in Chapultepec[3] and the first to make war against them were the people of Xaltocan. This was the beginning of a long enmity between the two peoples. The Otomí kingdom continued to flourish until the end of the 14th century when it fell to the Mexica-dominated alliance (Torquemada, 1969). Its destruction marks the end of the political importance of the Otomí. Part of the population fled toward the east and south. Subsequently the Mexica-dominated alliance acquired their land. The result was an increase of the Nahuatl element in Otomí regions. Subsequently the Mexica included Otomís in the movement of peoples which they carried out in order to consolidate their power in the territories they kept adding to their empire by means of war. As the Mexica conquered more and more territory they completely subjected the Otomí who had to pay tribute to them.

There were other territories in central Mexico which the Otomí also inhabited, but they were gradually forced to migrate to the least desirable lands and the population of Nahuatl speakers increased in the former Otomí territories. By the time of the arrival of the Spanish, however, the Otomí still occupied three residential sections of Mexico City. To the north of the Mexica capital Otomí was also spoken and its speakers predominated in the region to the north of the Basin of Mexico, which is roughly equivalent to the Mezquital Valley in the state of Hidalgo. There were Otomí towns in parts of the fertile lands of the Huasteca[4] area as well. In the highlands of Puebla there were also Otomí speakers but they shared the territory with speakers of Nahuatl and Totonac. Some Otomí lived in the area between Tetzcoco (Mexico) and Tulancingo (Hidalgo). Tlaxcala was Nahuatl-dominated by the 16th century but there were also Otomí chiefly to the east of the Malinche mountains. In Michoacán they reached as far as the Balsas river to the southeast of the present-day western states of Jalisco and Colima (Carrasco, 1950; Lastra, 1992a).

The extent of Otomí territory denotes their former importance. They settled before the Mexica who were the last to arrive in Mesoamerica from the north. Other speakers of Nahuatl had settled in parts of the centre of Mexico long before the Mexica did and they shared some territories with the Otomí. Even today it is possible to find contiguous towns where one of the languages is spoken in one town and the other in the town next to it. The people celebrate the same fiestas and trade with one another, but there is little intermarriage and the ethnic groups maintain their separate identities.

In former times the Otomí seem to have transmitted many cultural traits to the Mexica, but the latter have never acknowledged this. It is well-known that they had codices burnt so that people would not know some of the facts of their own history. The indebtedness to the Otomí must have gone up in smoke! From then on history could be re-written and the Otomí were depicted as lowly, despicable and stupid. This view was subsequently passed on to the Spanish conquerors, who swallowed the Mexica story without much reflection. Fray Bernardino de Sahagún, who enjoys the reputation of being the first ethnographer, was a Franciscan Friar who took it upon himself to find out everything he could about the religion and the culture that he and his fellow-countrymen were intent upon destroying. He gathered information from elders who belonged to the Mexica elite and consequently the Otomí were portrayed in the most disparaging terms.

Ancient Mexican history thus has a bearing on the present-day language situation because one of the reasons why some Otomí are shifting their language is due to the reputation fabricated by the Mexica after the fall of Xaltocan in the 14th century, a reputation believed and repeated by the Spaniards and later on by Spanish-speaking Mexicans.

Nahuatl seems to have been a lingua franca even before the establishment of the Mexica (Aztec) empire. The names of people and places, for instance, have usually come down to us in that language. The majority of the names of the municipalities and towns that we mention below in connection with the statistics of language shift have a Nahuatl origin. After the Mexica rose to power their language became even more prestigious and bilingualism (local language/Nahuatl) seems to have been common at least among the elites. The Otomí who fled to other lands when the Mexica destroyed their towns often but not always lost their language and their identity.

Tlaxcala was an independent state, which the Mexica never conquered and there were many Otomí there, chiefly as defenders of the frontiers. Tlaxcaltecans and Tlaxcala Otomís joined Cortés against the Mexica not realising that after a while their contribution would be forgotten. But due to the Conquest the Otomí were able to expand and be conquerors themselves. They founded the town of Querétaro and other towns in that region and in what was to become the state of Guanajuato. These migrants had already been converted to Catholicism and seem to have accepted the Faith willingly. Nevertheless many ancient customs still survive both among them and among the Otomí who never moved from their former settlements. Galinier (1979, 1990) the best modern ethnographer of the group, describes many customs and beliefs of the Puebla highlands and is able to reconstruct their world-view which maintains their ancient philosophy of life together with some apparently Christian ways.

With the Spanish Conquest the *encomienda* was instituted. It was a system which supposedly helped the Indians but which permitted the person in charge of a group to utilise their labour. Some towns were called Indian Republics and there the Indians could govern themselves, and in many cases aspects of pre-Hispanic organisation were preserved.

During the colonial period, aside from the regions where there were Otomí speakers interspersed with Nahuatl and Spanish speakers, the main areas where the language was spoken were the newly settled ones in Guanajuato and Querétaro, the Mezquital valley, the highlands area of Puebla, Veracruz, and Hidalgo, the Toluca valley and two enclaves, one in Michoacán and the other in Tlaxcala. Most of these people were farmers.

The comments that follow refer mostly to the Mezquital valley. The lands there were so dry that the people also hired themselves as day labourers and they made use of agave to produce syrups and a traditional fermented drink called *pulque*. At first the colonial government forbade pulque, but later on it taxed it. Rich landowners quickly took over this business and the Otomí were forced to use the agave drink only for their own use. Agave fibres and those of other plants were used to make cords, baskets and other products, which they sold through intermediaries who profited the most. They also cut wood, made charcoal and lime.

The Spaniards developed the silver mines in the neighbourhood, but not many Otomí became miners unless the Spaniards forced them to. The Spanish speakers owned the best lands and they used them for cattle raising.

During the War of Independence the Otomís were almost always on the side of independence because they resented the Spaniards who had taken their lands. With independence the Mezquital was divided and sold to native descendants of the Spaniards. The Indians continued to be hired hands.

During the Revolution against the dictator Porfirio Díaz the Otomís of the Mezquital did not fight for land. They still have a marginal position and they attribute their situation to illiteracy and to the lack of help from the government but not to their being exploited by non-Otomís.

Otomí participation in politics has been non-existent until recent years. In the Mezquital a government agency set up in the 1940s and 1950s was supposed to educate and help the Indians economically, but it didn't really succeed. The people still farm a little, work as day labourers and make use of the products which they gather. It is an economy of subsistence without profits or capital. All this within a capitalistic system where labour and land are irrationally exploited by those in control of the economy. Agriculture may be profitable where there is irrigation, but Indian lands mostly do not have irrigation (Mendizabal, 1947; Nolasco, 1966).

There have been confrontations between family and school and the influence of the family has diminished and bilingualism has increased. Religion has diminished in its importance particularly where there is irrigation. Traditional celebrations give way to dances, sports and commercialisation. In many places Evangelism has been introduced. The converts read the Bible in Spanish and comment on it in Otomí (Franco and Manuel, 1992).

Since independence the government in general adopted an attitude of looking down upon all living Indians while admiring pre-Hispanic monuments and art particularly Aztec and Maya ones. Thus the lack of prestige of the Otomí continued. This attitude was even adopted by archaeologists who did not begin to try to look for evidence of ancient Otomí way of life until very recently. It is definitely the attitude of school teachers even of the so-called bilingual ones. Mexico is supposedly a pluricultural state. These are high-sounding words, but there is very little evidence of its existence. The mainstream dominates and permeates every aspect of life even in remote towns where television and radio come with electricity, Western medicine with government clinics, Spanish with literacy. Other factors contributing to language shift are migration to cities, work in cities away from Otomí centres, temporary migration to the United States, commerce, Spanish-speaking migrants who come to live in indigenous communities, and so on. Of course, reversing language shift does not mean the denial of modernity, but Otomí is associated with backwardness not only in the minds of government officials but also in the minds of some of the speakers themselves.

However, a lot of non-material culture is still preserved. Otomí songs are heard when people go up the Hueyamelucan hill (in the state of Mexico about 80 kilometres from Mexico City) on Saturday nights to pray; I collected a prayer to the Earth Mother in Guanajuato where the language is practically extinct; tales are still known by elders and enjoyed by young people who don't have television and still understand the language; Galinier has been able to reconstruct Otomí philosophy, but I doubt that ordinary Otomí know their history, not even the summary I have given above. At school Mexican history includes a few words about the Olmecs, a few more about Teotihuacan, some Aztec history, and students are told that the Maya knew the concept of 'zero', had a writing system and built beautiful buildings, but not much else. Otomís are weak and despised but persistent. If they were told about their history and if non-Otomí, who do not understand their culture or their needs were to stop managing their education perhaps the language and the culture could survive. We will come back to the issue of education later on.

Language Shift

In this section the appalling statistics of language shift are reviewed. According to the last census (1990) there are 280,238 speakers of Otomí. This includes monolinguals and bilinguals. Their number is lower than it was in 1980 when there were 306,190 speakers. The territory where the language is spoken has shrunk and the percentage of Otomí speakers to the population of each municipality is smaller than it was before (Lastra, 1994).

Let us consider only the censuses taken since independence. The first was taken in 1895. The territory of each state was divided into districts which later were subdivided into municipalities (roughly equivalent to counties). The language habitually used by the people was given for each district together with the total population. The next census was taken in 1900 when the division into municipalities had been made, but luckily the names of the former districts are also given which makes some comparisons possible.

From such comparisons we note that according to the 1895 census there were speakers of Otomí in eight states including San Luis Potosí which had six districts with a small Otomí population. The district with the largest population was Tamazunchale, situated near the border of Querétaro; it only had 204 speakers of Otomí. By the time of the 1900 census we find no speakers left in this district. The district of Tancanhuitz, which had 175 speakers according to the former census shows an increase in the absolute number of speakers (388), but the figure amounts to less than 1%.

The 1910 census has no information on languages. The next census was taken in 1921 and it lists only total numbers of Otomí speakers for states. The 1930 census only registers monolinguals. Comparison of the figures in these two censuses shows that the number of monolinguals is smaller in 1930 than the total number of speakers was previously, but we are left with many questions since the figures are not really comparable. The 1940 and the 1950 censuses asked if people spoke an Indian language, but without specifying which one.

The following census, that is the one for 1960, lists the information by municipality giving the number of bilinguals and monolinguals older than five years and the name of the language. The format of the censuses has not changed significantly since then, which simplifies comparison. On the other hand, the comparison with the 1900 figures is much harder. In Table 6.1 I converted the census figures into percentages in order to show that the proportion of speakers of Otomí has progressively diminished even though in some cases absolute numbers have increased. One has to keep in mind that the 1900 census does not specify age, while the 1960–1990

Table 6.1 Comparison of percentages of Otomí population by municipality: based on census figures for 1900–1990

	1900	1960	1970	1980	1990
Guanajuato					
1. Allende	7%	–	–	2%	1%
2. Apaseo el Alto	3%	–	–	–	–
3. Comonfort	29%	–	–	1%	–
4. Cortazar	–	–	–	1%	–
5. Dolores	2%	–	–	1%	–
6. Villagrán	–	–	–	1%	–
Querétaro					
1. Amealco	28%	36%	25%	32%	28%
2. Cadereyta	36%	9%	6%	5%	2%
3. Peñamiller	6%	–	–	–	–
4. Querétaro	4%	–	–	–	–
5. San Juan del Río	3%	–	–	–	–
6. Tequisquiapan	5%	–	–	–	–
7. Tolimán	67%	33%	24%	35%	28%
Hidalgo					
1. Actopan	28%	66%	13%	11%	6%
2. Alfajayucan	66%	53%	31%	33%	25%
3. Arenal	14%	?	3%	3%	1%
4. Atotonilco el Grande	7%	2%	–	–	–
5. Cardonal	54%	78%	47%	71%	66%
6. Chilcuautla	62%	50%	70%	67%	53%
7. Franciso I. Madero	–	11%	9%	6%	3%
8. Huautla	24%	–	–	–	–
9. Huehuetla	38%	70%	45%	44%	55%
10. Huichapan	11%	17%	3%	2%	–
11. Itzmiquilpan	82%	96%	56%	63%	54%
12. Metztitlán	14%	–	12%	13%	12%
13. Mixquiahuala	38%	–	5%	4%	2%
14. Nicolás Flores	–	96%	70%	64%	59%
15. San Bartolo Tutotepec	52%	68%	47%	45%	45%
16. San Salvador	78%	39%	44%	36%	29%
17. Santiago	82%	93%	56%	70%	58%
18. Tasquillo	63%	60%	51%	55%	47%

Table 6.1 (*cont.*) Comparison of percentages of Otomí population by municipality: based on census figures for 1900–1990

	1900	1960	1970	1980	1990
19. Tecozautla	44%	19%	12%	13%	7%
20. Tenango de Doria	41%	36%	23%	35%	32%
21. Tepeji del Río	10%	–	5%	6%	6%
22. Tepetitlán	9%	–	4%	–	1%
23. Tezontepec	2%	5%	–	–	–
24. Tlaxcoapan	12%	–	–	–	–
25. Tula	11%	–	–	–	–
26. Tulancingo	8%	–	35%	3%	3%
27. Zimapán	41%	50%	25%	24%	14%
Puebla					
1. Chila Honey	–	5%	11%	11%	9%
2. Metlatoyuca	–	15%	1%	1%	1%
3. Jalpan	–	22%	4%	3%	3%
4. Pantepec	–	33%	12%	13%	13%
5. Tlaxco	–	–	8%	8%	5%
6. Venustiano Carranza	–	–	1%	2%	2%
7. Huauchinango	20%				
8. Pahuatlán		–	–	17%	19%
9. Xicotepec	4%	–	–	–	–
10. Tlahuilotepec	6%	–	–	–	–
11. Naupan	4%	–	–	–	–
Veracruz					
1. Huayacocotla	22%	5%	–	–	–
2. Ixhuatlán	31%	69%	10%	15%	14%
3. Tlachichilco	38%	31%	9%	16%	17%
4. Zacualpan	50%	9%	2%	3%	1%
5. Zontecomatlán	40%	45%	12%	14%	11%
6. Espinal		1%	–	–	–
7. Temapache		11%	–	–	–
8. Texcatepec		58%	38%	75%	72%
9. Tihuatlán		6%	–	–	–
Michoacán					
1. Zitácuaro	9%	4%	1%	–	–
México					

Table 6.1 (*cont.*) Comparison of percentages of Otomí population by municipality: based on census figures for 1900–1990

	1900	1960	1970	1980	1990
1. Acambay	22%	35%	29%	30%	23%
2. Aculco	3%	22%	14%	17%	9%
3. Amanalco	–	–	23%	18%	10%
4. Capulhuac	6%	–	–	–	–
5. Chapa de Mota	18%	54%	37%	29%	23%
6. Huixquilucan	26%	15%	4%	2%	1%
7. Jilotepec	3%	–	–	1%	–
8. Jilotzingo	–	–	–	1%	–
9. Jiquipilco	11%	27%	29%	27%	16%
10. Lerma	39%	–	16%	8%	5%
11. San Bartolo Morelos	50%	66%	47%	42%	31%
12. Naucalpan	6%	5%	1%	–	–
13. Nicolás Romero	11%	–	2%	–	–
14. Ocoyoacac	42%	2%	6%	2%	1%
15. Otzolotepec	46%	28%	25%	25%	13%
16. Polotitlán	3%	–	–	–	–
17. San José Malacatepec	11%				
18. Temascalcingo	7%	1%	5%	4%	2%
19. Temoaya	71%	66%	58%	55%	46%
20. Tianguistenco	8%	–	4%	2%	2%
21. Timilpan	23%	17%	15%	10%	7%
22. Tlalnepantla	1%	–	–	–	–
23. Toluca	2%	9%	7%	4%	4%
24. Villa del Carbón	6%	–	7%	4%	1%
25. Xonacatlán	29%	14%	8%	7%	5%
26. Zinacantepec	33%	–	3%	1%	1%
Tlaxcala					
1. Ixtenco	54%	13%	24%	18%	14%

censuses consider the population which is five years or older. The table lists municipalities with a number which is keyed to Figure 6.1.[5] In the table we list only those municipalities which have 1% Otomí population or above. The figure shows other municipalities not included in the table which have a very low number of speakers.

Examining the data presented in Table 6.1 one can see that the percent-

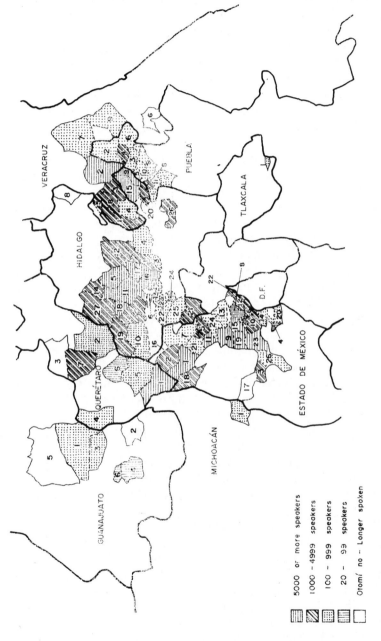

Figure 6.1 Present-day distribution of Otomí speakers (1990)

ages of Otomí speakers diminish as the years go by, so much so that some municipalities which had speakers at the beginning of the century no longer have them. The present-day distribution of the Otomí population can be seen in Figure 6.1.[6] The figure includes municipalities which have between 20 and 99 speakers; 100–999; 1000–4999; over 5000. It is easy to see that communities with a very low number of speakers are located in the municipalities that only have between 20 and 99 speakers. Such municipalities appear in the figure because their number is very large and they are the ones where the language will probably disappear within a generation or so.

In Guanajuato there were six municipalities in 1900 which had between 1% and 29%, now only one remains and it has 1%. All of the speakers are old people, which means that after their generation passes away the language will be gone in that state.

In Querétaro at the beginning of the century there were seven municipalities with Otomí population (between 67% and 3%), and now there are three, two with 28% and the other with 2%.

Hidalgo had 27 municipalities where the language was spoken in 1900; now there are 21, 3 of them with only 1%. In 1900 13 of the municipalities had over 30% speakers of the language, now only 9 of them have that many.

Puebla and Veracruz have suffered many changes in the nomenclature because of the creation of new municipalities so that the comparison is difficult to make.

In Zitácuaro, Michoacán the Otomí population was 9% and now it is less than 1% and the speakers are all old people.

In the state of Mexico at the beginning of the century 26 municipalities had over 1% Otomí population; now there are 18 and 4 of them have only 1%. The highest percentage was 71% and now it is 46%.

In Ixtenco, Tlaxcala, Otomí is no longer spoken by young people, only 14% of the population speaks it and they are all over 60 while in 1900 more than half of the population spoke the language.

As far as knowing 'whether the number of speakers has dropped because the number of speakers who *can* speak has decreased or because the number who *want* to speak has decreased' (Fishman: 1991:49) is concerned, unfortunately the latter is probably what has happened owing to centuries of hearing that they are inferior, because of their bad experiences in school and due to the necessity of finding jobs outside the community for which Spanish is necessary and the mistaken view that bilingualism is difficult and it is better to shift completely to Spanish.

Schooling in Spanish is probably the main cause of language shift. In colonial times, friars generally used Indian languages to evangelise and educate Indians, but after independence public education in Spanish was instituted throughout the country. Language policy has changed from administration to administration, but the main language of instruction has remained Spanish. At present, education is being decentralised, meaning, theoretically, that states will have more control over education than the federal government: but even so the Ministry of Education still has ample control. In indigenous communities parents can register their children in regular schools or in so-called bilingual schools. The latter are managed by an agency of the ministry called Dirección General de Educación Indígena (DGEI). It has few resources, politics plays a large part in its appointments, and consequently it has not been very successful in maintaining indigenous languages. Poor administration results, for instance, in cases where bilingual teachers in language A are assigned to community Z.

Language shift has also occurred because of human intervention. For instance, in San Miguel Allende, Guanajuato, a dam was built in the 1970s and people of many small villages were relocated. This contributed to the abandonment of the language. In an area of the valley of Toluca, some 40 years ago, water was pumped from a marshy area which was part of the source of the river Lerma in order to add to the supply of Mexico City. A whole way of life thus came to an end: no more gathering of many edible weeds, no more fishing, or collecting a type of local shrimp. As the story goes, a mermaid (an ancient water goddess) who had protected her children from time immemorial left and the water dried up. Now the people farm there but they are nostalgic about their lost resources and do not speak Otomí among themselves because even though some adults still speak the language, most of their children do not.

Another cause of language shift is the literal invasion of their territory by speakers of Spanish. Members of the Otomí minority are socially disadvantaged, that is less economically and educationally fortunate than the Spanish-speaking population surrounding them. 'In many cases they have been peripheralised even while remaining in their traditional areas of residence' (Fishman, 1991: 59).

Others who emigrate to Toluca, Pachuca, Puebla, Tulancingo, or Mexico City are worse-off. If they are lucky they can find housing near other Otomís, but they have to work in a completely Spanish-speaking environment and their children will not even learn the parental language. Still others migrate or seek temporary jobs in the United States where their lingua franca will be Spanish.

They are poor and less educated than the average Spanish monolingual. Their language is the symbol of backwardness, but abandoning the language is even worse because they lose their identity and their culture. On the other hand, there are many cases of people who succeed in climbing the social ladder, such as the relative of an old Otomí from Ixtenco who is a successful lawyer in Puebla, and the son of another man who is a teacher in Toluca. These people have no regrets, but they could have been just as successful if in addition to acquiring Spanish they had kept their former language.

Economic mobility requiring the official language can and should be available to those Otomís who wish to acquire Spanish but retain their language and culture (cf. Fishman, 1991: 63). Some people will prefer to join the mainstream, but those who want to preserve their language and be bilingual should have that option. Attitudes of teachers and other mainstream people have to be changed. The trouble is the Otomí in general are so poor that they can devote very little time to RLS efforts. Also, they are used to having schools, libraries, sports and such be managed by the government and therefore in Spanish and not by the indigenous people. Mexico is, constitutionally, a federal republic, but in practice the central government in Mexico City has much more power than the state governments. Currently some changes are being made and supposedly state governments are gaining more control. In turn, municipalities ought to gain more control over local matters and this apparently has become possible in many cases. But if people want to be involved in local government, they have to participate, and again, many of the speakers of indigenous languages do not because of their poverty and lack of education, and also because it has been customary for the local mestizos (usually monolingual in the official language) not to take them into account for any decisions that have to be made.

Graded Intergenerational Disruption Scale

As Fishman (1991) argues, intergenerational mother-tongue transmission is essential if a language is to be maintained. In order to help people interested in reversing language shift he sets up a typology called the 'GIDS scale'. In this chapter this scale serves as a useful point for comparison. In what follows the Otomí areas going roughly from north to south will be given a GIDS scale.

In Guanajuato the language is practically extinct. No children learn it. Only a few scattered old people know it (in some few cases, very well). No one has made a detailed study of the situation, but I am basing these comments on my own experience. San Miguel Allende is the only municipality where 1% of the population speaks the language. The speakers may be a handful in each village so that most of the villages would be classified as Stage 8 (vestigial use; language needs documentation) on the GIDS scale.

Perhaps Don Francisco is in Stage 7. (Most users of the language are ethnolinguistically active, but they are beyond child-bearing age.) There are no RLS efforts apparent in the municipality. The dialect has hardly been described except for a few remarks in Lastra (1994–95). There are two old people in the municipality of Villagrán, a few more in Comonfort, and there may be some in Cortazar.

In Querétaro there are two municipalities where the language is quite healthy, Amealco and Tolimán. I would classify them as GIDS 4b (schools supported by the government) because there are bilingual schools functioning there. The Amealco dialect, more precisely that of Santiago Metzquititlan, has been described and there is a dictionary (Hekking and Andrés de Jesús, 1984, 1989). Furthermore Hekking (1995) has also described the linguistic situation very ably. The Tolimán dialect is being worked on by Hekking as well. Moreover, there is an incipient association of enthusiastic bilingual teachers whose RLS efforts are to be commended.

In the Puebla highlands, I only know of the situation in the famous town of San Pablito in the municipality of Pahuatlán. Nahuatl is also spoken in this municipality. San Pablito is famous because the Otomís there make bark paper by hand and sell it quite profitably to Nahuatl artists in the state of Guerrero and to artists the world over. In addition the women work in embroidery and make artifacts with small beads. Otomí in the town would definitely be classified Stage 4a, but the bilingual school is only one or two years old. The whole town is devoted to paper-making and the language used is Otomí. The women dress in traditional garb and are monolingual in Otomí or bilingual but Otomí-dominant. Children play using the local language. Otomí is used in loud speakers (which are about the only media used) so the town could possibly be classified as Stage 2 (language used in government services and mass media). The language and the culture are vigorous and not stagnant. In a brief visit I became aware of change agents on behalf of persistence; it is the only place where I have found examples of leaders, aware of the necessity of change and persistence, who are not teachers. One of them is making efforts for archaeologists to excavate a cave where there are petroglyphs, which first served as models for some of the designs used in embroidery. The development of a tourist centre would help the economy. The other change agent is a young man who travels constantly to Europe and the United States giving demonstrations of bark-paper products and embroidery. He is well educated and proud of his heritage.

The town has attracted the attention of anthropologists, but not of linguists. The dialect is a conservative one in phonology and grammar; that is, the phonology is close to what an older form of the language must have been like and the grammar preserves categories which have disappeared: for instance, in the Mezquital Valley; very few Spanish loans are heard. There is valuable Otomí terminology for paper-making and for religious rites, so it should be thoroughly described.

Texcatepec, Veracruz, also in the highlands, is the municipality with the highest percentage of Otomí speakers in the country. It is governed by Otomís, which is a rare phenomenon, and the government hasn't even bothered to establish bilingual schools, so for the time being it is 'safe' and can easily be classified in GIDS 2. There is a radio station in Huayacocotla which uses Otomí at least part of the time. The dialect has not been described; it seems to be fairly conservative. I have no information about the other municipalities in the highlands of Veracruz.

Hidalgo is the state with the largest number of Otomí speakers. It has two areas: the Mezquital valley and the highlands. The Mezquital valley is probably also GIDS Stage 4b and to a certain extent GIDS Stage 3 (used in the lower work spheres) and even Stage2 (radio) at least in some municipalities. In this area the dialect has been the subject of books and articles by linguists and amateurs as well. There is a small dictionary (Wallis & Lanier, 1956), another written by native speakers, and one very complete one written in collaboration by native speakers and linguists in preparation under Doris Bartholomew's supervision; it circulates in photocopies, but will soon be printed by the University of Hidalgo. In Itzmiquilpan there are people interested in language maintenance. Their activities will be mentioned below.

In the area of the highlands of this same state, the GIDS scale would be 6 or 4b depending on the municipality. I am only familiar with the town of Santa Ana Hueytlalpan on the way toward the highlands in the municipality of Tulancingo. People who are about 25 or older speak the language well and children understand it but as far as I know the language is not taught in schools at all. It could be classified as Stage 6 but in danger of being 7. The dialect is a conservative one which has not been described.

The state of Mexico has places which are Stage 7 and are in danger of being 8 such as Huixquilucan, Acazulco in Ocoyoacac, and Tilapa in Tianguistenco. Others are definitely Stage 6 and some have bilingual schools so they can be considered 4b. There is an association of teachers in charge of making uniform the writing systems not only of Otomí, but also of other languages spoken in the State, and of preparing teaching materials, so we can say that there are some organised RLS efforts.

In addition, Guillermo Linarte Martínez (1998), of Acazulco in Ocoyoacac, has made some individual efforts to preserve the customs at religious holidays. These include traditional dances which in that region are called *danza de arrieros*. Mr Linarte participated in a contest and won a prize which enabled him to publish a book about the dances which includes a prayer to the patron saint (San Jerónimo) in Otomí and the speeches which were customarily spoken in Otomí when the dance organisers invited people to participate going from house to house. Linarte and a group of friends are interested in RLS as well as in preserving the local religious traditions.

The phonology and verb morphology of Temoaya Otomí have been studied by Andrews (1949, 1993), and the dialect of San Andrés Cuexcontitlan, in the municipality of Toluca, is described in Lastra (1992b).

Zitácuaro is the name of the municipality where the San Felipe los Alzati is located. Here some old people speak the language well but have not been able to transmit it to their children; there are two other localities where the situation is reportedly the same, that is, the GIDS classification would be 8. There are no RLS efforts going on.

Ixtenco is the only municipality in Tlaxcala where the language is still spoken. It would be 7 in the GIDS scale; people aged 60 or over speak it. The dialect has been studied in Lastra (1997). There is one teacher interested in maintaining the language and one native speaker who teaches children: he has had no training in language teaching, but at least the language is not looked-down upon by all of the townspeople.

Intergenerational Transmission Status, 1988–98

Very little can be said in respect to the intergenerational transmission status of Otomí because of the lack of studies. Furthermore, the evidence is contradictory: we have seen the decline in the number of speakers, but at the same time the persistence is admirable. It is due to the willingness of the people to maintain their culture in spite of the generally hostile attitude (or at least benevolent but never admiring attitude) surrounding them.

On the other hand, there is a countercurrent among some of the authorities to encourage indigenous languages to live. I am referring to the amendment to the Constitution (article 4) which reads: 'The Mexican nation has a pluricultural composition based originally on its indigenous peoples' and 'the law will protect and promote the development of its languages, cultures, usages, customs and resources, and specific forms of social organisation and will guarantee that its constituents will have effective access to the jurisdiction of the state' (my translation).

There have always been a lot of unimplemented plans and wishful thinking on the part of the government and very little action as far as the education of minorities goes. But writing this amendment into the Constitution gives people who may be interested in reversing language shift a possible legal foothold. It is yet too early to tell whether this declaration will make any difference or not, but quite informally I think it has. People are not so ashamed of their languages as they used to be; there are more bilingual schools; books are distributed in the schools instead of remaining in government warehouses, as was the case with primers formerly. A few bilingual teachers (very few) have received proper training. There is a Masters degree being offered to speakers of Indian languages at CIESAS (Centro de Investigaciones y Estudios Superiores en Antropología Social in Mexico City). One hears of students of Anthropology and Linguistics who are native speakers of Indian Languages. For a while there was very little interest in linguistic fieldwork, I think that interest has been renewed. There are occasionally small newspapers and also occasionally articles about Indian cultures in national newspapers.

In 1995 the First Colloquium on Otopames took place in Querétaro. This was a national event organised by UNAM (Universidadad Nacional Autónoma de México), INAH (Instituto Nacional de Antropología e Historia) and several state universities and centres. The following year a state colloquium took place at the University of the State of Mexico in Toluca. In 1997 another national colloquium took place in Mexico City and this year the third state colloquium was held at the University of Hidalgo in Pachuca. The third national one is to be held in Toluca. The result of the two first colloquia has been a new periodical entitled *Estudios de cultura otopame* published by the Instituto de Investigaciones Antropológicas of the UNAM (Lastra & Quezada, 1998). These colloquia are witness to the interest in Otopamean studies. Indians have attended all except the Mexico City one. To my mind these colloquia are important in building up Indian morale and showing them that not all mainstream people despise them.

Also the Chiapas phenomenon has occurred. There have been rebellions before, but none have had the impact of this one with television and internet. Indians now have access to television and the fact that some Tzeltales have supported the rebellion and hold the army in check must be a source of pride and glee for any Indian.

The facts mentioned have to do indirectly with intergenerational transmission because a positive attitude toward the language is necessary for any parent to transmit it to his or her child. Therefore all of the above factors should have contributed to encourage people to use it with their children and thus transmit it to them.

Successes and Failures During the Last Decade

Due to the lack of studies it would be impossible to review successes and failures in the last decade for the whole Otomí-speaking area. It can be done for the Mezquital area which attracts students more than other regions and for which we can survey what the situation was like approximately 10 years ago.

Claro and Botho (1982) regret the fact that schools teach Spanish and contribute to people giving up their language. They complain about the low status of Otomí and of Indians in general. In my opinion the negative attitude that the Otomís themselves had of their language is as much to blame as the negative attitude of Spanish speakers.

Coronado *et al.*, (1982) also refer to a period when Spanish was taught as a foreign language in the Mezquital. They examine the effect of the policy in two Mezquital communities, Remedios (which in 1982 was 74% bilingual) and Ocotzá (which was 91% bilingual). Remedios had had a complete primary school for 25 years and Ocotzá only had a school with the first three elementary grades for seven years. Remedios has 1500 inhabitants; it is a Catholic village with private property. Ocotzá has 400 inhabitants, it is Pentecostal and the land is held in common in an *ejido*.

The authors believe that a greater or lesser resistance to language loss is associated with a greater or lesser social cohesion in which language plays a primary role. To the degree that the group is organised differently from the mainstream the language becomes not only a means of communication but a central part of the organisation itself.

Spanish has been learned only minimally. The speakers do not use Otomí in certain contexts but Spanish has not been developed to the extent that it can be used effectively in those contexts. Without Otomí there is a lack of identity; people migrate and they are not accepted socially in their new abodes because they are poor and ignorant and speak poor Spanish.

In Ocotzá kinship is useful for getting a job. In Remedios most people are hired hands and there is not enough land, less land per family in comparison to Ocotzá. In both places children are addressed in Spanish, but in Ocotzá they learn Otomí when they play but in Remedios they don't. In Ocotzá migrants who return still speak Otomí; in Remedios they are ashamed to. In Remedios people have a hard time understanding and speaking Spanish while at the same time the use of Otomí is being reduced. The control of Spanish is better in Ocotzá than in Remedios and at the same time the vitality of Otomí is greater in Ocotzá than in Remedios.

While the teaching of Spanish in school has not fulfilled its goal, it has contributed to the loss of Otomí. Schooling has been instrumental in producing marginal individuals. This short article by Coronado, Ramos and Tellez is very moving. To my mind it shows that formal Western-style education is not a solution to end marginality and that 'uniformation is never an optimum human solution. It necessarily involves subjugation of the weak by the strong; of the few by the many' (Fishman, 1991: 31).

Coronado *et al.*, (1984) further examine the situation in Ocotzá emphasising the fact that the children learn Spanish in an abnormal way because they learn it from their Otomí-dominant parents who do not transmit their native language to them. The Spanish learned in school is a series of memorised songs and riddles. They also memorise church songs and radio commercials. They hardly ever listen to Radio Mezquital, a government-sponsored station which combines Otomí with the most boring aspects of school learning. There is no code-switching which is evidence of the poor control of the languages which the children have and of the poor Spanish spoken by the mothers.

Language Policy in Independent Mexico

Language policy in Mexico can be summarised as a tendency to unify the country linguistically and make native languages disappear. The policy is based on the relations established by the indigenous groups with Spanish-speaking sectors which in turn are based on economic relations and social discrimination transmitted by the media, religion and primarily by the educational system. Since 1964 there is supposedly 'bilingual and bicultural education'. It has amounted to making the communicative barrier between teachers and students less abrupt, but it isn't a real system of bilingual education and it certainly is not bicultural: the teaching materials are inadequate, the teachers are not qualified and above all their attitude is negative. What they do is use the native language to teach Spanish.

Coronado *et al.*, (1981) examine the language and educational situation in various Mezquital communities. The National Indigenist Institute (INI) sponsored pre-schools for children in 60 communities. The teachers were middle-school graduates with hardly any training. In the regular schools Spanish is the medium of instruction and the children have had no training in Spanish at all. The groups are very large, teachers do not remain in the same town for long, and the index of school desertion is very high. The texts used in the bilingual schools vary in quality, a couple of them being adequate but most are not graded properly and in the worst one we read: 'The Indian while learning to read his language simultaneously learns to read the national language. The difference is that he understands what he reads in his own language while he doesn't yet understand the other one' (quoted in Coronado *et al.*, 1981: 127), and my translation).

The above extracts give an idea of the backwardness of the pedagogy employed and clearly emphazise the low opinion that the mainstream members have of the minority, the poverty of the people, and their marginalisation.

In the last decade the situation has not improved very much as far as attitudes are concerned. There are many more schools which have presumably contributed to the increase of bilingualism. However, an important development has been the establishment of the 'Academia de la Lengua Ñahñú'. The word Ñahñú is the Otomí word for the language and the ethnic group in the dialect of the Mezquital. The academy was founded by graduates of a special BA programme in 'Ethnolinguistics' sponsored by CIESAS (Centro de Investigaciones y Estudios Superiores en Antropología Social in Mexico City), which functioned in Pátzcuaro, Michoacán in the 1970s. It had political overtones and was not as academic as one would have wished, but still it gave some Indian teachers an opportunity to acquire higher education including some knowledge of linguistics, social anthropology, and language teaching.

The purpose of the Academy, founded in 1986 with 16 members, is to reverse language shift. At first it was a voluntary group of bilingual teachers, but as of 1989 they are officially recognised in the sense that their salaries as teachers are paid for, but instead of each member being assigned to a school as a regular teacher they can devote themselves to the activities which they consider will foster RLS. They have been given the use of a large room in a government building outside Itzmiquilpan which they use for their work.

According to the Academy members, the main problem they face is the negative attitude of the so-called bilingual teachers, many of whom do not know how to write in Otomí. The Academy sponsored a regional forum for the regularisation of Otomí orthography; it organises courses in reading and writing for adults; it organised a workshop to write stories with the parents of school children in 1994–95; it sponsors song contests, spreads the knowledge of indigenous rights, and sells cassettes of Otomí stories. Currently, for instance, they are preparing two cassettes, one of Ñahñú stories and another one of Ñahñú songs.

The Academy members have been in charge of advising as to language matters in 10 pilot schools in the Mezquital since 1991. They developed a plan for the preparation of teaching materials which the DGEI (Dirección General de Educación Indígena), the government agency in charge of bilingual schools nationwide, did not accept in 1992, but which was modified and accepted in 1993. As a result, language textbooks were prepared for the first four years of primary school. These were printed, but the DGEI head was changed and, as a result, the books could not be used initially but now they do have books which are distributed to all the bilingual schools of the Mezquital. There are 1800 bilingual teachers: not all of them use the books, but some 40% do. Of course not all the schools are 'bilingual'; most are regular schools where Spanish is the medium of instruction for every child regardless of his language background.

Among other developments, there is one close to their hearts: this is the general acceptance of the word Ñahñú in the area. For instance, the vans used for public transportation have signs with this word in them. A few stores have signs written in the language. Radio Mezquital offers more programmes in Otomí. There is another radio station situated in Cardonal sponsored by INI. The academy members asked the radio speakers not to call Otomís 'ñahñucitos', with the Spanish diminutive, which they consider demeaning, but to use the Otomí diminutive ci- which is also a reverential. The Academy has lately received the help of some Catholic German missionaries who live in El Cardonal. They have prepared songs, stories, prayers and a translation of the mass into Ñahñú. As a whole, the group seems very optimistic, and intends to go on with its work in spite of all the odds.

All members of this enthusiastic group are hard working and influential. To my mind they have to be made aware of the fact that school-learning is not all there is to RLS. Also, they should not fall into the trap of folklorising the language by making too much of those songs that can easily be memorised. Language is for communication about any subject. The Academy members think that the bilingual situation is stable and that children are learning Otomí in the normal way; but I think they should carry on more activities to turn the more or less passive attitude of the people into an active one of love and admiration for their own language and identity. They have to be reminded of the fact that language is a symbol fundamental to the preservation of culture. Culture and language should not remain static, they have to evolve and be adapted so they can survive in this modern world. At the same time, the Academy members have to realise that their dialect is not the standard language. There is no standard and the other dialects deserve the same respect as their own.

Conclusions

The main thesis of Fishman (1991) is that normal intergenerational transmission of language is the *sine qua* non of language maintenance. With this I agree wholeheartedly. Whenever parents decide to speak to their children in the official language (often to 'help them in school') they doom the language in their community and at the same time they doom their culture. Usually they don't realise what is happening and when they slip into the native language they wonder why the children don't respond or are unwilling to learn their language!

Otomí is vigorous in the communities where the language is transmitted normally, *regardless of the presence or absence of bilingual schools*. As a whole, schools have been responsible for language shift, but the primary cause is the negative attitude toward the Otomí language held by the dominant classes and by many of the Otomí speakers themselves. If we could contribute to change these attitudes, the speakers themselves would continue to speak to their children in the language in Otomí in those communities which are now at Stage 6. More strenuous efforts would be necessary in areas now at Stage 7 and 8, but the possibility is there and it is to be hoped that enlightened speakers will lead the way for the preservation of this ancient culture.

Notes

1. In Spanish, stress falls on the last syllable of the word, e.g. beber, unless the word ends in a vowel, n or s in which case the stress falls on the next-to-last syllable as in comes, cantaba. All exceptions to this rule have a written stress mark on the vowel to be stressed: fértil, mención, espíritu. In Mexican Spanish there are many loan words from Nahuatl, the language of the Mexicas (Aztecs). Many of these loans are place names; they are stressed following Spanish rules.
2. The present-day location of the town of Xaltocan is in the State of Mexico.
3. A hill which is now a famous park within Mexico City.
4. The lowlands located in the present-day states of San Luis Potosí, Hidalgo, Veracruz and Tamaulipas.
5. Mexico City appears in Figure 6.1 as D.F. (Distrito Federal). The state of Mexico appears as MÉXICO.
6. Figure 6.1 shows municipalities with Otomí population above 20. The table only lists those which had more than 1% Otomí population at some point. Census figures, of course, do not discriminate between those municipalities which have been traditionally Otomí and those with recent Otomí migration. Some of the latter may appear in Figure 6.1 but not in Table 6.1.

References

Andrews, H. (1949) Phonemes and morphophonemes of Temoayan Otomí. *International Journal of American Linguistics* 15, 213–22.
Andrews, H. (1993) *The Function of Verb Prefixes in South-western Otomi*. Dallas: Summer Institute of Linguistics and University of Texas, Arlington.
Carrasco Pizana, P. (1950) *Los otomíes*. Cultura e historia prehispánica de los pueb-

los mesoamericanos de habla otomiana. Facsimile edition, México: Bibliotéca enciclopédica del Estado de México, 1979.

Claro, M.G. and Botho, A.M. (1982) *¿Qué Somos Los Maestros Bilingües en el Valle del Mezquital?* México: Secretaría de Educación Pública and Instituto Nacional Indigenista.

Coronado, G., Ramos, M.T. and Tellez, F.J. (1982) Castellanización formal: Un método para el desaprendizaje. *Cuicuilco. Revista de la Escuela Nacional de Antropología* e Historia 9, 19–29.

Coronado, G., Ramos, M.T. and Tellez, F.J. (1984) *Continuidad y Cambio en una Comunidad Bilingüe*. México: Centro de Investigaciones y Estudios Superiores en Antropología Social .

Coronado, G., Franco, V.M. and Muñoz, H. (1981) *Bilingüismo y Educación en el Valle del Mezquital*. México: Cuadernos de la Casa Chata.

Fishman, J.A. (1991) *Reversing Language Shift. Theoretical and Empirical Foundations of Assistance to Threatened Languages*. Clevedon: Multilingual Matters.

Franco, P. and Manuel, V. (1992) *Grupo doméstico y reproducción social. Parentesco, economía e ideología en una comunidad otomí del Valle del Mezquital*. México: Centro de Investigaciones y Estudios Superiores en Antropología Social.

Galinier, J. (1979) *N'yûhû Les indiens otomis. Hiérarchie social et tradition dans le Sud de la Huasteca*. Mexico: Mission Archeologique et Etnologique Française en Mexique. Spanish translation: *Pueblos de la Sierra Madre. Etnografía de la comunidad otomí*. México: Centre d'Etudes Mexicaines et Centramericaines and Instituto Nacional Indigenista, 1987.

Galinier, J. (1990) *La mitad del mundo. Cuerpo y cosmos en los rituales otomíes*. México: Instituto de Investigaciones Antropológicas, Universidad Nacional Autónoma de México.

Hekking, E. (1995) *El otomí de Santiago Mexquititlán: desplazamiento lingüístico, préstamos y cambios gramaticales*. Amsterdam: IFOTT (Institute for Functional Research into Language and Language Use.

Hekking, E. and Andrés de Jesús, S. (1984) *Gramática otomí*. Querétaro: Universidad Autónoma de Querétaro.

Hekking, E. and Andrés de Jesús, S. (1989) *Diccionario español-otomí de Santiago Mexquititlán*. Querétaro: Universidad Autónoma de Querétaro.

Lastra, Y. (1992a) Estudios antiguos y modernos sobre el otomí. In R. Barriga Villanueva and J. García Fajardo (eds) *Reflexiones Lingüísticas y Literarias Vol 1. Lingüística*. México: El Colegio de México. Enlarged version, *Anales de Antropología* 29, 453–89.

Lastra, Y. (1992b) *El otomí de Toluca*. México: Instituto de Investigaciones Antropológicas, Universidad Nacional Autónoma de México.

Lastra, Y. (1994) ¿Es el otomí una lengua amenazada? 48th International Congress of Americanists, Stockholm and Upsala, 4–9 July 1994.

Lastra, Y. (1994–95) La lengua otomí en Guanajuato y Querétaro. *Cuadernos del Sur, Letras* No 26, 59–66, Bahía Blanca, Argentina.

Lastra, Y. (1997) *El otomí de Ixtenco*. México: Instituto de Investigaciones Antropológicas, Universidad Nacional Autónoma de México.

Lastra, Y. and Quezada, N. (eds) (1998) *Estudios de Cultura Otopame* I.

Linarte Martínez, G. (1998) *La Danza de Los Arrieros*. Toluca, México: Norte/Sur.

Mendizabal, M.O. (1947) Evolución económica y social del Valle del Mezquital. *Obras Completas* VI, 7–150 México: Talleres Gráficos de la Nación.

Nolasco, A.M. (1966) Los otomíes del Mezquital. Epoca post-revolucionaria. In *Homenaje a Roberto J. Weitlaner*, 637–658 México: Instituto Nacional de Antropología e Historia.

Torquemada, fray Juan de (1969) *Monarquía Indiana*. México: Porrúa [1615 1st printing].

Wallis, E. and Lanier, N. (1956) *Diccionario castellano-otomí, otomí-castellano*. Itzmiquilpan, México: Ediciones del Patrimonio Indígena del Valle del Mezquital y del Instituto Lingüístico de Verano.

Chapter 7

Reversing Quechua Language Shift in South America

N.H. HORNBERGER and K.A. KING

This chapter is dedicated in loving memory of Faustino Espinoza Navarro, b. 15 December 1905, d. 15 January 2000, Cusco, Peru, lifelong champion of the Quechua language.

Introduction

Quechua is a threatened language (Dorian, 1998: 4). Yet with 8 to 12 million speakers (Grinevald, 1998: 128), most of them concentrated in the Andean highlands of Peru, Bolivia and Ecuador, Quechua is also the most widely spoken indigenous language in the Americas. When the status of Quechua is compared with that of the hundreds of languages in the world which have only a few dozen elderly native speakers and no active community of language learners or users, Quechua may appear to be a safe, even robust language. After all, one might well ask, how can a language with millions of speakers possibly be endangered?

Quechua as threatened language

The relatively large number of Quechua speakers obscures the unfavourable social and political circumstances under which Quechua has endured for many of the last 500 years. While in the initial stages of the Spanish conquest Quechua was used by Spaniards and indigenous persons as a lingua franca, this period was short-lived (Cerrón-Palomino, 1989, 1997: 55; Botero, 1991: 115; Haboud, 1996: 57). A decree from the Spanish crown in the second half of the 18th century mandating compulsory Castilianisation of native Americans marked the end of toleration of indigenous languages (von Gleich, 1992: 49; Cerrón-Palomino, 1997: 57). As the Spaniards solidified their control of the region in subsequent decades, the Spanish language spread and became revered as the language of power and prestige, while the 'Indian population and their language(s) were further denigrated' (Haboud, 1996: 25). Although formal measures to instruct Spanish were generally ineffective, the indigenous population learned the dominant language informally for social survival and acquired it as part of the biological and cultural process of mestisation (von Gleich, 1992: 49–50; see also Heath, 1982).

As the nations of Ecuador, Peru and Bolivia gained their independence from Spain in the 1820s and 1830s, Spanish continued to reign as the official language; Quechua and other indigenous languages were at best ignored, and at worst, actively oppressed. Indeed, throughout much of the region's post-colonial history, governmental policy concerning the indigenous sectors has remained relatively unchanged: shift away from indigenous languages and cultures has long been either an implicit or explicit goal (Mannheim, 1984: 303). This 'clearly assimilationist' language policy has resulted in the current 'linguistic shame and self-negation' among many incipient bilinguals (von Gleich, 1992: 51). As Coronel-Molina notes, 'it took centuries to devalue the language; it may take centuries again to totally revalorise it' (1999: 168).

Recent decades in the major Andean countries have been marked by the rise of indigenous political organisations and the implementation of political reforms targeting the indigenous sectors.[1] Yet while there has been substantial progress on some levels, the Quechua language and Quechua speakers generally remain powerless and marginalised within their national contexts. Quechua continues to be strongly linked with the rural, uneducated and poor, while Spanish remains the primary language of national and international communication, literacy and education, and professional and academic success. What Mannheim has noted for Southern Peruvian Quechua has long been characteristic of all Quechua varieties, namely that 'formal political participation and economic mobility both depend not on overcoming the stigma attached to the language, but on abandoning altogether the language and the cultural universe that accompanies it in favor of an alien language and culture' (1984: 292).

Given that Quechua is clearly 'the loser in the language and culture contact resulting from the Spanish conquest' (von Gleich, 1994: 78), its current precarious state is hardly surprising. While the position of Quechua varies greatly from one community and region to the next, there are substantial sociolinguistic data which indicate that Quechua is indeed a declining and threatened language. In Peru, for example, figures from the official census reveal that Quechua monolingualism is steadily giving way to temporary, subtractive bilingualism in one generation, followed by Spanish monolingualism in the next. As the percent of Quechua monolinguals has declined (from 31% in 1940, to 17% in 1961, to 11% in 1982), the percent of bilinguals has held almost constant, and the percent of Spanish monolinguals has risen (from 50% in 1940, to 65% in 1961, to 72% in 1982) (von Gleich, 1992: 59). Data from Bolivia suggest a similar pattern. While 36.5% of the population reported using Quechua most frequently in 1950, only 25.7% did in 1976. During that same period, the number of Bolivians who reportedly used primarily Spanish doubled (from 26% in 1950 to 54.1% in 1976) (von Gleich, 1994: 90). Recent sociolinguistic surveys in the Ecuadorian highlands also provide evidence that language shift is well underway. Haboud, for example, finds that the indigenous household, traditionally an exclusively Quechua domain, has largely become a 'bilingual space', where, at the expense of Quechua, Spanish is now regularly employed (1996: 175).

Correspondingly, ethnographic investigations provide insight into the patterns of community language use leading to language shift in the Andes. Although conducted in different areas, comparison of Hornberger's (1988) study of language use in the mid-1980s with King's investigation (1997; to appear) of the mid-1990s reveals the processes at work in the slow, but steady decline of Quechua. Hornberger's data, collected in highland communities in Puno, Peru, revealed that although use of Spanish was increasing, there were clearly defined domains of use for both Quechua and Spanish. Hornberger reports that Quechua was used consistently in discourse between and among community members in home and traditional community settings, while Spanish was reserved for communication with non-members and in formal, non-traditional settings (e.g. during school hours). King's data, in contrast, reveal that even the more remote and isolated of the two communities she studied in highland Saraguro, Ecuador could no longer be considered diglossic. While Quechua is often selected for communication between and among elders, for kidding and making jokes, and at certain traditional community events, 'Spanish has made in-roads into seemingly every speech situation, and presently, only what might be the *traces* of former domains are left' (King, 1999: 25). There is no longer a 'safe' space, for instance, in the home, in the community, or among family, for Quechua to be used exclusively and therefore ensured transmission to younger generations. The limited bilingualism which exists is extremely unstable and likely a transitional phase leading to Spanish monolingualism. Thus, in the communities studied by Hornberger and King, and in many other Andean regions as well, shift away from Quechua takes place domain by domain, as Spanish encroaches into every arena of use.[2]

The diversity of Quechua language contexts

If one aspect of Quechua's unusualness lies in its large number of speakers, yet precarious status, a second lies in its remarkable diversity.

This diversity runs along at least three related lines: linguistic diversity (in terms of the multiple varieties which exist), geographic diversity (in terms of the range of contexts of use of the language), and a particular type of sociolinguistic diversity (in terms of varied levels of contact with other languages).

Linguistically, Quechua has been characterised as 'a group of varieties within a language family, but lacking the superstructure of parents and grandparents' (von Gleich, 1994: 81). While many of the original languages of the Andes have disappeared (Grinevald, 1998: 129), Kaufman (1994) argues that Quechua consists of 17 'emergent' languages, that is, 17 Quechua varieties, each with three to five centuries of diversification (in Grinevald, 1998: 129). Given the difficult and controversial nature of classifying language varieties, there is little agreement concerning the total number of varieties. However, based on phonological and lexical data, two main groups of Quechua have traditionally been recognised: Quechua I (Torero, 1974), also known as Quechua B (Parker, 1973), which is spoken in central Peru; and Quechua II (a.k.a. Quechua A), which consists of many other varieties found to the south and north of Quechua I, in Ecuador, Bolivia, Chile, and Argentina, and southern and northern Peru.

Linguistic classification of Quechua is complicated by the fact that it is spoken in a half dozen Andean nations, each of which has treated the language somewhat differently. In Peru, for example, dictionaries and grammar books were published in the 1970s for six distinct Peruvian dialects: Ancash-Huailas, Ayacucho-Chanca, Cajamarca-Cañaris, Cuzco-Collao, Junín-Huanca, and San Martín (de Vries, 1988: 108–9; Hornberger, 1988: 30–1; Cerrón-Palomino, 1997: 61). The Bolivian government took quite a different approach: in 1980, the government approved a 'Unified Alphabet', which serves as the standard system for both Quechua and Aymara. In Ecuador, in contrast, an Ecuadorian 'National Unified Alphabet' was established for all Quichua varieties in the country as part of the National Quichua Literacy Conference in 1980.[3] Known as *Quichua Unificado*, this form diverged linguistically from what was commonly used in Bolivia and Peru. As Montaluisa describes, the decisions surrounding the establishment of Ecuadorian *Quichua Unificado* were made largely independent of either scientific or previously established international criteria (1980; in de Vries, 1988: 61).[4]

Non-governmental organisations, such as the Summer Institute for Linguistics (SIL), have further emphasised the diversity of Quechua varieties. SIL's catalogue of world languages, *Ethnologue*, lists 47 different Quechua languages belonging to the 'Quechuan language family'. Some of these, such as Quechua-Yauyos of the Department of Lima, are further dissected and described as 'cover terms' for many different 'one-village varieties' (Grimes, 1996).

Geographically, the situation of Quechua speakers is equally complex. Quechua reside in Peru, Bolivia and Ecuador, with smaller numbers in Argentina, Colombia, and Brazil.[5] While the rural Andean highlands have been the traditional stronghold of the language, there are substantial numbers of Quechua speakers, and indeed, whole communities, who reside in a variety of different non-highland, non-rural settings.

Massive migration over the last 50 years has transformed all Andean countries, to a greater or lesser extent, from largely rural nations to primarily urban ones. Official census figures for Peru, for example, reveal how pronounced this shift has been: in 1940, 35% of the population resided in urban areas, 65% in rural sectors; by 1982 these numbers were reversed, with 65% of the country counting as urban and 35% as rural (von Gleich, 1992: 59). Quechua speakers have been a major part of this trend, leaving their communities for positions as domestic, construction, or factory workers in the cities. Furthermore, in Peru, the violence and fear which accompanied the *Sendero Luminoso* 'Shining Path' revolutionary guerrilla movement intensified this trend in some regions, as many Quechua highlanders fled their communities for shanty towns surrounding Lima and other major cities in the 1980s.

In addition, there are also Quechua communities which have long existed in the lowland Amazon regions. The 'Quichua del Oriente', for example, number approximately 60,000 and have subsisted in the Ecuadorian provinces of Napo and Pastaza much like (and sometimes in close contact with) other Amazonian groups such as the Shuar and the Huarani (Benítez & Garcés, 1992: 176–80). Other Quechua, such as the Saraguros of the southern Ecuadorian highlands, have slowly migrated eastward, either cyclically or permanently, into the Amazonian lowlands to raise cattle. Lastly, a much smaller number of Quechua speakers travel and reside abroad in US and European cities as students, musicians, and business persons.

The geographic diversity of Quechua speakers and communities results in great variation in the amount, duration, and intensity of contact with speakers of indigenous languages such as Aymara and Huarani, as well as speakers of European languages such as Spanish and English. The number of language contact scenarios is nearly as great as the number of Quechua speaking communities. There are, for example, Quechua who live in major urban centres, interacting almost exclusively in Spanish; Quechua who live in large *pueblos jovenes* 'shanty towns' surrounding major cities, whose traditional patterns of language use disappeared with their move and the loss of physical boundary domains, and who increasingly use Spanish; Quechua who live in close contact with speakers of Aymara or other indigenous languages; and there are still a limited number of Quechua who reside in remote, monolingual Quechua communities, with limited contact with non-Quechua. Furthermore, as Cerrón-Palomino (1997: 52, 62) has pointed out, Quechua continues to spread in some areas (the Ecuadorian Amazon or northern Potosí in Bolivia, for example), even while it is on the verge of extinction in others (for example, the Peruvian Quechua varieties of Chachapoyas, Cajatambo, Huaral, Yauyos, and Valle del Mantaro). The degree of change in different regions is so varied and the range of sociolinguistic situations is so great that at the turn of the 20th century it is difficult to describe a 'typical Quechua community'. Quechua is characterised, then, not only by its precarious linguistic status, but by the remarkable diversity of its communities.

Quechua in Relation to the Graded Intergenerational Disruption Scale

The Graded Intergenerational Disruption Scale (GIDS) (Fishman, 1990, 1991) is designed to provide a means of assessing the status of a language, the prospects of intergenerational transmission of the language, and, by implication, the level of success of efforts to maintain and revitalise the threatened language. In Fishman's words, the scale is appropriate for determining 'the intergenerational continuity and maintenance prospects of a language *network or community*' (1991: 87; emphasis ours).

While 'speech networks' and 'speech communities' have been defined somewhat differently by various scholars (e.g. Hymes, 1972; Labov, 1972; Milroy, 1987), most definitions demand that members of a given speech community share norms for interacting in the language, attitudes concerning language use, or the use of a specific variety, typically developed by engaging in regular interaction. Given the linguistic, geographic, and sociolinguistic diversity of Quechua communities, by most definitions, Quechua speakers do not constitute one language network or one language community.[6] Hence, it is impossible to outline uniformly the situation of the language; to do so would entail making over-simplified and at least partially inaccurate generalisations.

Similarly, Quechua language revitalisation and maintenance efforts are underway in many regions, and in some cases, have been for multiple decades. These efforts to reverse Quechua language shift have been far from uniform, varying in goals, means, intensity, duration, and results. Because of this dramatic diversity, it is not feasible to detail and analyse all of the efforts and their impact as it might be for a language with a smaller number of speakers and more unified functional distribution. It is thus impossible completely and accurately to describe the situation of Quechua, a language spoken by at least eight million people in thousands of communities, in terms of the GIDS or any other framework.

It is, however, possible to provide sketches of some of the diverse language revitalisation activities taking place on behalf of Quechua in different communities and analyse them in terms of Fishman's framework. In what follows, we discuss the range of uses of Quechua and types of RLS attempts in relation to the GIDS scale, drawing from multiple regions and contexts and illustrating the diversity of efforts being undertaken at a variety of levels on the behalf of Quechua. We conclude with some comments about both the status of Quechua language revitalisation efforts and the validity of the GIDS framework.

Revitalisation attempts illustrative of each GIDS stage

Stage 8: Reconstructing Quechua

The major goal at this stage of revitalisation efforts is 'to reassemble the language itself and to build up a core of those who have at least some knowledge of it' (Fishman, 1991: 90). Fishman suggests that the process of reconstruction may begin with piecing together folksongs, proverbs, folktales and formulaic expressions collected from the few remaining users of the language and subsequently, on the basis of these, assembling partial phonologies, grammars, and lexicons (1991: 88). Re-establishing community norms not only of grammar and phonology, but also of 'intonation and prosody . . . and semantic typologies is highly desirable' (1991: 397).

Given the diversity of Quechua communities described above, Quechua activists[7] who recognise and seek to address the threat to the language in their own community or region generally have had the option of seeking out more isolated, rural, inaccessible locations where Quechua is still spoken. This has been the recourse and resource which, for example, Faustino Espinoza Navarro (b. 1905–d. 2000) cultivated throughout a lifetime dedicated to promoting and revitalising Quechua. Beginning from his years as a functionary with various governmental ministries in the first half of the last century and continuing throughout his life, Espinoza relished travelling and working in remote highland communities throughout Peru, where, he said, 'speaking well with those who don't know Spanish, I acquired a better, clearer form of the language of the Inca' (Hornberger, 1994: 245). As a result of his efforts spanning nearly a century, he was widely recognised in Cusco as the most eloquent speaker of Quechua when he was alive, not only for his enormous working vocabulary, but also for the elegance of his sentence structure, intonation and prosody, which found expression in invited public speeches, radio broadcasts, and video appearances.

Visiting the *campo* 'countryside' and seeking out monolingual Quechua speakers is also a principal means of cultivating and revitalising Quechua linguistic and cultural knowledge for Rufino Chuquimamani of Puno, Peru. Like Espinoza, Chuquimamani seeks to document Quechua lexicon, and in particular is interested in semantic domains central to rural life (Chuquimamani, 1988; Hornberger, 1994: 249). In addition, in his zeal to investigate and document Quechua knowledge, he asks for stories wherever he goes; some of these have been published in volumes produced by the Experimental Bilingual Education Project of Puno with the express purpose of cultivating a Quechua-literate adult population (Chuquimamani, 1983, 1984).

The efforts of these two Peruvian Quechua activists devoting their own unpaid time to reconstructing Quechua lexicon and oral literature are consistent with those of others in this century such as Jorge Lira (Hornberger, 1992: 443), and indeed of efforts extending back to the 16th century arrival of the Spanish and the first publication of dictionaries and oral traditions (e.g. Gonzalez Holguín, Domingo de Santo Tomás, Guaman Poma, Garcilaso de la Vega, The Huarochiri Manuscript; see Adelaar, 1991, for references). Given Quechua's centuries-long history as an oppressed language (Albó, 1977: 5), surviving under threat, the reconstruction and documentation of Quechua language and literature is an ongoing and never-ending uphill battle. And given that there is extremely limited state support for the work of Quechua language activists, and that the vast majority of their efforts have been self-initiated and self-supported, they seem to exemplify well Fishman's admonition that 'the road to RLS is a long and difficult one . . . paved with self-sacrifice' (1991: 98).

Stage 7: Cultural interaction in Quechua

At Stage 7 of the GIDS, 'most users of Xish [Quechua] are a socially integrated and ethnolinguistically active population, but they are beyond child-bearing age' (Fishman, 1991: 89). The major goal at Stage 7 of the GIDS is to develop a younger cohort of Quechua-as-a-second-language learners who will eventually become regular Quechua users. Since the ultimate aim of language reversal is to re-establish intergenerational transmission, it is important that these new Quechua learners and users be young enough to bear children to whom they can eventually transmit the language as a mother tongue. The development of this younger cohort of language learners and users, according to Fishman, happens through the establishment of 'a variety of youth groups, young people's associations, young parent groups and, finally, residential communities or neighborhoods all of which utilise (or lead to the utilisation of) Xish [Quechua]' (1991: 91).

In some Quechua communities, these sorts of youth groups are well established and very active. For example, among the Saraguros, a group of about 20,000 who reside principally in the southern Ecuadorian Andes, youth organisations, primarily focused on music and dance, have been popular for at least four decades. Despite the fact that the Saraguros are in the late stages of shift away from their once native Quechua and are now primarily Spanish dominant, the Saraguros continue to maintain a long tradition of forming youth-oriented cultural groups.

One of the first of these organisations, *Grupo Intiñan* 'Sunroad Group', was formed in the late 1950s with the support of two non-Saraguros (Volinsky, 1996: 11). *Grupo Intiñan* performed traditional Saraguro music, dance, oration and poetry, and enjoyed popular success both within Saraguro and in national venues. In addition to reviving traditional Saraguro performance arts, *Grupo Intiñan* was effective in spreading an indigenous Saraguro perspective by 'discussing the social injustice and exploitation suffered by the Saraguros' during the performances of orations (Belote & Belote, 1981: 469). In the 1970s *Grupo Intiñan* evolved into the *Grupo Artístico Cultural Saraguro* 'Artistic Culture Group Saraguro' and was legally recognised as an indigenous organisation (Volinsky, 1996: 12). Since that time, the group has continued to promote Saraguro culture by performing at various youth events in the region.

The group has also been influential in the establishment of other cultural groups such as *Grupo Rumiñahui* 'Stone-eye Group'[8] a youth organisation which aims to 'rescue, promote, and revitalise what they considered to be the cultural patrimony of the Saraguros' (Volinsky, 1996: 13). There are currently numerous other youth-oriented cultural organisations which perform traditional Saraguro music and dance. While the membership and participation in the organisations are somewhat fluid, many young Saraguros have participated over the years and performances continue to be well attended by young and old alike.

Language plays an important symbolic role in many of the cultural performances. While in recent decades the audience, as well as the performers, have tended to be Spanish dominant if not Spanish monolingual, most groups make an effort to use Quechua in their lyrics, in their poetry, or in the formal announcements to the audience. However, given the sporadic use of the language and lack of regularity of the performances, it is doubtful that much real language learning takes place. As Fishman notes (1991: 398), these sorts of 'special events' are precisely that; and as such they are not likely to impact everyday language use. Yet such symbolic use of the language at least provides some exposure to Quechua, possibly raising ethnolinguistic consciousness among young Saraguros and perhaps indirectly contributing to the formation of future Quechua learners.

While the Saraguro cultural groups provide a clear example of Stage 7 efforts, two points concerning these activities should be made clear. First, these groups have not developed into the 'young parent groups and, finally, residential communities or neighborhoods' which use Quechua that Fishman's model suggests (1991: 91). Indeed, cultural groups in Saraguro have been active for four decades and have yet to take these next important steps. The second point directly concerns Fishman's emphasis on the role of the elder generation in organising and actively participating in these activities. In Saraguro, the cultural activities are typically organised by the *younger* generations, not the elders. Cultural interaction is not taking place exclusively among the 'old-timers' (Fishman, 1991: 398). Indeed, the most active and vocal promoters and users of the language are members of the younger generation who are in their teens or twenties. It is not the case that they are 'young guests', who are simply passive observers at this stage, as Fishman describes (1991: 398), but rather, the young are the primary performers, organisers, and participants in these cultural events. The Saraguro case, then, suggests that the role of the younger and often highly politicised generation may be insufficiently stressed in the framework.

Stage 6: Intergenerational and demographically concentrated home-family-neighbourhood transmission

Stage 6 of the GIDS, according to Fishman (1991: 93–5), is not only the most difficult stage, but also the most crucial. At this stage, the threatened language becomes 'the normal language of informal, spoken interaction between and within all three generations of the family', as well as the 'language of interfamily interaction, of interaction with playmates, neighbors, friends and acquaintances' (1991: 92–3). It cannot be over-stressed how difficult the attainment of this stage is once it is lost.

Returning once again to the communities of Saraguro in southern Ecuador, despite the intensive efforts at schools, among various community and political organisations, and, as discussed above, by cultural groups, regular, everyday use of the languages in homes and neighbourhoods among young adults and children remains exceedingly rare.

Saraguro parents, many of whom are Spanish dominant with limited Quechua skills, speak of their desire to transmit the language to their children, but find it very difficult to use the language consistently at home. The reasons behind this phenomenon are complex. Saraguro parents explain the dearth of Quechua use in the home as a result of their lack of Quechua skills; their lack of confidence in using the language; their children's resistance to Quechua; and the force of habit. Some Saraguro parents who are strongly committed to Quechua revitalisation do use Quechua occasionally with their children informally, as well as more formally in order to teach them new words (King, 1999). Yet even these unusually dedicated parents report being unable to use the language routinely.

Similarly, Haboud (1996), in her large-scale sociolinguistic survey of the Ecuadorian Andes finds that even some of the most committed bilingual education professionals experience difficulty in regularly using the language at home. She quotes one such individual who observes: '[My children] ... talk to me in Quichua and want me to talk to them but I am not able to, it is the habit, you know, even if I want to [. . .]. It is contradictory because, you know, I have taught Quichua and various things in Quichua for a long time. I am as one would say, an expert in the language (Quichua), but I cannot teach it to my own children' (Haboud, 1996: 178).

Both Haboud's data and the Saraguro case make clear how difficult and unlikely attainment of intergenerational transmission of Quechua is, and give us cause to question the position of Stage 6 on the framework. In the GIDS, Stage 6 is framed as following the reconstruction of the language (Stage 8) and its use in cultural activities (Stage 7). The Quechua case suggests that attainment of these two prior stages may be necessary, but not sufficient to support intergenerational transmission of Quechua. In other words, attainment of Stage 6 may require, at least in some cases, the concomitant support of activities at higher GIDS stages.

Stage 5: Schools for literacy acquisition, for the old and for the young and not in lieu of compulsory education

Stage 5 deals with educational efforts that are 'entirely [Quechua], primarily literacy-focused, socialisation-related and entirely under intra-communal control' (Fishman, 1991: 98). The goal is the attainment of a 'guided literacy'; the agencies of this literacy acquisition, for example, may be the home, a local religious unit, or a local literacy programme; and these efforts characteristically do not receive government funding nor satisfy compulsory education requirements (1991: 97).

Returning again to Cusco, Peru for illustration, we will briefly consider three institutions and the degree to which they meet these criteria: the

Iglesia Evangelica Peruana 'Evangelical Church of Peru' (IEP); the *Academia [Peruana] de la Lengua Quechu*a '[Peruvian] Academy of the Quechua Language' (ALQ); and a non-governmental organisation, *Centro Andino de Educación y Promoción* 'Andean Center for Education and Promotion' (CADEP). All three institutions promote Quechua literacy, and do so without government funding and outside the compulsory education system; however, a focus on literacy, a fostering of socialisation into Quechua ways, and control by Quechua speakers are not consistently present in every case.

Maria de Centeno, already literate in Spanish, became literate in Quechua through her association with the Evangelical Church of Peru. She first began to attend the IEP at age 13 and was baptised at age 18 (in 1943). Missionaries asked her to use her knowledge of spoken Quechua to serve as interpreter at church conventions and to teach pastors' wives at semi-annual two-week Bible Institutes. Then one day, she was asked to give the closing address at the Bible Institute. 'As she tells it, she set out to prepare her message with the intention of writing it in Spanish and then translating into Quechua as she spoke. However, at one point, asking God's help . . . she began to write directly in Quechua, to the best of her knowledge. . . . From that time on, .. she knew how to prepare her messages directly in Quechua. She bought the Quechua New Testament and began to draw her messages directly from the Quechua text . . . [S]he learned to read Quechua and now can read, not only the Bible, but also the Quechua songbook . . . [S]he remains dedicated to teaching in Quechua; she teaches a lesson every other Monday afternoon for the Women's League and a women's Bible class every Sunday morning' (Hornberger, 1994: 247). Maria's case, representative of thousands like her in the Andes, illustrates the role of the IEP (and other evangelical Christian churches) in fostering Quechua literacy acquisition, with a primary goal of socialisation to Christianity (albeit a Quechua expression of Christianity) rather than to Quechua culture *per se*, and with a pattern of control involving missionaries' systematic devolution of leadership positions to local Quechua (and Spanish) -speaking Christians.

In contrast, the Academy of the Quechua Language has perhaps less of a role in directly promoting Quechua literacy acquisition than the IEP, but has a more primary orientation to fostering Quechua language and culture and a more immediate control by local Quechua speakers (albeit urban, bilingual 'mestizo intellectuals' rather than 'rural Indian' monolingual Quechua speakers, cf. Niño-Murcia, 1997: 134, 147). The ALQ, founded in 1953, regularly offers Quechua instruction, publishes books and journals in

Quechua, sponsors an annual competition of Quechua literary works (drama, poetry, short stories, novels), and broadcasts programmes promoting Quechua on local radio networks (Hornberger, 1994: 245; Niño-Murcia, 1997: 148), all without government support and outside the formal educational system.

More recent institutional efforts to promote Quechua literacy are those of CADEP and other non-governmental organisations implementing mother tongue adult literacy programmes in rural communities of the department of Cusco beginning in the 1990s. The CADEP literacy projects, for example, explicitly seek to foster literacy acquisition in Quechua (as a first literacy), using culturally relevant materials for rural Quechua speakers and in particular for women, and working with existing local leadership organisations, such as the Federation of Peasant Women of Anta (FEMCA) (Chirinos, 1996: 251–65).

Although each of the above efforts falls somewhat short of a total commitment to Quechua literacy acquisition, Quechua socialisation, and Quechua community control, they do nevertheless contribute to facilitating and fostering intragroup communication and goal attainment for Quechua speakers. Furthermore, despite Fishman's admonition to the contrary (1991: 96), these efforts afford group members some degree of social mobility in the wider society, at least for those in leadership positions in the institutions: the CADEP programme contributes to the empowerment of FEMCA's leadership, the ALQ and its activities afford its members access to symbolic cultural capital (Niño-Murcia, 1997: 147), and the IEP's evangelisation efforts continuously recruit new leaders from among its members. It is still true, though, that in this, the last stage in the 'first and most difficult phase of RLS' (Fishman, 1991: 98), it is primarily internal rather than external reward that must sustain the efforts of Quechua speakers for the revitalisation of their language.

Stage 4: Schools in lieu of compulsory education

Stage 4 of the GIDS focuses on use of Quechua in lower education systems which meet the requirements of state compulsory education laws. There are two forms which schooling may take at this stage of the GIDS: type a, which is substantially under Quechua curricular and staffing control; and type b, which offers some instruction via Quechua, but is substantially under state control. Type a schooling entails community organisation and, often, community capital in order to develop a 'cultural space' to educate the community's children in the manner which the community, not the state, deems appropriate (Fishman, 1991: 100). Type b involves greater compromise on the part of the state primarily since this education will be 'conducted and paid for out of general tax funds' (Fishman, 1991: 100), even while some instruction is carried out in Quechua.

The Saraguros once again provide a useful example to illustrate how these two steps have developed as part of community based efforts to maintain and revitalise Quechua, but also in conjunction with national policy changes and government compromises. Type a schools, those which are organised and run by community members, but recognised as meeting state educational requirements, have existed in Saraguro[9] for 15 years. These schools, known as *escuelas activas* 'active schools' were formed in three Saraguro communities in the mid-1980s by a small group of indigenous teachers in response to what they saw to be the generally inadequate and often detrimental teaching methodologies of traditional state schools. The teachers felt the methodology of the traditional schools was lacking in two respects: the schools were unconcerned with the individual, intellectual, and emotional needs of the indigenous students, and they failed to support or, in the opinion of some, actually undermined, indigenous Quechua culture and language.

With financial and technical assistance from an international organisation, but also through use of their own personal funds, this group of local indigenous teachers established *escuelas activas* in three Saraguro communities. Similar in some ways to Montessori schools, the active schools' pedagogical philosophy and practice are based on the theory that children learn best through 'hands-on' self-directed manipulation of pedagogical materials. Instruction is individualised and for the most part, teachers attempt to serve primarily as guides, respecting the child's level of intellectual and emotional development. Emphasis is also given to supporting indigenous culture. One of the principal goals of the school is to recapture and revitalise the traditional ways of the community, including dress, language, food, and lifestyle. Although currently the teachers' salaries at the active schools are paid for by the state, much of the cost and all of the initiative for the development of these schools came from the Saraguro communities. The state has tolerated their existence, but has not fully supported them.

In 1989, policy shifts at the national level brought major changes to education in Saraguro, not just for the active schools in Saraguro, but for all schools serving indigenous populations. Type b schools, those which include Quechua language and culture, yet are financed by and incorporated into the state system, arose in Saraguro as part of national-level gains hard won by indigenous political groups. In November of 1989, after a decade of pressure, the *Dirección Nacional de Educación Intercultural Indígena Bilingüe* 'National Directorate of Bilingual Intercultural Indigenous Education' (DINEIIB) was established by the federal government. An arm of (what was then) the Ministry of Education and Culture, DINEIIB was created to administer schools in indigenous areas.[10] At the local level this meant that in all areas where more than half of the school-age population identifies as indigenous, schooling is directed by the regional indigenous education directorate which reports to DINEIIB. In Saraguro this resulted in dramatic changes. One of the two local indigenous political organisations became responsible for administering all indigenous education in the region, including making hiring and promotion decisions, conducting staff development sessions, and setting some aspects of the schools' curricula. While controlled by indigenous persons at the local level, the schools are part of the national education system, ultimately reporting not just to DINEIIB, but to the national education ministry. Thus, the creation of DINEIIB resulted in the emergence of schools which approximated type b; although they are administered locally by Quechua, the schools are ultimately controlled and financed by the state.

For both the type a (active) schools and the type b (DINEIIB) schools in Saraguro, issues of language and culture are at the forefront of planning and politics. Teachers and administrators at both types of schools are concerned about instruction of Quechua-as-a-second language in particular and the revitalisation of Quechua in general. Some schools of both types attempt to teach and use Quechua with varying degrees of regularity and success. It is important to note that no schools in Saraguro, however, have established immersion programmes where Quechua is used as the language of instruction for all, or even part of the day.

The Saraguro case brings two important points to the surface. First, indigenous control of schools does not necessarily ensure that the indigenous language will be emphasised, or even included. There are schools in Saraguro, for example, which although run by indigenous Saraguros, do not regularly teach Quechua. The second point is that the control and financing of schooling may be too complex to be neatly dichotomised into only two types. As the Saraguro case illustrates, there are complex and fine gradations of government support, control, and financing of indigenous education. And looking beyond Saraguro, there are numerous indigenous language education programmes which cannot be clearly designated as type a or as type b. One such well known example is the multinational, Bilingual Intercultural Education Project (known by its Spanish acronym PEBI) which was largely funded and designed by a German organisation, but which also cooperated and collaborated with the education ministries of several Andean governments, and in some instances with indigenous organisations.[11] PEBI schools were thus neither under the direct control of

Quechua communities, nor the national governments. Both the local Saraguro case and the multinational PEBI example suggest that the two GIDS sub-stages may be insufficient to capture the diverse configurations of community and government involvement in education.

Stage 3: The local/regional (i.e. non-neighbourhood) work sphere, both among Quechua and non-Quechua

Stage 3 on the GIDS emphasises the use of Quechua in work spheres which are outside of the traditional Quechua communities and involves interaction between indigenous and non-indigenous persons in the threatened language. For the most part, this stage has not yet been reached for Quechua. Regular use of Quechua outside of traditional indigenous contexts is unusual; use of Quechua by non-indigenous persons is exceedingly rare. Despite these facts and the continued stigmatisation of indigenous languages in much of South America which lies behind them, Quechua has gained some ground in recent years.

Quechua has become popular among businesses which cater to foreign tourists and certain upper-class sectors of the national population. A stroll down the streets of the commercial sectors of Quito or Cusco, for example, reveals a large number of tourist agencies, souvenir shops and art galleries with Quechua names. In large open-air markets, such as those of Otavalo, Ecuador and Chinchero and Pisaq, Peru, where indigenous retailers sell sweaters, weavings, blankets, bags and other goods to national and international tourists alike, Quechua is used both as a promotional tool and for conversation among vendors. In thriving, urban commercial centres such as Juliaca, Peru and Cochabamba, Bolivia, where large numbers of rural Quechua speakers migrate both cyclically and permanently, transactions in both street markets and commercial establishments commonly occur in Quechua. These transactions in Quechua embrace all types of commerce: including food, clothing, electronics, hardware, appliances, automotive, among others.

The use of Quechua in these work spheres is one indicator of its status and caché in certain circles. However, it is important to note that Quechua remains outside of the traditional channels of authority and power. Quechua is still not used regularly, for example, for formal interaction in banks, police stations or, as noted below, in government offices. Furthermore, the crucial point should not be overlooked that use of Quechua among non-indigenous persons is extremely uncommon. And despite the fashionability of Quechua in some contexts, the burden of bilingualism continues to fall uniformly on indigenous shoulders.

Stage 2: Local/regional mass media and governmental services

At the level of local government and mass media (Stage 2), the use of Quechua is even less noticeable than in the education and work domains (Stages 4 and 3). Fishman notes that this stage, and Stage 1 which follows, are reached by relatively few RLS movements, since they involve 'taking on the most powerful and most central institutions and processes of the polity' (1991: 106). Nevertheless, there are some instances of Quechua use in these domains, which can be seen as exceptions proving the rule.

In Peru, for example, Quechua is in use at local health posts in rural communities. These posts, set up by the Ministry of Health, are often staffed by local community members trained as health promoters who use Quechua in interaction with their fellow community members. There is also radio programming in Quechua by regional radio stations (e.g. Radio Tawantinsuyu in Cusco or Radio Kollasuyu in Puno), directed mainly to rural community members and broadcast at hours of the day suited to their agricultural work cycle (such as the early morning hours when most urban dwellers are still asleep) (see also Hornberger, 1988: 170–1). Both these cases exemplify the marginality of Quechua in these domains, as well as the lack of control of Quechua community members over these uses of Quechua.

Grade 1: Higher education, occupational, governmental, and mass media efforts

What use there is of Quechua in local level government or mass media emanates primarily from national or international level initiatives and thus falls under Stage 1. The paradox here is that, while Fishman emphasises that Stage 1 'essentially represents the arrival of the pursuit of cultural autonomy' (1991: 107), for Quechuas this is not the case. Even when Quechua is put to use for national and international educational, occupational, governmental, and mass media purposes, it is very often still out of Quechua speakers' control.

For example, in the higher education domain, Quechua is widely available as an academic subject in universities and institutes worldwide, including more than a dozen sites in the United States, and several in Britain, Germany, Japan, and elsewhere.[12] It is also offered in universities and institutes in Ecuador, Bolivia, and Peru.[13] Indeed 'the Chair of Quechua studies at the University of San Marcos, Lima, dates back more than four hundred years' (Grinevald, 1998: 147). Yet none of these efforts is primarily initiated and controlled by Quechua speakers, but rather by interested linguists or anthropologists, who often employ native Quechua speakers as instructors. Furthermore, the availability of these courses to indigenous Quechuas is highly limited, for socioeconomic reasons.[14]

Similarly, there is by now, dating from the 1960s, a considerable accumulation of top-down national and international initiatives to introduce Quechua as subject and medium of instruction in primary education in Peru, Ecuador, and Bolivia; yet again few of these are in the hands of Quechua speakers.[15] One clear exception to this pattern is the creation of the DINEIIB in Ecuador (mentioned above), which has empowered indigenous Ecuadorians to formulate and implement school policy, curriculum, and staffing in the indigenous sectors of the population.[16]

One such top-down initiative which was originally intended to raise the status of Quechua not only in the schools, but also in government, occupational, and media spheres as well, was the 1975 Officialisation of Quechua in Peru which made Quechua an official language of Peru, co-equal with Spanish, and specified that it would be taught at all levels of education beginning in 1976 and used in all court actions involving Quechua speakers beginning in 1977; these innovations were to be implemented by various ministries of the government. The decree was immediately followed by the launching of a national daily Quechua newspaper by one of Peru's major dailies (*Cronicawan*, published by *La Crónica*), an effort which was unfortunately short-lived due primarily to a lack of readership. The reaction of Peru's Spanish-speaking majority against Quechua Officialisation is by now well known. In fact, it was in part because of the Spanish-speaking majority's resistance that the implementation of this language policy fell far short of the stated goals. Indeed, as Coronel-Molina has pointed out, if real progress is to be made in reversing language shift from Quechua to Spanish, it is not primarily Quechua speakers who should be the target of revalorisation efforts, but rather the hegemonic Spanish-speaking majority (1999: 177).

Coronel-Molina also points to the shameful irony in the fact that, while denigrated in its home countries, Quechua is valued internationally, as evidenced for example in its spread on the electronic media, with 'numerous webpages on the internet, as well as a host of Quechua software programs' (1999: 171). He goes on to describe 'a new radio programming effort, . . . Ñuqanchik, . . . distributed via e-mail and the internet to radio stations throughout the Andean region, as well as maintaining a web site on the World Wide Web' (1999: 171–172). In light of developments such as these, he notes the paradox that 'it is more likely that Quechua speakers, given the proper technology, could communicate with foreigners from around the globe than with the majority of their own countrymen' (1999: 171).

The international prestige of Quechua is indeed a double-edged sword for Quechua revitalisation efforts, especially *vis-à-vis* the braindrain that Fishman alludes to as a possible threat once Stage 2 is reached (1991: 106). Quechua activists in leadership positions can on the one hand receive invaluable moral, intellectual, and financial support from beyond their national boundaries to advance the cause of Quechua revitalisation at home; but on the other, they may also find themselves crossing those national boundaries to seek more favourable venues for their efforts, thereby leaving their own national compatriots to fend for themselves. To the extent that reversing Quechua language shift is truly an international endeavour, this is all to the good, but to the extent that it also requires community-level fostering of intergenerational interaction in Quechua, an internationally mobile leadership cannot provide the necessary day-to-day modelling and practice of Quechua discourse.

Indeed, an internationally mobile Quechua activist leadership becomes peculiarly susceptible to the question Fishman poses, of whether having reached this stage, the promoters of Xish [Quechua] 'are now merely moderns, like all other moderns, but in Xish?' (1991: 108). While this question has not really arisen in any great measure for the vast majority of Quechua speakers, it is very much present for those who have pursued international avenues for reversing Quechua language shift; ironically so, since they pursued those avenues in most cases because they were the only possible routes to promoting Quechua.

Conclusion

As is clear from the above discussion, the process of reversing Quechua language shift in the Andes is highly complicated and difficult to summarise neatly. While the GIDS framework is helpful for organising and analysing various efforts taking place at different levels and in different Quechua communities, the Quechua case also serves to highlight some unanswered questions implicit in the framework. In the paragraphs that follow, we briefly touch on some of these unresolved issues, organised around the questions: who? what? when? and where?

Who?

Who are the activists that carry out RLS? The GIDS framework tends to assume that pro-RLSers are in all cases members of the language community and furthermore that RLS often begins with the older generation (1991: 391, 98). We have seen in the Quechua case, however, that non-Quechua entities such as international linguists, non-governmental organisations, and missionary churches may also be effectively involved in, and indeed initiators of, RLS efforts. Yet, as Grinevald points out, throughout South America, the lack of locally based, indigenous language projects is problematic, and the need for truly collaborative linguistic efforts is real (1998: 147–59). Furthermore, we have also noted the important role that the younger, often highly politicised, generation may play in RLS in promoting cultural activities which highlight the use of Quechua, as well as in their important potential choice to raise their children in Quechua-speaking households.

A more profound issue, perhaps, is the question of who the Quechua activists are or become as they carry out RLS efforts. To what degree is it possible for Quechua people, who have for centuries made up the rural, poor, and marginalised sectors of their societies, to be engaged in higher level RLS activities such as those represented in Stages 4–1 and still be authentically Quechua? Luykx has written about indigenous teachers in Bolivia, part of whose 'socialisation [as teachers] involve[s] coming to grips with the fact that the achievement of professional status [will] distance them from their ethnic and class origins, while simultaneously requiring them to live and work among those from whom they [have] differentiated themselves' (1996: 246). The Quechua activists' plight seems similar. As Fishman suggests, the question of authenticity, and the tensions between traditionalists' and modernists' responses to it, is perhaps an unending, but not necessarily unproductive, unresolved issue in RLS (1991: 109).

What?

What are the stages of RLS? Although the GIDS is intended as a quasi-implicational scale (Fishman, 1991: 87), in some cases the discreteness and sequencing of the stages in actual RLS efforts is not clear-cut. In the Quechua case, for example, we saw that schooling administration issues within Stage 4 are too complex to be neatly divided up into 'a' and 'b', and could perhaps be more usefully conceptualised as a continuum. Similarly, Stage 8 and Stage 1 appear to overlap somewhat in view of the fact that adult acquisition of Quechua (Stage 8) occurs very often in institutions of higher education or teacher professional development (Stage 1). Fishman has noted that the GIDS framework represents a 'heuristic theoretical stance, rather than a fully proven verity' (1991: 396). The Quechua case suggests that the stages are perhaps best seen as exactly that – a useful heuristic, rather than a step-by-step prescription.

When?

When are the stages of RLS to be carried out? This question also addresses the discreteness and sequencing of the stages, and in particular the relationship of Stage 6 to all the rest. It seems to us that, from both a theoretical and practical standpoint, Stage 6, the attainment of intergenerational informal oralcy, stands outside the other stages, as a central focus before, during, and after all other RLS efforts.

Stage 6, according to Fishman, is the 'heart of the entire inter-generational transmission pursuit and the *sine qua non* of the initial stages thereof' (1991: 398). The centrality of Stage 6 to the language revitalisation endeavour is partly based on the premise that functional differentiation between languages leads to stable bilingualism within a community. Fishman notes that an RLS focus on Stages 8 through 5 'presumes a stable bilingual model of . . . society in which . . . diglossia is attained and main-tained' (1991: 400). Luykx (1998) has recently argued, with reference to the Andean case, that it is precisely diglossia's functional differentiation that allows for the maintenance of bilingualism. In a related case of a threatened language, native Montagnais in Quebec, Drapeau raises the question whether code-switching, which 'may be construed as a manifestation of balanced bilingual competence on the part of middle-aged adults', when it occurs in caretaker speech instead 'turns into erosion of lexical skills among the younger generation' (1995: 163). All of this suggests that use of Quechua in the home is the most important effort Quechua activists can undertake. And yet, we have seen how hard it is for many of them to carry it out.

The ordering of Stage 6 in the scale implies that it must take precedence over Stages 5 through 1; repeatedly Fishman tells us that Stages 4 through 1 must be linked to Stage 6 (1991: 402–4). Yet, we have seen that, for better or for worse, reversing Quechua language shift in the Andes has not neatly climbed up the RLS stages of the framework. Rather, in at least some Andean communities, Quechua has been promoted, used and (to some extent) acquired in public, often culturally symbolic and political domains first and foremost, with daily face-to-face household interaction in Quechua remaining an elusive goal. Given this practical reality, must we assume that all the other Quechua RLS efforts are in vain? Rather, it seems important to locate this all-important dimension of RLS outside the stages, as either an overarching or underpinning essential to all of them, to be pursued at all times.

In a similar vein, Fettes (1997) has suggested that effective language renewal practices are best conceived of as a 'triple braid' interwoven of three discursive strands: (1) 'critical literacy', or what Fishman would likely term initial ideological clarification; (2) 'local knowledges', Fish-man's institutional domain; and (3) 'living relationships', Fishman's Stage 6. The concept of the braid is meant to remind us that 'one approach is never enough. Only when woven together can the strands endure' (1997: 315). Furthermore, concerning Stage 6 in particular, Fettes suggests, as we do above, that it is best conceptualised as a long-term and perhaps over-arching goal, noting that 'any meaningful long-term relationship conducted in the language helps to establish an intergenerational network of relationships, which clearly at some stage should involve children but which may not reattain the stage of stable transmission as a first language for years, possibly even generations' (1997: 311).

Where?

Where are RLS efforts carried out? We return here to the tremendous linguistic, sociolinguistic, and geographical diversity that characterises Quechua, with its several million speakers spread across several national boundaries. In this, the case of Quechua shares similarities with that of the Mayan languages in Guatemala, Mexico, and Belize (England, 1998; Grinevald, 1998: 140) and the Eskimo languages in Alaska (US), Canada, Greenland, and Russia (Iutzi-Mitchell & Graburn, 1993). A recent status and prospectus report on Eskimo languages included recommendations which seem relevant for the Quechua case as well, and which suggest considerations for RLS in general.

Top among these is the continuing need for focused understanding of the status and processes of Quechua language shift and revitalisation in specific communities and regions. With regard to the Eskimo languages, Krauss calls for 'focused research ... on the social, cultural, and linguistic processes of the ever-shifting boundaries between the simply endangered Eskimo language regions and those where the languages have become moribund' and Gumperz urges the use of 'ethnography of communication in order to discover the discursive uses to which Eskimo people put the colonial [and indigenous] languages when speaking with each other' (Krauss and Gumperz as reported in Iutzi-Mitchell & Graburn, 1993: 130). Above, we used our own ethnographies of communication to corroborate large-scale language surveys, as well as to illuminate some of the processes at work in language shift (Hornberger, 1988; King, to appear). This kind of detailed description of how languages are currently being used and valued within specific communities can provide a sound basis for planning to reverse shift.

However, a focus on social, cultural, and linguistic processes in these communities is insufficient – economic processes are crucial as well. Indeed, Grenoble and Whaley suggest that 'economics ... may be the single strongest force influencing the fate of endangered languages' and they go on to note the role of economics in the pressure to assimilate to the economically dominant culture and the availability of published materials, schools, teachers, radio and television broadcasting (1998: 52–3). An example from aboriginal Australia, reported by Haviland (in Tomei, 1995), graphically demonstrates the impact of politico-economic forces on endangered languages. The Guugu Yimidhirr-speaking community of Hopevale in Queensland was founded by missionaries in 1886 with the purpose of educating and protecting remnants of Aboriginal tribes from the area. Major language shift did not take place until World War II, when the entire population of the mission was, without warning, suddenly evacuated to an inland Aboriginal settlement; they were eventually permitted to return in the early 1950s, but to a site about 25 kilometres inland from the original location. By then, the balance between English and Guugu Yimidhirr had been disrupted; and by late 1983, the Aboriginal language was in danger of disappearing. However, this changed with the passing of a new Aboriginal Land Act which made provisions for Aboriginal claims to certain lands in Queensland, with the result that 'young people who had given up speaking Guugu Yimidhirr ha[ve] begun to speak it again, seeing the language as a necessary part of making a land claim on traditional lands' (Tomei, 1995: 181–2). In this case, the question of 'where?' is quite literal: specifically, where are the people and their language in relation to their lands? In light of Quechuas' centuries of marginalisation to the most remote Andean highlands, their increasing migration from rural communities to urban and coastal areas in search of employment, and a language ideology which ties the language very closely to the rural community (Hornberger, 1988: 100), the question of land is a highly significant one for the future of Quechua as well.[17]

Beyond the need for focused research about the specifics of specific communities, 'another key to minority language survival, Krauss said, is the creation of new notions of nationhood, cross-cutting the nation state. If the Inuit of Greenland, Canada, and northern Alaska can come to see themselves as one people, . . . then perhaps through common effort and shared resources they will be able to achieve their goal of survival, as a people with their own language and culture, through the twenty-first century' (Iutzi-Mitchell & Graburn, 1993: 131). The same could be said for Quechua. Not only are Quechua speakers present across several nation-states, but we have also seen evidence of a worldwide extension of Quechua through electronic media and courses of study at institutions of higher education. Efforts to reverse Quechua language shift will have to take into account, not just the local reality of specific Quechua communities, but also the multinational character of Quechua use and the global reality of Quechua's place in the world.

Along these lines, Grenoble and Whaley, building on the work of Edwards (1992), consider the merits of a typology of endangered languages which 'distinguishes between micro-level (community-internal) variables and macro-level (community-external) variables' and which 'further organises macro-level variables at a number of levels: Local, Regional, National, and Extra-National' (1998: 52). Similarly, in a recent consideration of bilingual education efforts in Peru over the past half century, Freeland concludes that we need to reconsider the roles of institutions at each level – global, national, and local. Noting that international multilateral organisations are too large and too influenced by prevailing economic ideology to be sensitive to local realities, nation-states are too weak, and NGOs are too small and too localised to be more than initiators and pump-primers, she argues for targeting efforts to the development of institutions occupying an intermediate level between international and domestic, global and national (1996: 184–5). A recent initiative along these lines is the *Programa de Formación en Educación Intercultural Bilingüe para los Paises Andinos* 'Andean Program in Bilingual Intercultural Education' (PROEIB-Andes), a regional MA programme sponsored by a five-nation consortium with coordination between Ministries of Education, universities, and indigenous organisations (Bolivia, Chile, Colombia, Ecuador, and Peru), established at the University of San Simón in Cochabamba, Bolivia, in 1997. Efforts such as these for Quechua and other South American languages (Grinevald, 1998: 149–50), as indeed for Eskimo, Mayan, or other endangered languages, hold much promise for reversing language shift.

Not only do efforts such as PROEIB-Andes cut across nation-state boundaries, taking into account ethnolinguistically based concepts of nationhood, but they also, directly or indirectly, continue the tradition of working to reverse Quechua language shift at multiple stages simultaneously. For example, the MA programme not only involves use of Quechua in higher education (Stage 1) and promotes its use in the work sphere (Stage 3) and in public schools (Stage 4), but it also continues the process of reconstruction of the language and adult acquisition of Quechua (Stage 8), as well as facilitating cultural interaction in the language (Stage 7). Given the tremendous linguistic, sociolinguistic, and geographic diversity of Quechua outlined above, coupled with the language's unfavourable odds for long-term survival, efforts like this, which target many of Fishman's stages concurrently, seem to hold the most hope for the uncertain future of the language.[18]

Notes

1. For example, Quechua enjoyed legal recognition as an official language of Peru

under Velasco Alvarado's presidency in the 1970s; Ecuador saw the rise of a powerful national political organization in the early 1980s, CONAIE, which continues to represent the indigenous population of that country; and the Bolivian government passed sweeping educational reforms in the 1990s, many of which were directed at improving educational services for the indigenous population. See Hornberger (2000) for further discussion of these developments.

2. Coronel-Molina (1997) presents an overview of the threatened status of Quechua in Peruvian society, reviewing the functional domains that Quechua currently does or does not serve, in terms of Stewart's (1968) 10 language functions.

3. Quechua is the term used to refer to the varieties spoken in Peru, Bolivia, and parts of northern Chile; it is also the cover term for all varieties of the language. Quichua is used exclusively for varieties in Ecuador. The difference in terms has to do with the differing phonological evolution of the language in Ecuador, as compared to the other countries. In the former case, the uvular stop /q/ has been lost, and with it the lowering of the /i/ vowel to /e/ in proximity to the /q/.

4. Ecuadorian Quichua planners, for example, rejected the use of the Bolivian and Peruvian 'k' and favoured instead 'c' and 'q', and likewise they rejected the 'w' in favour of 'hu'.

5. The distribution of Quechua speakers is estimated as follows: Peru (4,402,023), Ecuador (2,233,000), Bolivia (1,594,000), Argentina (120,000), Colombia (4,402), and Brazil (700) (Cerrón-Palomino, 1987: 76).

6. Saville-Troike (1989: 18), however, would probably consider Quechua speakers to be a speech community since they comprise a racial and ethnic group, one of the possible definitional criteria she cites.

7. We use the term activists to refer to those actively engaged in promoting the Quechua language and its revitalisation; our term is equivalent to Fishman's 'pro-RLS advocates' or 'pro-RLSers'.

8. Rumiñahui was a loyal Inca general during the initial phase of the Spanish conquest and is also the name of a character in the colonial Quechua drama, *Ollanta*, revived in this century and currently performed annually in the town of Ollantaytambo in Cusco's Sacred Valley.

9. 'Saraguro' refers to a particular group of Quechua people, but also to the parish in which they live. For more information on the Saraguros, see Belote and Belote (1994) or URL [www.saraguro.org].

10. The name has since changed to the *Dirección Nacional de Educación Intercultural Bilingüe* 'National Directorate of Bilingual Intercultural Education' (DINEIB).

11. See Hornberger (1988) for more information on PEBI (PEEB) in Peru.

12. In the United States, this includes past and present offerings at Cornell University, Stanford University, University of California at Los Angeles, University of Illinois at Urbana-Champaign, University of New Mexico, University of Pittsburgh, University of Texas at Austin, University of Wisconsin at Madison. European universities include Liverpool, St Andrew's, London, Bonn, and Hamburg.

13. These include, for example, the Instituto de Idiomas Maryknoll and the Universidad de San Simón in Cochabamba, Bolivia; the Instituto de Pastoral Andina in Cusco, Peru; and the Universidad de Cuenca, Ecuador.

14. Compare the case of Hawaiian: A recent bill introduced in the Hawaiian legisla-

ture would waive tuition for any Hawaiian enrolled in a Hawaiian language course (Kapono, 1994: 131). For Quechua speakers, such an initiative would only begin to address issues of access (Grenoble & Whaley, 1998: 53).

15. See Hornberger (2000) for an overview of recent initiatives in Peru, Ecuador, and Bolivia, and for additional references on earlier initiatives.
16. See Hornberger (1996) for more on both top-down and bottom-up efforts to promote Quechua literacy in the Andes.
17. Teresa McCarty has also recently raised these issues for the case of Navajo in the US (McCarty, in preparation).
18. We would like to thank Kenneth Hyltenstam and other seminar participants at the Centre for Research on Bilingualism at Stockholm Univerisity for their thoughtful comments on an earlier version of this paper. This paper was also presented at the Conference on Nationalism, Identity and Minority Rights, University of Bristol, UK, September 1999.

References

Adelaar, W.F H. (1991) The endangered languages problem: South America. In R.H. Robin and E.M. Uhlenbeck (eds) *Endangered Languages* (pp. 45–91). London: Berg Publishers.

Albó, X. (1977) *El Futuro de Los Idiomas Oprimidos en Los Andes*. Lima: Centro de Investigación de Lingüística Aplicada.

Belote, L. and Belote, J. (1981) Development in spite of itself: The Saraguro case. In N.E. Whitten, Jr (ed.) *Cultural Transformations and Ethnicity in Modern Ecuador* (pp. 450–76). Urbana-Champaign, IL: University of Illinois Press.

Belote, L. and Belote, J. (eds) (1994) *Los Saraguros. Fiesta y Ritualidad*. Quito: Abya-Yala; Universidad Politécnica Salesiana.

Benítez, L. and Garcés, A. (1992) *Culturas Ecuatorianas Ayer y Hoy*. Sixth edition, Quito: Abya-Yala.

Botero, L.F. (1991) La iglesia y el Indio en la colonia. In J. Botasso (ed.) *Política Indigenista de la Iglesia en la Colonia* (pp. 55–144). Quito, Ecuador: Abya-Yala, MLAL.

Cerrón-Palomino, R. (1987) *Lingüística Quechua*. Cusco: Centro de Estudios Rurales Andinos Bartolomé de Las Casas.

Cerrón-Palomino, R. (1989) Language policy in Peru: a historical overview. *International Journal of the Sociology of Language* 77, 11–33.

Cerrón-Palomino, R. (1997) Pasado y presente del quechua. *Yachay Wasi* 4, 49–64.

Chirinos, A. (1996) An experience of indigenous literacy in Peru. In N.H. Hornberger (ed.) *Indigenous Literacies in the Americas: Language Planning from the Bottom up* (pp. 251–65). Berlin: Mouton.

Chuquimamani Valer, R. (1983) *Unay Pachas: Qheshwa Simipi Qollasuyu Aranwaykuna* (Vol. 1). Lima, Peru: Proyecto Experimental de Educación Bilingüe / Puno.

Chuquimamani Valer, R. (1984) *Unay Pachas: Qhishwa Simipi Qullasuyu Hawariykuna* (Vol. 2). Cusco, Peru: Centro de Estudios Rurales Andinos 'Bartolomé de las Casas'.

Chuquimamani Valer, R. (1988) Una muestra del conflicto lingüístico nacional en el habla de los sollocoteños: El caso del parto. In L.E. López (ed.) *Pesquisas en*

Lingüística Andina, (pp. 163–80). Lima-Puno, Peru: CONCYTEC/UNA-Puno/ GTZ.

Coronel-Molina, S. (1997). Language policy: Status planning for the Quechua language in Peru. *Working Papers in Educational Linguistics* 13(1), 31–48.

Coronel-Molina, S. (1999) Functional domains of the Quechua language in Peru: Issues of status planning. *International Journal of Bilingual Education and Bilingualism* 2(3), 166–180.

de Vries, L. (1988) *Política Lingüística en Ecuador, Peru y Bolivia*. Quito, Ecuador: Proyecto EBI-CEDIME.

Dorian, N. (1998) Western language ideologies and small-language prospects. In L. Grenoble and L. Whaley (eds) *Endangered Languages: Current Issues and Future Prospects* (pp. 3–21). Cambridge: Cambridge University Press.

Drapeau, L. (1995) Code switching in caretaker speech and bilingual competence in a native village of northern Quebec. *International Journal of the Sociology of Language* 113, 157–64.

Edwards, J. (1992) Sociopolitical aspects of language maintenance and loss: Towards a typology of minority language situations. In W. Fase, K. Jaspaert and S. Kroon (eds) *Maintenance and Loss of Minority Languages* (pp. 37–54). Amsterdam: John Benjamins.

England, N.C. (1998) Mayan efforts toward language preservation. In L. Grenoble and L. Whaley (eds) *Endangered Languages: Current Issues and Future Prospects* (pp. 99–116). Cambridge: Cambridge University Press.

Fettes, M. (1997) Stabilizing what? An ecological approach to language renewal. In Jon Reyhner (ed.) *Teaching Indigenous Languages* (pp. 301–18). Flagstaff: Northern Arizona University and Center for Excellence in Education.

Fishman, J.A. (1990) What is reversing language shift (RLS) and how can it succeed? *Journal of Multilingual and Multicultural Development* 11(1 & 2), 5–35.

Fishman. J.A. (1991) *Reversing Language Shift*. Clevedon: Multilingual Matters.

Freeland, J. (1996) The global, the national and the local: Forces in the development of education for indigenous peoples – the case of Peru. *Compare* 26(2), 167–95.

Grenoble, L. and Whaley. L. (1998) Toward a typology of language endangerment. In L. Grenoble and L. Whaley (eds) *Endangered Languages: Current Issues and Future Prospects* (pp. 22–54). Cambridge: Cambridge University Press.

Grimes B.F. (ed.) (1996) *Ethnologue*. Dallas, TX: Summer Institute of Linguistics, Inc. [WWW Document] URL http:// www.sil.org/ ethnologue/ ethnologue.html.

Grinevald, C. (1998) Language endangerment in South America: A programmatic approach. In L. Grenoble and L. Whaley (eds) *Endangered Languages: Current Issues and Future Prospects* (pp. 124–59). Cambridge: Cambridge University Press.

Haboud, M.I. (1996) Quichua and Spanish in the Ecuadorian highlands: The effects of long-term contact. Unpublished doctoral dissertation, University of Oregon, OR.

Heath, S.B. (1982) Castilian colonization and indigenous languages: The cases of Quechua and Aymara. In R. Cooper (ed.) *Language Spread: Studies in Diffusion and Social Change* (pp. 118–147). Bloomington: Indiana University Press/C.A.L., Washington, DC.

Hornberger, N.H. (1988) *Bilingual Education and Language Maintenance: A Southern Peruvian Quechua Case*. Berlin: Mouton.

Hornberger, N.H. (1992) Verse analysis of 'The Condor and the Shepherdess.' In B.

Swann (ed.) *On the Translation of Native American Literatures* (pp. 441–69). Washington, DC : Smithsonian Institution Press.

Hornberger, N.H. (1994) Continua of biliteracy: Quechua literacy and empowerment in Peru. In L. Verhoeven (ed.) *Functional Literacy: Theoretical Issues and Educational Implications* (pp. 237–56). Philadelphia: John Benjamins.

Hornberger, N.H. (ed.) (1996) *Indigenous Literacies in the Americas: Language Planning from the Bottom up.* Berlin: Mouton.

Hornberger, N.H. (2000) Bilingual education policy and practice in the Andes: Ideological paradox and intercultural possibility. *Anthropology and Education Quarterly* 31(2), 173–201.

Hymes, D. (1972) Models of the interaction of language and social life. In J. Gumperz and D. Hymes (eds) *Directions in Sociolinguistics: Ethnography of Communication* (pp. 35–71). New York: Holt, Rinehart & Winston.

Iutzi-Mitchell, R. and Graburn, N.H.H. (1993) Language and educational policy in the North: Status and prospectus report on the Eskimo-Aleut languages from an International Symposium. *International Journal of the Sociology of Language* 99, 123–32.

Kapono, E. (1994) Hawaiian language revitalization and immersion education. *International Journal of the Sociology of Language* 112, 121–35.

Kaufman, T. (1994) The native languages of Latin America. In C. Moseley and R.E. Asher (eds) *Atlas of the World's Languages* (pp. 31–76). London and New York: Routledge.

King, K.A. (1997). Language revitalization in the Andes: Quichua instruction, use, and identity in Saraguro, Ecuador. Unpublished doctoral dissertation, University of Pennsylvania, Philadelphia, PA.

King, K.A. (1999) Language revitalisation processes and prospects: Quichua in the Ecuadorian Andes. *Language and Education* 13(1), 17–37.

King, K.A. (to appear) *Language Revitalisation Processes and Prospects: Quichua in the Andes.* Clevedon, England: Multilingual Matters.

Labov, W. (1972) On the mechanism of linguistic change. In J. Gumperz and D. Hymes (eds.) *Directions in Sociolinguistics: Ethnography of Communication* (pp. 512–38). New York: Holt, Rinehart & Winston.

Luykx, A. (1996) From indios to profesionales: Stereotypes and student resistance in Bolivian teacher training. In B. Levinson, D. Foley and D. Holland (eds.) *The Cultural Production of the Educated Person: Critical Ethnographies of Schooling and Local Practice* (pp. 239–72). Albany, NY: SUNY Press.

Luykx, A. (1998) La diferencia funcional de códigos y el futuro de las lenguas minoritarias. In L.E. López and I. Jung (eds) *Sobre la Huellas de la Voz: Sociolinguística de la Oralidad y la Escritura en su Relación con la Educación* (pp. 192–212). Madrid: Ediciones Morata.

Mannheim, B. (1984) Una nación acorralada: Southern Peruvian Quechua language planning and politics in a historical perspective. *Language in Society* 13, 291–309.

McCarty, T.L. (in preparation) *A Place to be Navajo.* Unpublished manuscript.

Milroy, L. (1987) *Language and Social Networks.* Oxford: Basil Blackwell.

Montaluisa, L.O. (1980) Historia de la escritura del Quichua. *Revista de la Universidad Católica del Ecuador* 28, 121–45.

Niño-Murcia, Mercedes (1997) Linguistic purism in Cuzco, Peru: A historical perspective. *Language Problems and Language Planning* 21(2), 134–61.

Parker, G.J. (1973) Clasificación genética de los dialectos quechuas. *Revista del Museo Nacional* 32, 241–52.

Saville-Troike, M. (1989) *The Ethnography of Communication: An Introduction.* New York, NY: Basil Blackwell.

Stewart, W. (1968) A sociolinguistic typology for describing national multilingualism. In J. Fishman (ed.) *Readings in the Sociology of Language* (pp. 531–45). The Hague: Mouton.

Tomei, J. (1995) The practice of preservation: Views from linguists working with language renewal. A report on a session of the 1993 Meeting of the American Anthropological Association. *International Journal of the Sociology of Language* 115, 173–82.

Torero, A. (1974) *El Quichua y la Historia Social Andina.* Lima, Peru: Universidad Ricardo Palma.

Volinsky, N. (1996) Standing up: Violin performance technique and Saraguro ethnic resurgence. In-progress dissertation draft. University of Illinois, IL.

von Gleich, U. (1992) Changes in the status and function of Quechua. In U. Ammon and M. Hellinger (eds) *Status Changes of Languages* (pp. 43–64). New York: Walter de Gruyter.

von Gleich, U. (1994) Language spread policy: The case of Quechua in the Andean republics of Bolivia, Ecuador, and Peru. *International Journal of the Sociology of Language* 107, 77–113.

Chapter 8

Irish Language Production and Reproduction 1981-1996

P. Ó RIAGÁIN

Introduction

In *Reversing Language Shift*, Fishman (1991: 1) attempts to 'diagnose' the difficulties with reverse language shift policies, and 'to prescribe ameliorative and restorative efforts in a sociolinguistically informed way'. The eight-'*stage*' model he developed to structure policy options suggests some kind of evolutionary rationale or temporal sequence and there is more than one suggestion in the text that Fishman intends his readers to understand his model in this way. For example, he speaks of the need to 'attain' certain stages and to 'transcend' others. Viewed this way, there are some difficulties applying the model to the Irish situation, as Fishman himself acknowledged (p. 122).

While the Irish case can be seen to have some parallels with other minority language situations in Europe – Wales, Catalonia, the Basque Country, Friesland, etc., Ireland also differs from most, if not all, of these examples. Unlike other minority language situations, in Ireland the state tried to deal with its minority language problem by seeking to re-establish it as a national language. No other minority language problem in Europe was tackled in this way, although the cases of the regional languages in Spain have in recent decades shown some similarities. While that particular element of the language policy has not succeeded, it gave the overall policy adopted by the newly independent Irish government in 1922 a unique shape and character.

In the 1926 Census of Population, some 18% of the population of the state were returned as Irish-speakers. The *Gaeltacht Commission* (1926) estimated that nearly half of these were concentrated in western areas and, within that region, roughly half again lived in core Irish-speaking districts (The Gaeltacht), i.e. about 5% of the total population in the state. (Recent research (Ó Riagáin, 1997, Part II) has shown that even that latter figure was an overestimate – 3% might be a more accurate estimate .)

Despite the marked regional bias in the distribution of Irish-speakers at the time towards western areas, the Irish state did not legislate for a bilingual policy organised on territorial lines. It did not designate two language regions, one Irish-speaking and the other English-speaking, within which each language would be defined as the norm. While an Irish-speaking region was defined ('The Gaeltacht') and special measures were formulated to deal with it, Irish language policy applied to the state as a whole and not just a region of it. Of course, outside the Irish-speaking areas, Irish speakers formed negligible proportions of an almost entirely English-speaking population. In this region, the bilingual policy was not, therefore, one designed to meet the needs of an already existing bilingual community, but rather it sought to create one. The policy was, in that qualified sense, one of language revival.

Thus from the outset, it seems fair to say that Irish language policy incorporated, to varying degrees, practically all of the 'stages' in Fishman's model. There was no gradual progression from one stage to the next. Irish language policy over the 20th century includes, for all or part of the period, policies that were directed at economic development in the Irish-speaking areas, language teaching in the schools, recruitment procedures in the public sector, language standardisation, radio and television services, together with a myriad of other less important policies to promote and extend the use of Irish. Some of these policies are or were 'universal type' policies, that is, designed to affect all members of the public, while others selectively target particular geographic or social groups. To reverse the process of language shift, the state had to try to create pressures of sufficient persuasiveness in advance of society itself generating such pressures. Drawing on the theoretical framework developed by Bourdieu (1991), it may be said that the state used its authority to change the structure of the *language market* prevailing in Ireland in order to enhance the symbolic, cultural and economic value attaching to competence to speak Irish. This affected both the national language market and the internal language market of the Gaeltacht areas and had real economic and political effects.

However, while he frequently presents his stages as actual 'way-stations' on the road to successful reverse language shift, at other times Fishman appears to be largely, and at times very perceptively, assessing the relative importance of a number of common language planning objectives. For example, when discussing Stage 6, he emphasises that 'unlike other stages, when it (Stage 6) is transcended it is not merely 'left behind'; on the contrary: all subsequent stages must be diligently tied back to and connected with Stage 6 if they are to contribute to the living reality of RLS'. It is easy to see what Fishman is emphasising here. At Stage 6 a 'self-priming intergenerational transmissability system' is established because the minority language is (or has become) dominant in at least some neighbourhood and family clusters. This correctly asserts the primacy of language reproduction over language production, and with this proposition most Irish speakers would, I think, agree. They would also agree with Fishman that, when measured against this criterion, Irish language policy has only had limited success.

However, while the effort to re-establish Irish as a national language has not been successful, neither can the impact of Irish language policy be described as negligible. Not only did it slow down a long-established process of language shift, but it clearly altered the spatial and social structure of bilingualism in Ireland. After 70 years, the linguistic division of labour has changed to the extent that, while the original communities of Irish-speakers have declined in both absolute and relative terms, there has been an increase in the proportions of Irish-speakers in some, mainly middle-class, groups elsewhere.

The policies which have effected those changes have largely been policies which Fishman sees as characteristic of Stages 4 to 1. However, in his discussion of the Irish case in *Reversing Language Shift*, Fishman chose to place his emphasis on some, largely voluntary, programmes aimed at Stage 6 objectives. To present a more rounded picture, in later sections of this paper I would like to examine more fully the impact of formal state policies, bearing in mind, of course, Fishman's strictures that the impact of these must always be related to Stage 6 objectives. As an introduction to this discussion, I will first review the data on language reproduction and production which has become available since Fishman undertook his assessment of the Irish experience. At the very outset, however, it is necessary to digress briefly in order to say something about the data available in Ireland on the language situation.

Data

Ireland's census language question provides one of the oldest continuous series of regularly collected, standard public statistics on any language in the world. Apart from two 15 year intervals, it has been included every ten years in the national census of population since 1851. However, until 1996 the main part of the question, as put to census respondents, simply asks if they can speak Irish only or Irish and English. While, as a measure of language proficiency, the language question in the census is neither very precise nor informative, recent research has shown that the margin of error in census data does not invalidate its use for the purposes of analysis (Ó Riagáin, 1997). However, it should also be noted that the language ability question asked in the Census of Population includes a less well known option – 'Read but cannot speak Irish' – which has only been reported in published returns in recent censuses. This is presumably because it is only in the past 20 years or so that the Central Statistics Office have found a significant number of respondents choosing this option. In the 1986 Census of Population some 330,272 persons (10% of the total population) reported that, while they could read Irish, they could not speak it! This rather unusual linguistic situation, which reflects the emphasis on literacy skills in school programmes, is confirmed by the evidence of survey research (Ó Riagáin & Ó Gliasáin, 1994).

In the 1996 Census of Population, the language question was changed to a significant degree. The ability question was shortened to a simple 'Can the person speak Irish? (Yes/No). But if the answer was 'yes', the census then asked 'Does the person speak Irish daily, weekly, less often or never'. The results, which were published only when this paper was in the final stages of writing, were somewhat surprising and perplexing. While the census confirmed earlier survey findings that a large proportion of those claiming an ability to speak Irish do not, in fact, use it on a regular basis, the total percentage of such persons in the state rose from 32.5% to 41.1% between 1991 and 1996 – the highest intercensal increase since 1926. It will require some detailed analysis, and probably further survey work, to explain this unexpected finding, but my own hypothesis is that respondents who had previously chosen the 'read but cannot speak Irish option' as a way of recording weak speaking skills, in the 1996 census chose to return themselves as 'Irish-speakers' rather than declare themselves as knowing no Irish at all.

Apart from language data in the Census of Population and a small range of other relevant statistics produced by certain government departments (e.g. school examination results), practically all of the data available to the researcher who wishes to examine the foregoing research issues has been collected by means of specially designed surveys. The main national surveys were conducted in 1973, 1983 and 1993. A large proportion of the questions originally formulated for the 1973 survey were repeated in the 1983 and 1993 surveys and thus provide a bank of directly comparable data. These questions may be grouped into five large categories: (1) Ability or proficiency in Irish; (2) Acquisition of Irish; (3) Use of Irish; (4) Attitudes to Irish, and (5) Social and demographic characteristics of the respondents. (Full details of the questionnaires may be found in CILAR, 1975 and Ó Riagáin, 1992.)

The Irish Language 1981–1996: An Overview

While the proportion of persons claiming the ability to speak Irish has increased consistently throughout the 20th century, the regional distribution has changed radically. As can be seen from the percentages in Table 8.1, there has been a gradual convergence in the pattern of regional variations.

In the mid-19th century, the regions in the south and west contained the most extensive Irish-speaking districts but these were, even then, contracting. Since 1926, there has been a gradual, but continual, revival in the ratios of Irish-speakers, particularly among residents of the eastern region. As there has also been a shift in the regional distribution of population over the period towards the east (and to towns generally), the combined result of these two trends has been to move the spatial concentration of Irish-speakers eastwards as well.

About 50% of Irish-speakers now reside in Leinster (including Dublin), compared with about 5% in 1851. Therefore, the overall trend has been for the proportion of Irish-speakers in all regions to move towards the national average.

Table 8.2, which presents the percentages of Irish-speakers (as defined in census data) in each age-group, allows the changes in patterns of language reproduction since 1926 to be broadly identified. The age-specific data shows that the national increase in the proportion of Irish-speakers was primarily caused by a continual improvement – since the 1920s – in the proportion of young adult cohorts claiming the ability to speak Irish.

The pattern for 1926 is bi-modal, peaking around the 10–20 year-old group and again among the over 65s. It is clear that, even then, two processes of language change were operating. The relatively higher

Table 8.1 Percentage of persons claiming the ability to speak Irish by region 1851–1991 (selected years)

Year	Leinster (East) (%)	Munster (South) (%)	Connacht (West) (%)	Ulster (North-west) (%)	State (%)
1851	3.5	43.9	50.8	17.0	29.1
1901	2.3	25.7	38.0	20.7	19.2
1946	15.1	22.0	33.2	26.0	21.2
1981	28.1	34.6	38.8	30.8	31.6
1991	30.5	36.3	40.1	32.0	32.5
1996	37.4	45.4	48.2	39.3	41.1

Source: Census of Population

Table 8.2 Percentage of persons with ability to speak Irish by age-group (selected years 1926–96)

Age group	1926 (%)	1946 (%)	1981 (%)	1996 (%)
3–4	4.6	4.1	4.9	10.0
5–9	19.8	21.6	27.8	48.2
10–14	39.2	47.5	50.8	68.0
15–19	27.6	43.4	51.0	68.0
20–24	15.8	32.2	40.0	51.7
25–34	13.2	20.8	32.8	37.3
35–44	11.9	11.2	30.0	39.8
45–54	13.7	10.0	28.3	37.1
55–64	16.9	9.5	22.9	32.9
65+	25.1	11.9	13.0	27.7
Total (over 3 years)	18.3	21.2	31.6	43.5

Source: Census of Population

percentages among the older age-groups reflects the typical pattern found in communities where a language is in decline, while the higher percentages within younger age-groups reflects in initial impact of revival strategies. By 1991, the pattern revealed by census data had become most unusual, if not unique, as compared to other minority language situations. The largest proportion of Irish-speakers is to be found in the 10–20 year-old age-groups, after which it consistently becomes smaller. As regards the absolute percentages of Irish-speakers in each age-group, it is clear from earlier remarks that I would treat the increases recorded in the 1996 Census with caution – due to changes in the census question. If my hypothesis is correct, then these increases are largely due to persons with weak speaking skills – mostly of school-going age – now being returned as Irish-speakers. This hypothesis receives some indirect confirmation from the survey results, which, however, measure adult abilities only (i.e. over 18 years).

The three national language surveys (1973–93) asked a number of questions about the respondents' own ability in Irish at different periods of their lives, as well as questions about the Irish-speaking abilities of various members of their families. The speaking ability question, which was devised by CILAR (1975: 116), asked respondents to rate their ability to cope with normal conversations in Irish on a six-point scale and the same question was used in all three surveys. Rather than use categories such as 'poor', 'fair', 'good', etc. the question was phrased to offer the respondent somewhat more guidance. Respondents were asked if they knew 'No

Table 8.3 Ability to speak Irish

Ability level	1973 (%)	1983 (%)	1993 (%)
1. No Irish	21	16	18
2. The Odd Word	27	32	32
3. A Few Simple Sentences	22	19	17
4. Parts of Conversations	17	20	22
5. Most Conversations	10	10	9
6. Native speaker ability	3	3	2
Total	100	100	100

Irish', the 'Odd Word', a 'Few Simple Sentences', enough for 'Parts of Conversations', for 'Most Conversations' or, finally, if they regarded themselves as 'Native Speakers'. The replies (Table 8.3) suggest a far more variable picture than that revealed by the census reports.

In each survey, about half of the sample said that they had little or no Irish, about 40% felt that they could manage a few simple sentences or parts of conversations, and just over 10% said that they could handle most or all conversational situations. It can be seen from the table that there has been little or no change in the 20 years since 1973. Even combining the top or bottom *three* points of the scale in the three surveys produces a statistically insignificant variation of only three percentage points.

The survey evidence would suggest that only about 5% of the national population use Irish as their first or main language. A further 10% use Irish regularly but less intensively in conversation or reading. In the state generally, these levels would appear to have remained stable over recent decades. As opposed to these relatively low ratios of spoken or active use of Irish, the ratios of passive use, primarily listening/watching Irish language radio and television programmes, are considerably higher. About 12% of the population watch some Irish language programme weekly (this figure would appear to have increased to about 20% since the new Irish language television station began broadcasting in 1996). The new 1996 Census of Population data on language use are in accord with these findings. On average, about 10% of the population said that they used Irish on a daily basis, but this percentage ranges from 27–36% for school-going groups, to about 3% for age-groups over 20 years.

The age-specific language data in the census shows that the national increase in the proportion of Irish-speakers was primarily caused by a continual improvement – since the 1920s – in the proportion of young adult cohorts able to speak Irish. Although over time the proportion of Irish-speakers in older adult cohorts also improved and continues to improve, the improvement is much smaller than the ratio of Irish-speakers in school-age cohorts would suggest. The constant 'slippage' from the relatively high levels of ability attained at school as the cohort moved into adulthood clearly reflects the low incidence of bilingualism in society.

However, it should also be noted that in the small Gaeltacht districts the use of Irish as measured by language surveys is still very much higher than the national average. The 1996 Census would suggest that 43% of persons resident in this area speak Irish on a daily basis – compared to 10% nationally. However, this relatively high ratio may be declining. In 1973, which is the last year in which all areas were surveyed, frequent and extensive home use of Irish was reported by about 60% of respondents (as compared to 5% nationally in that particular survey) and differences in work and social contexts are of the same order. For obvious reasons, the 1973 survey and 1996 census figures cannot be directly compared, although there is other evidence to suggest that language shift continues to occur in these areas (Ó Riagáin, 1997)

Except in Gaeltacht areas, bilingualism in Ireland is based rather loosely on a thin distribution of family and social networks which have a degree of underpinning from a variety of state policies in education, work-place and media institutions. But these networks are dispersed and weakly established and are very vulnerable to the loss of members over time as they are not sufficiently large or vibrant enough to easily attract and retain replacements.

Overall, if 'stability tending towards slight improvement' describes the trend with Irish speaking and reading abilities, then 'stability tending towards slight decline' might be a fair way of summarising the evidence on levels of use of Irish over the period 1981–1996. The rather complex mixture of success and failure, of growth and decline to be found in the present bilingual pattern indicates that while falling far short of the original policy objective, some modest element of revival and maintenance is still being accomplished.

Bilingual Reproduction

Not surprisingly, the ability of Irish-speaking networks to reproduce themselves is limited by their distribution, number and size in an English-speaking environment. Overall, both within and outside the Gaeltacht, bilingual reproduction is extremely problematical.

Even on census evidence, it is clear that Irish is not being maintained in its traditional core-area – the Gaeltacht (Ó Riagáin, 1992, 1997). The weakening rate of bilingual reproduction in these areas has not, however, been a continuous process. Up until about 1960 the degree of continuity with pre–1926 patterns was considerable, although concealed by the rather ambitious and optimistic way in which the Gaeltacht had been defined in 1926. However Ó Riagáin has shown that in the 1970s and 1980s the Irish-speaking core, which had remained stable over the period 1926 to 1956, had itself become unstable and was showing signs of substantial and rapid language shift. Not only is the number of marriages among fluent Irish-speakers in decline, but there is also evidence to suggest that some parents with high ability in Irish have become less efficient in reproducing children with equally high levels of Irish in recent decades.

Outside of the Gaeltacht, both survey and census data would indicate that only about 4% of households are Irish-speaking (The 1996 Census suggests that only 5% of 3–4 year-olds – i.e. the pre-school group – are reported to speak Irish on a daily basis). If this is accepted as a reasonably accurate measure of the extent of active home bilingualism in the community, the task of maintaining that low level requires the production in each generation of a substantially higher proportion of people with the potential to participate actively in Irish-speaking networks. This is because in a situation where Irish-speakers are distributed widely in the English-speaking areas a high degree of loss across the life-cycle is to be expected (APC, 1986: ix). While bilingualism, so measured, appears to be relatively stable, only one-quarter of those who grew up in Irish language homes use Irish with the same intensity in their current homes.

Apart from the bilingual output of the schools and the small minority of Irish-speaking homes, it also appears that some element of home bilingualism derives from a group who did not have an Irish language home background, and did not appear to have had any strong association with Irish during their school years. How and why this group began to use Irish in their adult years is not clear from the research, but in the past it appears that Irish began to be used 'on marriage or on the establishment of their own households' (CILAR, 1975: 212). This group includes many of the small but growing minority of parents who have chosen Irish medium education for their children, and there is evidence to suggest that these schools help to establish some degree of home bilingualism and to introduce parents to Irish-speaking networks.

Despite their small size, therefore, there is evidence that Irish-speaking networks possess some capacity to recruit new members. This must be set against their apparent inability to secure a permanent character, to ensure efficient reproduction of bilinguals and to absorb all of the bilingual output of homes and schools.

Bilingual Production

The maintenance of more or less stable rates of bilingualism over recent decades is therefore due more to the capacity of the schools to produce competent bilinguals rather than the capacity of the bilingual community to reproduce itself. Until recently, the educational system would appear to have been able to fulfil this task. However, more recently the pattern appears to have been changing.

Most Irish children learn Irish in both primary and post-primary school as a subject, but despite some 13 years' experience in the case of the average child, these programmes do not generally produce highly competent active users of Irish. When they do, they are usually among those who stay in the system the longest and take the academically most demanding syllabus, or else among the small minority who attend all-Irish schools .

Paradoxically, in a period when Irish language policy in the schools generally is experiencing considerable difficulties, the number of Irish immersion primary schools in English speaking areas continues to grow. In 1981, there were 28 such schools. In 1991, this figure had risen to 66 and it is now over 100. As a consequence, the proportion of children receiving this type of education has increased from 5% to 8%.

The position in mainstream schools is not so healthy. In these schools Irish is taught as a subject only. In 1993, nearly three-quarters of current users of Irish had post-primary schooling and nearly half had taken the higher level course in Irish. However, since 1980 only 10–15% of a cohort opt for the higher level courses in Irish in post-primary schools and even after 13 years' study of the subject the speaking ability of the majority of the cohort is only moderate or, in the case of a growing minority, negligible (Ó Riagáin, 1997).

Notwithstanding the trends in examination performance, there has been a clear rise since the 1960s in the proportion of the *total* cohort which now receives some certification in Irish at Leaving Certificate level. It has grown from 17% in 1963 to 59% in 1991. The pattern which has developed in the school system reveals the operation of two processes, the more significant being the increase in post-primary participation rates since 1966. This was able to compensate for the decline in the proportions achieving higher grades in public examinations and for the combined increase in the proportions failing or not taking Irish. The education system, therefore, is producing *larger numbers* of graduates with high qualifications in Irish, but it is realising the potential of a *smaller proportion* of candidates than in former years. This appears particularly true of male students, whose representation among higher level Irish candidates has declined in recent years while that of female students has increased.

In tandem with the growth of second level education, the third-level sector has expanded enormously since 1996. Numbers in third-level education have increased from 21,000 in 1965 to about 75,000 in 1991/92. Student intake in 1991/92 was close to 26,000, representing almost 40% of the age-group. About half of the intake proceed to degree-level programmes (DOE, 1992: 183). Thus the continuing requirement to have a pass in Irish, at Leaving Certificate level, for entry to the constituent colleges of the National University of Ireland and the Teacher Training Colleges maintains some support for the language. In addition to the entrance requirement, note must be taken of the extremely competitive nature of the entry process to the third-level system. Applications greatly outnumber the available places. Places are allocated on the basis of the grades awarded in the Leaving Certificate examinations, with more points being allocated for Higher level courses than Lower. As Irish must be included in the set of six subjects upon which the points score in calculated for entry to the national University and Teacher Colleges, it is obviously in the interests of those students seeking places to score highly on the Irish paper.

Just half of those with a higher grade in Irish went on to third-level education, compared to one-quarter of those with a Pass grade. An analysis conducted by the Advisory Planning Committee (APC, 1986) of the educational attainments of applicants for third-level places would suggest that the position has become more complex with growth in the range of third level institutions. These now include a number of new universities, Technical Colleges and Institutes of Technology. None of these new institutions insist on an Irish qualification on entry and neither does the oldest university in Dublin, Trinity College. Thus, while a high proportion of those selecting the Higher level paper in the Leaving Certificate examination transfer to third-level (usually university) education, a significant and growing proportion of pupils who have selected the Pass level course or who do now select Irish at all appear to have the academic ability to attain third-level places (APC, 1986: 50).

The relationship between third-level education and achievement levels in Irish, which has worked to the advantage of Irish in the post-primary system has, however, certain sociodemographic implications (APC, 1986: 31; see also Ó Riagáin, 1997). Although only a minority of post-primary graduates proceed to third-level education, this minority is not randomly determined. Access to education, particularly third-level education, is in large part determined by social class (Breen *et al.*, 1990: 131)

Whereas over one-third of respondents in the top two classes proceeded to third-level education, this was true for only about one-twentieth of those from the two lowest classes. The consequences of these inequalities for social policy are, of course, the subject of much political debate but, as the foregoing analysis would suggest, they are also reflected in the class profile of those who study Irish at the most advanced level in the post-primary sector

The degree of social polarisation is pronounced. Although respondents from families in the top three classes constitute just 38% of the total sample, they account for nearly three-quarters (71%) of the Higher level Irish graduates. However, within the upper classes some changes have been occurring in recent years. While the achievement levels of those from families in Classes II to IV appear to be improving, that of Class I is weakening. This is not due to any lessening in the propensity of families in this class to educate their chilren to the third-level. The contrary, in fact, is the case. Among the younger age-group in this class, nearly half (45%) had received third-level education, compared to 27% of the older group. It would thus appear, as APC (1986: 44) has suggested, that for this group in particular, the educational decisions taken by students and families involve the adoption of a strategy which increasingly does not include Higher level Irish or any Irish at all. As this group includes the elite elements in Irish society, this tendency clearly has implications for the long-term societal support for Irish.

Furthermore, now that the major expansion in post-primary education participation has run its course, the continued reliance on current schooling procedures as a means of generating competence in Irish places the language in a very vulnerable position.

Explaining Bilingual Patterns and Trends

Language policy is formulated, implemented and accomplishes its results within a complex interrelated set of economic, social and political processes which include, inter alia, the operation of other state policies. The modernisation of Irish society, a process which developed slowly prior to 1960, exerted a powerful influence in subsequent years. With the rapid growth of economic prosperity since 1960 has come a widening of economic, political, demographic and cultural contacts and influences as Ireland became more comprehensively incorporated within the framework of international capitalism. These external influences, with their various and differentiated impacts on Irish society have created severe problems for policies designed to maintain Irish as a minority language.

Irish language policy, particularly in the period 1922–60, succeeded to the extent it directly or indirectly changed the 'rules' of the social mobility process. It is the relationship between educational qualifications and the labour market – and not pedagogic factors *per se* – which is crucial to an understanding the effectiveness of Irish language policies in the schools. The Irish economy before 1960 was dominated by family businesses – mostly in farming – and the self-employed. Job opportunities for those with, in Bourdieu's terms, cultural rather than economic capital, were very limited (Bourdieu, 1991). Therefore, participation rates in post-primary education were low. Yet research studies have consistently shown that the education system's capacity to produce competent bilinguals was closely related to the number of years an individual spent in school and, of course, the type of language programme followed. Of these two variables, the duration of education has proved to be the more relevant for the majority of pupils. Notwithstanding the influence of other factors, it remains the case that most of those with high levels of ability in Irish had remained in school at until the end of post-primary education.

The selective impact of language policy in the schools was reinforced by policies regulating entry to the professions (via third-level education) or the public service. As a consequence the percentages of Irish-speakers in both sets of occupations increased after 1922. But Irish language policy was relatively ineffectual in the case of those labour market sectors where entry depended on inheritance rather than educational qualifications. Thus the very limited degree of social mobility in Ireland in these early decades placed some severe limitations on the social impact of Irish language policy.

However, Irish society has changed considerably since 1960. The new economic policy, which was elaborated in a series of economic development programmes between 1960 and the early 1970s, placed emphasis on export markets and foreign industrial investment. Education was primarily seen as a form of investment within context of economic growth. In short, the modern industry targeted by the economic programmes were perceived to require a well-educated labour force. A range of new policies led to huge increases in second-level participation rates, and simultaneously the number and range of third-level institutions was widened. Meanwhile, as a more direct consequence of the economic programmes, the range of employment opportunities outside the professions and the public sector expanded. Thus the relationship between education and the labour market was strengthened, but the state was unable to adapt the scope of its language policies to regulate these new developments. In fact, it effectively gave up the struggle. In 1973, Irish ceased to be a compulsory subject for examinations or a requirement for entry to the public service. These societal trends severely reduced the institutional support for Irish and the reproduction of high levels of ability in certain key social groups.

However, some elements of the original policy continue to operate. Irish must still be included on the curriculum of schools in receipt of state support and it remains necessary for entry to the four colleges of the National University of Ireland. As post-primary education became more widely available, children from the upper classes increasingly sought third-level education. Thus, the Irish language requirement for entry to the universities maintained the class element in language reproduction, but with rising participation rates in both second and third-level education, the class base has widened.

It is important to note that, while the Gaeltacht is located in peripheral rural areas, it too was directly affected by these changes in occupational structures. As late as 1961 nearly three-quarters of males in these areas were working in agriculture, but by 1981 agriculture was employing less than half of the workforce, while other sectors had grown proportionately and in absolute terms.

Social Reproduction and Irish-speaking Networks

The significance of socioeconomic trends for language reproduction arises from their impact of Irish-speaking networks and communities. The available research evidence indicates that the small farm economy of Gaeltacht areas supported a pattern of social networks which were very localised and restricted in spatial scope in the first half of this century. The relative stability of these network boundaries was an important factor in sustaining Irish-speaking communities. However, state policies were not able to maintain population levels. By the early 1980s, the population had been halved and major structural changes had occurred within the community. As economic development began to percolate into rural areas in the post–1960 period, the minimum threshold population levels were no longer available in many rural communities to support traditional activities (primary school, parish, etc.), even less so new functions, e.g. post-primary education. The growth in non-agricultural employment had resulted in increases in commuting to and from towns. This, combined with the growth in post-primary education (also centred in the towns), changes in shopping and recreation patterns, and shifts in migration patterns all signified a major transformation of social network patterns which occasioned significant changes in patterns of bilingualism.

These developments in the structure of the community which served to intensify the frequency of interactions between Irish-speakers and English-speakers, or to increase the probability of young people working outside the community, served to diminish the possibility of maintaining Irish. For example, network changes resulting from both in-migration and return migration have been increasing in importance in recent decades. There was also a growing involvement in social and occupational networks outside of the Irish-speaking area, As a consequence, the overall proportion of married couples with joint native-speaker ability in Irish has been declining. These homes are substantially more efficient in reproducing similarly competent Irish-speakers than are homes in which only one or no parent is a native-speaker.

Outside of Gaeltacht areas, the relationship between social class and Irish has been a significant factor in the formation of Irish-speaking networks in these English language regions. Because of the relationship between social class and the housing market, the spatial distribution of bilinguals varies with the class character of residential areas and, therefore, spatial variations in the distribution of Irish-speakers are apparent in large urban areas. One of the few studies of Irish-speaking networks in urban areas found a strong relationship between the distribution of Irish language schools and the sociospatial concentrations of Irish-speakers (Ó Riagáin, 1997). Thus it seems plausible to argue that the social concentration of high ability Irish speakers within the middle-classes and, in particular, within the public sector provides the potential, at least, for the formation and maintenance of Irish-speaking networks. For network forming institutions, like schools, to become viable operations, they require sufficiently large numbers of supportive parents within a reasonable catchment area. But once the school is established in an area, all the indications suggest that it had an importance far beyond its basic aim of educating children through Irish. The capacity of the school-based networks to attract 'novice' or 'reluctant' bilinguals is evidence that Irish-speaking networks are capable, in these circumstances at least, of recruiting new members. This must be set against their acknowledged inability to secure a permanent character that could ensure the reproduction of Irish speakers and absorb the bilingual output of homes and schools (APC, 1988: 31).

Current Policy Dilemmas and Future Directions

At the political level it is not surprising, therefore, to find state agencies in the 1980s and 1990s speaking more of survival rather than revival. While Bord na Gaeilge (Irish Language Board) continues to present bilingualism as a model of language choice for Irish society as whole, the practical focus of its programme is directed at the provision of certain basic state services in and through Irish, i.e. Irish language schools, television and radio stations, sections of public offices, etc. One can detect in this approach the beginnings of a more selective strategy – that of institutional parallelism.

For example, the state broadcasting organisations have always experienced considerable difficulties in trying to find a balance between their budgetary responsibilities and the programming requirements of a scattered linguistic minority, whose bilingual competences, social background and interests are also very variable. These operational problems are compounded by others which relate to the ideological character and strategic shape of the state's language policy. The broadcasting system is expected at one and the same time to reinforce both the revival and maintenance elements of the strategy, but these objectives envisage somewhat different target audiences with very different requirements. These issues form a set of related co-ordinates around which Irish language broadcasting has been organised.

The principal re-alignment of broadcasting policy over the past two decades has been a move towards the maintenance pole of the overall stategy and a consequent weakening emphasis on the revival dimension. This is most clearly seen in the fact that Raidio na Gaeltachta – originally a local station serving Irish-speaking areas on the western coast – now carries the overwhelming bulk of national radio programming in Irish. It is important to recognise, however, that this shift also eases operational and ideological problems. The programmers are offered a more clearly defined audience (even if it constitutes only part of the bilingual population), and as the focus is directed towards the day-to-day problems of the Gaeltacht community the programme makers can justifiably dodge the more tricky ideological issues.

Television programming in Irish has been moving in the same direction. At present, such programming has already been moved to the less popular of the two national channels. Although an Irish language television station was established in 1996, the long-term implications of this for Irish language programming on other channels is unclear. If television programming for the Irish language in any significant way follows the pattern of radio programming, then it can be concluded that the earlier role of helping to create bilingual communities will have been abandoned. The underlying principle will become one of servicing the existing bilingual population.

One can also detect some signs of a similar development within the education system. The long-term drift from the objective of Irish language medium education for all seemed to have receded to the last line of defence in 1973, when Irish ceased to be a compulsory subject in state examinations, but was retained as a required subject on the curriculum of schools in receipt of state funds. But the pattern of recent examination results in Irish – which show a growing percentage of pupils failing or not taking the paper – together with a number of recent policy decisions, suggest that this line is itself showing signs of erosion. While the government is careful to support the expanding all-Irish school movement, it has also relaxed further the requirements for pupils to study Irish and the requirements for teachers to have a professional competence in Irish. The proposals to restructure the National University of Ireland raise questions about the continued status of Irish as a required matriculation subject. There is now a clear possiblity that Irish as a school subject will revert to its pre-independence status as a voluntary subject.

There are dangers in this development. Tovey (1988: 67) points out that the more policy singles out 'Irish-speakers' as the target for language policies on the grounds of their rights as a minority group, the less plausible it becomes to sustain existing policies to revive Irish. Nor is it easy, in political terms, to move from a universal policy, which has been in operation for 70 years, to one which is more selective without severely damaging public confidence in the overall policy objective.

There is another consideration. The stability of current Irish usage is dependent on the stability of the social networks of users, that is, on the series of interlinked social relationships that may grow out of contacts in an institutional setting, but whose survival depends on the achievement of some degree of friendship, intimacy and interpersonal knowledge among participants. It seems unlikely that these are strong enough at present to guarantee the reproduction of spoken Irish, or its expansion, into the next generation. A policy built around the provision of state services to Irish-speakers may find that they do not exist in large enough numbers nor are they sufficiently concentrated to meet the operational thresholds required to make these services viable.

In all of these respects, one feels that Irish language policy is now at a critical stage. The way forward is no longer clear. To further confuse the issue, Irish language policy has emerged as a key element in the Northern Ireland peace process. Under the terms of the peace agreement concluded in April 1998, a new all-Ireland language policy unit is to be established to oversee language policy in both the Republic and Northern Ireland. This will bring together, as part of one policy operation, two very diferent Irish language situations. The Irish language is very much part of the nationalist programme in Northern Ireland, while the Republic has already moved into a post-nationalist phase. On the other hand, despite all the foregoing analysis of its weaknesses, the Irish language is considerably stronger in the Republic than it is in Northern Ireland. It remains to be seen whether the political impulse from the North will give language policy a lift, or whether the practical situation in the North will operate to further dilute the policy in the Republic. For example, the Irish language is an optional subject in Northern schools, while it is still a required subject in all schools in the Republic. It remains to be seen how this will work out.

Conclusions

As opposed to Fishman's evolutionary universalistic approach I would wish to argue that before we can place policy interventions on a sound theoretical footing, we need to much more systematically account for varia-tions within and between in language shift situations and seriously and explicitly to locate these situations in time and space (Giddens, 1984). This inevitably means linking local interaction sytems, within which language behaviour occurs (and which are the main focus of Fishman's overview), to the wider economic and social systems which impinge upon them (Gal, 1988, 1989; Bourdieu, 1991). There is nothing in Fishman's model to indi-cate how variables of an economic, social or spatial nature are to be incor-porated for either analytical or prescriptive purposes. Yet clearly these issues have had an important bearing on the way language shift evolved and formed part of the Irish government's response to these issues. The complex sequence of maintence, shift, revival, etc. apparent in Ireland over this century is intimately related to changes in the economic base of the community within the wider society. Unless we can understand how different social groups and categories vary in their response to broadly similar external circumstances, 'use existing sets of relationships and resources and reinterpret traditional norms and values' (Long, 1977), we cannot begin to evaluate the potential effectiveness of different kinds of policy interventions.

There is a further point to be made. As Glyn Lewis (1983) pointed out many years ago, it is necessary to avoid the tendency, only too apparent in many discussions of language planning and policy, to regard the process as autonomous. The social uses of language owe their specifically social value to the fact that they are organised in systems of social interaction which reproduce the system of social differences (Bourdieu, 1991). The state plays a very dominant role in shaping the socioeconomic development and thus it is necessary to examine policies which relate to economic, and social (particularly education) issues, and whose intent was not at all language oriented, but which greatly affect the operation of language policy. It is probable that, in total, their consequences for language maintenance objectives are extensive and of more importance than language policies *per se*. As Pierre Bourdieu observes, 'those who seek to defend a threatened language, . . . are obliged to wage a total struggle. One cannot save the value of a competence unless one saves the market, in other words, the whole set of political and social conditions of production of the producers / consumers.' (Bourdieu, 1991: 57)

Note

1. This chapter revises and updates sections of my book *Language Policy and Social Reproduction: Ireland 1893–1993*. (Oxford Studies in Language Contact). Oxford, Clarendon Press.

References

Advisory Planning Committee (1986) *Irish and the Education System: An Analysis of Examination Results*. Dublin: Bord na Gaeilge.
Advisory Planning Committee (1988) *The Irish Language in a Changing Society: Shaping the Future*. Dublin, Bord na Gaeilge.
Bourdieu, P. (1991) *Language and Symbolic Power* (edited and introduced by J.B. Thompson). Cambridge: Polity Press.
Breen, R., Hannan, D.F., Rottman, D.B. and Whelan, C.T. (1990) *Understanding Contemporary Ireland: State, Class and Development in the Republic of Ireland*. Dublin: Gill & Macmillan.
Committee on Irish Language Attitudes Research (CILAR) (1975) *Report*. Dublin: The Stationery Office.
Department of Education. *Education in a Changing World* (Green Paper) (1992) Dublin: Government Publications Office.
Fishman, J.A. (1991) *Reversing Language Shift: Theoretical and Empirical Foundations of Assistance to Threatened Languages*. Clevedon: Multilingual Matters.
(Gaeltacht Commission) Commission of Inquiry into the Preservation of the Gaeltacht, (1926) *Final Report*. Stationery Office: Dublin.
Gal, S. (1988) The political economy of code choice. In M. Heller (ed.) *Codeswitching: Anthropological and Sociolinguistic Perspectives*. Berlin, Mouton de Gruyter.
Gal, S. (1989) Language and political economy. *Annual Review of Anthropology* 18, 345–67.
Giddens, A. (1984) *The Constitution of Society*. Cambridge: Polity Press.
Lewis, G. (1983) Implementation of language planning in the Soviet Union'. In J. Cobarrubias and J.A. Fishman (eds) *Progress in Language Planning: International Perspectives*. Berlin, Mouton.
Long N. (1977) *An Introduction to the Sociology of Rural Development*. London: Tavistock.
Ó Riagáin, P. (1992) *Language Maintenance and Language Shift as Strategies of Social Reproduction: Irish in the Corca Dhuibhne Gaeltacht 1926–86*. Institiúid Teangeolaíochta Éireann.

Ó Riagáin, P. (1997) *Language Policy and Social Reproduction: Ireland 1893–1993*. (Oxford Studies in Language Contact). Oxford, Clarendon Press.

Ó Riagáin, P. & O Gliasáin, M. (1979) *All-Irish Primary Schools in the Dublin Area: A Sociological and Spatial Analysis of the Impact of all-Irish Schools on Home and Social Use of Irish*. Dublin: Linguistics Institute of Ireland.

Ó Riagáin, P. and O Gliasáin, M. (1994) *National Survey on Languages 1993: Preliminary Report*. Research Report 18. Dublin: Institiuid Teangeolaiochta Éireann.

Tovey H. (1988) The State and the Irish language: the role of Bord na Gaeilge. *International Journal of the Sociology of Language* 70, 53–68.

Chapter 9

A Frisian Update of Reversing Language Shift

D. GORTER

Introduction

The general meeting of the Provincial Council of Friesland on 24 April 1985 was an important milestone for language policy for the Frisian language. On that day the politicians adopted the conclusions and recommendations of the language planning report *'Fan Geunst nei Rjocht'* (From favour to right), a title significant of the message they wanted to get across. The Frisian provincial representatives were well aware that their acceptance of this report was going against the views of the central state government. The vote symbolised the wide divergence on the development of a language policy for Frisian as a minority language (Van Dijk, 1987). As a solution to the ensuing deadlock – in good Dutch tradition – a compromise was worked out between both layers of government. It took shape in the form of a *covenant*. However, that document was only going to be signed after four years of long and tedious negotiations. Then, on top of all that, the highest court in the Netherlands rejected the heart of the covenant within a year, when it found the provisions for translations of official documents not applicable. Although there were no provisions on official language use in the system of laws, the court ruled that Dutch had to be taken for granted as the only language of all administrative affairs, until a law specifically would declare otherwise. In retrospect, the debate in April 1985 demarcates the end point of a process, which began in the mid-1960s, of increased political priority for language matters. In the 1990s issues surrounding the promotion of the Frisian language have gradually become less of a priority and are more and more incorporated into the daily business of 'doing politics'.

At the threshold of the new millennium, on the basis of survey research (Gorter & Jonkman, 1995b), one may claim that in absolute numbers the Frisian language has more speakers than ever before.[1] Even though such a statement has limited scientific value, it scores well in the media and it also gives new heart to RLS activists. The claim about the absolute number of speakers also partially answers the main question of this article. On the surface things have not really changed in the position of the Frisian language over the last 25 years. The basic percentages of people who have the ability to understand (94%), speak (74%), read (67%) or write (17%) Frisian have remained more or less the same. Those four percentages have only changed a little between the first general sociolinguistic survey of 1967 (Pietersen, 1969) and the most recent one of 1994. Gorter and Jonkman (1995b: 55) concluded that the preliminary results of their survey, in terms of language ability, usage in intimate and more public settings and language attitudes, point to a stable situation for the Frisian language.

In this article I will look back over a period of roughly a decade and a half of Reversing Language Shift efforts on behalf of Frisian, in order to update the chapter on Frisian by Fishman (1991).[2] I will first characterise this period of well over a decade by three major developments: (1) internation- alisation in a European context, (2) legitimisation inside a framework of laws and regulations, and (3) stabilisation of the language situation. Subse- quently, I will discuss step by step each of the eight stages of the GIDS model as Fishman presented them in his RLS book. I will apply the model again to Frisian using the most recent data.

Internationalisation

'*Europe*' has become part and parcel of the everyday reality of speakers of Frisian. This is true in the general sense as it would be for many inhabit- ants of the member states of the European Union (think only of the intro- duction of the common currency the 'Euro'). It is also true in the sense that the Frisian language has become officially recognised as a European, autochthonous minority language in the *Charter for Regional or Minority Languages* of the Council of Europe. The international context is conspicu- ously missing from Fishman's model of the GIDS, even from the highest Stage 1, which is limited to 'nationwide levels'. However, in my opinion the developments of European unification, in particular those aimed at the promotion of minority languages, do hold relevance for the way in which RLS efforts take place, also for the Frisian case. I can mention a few of those developments.

Numerous publications, symposia, study days, letters to the editor and discussion programmes have been filled with the consequences for the Dutch language of a 'Europe without borders'. Leading up to the magic year '1992', a lasting public debate arose in the Netherlands surrounding issues of national identity and language. Many opinion leaders have painted a bleak future for Dutch. According to some, Dutch itself was likely to become some sort of threatened minority language. Or, as was sometimes said, the future position of Dutch in Europe can be compared to the position of Frisian as a minority language in the Netherlands. It has to be admitted that in line with the general lack of pride about their national language, quite a few people in the Netherlands would not mind at all if Dutch were cast in such a subordinate role, or even completely disappear and be replaced by English as a common language. Others rightfully point out that the chances of Dutch disappearing in the short run are quite small, as the language has some 20 million speakers and a strong infrastructure in two national states, the Netherlands and Belgium. This debate on national language and identity started in the late 1980s and has continued for over a decade now. As recently as 1998, the European Cultural Foundation (based in Amsterdam)[3] launched a new programme under the title 'Which languages for Europe?'. This programme is mainly concerned with the problems of the use of a multitude of languages in the institutions of the European Union (with 11 official languages). The programme also deals with ways to maintain the pluralinguality of Europe as a whole and it devotes some attention to minority languages such as Frisian. Another recent example is the initiative of the Dutch Language Union (*Nederlandse Taalunie*), which is the joint Belgian–Dutch governmental body responsible for the development of the Dutch Standard language. Early in 1999 this organisation initiated a project to discuss the 'Institutional Status and Use of National Languages in Europe'. The project emphasises the contributions that smaller national languages such as Dutch can make to a European language policy. It is feared that these languages may become 'crushed between the smaller minority languages and the "big three" (English, French and German)'.

Another development, which has already been mentioned, is the European *Charter for Minority or Regional Languages* of the Council of Europe. After about 10 years of preparatory work the Charter was opened for signature by the member states in 1992. The Netherlands were among the first signatories. After ratification by five member states the Charter became effective in 1998. The Charter has been fully ratified for Frisian.

An important outcome of the process of internationalisation is the enormous increase in contacts among speakers of minority languages across Europe. Since the beginning of the 1980s the European Union has taken a lively interest in the question of minority languages. One significant measure was the introduction of a special budget line in 1982. This budget line enables support of projects to preserve and promote minority languages. For instance, the first international conference organised from this budget line took place in Ljouwert (Friesland) in 1985. Later on many projects were carried out in Friesland with European Union support, among them the Mercator-Education project.[4]

Although we may observe a general increase in awareness of the importance of language issues in the Netherlands, this has not really changed the basic attitude of the majority of politicians and civil servants towards Frisian. Ignorance seems to dominate and, even when there may be some goodwill, this is not easily translated into positive measures for Frisian.

Legal Framework

Alexander Schmidt (1997: 30) of the Max Planck institute of International Law in Heidelberg recently concluded: 'the Frisian language underwent an important increase in prestige'. In his article he describes what has happened in Friesland in terms of building a legal framework over the last decade. This legal framework can be summarised in four parts: (1) the Covenants between the State and the Province in 1989 and 1993; (2) the General Act on Administrative law in 1995; (3) the Act on Frisian in the Courts in 1997; and finally (4) the European Charter for Regional or Minority Languages in 1998. Each of these four parts of the legal framework will be briefly amplified below.

(1) In 1989 a *Covenant* on Frisian language policy was entered into between the State and the Province (as referred to in my introduction). The covenant was renewed in 1993 and negotiations began in 1998 for a new covenant with a long-term perspective of at least 10 years. These covenants include provisions for education, media, culture and scientific research, but also for public administration and the use of Frisian in the courts. Every section contains specific agreements and provisions for a budget for several parts of the 'infra-structure' of the Frisian language. Thus, for instance, arrangements are outlined for the only professional theatre company *'Tryater'*, the broadcasting organisation *'Omrop Fryslân'* and the centre for scientific research – the *'Fryske Akademy'*. The advantage of a covenant is clear. It provides an exception and protection to statewide rules which otherwise would not easily apply to Frisian organisations. It also provides some safeguard against cutbacks. On the negative side one has to mention that the covenant has a limited duration and has to be renegotiated again and again. Moreover, it is only a weak form of legal protection and provided no guarantee. This was almost immediately made clear by the rejection by the highest court of the arrangements in the first covenant about the use of Frisian in public administration, which made the new legislation of 1995 necessary.

(2) Until recently the official language of the Netherlands was not established by law. Therefore, a motion was introduced in parliament to change the constitution, which is also a sign of the increased language awareness in the Netherlands. However, in the debate over the protection of Dutch, nothing even remotely near a two-thirds majority was to be found among the parliamentarians. The majority did rightfully think that formulating a phrase such as 'Dutch is the language of the Netherlands' would not in any way protect the language in a unified Europe. Thus the constitution was not going to be changed. A compromise was found in changing the Act on Administrative Law. In 1995 regulations were accepted that Dutch is declared to be the official language of public administration. Frisian has picked some fruits of this debate, as it has been included with some specific provisions in the same law. The Act has made it possible to use Frisian in most administrative affairs, both in written and in spoken form.

Still, such legal arrangements are only a first step, as can be illustrated by an example from the practice of language policy. As part of their language policy, the provincial government and many municipalities in Friesland ostensibly accept the rule of 'following language choice'. This means that local government does not want to take the first step when using Frisian, and, in principle, only gives an answer in Frisian when addressed in that language. However, some research among civil servants showed what happens in reality. Of the few letters written by citizens in Frisian (less than 5% of all letters), these letters were *not* answered in Frisian in about two-thirds of cases (Gorter & Jonkman, 1994). There are several reasons why they were not answered in Frisian. I can give a few examples. The civil servant who had to write the answering letter could not write Frisian and he did not want to go to the translation service. Perhaps he just took an old example from his files of a similar case, or he was insecure about the Frisian legal terminology. He may also have felt that a Frisian letter would be disapproved of by his colleagues, etc. (Gorter, 1993). In this way, many practical reasons make civil servants almost always choose Dutch. Thus far, little has been done to change this phenomenon of 'silent obstruction', neither by the provincial administration nor by the municipalities.

(3) Similar problems existed with the official use of Frisian in the courts. Frisian was allowed to a limited extent by a law dating from 1956. According to that law, if one insisted, one could use Frisian before a court, at least when the presiding judge allowed one to do so. Therefore, only in a few cases would a person actually use the Frisian language. In 1997 a new law became effective which contains better provisions. Today, one does indeed have the full right to use the Frisian language in court. Whether many persons will now actually use it remains uncertain, seeing the hardi-

ness of traditions. Practice will tell how this law works and what jurisprudence will need to be added in order to implement it.

(4) The European *Charter for Regional or Minority Languages* is perceived
as quite important by the Dutch State. After signing it in 1992, the Netherlands were among the first to ratify the Charter in 1995.[5] One reason why
the Dutch government wanted to be among the first signatories was the
opportunity to play a leading role in European moral affairs, a role which it
likes to play anyway. Thus, parliamentarians mentioned in their statements the importance of supporting the Charter in the light of developments of new democracies in Central Europe. Another reason was that by
codifying the existing situation for Frisian it was possible to realise some
minimal Frisian aspirations.

The Charter consists of three parts. Part I contains general considerations; in Part II the languages are entered for which the Charter will be
applied; and Part III consists of a long list of more than 90 articles with
specific provisions to preserve and promote minority or regional
languages. When a state decides to sign Part III for a specified minority
language, it has to choose a minimum of 35 articles which it will apply. In
the case of the Netherlands five languages were brought under Part II
(along with Frisian, the languages are Low-Saxon, Limburgish, Romani
and Yiddish)[6] but Part III has only been applied to Frisian. The approach
chosen by the Netherlands is one of *codification*. The Charter was ratified by
the Netherlands in such a way that specific provisions were chosen which
were already being implemented.

Thus, the Charter affirms existing language policy drawn from the covenants and existing laws. Still it has a positive *symbolic* effect because the
Dutch member state is binding itself in this way to international law. It also
becomes more difficult to reverse existing measures. For Frisian RLS activists the hope of the Charter is that in the future it will be possible to sign
additional provisions.

Stable Language Relationships

The common expectation in Friesland seems to be that the Frisian
language is decreasing in use. There is a general sense of a 'threatened
language' underlying the development of language policy and all kinds of
other RLS efforts. In 1994 the Fryske Akademy carried out a new language
survey among the population, in which many questions were repeated
from earlier surveys in 1967 and 1980. The first results were eagerly
awaited, but they were also quite surprising to many people. The survey
did *not* find that Frisian was diminishing in use. Stability over the last

Table 9.1 Home language 1967, 1980 and 1994

	1967 (%)	1980 (%)	1994 (%)
Frisian	71	56	55
Dutch	13	33	34
Dialect	16	11	10
Total	100	100	99

decade proved to be a characteristic of the language relationships in many ways. This can be illustrated by a central variable such as home language. The proportions for 'language usually spoken at home' are shown in the Table 9.1.

The outcomes of the table do make clear that the use of Frisian as a home language declined sharply between 1967 and 1980, from 71% to 56%.[7] Dutch as a home language in Friesland increased substantially between 1967 and 1980 to about one-third, but afterwards remained at about the same level. Migration is an important factor is this regard (see below).

Compared to home language, on average, the figures for proficiency in Frisian have changed less over time. In 1980 and 1994, three-quarters of the Frisian population could speak Frisian, whereas in the period 1967–80 a decrease of about 10% in speaking Frisian occurred. For understanding and reading Frisian the decline was small, within margins of error of the samples. Ability to write remained stable for the period 1967–80, while from 1980–94 an increase of over 5% was observed.

The distribution of language use of Frisian over different social domains shows an uneven pattern. A majority of the population habitually uses Frisian in the domains of the family, work and the village. Frisian holds a relative strong position there. In the more formal domains of education, media, public administration and law, the use of Frisian has made some inroads during the last decades, but overall it is still fairly limited.

Figure 9.1 contains a summary of 12 situations in public life for which the respondents have stated the language they ordinarily use. The situations can be distinguished according to the degree of formality and the familiarity with the interlocutor. A cross-tabulation has been made with language background: those respondents who have learned Frisian as their first language (L1) are distinguished from those who indicated that they could speak Frisian, but it was not their mother tongue (L2) (those who cannot speak Frisian are excluded).

At the bottom of the figure we find that 85% of Frisian L1-speakers habitually speak Frisian in the shop where they do their daily shopping, whereas only 42% of L2-speakers use Frisian. So language background

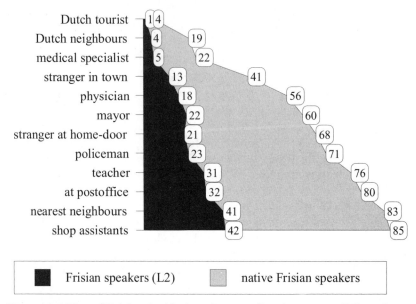

Figure 9.1 Use of Frisian in 12 situations: as first language (L1) and as second language (L2)

seems to determine much more which language will be used in public than language ability by itself. In climbing this 'mountain graph' the gap between L1 and L2 speakers narrows in terms of the percentage that does use Frisian in the selected situations. For instance, when we look at language used with a medical specialist all seem to agree that this is a formal situation with status differences between both interlocutors and thus less 'fit' for Frisian.

Still, in the situation of language spoken with Dutch neighbours second-language learners barely use Frisian with their Dutch-speaking neighbours, where first language speakers do so in about one-fifth of the cases (19%). At the top of the graph there is very small difference between first-language speakers and second-language speakers of Frisian. Speaking to a 'Dutch tourist' is obviously something for which Frisian cannot be used. Of course, these results have informed us only about a limited number of situations of language choice. It is quite obvious that the language of the interlocutor is an important factor. Language choice is 'person bound'.

On the basis of systematic participant observation a set of four rules for interactional language behaviour has been formulated which is a sort of 'linguistic etiquette' (Gorter, 1993: 167–81). The first rule is: [1] 'Dutch is the common language for everyone'. This rule does not take bilingualism into consideration. Because everyone can speak Dutch, everyone could – theoretically – act in accordance with this rule. There is a second, contrasting rule, which is [2] 'Everyone may speak his/her own language'. Because almost all inhabitants can understand Frisian, in principle all Frisian-speakers could act in accordance with such a norm and speak Frisian all the time without making communication impossible. However, the rule of the right to speak their own language is only applied cautiously. Thus, additionally, a third rule can be formulated: [3] 'Frisians must speak Dutch to Dutch-speakers and only Frisian to Frisian-speakers'. This rule seems quite simple and straightforward but, as could be shown, is not without problems when applied. For instance, second-language learners are a complicating factor. In case of a conversation with three or more participants still another rule is put forward: [4] 'A speaker will have to accommodate to the language of conversation in the company of others'. There is a preference for one language in one conversation (Feitsma, 1984).

These four rules do not predict the language choice precisely in all cases. Interaction generally is a process of negotiation where not everything is arranged beforehand. The rules are part of the normative ideas about appropriate language use: what language is marked in certain cases and what is not. Frisian is usually the noticeable, the marked language and Dutch is the expected, the unmarked language. This is an indication of an underlying power process. Dutch sets the tone in the community, a fact which is very much taken for granted. The persistent alternation of Frisian and Dutch in one conversation usually costs an extra effort. A person who continues to speak Frisian to a non-Frisian person runs the risk of being labelled a 'Frisian activist' or, in other situations, as 'someone who can't even properly speak Dutch'.

The language situation is faced with a paradox: there is stability for the minority language Frisian, but at the same time an increase in the presence of the dominant language Dutch. One of the reasons is that bilingual speakers have learned to speak and use Dutch better, but at the same time have not 'unlearned' their Frisian.

GIDS Stages for Frisian

In my description of the eight stages of the GIDS (Graded Intergenerational Disruption Scale) I will follow Fishman's description of Frisian RLS efforts and update or criticise it where necessary. In his chapter Fishman (1991: 149) states that the province of Friesland as a 'moderately prosperous region' has 'as a result . . . experienced relatively more in-migration than out-migration for many years.' This seems to be too general, because this was only true during the 1970s. During the 1980s and 1990s the migration pattern changed again to what it had been for over a century: more people leaving than settling.

From 1960 till today the number of persons leaving the province every year has remained fairly constant, averaging ±25,000. However, the number of newcomers has fluctuated from just over 20,000 in 1960, going up to a high point of almost 35,000 in 1974, decreasing to 22,000 in 1984 and settling at almost 27,000 in 1997. The outcome has been a surplus of immigrants between 1971 and 1982 and a negative departure balance in most other years. During the last two years (1997 and 1998) there was a slight positive balance again, mainly due to higher figures for immigrants from abroad (refugees). The population has increased from 508,000 in 1980, 580,000 in 1990, to 621,000 in 1999. Growth has come predominantly from a surplus of births.

There is also internal migration in the province, to and from the countryside. Living in towns has become more important. The effect of this relocation of the population on the distribution of the language has been substantial. Both processes of migration have made geographic differences related to language less distinct.

Stages 8 and 7: Reassembling Xish, learning it as a second language during adulthood and enriching the ethnocultural and ethnolinguistic experiences of those who are already Xish-speaking

As Fishman says, Frisian RLS efforts are 'more focused on stage 7 than 8'. The Frisian 'language is still well and naturally spoken by . . . speech networks engaged in many activities'. Stage 8 is not really at stake in the Frisian case, notwithstanding discussions on the quality and development of the standard language, where some seem to oppose the re-introduction of older speech forms.

The expressions of culture mentioned by Fishman (theatre, Frisian festival, film, music and literary evenings) do, in a sense, flourish more than ever. For instance, open-air theatre performances in Frisian are enormously popular: the most famous annual theatre in Jorwert has a series of 10 evenings, for which tickets are sold out through special phone-lines within hours. In literature there are still no real literary 'big young talents' or 'discoveries', but there is an ongoing discussion between the older 'grey-hair' establishment (over 50) and a younger generation (under 40), which seems to gain momentum and may become quite interesting. Because open-air theatre and also music are so popular, today it would be harder to conclude that 'most of stage 7 reaches only those already committed to Frisian' as Fishman did. One of the 'breakthroughs' for Frisian has been its remarkable acceptance in pop music over the Netherlands as a whole: two top-10 hits over the last two years. Also the language has been used as a commercial gimmick in Dutch TV and radio, stressing humour for selling a traditional Frisian alcoholic beverage. Part of the reason for this success certainly lies in the 'Eleven cities tours' (*Alvestêdetocht*) in 1985, 1986, and 1997. This ice-skating tour of some 200 kilometres can only be organised in very severe winters. These tours were mass media events of mega size and as a result the province of Friesland, but also the Frisian language and culture, became a bit more popular in the rest of the Netherlands.

Stage 6: The intergenerational, demographically concentrated family-home-neighbourhood-community sphere: the basis of transmission

The slow decline of percentages of mother-tongue speakers in the traditional rural areas has continued and there has been a slight increase in the towns. Today, on average some 70% in the countryside and some 40% in the towns are Frisian L1 speakers. This means that the speakers are geographically more evenly distributed (during the 1950s these percentages were over 90 and below 30, respectively). Migration from rural areas to the towns is, of course, an important factor. It also means that almost all neighbourhoods and most families have become linguistically mixed. Here lies a potentially dangerous situation for Frisian, because research tells us also that in mixed marriages by far the majority will opt for Dutch as the language for the next generation. Against this goes the finding that quite a few persons learn to speak Frisian as second language (20% of the total population) and will use it to some degree, even if much less than first-language speakers. Another surprising finding was that Frisian-speaking parents, on average, have slightly more children than non-Frisian speakers, this birth surplus has compensated somewhat for the loss due to mixed families (Gorter and Jonkman, 1995a).

Also of some apparent importance is a process of 'mental urbanisation' of the rural areas (Van der Vaart, 1999; Mak,1997) which leads to further Dutchification of everyday life. As Fishman already rightfully observed, the few cultural manifestations of Frisians 'cannot repair damage to foundations'. Similarly the religious domain cannot do much repair. In particular not because there have been few if any changes in the use of Frisian in the church (which is generally low), although an organisation of ministers is rather active.

Stage 5: Schools for children (that do not meet the requirements of compulsory education) and courses in language and literacy acquisition for adults

In his original chapter Fishman (p. 166) mentions the Afûk organisation that provides adult courses in the Frisian language. Ten years ago Afûk was perhaps a somewhat old-fashioned operation, but it now has renewed its courses and has diversified its products, also catering for special target groups such as legal professionals, workers in health care and an intensive course for foreigners. Afûk is also working on a general course on CD-ROM, but, other than advertising its products, is not yet active with courses through the Internet, although this can be expected in the years to come.

As Fishman (p. 166) states 'every RLS movement will have its "great dictionary" project'. When he wrote his chapter the *Larger Frisian Dictionary* had published five volumes. Ten years later there are 15 and the Fryske Akademy has almost finished this monument to the language. In total either 22 or 23 volumes will appear. Other more applied dictionary projects are also nearing completion, such as the Frisian–Frisian desk dictionary and the Frisian–English dictionary. In 1985 work began on the establishment of a Language Data Bank for Frisian, which now contains over 15 million tokens from written texts. A reverse dictionary and a spell-checker were the few directly usable products of the Language Data Bank. In terms of computational linguistics results are below original expectations. Of more recent date, a new project has begun in the field of spoken language. Following the model and procedures for the Corpus of Spoken Dutch, a major project in the Netherlands launched in 1998, the Fryske Akademy is attempting to set up a parallel, although smaller project for a Corpus of Spoken Frisian. This will result in a cross-section of the Frisian language as it is in use by the end of the 20th century. Probably it will also have some new applications in speech technology. The relevance of this work lies in keeping a language such as Frisian at least in a minimal way up to date with so many new technological developments related to language.

Stage 4a: Schools in lieu of compulsory education and fully under RLS control

In his chapter Fishman (p. 169–71) outlines a brief historical account of developments in education, which I will not have to repeat here. There have not been serious new developments in the teaching of Frisian in primary schools during the last few years (Zondag, 1993). The great majority of primary schools comply with the requirement that they teach the subject of Frisian. A survey by the Inspectorate in 1988 showed that about 30–45 minutes a week were spent on teaching Frisian as a subject. The same survey told us that one-fifth of the primary schools used Frisian as a medium of instruction with other subjects. In 1993 the central government published official 'key objectives' for Frisian, which describe the knowledge and skills pupils should have at the end of primary school. It was striking that the objectives for Frisian and Dutch were exactly the same.

Although the data were collected before the key objectives were published, studies by De Jong and Riemersma (1994) and Ytsma (1995), made it very clear that school practice was not reaching those ideal objectives for Frisian at all. The studies, however, reaffirmed the conclusion that teaching Frisian as a subject or using Frisian as a medium of instruction has no detrimental effect upon the results obtained in Dutch. Children in Friesland, on average, have the same level of achievement in Dutch at the end of primary school as do other children in the rest of the Netherlands. Their achievements in Frisian tend to lag behind their achievements in Dutch.

A seeming 'breakthrough' came in 1993 when Frisian became a compulsory subject in the first, basic stage of secondary education. But the obligation turned out to be light as a feather. Much dissatisfaction remains among RLS activists and responsible policy-makers about such a minimal implementation.

Type 4b schools: The object of RLS affection as a distinctly part-time 'guest' in the public school arena

There were no alternative schools of their own of whatever type. In 1989 an initiative was taken by a group of parents to establish all-Frisian language playgroups ('*pjutteboartersplakken*'), aiming both at Frisian-speaking and Dutch-speaking children. The first playgroups were established in larger towns because parents were dissatisfied with the fact that existing pre-school provisions took no account of the Frisian language background of their children. In 1999 the Frisian playgroups organisation was responsible for 11 groups; not a very spectacular number considering that over 200 other playgroups exist in Friesland. As Fishman (p. 173) concluded 'The many weaknesses of Frisian that we have encountered at levels 6, 5 and 4 constitute a very serious handicap [to] future possibilities in the RLS arena, particularly insofar as the improvement of the inter-generational transmissibility of the language is concerned.'

A new development in 1998 was an experiment with 'trilingual education'. That is, some primary schools have started to develop a curriculum where Frisian and Dutch are used on a 50–50 basis during the first 5–6 grades and English is introduced as subject and medium at the upper stage as a third language for about 20% of teaching time. This experiment is being scrutinised by intensive research (Ytsma, 1999), but it is premature to predict any of the outcomes.

Stage 3: The world of work, both within the ethnolinguistic community (among other Xmen), as well as outside it (among Ymen)

Frisian plays a small role in trade and industry (Fishman, p. 173). As a spoken language its use is quite common on the workfloor, but may be quite exceptional at the management level. In all kinds of client-service situations, with unknown interlocutors, there is an expectation that Frisian will be understood. The figure of 94% of the population being able to understand the language, makes clear why this expectation is almost always fulfilled. Every now and then there may be a small riot over this issue. For instance, in a public meeting when someone asks that Dutch be used. Whereas 30 years ago the chairman of such a meeting would immediately yield to a request for Dutch, today such concession runs the risk of protests by Frisian speakers and usually some negotation takes place. Spoken Frisian may be generally accepted, written Frisian still stands out as something special. Thus, in some advertisements that fact is used to attract attention. All in all Frisian is spoken in the work environment, outside the neighbourhood, without any problems, but the domain of work is not an area of any RLS efforts, except for civil servants and teachers.

Stage 2: Xish in regional mass media and government services

Quite a bit of energy in Frisian has been devoted to developments in the domains of media (Radio/TV) and the government ('official domain'). For this reason I will discuss it more elaborately. 'Radio Fryslân' had 20 hours per week in 1988 and almost no TV (30 hours *per year*). Ten years later the media position has improved substantially. Today there are daily TV broadcasts in Frisian (one hour original production early in the evening of every day, with reruns). These broadcasts are quite popular: the 'viewer-density' is the highest of all channels in Friesland at that hour. This is regarded a big success by most RLS activists. Opinions differ on how much it serves as an example and influences the use of Frisian by its speakers. Moreover, in both regional newspapers the same weak position of 10 or 20 years ago still continues, where Frisian is used very marginally in less than 5% of all texts. Frisian is just a prominent 'topic' for regional journalists, especially for 'human interest' (e.g. a student from Vienna writing a doctoral thesis on Frisian) or a 'riot' (e.g. civil servants protesting against the language policy for Frisian). In 1999 a new monthly magazine will be launched. There are some prudent developments in multimedia (e.g. a CD-ROM with the history of Friesland). On the Internet there is a 'Frisian ribbon campaign' promoting the use of Frisian for web pages, there is even an all-Frisian search engine ('Frysyk'), but not yet any on-line course in Frisian or even an on-line dictionary.

As Fishman (p. 177) rightly observed 'a great deal of attention has been given to the legalistic niceties of language legislation and policy statements, and the overcoming of Dutch resistance in these areas is greatly stressed as a matter of principle'. The legal framework which has been described above is the outcome of this 'attention' and may be seen as a victory over Dutch resistance. However, Fishman also already observed that the 'implementation of new opportunities leaves much to be desired'. Policy plans have been retarded and plans have not been implemented (a lot of attention was given to the highly symbolic, but really non-issue of Frisian place-names). Language policy has lost its prominence on the political agenda. The Charter for European minority or regional languages was important to keep policy development going. That Charter is mainly of symbolic importance to Frisian, but at the same time the Dutch government has recognised 'Low Saxon' (a collection of dialects), among others, as a regional language. Such recognition has stimulated new initiatives in other regions of the Netherlands, but at the same time has helped to keep Frisian ambitions down.

'The Hague' (the central state government) has acceded to demands from the provincial government very slowly and especially when it would cost little to nothing. Fishman used the term 'blockage' , which might be less applicable these days. A turn of policy in The Hague took place in the period 1989–93 when there was an Under-Minister for the Interior who was of Frisian descent and who was proud of it. Moreover, she was made explicitly responsible for 'coordinating Frisian affairs' at the central state level. The Council of Frisian movement, an organisation of volunteers, has attracted some young persons, but has not yet been able to obtain a clear new profile. Activism for Frisian RLS efforts still has quite a low profile.

Stage 1: Government, employment and education at the highest levels

Fishman (p. 178) observed that the Frisian scene was far less promising and far less coordinated and vigorous than the Basque counterpart, considering the highest levels. Not much has changed and there still is no 'well-considered set of urgent priorities' defined by the Frisians themselves. Language policy plans have to a large degree indeed been 'public posturing and the adoption of well-meaning and good-sounding resolutions'; implementation has turned out to be difficult.

There is still no 'leading intellectual centre' in Friesland because the plans for a university have failed. Even where the differences between colleges for higher vocational training and universities are becoming smaller, the three institutions for higher education in the capital of Friesland have not provided anything like 'intellectual leadership' to the community. They are involved in a 'battle to attract students' from all over the Netherlands (or from abroad), thus Frisian is usually more seen as a nuisance than as an asset.

Cutbacks in Dutch higher education have resulted in the disappearance of two of the five chairs in Frisian linguistics outside Friesland. The full chair at the University of Amsterdam could be saved through close collaboration with the Fryske Akademy and fulfils more or less the function of a Frisian embassy in the Dutch capital.[8] During the 1990s four doctoral dissertations were published in Frisian and another eight dealt with a specific Frisian topic from linguistics or literature studies. The Fryske Akademy underwent a small reduction of staff, notwithstanding a very positive peer review by a committee of international experts in 1995.

General Conclusion

As far as the effect of the RLS book by Fishman is concerned, I find it hard to judge its impact. The chapter on Frisian and Basque was translated into Frisian and separately published, but it did not get any further attention in the public debate. The provincial advisory body on Frisian (*Berie foar it Frysk*) has looked into it seriously. I have come across it several times in the 'scientific literature', but it has not become a 'handbook' for RLS activists. Fishman (p. 180) concluded that things may not be entirely bleak for Frisian. 'The basic problem seems to be in activating the goodwill'. This is most certainly the case and I doubt whether much has changed over the last decade. 'The struggle is far from over. Indeed, it may go on forever, ineffective though it may generally be insofar as intergenerational transmissibility of Frisian as mother tongue is concerned' (p. 181).

My conclusion is that things have, on the whole, not gotten worse for Frisian. Of course, there are also some real threats today, especially in mixed families and neighbourhoods as well as for the continued erosion of the language itself. The quality of the language is deteriorating and Frisian may at a certain point run the risk of dissolving into Dutch. In Friesland both languages are used and they are sometimes in conflict. The norms for language use can also be seen in terms of a power process. The Frisian speakers are still a quantitative majority in their own area, but the Dutch speakers are the group with most power. There is an unequal chance for Frisian speakers to realise their language preference *vis-à-vis* the Dutch speakers. So, the rule that 'everyone may speak his/her own language' is really restricted in practice. Dutch is the common language of everyone because all Frisian-speakers are bilingual and most Dutch-speakers are only passively bilingual. You can always say as a kind of powerplay, 'let us all speak Dutch' and only few diehards will not comply. Frisian is allowed, and its use must be possible, but other mechanisms are doing the work of constraining its use.

The well-known concept of *diglossia* may still be of some use to describe the relationship between Frisian and Dutch. Application of the concept is a matter of some debate among scholars of the Frisian language situation (Gorter, 1993: 24–7). It is clear that the older static 'division of functions' between the two languages has given way to new patterns. There used to be some sort of stable diglossia relationship, where Dutch was the higher and more prestigious language, and Frisian was the language of the home and of the family. Today Dutch enters into and cannot be kept out of the intimate spheres of the home, friends, family and neighbourhood. At the same time Frisian seeks to 'conquer' some of the higher domains of education, media and public administration. Frisian has made inroads in areas where it was not used 50 years ago. This implies that it is far less clear what language to use, at what moment in time, or who is going or not going to use Frisian. Dutch is the language that is taken for granted, Frisian is the marked language most, but not all, of the time. Conscious speakers of Frisian or RLS activists may find themselves frequently in a situation of 'competing bilingualism'. However, as a written language Frisian has remained quite marginal, thus there is still a diglossic distribution between spoken and written language functions. A number of structural power processes work against the use of Frisian. This is not only at the level of society as a whole, but also in personal interaction between people. It implies at the same time that, in these conflicts between the two language groups, some positive tensions are also created that lead to more dynamism in society, a dynamism which is lacking in monolingual societies.

Notes

1. The province of Friesland has roughly 340,000 mother-tongue speakers of Frisian or 460,000 inhabitants who claim to have at least 'reasonable proficiency'. Respectively 55% and 74% of 621,000 inhabitants (1 January 1999). Take note, these percentages are based on survey-research among the population of 12 years and older from 1994. The sample size was 1368 successful interviews.
2. Fishman's chapter in the original RLS book on Frisian (and Basque) was based on visits to Friesland in 1982, 1983 and 1989 (Fishman, 1991: 183). Mine is based

on (almost) continuous presence as a professional sociologist of language, working for the Fryske Akademy (and since 1994 part-time for the University of Amsterdam). Fishman's chapter was translated into Frisian and published in the scientific journal of the Fryske Akademy, *It Beaken* (jrg 53, 1991, nr 3/4, pp. 120–49). Comments were added by Jansma, Jelsma, and Van Rijn and by Van der Plank (pp. 150–60). Even though *It Beaken* has a circulation of 3000, to my knowledge, it did not attract any further response.

3. In cooperation with the European Parliament and the Ministry for Culture of Luxembourg; based on a 'need for improved communication'.

4. The Mercator Education project is concerned with information, documentation and research in the field of education involving autochthonous minority languages in the European Union. It is part of a network including Mercator Media and Mercator Legislation. For further information: www.fa.knaw.nl\mercator.

5. There are eight member states of the Council of Europe, thus far, that have ratified: Finland, Norway, Hungary, the Netherlands, Croatia, Liechtenstein, Switzerland and Germany.

6. From this list it becomes clear that certain variants that were earlier regarded as dialects have now been officially declared (regional) languages.

7. One point of caution is in place: the 71% comes from the sample by Pietersen where Frisian may have been somewhat oversampled. Due to random draw he did not include a number of municipalities where less Frisian has traditionally been spoken, whereas in 1980 and 1994 all municipalities were represented proportionally.

8. Although right next door to the university building in the centre of Amsterdam there is an arts gallery cum antiques and books shop that is literally called the 'Embassy of Friesland' (*Ambassade van Friesland*).

References

Dijk, K.J. van (1987) Language policy in Fryslân: Diverging concepts. *International Journal of the Sociology of Language* 64, 37–45.

Feitsma, A. (1984) Interlingual communication Dutch-Frisian, a model for Scotland? In D. Strauss and H.W. Drescher (eds) *Scottish Language and Literature, Medieval and Renaissance* (pp. 55–62). Frankfurt.

Fishman, J.A. (1991) *Reversing Language Shift* (in particular the chapter: The Cases of Basque and Frisian). Clevedon: Multilingual Matters.

Gorter, D. (1993) *Taal fan klerken en klanten*. Ljouwert/Leeuwarden: Fryske Akademy.

Gorter, D. *et al.* (1984) *Taal yn Fryslân*. Ljouwert: Fryske Akademy.

Gorter, D. and Jonkman, R.J. (1994) Taal op it wurk fan provinsjale amtenaren. Ljouwert: Fryske Akademy.

Gorter, D. and Jonkman, R.J. (1995a) Enkele veranderingsprocessen binnen de taalverhoudingen in Friesland. In E. Huls and J. Klatter-Folmer (eds) *Artikelen van de Tweede Sociolinguïstische Conferentie* (pp. 217–28) Tilburg.

Gorter, D. and Jonkman, R.J. (1995b) *Taal yn Fryslân: op 'e nij besjoen*. Ljouwert/Leeuwarden: Fryske Akademy.

Jansma, L,G., Jelsma, G.H. and van Rijn, J.G. (1991) It fuortbestean fan de Fryske taalminderheid. *It Beaken*, jrg 53, nr 3/4, 150–55.

Jong, S. de, and Riemersma, A.M.J. (1994) *Taalpeiling yn Fryslân.* Ljouwert/ Leeuwarden: Fryske Akademy.

Mak, G. (1997) *Hoe God verdween uit Jorwerd.* Amsterdam: Atlas.

Pietersen, L. (1969) *De Friezen en hun taal.* Drachten: Laverman.

Plank, P. van der (1991) De ferhâlding tusken taalpolityk, aktivisme en boppelaach yn Fryslân. *It Beaken,* jrg 53, nr 3/4, 156–60.

Schmidt, A. (1997) Die friesische Sprache im Verwaltungsverfahren und vor Gericht-Neuregelungen in den Niederländen zur Förderung einer Minderheitensprache. *Europa Ethnica,* 1–2, 54 jrg, 30–9.

Vaart, J.H.P. van der (1999) Boerderijen en platteland in verandering. Ljouwert/ Leeuwarden: Fryske Akademy.

Ytsma, J. (1995) *Frisian as First and Second Language.* Ljouwert/Leeuwarden: Fryske Akademy.

Ytsma, J. (1999) Tweetaligheid bij kleuters in Friesland. In E. Huls and B. Weltens (eds) *Artikelen van de derde sociolinguïstische conferentie* (pp. 497–508). Delft: Eburon.

Zondag, K. (ed.) (1993) *Bilingual Education in Friesland (Facts and Prospects).* Ljouwert/Leeuwarden: GCO-Fryslân.

Chapter 10

Reversing Language Shift: The Case of Basque

M.-J. AZURMENDI, E. BACHOC and F. ZABALETA

Fishman's 1991 publication, *Reversing Language Shift* (RLS), marked an important milestone in the sociology of languages and linguistic groups. It was also important for Euskara (the Basque language) and for the *Euskaldun* (Basque speaking) group, included in his RLS model. This work has several aims. One is to describe the situation of Euskara in 1999, to compare it with Fishman's 1991 description and to establish its evolution in the 1990s. Another goal is to diagnose the situation of Euskara according to the RLS model.

This discussion predominantly takes on the sociological theoretical perspective of the 'graded intergenerational disruption scale in eight stages' (GIDS), Fishman's RLS model (1991). It will attempt to show some empirical information reflecting the present situation of Euskara today and its development in recent years. There are several descriptive studies to refer to, most of them fragmentary and dispersed. However, rare are the ones that apply a theoretical model and a general perspective for the different situations in the Basque Country. In this sense, Fishman's 1991 paper on The Case of Basque was something of a first with respect to Euskara. The main sources will be the results of the following two empirical studies: *Encuesta Sociolingüística de Euskal Herria: La continuidad del Euskara I* (A Sociolinguistic Survey of the Basque Country: The Continuity of Euskara I) (Basque Government, 1991) (ES-1991) and the *Encuesta Sociolingüística de Euskal Herria: La continuidad del Euskara II* (A Sociolinguistic Survey of the Basque Country: The Continuity of Euskara II) (Basque Government, 1996) (ES-1996). Both surveys have the same empirical design and cover all three Basque political territories: the Basque Autonomous Community (BAC), the Navarrese Autonomous Community (NAC) and Iparralde (Basque territories within France); this will simplify comparison between the data offered. Only bibliographical references directly related to data and empirical results having to do with Euskara will be cited.

The Social Situation of Euskara in the 1990s

Territorialisation of the Basque Country

It may be useful here to remind readers of the Basque Country's political and territorial differences, being divided between Spain and France. In Spain the southern Basque Country is further broken down into two Autonomous Communities: the BAC comprises the territories of Araba, Bizkaia and Gipuzkoa, and the NAC, the territory of Nafarroa (Navarre). Each of these political divisions has its own government and parliament (as of 1979 in the BAC and 1980 in the NAC) and therefore each applies its own linguistic policies. The French northern Basque Country, or Iparralde, is made up of the Basque territories of Benafarroa, Lapurdi and Zuberoa, where they are not recognised officially as a group, nor are they any kind of political–administrative unit within France, and, therefore, cannot apply linguistic policies of their own. (In Fishman, 1991, a map of the Basque Country can be seen in figure 6.1, p. 151, and in figure 6.2, p. 153.) This political-territorial division is directly reflected in the situation of Euskara.

In the BAC, the Basic Law for the Normalisation of the Basque Language (1982) set down a single linguistic plan for its three territories, designing a single Euskara recovery and normalisation plan. It is based on the shared official status of the two languages: Euskara and Spanish. This joint official status opens the doors to equal formal treatment for both languages. The official Autonomous Community status foments the recovery and normalisation of Euskara throughout the BAC.

In the NAC, the Law of the Basque Language (1986), establishes three linguistic areas, and creates a different linguistic policy for each. In the Euskara-speaking area, lightly populated and rural, approximately 75% of the inhabitants are *Euskaldunes* (Euskara speakers). Linguistic policy calls for official status for both Euskara and Spanish in this area and its approach is somewhere between maintenance and recovery of Euskara. The non-Euskara-speaking area is more populated, semi-rural and somewhat industrial. Here, the presence of Euskara is not formally recognised and therefore there is no linguistic policy. The official position with respect to Euskara here fluctuates between tolerance and prohibition. Finally, the mixed area around the capital of Iruñea/Pamplona is the most important quantitatively, as it accounts for more than half of Navarre's total population. Qualitatively it is the most active and innovative, dedicated to industry, trade and services. Approximately 15% of the population are

Euskaldunes and there is a linguistic policy which supports Euskara to a certain degree.

In addition to the official linguistic policies in the BAC and the NAC, there is also the Spanish central government´s policy. Here, only Spanish is recognised as the official language of the country, although it allows each Autonomous Community having its 'own language' to establish shared official status and to develop its own internal linguistic policy.

In France there is no official recognition of any language other than French (specifically laid down in the 1994-revision of the French Constitution), nor of any cultural-linguistic group other than the French. Hence, the official position in Iparralde with respect to Euskara is either prohibition or tolerance. This means that virtually all of the activity related to the promotion and recovery of Euskara stems from voluntary initiative, as can be seen in primary education, road signs, songs and books, folk expressions, etc. In 1994 the semi-official Institut Culturel Basque / Euskal Kultur Erakundea (the Basque Cultural Institute) was created and became the most important organisation for the promotion of Euskara.

Table 10.1 shows the percentage of *Euskaldunes* (Basque speakers) in the different Basque territories in 1991 (ES-1991) and 1996 (ES-1996), with an end to establishing Euskara loss or recovery trends.

Table 10.1 implies the degree of loss suffered by Euskara, and, as a consequence, its status as minority language within the Basque Country itself. Various factors confirm this loss: there are virtually no Basque-speaking monolinguals, the majority of the population is *Erdaldun* monolingual (Spanish-speaking or French-speaking only) and furthermore, the Euskaldunes are almost all bilingual. But what is most important now is to point out the trends between 1991 and 1996. Similar to what was seen in the 1980s, these trends show an increase in Euskaldunes, particularly in the BAC but also in the NAC. However, there has been a decrease in Iparralde. The differences between the three Basque political territories are clear. The greatest rate of recovery of Euskara in the BAC is interpreted, at least in part, as a consequence of a linguistic policy at aiming recovery and normalisation of Euskara. In the NAC, recovery of Euskara also took place, in spite of the different linguistic policies there. However, in Iparralde there was a rise in the Euskara-loss rate due, in part, to the fact that voluntary initiative efforts promoting Euskara are not enough. They do not make up for the lack of an official linguistic policy to foment Euskara, and do not suffice even to maintain the language.

These different results tend to be interpreted as reflections of the different degrees of the Basque linguistic group's political power and self-government in the three Basque territories. That is, if we go back to the

Table 10.1 Linguistic competence in Euskara and/or Erdara, by political territories, in 1991 and 1996 (absolute and %)

	1991				1996			
	Total	*BAC*	*NAC*	*Iparralde*	*Total*	*BAC*	*NAC*	*Iparralde*
Euskara Monolinguals	23,500	17,900	2,700	2,900	12,400	9,800	1,100	1,500
	1.0	1.0	0.7	1.4	0.5	0.6	0.6	0.7
Active Bilinguals	505,200	401,500	37,500	66,200	534,100	438,400	41,000	54,700
	21.4	23.1	8.9	32.7	22.0	24.7	9.4	25.7
Passive Bilinguals	182,700	148,700	19,300	14,700	352,900	290,200	42,800	19,800
	8.4	8.5	4.6	7.0	14.5	16.3	9.8	9.3
Erdara Monolinguals	1,659,800	1,173,500	361,200	125,100	1,528,700	1,040,000	352,300	136,400
	69.9	67.4	85.9	58.8	63.0	58.5	80.6	64.2
	2,371,200	1,741,600	420,700	208,900	2,428,100	1,778,500	437,200	212,400
	100	100	100	100	100	100	100	100

(*Source*: Sociolinguistic Survey, 1991 and 1996; ES-1991, ES-1996.)
Euskara = Basque language; Erdara = Spanish (in BAC and NAC) or French (in Iparralde); BAC = Basque Autonomous Community (Spain); NAC = Navarrese Autonomous Community (Spain); Iparralde = Basque territories (France)

theory of relative power or relative ethnolinguistic vitality to explain this situation, we would have to underline the importance of 'institutional backing and control' (Azurmendi, 1998), in stimulating Euskara loss/ recovery. This interpretation relates to and/or reinforces other political demands pertaining to power and greater self-rule. Some of these demands include changing the Spanish and French Constitutions, recognising Basque decision-making powers, unification of the Basque territories into a single political and administrative entity, and even codependence or political independence within the framework of the European Union, etc.

The cultural-linguistic heterogeneity of the Basque Country

The Basque Country reveals a great deal of internal heterogeneity in terms of history, demographics, socioeconomics, language, culture and ideology. This heterogeneity is important in order to explain the processes of the loss and recovery of Euskara in each of the eight stages suggested in the GIDS model. This chapter will show some of the aspects of this cultural–linguistic heterogeneity derived mainly from its situation of contact between two ethnic groups: on the one hand we have the autochthonous indigenous group of the Basque Country, those who make it possible to continue talking about the 'case of Basque' and, on the other, the Spanish-origin group, in the BAC and the NAC, or of French origin in Iparralde. In the BAC, the most densely populated Basque political territory and the one taking in the highest proportion of immigrants, approximately half of today's population is of first- and second-generation Spanish origin (Ruiz de Olabuenaga & Blanco, 1994). The level of cultural–linguistic integration of these people in the Basque Country, for a variety of reasons, has been very poor. Repercussion in the present-day situation of Euskara has been substantial, as can be seen in Table 10.2.

The data in Table 10.2 shows a disturbing situation from the point of view of the intergenerational transmission of Euskara. This transmission seems to be moderately successful in the case of natives (born in the Basque Country) whose parents are also natives, but not otherwise.

All in all, ES-1991 results show the prevailing sociodemographic characteristics of the four linguistic types taken into consideration, both as a whole and by political territories. These characteristics are as follows:

- The 'monolingual *Euskaldunes*' (Euskara speakers) and the 'active bilinguals' (the most significant linguistic types in terms of Euskara transmission) are over 35 (64%), almost always natives (97%), speak Euskara as their first language (L1) (86%), live primarily in the BAC (79%) and in the territory of Gipuzkoa (46%),

Table 10.2 Linguistic competence in Euskara and/or Erdara, according to ethnographic origin and by political territories, in 1991(%)

		Natives (Born in the Basque Country)				Spanish immigrants (First generation)
		Total	Native parents	Native father/mother	Immigrant parents	
Euskara Monolinguals	Total	1	2	0	0	0
	BAC	1	2	0	0	0
	NAC	1	1	0	0	0
	Iparralde	1	2	0	0	0
Active Bilinguals	Total	21	38	10	4	1
	BAC	23	46	12	4	1
	NAC	9	16	2	1	0
	Iparralde	33	50	12	3	3
Passive Bilinguals	Total	8	9	12	12	2
	BAC	9	10	14	15	2
	NAC	5	3	2	4	4
	Iparralde	7	10	12	4	1
Erdara Monolinguals	Total	70	51	78	83	97
	BAC	67	42	74	81	97
	NAC	86	80	96	95	96
	Iparralde	59	38	76	94	96
Total/political territory:		100	100	100	100	100

(Source: Sociolinguistic Survey, 1991; ES-1991).
Euskara = Basque language; Erdara = Spanish (in BAC and NAC) or French (in Iparralde); BAC = Basque Autonomous Community (Spain); NAC = Navarrese Autonomous Community (Spain); Iparralde = Basque territories (France); Total/political territories = total in each political territory: BAC, CAN or Iparralde

live in relatively high Euskara-speaking sociolinguistic areas (60%
in areas with a proportion of Euskara speakers of more than 45%),
have a basic or high school education (57%), mainly work for somebody else or are retired (55%) and have a medium to lower-medium
socioprofessional level (61%).

- The 'passive bilinguals' are young people between 16 and 24 years of
  age (46%), native (63%), speak Spanish as L1 (76%), live mainly in the
  BAC (82%) and in the territory of Bizkaia (40%), live in low Euskara-
  speaking sociolinguistic areas (54% live in areas with a proportion of
  Euskara speakers lower than 20%), have a basic or high school education (64%), work for somebody else or are students (68%), and have a
  medium-low to medium socioprofessional level (63%).

- The 'monolingual *Erdaldunes*' (non-Basque speakers: Spanish- or
  French-speaking) are over 35 (64%), are both immigrants (40%) and
  natives (39%), speak Spanish as their L1 (95%), also live in the BAC
  (71%) and in the territory of Bizkaia (44%), live in relatively low
  Euskara-speaking sociolinguistic areas (79% in areas with a proportion of Euskara speakers lower than 20%), have basic education
  (46%), work for somebody else or are housewives (60%), and have a
  medium-low or low socioprofessional level (58%).

The results of ES-1996 would seem to indicate a relatively similar situation, although the overall tone is somewhat more favourable towards
Euskara.

One of the limitations of both ES-1991 and ES-1996 lies in the fact that
they only take into account the over–16s. Therefore, they do not reflect the
most important outcome of the Euskara recovery process, the result of the
educational system efforts in the BAC and the NAC, as demonstrated by
the Censuses of 1981 and 1991.

The intergenerational transmission of Euskara as an L1

As proposed in the GIDS model, a language can be considered to be
undergoing a clear process of recovery when it succeeds in being informally transmitted as an L1; that is, through the child's earliest and most
immediate home-family-neighbourhood socialisation process. For this
reason in ES-1991 and ES-1996, which have tried to apply the Fishman
model, territoriality has been stressed for the purpose of studying the
impact of the linguistic policies applied in the different Basque political
territories. The mother tongue or first language (L1) has also been taken
into account as well as the sociodemographic characteristics of people
who have started speaking Euskara, and those who have stopped.

One of the most positive changes seen over the last two decades has been the reversal in the process of the loss of Euskara transmission as an L1 within the family. This has particularly been the case in the BAC, and has also occurred in the NAC, although not in Iparralde. According to ES-1991 this process reversal was seen in the 16 and 24-year-old group in the BAC, meaning that it precedes the effect of the linguistic policy carried out since the 1980s. In the NAC the reversal was seen in 3–15-year-olds as a result, or at least partly so, of the linguistic policy developed there (Table 10.3).

In terms of the transmission of Euskara as an L1, Table 10.3 shows huge differences between the BAC and the NAC, on one hand, and Iparralde on the other. In the BAC and the NAC, with two Euskara-speaking parents Euskara is generally transmitted to children as an L1, this being particularly pronounced in the 1980s. In addition, Euskara is usually the only L1 transmitted. This situation is attributed to the impact of the linguistic policies in both Basque political territories, owing mainly to the increase in power and control of Basque institutions (Azurmendi, 1998) and to the priority of the educational systems in transmitting Euskara (Zabaleta, 1996). In Iparralde, the loss of this transmission is continual, as a consequence, at least in part, of the lack of a Euskara-fomenting linguistic policy.

ES-1996 results show the prevalent characteristics of the three linguistic groups depending on their L1:

- People whose L1 is Euskara are generally Basque Country natives, who have two Euskara-speaking parents; their family and social environment is largely Basque-speaking; they are highly interested in Euskara and are in favour of its promotion. To a lesser degree, they live in towns of less than 25,000 inhabitants and have an average age slightly higher than the population as a whole

- People who have two L1s, Euskara and Spanish, are Basque Country natives, only half of whom have two Euskara-speaking parents; their family and social environment is only partially Basque-speaking; they are interested in Euskara and are in favour of its promotion. Their average age is slightly lower than the population as a whole and, due to being younger, have a much higher educational level than the average population.

- People whose L1 is Spanish (78% of the population of the total Basque Country) are the sons and daughters of non-Euskara-speaking parents, one-third of whom are immigrants and nearly another third the children of immigrants; their family and social environment is

Table 10.3 Transmission of Euskara and/or Erdara, as first language (L1), in 1996 (%) (Read vertically)

	Euskara L1			Euskara and Erdara L1			Erdara L1		
	BAC	NAC	Iparralde	BAC	NAC	Iparralde	BAC	NAC	Iparralde
Age:									
25–34	16	6	16	5	2	7	79	92	77
16–24	17	6	11	5	1	10	78	93	79
3–15	22	8	6	8	4	14	70	88	80
Compet. Eusk. Parents:									
Both Eusk.-speaking	83	65	72	8	7	11	9	28	17
One Eusk.-speaking	19	15	11	18	14	10	63	72	79
Compet. Eusk. Parents with children 3–15:									
Both Eusk.-speaking	94	93	35	6	5	41	0	2	24
One Eusk.-speaking	50	44	5	38	37	39	12	20	56

(*Source:* Sociolinguistic Survey, 1996; ES-1996).
Euskara = Basque language; Erdara = Spanish (in BAC and NAC) or French (in Iparralde); L1 = first language; Compet. Eusk. = Competent in Euskara; Eusk.-sp. = Euskara-speaking; BAC = Basque Autonomous Community (Spain); NAC = Navarrese Autonomous Community (Spain); Iparralde = Basque territories (France)

largely Spanish-speaking; most of them live in towns of over ?
inhabitants, and a quarter are against promoting the use of Euskara.

The intergenerational transmission of Euskara as an L2

The greatest efforts made in favour of Euskara have always been chan-
nelled through the educational system. One of the most interesting effects
was the creation of *ikastolas* (schools in Euskara for pre-school, primary and
secondary education) in the 1960s. These schools became the most important transmitters of Euskara as an L2. The other public school programmes
which were developed during the early 1980s in the BAC and the NAC
strengthened the tendency, leading to the possibility of different linguistic
models of teaching in these phases:

- 'Model D': material taught in Euskara, with Spanish as an additional
  subject, following the experience of the *ikastolas*.
- 'Model B': bilingual.
- 'Model A': taught in Spanish, with Euskara as a subject.

'Model X', which uses Spanish as the sole teaching language, was typical of
the pre-autonomy political era. In Iparralde, along with the voluntarily
instituted, Model D-type *ikastolas*, there have been signs of doors being
opened in the 1990s to the possibility of introducing Models A and B into
the public schools.

From the point of view of the transmission of Euskara, the most significant fact is the tendency towards pro-Euskara linguistic models, mainly in
the BAC at the pre-school and primary school levels. In the 1990–91 school
year each of the three linguistic models accounted for a third of the children. In the 1998–99 school year 56% of students studied under Model D,
31% under Model B and only 13% under Model A. In the same territory,
data for the 1998–99 school year indicates 37% of secondary students, 70%
of primary school students and 87% of pre-school students studying under
Models D and B (EUSTAT, 1998). The same trend, although weaker, can be
seen in the NAC and even in Iparralde. Table 10.4 (Etxeberria, 1999) shows
the present situation of the linguistic models.

One of the changes in the 1990s has been the incorporation of many of
the *ikastolas* into the public school system. This change has had positive
aspects, such as an increase of Euskara and Basque culture in the public
schools. However, it has also had negative aspects such as the presence of
pro-*Euskaldun* intragroup conflict between some of the more radical social
groups and the more moderate government of the BAC. This conflict
remains partially unresolved today.

Table 10.4 Schooling in the different linguistic models, in preschool, in the 1997–98 school year (%)

	BAC	NAC	Iparralde
Model D (in Euskara + Erdara subject)	55	25	5
Model B (Bilingual)	28		10
Model A (in Erdara + Euskara subject)	16	25	7
Model X (in Erdara)	1	50	78
	100	100	100

(*Source*: Etxeberria, 1999).
Euskara = Basque language; Erdara = Spanish (in BAC and NAC) or French (in Iparralde); BAC = Basque Autonomous Community (Spain); NAC = Navarrese Autonomous Community (Spain); Iparralde = Basque territories (France); Model D = Linguistic model in which schooling is done in Euskara with Erdara as a subject: preschool, primary and secondary stages; Model B = Linguistic model with schooling in Euskara and Erdara: preschool, primary and secondary stages; Model A = Linguistic model with schooling in Erdara, with Euskara as a subject: preschool, primary and secondary stages; Model X = Linguistic model with schooling in Erdara: preschool, primary and secondary stages

At the university level there has also been an increase in courses being taught in Euskara, especially at public universities. In the BAC, there has been a continual 2% annual increase. In the 1998–99 school year 33% of the nearly 65,000 students at the University of the Basque Country (UPV/EHU) studies totally or partially in Euskara. The II Plan for Normalisation of the Use of Euskara in the UPV/EHU (1999), which will be set in motion during the 1999–2000 school year, will increase the use of Euskara at all levels: teaching, lecturers, university materials, and so on. This tendency is still fairly weak at the Public University of Navarre in the NAC. The rise in the presence of Euskara at this level has served to increase its status and prestige and also to impel the modernisation of the corpus of Euskara and its adaptation to the world of science and technology.

At the university level, we must also mention the Udal Euskal Unibertsitatea (UEU, or Basque Summer University), which got underway in the mid-1960s thanks to voluntary initiative, and which was the first university experience totally in Euskara.

Basquisation and Euskara literacy in adults (aged 16 upwards)

This has been the most important goal after pre-university educational Basquisation, and has required the most amount of effort in terms of the linguistic policies applied in the BAC and the NAC. Parallel to the *ikastolas* and the UEU, *Euskaltegis* (centres specifically created to foster Basquisation and teach Euskara literacy to adults) first arose in the mid-1960s. They are centres for transmitting Euskara as a second language (L2) to adults. There is a growing number in the BAC, whereas in other Basque territories there are relatively few. In the BAC, the number of students in these centres has grown from 41,000 in the 1991–92 school year to almost 45,000 in 1995–96. (HABE, 1998; Arratibel, in press).

The prevailing sociodemographic characteristics of *Euskaltegi* students for the 1995–96 school year show that they are between 21 and 30 years of age (44.2%); are mostly women (63.9%); live in Gipuzkoa (the most Euskara-speaking territory) (55.7%); are university students (31.3%) or unemployed workers (25.2%); have a high school (36.7%) or university education (undergraduates, 22.5%); and are students of private officially approved *Euskaltegis* (which are therefore officially controlled and subsidised) (54%) (Arratibel, in press). Furthermore, most students starting the courses follow through to the end (83%), signing up each year until they reach the level of competence required for that level (Arratibel, 1999).

The Use of Euskara and its transmission

In the above sections we have described the situation as to the knowledge of Euskara. This is important, since without it, using the language would be impossible. But what is really important is to describe use *per se*, that is, the extent to which a person is capable of living in Euskara. This was obvious right from the start for the planners of Euskara recovery, both via official institutions with their linguistic policies, and via voluntary initiatives, especially in the BAC. The BAC Basic Law for the Normalisation of the Use of Euskara (1982) explicitly refers to the normalisation of the 'use' of Euskara. This is why in this analysis we must highlight use rather than knowledge alone (Table 10.5).

The results of Table 10.5 (ES-1996) show that Euskara speakers use Euskara to a larger extent in some environments than in others. It is important to remember that language-use norms in the Basque Country tend to linguistically accommodate non-Euskara speakers, meaning that if there is only one person who does not speak Euskara, the rest will switch to Spanish or French. As a result of this social norm, the use of Euskara in the different environments corresponds to the level of knowledge in the different environments: Euskara is better known where it is more often used. In addition, Euskara is proportionally used to a greater extent with children: parents with their children and teachers with their students,

Table 10.5 Use of Euskara and Erdara in different social environments (only for speakers of Euskara), by regions, in 1996(%) (read horizontally)

	BAC			NAC			Iparralde		
	Principally in Euskara	*In both Euskara and Erdara*	*Principally in Erdara*	*Principally in Euskara*	*In both Euskara and Erdara*	*Principally in Erdara*	*Principally in Euskara*	*In both Euskara and Erdara*	*Principally in Erdara*
FAMILY									
WITH: Mother	56	7	37	52	6	42	53	29	18
Father	53	6	42	47	6	47	56	22	22
Husband/wife	51	11	39	48	10	42	45	12	43
Children	73	12	15	65	11	24	37	16	48
AT HOME	48	18	34	46	16	38	35	22	44
COMMUNITY									
WITH: Friends	49	20	30	51	16	33	44	19	37
Merchants	48	17	36	39	10	51	21	15	64
At work	45	18	37	51	11	38	32	15	54
Market	78	7	7	68	6	26	73	14	14
Priest	74	10	10	67	4	29	64	15	21
SOCIETY									
IN: Banks	56	14	30	43	8	50	19	13	67
Town Hall	59	15	25	49	7	43	31	14	54
Child's teacher	85	7	8	76	6	18	21	11	68
Health Services	33	15	52	34	10	56	9	12	79

(*Source*: Sociolinguistic Survey, 1996; ES-1996)
Euskara = Basque language; Erdara = Spanish (in BAC and NAC) or French (in Iparralde); BAC = Basque Autonomous Community (Spain);
NAC = Navarrese Autonomous Community (Spain); Iparralde = Basque territories (France)

reflecting an awareness of the importance of the intergenerational transmission of Euskara.

Other results of ES-1996 underline the importance of the factors explaining the use of Euskara:

- Sociostructural and sociodemographic factors are the most significant, the most noteworthy of which are the density of Euskara speakers, in both sociolinguistic areas and spheres, and each individual's social network.
- Psycholinguistic factors are second in importance. The relative higher or lower linguistic competence in Euskara as compared to Spanish or French also determines the amount of Euskara used.
- Psychosocial factors (i.e. attitude or identity) are in third place.

These results appear to be consistent with others coming from different psychosociolinguistic research projects (SIADECO, 1991; Arratibel, 1999; García, 2000). These results are important for Euskara recovery planners.

The Psychosocial Situation of Euskara

It is useful to understand the social situation of Euskara, also from a psychosocial perspective. This is a more complex task owing to the amount and heterogeneity of the interpretations that exist today concerning Euskara. But this psychosocial perspective seems to be important in the case of Basque. Among other reasons is the fact that linguistic policies and planning attach more importance to the person than to the group, and are based on personal choice and will (Azurmendi, 1997a).

ES-1991 and ES-1996 looked at aspects such as interest, attitude, motivation and identity with respect to Euskara. Some of the results concerning attitudes are shown in Table 10.6.

These results show that attitudes are predominantly pro-Euskara in the BAC and Iparralde, while unfavourable in the NAC. However, favourable attitudes are on the rise in the NAC and in Iparralde, while the tendency is towards indifference (neither favourable nor unfavourable) in the BAC. In terms of the transmission of Euskara, it should be pointed out that the most favourable attitudes revolve around the idea that it is 'essential for all children to learn Euskara'.

The prevailing sociodemographic characteristics of the three attitudinal types obtained in ES-1996 are as follows:

- Nearly half of the people with pro-Euskara attitudes are Euskara-

Table 10.6 Attitudes promoting Euskara (Basque language), by political
territories, in 1991 and 1996 (%)

	1991				1996			
	BAC	NAC	Iparralde	Total	BAC	NAC	Iparralde	Total
(Very) favorable	52	23	45	47	46	38	49	45
Neither favourable nor disfavourable	30	24	41	30	38	30	39	37
(Very) unfavorable	19	54	14	24	16	32	13	18
	100	100	100	100	100	100	100	100

(Source: Sociolinguistic Survey, 1991 and 1996; ES-1991, ES-1996).
BAC = Basque Autonomous Community (Spain); NAC = Navarrese Autonomous Community (Spain); Iparralde = Basque territories (France)

speaking; they prefer having their children go to school under B
(bilingual) or D (Euskara) linguistic models; a third of them have
studied Euskara outside of school; most are Basque Country natives;
and half have a predominantly *Euskaldun* family and social environment.

- People with unfavourable attitudes are mostly *Erdaldunes* (non-
Euskara-speaking), with a predominantly *Erdaldun* family and social
environment; they mainly live in urban areas; their interest in
Euskara is scarce or non-existent; they generally intend to send their
children to B or D linguistic teaching models; and more than half are
immigrants or the children of immigrants.

- The sociolinguistic characteristics of people with neither favourable
nor unfavourable attitudes are fairly similar to the unfavourable-atti-
tude group, with the difference that their interest in Euskara is
greater.

Reversing Basque Shift, in Eight Stages

The following section will attempt to interpret the data presented in the
previous section, as well as other Euskara-related data, according to the
GIDS model in eight stages and to RLS (Fishman, 1991). Several questions
are emphasised in this model, including the importance of linguistic planning and of clarification of pre-existing ideology, the gradual nature of
linguistic loss and recovery processes, the centrality of intergenerational

transmission and the importance of voluntary initiatives along with official initiatives (government control and backing).

The ideology accompanying Euskara recovery

Explicit ideology has always accompanied the Euskara recovery process and becomes even more crucial as the process moves forward, as has been seen in the 1990s. With regard to the ideology coming from inside the Basque Country, different aspects can be seen in terms of previous ideological clarification and later ideological evolution. Two ideological macro-types can also be seen: favourable, or pro-Euskaldun and unfavourable, or anti-Euskaldun. Three sources can also be distinguished: voluntary initiative, official initiative (parliament, government and judicial) and semi-official initiative (political parties, labour unions, the Catholic Church, and so on). The two predominant issues are the final goals to be attained and the procedures to be used. The degree of homogeneity, versatility and dynamics is substantially greater in anti-Euskaldun than in the pro-Euskaldun ideology (Azurmendi, 1997b). Here, because of its repercussions on the ideology produced inside the Basque Country, we should also mention the generally anti-Euskaldun ideology coming from voluntary, official and semi-official initiatives originating outside the Basque Country. This leads us to consider ideology as both intra- and intergroup.

Previous ideological clarification, on the official level, was set down in the Spanish Constitution of 1978 and in the Autonomy Statutes of the BAC (1979) and the NAC (1980), although nothing similar exists in Iparralde. This clarification established Spanish as the only official language for the whole of Spain, and therefore the need for everyone to know it and use it, while the other languages within Spain could also be maintained and protected. It also states that the Autonomous Communities having their 'own languages' (such as Euskara in the BAC and the NAC) may recognise them as official languages, draw up legislation and establish linguistic policies for their protection and promotion. Another very different matter is the ideology accompanying the Euskara recovery process through the 1980s and 1990s.

The ideology seen in the last 20 years indicates a very heterogeneous situation, but could be divided into three more polarised groups, especially in the BAC (Azurmendi, 1997b):

- The most radically pro-Euskaldun ideology wants to see society-wide Euskara monolingualism throughout the Basque Country, and generalised individual multilingualism with regard to other languages (Spanish and/or French, English and others), plus the transmission of Euskara as L1. As far as the procedures to follow, it believes that using Euskara must be a necessity and an obligation, applied mainly to the younger population. This ideology stems from certain voluntary and semi-official initiatives from inside the Basque Country.

- The most radically anti-Euskaldun ideology wants to see society-wide Spanish monolingualism in the BAC and the NAC, or French in Iparralde, although it does make a few concessions to bilingualism. At the same time, it favours generalised individual multilingualism with regard to other languages (English, French/Spanish, etc., or Euskara). For this reason, the transmission of Spanish/French as L1 must be ensured by maintaining the compulsory nature of knowing and using Spanish/French. This ideology comes from some voluntary and semi-official initiatives, from inside the Basque Country, and also from all types of initiatives from outside the Basque Country.

- The symmetry ideology wants to see a balance between pro-Euskaldun and pro-Spanish/French. The idea is to overcome the ongoing conflict between languages and linguistic groups. The goals are symmetrical societal bilingualism in Euskara and Spanish/French, and generalised individual multilingualism (with regard to these two languages, English and others). It strives for both Euskara and Spanish/French to be transmitted as L1. The procedures to be followed involve ensuring the necessity and obligation of both languages, mainly by BAC autonomous official initiative (parliamentary and governmental), reflected in linguistic policy. This view also comes from some voluntary and semi-official initiatives from within the Basque Country.

Stages 8 and 7 on the GIDS (Graded Intergenerational Disruption Scale)

Stages 8 to 5 on the GIDS are the minimum needed to guarantee the natural intergenerational transmission of a language and ensure the RLS process. They are also the stages of diglossia consolidation, guaranteeing the use of Euskara at least in the spheres most closely related to people: the home-family-neighbourhood-community.

Stage 8 proposes reconstructing Xish (Euskara) and adult acquisition of XSL (Euskara as L2). And Stage 7 proposes the cultural interaction in Xish primarily involving the community based older generation. The most significant difference between these two stages lies in the intergenerational transmission of the language. Goals are of two kinds. From the point of view of corpus planning of Euskara: reunification, standardisation and modernisation of Euskara, and at the same time recovery and revitalisation of cultural tradition in Euskara. And from the point of view of status planning: reunification, recovery and revitalisation of the use and users of Euskara. It can be said that these two stages are being met successfully, particularly in the BAC. The situation pointed out by Fishman in 1991 (pp. 158–61) has improved in the 1990s. Below are some examples of this, referring particularly to the BAC.

In terms of the corpus of Euskara, in the 1990s, aspects such as 'recovery' and 'authentification' were emphasised through an historic dictionary. 'Modernisation' was also underlined via specific dictionaries for different areas (media, administration, commerce, finance, etc.), and by means of specific dictionaries for the different fields of knowledge (science and technology). In addition to the semi-official institutions already in existence (Euskaltzaindia, UZEI, ELHUYAR, etc.), new ones have been created, such as the University of the Basque Country (UPV/EHU) Institute of Euskara, in 1998. Concerns for the quality and use of Euskara have mounted, bringing about the need for new research.

With regard to the status of Euskara, initiatives already in existence have been stepped up. Publications in Euskara, although still predominantly literary or educational, amount to over 1000 books per year (according to the Annual Basque Book, Record and Video Fair of Durango, in the BAC). Literature is attracting more readers and therefore has become less dependent on government subsidies. In fact, Basque literature is gaining international prestige and acclaim, with works often being translated into other languages. New, mostly monthly, bulletins, are being put out either in Euskara or bilingually, such as the Council on Linguistic Policy's *Berripapera*, the UPV/EHU's *Campus*, Eusko Ikaskuntza's *Asmoz ta Jakitez*, the Donostia-San Sebastián Town Council's *Arkupe*, etc. In terms of daily newspapers, the *Egunkaria* is written totally in Euskara and Euskara is being increasingly used in the remaining papers, particularly in the new paper, *Gara*. Radio and TV audiences in Euskara have also risen. All of this has added to the status of Euskara, both inside and outside the Basque Country.

In sum, it can be said that these efforts are being maintained and augmented in the BAC, have been initiated in the NAC, and are still in their initial stages in Iparralde. All of these initiatives encourage the use of Euskara in community environments, and therefore act as a bridge between these stages and Stage 6 on the GIDS.

Stage 6 on the GIDS

This is the stage concerned with intergenerational oralcy and demo-graphic concentration in the home-family-neighbourhood-community: the basis of mother-tongue transmission. The home-family-neighbour-hood-community environment can be viewed apart from the school environment. All of these spheres have undergone a certain amount of change in the 1990s, particularly in the BAC. One of these changes concerns the mounting interdependence between all of these spheres of daily life and linguistic behaviour.

In the school system, two new experiences should be highlighted. The first, not compulsory but commonplace, is that of children beginning pre-school at the age of two in Euskara. The second is the teaching of English at the age of four, still within the pre-school stage. Both of these are societal initiatives which originates in 1995 as experimental projects in the *ikastolas*. Their main goals were to facilitate the transmission of Euskara, almost as an L1, and to acquire English as an L2, in an attempt to reach maximum levels of linguistic and communicative competence. The idea was to ensure the intergenerational transmission of Euskara as an L1, in addition to attaining generalised individual multilingualism. After a positive evaluation of both experiences, these projects will be set into motion on a broader scale as of the 1999–2000 school year, in the rest of the *ikastolas*, as well as in the public school system; hence they will reach virtually all children.

These innovations in the area of education will boost the current trend of interdependence between education and the home-neighbourhood-community sphere, with respect to the intergenerational transmission of Euskara. Families consist less and less of captive audiences, and share more and more with other areas in the initial socialisation of children. There are increasingly more curricular and extra-curricular activities, especially in pre-school (2-to-5-year-olds) and primary school (6-to-12-year-olds). All of this encourages multiple parent-children, parent-teacher, parent-parent and children–children relationships. The general population is aware of the importance of early, generalised Basquisation. Therefore, we can predict success in these joint initiatives, at least in the BAC. All of these process are not yet available in the NAC and are unheard of in Iparralde.

As far as teenagers and children are concerned, awareness in fostering the use of Euskara has also grown. One example of this is the increase in activities in Euskara organised for young people and adults by the govern-ment-sponsored *casas de cultura*, or cultural centres. The 1990s have seen these cultural centres being opened in virtually every city neighbourhood, and in small municipalities, for the purpose of organising cultural, sports and leisure activities. But these initiatives have been both a blessing and a curse to daily life in Euskara and to intergenerational transmission. In fact, so far they have been more effective in ensuring the generalised transmission of Spanish than of Euskara.

There are other aspects introduced by Fishman (1991) in Stage 6, related to daily life and the immediate environment, such as linguistic landscape: place-names and anthroponymy, street and road signs, shop and building names, advertising, and so on. These aspects of the recovery process of Euskara have not yet seen much progress.

To summarise, this stage is clearly being focused upon in the BAC, although not to the same extent in all spheres. In the NAC, its implementation is still weak. In Iparralde, sadly enough, Euskara continues to decline, except in terms of linguistic landscape, where Euskara has made its biggest strides.

Stage 5 on the GIDS

This is the stage of school for literacy acquisition, for the old and for the young, and not in lieu of compulsory education by focusing on intragroup resources and processes with respect to its acquisition, its content and its control. Therefore, these goals are, to a certain extent, the same as the goals in previous stages. In terms of these goals, too, the situation of Euskara has improved in the 1990s.

One of the problems detected in the 1990s research deals with the level of competence in Euskara. The increase in Basque-speakers is one thing, but the increase in competent Basque-speakers is another altogether (Tables 10.1 and 10.2). This is important because it is directly related to the use of Euskara. Recalling information offered previously, the results of ES-1991 and ES-1996 show that Euskara is used when competence in Euskara is equal to or greater than that of competence in *Erdara* (Spanish or French). But ES-1996 also shows that out of 21% of the active bilinguals in the Basque Country (Table 10.1), 32% are balanced bilinguals and 30% are bilinguals with predominance in Euskara, while 38% are bilinguals with predominance in *Erdara*.

Etxeberria (1999), after analysing the 39 studies done on pre-university education in the BAC, comes to some alarming conclusions. Only linguistic Model D guarantees a good enough level of competence in primary education to be able to go on studying under Model D in secondary school. Model B ensures quite a good level of competence in primary education, but not good enough to go on to Model D in secondary school. Following Model A in primary school, students 'barely reach a rudimentary colloquial level of Euskara and are generally incapable of using Euskara as a work tool in the classroom' (Etxeberria, 1999: 218). However, none of these linguistic models influence the acquisition of Spanish, whose high level of competency is always guaranteed. For this reason, after 15 years of experience in linguistic educational models, there has been a need to revise and change educational planning. The innovation of beginning preschool in Euskara at the age of two and teaching English at four can be seen as one way of responding to this need.

In the process of adult Basquisation a similar problem was detected. Adults acquire a higher level of linguistic competence in written skills (reading and writing) than in oral skills (understanding and speaking) (Arratibel, 1999), typical in the formal acquisition of foreign L2 languages. This means that learners are not taking full advantage of the close proximity of Euskara, and hence, are not using informal language acquisition processes.

In short, the achievements in Stage 5 are not very favourable as far as natural intergenerational Euskara transmission is concerned. In addition, Stage 5 on the GIDS is being carried out currently only in the BAC, is just getting underway in the NAC and barely exists in Iparralde.

Stage 4 on the GIDS

Stage 4 is the beginning of the second phase of the RLS process. The goal in this stage is also related to the educational system. Fishman points out two types of schooling: Type 4a consists of schooling in lieu of compulsory education and substantially under Xish (Euskara) curricular and staffing control. Whereas Type 4b, offers public schools for Xish children, providing some instruction via Xish, but substantially under Yish (Spanish) curricular and staffing control. In Type 4a the task lies in making sure that the efforts and achievements of Basque schools, the *ikastolas* in this case, spread into extracurricular activities, so that intergenerational transmission can take place. In Type 4b, the difficulty lies in the fact that the *Euskaldun* linguistic group needs the approval of the other linguistic group, which continues to be the ultimate decision-maker in all important educational aspects. These goals partially overlap with the goals of previous stages on the GIDS.

The situation described by Fishman in the 1980s with regard to Euskara (1991: 167–73) has improved in the 1990s. The goals for Type 4a are being implemented as are the 4b goals, although the latter are always controversial. For this reason, the difficulties described still exist. This is the situation in the BAC. In the other Basque territories, the Euskara recovery process, in terms of these goals, is still weak and uncertain.

Stage 3 on the GIDS

Stage 3 pursues the use of Euskara in the lower work sphere (outside of the Basque neighbourhood-community), involving interaction between the Basque group and the Spanish group. Fishman distinguishes two different situations. First, there are the companies controlled by the *Euskaldun* group, but revolving around the needs of the *Erdaldun* group, in which internal communication can be carried out in Euskara. Then there are the companies controlled by the *Erdaldun* group, serving the needs of the *Euskaldun* group; the *Euskaldun* group can always fall back on 'the customer is always right' principle to get the conversation to switch to Euskara. Fishman's differentiation is important in terms of analysis, but in the case of Basque is difficult to use empirically due to the predominance of more varied situations.

The situation of Euskara described by Fishman (1991: 173) has improved in the 1990s. The first experiences planned for Basquisation and / or to boost the use of Euskara as a work-sphere language in private industry, began in the 1990s, once again in the BAC. The Québec model of self-managed linguistic planning was followed. The first experiences are being carried out in high-density Basque-speaking sociolinguistic areas so as to facilitate success. The companies are relatively large and impor-tant so as to be able to set an example for other companies. Some of the companies selected belong to the Mondragón Grupo, a truly substantial corporate group in the BAC.

The goals in this stage involve difficulties of all types: inertia, pragmatic issues, social rules regarding the choice of which language to use, and so on. For example, from the ideological point of view, the consideration of Euskara as a 'working language' is still a matter of debate. The *Euskaldun* linguistic group demands this, while the *Erdaldun* linguistic group either rejects or simply tolerates it, with the excuse that it could foster discrimina-tion and intergroup conflict.

This stage is still in the initial phase. The General Plan for the Revitalisation of Euskara (Eusko Jaurlaritza / Gobierno Vasco, 1998), for the BAC, and the General Plan for the Normalisation of Euskara (Euskararen Gizarte Erakundeen Kontseilua, 1999), for the Basque Country, include plans for incorporating Basque into the workplace.

Stage 2 on the GIDS

Stage 2 involves the implementation of Euskara in lower governmental services and mass media but not in the higher spheres of either. This is an interesting stage, because it means taking part in the world of politics, of institutional support and control, and participating in making decisions about and having authority over the distribution of available public resources. But it is also a difficult stage because it is basically a philosoph-ical/ideological position and, as such, it requires constant philosophical/ ideological restatement and updating if it is to remain effective.

The situation described by Fishman (1991: 174–75) has also improved, at least in the BAC, with a significant presence of pro-Euskaldun political parties. However, this is not the case in the NAC, where there is a majority of anti-Euskaldun political parties. This process has not even gotten underway in Iparralde. However, the advances attained have also given rise to an increase in polarised ideologies. In the pro-*Euskaldun* group, the conflict is between the more radical voluntarily initiated positions and the more moderate, coming from both voluntary and official initiatives. The recent 1999 agreement signed jointly by the BAC's Council on Linguistic Policy and the voluntarily-initiated Euskararen Gizarte Eradundeen Kontseilua, can be seen as a giant step toward internal social consensus. The anti-*Euskaldun* group wants to remain the dominant group and assimi-late the Euskaldun group; therefore any advance in the recovery process of Euskara is viewed as contrary to their aims

Stage 1 on the GIDS

Stage 1 seeks some use of Euskara in higher level educational, occupa-tional, governmental and media efforts, but without the additional safety provided by political independence. This is the final stage of the GIDS model, and represents the highest level of cultural autonomy (but not inde-pendence), for Euskara and the *Euskaldun* group. Once more we would have to say that there has been progress, especially in the BAC. But this does not necessarily mean the end of RLS problems, neither from the stand-point of the pro-*Euskaldun* group, which may ultimately aspire to be the only official language and culture in the Basque Country, nor from the point of view of the anti-*Euskaldun* group, which may not want to relin-quish Spanish linguistic and cultural dominance over Euskara.

Conclusion

Summing up, the following conclusions can be reached from this presentation:

(1) The process of recovery of Euskara has moved forward in the 1990s, although it has not been equal throughout all of the Basque political territories. Although some new initiatives have been started, most advances were based on initiatives already developed in the previous

decade. The most important results have more to do with the acquisition of Euskara than with its use, mainly due to education (pre-university and university), and also through the Basquisation of adults. From the point of view of the GIDS model, there has been more quantitative than qualitative progress.

(2)   The GIDS model proposed by Fishman (1991), as a gradual process in two phases and eight stages, has only been applied in part in the case of Basque. The process followed for the recovery and normalisation of Euskara has not been entirely linear, but rather spiral, and with some overlapping. That is, goals corresponding to different stages on the GIDS model have been pursued simultaneously. The GIDS model has been followed in terms of establishing priority goals for the recovery and normalisation of the use of Euskara in the home-family-neighbourhood-community spheres, and the intergenerational transmission of Euskara as an L1. These goals have been present throughout the entire Euskara recovery process. There are different reasons for this, some of which have already pointed out in this paper. But there is still not enough research on the matter.

(3)   The GIDS model places emphasis on intragroup process: Xish-to-Xmen. But in the case of Basque, the reality is more complex, both in the make-up of the groups and in the processes, which are both intragroup and intergroup. With regard to Euskara (Xish), in the Basque Country there is the *Euskaldun* (Xmen) group and the Erdaldun (Ymen) group. But there is also the pro-Euskaldun group (Xmen+Ymen-via-Xish) and the anti-*Euskaldun* group (Xmen+Ymen-via-Yish). Both types of groups are interwoven and partially overlapping. In addition, from outside the Basque Country there is also an anti-*Euskaldun* group (Ymen-via-Yish). This is why the relationships to be considered are so complex. With regard to the recovery of Euskara, the most pertinent groups are the pro-Euskaldun and the anti-Euskaldun groups, and not simply the Euskaldun and the Erdaldun (non-Euskaldun) groups.

(4)   The GIDS is predominantly sociological, although concessions are made to the psychosocial perspective, especially through the importance placed on identity. In this sense, the experience of the case of Basque fits well in this model. In spite of this, it seems that the psychosocial perspective plays a more important role in the case of Basque, as can be seen in some of the research carried out (Azurmendi, 1997a; Azurmendi & Bourhis, 1998; Azurmendi *et al.*, 1998). Linguistic policies today plan the recovery of Euskara as a right and not an obligation, an individual right based on the principal of the individual and

not the territory. This may be why the general population thinks that 'the will to be Basque' is the most important factor in considering oneself really Basque (more so than being Basque-speaking) (Azurmendi *et al.*, 1993). This explains the importance of this way of thinking during the process of recovery of Euskara and why it has increased as recovery advances.

(5) The enormous differences existing today between the Basque territories (ES-1991, 1996; Zabaleta, 1996; Bachoc, 1998) allow us to make an internal, diachronic and synchronous comparison, which can be interpreted from the GIDS point of view. One of the interpretations refers to the predominance of intergroup relationships and their impact on intragroup relationships, both in the pro-*Euskaldun* and the anti-*Euskaldun* groups. Another interpretation is the importance of political power in developing successful linguistic planning and policy. Yet another interpretation speaks to the importance of political and territorial unity in order to draw up a single linguistic policy.

(6) To finish up, the most important conclusion should refer to a general assessment of the process followed in the Basque Country in the 1990s, according to the GIDS model. From the standpoint of GIDS predictions, we would have to say that changes have not been very significant, in the sense that they have not been effective enough to ensure the goals in Stage 6. We are looking more at quantitative than qualitative changes. Therefore, the situation of Euskara in the GIDS model proposed by Fishman in 1991 (p. 405) has changed very little by 1999 as far as the BAC is concerned. The situation in the other territories is even weaker or still. But the perspective of the GIDS model is effective in understanding the processes related to Euskara and its evolution.

References

Arratibel, N. (1999) *Helduen Euskalduntzean Eragiten Duten Prozesu Psikosozialak: Motibazioaren Errola.* Donostia/San Sebastián: UPV/EHU, Tesis doctoral.
Azurmendi, M.-J. (1997a) Psicología social y planificación lingüística. In *Actes del Congrés Europeu sobre Planificació Lingüística, Barcelona, 1995.* Barcelona: Generalitat de Catalunya.
Azurmendi, M.-J. (1997b) Lengua, identidad y nacionalismo. *Curso de Verano de la Universidad Complutense, 1997: Lenguas y Nacionalismos en España y en Europa.* El Escorial: Universidad Complutense.
Azurmendi, M.-J. (1998) Importancia del 'soporte institucional' para la normalización del uso del Euskara. In *Actes de la Cinquena Trobada de Sociolingüistes Catalans, Barcelona, 1997.* Barcelona: Generalitat de Catalunya.
Azurmendi, M.-J. and Bourhis, R.Y. (1998) Presentación del Proyecto de investigación 'ICYLCABE–1996': Identidades culturales y lingüísticas en las

Comunidades Autónomas bilingües (CAB) de España. *Revista de Psicología Social* 13, 3, 545–58.

Azurmendi, M.-J., Bourhis, R.Y., Ros, M. and Garcia, I. (1998) Identidad etno-lingüística y construcción de ciudadanía en las Comunidades Autónomas bilingües (CAB) de España. *Revista de Psicología Social 13(3)*, 559–89.

Azurmendi, M.-J., Espi, M.J., Garcia, I., Gonzalez, J.L. and Muñoz, I. (1993) Lengua e identidad social en el País Vasco. In B. González and A. Guil (comps.) *Psicología Cultural* (IV Congreso Nacional de Psicología Social). Sevilla: Eudema.

Bachoc, E. (1998) *L'Avenir de la Langue Basque (Euskara) en Pays Basque de France.* Bayonne/Baiona: Institut Culturel Basque/Euskal Kultur Erakundea.

Etxeberria, F. (1999) *Bilingüismo y Educación en el País Vasco.*

Euskararen Gizarte Erakundeen Kontseilua (1999) *Euskara Normalizatzeko Plan Nagusia.* Donostia/San Sebastián: Euskararen Kontseilua.

Eusko Jaurlaritza/Gobierno Vasco (1998) *Euskara Biziberritzeko Plan Nagusia.* Vitoria/Gasteiz: Eusko Jaurlaritza/Gobierno Vasco.

Eusko Jaurlaritza/Gobierno Vasco and Nafarroako Gobernua/Gobierno de Navarra (1991) *Encuesta Sociolingüística. La Continuidad del Euskara I.* (ES-1991). Vitoria/Gasteiz: Eusko Jaurlaritza/Gobierno Vasco.

Eusko Jaurlaritza/Gobierno Vasco, Gobierno de Navarra/Nafarroako Gobernua and Institut Culturel Basque/Euskal Kultur Erakundea (1996). *Encuesta Sociolingüística. La Continuidad del Euskara II.* (ES-1996). Vitoria/Gasteiz: Eusko Jaurlaritza/Gobierno Vasco.

EUSTAT (1998) *Anuario Estadístico Vasco.* Vitoria/Gasteiz: EUSTAT.

Fishman, J.A. (1991) *Reversing Language Shift. Theoretical and Empirical Foundations of Assistance to Threatened Languages.* Clevedon: Multilingual Matters.

Garcia, I. (2000) *Euskararen Erabileran Eragiten Duten Brozesin Psikosozialak: Identitate Etnolinguistikoaren Gorratzia.* Donostia/San Sebastián: UPV/EHU, Tesis doctoral.

HABE (1998) Statistical data. Donostia/San Sebastián: HABE.

Ley Básica de Normalización del Uso del Euskara, 1982. Vitoria/Gasteiz: Eusko Jaurlaritza/Gobierno Vasco.

Ley Foral del Vascuence, 1986. Pamplona/Iruñea: Gobierno de Navarra.

Ruiz de Olabuenaga, J.I. and Blanco, M.C. (1994) *La Inmigración Vasca. Análisis Trigeneracional de 150 Años de Inmigración.* Bilbao: Universidad de Deusto.

SIADECO (1991) *Euskararekiko Eritzi eta Jarrerak.* (Report).

Universidad del País Vasco/Euskal Herriko Unibertsitatea (UPV/EHU) (1999). *II Plan de Normalización del Uso del Euskara en la UPV/EHU.* Leioa: UPV/EHU.

Zabaleta, F. (1995) El factor educativo en el conocimiento y uso del euskara en Navarra. In *Actes del Simposi de Demolingüística.* Barcelona: Generalitat de Catalunya.

Zabaleta, F. (1996) *Nafarroako Mapa Soziolinguistikoa, 1991. Biztanleria Euskaldunaren Dinamika eta Bilakaera/Mapa Sociolingüístico de Navarra, 1991. Dinámica y Evolución de la Población Vascófona.* Pamplona/Iruñea: Gobierno de Navarra.

Chapter 11
Catalan a Decade Later

M. STRUBELL[1]

Introduction

When Professor Fishman discussed the case of Catalan (in Catalonia, as the state of the language in other areas is far less healthy) in his book *Reversing Language Shift*, he classified it at Stage 1[2] on his Graded Intergenerational Disruption Scale (GIDS). While regretting that an overall view of all Catalan-speaking lands cannot be given here, the author of this chapter will revisit the same area, 10 years on, to judge whether Catalan remains at Stage 1. There is also a second request by Fishman: to 'use, modify, critique or abandon the RLS "theory" proposed in my 1991 book'.

Research on Language Shift and its Reversal

General

Let us look first at the second part of Professor Fishman's request: a critique of the RLS theory.

A number of Fishman's statements ring truer today, at least in the Catalan context, than they did when RLS was published in 1991. The issue of a 'sufficiently refined taxonomy of language status planning to explicitly provide for the consideration of RLS activity' (Fishman, 1991: 381) is one.

A second issue is the apparently endemic neglect of RLS as a research topic in the social sciences. There are of course notable exceptions. Yet it is extraordinary that such an easily observed and recorded social phenomenon – language choice among individuals – has not yet become the benchmark for theoretical innovation in these fields. Fishman offers a plausible reason for this:

> RLS is an activity of minorities, frequently powerless, unpopular with outsiders and querulous among themselves [. . . It strikes many] otherwise intelligent social scientists as 'unnatural', i.e. as counter to some supposedly 'natural' drift of historical events or the 'obvious' direction of social change. (Fishman, 1991: 382)

This lack of interest is especially surprising given that RLS-efforts 'are characteristically socially patterned and organised activities of the type that sociologists refer to as "social movements".' (Fishman, 1991: 382).

Fishman (1991: 383) also underlines the commitment[3] involved in RLS efforts, which the mainstream may view with fear, suspicion and rejection, as bordering on the irrational and the mystic. We shall see below how Catalan language planning is sometimes portrayed in the rest of the Spain as being a fanatical mania.

What Fishman refers to as 'ethnicity' is usually, in Europe, termed 'nationalism', the will to exist on the part of stateless nations. Since nationalism has fuelled a wide range of claims, is more a sentiment than an ideology and is not based on common premises (e.g. Conversi 1997), it is perhaps not surprising that social scientists seem bewildered and regard it as an anomaly, rather than as one of the prime motivating forces of mankind in the present age (Fishman, 1991: 384). RLS theory as presented raises some questions which deserve further attention.

The causes of intergenerational transmission in minority language situations

Among monolinguals this issue is not relevant, but it is, and very much so, among bilingual people, especially young couples starting to raise a family. There can surely be two main factors behind the choice to be made: language group loyalty and the perception of language usefulness. RLS theory has hitherto concentrated – as might be expected if built on the foundations of cases of extreme minoritisation – on integrative, or identity, factors. However, as we move along the scale towards the least disrupted values, the pragmatic worth of the language increases. Fishman makes some direct allowance for this:

> Clearly, there is and must be an economic basis to Xish life and to the advancement of RLS. [...] In Stage 3 [...] this already important lower work sphere is attended to additionally along two different lines [...]. On the one hand, Xish-controlled and staffed enterprises and services seek to meet the needs of the Yish market; on the other hand, Yish-controlled enterprises and services seek to meet the needs of the Xish market. (Fishman, 1991: 103–4)

Let us look at several other economic factors relevant in intergenerational language choice.

(1) The perceived *usefulness of the language for social advancement* is crucial (Colomer, 1996). Parents want the best for their children. They do not want them to be held back, or subject to ridicule or abuse, the way they may feel

they themselves have been. The significance of this factor in language reproduction was underlined in the Euromosaic report (Nelde *et al.*, 1996). In dealing with subordinated languages, it would seem reasonable to suggest that at high levels of disruption, the affective, identity appeal for intergenerational language transmission is more powerful, and that lower down the scale, pragmatic motives take over or at least are added to the decision-making process.

It is thus essential to study the role each language plays in the labour market which most school-leavers will be entering. It may be local, if there are new jobs available; it may be outside the linguistic area, in which case it will be less likely that the family will speak the subordinate language (which may well be viewed as less useful) to their children.

(2) The Euromosaic report also drew attention to the degree of *linguistic homogeneity or heterogeneity* in families. Economic factors are absolutely crucial in population movements, and provided the social integration of new arrivals is facilitated, such immigration usually leads to some degree of intermarriage. Whether the offspring of such marriages are bilingual in both parents' languages, or have only one of the two as their home language, will certainly have a large impact on the future of the subordinate language whenever such families are numerous.

Intergenerational transmission of the language is of course not the only short-term mechanism for a language community to survive. Other agents can help to produce the language, principally the school, the media and the community or neighbourhood. RLS efforts are also directed, in the more powerful and geographically concentrated minorities, towards the linguistic recruitment of in-coming families and their offspring. This is critical where the local socioeconomic climate is attracting outsiders. Nelde *et al.*, (1996) dwell at some length on the various agents.

The influence of the mass media

The Catalan experience shows the great importance, on several scores, of the mass media. The existence of printed or, especially, audio-visual media in a language firstly helps to create a sense of community among those who consume such media. Secondly, it provides a formal model of language which may well help to improve levels of competence in the community. Thirdly, it helps to generate discourse within the community. Finally, it offers considerable job opportunities to speakers of the language (as has also happened in Ireland, Scotland and Wales, following the setting-up of television channels in the respective languages).

However, the mainstream media may also be players in the process. We shall see below how Madrid-based media had a clearly detrimental effect on public opinion and perceptions of the language situation in Catalonia and the policies being pursued, in the period 1993–97. In this context, Fishman's statement about achieving ethnocultural separation perhaps underestimates the penetration that Yish media can achieve:

> Those RLS movements that safely secure stage 5 and below can remain intergenerationally secure, provided they can maintain sufficient ethnocultural separation from Yish encroachment on their own family-home-neighbourhood-community intragroup institutional bases. (Fishman 1991: 105)

The political climate

The view of the dominant (or 'majority') language group with regard to RLS efforts is greatly important, for given its access to power (and particularly to public opinion) it can place serious obstacles in the way of such a process. Fortunately, in Europe there is an ongoing and unparalleled process of unification which will tend to lessen such obstacles. The European Union, founded in the 1950s with six members, now has 15, and six central and eastern European countries may soon join. Though the effects on a language such as Catalan may be marginal, there is an interesting and promising discourse developing. In order for citizens to embrace the idea of Europe, and accept historical foes as friends, cultural diversity and tolerance have to be promoted, as the only way to move to greater European integration and unity. In such a climate, the tolerance of multilingualism that was for so long denied Catalan, Basque and Galician in Spain can surely have a beneficial effort on RLS-efforts.

Demographic considerations

Declining numbers of speakers may not result simply from language shift inside families, i.e. from intergenerational transmission ceasing. Low birth rates, or high infant mortality, may also have significant effects.

In Catalonia there has been concern for decades about the low birth rate (the small average number of children that each woman has). Over the past 20 years there has been a dramatic decline in the birth rate and general fertility of the population in both Spain and Catalonia. It is estimated that women are now having an average of under 1.2 children, well below the replacement level, usually put at 2.1.[4] Annual births in Catalonia have halved, and many schools have closed down. The typical dumb-bell-shaped distribution of the population is developing a tapering base. In 1996 the numbers of births and deaths were almost identical (54,602 and 53,433 respectively).

Though there is no specific research on the issue, several studies suggest tangentially that the average number of children born to native Catalan-speakers continues to be lower than among Spanish-speaking incomers. This would explain why the percentage of native Spanish-speakers in primary schools is higher than it is in the general population. This trend obviously has serious implications indeed for the future of the Catalan language community, given its weak powers of linguistic linguistic recruitment, on the one hand, and assimilation, on the other.

Though levels of immigration from Spanish-speaking Spain have, since 1975, been well below those of the 1950s and, especially, the 1960s, there is still a steady annual flux of about 20,000 moving each way. Most of those leaving Catalonia are apparently non-Catalan-born, which reduces the negative impact of such movements on the overall linguistic situation in Catalonia.

There is also a smaller, but growing, proportion of migrants from the Third World, mostly from west Africa and Morocco. Exact figures are impossible, for many are illegal migrants and are not on the census (Hall, 1997). But they still amount to less than 2% of the whole population. The question remains of whether their linguistic integration will be just to Spanish, to both Catalan and Spanish, or just to Catalan.

RLS and language planning in Catalonia

Let us now move to the other part of our task: to review the past decade. A number of crucial statements made by Fishman are clearly verified in the Catalan context. (1) the important role of language, (2) bilingualism and language shift, (3) the crucial role of family transmission, (4) the indirect relationship between language policy and the family, (5) concern about the language commitment of young Catalans, (6) the passive acceptance of the language situation, (7) the need for steps to increase social language use, (8) the need for civil society to be active, (9) policy as official commitment and example, (10) the need to relegitimise the language policy.

The important role of language

Fishman describes the salience of language and language issues among supporters of RLS: 'Ethnolinguistic persistence involves a basic continuity in the meaning of symbols. For RLSers a given language is the first and foremost of these symbols, as is their interpretation of that language as being truly fundamental to identity and continuity' (Fishman, 1991: 387; see also Conversi, 1997).

Marí (1996: 18) also underlines the central role that language and culture enjoy, as the result of the *historical definition* of a collective identity, as the *repertoire* of available options to freely define each individual's identity and the position of each person before the world, and as the symbolic *vehicle* of socialisation and of the integration of one's own personality.

Bilingualism and language shift

In Fishman's chapter on 'Three success stories (more or less): Modern Hebrew, French in Quebec and Catalan in Spain',[5] he refers in detail to 'three language-and-culture settings which [...] have traversed the most sensitive and dangerous sections of the difficult path from "essentially problematic" to "essentially non-problematic" within the lifetimes of individuals still alive today (Fishman, 1991: 287). In reference to Catalan he describes the government's policy as a 'triple balancing act': attaining . . .

> the symbolic promotion and the functional institutionalisation of Catalan in [...] the most influential and powerful areas of modern life [; 2. overcoming] the legacy of mother-tongue illiteracy and inferiority that many native, middle-class Catalans have inherited from the Franco years [. . . and 3.] activating the passive Catalan that Spanish speakers quickly acquire. (Fishman, 1991: 299)

Catalan sociolinguistics has long been wary about the possibilities, in practice, of personal bilingualism in a given society being a stable and long-lasting social phenomenon. Valencians such as Lluís-Vicent Aracil and Rafael-Lluís Ninyoles have witnessed a three-generation shift in the larger cities of Valencia, from Catalan monolingualism in the first generation, through a bilingual second generation, to a third generation practically monolingual in the state language. While the author shares this profound doubt, it may be that given certain circumstances, such as those that apply to the survival and recovery of Hebrew (in which, outside Israel itself Jews have over the centuries retained very specific, if limited, functions for the language, in the fields of religious life, literature and popular culture), bilingual situations can be stable. However, few would claim that such circumstances prevail in the Catalan context. Prats, for instance, claims that history shows us that language conflicts are resolved either through language shift or through language normalisation. They always pass, he claims, through a phase of bilingualism which leads on to shift almost inexorably. 'To defy history, leading people to believe that we shall be the first to maintain the balanced coexistence of two languages in a given territory, is an error which will be paid for dearly' (1990: 23).

Such a stance would require that the former subordinate language displace the formerly dominant language, rather than aiming at an impossible balance; so what Fishman termed 'success stories' in RLS can only be successful in the long run if their aim is a monolingual society such as is being achieved in Israel. However, the prospects of such a society in western Europe are bleak even in large countries such as Italy or Germany, as the need for international languages such as English or French is increasingly clear. So it is hard to envisage a language policy that could indeed displace Spanish and leave Catalan in a totally consolidated and safe position, given the deeply rooted habits still prevalent in Catalonia, as well as the high proportion of the population whose family origins, unlike the situation say 50 years ago, are monolithically Spanish-speaking.

There are certainly signs that language choice norms are more flexible than they used to be (Vallverdú, 1998: 61–4). Yet the changes that had been hoped for in such norms for interethnolinguistic contacts have been slight, and the dominant position of Spanish in Barcelona seems unchallenged. According to Boix (1993: 211), despite the introduction of new language choice norms which are more favourable towards Catalan, the demographic context and the more general cultural patterns support the predominance of Spanish in interpersonal relations. This is further increased by the fact that most Catalans nowadays speak Spanish with little or no accent, thus even leading to conversations between Catalan-speaking strangers often taking place in Spanish (Flaquer, 1996: 177–8).

How true, in the context of Catalan, is Fishman's statement (1991: 108) that 'even in the heartland and even with cultural autonomy the pressures from Yish may still be omnipresent'!

Some argue that Catalan has put up with similar situations before and can come through relatively unscathed. Others disagree. Prats *et al.*, for instance (1990: 60–2), believe that 'the danger threatening the Catalan language today [. . .] has no equivalent in earlier situations, as it now rests upon an unprecedented situation: in the complete, definitive extension of social bilingualism in the Catalan-speaking community'. In their view, social bilingualism is by definition unstable, and that the imbalance between the two languages in contact gives rise to a set of attitudes which are disastrous for Catalan. 'In all segments of social life Spanish becomes *de facto* the only language of communication which is truly indispensable, necessary', they claim. 'There are never any domains where Catalan is the only language used, exposed as it is to the bilingualisation of its users.'

The crucial role of family language transmission

The absolutely crucial role of intergenerational transmission is underlined by several Catalan researchers. Boix (1993: 34) for instance states that the plight of a minoritised language becomes virtually irreversible when it ceases to be transmitted intergenerationally, when the 'cobweb' which for generations has linked the use of a language to various fields of everyday activity of a community is broken.

Another, Valencian, sociolinguist is equally clear in his opinion. 'The end-causes of the extinction of a language are to be found in the interruption of its intergenerational transmission, a phenomenon of which we have good illustrations in languages such as Occitan or even in Catalan itself' (Montoya-Abat, 1996: 215). His mention of Catalan refers to some cities in the southernmost part of the Catalan-speaking lands, such as Alacant (*Alicante*) or the totally hispanified Oriola (*Orihuela*).

Of Stage 6 ('the attainment of intergenerational informal oralcy and its demographic concentration and institutional reinforcement'; Fishman, 1991: 92), Fishman says (p. 399) that '*if this stage is not satisfied, all else can amount to little more than biding time,*[6] at best generation by generation, without a natural, self-priming social mechanism having been engendered thereby.' On re-reading this passage several thoughts spring to mind. Surely it is not just RLS proponents that aim to achieve a change in the linguistic child-rearing practices of citizens. A process of language shift as dramatically successful as that undertaken by the French republicans broke the back of the so-called 'regional languages' when the first whole generation of adult speakers of Occitan, or Dutch or Breton or Catalan decided to speak to their children only in French.

It is true that the Occitan *Calandretas*, the Catalan *Bressola* schools and the *Arrels* educational movement do a great deal to keep their languages alive: but it is very uphill work if most of their pupils speak only French at home. The Welsh and the Basques (in Spain) have made great strides, achieving quite high proportions of bilingual schooling for children, and the number of people fluent in these languages has recently stabilised thanks to the growing proficiency of the younger generation. Nevertheless, the starting point is very low: perhaps only 12–15% of young children have Welsh or Basque as their main home language.

An overarching model of sociolinguistic change is needed which can cope with RLS in a lesser-used or 'minority' language such as Irish or Welsh or, more recently, Latvian or Estonian, and the spread of a 'national' or imperial language such as Latin, French, Russian or English, whilst incorporating Fishman's reference to 'a natural, self-priming social mechanism'. The model would perceive of societal language status changes as processes which can become self-maintaining, perhaps through feedback mechanisms. It would then look at the obstacles that prevent such a 'natural' process taking place. It would also lead to simple formulations of language policy, as deliberate procedures to remove obstacles to natural changes occurring. We shall return to such a model towards the end of the chapter.

The indirect relationship between language policy and the family

The need for a sturdy language policy overflows into the family domain, though only as an indirect result thereof, according to Torres (1994: 47), who argues that an intensification of the policy of linguistic normalisation is needed, among other important motives, to help maintain in as crucial a domain as the family a sufficiently high presence of Catalan to ensure its future.

Bastardas explains the relationship between language policy and expected changes in individual behaviour. There seems to be a dynamic relationship between the spread of the use of the standard autochthonous variety in communications which Corbeil (1980) calls *institutionalised*,[7] and the later effects of language shift or normalisation which can be observed in *individualised* communications.[8] In Bastardas' view, if and when the normalisation process is perceived as successful and irreversible, the private behaviour of individuals – individualised communications – will tend to adapt accordingly: though probably only very gradually (Bastardas, 1994: 35; see also Fishman, 1991: 404). Given the complexity of the many other intervening socio-environmental factors, and the importance of this issue, Bastardas (personal communication, February 1999) calls for urgent research.

It is clear that the nature of language planning changes substantially as we move up the GIDS from Stage 7 to Stage 1. Planning at Stage 7 is an unofficial, social, group activity. A good example is the extraordinary case of Cornish, which has literally been resuscitated in this century, several generations after the last speaker of the language died. Planning at Stage 1, on the other hand, is official, often legally legitimated, and affects institutional bodies and services, as Fishman (1991: 381) reminds us: 'Language "status planning", of which RLS is a sub-category, is overly identified with central government efforts, hardly the most likely or the most sympathetic auspices for minority-RLS efforts'. Now, the way people bring up their families – including the language they choose – is not for the authorities to decide. Policies may influence language attitudes through a discourse that can be perceived through the language behaviour of politicians, government bodies and civil servants (particularly teachers); and through legislation. But such measures cannot legitimately intervene in people's domestic lives and decisions: any influence is much more subtle, and therefore long term, in nature. In Catalonia, older people still remember the savage repression of the language following the Spanish Civil War of 1936–39

(Benet, 1973; Ferrer i Gironès, 1985): yet the authorities could not force people to use Spanish at home. Such a change took place mainly in social and ideological circles either close to the regime or keen to take advantage of the situation for their own economic advancement.

Concern about the language commitment of young Catalans

Fishman practises what he preaches in reminding readers (1991: 386) that those committed to RLS are subject to bouts of depression or pessimism in the face of negative facts: he describes the 'diminution in the numbers or proportions of speakers' as 'constant', which may be so in immigrant communities but is not always the case (namely the Catalans, the Welsh).

Some books on the language situation in Catalonia, published since *Reversing Language Shift* appeared, have quite dramatic titles and reflect the concern about the future of the language: references are made to a 'controversial future' for Catalan (Vallverdú, 1990); to an 'interrupted language' (Montoya-Abat, 1996); to 'choosing not being betraying' (Boix, 1993); to a 'language war' (Voltas, 1996); to Catalan being a 'public or a private language' (Flaquer, 1996); and to an 'improbable normality' (Branchadell, 1998).

Fishman (1991: 108) argues against head-in-the-sand reactions: 'It is unwise to disregard the pessimism of the pessimists, the alarms of those who constantly "view with alarm" the state of health of Xish language-in-culture. Yish, the constant competitor, is always part of the local "heartland" scene too, not to mention that its undisputed domination in all other parts of the polity [. . .] also remains inviolate.' His message is grim: 'Eternal watchfulness is the price of RLS and that price must be paid at stage 1 too'.

In Catalonia there is particular concern about the language attitudes of young people. Larreula (1998: 20) has recently written that the offspring of those who arrived in the 1950s and the 1960s from Spanish-speaking Spain fully identify themselves as Catalans, yet perceive that most Catalans communicate naturally in Spanish. As a result, he continues, they may view the language of the institutions and the school (Catalan) as artificially fostered by those in power. Such a policy might be construed as favouring a minority simply because Catalan is its family language. The fact, Larreula concludes, that Catalan is not the clearest sign of identity among most young people who fully identify themselves as Catalans, fills many people with anxiety, frustration and pain.

Faced with massive immigration and low birth rates, the only long-term hope for Catalan is to recruit new speakers among the immigrant groups.

There is growing evidence that this recruitment is at least partly taking place. Comes *et al.*, (1995), for instance, looked at 11 to 14-year-old Spanish-speaking pupils throughout Catalonia. It may be premature to look at the language habits of youngsters who have not yet left school; nevertheless, the attitudes found were very positive, and language habits are beginning to change: 50% claim to speak Catalan 'a lot' or 'quite a lot', and only 7% said 'not at all' (table 42: 118): 58% claimed they could hold a conversation completely in Catalan (table 41: 117). To speak with their Catalan friends, 14% said they use Catalan, while 47% said both Catalan and Spanish (table 24: 98).

Flaquer (1996: 61–2) argues forcefully that the recent process of economic and political modernisation has given immigrants a new status and dignity as citizens rather than subjects, and that this, coupled with greater mobility and the impact of television, has radically reduced the level of linguistic integration among Spanish-speaking incomers to Catalonia.

The passive acceptance of the language situation

Boix (1993) and Bastardas (1994: 39) believe that appropriate language choice norms are crucial in any process of language status change. During periods of crisis and of rapid changes in which language market tensions are strong, Boix argues, some people will probably realise that the language use norms that regulate their code changes can be changed, and wish to do so. Beside these sectors with language loyalty, however, other members of the subordinated community continue to perceive the language use norms in a non-conflictual manner and have internalised them so much that they consider them natural and immutable.

Boix is concerned that the lack of clear language-use guidelines favourable to the recovery of Catalan, among youngsters in Barcelona, is an ominous sign for its future. They accept quite happily being spoken to in Catalan or in Spanish. He detects no perceived need for any voluntary (personal or group) attempt to modify the norms. Boix thinks that this contemporising approach is, as a Quebec policy-maker said of youngsters in his own country, a sign of 'a poor knowledge of the linguistic situation [. . .] and of a false feeling of security' (Plourde, 1985: 303). 'Despite all the advances in the dissemination of Catalan in Barcelona and the introduction of new language use norms which are favourable to Catalan', Boix (1993: 211) concludes, 'the demographic context and the more general cultural traits favour the dominance of Spanish in interpersonal relations.'

This conformity is also underlined by Flaquer (1996: 353), who realises that it is the citizens, in the last analysis, who will decide the future of the language and are the true architects of any change in the linguistic habits of the population. He is surprised at the passivity and lack of interest that both political leaders and the Catalan-speaking community as a whole display towards these issues. Flaquer calls for a public discussion which will allow Catalans to calibrate and investigate which options they have.

The need for steps to increase social language use

Aymà stresses the need to act outside institutional areas, to counteract the drop in the social, interpersonal use of Catalan which has resulted from the incorporation into Catalan society of the offspring of the Spanish-speaking migrants of 1950–75. Policies on providing for the needs of the Catalan-speakers in the field of cultural industries, the media and in dealings with the public authorities are not enough. There is a danger of:

> tipping the concept of normalisation too far in the direction of satisfying Catalan-speakers' demands for consumption (of and in) Catalan, with the aid of protective linguistic rights, and of not producing, on the other hand, sufficient generating activity to achieve language change on the part of the Spanish-speakers. (Aymà 1993: 88–9)

The need for civil society to be active

Some, in describing RLS as a political task, seem to suggest that the rest of society need not be committed to participating. Prats *et al.* (1990: 75) analyse two main threats to the survival of Catalan – a direct one, the passage to Spanish and an indirect one, following the path of progressive linguistic empoverishment – and demand a political project capable of creating the conditions which will ensure language normalisation throughout the territory. In the opinion of Prats *et al.* (1990), some sociolinguists do not fully appreciate that 'preventing the retreat of Catalan, so often blurred by the (limited) access to some high-prestige domains, is a political task.'

A leading Catalan sociolinguist, Vallverdú, vehemently criticises those who call for still more dynamic policies while seemingly not accepting their own share of responsibility in the process. He finds it shameful that among those who call for a radically new language policy with an almost exclusive use of Catalan, some have given up practising passive bilingualism:

> under the pretext that they do not want to be 'martyrs' or 'heroes', that they only want 'to live in peace', they discharge their own responsibility upon the institutions – Generalitat, local councils, etc. – as if everything depended on political decisions from 'up top" (Vallverdú, 1990: 84)

There has indeed been a constant insistence that a language policy should not have to rely on 'volunteers' or committed 'martyrs'. I contend that this belief seriously weakens the Catalan process, yet in other Catalan-speaking lands (the Balearic Islands and Valencia, in particular) social movements supporting the language are far more dynamic and active.

Flaquer has pointed out (1996: 355–6) that there is a risk of a divorce developing between official circles (which invest in support of the Catalan language) and the man in the street, unless the necessary effort is actively supported by civil society, including the citizens themselves. The success of the language policy will, in his opinion, occur by means of the steady incorporation to the use of Catalan by the large number of residents born outside Catalonia, or Spanish-speakers who hitherto have felt no need to do so. In his view, the former social pressure for the cultural integration of incomers has been displaced by institutional pressure, which, he claims, is much less effective than community pressure and may be perceived as an imposition. Flaquer stresses that it is up to the citizens of Catalonia to decide the future of the language; unless they actively defend Catalan in daily life and stop relying on institutional campaigns, it could well be threatened. (Flaquer, 1996: 357)

Language policy as official commitment and example

Several authors, and particularly politicians, have stressed the exemplary role of the language policy and practice of the Catalan government (*Generalitat de Catalunya*). The present director general, Lluís Jou, has written that the 1998 Linguistic Policy Act is 'a message of the political will of the Generalitat to continue impelling the process of recovery and presence of Catalan in all fields and all segments of social life and a commitment on the part of the Catalan institutions to the language of the country' (Jou, 1998: 22).

Many have stressed that legislation alone cannot save a language. Apart from the participation of what is often called 'civil society', the need for intelligent and ingenious measures by language planning policy implementers, and the need for institutions – including researchers – to work together, have also been pointed to. According to Bastardas (1994: 38) 'the study of and research on the elements of persistence and strategies of change, real controlled and evaluated experimentation, and the wholly scientific attitude of questioning the very representations of the planners and militants, are aspects of great importance in the success or failure of sociolinguistic planning'.

The need to relegitimise the language policy

The theoretical bases for the present language policy in Catalonia need to be renovated and publicly disseminated for several reasons. Firstly, opposition to such a policy, which was fairly disorganised in 1981 when the first attempt to pre-empt the re-catalanisation policy was made (a *Manifiesto* published in a Madrid newspaper just a few days after the attempted coup of 23 February), is much better articulated now, and was particularly virulent in nature between 1993 and 1997, to try first to bring down the Socialist government in Madrid, and later, to block the Catalan language policy Bill (enacted in January 1998). The political context of these attacks has been described elsewhere (Strubell, 1998a, 1999). Voltas has traced the history and development of the movement. Not since 1981, he wrote (Voltas, 1996: 11), had the people, interests and associations who organised the 1994 revolt against the Generalitat's language policy been at all successful. This time, Catalan civil society and the nationalist world in general were unable to articulate an organised response: the 1981 *Manifiesto* was neutralised, among other things, by the formation of a dynamic NGO committed to promoting the Catalan language, *la Crida a la Solidaritat*,[9] while the 1994 one arrived after the dissolution of this organisation of linguistic self-defence.

On 12 September 1993, the main right-wing Madrid daily newspaper plastered the following headline across its front page, under a photograph of the king of Spain in full military regalia: 'Igual que Franco, pero al revés: Persecución del castellano en Cataluña'.[10] Voltas described his reaction thus:

> The front page of *ABC* had all the makings of something else: the start of a crusade which was to be taken up as if it were their own by many of the mass media throughout Spain and which was to focus the limelight of political life in this country for the following two years. (Voltas, 1996: 28)

The text in the paper's leading article was a head-on attack on the *Generalitat*'s language policy, describing it as the same, in reverse, as what had been done under the dictatorship, including a campaign of 'persecution' against Spanish, in an attempt to 'eradicate' it.

The *Generalitat* decided to publicly ignore such attacks. However, while this helped to prevent a mud-slinging contest, the perceived legitimacy of Catalonia's language policy suffered, since replies by intellectuals (e.g. Branchadell, 1997) had little effect on public opinion. There is a clear need to relegitimise the aims of the policy, for the main actor and agent is the Catalan-speaking community, which has retreated into a defensive role instead of still actively supporting the process.

There is another reason for renovating the RLS discourse in Catalonia.

Flaquer (1996: 355) has pointed out that as time goes by, the continual reference to political repression in the past will have less and less explanatory appeal, so a new discourse is needed to relegitimise a policy which promotes the Catalan language. The author feels that in the present context there is certainly a place for a policy to neutralise the (linguistic) effects of globalisation – not just for Catalan, but for Danish, Dutch or Greek as well – but Flaquer's point is nevertheless important.

Some have tried to criticise Catalonia's language policy on neo-liberal grounds. However, appeals to liberalism have been significantly one-sided, and have ignored the much more numerous and more stringent norms imposing the use of Spanish. A legal specialist claims that whoever favours non-intervention in relation to threatened languages either considers that the linguistic heritage is not a common value needing active protection, or else defends that conflicts be resolved according to the law of the strongest, 'provided the language in danger of extinction is not their own' (Solé, 1998: 11). He discounts appeals to linguistic liberalism in debates on norms, such as the recent Linguistic Policy Act, which are attempts to protect languages from the 'overwhelming and predatory might of other stronger ones. As has been repeated pointed out,' Solé recalls, 'those who call out against quotas and sanctions in the Catalan Linguistic Policy Act have said nothing against the two hundred Spanish pre-constitutional and post-constitutional norms which impose Spanish.' A recent one is a Royal Decree[11] which makes Spanish compulsory on part of the information relating to cosmetic products. It makes things worse by allowing the use of French or English instead of Spanish . . . but not Catalan.

Catalan in Catalonia: A Brief Overview (1988-98)

In this part of the chapter we shall reconsider first of all Fishman's classification of Catalan in Spain at Stage 1, and then look at the specific development of Catalan in Catalonia, in the 10-year span that the book covers.

Fishman (1991, fig 14.2: 405) stated his opinion that the following stages on the Graded Intergenerational Dislocation Scale (GIDS) were receiving most attention in RLS-efforts:

Stage 1: Some use of Xish in higher level educational, occupational, governmental and media efforts (but without the additional safety provided by political independence)
Stage 1 essentially represents the arrival of the pursuit of cultural autonomy for those who have pursued the vision of Xmen-via-Xish.

[The language's] spokesmen and representatives would become responsible for planning, conducting and evaluating such activities ... Even if this stage is attained, there will inevitably be some pro-RLSers who are still dissatisfied, perhaps because Xish is not the sole and official and ethno-national language of the region, [...] or perhaps because even in the 'heartland' and even with cultural autonomy the pressures from Dish may still be omnipresent. (Fishman 1991: 107–8)

Whereas Stage 1 can make a definite contribution to RLS, this contribution must be successfully translated into intergenerationally transmissible Stage 6 processes and interactions before it will have more than bureaucracy-building and elite-building effects. (Fishman, 1991: 404)

He placed Catalan at this stage.

Stage 2: Xish in lower governmental services and mass media but not in the higher spheres of either. Plenty of work is still being done at this level as well.

Stage 3: use of Xish in the lower work sphere (outside of the Xish neighbourhood/community) involving interaction between Xmen and Ymen. Such interactions may be increasing: but the use of Catalan is such contexts is perhaps no longer recovering.

There seems to be no reason for placing Catalan in Catalonia anywhere other than at Stage 1. However, in the Balearic Islands and Valencia, where well over a third of all Catalan-speakers live, the intergenerational transmission of Catalan foreseen at Stage 6 and above is certainly not guaranteed at present in urban areas.

We shall now look at language competence, language quality and a few aspects of language use in Catalonia. Much of the following data comes from a recent overview (Romaní and Strubell, 1998).

Competence in the language

The census data for 1986 and 1996 in Catalonia show how many people report they can understand, speak, read and/or write the language. In all four aspects the increase has been great. Comprehension is approaching 100%. In terms of the numbers of the other three competences there has been a remarkable increase over this period, with rises in the percentages of between 11 and 14 points. Literacy has grown especially rapidly (Table 11.1).

In a country with just over six million inhabitants, such improvements are spectacular and are probably unrivalled anywhere in the world. They

Table 11.1 Proportion of population of Catalonia recorded as being able to understand, speak, read and write Catalan in 1986 and 1996 (official statistics)

	1986		1996		Increase	
Can understand Catalan	5,287,200	90.3%	5,683,237	95.0%	396,037	4.7
Can speak Catalan	3,747,813	64.0%	4,506,512	75.3%	758,699	11.3
Can read Catalan	3,542,012	60.5%	4,330,251	72.4%	788,239	11.9
Can write Catalan	1,844,493	31.5%	2,743,326	45.8%	898,833	14.4
Total (aged 2 or more)	5,856,435		5,984,334		127,899	

Table 11.2 Proportion of population of Catalonia recorded as being able to speak Catalan, by age-group (official 1986, 1991 and 1996 statistics)

Age group (years)	1986 (%)	1991 (%)	1996 (%)
From 2 to 14	62.2	77.9	83.6
From 15 to 29	72.6	79.1	90.4
From 30 to 44	60.6	64.1	74.9
From 45 to 64	59.5	57.7	63.0
More than 64	64.2	62.6	61.9

stand as a fitting tribute to the work being done in schools, since the changes have occurred above all among young people (Table 11.2).

The rise in oral fluency between 1986 and 1996 is clearly visible: it is concentrated in the 2–14 year age group (a 21.4 point rise) and continues in the 15–29 year age group (a 17.8 point increase) and in the 30–44 year age group (a 14.3 point increase). The overall impression, which is even clearer when looking at literacy-related competence, is that of a tidal wave sweeping up from the school-age groups, peaking at 15–19, and then gradually declining with age. After each successive five-year period the wave peaks at a higher level, and its effect spreads across into older groups as the cohorts age.

The learning process is also taking place, naturally enough, among recent arrivals to Catalonia. The improvement in the period between 1986 and 1991 was clear: even among the (extraordinarily large number of) non-Catalan-born people who had arrived in the 1960s there was a noticeable

Table 11.3 Percentage claiming oral fluency in Catalan (official statistics)

Period of arrival	1986 census	1991 census
1920 and earlier	77.5	77.7
1921–1930	69.6	69.5
1931–1940	58.5	55.8
1941–1950	44.3	42.6
1951–1960	33.0	33.7
1961–1965	23.7	27.0
1966–1970	24.2	28.8
1971–1975	25.1	34.6
1976–1980	30.9	39.3
1981–1985	25.6	41.1
1986–1991	–	30.2

overall increase in the proportion of those claiming oral fluency during the five-year period. There was no significant increase among those who arrived before 1960 (most of whom were at least in their fifties in 1991); but the increase was very marked among those who arrived in the 1970s. The base-line is also improving: there is a rise in the percentage of the latest cohort of arrivals that claim oral fluency within the space of 0–5 years (Table 11.3).

Little reference has been made to the other highly populated Catalan-speaking areas in Spain. Neither the Valencian nor the Balearic Islands governments included a language item in their 1996 municipal censuses. However, it seems probable that in neither qualitative nor quantitative terms have competence in, or use of, the language, increased as much in these two areas; and recent events can hardly prove positive for the language in Valencia (Strubell, 1998c).

The quality of the language

A brief reference to the issue of the degradation of the language has already been made (Prats *et al.* 1990: 75). There is a danger of the specific features of Catalan, in phonetics, in grammar and syntax, and in lexicon, gradually being lost, and of Catalan becoming, in effect, a mere dialect of another language (Spanish).

Has the quality of the language used in Catalonia improved between 1986 and 1996? Even giving full credence to the census data themselves, a growing proportion of the population speak Catalan as a second, not first, language, or can even be classed as *ambilinguals* (Vallverdú, 1998: 30). Since nearly all learners are native Spanish-speakers (unlike countries like the United States or Canada, where the linguistic background of immigrants is varied), a decline in the quality of Catalan is unavoidable – in lexicon, phonetics, grammar – on account of interference from Spanish. (This has been going on much longer in Valencia, south of Catalonia, where schooling in Catalan is more recent and less widespread, and where the colloquial language has many, many hundreds of loan-words from Spanish.)

As regards the level of literacy, things are somewhat better. Never before have so many people been able to read and write Catalan. Whether they actually do so or not should more appropriately be answered in the next section. Suffice it to say that one of the two leading Spanish-language newspapers in Catalonia, *El Periódico de Catalunya*, decided to start issuing a Catalan-language edition in parallel in October 1997, and are very satisfied that this edition is accounting for 40–42% of their sales. Their market research revealed a growing number of potential readers, to whom they have successfully offered their product.

Incidentally, as far as proficiency in Spanish is concerned, research (e.g. Consell 1998) shows that average levels, though not as high as in some monolingual regions, are higher than in several; there is therefore no cause for concern on this score.

The use of the language

Romaní and Strubell (1998: 809–10) quote research results which suggest increases in the overall intergenerational use of Catalan. These changes are primarily due to first-generation Catalans: their average self-estimated use of Catalan, on a 0–10 scale, was 1.31 with parents, and 4.08 with offspring.

In the metropolitan area of Barcelona, where over half the population (and a much higher proportion of non-Catalan-born residents) live, only 18% of couples had different first languages. According to a 1986 survey, 98% of the offspring of Catalan-speaking parents were returned as being themselves Catalan-speaking; the figure was 97% among the offspring of Spanish-speaking parents (Subirats, 1990: 28). Vila (1993) considers that linguistically mixed couples have a crucial role in deciding the future of Catalan in the region. The 1986 and 1990 surveys in the above-mentioned area suggest that unlike the situation in the 1970s, such linguistically heterogeneous couples now grant Catalan a more substantial place than Spanish, as shown by the first language of the offspring, and that for the first time, a large number of young people are being brought up as natural bilinguals (Table 11.4).

Table 11.4 Percentage of young people brought up as natural bilinguals

		Catalan (%)	Both (%)	Spanish(%)
1986	Metropolitan area	45	22	33
1990	Metropolitan region	36	45	20

Source: Vila (1993:13)

No trend should be sought from these diachronic figures: the questions regarding subject's main language were slightly different, and the two areas were not identical. However, as stated above, the persistence of negative interethnolinguistic language choice norms (e.g. Bastardas, 1994), and the sheer demographic weight of non-Catalan-speakers living in and around Barcelona, make the future of the language, even in its heartland, much less secure than many believe.

Closing Section: A Model of Language Status Change

Of stage 6,[13] Fishman says that *'if this stage is not satisfied, all else can amount to little more than biding time,*[14] at best generation by generation, without a natural, self-priming social mechanism having been engendered thereby' (Fishman, 1991: 399). In fact, however, surely it is not just RLS proponents that aim to achieve a change in the linguistic child-rearing practices of citizens. The dramatically successful language shift achieved by the French republicans broke the back of the so-called 'regional languages' when the first whole generation of adult speakers of Occitan, Dutch, Breton or Catalan decided to speak to their children only in French. There is perhaps more in common than meets the eye between RLS and these traditional policies regarding national languages.

I am at present developing a circular model to describe social processes of language status change, both LS and RLS. There is a great deal of feedbacking in any process of social change, including RLS. The identification of obstacles to such processes, and designing ways of overcoming (or sidetracking) them, is probably the main task of language planners. The main idea is that learning a language, using it, and having positive perceptions and motivation to further increase its study and use, are linked together to form a 'natural, self-priming social mechanism', but that the passage from one to the next may be blocked by external or internal factors. The motivation, and the learning of the language, are related to the function or domain: it is not the same to regard the individual as a consumer of products, as a member of a labour market, or as a member of a local community.

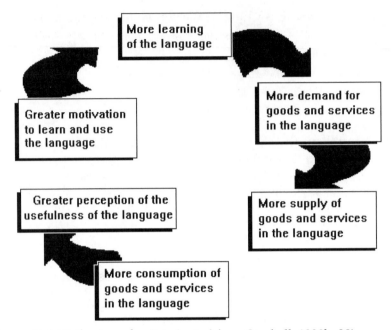

Figure 11.1 'Catherine wheel' (adapted from Strubell, 1998b: 28)

Each of these makes special demands upon language use, which may be passive or active, or both. An early draft of the model, which the author terms the 'Catherine wheel' to convey the objective of a self-perpetuating change, has been published recently (Strubell, 1998b). (See Figure 11.1.)

The 'Catherine wheel' model views the individual as the centre of any process of democratic social change. In the illustration, the individual is taken as a consumer. Any of the six steps may be subject to blockage, and it is the task of language policymakers to overcome the causes of blockage with specific measures where they are required. However, more often than not the measures are neither directly linguistic in nature, nor can they be adopted by language planners on their own.

In the Catalan case I feel that there are growing obstacles in the 'pragmatic' fields of perception and motivation. These are crucial areas; despite considerable interest displayed in our experience among Quebec language planners, for instance, Catalonia's language planners have tended to neglect them in recent years, relying perhaps more than is advisable on legislation.

Thus, a public discourse to relegitimise the language policy, and to convince the populace of the importance of working together in everyday life to fully restore the language, would I am sure pay handsome dividends and allow us to look forward to the next 10 years with high hopes.

Notes

1. The author would like to express his gratitude for the many remarks and suggestions made to an earlier draft by A. Bastardas, D. Conversi, L. Flaquer, B. Montoya, A. Rossich, F. Vallverdú and Professor J.A. Fishman.
2. 'Some use of Xish in higher level educational, occupational, governmental and media efforts (but without the additional safety net provided by political independence' (Fishman, 1991: 107).
3. 'A very palpable degree of affect, a sentimental (rather than merely an instrumental) bonding, a stress on real or putative ethno-kinship, an aspiration toward consciousness and identity (re)formation, a heightened degree of altruistic self-sacrifice and a disregard for "least effort" advantages'.
4. The causes of this decline are beyond the scope of this paper to consider, though they probably include working-womanhood, an endangered welfare state and job uncertainty.
5. Published in a Catalan translation in 1993 (Fishman, 1993).
6. The italics are Fishman's.
7. That is, those which are usual in public spheres, generally corresponding to the organisations into which a modern society is structured.
8. That is, those produced by people as private individuals.
9. Literally, '*Call to Solidarity [in Defence of the Catalan Language, Cultura and Nation]*'.
10. 'Just like Franco, but the other way round: Persecution of Spanish in Catalonia'.
11. No. 1599/1998, of 17 October.
12. 'The attainment of intergenerational informal oralcy and its demographic concentration and institutional reinforcement' (Fishman, 1991: 92).
13. The italics are Fishman's.

References

Aymà, J.M. (1993) Estendre l'ús interpersonal del català (per, i) conservar-ne la qualitat. *Revista de llengua i dret*, núm. 20, 87–94.

Bastardas, A. (1994) Persistència i canvi en el comportament lingüístic: la planificació lingüística. *Treballs de Sociolingüística Catalana*, núm. 12, 31–9.

Benet, J. (1973) *Catalunya sota el Règim Franquista*. Paris: Edicions Catalanes de Par s.

Boix i Fuster, E. (1993) *Triar no és trair. Identitat i llengua en els joves de Barcelona*. Edicions 62, Barcelona.

Branchadell, A. (1997) *Liberalisme i política lingüística*. Barcelona: Empúries.

Branchadell, A. (1998) *La normalitat improbable*. Barcelona: Empúries.

Colomer, J.M. (1996) *La utilitat del bilingüisme*. Barcelona: Edicions 62.

Comes, G., Jiménez, B. and Alcaraz, V. (1995) *La llengua catalana i els castellanoparlants de 10 a 15 anys*. Barcelona: Columna Edicions.

Consell Superior d'Avaluació del Sistema Educatiu (1998) *Resultats acadèmics de l'alumnat de 14 i 16 anys a Catalunya*. Informes d'avaluació, 2. Consell Superior d'Avaluació del Sistema Educatiu, Departament d'Ensenyament, Generalitat de Catalunya, Barcelona.

Conversi, D. (1997) *The Basques, the Catalans and Spain. Alternative Routes to Nationalist Mobilisation.*London: Hurst & Co.

Corbeil, J.C. (1990) *L'aménagement linguistique du Québec.* Montreal: Guérin.

Ferrer i Gironès, F. (1985) *La persecució política de la llengua catalana.* Barcelona: Edicions 62.

Fishman, J.A. (1991) *Reversing Language Shift.* Clevedon: Multilingual Matters.

Fishman, J.A. (1993) Tres casos amb (més o menys) èxit: l'hebreu modern, el francès al Quebec i el català a Espanya. *Treballs de Sociolingüística Catalana* 11, 19–48.

Flaquer V.L. (1996) *El català, ¿llengua pública o privada?* Barcelona: Empúries.

Hall, J. (1997) Nascuts i vinguts a Catalunya: la població estrangera. In M. Reixach (ed.) *El coneixement del català. Anàlisi de les dades del cens lingüístic de 1991 de Catalunya, les Illes Balears i del País Valencià* (pp. 101–40). Barcelona: Departament de Cultura de la Generalitat de Catalunya.

Jou, L. (1998) Els principis de llengua pròpia i llengües oficials en l'articulat de la llei 1/1998, de 7 de gener, de política lingüística. *Revista de llengua i dret,* núm. 29, 7–22.

Larreula V. (1998) Enric. Identitat. Canvi de llengua i crisi d'identitat a Catalunya, *Escola Catalana,* Any XXXIII, Núm. 353, 18–20.

Marí, I. (1996) *Plurilingüisme europeu i llengua catalana.* Biblioteca Lingüística Catalana, Universitat de València, València.

Montoya-Abat, B. (1996) *Alacant. La llengua interrompuda.* València: Denes editorial.

Nelde, P., Strubell, M. and Williams, G. (1996) *Euromosaic: Production and reproduction of minority language communities in the European Union.* Luxembourg: Commission of the European Communities.

Plourde, M. (1985) L'attitude des jeunes face à la langue. In *La langue française au Québec. Conférences et al.locutions* (pp. 301–3). Quebec: Éditeur officiel du Québec.

Prats, M. (1990) Reflexió ignasiana sobre la normalització lingüística. In M. Prats, A. Rafanell and A. Rossich (eds) *El futur de la llengua catalana* (pp. 9–28). Barcelona: Empúries.

Prats, M., Rafanell, A. and Rossich, A. (1990) En l'esperança, contra l'esperança. In M. Prats, A. Rafanell and A. Rossich (eds) *El futur de la llengua catalana* (pp. 39–83). Barcelona: Empúries.

Romaní, J.-M. and Strubell, M. (1998) L'ús de la llengua a Catalunya. In S. Giner (coord.) *La Societat Catalana* (pp. 805–20). Barcelona: Institut d'Estadística de Catalunya, Generalitat de Catalunya.

Solé, J.-R. (1998) La legislació sobre llengües en el món, *Escola Catalana,* Any XXXIII, Núm. 351, 9–11.

Strubell i Trueta, M. (1998a) Language and diversity: The case of Catalonia. Paper read at the OSCE Seminar on *Launching the Oslo Recommendations on the Linguistic Rights of National Minorities,* Vienna, February.

Strubell, M. (1998b) Can sociolinguistic change be planned? In *Proceedings of the 1st European Conference 'Private Foreign Language Education in Europe. Its contribution to the Multilingual and Multicultural Aspect of the European Union'. Thessaloniki, November 1997* (pp. 23–31). Palso, Thessaloniki.

Strubell i Trueta, M. (1999) Language, democracy and devolution in Catalonia. *Current Issues in Language and Society* 5(3), 146–180.

Subirats, M. (ed.) (1990) *Enquesta metropolitana 1986. Condicions de vida i hàbits de la població de l'àrea metropolitana de Barcelona. Vol. 20: Transmissió i coneixements de la llengua catalana a l'àrea metropolitana de Barcelona.* Àrea metropolitana de Barcelona. Bellaterra: Institut d'Estudis Metropolitans.

Torres, J. (1994) Evolució de l'ús del català com a llengua familiar a Catalunya, *Treballs de Sociolingüística Catalana,* núm. 12, 41–7.

Vallverdú, F. (1990) *L'ús del català: Un futur controvertit.* Barcelona: Edicions 62.

Vallverdú, F. (1998) *Velles i noves qüestions sociolingüístiques.* Barcelona: Edicions 62.

Vila, F.X. (1993) Transmissió dels idiomes en les parelles lingüísticament mixtes. *Pubblicacions de l'Institut de Sociolingüística Catalana. Documents de Treball núm. 1.* Barcelona: Departament de Cultura de la Generalitat de Catalunya.

Voltas, E. (1996) *La guerra de la llengua.* Barcelona: Empúries.

Chapter 12

Saving Threatened Languages in Africa: A Case Study of Oko

E. ADEGBIJA

Introduction

The threat of death hangs over many languages in Africa, Asia and Latin America, which have an unenviable concentration of status-poor, officially inconsequential and functionally emaciated languages. All over the world, such languages are differently christened: 'minority', 'small-group', 'lesser-used', 'small population', etc. Sub-Saharan Africa alone has far more than 1700 languages and very little institutional attention is given to most of them (cf. Adegbija, 1994: 1, 1997). Over 90% of African languages, there-fore, exist as if they don't really exist; they live without being really alive. Living functional blood is being sucked out of them because they are consigned to low level functions in the national scheme of things.

This chapter attempts to relate and document the current inter-generational transmission status in uses and in attitudes of languages in Africa, using Oko, a Kwa language in Kogi State, Nigeria, as a specific case study. The chapter demonstrates that while Oko seems to be doing quite well in its own small village hinterland, this is not the case in larger cities and in other regions to which Oko-speaking immigrants have moved. Additionally, it will examine the 1991 intergenerational transmission theory proposed in Fishman (1991), with respect, particularly, to its adequacy or otherwise for the African context. As a prelude to this primary task, it is desirable first to investigate some of the principal causes of language shift in the African context. Put differently, why are several African languages under threat? Why are they likely to continue to be endangered? And what are some of the strategies for reversing language shift in the African context particularly?

For a proper understanding of why many African languages are constantly under threat a proper context and background of their present plight is a desideratum and our attention will now be focused on this.

Primary Sources of Threat to African Languages

The presence and prestige of ex-colonial languages

The very presence of European languages and the disproportional prestige associated with them overtly and covertly by virtue of the dynamic roles that they have played in national life since colonial times is a major threat to African languages, which, functionally, become insignificant by comparison. Ex-colonial languages began their lives in Africa as the masters' languages, and in most parts of Africa have continued to enjoy this enviable attitudinal posture. If anything, subsequent events all over the African sociolinguistic scenario have only served to entrench their being functionally placed on the pedestal, being attitudinally extolled, and being seen as inevitable both at the individual and societal level. The educational domain was, and still is, a major arena for the language shifting pull. Part of the evidence for this claim is that many children who have been to school have completely shifted away from their mother-tongues to the English language. In Nigeria, Ghana, Uganda, Kenya and many other African countries colonised by the British, for instance, to be educated is virtually synonymous with knowing and being able to use English. To be educated, in this sense, also provides a green card for some degree of membership in the power-brokering elite club. Membership in this club connotes being up there whereas non-membership is tantamount almost invariably to being down there. Given the fact that English has assumed many official roles in education, administration, the mass media, the judiciary and politics, its perceptual salience naturally impels and constrains a shift towards it wherever possible. The same can be said to be true of European languages such as French and Portuguese in other African countries. To know and be able to use them means power and well-being: not to, means impotence, voicelessness and, often, social and economic ill-health. The official dominance of ex-colonial languages is therefore a potent language shifting trigger constantly pulled by the desire of every individual to rise on the vertical and horizontal social and economic ladder.

The inferiority syndrome associated with Afrian languages

The official neglect of indigenous languages is another main source of threat to the existence of African languages that triggers language shift in African countries. Indigenous languages are officially considered unworthy of being used in official contexts because of their low developmental status. Their perceived unworthiness increases year after year as frontiers of knowledge continue to expand. This has been particularly so with French and Portuguese colonies, though somewhat less true of British and Belgian. The Portuguese and French deliberately trampled upon and indeed wanted African languages dead, as they were considered obstacles to their 'civilising mission'. Indigenous languages were conferred with an inferior status which, sadly, and due to the functions that indigenous languages are palpably seen as performing or not performing, have become accepted by many individual citizens of African countries. This inferiority syndrome or complex associated with indigenous languages, sadly, has stuck to the minds of many Africans, especially as far as indigenous languages are concerned in official domains, and so their impotence in such domains virtually appears to have become institutionised and canonised.

Officially and functionally recognised big or indegenous major languages make smaller languages seem insignificant

Big-population, officially and functionally recognised languages in Africa constitute a threat to small-population languages because their speakers are the power brokers and decision makers. They thus make decisions that favour big languages and threaten the very existence of small ones. Smaller languages are thereby made virtually irrelevant and functionally impotent at the societal level and even sometimes at the individual level. There is consequently a pull towards the major languages. The more powerful and functionally dominant the language, the more pressing its attraction and pull and the greater the tendency to shift towards it, given the fact that the pressure for social vertical mobility is virtually irresistible. This seems quite obvious when we examine the stature of European languages and of major African indigenous languages which have attracted many speakers. In the northern part of Nigeria, many speakers of other languages have been attracted to the Hausa language because of its functional dominance and power. Virtually every African country has regionally located major languages which pull and attract speakers of smaller languages to themselves because of their perceptual salience, functional dynamism and distinct ecological standing and weight in the national scheme of things. For instance, Mali has Bambara and Fulfulde; Gambia has Manding, Wolof and Fulfulde; Ethiopia has Amharic, Tigrinya and Galla; Congo Kinshasha (formerly Zaire) has Lingala, Luba, and Kongo; Malawi has Nyanja and Lomwe and Yao; Uganda has Runyankore, Luganda, Luo, Lugbara; Togo has Ewe and Kabiye; Benin has Fon-Ewe; Yoruba and Bariba; Kenya has Kikuyu, Swahili, Luhya, Luo and Kamba; Ghana has Dagbani, Ewe, Akan, Adangme, Nzema, Ga and Dagaari, while Nigeria has Hausa, Yoruba and Igbo. These major languages are like big fish that deliberately go out to swallow up the smaller languages (cf.

Batibo, 1992 with reference to Kenya). Their functional dominance in the national scheme of things dictates, willy nilly, that anyone who desires any meaningful participation in national life must learn to use at least one of them. Unhealthy rivalry between speakers of major languages also sometimes encourages a shift towards European languages, rather than vote for (or subject oneself to the language of) an intimidating and supposedly oppressive ethnolinguistic group. This does not mean, however, that any kind of bilingual acquisition will necessarily result in language shift.

In such an atmosphere, smallness in number of speakers of a language results in official neglect and denial of developmental attention. Moreover, it is often argued in many African countries that hunger, poverty, and war constitute more pressing priorities than the development of small languages, which, the argument normally goes, is contrary to the pragmatic and administrative need for maintaining unity in a multilingual polity. Moreover, undue attention to small languages, it is reasoned rather innocently, could cut them off from mainstream life. In most African countries, such logic has resulted in more and more attention being paid to bigger languages, and less and less attention to lesser-used languages: the rich thus become richer and the poor poorer. Many speakers of smaller languages thus shift to European languages or major languages simply as a survival ploy because they perceive that their own languages are threatened by extinction.

Low emotional, intellectual and functional investment in languages

Low emotional, intellectual and functional investment in one's own language is frequently a dominant cause for shifting to another language. A quick examination of the bottom-line language attitude determinants in sub-Saharan African countries will easily demonstrate why this has to be so. Among such attitudinal determinants identified in Adegbija (1994: 68–73) are: socio-historical forces relating to the African colonial heritage and the consequent association of colonial languages with power; the linguistic and social politics of complex and great multilingualism; the irresistible quest and pressures for social mobility in the individual, often associated with big languages and European languages; the functional dynamics inherent in languages, demonstrated by the fact that the prestige, respect and the value judgements made concerning a language tend to grow when a language is assigned significant functions and given official recognition; individual and societal pressures to survive, which often impinge on, and dictate attitudes towards particular languages. All such attitudinal factors, heavily, and, on the aggregate, overweighted in favour of European languages and big languages, tend to reduce the emotional, intellectual, functional and loyalty stake of speakers of small languages in their own languages, thereby diverting their attention, love, involvement and loyalty in the direction of both European languages and major languages, which are associated with achieving and being up there. Positive attitudinal stake in a language is a dominant factor in its maintenance both at the individual and societal level. Conversely, attitudinal doldrums with respect to a particular language constitute the principal precipitator of language shift.

The Sociolinguistic Atmosphere that puts Oko under Threat

The village of Oko, known to non-natives as Ogori, is inhabited by a small ethno-linguistic group in Nigeria. Formerly in Kwara State, the village has belonged to Kogi State since the state creation of 27 August 1991. Along with Magongo, another small village about three kilometres away, the people speak a very unique minority language, known to the native speakers as Oko, to outsiders as Ogori, but referred to as Osanyin in Magongo. The uniqueness of the Oko language lies in the fact that it shares very little with the languages of the immediately surrounding neighbours and also because only Ogori and Magongo (with perhaps less than 50,000 speakers, in all of Nigeria, and, most likely all over the world) speak this language; in the Nigerian context, this very fact is a potential source of threat.

An interesting fact about the Ogori-Magongo ethnic group is that although they are surrounded by different and relatively powerful language groups, they have, within their small village setting, stubbornly and doggedly stuck to their culture and language because of their pride in their language and have resisted every attempt, covert or overt, to assimilate them. Politically and for administrative convenience, most Nigerian governments have found it convenient to group Ogori-Magongo with the Okene Local Government area until 1996, when they were awarded a Local Government Area with the name 'Apafa Magongo'. This has increased contact with the Ebira, a much larger ethnic and language group that has often attempted to solidarise with the Ogori people, identifying them as part of Ebira. This has resulted in intermarriages. Moreover, many Oko people have learned to use the Ebira language in the attempt to interact with their Ebira neighbours. On the other hand, very few Ebira people ever learn how to use the Oko language because they see no need for it. This study is based on participant observation among the Ogori people as well as on informal interviews and interactions with native speakers of the Oko language.

Although no Yoruba community exists in the immediate neighbour-hood, many Oko people, intriguingly, and to the surprise of most neigh-bours, speak or understand Yoruba. It is sometimes considered a thing of pride for an Oko person to be able to speak Yoruba because it is one of Nige-ria's three major functionally and officially recognised languages. Many non-Ogorians, have, in fact constantly wondered how Oko people manage to be able to speak Yoruba. Yoruba forenames and surnames are also very common among Oko indigenes. Also, Yoruba is spoken along with Oko in the church. Pastors posted to Ogori by the Anglican Mission have been Yoruba-speaking. Thus, the reading of the Bible often occurs in Yoruba even though simultaneous translation into Oko while reading is occasion-ally done as well. The practice of reading the Bible in Yoruba constitutes a threat to Oko in the religious domain. Most of the local people who are able to read and need a Bible invariably buy a Yoruba Bible because there is none in Oko as yet. Moreover, the utility of a Yoruba Bible in the church context makes possession of a Yoruba Bible desirable. The church is thus the chief source of the transmission of the Yoruba language among the Ogori people. In addition, however, the youths and the educated elite in general have often had one cause or another to interact with the Yorubas by virtue of Ogori being a part of the former Kwara State, which had a very large concentration of speakers of Yoruba. Songs in churches are rendered in both Yoruba and Oko. Sermons are also frequently delivered in Yoruba, simply because many of the vicars cannot speak the Oko language. The use of Yoruba is beginning to infiltrate many Oko homes, though it is still uncommon in others. Children reared outside the community are particu-larly disadvantaged as far as speaking Oko is concerned because many of them return to Oko, not being able to communicate with their kith and kin who are not competent in the Yoruba language. Such children also have difficulty in interacting with other children in the Oko community. In the homes of such children, parents often have to speak either Yoruba or English even when they are within the Oko community. When these chil-dren also grow up and have children of their own, they invariably speak Yoruba or English, learned at school, to their own children even in their homes. The major threat to the Oko language, therefore, is among the younger generation who, invariably, have to emigrate to urban centres because jobs are not available within the Oko village setting. In such urban settings, there is no environmental enrichment for the use of the Oko language among children. Functionally, it is also seen to be irrelevant in the daily chores. Friends and acquaintances cannot speak it, it is not used in schools, it is not needed in interaction with peers, and even in many homes, many parents would rather speak English, in order to give their children a headstart in the educational domain, than speak Oko, which is perceived to be of no major utilitarian value.

Internally and for administrative convenience, the Ogori district is divided into seven sub-districts: Eni, Okesi, Udoba, Oshobane, Okigbo, Udo, Ileteju. Ebira is spoken by many people in the Oshobane sub-district of Ogori. It was principallly initially used in trade interactions with the Ebira people. There have been some inter-marriages between Ebira and Oko people and most people involved in such intermarriages have settled in Oshobane district, thus resulting in a heavy presence of the Ebira language in that sub-district of Ogori, and the transmission of Ebira there. This constitutes a big threat to the Oko language in such districts. However, the Ebira threat is not greater than the threat from English because Ebira does not have the national status that English has. It is also not quite relevant in the educational process.The utilitarian value of Ebira – in trade links, in interpersonal interactions with Ebira people, in communicating within some homes – has resulted in the language becoming more dominant among many Oko-speaking people even within the Oko community. Frequent interactions with the Ebiras has also been common over the years, especially because Ogori belonged in the past to the Okene local government area.

Another language that is perceptually salient, and thus constitutes a big threat to the Oko language is English. In official contexts, it is non-pareil. Many youths take pride in being able to speak English. In fact, they use it to exclude their parents from several conversations. Ability to speak English competently is a reflection of peer group pride in Ogori. The high regard for English is heightened by its international stature, the functional load it carries within Nigerian society, and the fact that it is required in interethnic interaction. English is also required for vertical upward social mobility. To achieve and be considered an achiever in the Oko community, one must be able to speak English. In most official domains, most Oko people, especially youths, are virtually incapable of functioning in the Oko language. The English language thus constitutes a major threat to the development of the Oko language.

Every Sunday morning, there is a worship service at the Anglican Church conducted in English. It is attended principally by youths and foreigners in the Ogori community. Ogori students also frequently speak English, both to display their achievement of the 'educated status' and to exclude from interactions some of their fellow Ogorians. Except for isolated instances, English is not commonly heard in homes. Those of the secondary school generation may, however, occasionally speak it among themselves in interpersonal interactions just to boost their ego. The working educated elite in the Oko village setting seem to insist often on the use of the Oko language, in which they take great pride. However, their counterparts that have emigrated to urban centres in search of jobs are unable to do so because their children are beginning to lose competence in the Oko language.

English, as an official language in Nigeria, carries with it a lot of prestige; Yoruba, as a language of a major ethnic group, is also very conspicuous in Nigeria; Ebira is the language of a former governing ethnic group that is also numerically superior to Oko. These are formidable ethnolinguistic forces that have remained a threat to the Oko competence of people of the younger generation. While Oko youths living within the village often appear to be able to weather such competition, their counterparts in urban centres have not been so lucky as they. The situation is so bad that some of them completely lose their competence in the Oko language. When such youths get married to non-Oko speaking spouses, the Oko language completely dies off in their own generation. Sometimes, Oko speakers are mistaken for people belonging to the Yoruba ethnic groups because they speak more of Yoruba than the Oko language.

Oko and the GIDS Scale

In this section, we shall attempt to document the current intergenerational transmission status in overt uses and attitudes of Oko, using the GIDS scale (Fishman, 1991) insofar as is possible, as a point of departure.

In his attempt to formulate a theory for RLS, Fishman (1991: 81–7) makes the very important point that RLS 'involves a prior value consensus among those who advocate, formulate, implement and evaluate it. Without such prior consensus, RLS *policy may become a bone of contention even among its own advocates* (Fishman, 1991: 82). He then proposes a Graded Intergenerational Disruption Scale) typology of threatened statuses, on analogy of the Richter Scale measures of the intensity of earthquakes. High numbers are intended to indicate stronger tremors or greater disruption of the established or normal geological strata and are, accordingly of greater threat to those living in the vicinity of the quake. Similarly, in the sociolinguistic disruption scale higher numbers are intended to 'imply greater disruption and therefore, more fundamental threat to the prospects for the language to be handed on intergenerationally' (Fishman, 1991: 87). The GIDS, according to Fishman, is a 'quasi-implicational scale' in that higher (more disrupted cores imply all or nearly all of the lesser degrees of disruption as well' (p. 87). We shall now attempt to evaluate the current intergenerational transmission status of Oko in particular and African languages in general on the basis of this scale.

Stage 8 on the GIDS (Graded Intergenerational Disruption Scale)

Most vestigial users of Xish are socially isolated old folks and Xish needs to be reassembled from their mouths and memories and taught to demographically unconcentrated adults

Ohiri-Aniche (1997: 75), observes that many Nigerian languages are dying because of the trend to bring up children as monolingual speakers of English. This is

> exerting a heavy affective price in that such children now hold our languages in disdain and feel ashamed to be associated with them. The situation is now such that in many urban schools even those children who understand local languages will pretend not to. Otherwise, they speak such languages at the peril of being mocked and jeered at by their peers . . . We need to pay attention to the damage being done to the psyche of Nigerian children who now are neither wholly 'European' nor Nigerian while also giving thought to the social malaise that this confusion of identities is engendering.

She continues by observing that the great danger inherent in this phenomenon is that

> when this generation of children become parents, they will not be able to pass on these languages to their own children. The result is that in a few generations, as the old people who know these languages die off, the languages also decline and eventually become extinct. This is the fate that has befallen many formerly flourishing languages of the world, the best examples being the native Indian languages of North and South America. (p. 75).

Some of the Nigerian languages cited as suffering such a fate, formerly spoken by some northern communities in Nigeria, include: Ashaganna, Feli of Baissa, Shirama, Ajanci, and Basa-Gumna. Others mentioned are Bassa Kontagora, with only 10 speakers left in 1987. An American linguist, Ron Shaefer, was also reported to have raised an alarm over Emai, spoken by a small community in Edo State, in the This Day newspaper of 31 March 1997:

> Emai language and the 30 different languages spoken in the area, would probably be dead by the year 2050 as none can serve as a lingua franca and are therefore being supplanted by English. (cf. Ohiri-Aniche, 1997: 75).

Ohiri-Aniche further reports a 1990 study in which she discovered that among the Primary and Secondary School children studied in five states in

Table 12.1 Percentage of JSS students not speaking their local language

Lagos State (Yoruba)	Imo State (Igbo)	Kano State (Hausa)	Gongola State (Minority Languages)	Rivers State (Minority Languages)	Average (Nigerian Languages)
2%	8%	1%	8%	14%	7%

Nigeria, a growing number are becoming non-speakers of local languages. The 1990 study revealed that among the Junior Secondary School students in five Nigerian states, those shown in Table 12.1 did not speak the ancestral language of their parents.

It is not surprising that minority languages have the largest percentages of students not speaking their local languages. Rivers State, for instance, has about 33 languages and most of them are minority languages. Ohiri-Aniche cites Afisimania who, in a 1991 doctoral dissertation, discovered that whereas 5% of educated adults interviewed in the state could not speak their local language, the figure had jumped to between 31.3% and 40.8% among the children of these adults and that this is a very significant difference in only one generation (Ohiri-Aniche 1997: 74). Given the dynamic role of European languages in education and their unique potential for pulling speakers of minority languages in particular, it is most likely that the situation in Africa as a whole will not be much different from this.

With respect to Stage 8 of GIDS, Oko, within the village setting, is not anywhere near this stage as a society or community of language speakers. However, this stage of GIDS might be considered somewhat applicable to some families of Oko speakers, especially those who have emigrated to urban centres. Among some of these people, neither the parents nor the children can speak the Oko language any longer. Generally, many speakers of African languages living in urban centres have completely abandoned their native languages and perhaps have lost contact with their kith and kin back home and shifted to the European language or a major indigenous language. For such categories of individuals, no trace of the language will probably be found within a few years.

Stage 7 on the GIDS

Most users of Xish are socially integrated and ethnolinguistically active population but they are beyond child-bearing age

This stage is not applicable to Oko in the village setting and as a community in totality. It is, of course, quite applicable to individual families that have migrated to urban centres and visit Oko only very occasionally.

Languages like Emai, referred to earlier, may be at this stage of the GIDS. The same may be true of Bassa-Kontagora, reported to have only 10 speakers in 1987.

Undoubtedly, many African languages are at Stages 8 and 7 of the GIDS and their survival is seriously threatened unless urgent RLS measures are taken.

Stage 6 on the GIDS

The attainment of intergenerational informal oralcy and its demographic concentration and institutional reinforcement

Oko, just like many of Africa's languages, may be placed on this stage of the GIDS within the Oko village setting. The family, within Ogori itself, and even among native speakers of Oko living in urban centres, may be said to be the locus and nerve centre of intergenerational transmission of the Oko language. However, the family as a transmission agency of Oko is seriously under threat, especially among Oko people in urban centres because people of the younger generation find no valid reason for continuing to speak the language in urban centres. Often, they have no one they can speak it to. Their parents do not speak it to them within the home setting *because they want them to do well at school.* Their peers do not know Oko and so interaction with them is often in English or in the major Nigerian language spoken in the particular urban centre. Several strategies may be employed to assist these non-retentive sub-groups in the promotion of the Oko language or for ensuring the transmission of the Oko language. Else- where, we have referred to these RLS devices as 'survival strategies' (cf. Adegbija, 1993a). Such RLS strategies are indeed of great importance because there are over 400 languages in Nigeria. The Nigerian government has not even given the officially designated three celebrity languages, Hausa, Yoruba and Igbo, the kind of developmental attention they deserve. The hope of languages on the lower rung of the minority ladder, because of numerical inferiority, is therefore a very meagre one. Internal efforts of the Oko people are needed to blow their own trumpet culturally and linguisti- cally and such efforts are therefore of immense sociolinguistic and RLS interest. Internally motivated RLS activists are usually immune to the apathy that commonly befalls projects that have a governmental tagging. Members of the Oko community in urban centres need to take their cultural and linguistic destinies into their own hands. Such RLS efforts, anchored within a particular Oko-speaking community in an urban centre and with a strong family base, have been grouped by Adegbija (1993a) into three types: cultural, linguistic or language related and political, with the first two being more critical in terms of their being 'totally internally generated and controlled'.

How Non-Retentive Oko Sub-groups Can be Assisted in Terms of RLS

Cultural RLS strategies in non-retentive Oko communities

The annual 'Ovia Osese Festival' is perhaps one of the most potent and perceptually salient device for the promotion, maintenance and transmission of the Oko language. With its base in individual families, it has, over the years, metamorphosed from a quietly celebrated local festival into a gargantuan cultural and linguistic carnival of state and national repute. It has often attracted the attention of the Nigerian Television Authority both at the state and local levels. Through the festival, the Oko people not only advertise, maintain and preserve their language and culture, but also celebrate and preserve their local prominence and their very existence as a cultural and linguistic minority. Its focus is on the initiation of girls into womanhood but it touches the very chords or 'okoness'. The occasion brings to Oko many important dignitaries and there is emphasis on the 'oke' song, with its sonorous 'eeeeeeeee' refrain. The occasion is marked by dancing, drumming and the singing of numerous songs in the Oko language. During the festival, the Oko people nurture and celebrate a sense of community and belongingness to a unique ethnolinguistic entity. Several family and community preparations precede the 'Ovia' festival. These include the rendition of 'Eregba' songs, the preparations of the maidens attaining womanhood through informal and formal as well as verbal and non-verbal interactions with parents on the values of womanhood; 'Ohenhenne', that is, the singing or reciting of the praise names of the clan to which a particular family that has a child celebrating the womanhood festival belongs, etc. The Eregba songs directly involve the men in the Ovia festival, since the Eregba artists, and a majority of its audience, are typically men. However, women also join Eregba song groups as new songs are created in the Oko language that are relevant to the history, culture, social life and the very essence and raison d'être of the Oko community. From this perspective, the Ovia festival constitutes a potent language maintenance and RLS device.

Unfortunately, however, many Oko sub-groups that have emigrated to urban areas have completely lost touch with the Ovia Osese festival. These sub-groups cease to practise the rituals and observances described above. For some, affinity with Christianity has made them to look down on many Oko cultural practices, which are considered unholy, immoral or ungodly.

Children in such family sub-groups grow up not knowing anything about the Ovia festival, and not being able to participate in the numerous rituals and cultural observances that perpetuate, promote and entrench the Oko language. When the children of such parents return to the Oko community, they are unable to communicate with their kith and kin. Although most festivals are of limited duration and constitute a departure from ordinary daily life, they are so effective in RLS because they bring the entire community together as one and create pleasant, long-lasting impressions about the togetherness and the very essence of the Oko community as an ethnolinguistic group.

Most clans in sub-districts within Ogori have their *'Ohenhenne'* or praise song, which is usually poetic in nature, as illustrated by the following praise song of the 'Okpowu' clan, with family members clustered in Okesi, Ileteju, Udoba and Eni districts:

Oko	English Gloss
Okpowu ro egben	Children of Okpowu
Alewere were	(no gloss: connotation of brightness, radiance and glory
Ecincin era	The fire of chaff
Ba ka ewu, ede jin yeeen	When attempting to quench it, it opens up and burns even much brighter

The above ohenhenne is used by the Okpowu clan and in individual families belonging to the clan for self-adulation and self-identification on festive occasions, at moments of crisis, and at moments of great achievements. In doing this, the Oko language is glorified, the culture it represents is exalted and the togetherness and identity as members of the micro-group, Okpowu clan, within the macro-culture, Oko, are emphasised, magnified and accentuated. This practice is passed on from one generation to another in individual families. Each clan has its praise song, frequently remembered in individual families and constantly recited in frequent festive moods and occasions.

RLS festivities in Oko are by no means limited to the Ovia festival which, one must admit, is non-pareil. *'Ogben esen'* (a ceremony that heralds the birth of a new baby, especially the very first) is another occasion in which every family can share a part at one time or the other. It also is a carnival experienced by verbal creativity and cultural awareness.

After the first child is born by a woman, married to a member of the Oko community, women sing songs and dance the distinctive rhythm of the Ogbenesen dance from house to house greeting each other as they join the smallest finger of the left hand and shout 'Odiororo', an exclamation of excitement in sharing the joys of a fellow member of the Oko community in contributing to the perpetuation of the community and a sign of gratitude to 'Osibina' (God), the giver of all good gifts.

Eregba, Ogun, Erimi and other related cultural songs are used to honour the departure (death) of aged members of the community. They are also common when traditional titles such as 'Osiako'; 'Uboro', 'Otaru', etc. are to be conferred on Oko indigenes who have made significant contributions to the growth and development of the community. In such festivals, proverbs, which normally punctuate day-to-day interpersonal interactions, are freely quoted and used and many children growing up in the community are able to learn their use in appropriate contexts.

In the Oko village setting, the frequent telling of 'Ogarega' or folktales during moonlit nights is another RLS intergenerational transmission device which the non-retentive sub-groups in urban centres could practise as a strategy for promoting the Oko language. Games like 'alele puepue' (a blindfolding game); 'eba', a traditional type of chess game, and 'Eto fomaya' (where are you taking me to); 'gbio' or riddles, which also serve as powerful means for transmitting Oko from parents to children, would be of interest to the children of parents in these non-retentive sub-groups and it would encourage and enable them, in urban settings, to observe more Oko cultural traits within their own homes and communities. The Ogori Descendants Union (ODU), which has branches in most urban centres in Nigeria where native speakers of Oko are found, is another language and cultral transmission organ. In fact, its primary purpose is to promote the identity and culture of the Ogori people. Thus, as an unwritten statute, its meetings, both in Ogori and in all the branches spread throughout Nigeria, are held through the medium of the Oko language. Unfortunately, however, in many urban settings, only very few natives of Oko attend these meetings that could be very useful as far as the promotion and transmission of the Oko language is concerned. In fact, young people rarely frequent such meetings, which are held largely among people of the older generation. Such customs and traditions are not passed on to the children of parents who have emigrated to urban centres. The rate of emigration will likely continue to increase because of better amenities, better jobs, and a more attractive modern life-style for Oko youths in urban centres.

Linguistic or language-based RLS strategies for non-retentive sub-groups

Adegbija (1993b: 9) makes the following pertinent observation:

Globally, language is the dynamite of thought. If you kill or render impotent a people's language, you can as well kill the people, but if you effectively plan or develop a people's language, you are laying treasures that can affect eternity and providing the people with tools of self-actualization, self-identity and self-promotion.

Commenting specifically on the Nigerian context, Agheyisi (1984: 234) makes the following unfortunately valid observation: 'Language planning, as a systematic programme of development has remained largely peripheral to the mainstream of national planning.' Language planning can help in saving threatened languages because of its potential for focusing attention on threatened languages and ensuring their continued use. We have observed earlier on that if lack of attention applies to the so-called 'major Nigerian languages', then it applies even more to the acutely minor minority languages such as Oko, and any language group that will survive or succeed in reversing language shift may do so by the skin of its teeth. In essence, those who speak that language have to show an active and dynamic interest in planning for the existence and survival of their own language. This kind of take-your-own destiny in your own hands attitude has again been displayed by the Oko community *in its own small-village hinterland* with respect to corpus planning and 'language promotion' (cf. Rubagumya, 1991). Encouragement of linguistic studies on different aspects of Oko constitutes a specfic aspect of corpus planning. Chumbow (1982) did an autosegmental analysis of vowel harmony in Oko, and was very much encouraged by native speakers of the language who served as informants. He, in turn, encouraged several undergraduate students to do their undergraduate projects on the Oko language. Adegbija (1989) did a study on aspects of the pragmatics of Oko. Adegbija (1993b) also focused on 'The graphicization of a small-group language: A case study of Oko'. Earlier on in the yearning to have a writing system for the language, an orthography of the language was devised by some non-linguist indigenes, examined with keen interest by the ODU and sent to linguists for scrutiny. The revision done on it has subsequently resulted in the preparation of try-out texts in the language, some original creations, others a translation of general and familiar texts such as *'Osibina Adura'* (Our Lord's Prayer) which is frequently recited in the homes of many Ogori Christians. As Adegbija (1993b: 153) remarks:

The graphicization of a language brings that language into fellowship with the world's community of languages that can do things, that can achieve, and that can tread in realms where the spoken language is incompetent to tread. It constitutes a basic prerequisite for the use of a language in education, in print, and in other realms of language functionality.

For a long time, *Asekee*, a magazine in the Oko language, was published by the Ogori Students Association. The word 'Asekee' connotes 'listen, there is an important message'. It is normally used when the town crier beats his gong round the town to announce an important message, often from the Ologori of Ogori, the village head, or one of the titled chiefs.

Also of interest in terms of its potential for RLS is the current trend in the patterns of naming among some Ogori people. Before the 1970s it was common for children to be given Yoruba first names such as Kayode, Oluwole, Ayo, Taiyewo, Kehinde, Ayodeji, Olorunfemi, etc. In fact, Yoruba surnames such as Abisoye, Akerejola, Atere, Aje, Adegbija, Asiribo, Abanikanda, etc., which are normally difficult to change because of the implications of changing surnames, are still very common and were almost the norm too. It is not surprising, therefore, to see people of the older generation answering to Yoruba forenames and surnames. This onomastic process has resulted in probing into and considerably enriching the lexicon of the Oko language recently. Although a few children, even in the past, were given distinct Oko names such as Osigbodi, Osebekwin, Osekafore, Oreka, etc., the trend of Oko-naming has become much more common and has been inherited by members of the new generation of Ogorians. Hence, vivid and striking new names in the language have been created. We now find many more individuals carrying very original distinctive and typically Okoish names such as Titiosibina, Tosibinaronmuro, Amadosibina, Osibinadinfenyan, Mosiefilemu, Igule, etc. Our investigations revealed that the trend in the giving of Oko names began in the 1960s and appeared to have increased in scope as a deliberate ethnic identity and RLS or language promotion strategy. Then, many of those rebelling against 'foreign' names had no children. Consequently, they demonstrated their reaction against non-Oko names given to them by their parents by giving themselves newly created or existing Oko names, different from the Yoruba or biblical names given to them by their parents. Some of these are illustrated by the instances shown in Table 12.2.

Today, most members of the Oko community living in Ogori tend to follow this pattern of naming. Unfortunately, however, this cannot be totally said to be equally true of those living in urban centres, many of

Table 12.2 Newly created names

Old Name	Self-given 'Okoish' names
Phillip (biblical source)	Mekamagba (It's mine that I see)
Ebenezer (biblical source)	Osebekwin (to God belongs thanks or kneeling)
Joshua (biblical source)	Imunefan (I ran and escaped)
Olorunfemi (Yoruba source)	Efurosibina (connotes 'outside God I'm helpless)
Victoria (English source)	Mosiforeba (my God has conquered them)

whom prefer Yoruba or biblical names. While the Yoruba names conform with the societies they live in, the biblical or Hebrew names are in line with the religion they practice. As in many other Nigerian and African communities, every name has a meaning relevant to the personal, interactions history, culture and life of the people. As the Oko-speaking community within the village is concerned, therefore, there is everything in a name and this explains the desire to ensure that children have 'Okoish' names that have a strong and palpable bearing on the maintenance, promotion and perpetuation of the Oko language and culture. Every child with an Oko name will, at the very least, be always reminded of his linguistic background and identity whenever the name is written or called. The giving of indigenous Okoish names bearing sociocultural import is therefore an indirect means for ensuring that the children remember their origin and that the language remains prominent, for we carry our names with all their connotations with us wherever we go. In essence, far from being a mere identity tag, naming for the Oko people, now, constitutes a means of audio and mobile culture and language promotion, and hence, subtly, an RLS effort. The Oko speaking sub-groups in urban centres would also need to apply such linguistic strategies for reversing language shift. Unfortunately, hard economic conditions have increased the barriers between those in urban settings and those in the Ogori village. Consequently, contact with the Oko language is being reduced both among the older and younger generation of Oko speaking sub-groups in urban centres. Whereas in the past, they visited home during festivals, and quite frequently, it has now become commonplace, for economic reasons, in particular, for many families not to have any contact with their kith and kin in the villages for several years on end. Space is also creating language distance and intergenerational transmission of the Oko language is the worse for it. In view of the increasing rate of emigration in search of jobs and a more prestigeous life-style, this distance is likely to continue to increase.

Politically-oriented RLS strategies for non-retentive sub-groups

Behind every successful RLS programme there is often a subtle and successful political manoeuvring at the individual, local, regional or national level or, sometimes, at all the levels combined. This is because language planning and the functional allocation to languages in multilingual contexts always have sharp political cutting edges. In the Ogori community, the politics behind the promotion of the Ogori language is played both within the community itself, to convert the uninitiated, and outside it. It also occurs at the individual, family, local, regional and national levels. For instance, at family levels within the Ogori village itself, children are frequently appealed to about the need to speak their language, to know it, to be proud of it and to get used to it. Fathers and mothers frequently engage in this kind of family politics as an RLS device. Through socialisation and informal education at home, this strategy can be extended to Ogori indigenes in urban centres whose children stand a greater risk of losing their competence in the Oko language because they have no daily access to it, and cannot find any utilitarian value in using it in urban centres. Children could be taught and encouraged from their earlier years to, for instance, pray in the language, interact with each other in the language on a daily basis, and to always insist on maintaining an Okoish identity wherever they go. Parents should encourage their children to interact with each other in the Oko language, especially in the home setting. Individual members of the Oko community, on their part, should use every opportunity to announce to interlocutors that they belong to the Oko community, and that their language is quite different and distinct from Yoruba, or Ebira, the larger ethnolinguistic community around them with which they are commonly linked.

At the regional and national levels, the politics behind the language should be played with greater dexterity and efficiency, principally by members of the ODU, which has branches all over Nigeria. Its members should meet more regularly and national meetings should be held more faithfully. Wranglings over chieftaincy affairs by rival clans have recently crippled the power of the ODU, which has been the major political organ of the Oko people. Such feuds among different clans laying claim to chieftaincy have distracted attention from the growth and development of the Oko language. Rival clans have taken each other to court and the entire village has been divided accordingly. This has made it difficult for members of the community to act as one force and has been a great drawback for interest in, and the development of the Oko language.

Political wranglings among rival clans have also reduced the publicity that the Oko language normally enjoys during the Ovia and other festivals within the community. This has been a great setback for Ogori identity and the promotion of the Oko language. The reversal of ethnicity annihilation and of language shift, previously created by political togetherness, has thus been seriously jeopardised, compromised and undermined.

Stage 5 on the GIDS

Xish literacy in home, school and community, but without taking extra-communal reinforcement of such literacy
Not many African languages have reached this level on the GIDS scale. Our language, Oko, certainly has not. Very few are literate in Oko, as its orthography is not yet very well publicised and so has not been learned by many of the indigenes. Moreover, the internal political wranglings over chieftaincy, referred to above, have constituted a serious setback for the marketing of the orthography and RLS efforts in general.

Nigerian languages such as Yoruba, Hausa, Igbo, may be said to have reached this level to a very limited extent. Limited because literacy in the languages among native speakers is at a very low rate, especially when compared with literacy in the English language. Even many speakers of the Yoruba language cannot read it. The same is true of virtually every other major African language. One principal reason why many African languages have not attained this level is that literacy in them is not required as 'a key to social mobility and to competitiveness in the modern work sphere' (Fishman, 1991: 96). In most African countries, except perhaps in Tanzania, to some degree, social mobility is possible only with literacy in the language of the former colonial master. Most African languages, for instance, have no newspapers in them. Of all languages in Nigeria, only Hausa, Yoruba and Igbo have newspapers published in them, and these are not published regularly or daily in all three languages. When literacy in an African language is conducted at the local level, participants often cannot see its functional value or utility and so tend eventually to get discouraged and give up the attempt at getting literate in the indigenous language. Many prefer literacy in the European languages, which make one to be counted among 'those who know book' (i.e. the educated or the knowledgeable).

Stage 4 on the GIDS

Xish in lower education (types a and b) that meets the requirements of compulsory education laws
Although the Nigerian National Policy on Education stipulates that the mother-tongues be used as media of public education at the lower levels of

education, very few schools follow this stipulation and no governmental sanctions have been applied on the majority of schools flouting it.

Governmental inertia with regard to applying sanctions could be because of awareness that a majority of languages have not been prepared for use in education at any level because no orthographies have been devised for them. Unofficially, and in reality, however, many teachers often discover that their pupils at the lower levels of education can neither understand them nor follow explanations in English and so have to carry out explanations in the indigenous languages. This observation most likely cuts across many African countries. In essence, most African languages have not even 'gained co-control of the lower . . . educational and lower work domains' officially. In fact, in many schools all over Africa, children are frequently penalised for speaking their mother-tongues, and not the language of the former colonial master, in the school environment. Consequently, children grow up cultivating the attitude of subtle distaste or outright hatred for their mother-tongues in the educational domain. Even if there is no hatred, the clear message being sent across, which affects the attitude built round the indigenous languages throughout life, and is very evident in the attitude of most Africans, is about the irrelevance, the lack of consequence, and the impotence of the indigenous languages for educational purposes. Given the fact that over 80% of African languages as yet have no orthographies, the prospect of their use at the lower rungs of the educational ladder remains very dim indeed in spite of the educational policies in many countries stipulating that they be so used.

Stage 3 on the GIDS

Use of Xish in the lower work sphere (outside of the Xish neighbourhood community) involving interaction between Xmen and Ymen

Again, Oko is not used in the lower work sphere. A majority of African languages similarly, are yet to arrive at this level. Whereas it is true that speakers of the same African language will most likely select to interact with each other in their mother-tongues even when they are in other communities in the lower work sphere, there would be no need, or rather no opportunity to use Xish outside of the neighbourhood community in interactions between Xmen and Ymen, simply because most Ymen probably do not understand Xish.

In most informal interactions even outside the neighbourhood, Xmen would most likely interact with each other in Xish. Thus, Oko people within the Ogori village would probably interact using the Oko language, both at the lower and higher work sphere in informal contexts and situations. This example needs to be copied by their counterparts in urban centres. In formal contexts, however, Oko is completely endangered because it is not used at all. Instead, English is most frequently used in formal interactions. The picture, in varying degrees in different countries, is virtually the same: namely, that indigenous languages are used in informal interactions even at the work sphere, and the language of the ex-colonial master is used in formal interactions and for official purposes whenever interactions with speakers of other languages are involved.

Stage 2 on the GIDS

Xish in lower governmental services and mass media but not higher spheres of either

Of all Nigerian languages, perhaps only Hausa, Yoruba and Igbo could be said to partially be at this stage on GIDS in that they have some newspapers being published in them. But they are not officially used even in lower governmental service even though, in reality, they function most in informal situations, just as is the case with most other indigenous languages. The principal difference between these three major languages and other Nigerian languages is that some form of written communication does occur in them at the lower governmental services, even though these could be rather sporadic and uncoordinated. They are used in political campaigns, advertisements, commercial jingles, etc. perhaps more frequently than other indigenous languages.

Stage 1 on the GIDS

Some use of Xish in higher level educational, occupational, governmental and media efforts (but without the additional safety provided by political independence)

Only very few major African languages have attained this stage on the GIDS scale. In Nigeria, Hausa, Yoruba and Igbo certainly are partially used in higher education, but mainly as subjects in the curriculum for those who wish to study them. For such people as well, they would often be used as medium in courses relating to the specific languages. Kiswahili in Tanzania, perhaps also in Kenya and Uganda, may also be said to have to some degree attained this level since, in Tanzania, for instance, it is often used as a medium of instruction in some aspects of higher education. Somali in Somalia is also used in some aspects of higher educational, occupational, governmental and mass media activities. In most previous French and Portuguese colonies, e.g. Togo, Benin, Angola, etc. the journey towards this stage of GIDS is still a very tortuous and bleak one. In general, perhaps over 95% of African languages have not yet reached this stage and are most unlikely to, given the present language planning postures and attitudes towards small languages within the continent.

Desirable RLS Strategies in Africa

Before concluding this paper, it would be in order to examine some specific RLS strategies that are particularly suitable and desirable for the African context. Adegbija (1997) proposes some concrete strategies for combatting RLS problems bedevilling the African continent in particular, which could also be relevant for, and have deep implications for other contexts in which RLS is either a major preoccupation, or is considered desirable. The strategies are intended for promoting and ensuring the survival of small languages and for combatting some of the problems responsible for their neglect. These strategies will now be briefly considered:

A strong basic commitment and developmental RLS philosophy

Such a philosophy: that all languages, no matter the number of their speakers, qualify for and should be given a chance to survive and grow to their optimum potential without being stifled by government policy actions, is a desideratum for RLS. Where there is first the will, a way can be found and nagging obstacles can be overcome and boldly confronted. Policies should be formulated that will require speakers of particular indigenous languages, at least, to be literate in their mother-tongues. Teachers would need to be trained to make this possible. In essence, just as vital economic resources, all languages should be treasured. There should be a vision to rescue all languages from extinction, death or the endangered languages list.

The establishment of national and local language-development coordinating bodies, committees or agencies

In every context, an RLS committee or body is required to assume responsibility for RLS. When a responsibility belongs to nobody, nobody will feel committed to it. Of course coordinating bodies are desirable for the formulation of policies rather than to stifle local and internally generated development efforts. A national agency is also required to orchestrate and encourage the reversal of language shift.

Deep involvement of the language communities concerned in development efforts

An Oko proverb is germane to this: 'When you do not attempt to carry your own load, you cannot expect assistance from anyone.' Another says: 'Only a child that knows how to wash his hands can eat with elders.' This proverbial hand washing is required by all communities desiring the reversal of language shift. Small language groups need to take their own destinies in their own hands before expecting to 'cross the periphery, oblivion and damnation hurdles and enter the crooked and narrow road to salvation' (Adegbija, 1997: 20). Communities concerned therefore need to be involved emotionally, intellectually and mentally in RLS efforts. In fact, to be maximally successful and effective, RLS efforts must be internally motivated and perpetuated. When the community has a stake in it, it will feel constrained to continue carrying its own load even when no assistance is forthcoming from other quarters.

Tapping all available resources and reducing language-development costs

If RLS is properly planned at the local and national levels, resources, both human and material, can be judiciously harnessed to meet RLS goals, especially given the fact that the excuse of scarcity of resources is often the alibi for lack of RLS initiatives at governmental quarters (cf. Adegbija, 1997 for details of available resources in most African countries that can assist RLS efforts).

Official institutionalisation of multilingualism

Opportunities for the use of a language in the public sector tend to promote its growth and boost its prestige. At the moment, Oko does not have such opportunities. Besides securing the use of endangered languages in the intimate spheres of family and community, which Fishman (1988: 12–13) likens to the stopping of the haemorrhaging of the vital arteries, there is the need to officially institutionalise their use, if they are to gain prestige or be lifted up from the lower rungs of the social ladder in the minds and psyche of many Africans. As a first step, bold attempts must be made to graphicise all African languages, for this is a deliberate language reversal ploy. Time should also be created for their use on radio and television. Use in the public sector will promote a language from the kith and kin domain to the public limelight and thus elevate its esteem and increase its functional stamina and utility calibre.

Conclusion

Every language is entitled to a buoyant life. A language that is deliberately used in the home and public sector, which its speakers are proud to be associated with, which has a vibrant culture that is consciously promoted and orchestrated into prominence, and which the younger generation is eager to use and be associated with, can never die. Conversely, a language that is restricted in use both in the private and public sectors, family, local, regional and national settings, which its speakers are ashamed of, which has no vibrant culture to boast of or exhibit, and which the younger generation would rather forget, is already dead, even if apparently living.

Given the GIDS, virtually every African language will, unfortunately, belong to the endangered language group, at one degree or another. In this paper, we have shown that Oko seems to be doing well in its own small village setting. This is, however, not the case in larger cities to which many Oko indigenes frequently emigrate, and would still need to continue emigrating, in search of jobs, a better life-style, better pay, etc. Such emigration will most likely intensify because the prospects of enough better-paying jobs in the village have remained dim for a very long time. Moreover, the younger generation is more ambitious about rising high and the available jobs within the village setting are not commensurate with the height of their ambitions. Immigrants, we have shown, find no motivation or encouragement to practise the customs and rituals of their kith and kin, the major avenue for promoting the Oko language, among their children, in urban centres. This thus creates an intergenerational gap in the transmission of the Oko language and constitutes a great threat to the growth, development and very existence of the Oko language. Consequently, children of such parents return home unable to communicate with their kith and kin in the Oko language. The Oko language is thus already dead among many individual city-dwelling indigenes, due to an extremely low intergenerational transmission status and is seriously under threat in most others. For the language to remain alive, its speakers both within the village and in urban centres must have a higher affective stake and deep emotional inventory in its survival, promotion and plight. As long as speakers of a language have a deep stake in its survival and a high emotional involvement and commitment to its existence, all the language shift agents and triggers in this world will not be able to kill their resolve.

Acknowledgements

I am grateful to Professor Joshua Fishman for detailed comments on earlier drafts of this chapter.

References

Adegbija, E. (1993a) The graphicization of a small language: The case of Oko. *International Journal of the Sociology of Language* 102, 153–73.

Adegbija, E. (1993b) Survival strategies for minority languages: the case of Oko. *ITL Review of Applied Linguistics* 103–4, 19–37.

Adegbija, E. (1994) *Language Attitudes in Sub-Saharan Africa: A Sociolinguistic Overview*. Clevedon: Multilingual Matters.

Adegbija, E. (1989) A comparative study of politeness phenomena in Nigerian English, Yoruba and Ogori. *Multilingua: Journal of Cross-cultural and Interlanguage Communication* 8(1), 57–80.

Adegbija, E. (1997) The identity, survival, and promotion of minority languages in Nigeria. *International Journal of the Sociology of Language* 125, 5–27.

Agheyisi, R.N. (1984) Minor languages in the Nigerian context: Prospects and problems. *Word* 35(3), 235–53.

Batibo, H.M. (1992) The conflict between elitist, national and ethnic loyalties in language attitude and use: The case of Tanzania. Lecture delivered at the University of Duisburg, March 1992.

Chumbow, B.S. (1982) Ogori vowel harmony: An autosegmental perspective. *Linguistic Analysis* 10(1), 61–93.

Fishman, J. (1988) Language spread and language policy for endangered languages. In P.H. Lowenberg (ed.) *Language Spread and Language Policy: Issues, Implications and Case Studies* (pp. 1–15). Washington, DC: Georgetown University Press.

Fishman, J. (1991) *Reversing Language Shift*. Clevedon: Multilingual Matters.

Ohiri-Aniche, C. (1997) Nigerian languages die. *Quarterly Review of Politics, Economics and Society* 1(2): 73–9.

Rubagumya, C.M. (1991) Language promotion for educational purposes: The example of Tanzania. *International Review of Education* 37(1), 67–85.

Chapter 13
Andamanese: Biological Challenge for Language Reversal

E. ANNAMALAI and V.GNANASUNDARAM

Geography

A cluster of islands running from north to south in the Bay of Bengal on the south-eastern side of the Indian sub-continent is the Andaman Islands. They lie between 10° 13 and 10° 30 N. latitudes and 90° 15 and 93° 10 E. longitudes. They are spread over an area of 6430 square kms and are separated from the Nicobar Islands in the south by the Ten Degree channel. The northernmost island of the Andaman Islands is at a distance of 9016 kms south-east of the confluence of the Hugli River in West Bengal, India, and at a distance of 193.12 kms south of Ca Negrais in Myanmar (Burma). The capital town Port Blair is at a distance of 1255.25 kms from Calcutta and 1190.88 kms from Chennai (Madras). The Andaman Islands are divided into Great Andaman Islands and Little Andaman Islands. The Little Andaman Islands are separated from Port Blair by 100 kms of sea.

In the Little Andaman Islands live the Onges. In Great Andaman Islands, Jarawas live in the South Andaman and Rutland Islands, Sentinels in the North Andaman Island and the Andamanese in the Strait Island.

Anthropology

Anthromorphically, the native population of the Andaman Islands is 'Negrito' (of South East Asian region according to Pandit 1976) and that of Nicobar Islands is 'Mangoloid'. The Andamanese belong to the former. Their population is estimated to have been between 5000 and 8000 in 1858 when the British Government of India founded a penal colony in Port Blair. They inhabited most of the Great Andaman Islands at that time.

The Andamanese comprised 10 different ethnic groups each with a separate speech form and a name (Brown 1914: 12). They were: (1) Aka Cari; (2) Aka Kora; (3) Aka Jeru; (4) Aka Bo; (5) Aka Kede; (6) Aka Kol; (7) Oko Juwoi; (8) Aka Pucikwar; (9) Aka Bea and (10) Aka Bale. These 10

309

groups may be classified into two broad divisions on the basis of cultural differences. They are the Northern group consisting of Cari, Kora, Bo and Jeru; and the Southern group consisting of Kede, Kol, Juwoi, Pucikwar, Bea and Bale. All were, however, lumped together by the British administrators under the name of Great Andamanese or Andamanese, for short. Brown (1948: 24–5) observes about the language of the Andamanese that

> although the natives themselves . . . recognise and give names to ten distinct languages, all of them are closely related. There is, on the whole, not a great deal of difference between two neighbouring languages. A man of Aka-Jeru tribe could understand without any great difficulty a man speaking Aka-Bo. On the other hand, many of the languages included two or even more distinct dialects.

This is to be expected as there was no or very little interaction between them. Brown (1914) observes, with reference to Bea and Jeru, that 'until the islands were occupied by Europeans by 1858, these two tribes did not know of each other's existence'. This is supported by Mann (1932: xxi), who says that 'in many cases no knowledge was possessed regarding tribes distant only fifteen or twenty miles'.

Demography

The Andamanese population started to decline from the middle of the 19th century when it became a penal colony. The native people were killed by the British soldiers during their punitive expeditions into the forests to claim land for settlement. When peace was established leading to interaction between the Andamanese and the non-tribal settlers, the former were introduced to tobacco, liquor and opium and exposed to new diseases, which became epidemic – pneumonia in 1868, syphillis in 1876, measles in 1877 and influenza in 1892 – killing a large number of the people (Awaradi, 1990: 227). In the earlier battles with the colonisers, most of the young men of reproductive age had died. Among the surviving Andamanese, the changed life style and food habits contributed to the deterioration of their health. For example, the clothes, which they often wore wet during hunting expeditions in the rain in the forest or in the sea, caused bronchial and pulmonary infections. When the Japanese occupied the Andaman islands from March 1942 to October 1942 during the second world war, they suspected the Andamanese to be spying for the British and massacred a good number of them.

Table 13.1 illustrates the decline of the population of the Andamanese in the first six decades of this century.

Table 13.1 Population decline in total

Year	1901	1911	1921	1931	1951
Population	625	453	209	90	23
Year	1961	1971	1975	1988	1998
Population	19	24	23	28	35

Figures from 1901 to 1971 are from the Census of India. The figures for 1975, 1988 and 1998 are from field work.

Table 13.2 Decline in the population of ethnic groups

	1901			1911			1921			1975
	Adult	Child	Total	Adult	Child	Total	Adult	Child	Total	Total
Aka-Cari	31	8	39	26	6	32	15	2	17	4
Aka-Kora	63	33	96	57	18	78	36	12	48	1
Aka-Bo	31	17	48	40	22	62	12	5	17	6
Aka-Jeru	178	40	218	143	37	180	84	17	101	11
Aka-Kede	54	5	59	28	4	32	16	0	16	0
Aka-Kol	8	3	11	2	0	2	0	0	0	0
Oko-Juwoi	40	8	48	9	0	9	5	0	5	0
Aka-Pucikwar (Bojigyah)	45	5	50	33	3	36	8	1	9	0
Aka-Bale	15	4	19	14	1	15	4	0	4	0
Aka-Bea	30	7	37	9	1	10	0	1	1	1
Total			625			453			209	23

Figures for the period 1901 to 1911 are from the census of India and are taken from Chakraborty (1990). Figures after 1921 are not available for different ethnic communities, and figures for 1975 are from field work.

The decline of population in different ethnic groups of Andamanese is given in Table 13.2.

When the 1961Census reported only 19 speakers of Andamanese scattered in many islands, the Government of India, pursuing a policy of preservation of tribes, collected them and placed them in 1970 in a small island called Strait Island in South Andaman. They were provided free shelter, clothing, food and medicine. These 19 people belonged to five ethnic groups namely, Jeru, Kora, Bo, Cari and Balwa, but were mixed with Karens of Burma and Oroans of Bihar, India (locally called Ranchis), who were brought by the British to the Andaman Islands as labourers. The policy of preservation has helped to increase somewhat the population of the Andamanese.

Table 13.3 Current age and sex-wise distribution

Age in years	Male	Female
0–4	2	1
5–9	2	1
10–14	2	3
15–24	3	4
25–44	6	5
45–54	1	0
55–64	1	2
65 and above	1	1
		Total 35

The age and sex-wise distribution of Andamanese population in 1998 taken from the field work is given in Table 13.3.

Language

The language is noted in the Census as 'an unclassified language spoken by a few remaining individuals of the tribe of the same name' (Nigam, 1972: 8) echoing Brown (1948: 495), who stated that 'the Andamanese languages constitute a separate family having no apparent affinity with any other family of languages'; and Colonel Temple, who observed that 'the Andaman languages are one group, they are like (i.e. connected with) no other group, they have no affinities by which we might infer their connection with any other known group' (quoted in Mann, 1932: 5). Other members of this yet unidentified language family are the Onges, Jarawas and Sentinels in the Andaman Islands (Manoharan, 1989: 8). Brown (1948) divides the Andmanese family of languages into two: (1) Northern group and (2) Southern group. Mann (1932: xxvii) divides them into three: South Andaman, Middle Andaman and North Andaman. Manoharan (1989: 173) groups them as shown in Figure 13.1.

All the speech forms, whether languages or dialects, that were genetically related and were spoken in the Great Andaman Islands are now lost except the one now called Andamanese.

The present native speakers of Andamanese claim that their language is of the Jeru group, the largest group. But, according to Manoharan (1989), the present language is a mixture of different extinct varieties with a high percentage of Jeru forms.

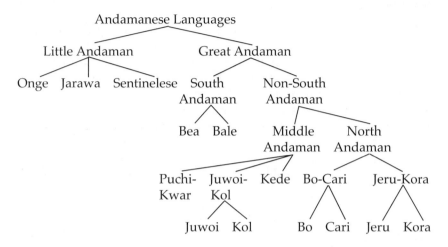

Figure 13.1 Andamanese languages

Social Organisation

The Andamanese were hunters in the forest and in the sea and food gatherers. Each ethnic group had a specific territory for hunting and gathering. Tropical forests supplied them with various types of fruits, roots and wild pigs. The sea was the source for tortoise, dugong and different types of fish including shell fish. They also collected the eggs of birds. They are now given free rice, wheat, cereals, etc. by the government. They have also been trained to grow in small plots sweet potato, tobacco, green pepper, pineapple, banana and papaya.

Marriage was originally within the ethnic group (Brown, 1948: 72–3) and 'was prohibited between siblings, step-brothers, step-sisters and between consanguineal relatives of the same generation, who were regarded as brothers and sisters' (Chakraborty, 1990: 18). The small size of the population does not allow them now to follow these normative rules. A woman is permitted to share her husband with another woman for reproduction and similarly a man is permitted to share his wife. The marriage rule is relaxed with regard to age also but the family remains the unit of social organisation. There are now seven families in the Strait Island. There is a chief selected by age by the community. Government reaches the people for developmental activities through him. This is the only hierarchical structure of the community.

Development

The government has constructed houses with tin roofs, brick walls and concrete floors for each family of the Andamanese in the Strait Island. Coconut trees have been planted as a cash crop and canoes have been given for fishing but they hardly use both. Besides the food, stitched clothes are given to them by the government. This kind of 'development from above' has made them lose their traditional skills. It has robbed them of their pride and purpose of life. It manifests itself at the individual level in different forms such as 'occasional fits of depression, bouts of drinking or the sporadic spree of visiting cinema theatres or video parlours at a stretch watching all shows available and at the end experiencing the void' (Awaradi, 1990: 241)

Grammar

The details of the grammar of the Andamanese language may be seen in Manoharan (1989). The grammar shows that the language does not exhibit features of attrition. There is no significant difference in the complexity of the grammar among the users of the language of all ages. There is however a difference in the active command of the vocabulary and code mixing with Hindi between older and younger generations.

Andamanese has a phonemic inventory of 7 vowels and 21 consonants; vowel length is phonemic. It has an elaborate pronominal system. The three person pronouns also distinguish number and respect and the first person plural pronouns distinguish inclusion and exclusion of the addressee. There are three deictic pronouns. There are nine cases. The verbs belong to 17 classes on the basis of the lexically determined allomorphs of the imperative suffix. Transitivity of the verb is expressed by derivational morphology. The finite verbs are not marked for gender and number. There is a three way tense system (past, present and future) and two-way aspectual system (durative and perfective). The word order is SOV. The modifier (like the adjective) precedes the head (like the noun).

In the lexicon, native vocabulary has been replaced by Hindi words even in the semantic domains of kinship, colour, numerals, etc. There is heavy borrowing from Hindi for culturally new objects and concepts such as sari, pants, cooked vegetable, frying pan, medicine, hospital, electricity, etc., as well as for numbers beyond three.

There is heavy code switching between Hindi and Andamanese and code mixing of Hindi in Andamanese particularly among the younger people. The borrowing and mixing at the lexical and structural levels do not necessarily indicate a shift towards language loss. They may indicate a pattern of language use of bilinguals and language change in a contact situation as long as they can be shown to be instances of convergence, a phenomenon well attested among the languages of the Indian sub-continent (Pandit, 1972, 1977). There is an increase in borrowing and mixing along generational lines and the younger generations borrow and mix more. If this trend continues to cover the entire lexicon and grammar and there is no sociolinguistic identification of it as the current Andamanese but as a variety of Hindi, then it will be possible to speak of language loss. At present, though there is resentment among the older generation about the excessive mixing of Hindi, it is accepted as a feature of Andamanese of the younger generation. The sociolingusitic identity of ethnicity through language, though weak among the younger generation, seems to gain ground as this generation grows older and strengthens its ties with the community.

Bilingualism

Constant contact with mainland people settled in the islands and with government officials in charge of tribal development has made Andamanese bilingual in Hindi. This bilingualism was necessary for their survival with changed occupations, cultural habits and social needs that are dependent on the mainlanders. Their basic needs of food and clothing are to be obtained from the market or government, which are controlled by the mainlanders. Their everyday food items include rice, wheat, oil and market vegetables and meat besides fish and other sea products, which they occasionally hunt on their own. They use cooking vessels like *tava*, 'frying pan', *kada:i* 'a kind of frying pan', *pati:la:* 'a kind of cooking vessel', etc. Men wear shirts, pants and *lungi* and women wear sari, blouse, *salwar, khameez* (both are girls' wear in the town) and they are purchased ready-made in the market. Linguistically they use Hindi words for cooking vessels mentioned above and other words pertaining to daily life like *capa:ti* 'a wheat bread', *sabji* 'vegetable curry', *bhuna:na:* 'frying', *se:ka:na:* 'roasting', *sa:ri* 'sari', *kami:c* 'khameez' and English words (through Hindi) *sart* 'shirt', *pE:nt* 'pants' etc.

All Andamanese (30 of them excepting the five children below the age of three) know two languages, namely Andamanese and Hindi. Bengali and Burmese are known besides these two languages to four and five persons respectively. All Bengali knowing persons except one are male in the age group of 40 and above. The earlier generation was in contact with Burmese and there was also intermarriage with the Burmese. This contact declined after the resettlement of Andamanese in Strait Island. The adult women under 40 studied in Hindi medium schools in Port Blair, where there were Bengali-speaking students. Marriage took place between Andamanese and mainlanders. The boy or the girl may be Andamanese (as in the case of a Muslim boy marrying an Andamanese girl and as in two cases of Andamanese marrying girls from Ranchi of Bihar). Such marriages are accepted by the community, as a spouse is not available for all eligible Andamanese boys and girls locally.

Whether this total bilingualism leads to language shift and loss of mother tongue is an important question for discussion. Andamanese of 40 plus (8 people of the elder group) have a good command of Andamanese. They could give effortlessly the equivalent Andamanese words for the Hindi borrowings that have replaced them. They could also produce freely sentences and texts in Andamanese. Men belonging to this age group also speak Hindi confidently. Women of this age group are hesitant to speak in Hindi, but their passive comprehension of Hindi is good. When questions are asked in Hindi they prefer to answering in Andamanese. Visits of these women to the main island are rare and when they go they are accompanied by men. This could be a reason for their less active command of Hindi.

People of 16–40 years (10 people) speak Andamanese fluently, but it is heavily mixed with Hindi. This group in both genders has the highest level of command of Hindi among the Andamanese. Children 3–15 years (12 people) were tested for the basic vocabulary items: 100 word list of Gudschinsky (1956) with respect to Andamanese and Hindi. The elicitation technique of naming and filling in the blank was used to test the vocabulary items in Andamanese and Hindi in their active command. Without giving any of the test lexical items directly either in Hindi or in Andamanese, cues were given (in Hindi as the investigators did not know Andamanese) in such a way that the child responded to the cue and gave the known word in Andamanese and in Hindi. The words not known to the child in either of the languages were left blank and they did not count. On the basis of the responded words, the percentage of words known to the child in Andamanese and in Hindi was calculated and it is given age-wise in Table 13.4.

Table 13.4 shows that the child starts with relatively a larger vocabulary in Hindi but there is a progression in the knowledge of words both in Andamanese and Hindi as the child grows up. The Andamanese vocabulary is acquired through the child's participation in the presently rare collective activities like fishing and turtle hunting and in cultural activities like the puberty ceremony. The Hindi vocabulary is acquired during visits to Port Blair with their parents, visits to hospitals for treatment and from watching Hindi movies. Hindi is learned in the school also. Children's

Table 13.4

Age group	Percentage of vocabulary given in Andamanese	Percentage of vocabulary given in Hindi
3–5	37	50
6–10	63	85
11–15	82	90

Hindi vocabulary is larger than the Andamanese vocabulary at any given time but the latter is neither stagnant nor regressive. Nevertheless, Hindi may be said to be dominant in their bilingualism in terms of the size of its vocabulary and variety of situations of use.

Hindi is also the language of literacy. Though Andamanese is written in Devanagari, the script used for Hindi, in the school primers prepared in 1994, it is not used for reading or writing in any communicative context. No other written material besides the primers is available in Andamanese. Hindi, being the language of literacy and of administration and market, is the language of prestige also.

The older group of Andamanese use only Andamanese among themselves. They prefer to use it with the younger groups, but switch to Hindi occasionally when, for instance, the children do not follow their instructions in Andamanese. These instructions may pertain even to performance of cultural rituals. The instructions are generally given by male elders and it may be said women always use Andamanese with the younger people. The middle group use mostly Andamanese with elders and among themselves. With children, they use both Andamanese and Hindi and code switching is common. Their Andamanese is mixed with Hindi more when they speak to the younger group.

The younger group use Hindi and Andamanese among themselves. The frequency of use of the two languages is in reverse order compared to the middle group. They try to speak only in Andamanese with the older group and speak both in Andamanese and Hindi with the middle group. They are, however, more confident in speaking Hindi. Code switching is more common when strangers are present. When secrecy is required in the presence of strangers, the younger group use Andamanese exclusively among themselves.

All Andamanese use Hindi in meetings with the administrative and hospital staff and with strangers in the bazaar. The inter-generational negative correlation with age in the use of Hindi, described above, has led some researchers to conclude that 'the Andamanese have learnt Hindi to the extent that it is replacing their tribal language, especially among the younger generation.' (Awaradi, 1990: 230).

Language Attitude

The language attitude survey conducted during 1996–97 in Strait Island with regard to Andamanese and Hindi gives the following results. The older people have positive attitudes towards Andamanese. They believe in the preservation of their language and culture for maintaining Andamanese identity. While they are satisfied with the use of Andamanese by the middle group, they are not happy with the Andamanese of the younger group that is mixed with Hindi. They want the younger group to improve their Andamanese. The older group, along with the middle group, emphasise the need for teaching Andamanese in the school and for writing books in it to impart their culture and heritage to the younger group. They also believe that the use of Andamanese in the school will improve the status of their language.

Regarding the attitude towards Hindi, men of the older group believe that learning Hindi is inevitable to overcome marginal existence. They, however, strongly feel that Hindi must not be used exclusively in their homes, in community gatherings and in cultural practices. This group feels that the dominance of Hindi will destroy the Andamanese language and culture. The women of this group are shy of speaking in Hindi, as mentioned above; they even refuse to acknowledge their knowledge of it. The older group accuses the middle group of discouraging the younger group from learning Andamanese by speaking frequently in Hindi at home.

The attitude of the middle group towards Andamanese is ambivalent. It is not as strongly positive as the older group, though they feel that there is a need to preserve Andamanese, to transmit it to their children and to teach it in school. They also support the view of the older group that for their survival and identity as Andamanese, preservation of their language is essential. They are more tolerant of the use of Hindi than the older group even in the home domain. For them, Hindi is the language of wider communication and of prestige and power, that gives them opportunities and contacts.

The younger group is extremely shy of speaking Andamanese, particularly in the presence of strangers (except when they want to be secretive). They tend not to acknowledge their knowledge of it. They prefer a mixed code of Hindi and Andamanese when they speak among themselves and when they speak to their elders. They are critical of the Hindi of the older group believing that it is not 'pure'. They tend to mix less of Andamanese in their Hindi in contrast to mixing more of Hindi in their Andamanese. As they grow older, however, there is an attitudinal change and they increasingly feel the Andamanese is important to give them an identity.

The above description of use and attitude among three age groups regarding Andamanese and Hindi shows that the entire community is positive about bilingualism and there is no loss of the mother tongue yet. The gradual decline in the use of and in the empathy for Andamanese down the age groups does not necessarily point towards ultimate loss of the mother tongue. This is because both the utility value of Hindi and the identity value of Andamanese are at work and there is increasing realisation of the need for identity and preservation cyclically, as persons grow older. The greatest threat to the language is the biological extinction of the community. The community tries to check or delay it by relaxing its reproductive rules, by allowing marriage outside the community and by raising the off-springs in relative isolation. The children born of such an inter-ethnic marriage are kept and raised as Andamanese, even if the outsider deserts the community and leaves the island. The mother tongue is preserved, though may be similarly mixed with the dominant language, for the identity of the community. The conscious efforts, though meagre, to preserve the language are described below.

Reversing Shift

The Andamanese language is not an instance of language loss to be revived. It is used, as described above, by the entire population, though that population is now quite small. The entire community is bilingual with a functional distribution of the two languages, Andamanese and Hindi, though the distribution is less categorical and more diffused along the generational line. The present situation is closer to Stage 6 of Fishman (1991) but not identical to it in which 'Xish is the normal language of informal, spoken interaction between and within all three generations of the family, with Yish being reversed for matters of greater formality and technicality than those that are the common fare of daily family life'.

Unlike the above stage, the boundary between formal and informal situations of language use is diffused. Hindi is used alternatively with Andamanese by the younger generation in informal domains like the family. The middle generation is compelled to use Hindi with children when their competence in Andamanese is wanting in domestic and ritual matters. Though there is a concern among the elder generation about this situation, there is no community action to change it other than lending passive support to the efforts of the government school to teach Andamanese to the children.

There has been a primary school in Strait Island from 1970, but not much learning takes place there. Subjects were taught earlier through the medium of English; the two languages taught were English and Hindi; there was no Andamanese. In 1996 the medium was changed to Hindi. At this time, Andamanese was introduced as a language and as a vehicle to transfer the students to the Hindi medium. The Central Institute of Indian Languages, in collaboration with the Tribal Welfare Department and the Education Department of Andaman Islands, prepared bilingual educational materials and trained teachers (who are not Andamanese). It will take a few years to evaluate their effectiveness with regard to the acquisition of competence, including literacy in Andamanese, by the children and developing a positive attitude towards their language.

The most specific feature of Andamanese is the small size of its population. Given its size, it cannot hope to rise to Stage 4 of Fishman's GID scale, where the use of Andamanese in work place outside the community, in governmental services and in the media at the local and lower levels must come into play. Stage 4a, where Andamanese is used in lower education as part of compulsory primary education, is now in emergence at the initiative of the government with the acceptance of the community, as mentioned above. But the bilingual education model used is not geared to mother tongue maintenance, though it is not averse to it. The support for maintenance must come from outside the school. But there is no opportunity for using the literacy skills in Andamanese even for personal purposes like letter writing, as this small community functions on face-to-face oral communication. For reading, there is no material other than the school primers. There is no religious factor in literacy learning for reading sacred materials. Recreational reading is nil in this community as it is deeply depressed about its endangered state. These factors prohibit Andamanese literacy at home and in the community from being practised by the community as proposed for Stage 5.

This raises the question of whether intergenerational orality and the demographic concentration of the community in one place, which are features of Stage 6 and possessed by the Andamanese, are sufficient to arrest language loss. The institutional reinforcement of language use, which is another feature of this stage, is limited to rituals, which are truncated, and to hunting expeditions, which are becoming rare. The demographic concentration is a forced one as a result of the government's policy of isolation of the community geographically. The isolation is also from market related economic activities, as the community's basic needs are provided free by the government. Nevertheless, the lure of attractions of the town (Port Blair) is strong, particularly among the younger generation, primarily driven by their depression to seek an outlet in self-indulgence. The boat trip to the town (Port Blair) is dependent on the service run by the government once a week, but the tendency to stay longer, and in a few cases permanently in the town, is increasing. Intergenerational oral transmission of language, as mentioned earlier, is getting weakened in terms of preference and competence among the younger generation.

There is no marked change in the Stage 6 in the last 10 years and so sliding into Stage 7 does not appear to be imminent. The major reason for this is the consciousness of the threat to their survival as a distinct community defined linguistically and culturally. The community strongly believes that its cultural distinctiveness and ethnic survival are not possible without keeping their language. But this consciousness may not help to overcome the biological threat to the community's survival and hence its language.[1]

Note

1. The field work was conducted by the second author with M.R Ranganatha and K.S Rajyashree of C.I.I.L. and we are grateful to them.

References

Awaradi, S.A. (1990) Computerised Master Plan (1991–2021) for the Welfare of the Primitive Tribes of Andaman & Nicobar Islands. Port Blair: Andaman & Nicobar Administration.

Basu (1952) A linguistic introduction to the Andamanese. *Bulletin of the Anthropological Survey of India* 1(2), 55–70.

Brown, R.A.R. (1914) Notes on the languages of the Andaman Islands. *Anthropos* 9 (36–52).

Brown, R.A.R. (1948) *The Andaman Islanders*. Chicago: Free Press.

Chakraborty, D.K. (1990) *The Great Andamanese: The ASI Andamanese and Nicobar Tribal Series*. Calcutta: Seagull Books.

Fishman, J. (1991) *Reversing Language Shift: Theoretic and Empirical Foundations of Assistance to Threatened Languages*. Clevedon: Multilingual Matters.

Gudschinsky, S.C. (1956) The ABC's of Lexico-statistics (Glottochronology). *Word* 12, 175–210.

Mann, E.H. (1932) *On the Aboriginal Inhabitants of the Andaman Islands*. London: Royal Anthropological Institute (reprint).

Manoharan, S. (1989) *A Descriptive and Comparative Study of the Andaman Language*. Calcutta: Anthropological Survey of India.

Nigam, R.C. (1972) *India: Language Handbook on Mother Tongues in Census*. New Delhi: Ministry of Home Affairs.

Pandit, P.B. (1972) *India as a Sociolinguistic Area*. Pune: University of Poona.
Pandit, P.B. (1977) *Language in a Plural Society*. Delhi: The Devraj Chanana Memorial
Committee.
Pandit, T.N. (1976) The original inhabitants of the Andaman & Nicobar islands.
Yojana (Journal of the Planning Commission of India) 20(13), (81–96).

Chapter 14

Akor Itak – Our Language, Your Language: Ainu in Japan

J.C. MAHER

Introduction

Efforts to reverse language shift, to preserve a mother tongue in decline, commonly make up a patchwork of the quotidien and the elegaic. The design of the effort can reveal many things: nostalgia, ethno-ideology and stereotype, language planning formulation and what-can-we-do strategies for repair. It may reveal a challenge to official propaganda-myths of the 'vanishing people' and 'dying language'. It may reveal *Gemeinschaft* aspirations, heightened contrastivity and adversarialness. Involving so many different people and change-agents a patchwork of shift differentials is likely inevitable. Involving so many different ideas and aspirations, a range of shift patterns can be expected. People have, as the saying goes, different agenda. Ainu has powerful symbolic resonance since it calls forth the socio-political landscape of the past, the good old days and bad old days, colonialism, forced-removal from land, schooling in Japanese and prohibition of the Ainu language. Also, in the matter of language revival, what constitutes 'transmission' to one person is not transmission to another. The issue is certainly ambiguous among Ainu speakers. If the call to arms to defend a language in danger displays *in extremis* epic heroism and occasionally ethnocentrism at one end of the revival spectrum, at the other pole it fosters genuine solidarity among people. Manifestos celebrate this:

> Even though I, as one Ainu, make tireless efforts for the language I cannot alone hold back the tide which washes over my language and hollows it out. But now there are many pebbles against the destructive waters and the number is growing. We have now started to build a breakwater, a sea wall. We are an ever-increasing rock. (Kayano, 1987, *Ainu Bunka Kiso Chishiki* [*The Ainu Culture: the Basic Knowledge*] pp. 14, 22, 25)

In spite of the usual sociolinguistic disarray about who is doing what and what needs to be done, in the case of Ainu revitalisation it is obvious, to even the casual observer, that the Ainu language is on the move and has made substantial gains both in grass-roots consciousness and at national policy level.

Optimism and Universalism

To pursue the water metaphor, the effort to crack open the lock-gates to provide an albeit narrow intergenerational channel of Ainu tradition comprises also the idea of the oppressiveness of mainstream Japanese tradition whose sea has been turbid, even devastating. Ainu language revival nevertheless evokes optimism, futurism, the sense of familial 'gathering', sometimes euphoria in the call to defence of the mother-tongue:

> We are getting better and better. Through this gathering around our language we can begin to make our first steps to the learning of Ainu. And with these steps we will bend all our effort on the road to the development of the Ainu language and the learning of it. (Introduction to 'Ainu Language Classes'. *The 4th Ainu Cultural Festival Hokkaido Utari-Kyokai* [Hokkaido Ainu Association]. Hokkaido, 1992: 15.)

The idea of minority language maintenance holds that mainstream identity is partial and tendentious and must irrevocably lead the individual to cultivate a more humane and rich social affiliation. The idea is, ineluctably, a search for sidestream roots which in turn comprises a wider existential desire for historical relevance. In this model, there is enclosed a universalism applicable to all men. The mother tongue bears a nature spirit, the protector of all. It is linked to earth-values. By contrast, mandatory mainstream identity engenders social confusion and throws the individual into a landscape of solitude and alienation. The mother tongue is a room of one's own:

> When an Ainu does it you might say it is only to be expected. But each time a Japanese and Ainu learn to speak Ainu together they participate in the joys of Ainu. They preserve not only the culture of Ainu but also the culture of a whole land, a whole earth, one village. (Kayano, 1987, *Yasashii Ainu-go* [Easy Ainu (1)] *Shiratori Nibutani Ainu-go Kyoshitsu* [Shiratori Nibutani Ainu language class])

The cultural renaissance of Ainu has been accompanied by a skirting of politico-historical frontiers in which the primordial affiliations to 'the indigenous' and the static-ethnic jostle for space with a re-forging of a political community. This is a community in which ethnic mobilisation is a strategic choice rather than an ontological given. If we were to point to a historical watershed wherein all of these issues coalesced it would begin in the mid-1980s.

Six years after Prime Minister Yasuhiro Nakasone's public comments (1986) that Japan has no 'racial minorities' – a *de rigeur* official statement invoking Japanese homogeneity – Giichi Nomura stepped up to speak before the General Assembly of the United Nations in New York. It coincided with the inauguration of the United Nations 'International Year of the Indigenous Peoples'. Nomura spoke of the ravaging, the marginalisation and discrimination suffered by the Ainu in Japan and concluded with words of thanks in Ainu. This version of history runs counter both to successive Japanese governments' master narrative of national homogeneity but also to a popular narrative of brave conquest of difficult virgin lands in the freezing north. Quite simply, the Ainu version flouts common sense in Japan. Siddle (1995, 1996) has traced brilliantly the construct 'indigenous people' in the global postwar movement for decolonisation, emphasising 'the making and remaking of Ainu identity by both the dominant Japanese and the Ainu themselves   ways in which competing versions of Ainu identity have been articulated and rearticulated during different historical periods and how these identities – 'racial' and 'ethnic' – have served to shape relations between Ainu and Japanese' (1996: 2). The historical racialisation of the Ainu spawned popular images of Ainu *minzoku* ('race' 'people', '*Volk*', 'ethnic group') as being an inferior racial group. Until recently, advertisements have invited tourists to visit 'real Ainu villages' where they can see the 'ancient customs of the famed hairy Ainu' (Siddle, 1995: 90; Narita & Hanazaki, 1975: 312). Meanwhile, the Ainu language is popularly misconstrued typologically ('Is it Japanese' 'Is it a dialect?'). At the same time, it retains a comfortable identity as a dead language. Mervio (1995: 51) succinctly elaborates the cultural representation of Japanese (Ainu and other minorities) in the political economy, thus: 'Not only in Japan is language an "ideological" issue and at the core of many discourses on race, cultural proximity and nationalism . . . one can find a strong tendency to place attention to language as a distinguishing feature'.

In Japan, in contrast to the *fin de siecle* propaganda of 'internationalisation' inducted by politicians of the ruling class of 1980, the search is on for a new paradigm of cultural pluralism involving the recognition of 'other' languages. In this new matrix, Ainu holds a central place. (I have elaborated the paradigm of multilingualism in Japan elsewhere outlining the dynamics of many community languages and major dialects, the role of multilingualism in trade, education and the professions and pointing to creole aspects of the historical origins of Japanese itself. See Maher, 1985, 1989, 1991a, 1991b, 1993, 1994, 1996, 1997, 1999; Maher & Honna, 1994; Maher & Macdonald, 1995; Maher & Yashiro, 1991). The search for a new paradigm has been powerfully assisted by the ever-widening crack between national and local views of what constitutes community, society. An oft-cited example (Tsunemoto, 1999) is the ruling of the Sapporo District Court of Hokkaido in 1997 which declared: (1) that the controversial flooding of Ainu lands for dam construction was illegal, that the Ainu are indeed 'indigenous people' by any recognised definitions of the term (ILO, Cobo Report), (2) that Article 27 of the UN Covenant on Civil and Political Rights which protects the cultural and linguistic rights of minority peoples is legally binding domestically. Finally, the Hokkaido court invoked Article 13 of the Japanese Constitution which makes the government responsible for protecting a minority member's cultural rights and stated that government's culpability and subsequent responsibilty for Ainu's forcible minoritisation is unequivocal. This decision was widely viewed as 'surprising, epoch-making' (Tsunemoto, 1999: 368) and gave an additional surge to an increasing optiminism and confidence about Ainu culture and the framework whose framework is, as Sasamura opines, *urespa mosir* – 'a land where all things grow helping each other' (Sasamura, 1999: 170).

Charting Language Shift and Revitalisation

Ainu is one of the languages of Japan. The Japanese archipelago, located off mainland Asia with which it has had linguistic contact throughout history, consists of approximately 3000 islands over which a variety of languages and dialects are spoken by a population of 121,000,000. The general population lives mostly in the densely populated coastal areas along four main islands of Honshu, Kyushu, Hokkaido and Shikoku. Typologically regarded as a language isolate, the Ainu language is of linguistic, historical and social significance in the history of Japan. Ainu is now spoken predominantly in Hokkaido, an island bordered in the north by Sakhalin and Siberia. The Nibutani valley in the Saru district of southern Hokkaido is considered to have the highest concentration of speakers and learners of Ainu in Japan.

The traditional Ainu-speaking areas have undergone massive language shift over the last 200 hundred years. An actual figure for the number of native speakers is not known (see below). There is much evidence of renewed interest in the study of Ainu at university, community centres and private institutions and the matter of Ainu RSL (Reversing Language Shift) represents a huge challenge with a typical snakes-and-ladders scenario, i.e. the problem of

- too much to be done urgently;
- much goodwill;
- much uncertainty;
- lack of coordination on how to achieve renewal;
- potentially rich resources with which to accomplish the task.

Ainu language rights are not a matter of a linguistic minority requesting government cooperation to recognise linguistic difference and offer support. The issues involve an uncomfortable interaction of centre and periphery. The imposing fact that Ainu is conceived 'primordially' (Fishman's term) as an indigenous language of the 'far north' – a local phenomenon like a dialect – rather than as a language of Japan is an issue of phenomenology which impacts upon language perceptions. I mentioned above that the territory of Hokkaido was for long the site of pioneer struggle and settlement, of snow and cold, the felling of trees and the clearing of forests. Hokkaido was for many generations controlled by the independent Matsumae elite, a clan whose interest was as much with the rich Russian north as with Edo-Tokyo. Hokkaido was long regarded with suspicion. The territory is geographically and politically distinctive as a region being administered, even now, in a somewhat different manner from that of other prefectures. The peripheral warlords did not perceive themselves as unequivocally Japanese but rather as independent entities. As the Daimyo Matsumae Kimihiro declared to the Jesuit missionary de Angelis in 1618 'Matsumae is not Japan' (quoted in Siddle, 1995: 34). In the modern nation-state of Japan, forged through nationalist wars and burnished with carefully crafted ethno-cultural narratives and history, the Daimyo's matter-of-fact statement is heard now as a thunder-clap. At the centre of the suspicion about 'Hokkaido' (formerly 'Ezo') lay the Ainu language: curiosity, nuisance, potential Trojan horse of foreign influence, important trade language. (Paradoxically, Ainu interpreters, Ainu-Russian-Japanese, likely provided the first gateway to international trade between Japan and the rest of the world. Mixed factors thus led to the formulation of language laws which accelerated language shift.) I suggest that shift factors can be traced from the beginning of the 19th century running continuously through the 1900s. However, with the complete cessation of anti-Ainu laws in the late 20th century (the drafting of pro-Ainu legislation and official structures in Hokkaido) events have also occurred that point unequivocally to revitalisation. The flow of events and laws which, I suggest, forged language shift, as well as the slowing down of shift and exertions towards revitalisation are shown in Chart 1.

Chart 1 A chronology of Ainu language law and revitalisation

1799   Ainu not subject to Japanese law since the edict of Hideyoshi (1593) and Ieyasu (1604) establish principle of *Ezo shidai* (Ainu sort out their own affairs). In practice, various regulations are set up by local contractors and Matsumae officials forbidding use of Japanese language and customs.

1799–1821   The *Bakufu* (Tokugawa Shogunate regime) take over adminis-tration of *Ezo-ch*i (Hokkaido) and reverse previous policy, encourage Japanisation (occasionally by force), particularly in stra-tegic areas like Etorofu. Matsumae-*han* (clan) regain position in 1821. Revert to previous policy of non-assimilation. Discourage the learning of Japanese.

1855   Bakufu again revise the former policy of cultural non-assimilation of the Ainu. Educational measures instituted to enable and encourage the Ainu to learn Japanese.

1869   Renaming of Ezo-chi (*Ezo-chi Kaisho*). On the formal establishment of the Colonial Mission to Hokkaido by the Japanese government, former Japanese names of *Ezo-chi* (Ainu – *Ainu Moshir*) to Hokkaido and *Kita Ezo-chi* (Ainu – *Rebun Moshir*) to Karafuto. Other regula-tions standardise Japanese characters for reading Ainu place names (e.g. Karafuto place names in Dec.1873 – *Karafuto Chimei moji Seitei*) (There seem to be no official names for these laws in the early *Kaitakushi* (pioneer) years; they are instead in the nature of procla-mations.)

1871   Ainu rituals (e.g. funeral customs, songs and dances) prohibited (*Kyudojin Tamamono Hei kin Moku*). Repeated in 1876 – *Kyudojin Kyoka Yutatsu, Kyudojin Mimiwa Irezumi Kinshi.*) This emasculates the cultural contexts for language encouraged. In this year Ainu are designated as *heimin* (common people).

1872   Land Regulation Ordinance (1872) *Jisho Kisoku*. Article 7 takes all land formerly used by Ainu, i.e. Ainu land use not recognised as ownership – *terra nullius*. Not directly concerned with language issues but in Ainu history a watershed in that the link between a culture and a territory in which it may thrive is finally severed.

1875 Karafuto-Kuriles Exchange Treaty (*Karafuto Chishima Kokan Joyaku*). Indigenes given three years to choose nationality, but Japanese quickly relocate 841 Ainu people to Tsuishikari in Hokkaido. Set up school with Japanese instruction only. Lifestyle totally different from that in Karafuto.

1877 Article 15 of the Hokkaido Land Certificates Publishing Regulations (*Hokkaido Jiken Hakko Jorei*) places all remaining mountains, forests and wilderness under the control of the government. Some Ainu are given tiny plots of land designated as 'third class' government controlled property under Article 16. By inhibiting access to traditional areas these laws inhibit social communication between Ainu speech communities.

1878 Standardisation of the category name for Ainu in the family register. (*Kyudojin Meisho Ittei*). The terms *Dojin, Komin, Kyu Ezojin* replaced by *Kyu Dojin* (former aborigine). The notion of a 'former people' and a *horobiyuku gengo* ('a language on the road to extinction') is first introduced.

1883 *Nemuro-ken Dojin Kyusaiho*. Relief Law grants Ainu small allotments, tools, etc. Start of concentration and relocation of Ainu into *hogochi* reservations set up under 1877 'Class Three' land regulation. Traditional communities broken up. Relocations have deleterious effect upon the maintenance of customs and speech forms.

1884 Ainu from Shumshu in N. Kuriles relocated to Shikotan. Aggressive language and religious (Buddhist) policy; these Ainu speak Russian and are Orthodox Christians. Russians have been in Shumshu since 1730s.

1885 *Sapporo-ken Dojin Kyusaiho*. (Same as for 1883 Relief laws).

1898 The *Hokkaido Kyu Dojin Hogo Ho* ('Hokkaido Former Aborigines Protection Act') proposed to the 13th Imperial Congress by Hokkaido Prefectural Government for the third time (Private Members Bills failed in 1893 and 1895). Passed in the House of Representatives. This far-reaching law includes educational provision for all Ainu children. The use of the Ainu language is not permittted in schools (this is not in law but was policy in practice). Japanese language education for all Ainu.

1899 The *Hokkaido Kyu Dojin Hogo Ho* (Hokkaido Former Aborigines Protection Act) promulgated and put into effect.

1901 The first Statute on Former Aborigine Children's Education.

(*Kyudojin Jido Kyoiku Kitei*). Ainu and Japanese children to be educated separately. Ainu education is inferior, much time spent on Japanese language learning. The Ainu education policy has a huge impact on Ainu language, by 1920s only very elderly Ainu cannot speak Japanese. First Regulations abolished 1908.

1916 Second Regulations for the Education of Former Native Children (*Kyudojin Jido Kyoiku Kitei*). Reintroduces shorter and inferior Ainu curriculum. Abolished 1922.

1919–1968 Revisions 1–5 of the 1899 Act (*Hokkaido Kyu dojin Hogo Ho*). 1919 revision increases health care provisions, subsequent revisions gradually whittle away at welfare and education provisions (Native Schools scrapped in 1937) until only Articles concerning allotments and communal property are left.

1925 Speech by Ainu activist and poet Iboshi Hokuto to the linguist Kindaichi's Tokyo Ainu Gakkai (Tokyo Ainu Study Group) estab-lishes context for future reclamation of Ainu culture and language. Attacks on 'dying race' stereotype, call for equality and justice, linkage with ethnic extinction in global context (e.g. Australian aborigine).

1973 First issue of Ainu newspaper *Anutari Ainu* containing references to the need for Ainu language revival.

1980 Declaration by the Japanese government that no linguistic minori-ties are present in Japan. 1980 Report on Human Rights in accor-dance with the International Covenant on Civil and Political Rights. Referring to Article 27 which recognises the existence of linguistic minorities and recognises the right 'to enjoy their own culture . . . or to use their own language'. The government states: 'Minorities of this kind mentioned in the covenant do not exist in Japan'.

1983 The first Ainu language class established by folklorist Shigeru Kayano in Nibutani, Hokkaido.

1984 *Hokkaido Utari Kyokai* (Hokkaido Utari Association) proposes the *Ainu Minzoku ni kan suru Horitsu* 'New Law for the Ainu' to replace the 1899 Act. This proposal comprises recommendations on the revival and maintenance of the Ainu language and makes reference to language 'rights' (Article 3). Also explicit policy recommenda-tions for revitalisation of Ainu Language.

1986 Prime Minister Nakasone's speech proclaiming Japan as a 'racially homogeneous nation' blessed with an absence of minorities and consequently possessing a 'high level of intellectual competence' unlike the United States with its black and other problematic racial minorities. These minorities have 'debilitated the intellectual level of the nation'. Ainu and other minorities in Japan, angered by this statement, reaffirm the need to assert their cultural, including linguistic, presence. Widely viewed by the Ainu as a watershed in their postwar history. The planning of language revitalisation measures begin: includes the setting up of *Ainu kyoshitsu* (private language schools or other facilities).

1987   The government reports on its 2nd Human Rights Report to the United Nations. In this document, the government officially recognises the existence of the Ainu people (as individuals, not as an ethnic minority). Denies the existence of any discrimination (regarding language, etc.).

1987   The first Ainu language class (*Ainugo Kyoshitsu*) to be financially supported by the Hokkaido Prefectural Government and the Government of Japan. Nibutani, Hokkaido.

1987   The first 'Ainu for Radio' Language Course established. Sapporo Radio, Hokkaido

1988   The *Utari Mondai Konwakai* proposes the necessity of enacting the *Ainu Shinpo* (Ainu New Law) consultative committee. The Hokkaido Prefectural Governor demands that the government enact the Ainu New Law. The New Law proposes specific measures to maintain and promote Ainu language education.

1989   The *Dai Ikkai Ainugo Benron Taikai* (1st Ainu Language Speech Contest) held in Tokyo, Japan.

1991   Government of Japan admit that Ainu exist as a minority as defined under Article 27 of UN International Covenant on Civil and Political Rights.

1993   International Year of the Indigenous Peoples. New momentum in the Ainu movement for language rights.

1994   Shigeru Kayano the first Ainu to become a member of the Diet (House of Counsellors). A leading figure in the Ainu language revival movement and a fluent speaker of Ainu delivers inauguration speech first in Ainu then Japanese.

1994   *Akor Itak* (Our Language) the first standard textbook on the Ainu language published in Hokkaido.

1994   The 'Hokkaido Ainu Culture Research Centre' established in Hokkaido by the Hokkaido Prefectural Government.

1997   Enactment of the Ainu Culture Promotion Law and abolition of the

1898 law. Formation of the Foundation for Research and Promotion of Ainu Culture.

The Graded Intergenerational Disruption Model

In the effort to reverse language shift, Ainu is on the weak side. Hitherto, there has been sociolinguistic disarray. The work of linguists has concentrated on informant-based analysis of lexico-grammar and phonology.The underpinning of much of this work has been an unquestioning acceptance that Ainu is inevitably doomed. Linguistic and anthropological work has thus been haloed with tragedy and heroism. This as well as the philosophy and situation underpinning fieldwork in Ainu has undoubtedly changed in a more engaging and positive manner as Nakagawa (1998) describes. The current future and prospect for Ainu lies in functional differentiation (e.g. ritual, greeting, archival) and vigorous ethnosymbolic usage as found in code-switching. DeChicchis, in his wide-ranging review of the 'current state of the Ainu language', is upbeat in a rather specific way: 'With thousands of Ainu singing and praying and greeting each other, and teaching their children these Ainu songs and prayers and greetings, it is also a safe bet that the Ainu language is not about to die' (1995: 118–19). There is surely an overall and ever-present and increasingly vigorous diglossia whereby transmissibility has been demonstrated in certain areas. Ainu has achieved some stability in the wake of pervasive language shift.

Stage 8 Most vestigial users are socially isolated and aged individuals. The reassembly of Ainu must take place from their mouths and memories and taught to demographically unconcentrated adults

The reassembly of the Ainu language model is the most salient stage in the Ainu language's path through contemporary society. The standard variety is now gathered around the Saru dialect of Nibutani (see below) and is in good repair (see Tamura 1956, 1960, 1970, 1974, 1981).

Fieldwork on the Ainu language continues with some vigour and the reconstruction of an effective Ainu standard (*sic* Standard Ainu) has focused on grammar. A landmark was reached in 1994 when *Akor Itak* 'Our Language' the first general textbook of the Ainu language was issued in Hokkaido. Arguably, the first 'modern' attempt to show everyday Ainu speech and organise it in some instructional format was Iwao Yoshida's *Ainu-go kaiwa-hen* (Conversation Guide in Ainu) (1915–16). Since then, the notion that Ainu cannot function as a language for real-world communication has been the prevalent view among students and scholars of Ainu –

until recently. The emphasis has shifted from focus on decline to practical measures for reconstruction.

Adopting a method used widely in modern language teaching / learning in Japan, an *Ainugo Benron Taikai* (Ainu Language Speech Contest) – the first such competition – was held in 1989. It received extensive media coverage – television and newspaper – and was attended by several hundred people including Ainu, Japanese and non-Japanese. Participants came from all parts of the Tokyo (Kanto) area and Hokkaido and their ages ranged from pre-school children of three years old to university students and workers. Speech contests continue to be held annually.

Yoneda (Honda) noted the need for linkage between Ainu language teaching and other foreign language instruction such as Japanese, Korean and English as foreign languages (*Kokuritsu Kokugo Kenkyujo* discussion, 1995). The absence of the sharing of expertise in materials production and methodology and the need for an established association of Ainu language teachers must be addressed in the future. Meanwhile, a series of video-cassettes was produced by an Ainu-based group (*Kamuyturano* Association, 1988) to provide instruction in conversational, situation-based Ainu. The materials deal with the customs and language of traditional everyday life of the Ainu including the construction of houses, cooking, greetings, leave-taking, and other formulaic expressions. Language material is organised not according to a graded structural syllabus but by means of situational contexts in which new vocabulary is presented. The vocabulary and paradigmatic forms which emerge from these situations are discussed in the accompanying text. On the screen appear both *katakana* (Japanese phonemic syllabary) and *romaji* (romanised) transcriptions with glosses in Japanese.

The textbooks used for teaching Ainu conversation and grammar employ *katakana* (unlike the older grammars such as Batchelor's which used romanised Ainu). Most written materials are remarkably similar in format, based on a phrase-book type approach and requiring memorisation rather than communicative manipulation. Word lists or labelled drawings of traditional Ainu implements for hunting, fishing, and cooking, as well as place-names are standard textbook presentation. The lack of activity based language learning could be attributed as much to the need for modernisation of the language itself as the formalism of the grammar-translation methods which is still in vogue in modern language teaching in Japan (see Honda, 1997).

There are now progressive approaches to Ainu language teaching instruction, for example through *manga* (cartoon) as in Yokoyama and

Chiri's little books *Ainu Itak* (1987) (Ainu Language Manual) and *Ainu Ukoyso-Itak* (1988) (Ainu Conversation Manual). Here, standard 'Greetings' situations situations typical to Japan and Japanese are employed, as when Ainu speakers are shown bowing. (Traditional Ainu greeting involves rubbing the palms of the hands together from side to side away from the body.) Dialogues in social context (travel, supermarket, television) are now routine in many instructional materials and illustrations typically include representations of Ainu cultural production such as the highly regarded Ainu kimono (e.g. embroidery, *appliqué*, handweaving; see cover designs by artist Sanae Ogawa for Maher & Macdonald, 1995). Nakagawa has constructed an important pathway not only in Ainu linguistics generally (data collection, analysis, pedagogy) but also in the orientation of Ainu language teaching towards the Chitose dialect (see his *Ainu-Japanese Dictionary: Chitose Dialect*, 1995 and *Express Ainu*, 1997 a self-study textbook for beginners). He notes: 'Although today the Chitose region is considered to be the centre of the Ainu language-revitalisation movement, serious study of the region's dialect began only in the late 1980s, prior to that time, few Ainu-language researchers knew that the area had so many Ainu speakers' (1999: 374).

Ainu language study has been propelled also by interest in the *kamui-yukar* and *oina*: the language of music and ceremony. The worldwide ethno-music/world-music boom, which employed the vernacular languages of Africa, South-East Asia and Europe, arrived in Japan in the 1980s and has had no small impact on Ainu music and dance. Along with the distinctive Okinawan music of the Japanese south, Ainu *yukar* has now emerged in modern format. An Ainu jazz musician *Moshiri* ('*mosir*' being the Ainu people's designation for the territory 'Hokkaido') has adapted Ainu songs such as *Kamuy Chikap* (God's Bird) for jazz. Likewise, some cultural events, the language of Ainu prayers and ceremonies are experiencing a renaissance. In the chanting of *iyaihumke* (lullabies) and two main types of song (*kamui-yukar* – totemic gods; *oina* – ancestral heroes) ritual language in Ainu is performed during the following ceremonies. These ceremonies, many of which, like the Fox God Ceremony from 1986, are being performed for the first time in several decades. This is summarised in Chart 2 (various sources).

Chart 2 Ritual language maintenance and revival

Kamui-nomi ('prayer of offering to the spirits')
Bekambe ('Water Caltropo Festival')
Upopo and *Tapkar* (dance of the Menoko ['Ainu women'])

Rimse Dance Songs
Shakushain Warrior Memorial Ceremony
Icharupa ('Memorial Ceremony for Ancestors')
Icharupa (Memorial for Ainu skeletons seized from Ainu burial places by universities)
Kunashiri-Menashi Ceremony (Commemorating Japanese invasion of Hokkaido 200 years before)
Chiron-up-Kamui-Iyomante ('Fox God Ceremony')
Kimun Kamui Iyomante ('God of the Mountain Bear Ceremony')
Ashiri-Cheppu-Nomi ('First Fish Ceremony')
Chipsanke ('Boat Launching Ceremony')

The 'Imeru' movement led by Ainu artist and activist Mieko Chikap has been involved in the resurgence of these traditional customs and traditions; the word *imeru* ('thunderbolt') is taken from an Ainu epic and symbolises activism and awareness.

Stage 7 Most users of Ainu are socially integrated individuals and an ethnolinguistically active population

The precise number of native speakers of Ainu is inconclusive, and the proposition that the Ainu language is 'virtually extinct' is questionable. The number is certainly small; according to Fujimura (1989: 37) possibly around 30, almost all in their eighties. (Speakers of Japanese in Japan number around 120 million). These are apparently drastic circumstances for the Ainu population, conservatively estimated by the Hokkaido Registration Office to be close to 25,000. The Hokkaido Ainu Association has been quoted as estimating the actual number to be 50–60,000 (Oda, 1984: 287). However, given the very long and formidable history of the Ainu people throughout Japan, not just in Hokkaido but in the Tohoku region also, the history of enforced assimilation and fear of admitting ethnic identity, a more likely estimation would involve much higher numbers of people throughout the entire archipelago who feel able to acknowledge their Ainu heritage. A more accurate figure, one might estimate, is five times the above. We just do not know.

Stage 7 must be treated carefully in the case of Ainu. Perennial problems arise at the level of definition of 'native speaker', crucially in ascertaining numbers and even more crucially in what constitutes 'ethno-linguistically active'. We revisit the numbers problem. The number of native speakers (broad definition) might safely be estimated to be less than 100 whilst some people would maintain that it is less than five. Ainu people avoid the numbers game – for good reason. It is not merely a matter of statistical interest. Talk of numbers is redolent of the anthropologist's myth of the dying race, the vanishing people (Maher, 1994; Sawai, 1998). Okuda (1998: 148) correctly warns: 'It is very difficult to estimate the number of speakers of the Ainu language. There is no official census and the number of speakers who are known by researchers or journalists is very small. But there are also many people who do not reveal their competence to speak the Ainu language . . . In 1988, it was said that the last three speakers of a certain dialect had died. But after their death, one or more other fluent speakers became known. The number also varies according to how competence is measured'. The most active user/learners are not native speakers but are rather second language speakers most of whom are adults.

Concerning the matter of categories of Ainu users and what constitutes an active user, a useful schemata is elaborated by DeChicchis (1995: 110). He distinguishes the main types of Ainu speakers: (1) archival Ainu speakers, 'members of a robust multigenerational Ainu speech commu- nity . . . Few of these people remain alive, however, the audio and video recordings of their speech are culturally esteemed as representing a gener- ally pure form of the Ainu language, and this has secured their influential role as models to be emulated by living speakers'; (2) old Ainu-Japanese bilinguals who, now elders, have a varied range of fluency and who as chil- dren and young adults spoke Ainu on a routine basis in a natural commu- nity setting   ; (3) token Ainu speakers who, as ethnic Ainu, consider themselves unable to speak Ainu but recall older relatives speaking Ainu and who possess a command of words and formulaic phrases for certain contexts; and finally, (4) second language learners (both ethnic Ainu and non-Ainu) who possess no personal memories of any Ainu speech commu- nity but who are studying and speaking Ainu as a second language. Atti- tudes and self-perception often distinguish categories (3) and (4). As DeChicchis notes: 'These younger second-language learners see them- selves as learning a new language. Even those who are ethnically Ainu do not view themselves as having lost a language. These younger second- language learners recognise their marginal abilities in Ainu, but they view these abilities as being a partial competency rather than as being a partial incompetence, and in this respects they differ from the token speakers. At Ainu cultural events, these younger second-language learners seem more willing to speak Ainu than do the generally older token Ainu speakers' (DeChicchis, 1995: 111).

There is a perceptual if not objective gap between the things some linguists have observed or passed on as a socio-linguistic canon and how the Ainu people view themselves (Toyoka, 1983). Pon's (1976) work, for example, is entitled *Ainu-go wa Ikite iru* [The Ainu Language is Alive] (see also Pon's assertions of Ainu language vitality, 1986).There is, in the first place, an intense self-awareness of a living history and heritage (Maher, 1991b) and at the same time doubts that Ainu can be revived *in toto* and therefore 'Is it worth bothering at all?' (R. Toyoka – personal communication).

The ethno-symbolic vitality of Ainu plays a role in revitalisation. Here the objective reality of a symbolic role in personal life uncouples traditional criteria on the existence or non-existence of a language. Replying to my question: 'Do you speak Ainu?' an Ainu woman replied after a long pause: 'That's a difficult question. I don't speak it and I can't understand it but I know it and I can sing in it. It's always kind of here, a voice inside. And it's never left me' (personal communication – Kyoko Kitahara). A holistic view of language existence ('presence'?) obliges sociolinguists to re-examine both traditional criteria of language vitality.

Stage 6 The attainment of intergenerational informal oralcy and its demographic concentration and institutional reinforcement

The stage of reconstituting Ainu is a difficult one and depends upon what elements are considered important in the preservation of Ainu culture. A survey of adult Ainu people living in Hokkaido (membership of the Ainu association – *Hokkaido Ainu Utari Kyokai* – is roughly 24,000) submitted to the Hokkaido government in 1994 gathered opinion on attitudes to the Ainu language. The 'Report on Existing Conditions of the Ainu People in Hokkaido' indicated that more hope and aspiration for the Ainu language exists than previously thought.

Q: 'What do you know about Ainu culture?'
A1: The Ainu language (37.3%)
A2: Wood carving (33.6%)

Q :'How much Ainu language do you speak?'
A1: I am able to speak it (0.8%)
A2: I can a little (5.4%)
A3: I cannot speak Ainu but have some knowledge of the language (37.1%)

Q: 'Would you yourself like to speak Ainu?'
A1: Yes, willingly (6.5.%)
A2: Yes, if the opportunity presented itself (56.9%)

The issue of what constitutes language knowledge is pointed out by leading folklorist and retired politician Shigeru Kayano (1993: 365) who has noted, for instance: 'When I go to a village for recording and tell a *wepeker* [traditional folktale] to people of my age they listen intently. Many say afterwards that although they cannot repeat it they can more or less understand the story. In short, they can comprehend Ainu although they cannot speak it. Those who have this comprehension can soon come to be able to speak the language. Sawai sums up the present situation as follows: 'Despite the fact that all Ainu speakers today speak Japanese as a result of language shift, they enjoy speaking and listening to the Ainu language on many occasions, at ceremonies, prayers, songs or oral traditions; they enjoy the Ainu language irrespective of fluency . . . ' (Sawai, 1998: 186).

Code-switching is normal in Ainu families. Sometimes this is what might be considered low-level, like lexical borrowing, and at other times it takes the form of vigorous code-mixing. Even dialectal differences between individuals from families can be perceived – 'R- san and I chat and as we talk and use Ainu words sometimes we realise that what I said was a word in my dialect and what R-san said was in her dialect' (Harumi Sawai – personal communication, 1996).

In 1997, after years of deliberation and controversy, the Japanese government enacted the *Ainu Shinpo* (Ainu New Law) formally *Ainu Bunka no Shinko narabi ni Ainu no Dento tou ni kansuru Chishiki no Fukyu oyobi Keihatsu ni kansuru Horitsu* (Act for the Promotion of Ainu Culture, the Dissemination of Knowledge of Ainu Tradition, and Educational Campaign). The new Act (hereafter APCL) contains the following flagship statement:

> This Act aims to bring to reality a society in which the ethnic pride of the Ainu people is respected, enhancing the development of diverse cultures in our nation by the implementation of measures for the promotion of Ainu culture (hereafter 'Ainu Traditions'), the dissemi-nation of knowledge about Ainu Traditions, and education of the nation ' (My translation)

The provisions of the law did not generally meet the demands of the Ainu people. Certainly, the new law does treat language as a defining character-istic of Ainu culture: 'The Ainu Culture in this Act means the Ainu language and cultural properties such as music, dance, crafts, and other cultural properties which have been inherited by the Ainu people, and other cultural properties developed from these' (Article 2, ACPL). The new law, however, provides for 'cultural revival' without addressing any of the social and political conditions which led to and which continue to provoke the debilitation of the Ainu language. Needless to say, the law received

Table 14.1 Development of new measures for the promotion of Ainu culture

Measures	Implementation
Comprehensive and practical research	Enhance the role of Hokkaido as research centre
	Establish research organisation and system including but going beyond ethnology, sociology, history, linguistics
	Establish Ainu Research Promotion Centre
	The training of young researchers
	Introduction of education about Ainu at Institutes of Higher Education
Promotion of the Ainu language	Establishment of regular Ainu language classes for systematic study
	Establishment of teacher training programmes
	Development of teaching materials
	Support for existing programmes at institutes of higher education
	Support for existing language classes at local level
	Ainu language-programmes (courses) on TV and radio
	Ainu language speech contest
Reproduction of traditional living space – promotion of Ainu culture	Establish suitable places and facilities (e.g. parks, exhibitions) for the display of Ainu culture
	Collection, translation, soring of Yukar and oral literature
	Training storytellers
	Preparation of manual for reproduction of Ainu lifestyle and culture
	Dispatching advisers on Ainu cultural activity
	Exhibitions of Ainu craftwork
	Promotion of the traditional performing arts
	Video displays of oral Ainu literature
	International exchange related to Ainu culture
	Presentation of the 'Ainu Cultural Award'
	Ainu Cultural Festival
Dissemination of understanding and knowledge about Ainu tradition	Publication of leaflets about the Ainu and textbooks for elementary – junior high school
	Maintenance of home page
	Ainu Culture Centre activities
	Seminars and lectures to disseminate knowledge

Adapted from the Report of the Experts Meeting on Ainu Affairs (1996) to Chief Cabinet Secretary. *Www.frpac.or.jp/english/Report.Report.html.* Jan. 2000 much criticism (see Nakagawa, 1999). Details that relate to language revival (measures and forms of implementation) are shown in Table 14.1.

Stage 5 Ainu literacy at home, school, community, but without taking on extra-communal reinforcement of such literacy

Renewed study of Ainu oral literature was given historical impetus by Kyosuke Kindaichi's eight-volume compilation of the *Yukar*, the *Yukarshu* (Kindaichi & Kannari, 1959–68) in collaboration with the Ainu reciter Matsu Kannari. Several books and pamphlets have been published explaining aspects of traditional life and language in Ainu communities (see Maher, 1991). Many of these are based on the Ainu oral tradition whereby the telling of stories was passed on from generation to generation expressed in Ainu as *Ek ipekoro ae pashikuma* or 'Come and eat and I will tell you the story'. Shigeru Kayano has been a major figure in the updating of this literature and indeed in the Ainu revival as a whole (1983, 1984a, 1984b, 1985a, 1985b, 1985c,1986a, 1986b,1987, 1988, 1989a). Books written for the general audience include *Ainu Nenoan Ainu* [An Ainu Tells his own Stories] (1989b) which is a description of Kayano's childhood in the Ainu commu- nity. Pamphlets on individual topics have been compiled by Kayano and printed by the Nibutani Bunka Shiryokan ('Nibutani Cultural Information Centre'), e.g. place-name descriptions, in particular the *Shishirimuka zoroi no chimei* ['Place-names along the Shishiri river'] (1985). Typical of the recent range of popular materials is The *Ainu Bunka no Kiso* ['Fundamental Ainu Culture'] (Ainu Minzoku Hakubutsukan, 1987) which sets out brief descriptions of the Ainu language, history of the people, hunting, food, houses, religious customs, songs and play, and so on. Other personal biog- raphies include that compiled by Hokkaido University's 1983 edition of Kura Sunasawa's *Ku sukup oruspe* ('My Life'). In this oral history, a speaker of the Ishikari Dialect of Ainu, (a dialect stretching roughly from Asahikawa to Sapporo), describes her life (she was born in 1897) and expe- riences with the Ainu language.

Stage 4 Ainu in lower education and community institutions

From the 1980s onwards, vigorous efforts have been made to increase the cultural vitality of Ainu in the form of the revival of traditional rituals, the development of teaching materials, language classes in community centres and some universities, and a body of Ainu-sponsored political proposals which touches upon language maintenance. The United Nations declaration on language rights in the Year of the Indigenous Peoples (1993) was a landmark in the history of language maintenance among the peripheral language communities in Japan. Supported by many other language minorities, the Ainu achieved significant progress in their struggle for language protection. Progress is a slippery concept. Farina Becsky (1999), in a comparison of educational regimes for minority languages in Venezuela (Pemon) and Japan (Ainu) cautions that an educational system (always the 'toy' of political interests) must make language diversity more understandable to all participants and a humanistic goal rather than a token of 'progress' if the aim of common society is to go beyond the mere highlighting of difference.

Ainu is not taught in any primary or secondary (public or private) schools of the Japanese educational system. It is, however, taught in language centres throughout Hokkaido, in some universities in Hokkaido and in Chiba National University on the outskirts of Tokyo.

In 1987, a commercial radio station in Hokkaido began broadcasting an Ainu-for-Radio language course (STV Radio 1988). The programmes are not broadcast nationwide but in Hokkaido only and they are aired between 6.05 and 6.20 on Sunday morning. Ainu for early risers. This is a significant advance for maintaining the presence of the Ainu language in Hokkaido. The audience rating is relatively high for that day and time: 0.1–0.2%. (Hatakeyama, 1990: 47). The programme aims to create public interest in both the language and the traditional Ainu outlook on nature and life. Sapporo Broadcasting Corporation received more than 1000 requests for textbooks in 1988 and of these 40 were from the Tokyo region outside the transmission area. In 1998, broadcasts were expanded to Sunday and Saturday morning (15 minutes) and on the STV internet home page. All the lecturers are Ainu and they (and their dialects) rotate in three-monthly cycles. The system is particularly useful in training and cultivating potential lecturers in Ainu.

At no other time in the history of Ainu studies in Japan have there been more courses on the Ainu language at university level. In the Tokyo area, a syllabus was formulated at Waseda University in 1975 and the language continues to be offered at the undergraduate level. Chiba National University is a centre for Ainu language studies, offering Ainu language instruction as well as linguistic analysis (Nakagawa, 1991). At International Christian University, Tokyo, there is thesis and research supervision on multilingualism including Ainu sociolinguistics. A handful of universities in Hokkaido already offer Ainu courses and instruction. Language learning classes have been held in the Nibutani Valley area for many years but this has been joined by a number of other *Ainugo kyoshitsu* (Ainu language classes) now in operation in community centres such as (in order of establishment) Nibutani (1987), Asahikawa (1987), Urakawa (1989), Kushiro (1989), Akan

(1991), Chitose (1991), Shizunai (1992), Mukawa (1992), Obihiro (1993), Shiranuka (1994), Noboribetsu (1996), Tomakomai (1997) and occasionally, language institutes in Tokyo (e.g. Shorin). The *Ainu Taimuzu* (Ainu Times) was launched in 1987 as a means of promoting literacy in Ainu. The text is entirely Ainu both romanised (*romaji*) and *katakana*.

In the RSL model applied to Ainu there is virtually no place in which the remaining stages are relevant. In this I refer to Stage 3 (the use of Ainu in the lower work sphere (outside of the Ainu neighbourhood community) involving interaction between Ainu and non-Ainu; Stage 2 (no use of Ainu in lower governmental services and mass media but not in the higher services of either) Stage 1 (no use of Ainu in higher level educational, occupational). However, there *is* governmental effort (see chronology above) to promote the study of Ainu (without the safety provided by political independence). I refer here to the (1997) Ainu Culture Promotion Law. It should be noted that when Kayano (above) was elected socialist member of the Diet in 1985 he gave his inaugural speech in Ainu – a massive symbolic gesture. Clearly, this indicates that any RSL model must assume that a language may move across stages simultaneously or 'stage-jump', in the sense that the Ainu language revitalisation is now receiving government support legislatively and institutionally without any conception that it will or can be used in public education or the media.

Conclusion

Stage-jumping the Ainu language reversal continuum is most visible in the political rationale advanced for the Ainu Culture Promotion Law enacted in the late 1990s.

In the RLS model, the early stages of 're-assembly' of a language is pressed by the need for reformulation of theoretical constructs surrounding the language. For an effective retooling of the Ainu language nothing less than a remaking of history is needed. Let me examine this further.

Hitherto, many historians have sought to select, emphasise and exclude in order to further elite interests, 'sometimes not even conscious of the fact that they further the interests of the state because they are so much part of the power system from within which they write' (Macdonald, 1995: 301). For the taming of history, Macdonald notes that 'in contemporary Japanese mythology, the past is revered, the nation glorified, and contradictions and conflicts, including discrimination, are concealed. Vast social and economic differences are obliterated. Certain practices are selected to symbolise 'traditional Japanese culture' (301). This idealised culture finds its highest expression in Kyoto – an elegant city which played court to Imperial culture – rather than Sapporo – the new and cold 'far north'). We sometimes hear that 'Japan has lost its culture' in keeping with the peripheralisation of other cultural experience. There is no space to elaborate on this theme here; suffice to note first that advocacy of cultural and linguistic pluralism in Japan is not a postmodern phenomenon but advocacy has a heritage; secondly, pluralism is usually conceptualised in Japan in the form of a centre-periphery dichotomy. If language shift is to be reversed, Ainu can draw upon traditional as well as new formulations. I will cite one such historical formulation.

The traditional movement to preserve and encourage *mingei* 'people's art' began in the late 19th century. In this movement, the machine became the metaphor for the capitalist-industrial mainstream with its 'speed, power, complete uniformity and precision' contrasting with the little handiwork of the regions, the craft of Ainu and Okinawan which alone could produce 'creativity, adaptability, freedom, heterogeneity' (Yanagi, 1982: 108, quoted in Steele, 1995). Fully aware of the tension between national and local allegiances, support for the ideals of the *mingei* movement coincided with founding the so-called *Shirakaba-ha* (White Birch Society) led by Yanagi Soetsu – a complex and paradoxical figure of imaginative but also authoritarian and romantic-nationalist tendency. These ideals embraced cultural pluralism incorporating language maintenance and freedom at the same time. In 1939, the push to eliminate local dialects and the Okinawan in particular – to be replaced by *hyojungo* (standard language) – was initiated by the Japanese government. There was opposition to this attack on local languages and a damning of the policy of centralisation. Fear of the periphery and (regional/cultural) fragmentation whereby the 'centre cannot hold' is not confined to Japan but has long been foregrounded in language politics. As Yanagi wrote in a document sent to the Office of Education on the Problem of the Okinawan Language: Standard Language and Okinawan Language are both languages of Japan. One is a language of the centre: the other is a language of the periphery. These two languages have a close connection with each other. It is our understanding that both should be respected as Japanese national languages' (Yanagi, 1981, Zenshu, 15: 148–9, in Steele, 1995). He continued:

Languages of the periphery are important elements in the national language ... Any weakness of the languages of the periphery is an indication of a weakness in the cultures of the periphery. Local areas that are vigorous normally have a vigorous lifestyle, and possess vigorous literature and music. If Japan were to be a country without languages of the periphery, this would surely transform Japan into a country with little that would be unique . . . Just the existence of the Japanese is important with regard to world culture; there are strong reasons for the existence of the languages of the periphery as they relate to Japanese culture' (Yanagi, 149).

Whilst Yanagi at no point questioned the rightness of the colonial status of either Koreans or Ainu he defended their cultural contribution and language rights. He held an exhibition of Ainu crafts in Tokyo in 1941 to demonstrate that the Ainu did not lead a 'cultureless existence' and to challenge the prevalent view that they should be left to wither away.

No less than in the 1880s when Ainu began performing the yukar and dances for mainland tourists who visited Hokkaido, Japan's 'wild north', there arises in the 21st century the question of the future role of 'Ainu tradition' in mediating cultural identity. The issue spirals into larger issues in the anthropology of tourism, the tradition of invented tradition. After all, the tourist trademark of the Ainu – wood carving of the bear – was an idea imported from Switzerland in the 1920s and that the 'exotic' Marimo festival at Lake Akan was first held only in 1950. This is no a criticism but rather witness to the ever-present globalisation of culture and the fabric of economic relations in micro-systems of society. The implications for language revival are complicated but the overall 'effect' is to arouse interest among Ainu and Japanese in the matter of cultural revival and maintenance.

At some stage of RLS there arises the need for political struggle. This is the case with Ainu. The campaign for legal recognition of the Ainu language as one of the authentic languages of Japan is very significant. This is the site of media attention and the concern of politicians both at the local and national level.

The Ainu people are very conscious of the connection between the struggle for recognition of human rights and maintenance of their language. This is typified in the wording of a petition by Tokyo's Ainu community, the Kanto Ainu Association: 'The government for the last 120 years has not recognised that Ainu people have the right to speak their native language in daily life. Ainu children wanting to learn the language must endure prejudice and bullying. It is ridiculous that we have to have lessons to learn our native language' (Kitahara, Kyoko, July 1990, Asahi Shinbun).

The official response by the government to these proposals has been slow but nevertheless forthcoming. There is now emerging the establishment of clear goals. For the Ainu language this is a positive step towards the integration of aims for ethnolinguistic revitalisation.

In the intergenerational transmission of Ainu the perennial issue of ownership of the language is crucial. Honda's observation is insightful in this regard. She has noted, firstly, the difficulty encountered by younger learners of Ainu whose normal learner errors (particularly pronunciation) are seized upon by older native-speakers. Nagging discourages younger learners who then categorise Ainu as the property of the old rather than the heritage of a coming, younger generation (Honda personal communication, 1994). There is also the fact that more and more Japanese and not just ethnic Ainu take up Ainu language study. There is a crossing of ethnic allegiances in which language and culture are floating variables in shifting ethno-linguistic boundaries. The role of Japanese participants in an Ainu language programme receives attention in Anderson and Iwasaki-Goodman's useful study (2000) of an Ainu language programme in the Nibutani community.

The sociolinguistic expression 'language transmission' is conceptually polyvalent. Among Ainu speakers attitudes towards transmission are indeed complex and varied and rich. An effective RSL will take this into account. An example from Okuda (1998), is worth noting here. This Ainu fieldworker worked with two old ladies who undoubtedly wished for the transmission of their mother-tongue, but what puzzled the linguist was that ideas of transmission differed considerably. One of his informants was eager to recite the oral literature and keen to translate Japanese into Ainu: 'It appears that she wished for the revival of her language in daily life or its bilingual use with the Japanese language' (Okuda, 1998: 144). The second informant was principally concerned with Ainu ritual speech and not in daily conversation. She resisted translating modern Japanese into Ainu and refused to translate separate lexical items into Ainu preferring instead to recite a complete piece of literature in which the word occurred. This Ainu speaker permitted the use of Japanese for Ainu rituals. Okuda noted that among many speakers he 'could not perceive any apparent wish for the transmission of their language to the next generation'.

What is somewhat unclear in the ascending RLS model is where the political and the historical fit in and where they can fit in comfortably. Political reformism and the rewriting of history are crucial factors in Ainu revitalisation.

Postcript

The last word in this paper belongs to the Ainu language itself. The tongue-twister 'Who is Greater' told by Sadamo Hiraga (in Kayano, 1986) contains a useful summary of the paradox faced by any language that is undergoing shift and revitalisation: a paradoxical, optimistic affirmation of the future.

346

Africa and Asia

Who is Greater?

A little wolf falls on the ice
For the ice is greater
The ice is greater but is thawed by the sun
For the sun is greater
The sun is greater but above are the clouds
For the clouds are greater
The clouds are greater but leak the rain
For the rain is greater
The rain is greater but falls on the ground
For the ground is greater
The ground is greater but is pierced by the trees
For the trees are greater
The trees are greater but are cut by the Ainu
For the Ainu are greater
The Ainu are greater but die in the end
Cry 'fussa, fussa' as the Ainu die
And the Ainu will return again.

[Note: 'fussa': a shout or call when felling trees]

References

Ainu Minzoku Hakubutsukan (1988) *Ainu Bunka no Kiso Chishiki*. Hokkaido: Ainu Minzoku Hakubutsukan.
Anderson, F. and Iwasaki-Goodman, M. (2000 forthcoming) Language and culture revitalization in a Hokkaido community. In Noguchi and Fotos (eds) *Studies in Japanese Bilingualism*, Chapter 4. Clevedon: Multilingual Matters.
Asahi Shinbun (newspaper) (1990) Ainugo o Ima ni Ikasu. 5 May, 29.
Batchelor, J. (1938) *An Ainu-English-Japanese Dictionary*. 4th edn.
Davis, G. (1987) The Ainu: Japan's indigenous 'Indians'. *Tokyo Journal* October: 7–9 and 18–19.
DeChicchis, J. (1995) The current state of the Ainu language. *Journal of Multilingual and Multicultural Development*. Also in *Multilingual Japan* (pp.103–24). Clevedon: Multilingual Matters.
Farina Becsky, V. (1999) *The Relation Between Endangered Languages Revival and Education for Mainstream Society with Refence to the Ainu (Japan) and the Pemon (Venezuela) Indigenous Groups*. MA Thesis, Kyoto University Graduate School of Education, Kyoto.
Hatakeyama, S. (1990) Attitudes towards the Ainu and its language. Unpublished MA thesis. International Christian University, Tokyo.
Honda, Y. (1992) Ainugo Kyoshitsu – Piratori [Piratori Ainu Language Class]. In Kubota, Kuritsubo, Noyama, Hino and Fujii (eds) *Kosho Bungaku 2: Ainu Bungaku* [Oral Literature 2: Ainu Literature]. Tokyo: Iwanami Shoten.
Imura, K. (1985) Ainugo wa ikinokoru ka. *Gengo* 14(2), 36–41. Kamuytorano Kyokai.

Imura, K. (1987) *Ainu go Kaiwa: shokkyuken*. Hokkaido: Kamuy torano Kyokai.

Kayano, S. (1983) *Okikurumi no boken*. Hokkaido: Kominshoten.

Kayano, S. (1984a) *Pasui wa ikimono*. Hokkaido: Hokuto Shuppan.

Kayano, S. (1984b) *Kitsune no Charanke*. Tokyo: Komine Shoten.

Kayano, S. (1985a) *Shishirimuka Zoroi no Chimei*. Hokkaido: Nibutani Ainu Bunka Shiryokan.

Kayano, S. (1985b) *The Romance of the Bear God: Ainu Folktales*. Tokyo: Taishukan.

Kayano, S. (1985c) *Hitotsubu no Sachipoporo*. Tokyo: Heibon.

Kayano, S. (1986a). *Ainu no Mingu*. Tokyo:Suzusawa Shoten.

Kayano, S. (1986b) *Kibori no Ookami*. Tokyo: Komine Shoten.

Kayano, S. (1987). *Ainugo Kaiwa*. Shokyuhen (Videotape and textbook).

Kayano, S. (1988) *Ainu no Hi*. Tokyo: Asahi Shinbunsha.

Kayano, S. (1989a) *Yasashii Ainugo (I)*. Hokkaido: Nibutani Ainugo Kyoshitsu.

Kayano, S. (1989b) *Takusan no fushigi: Ainu ne no an Ainu (An Ainu tells his own stories)*. Tokyo: Fukuinkan Shoten.

Kayano, S. (1993) Ainu ethnic and linguistic revival. In Loos and Osanai (eds) Nibutani AInugo Kyoshitsu Kohoshi (Sokango – 20) [Magazine of Kayano Shigeru's Dictionary of the Ainu language] (pp. 360–67). Tokyo: Sanseido.

Kindaichi, K. and Kannari, M. (1959–68) *Yukara-shu 1–8*. [Collection of Yukar]. Tokyo: Sanseido.

Macdonald, G. (1995) The politics of diversity in the nation-state. In J. Maher and G. Macdonald (eds) *Diversity in Japanese Culture and Language* (pp. 291–315). London and Sydney: Kegan Paul International.

Maher, J. (1985) The role of English as an international language of medicine. *Applied Linguistics* 5, 18–36.

Maher, J. (1989) Doctors who write: Language preference in medical communication in Japan. *International Journal of the Sociology of Language* 52, 230–42.

Maher, J. (1991a) Hashigaki [Preface]. In Maher and Yashiro (eds) *Nihon no Biringarizumu* (pp. iv–vii). Tokyo, Kenkyusha.

Maher, J. (1991b) Ainugo no Fukkatsu (The Ainu Language Revival). In Maher and Yashiro (eds) *Nihon no Biringarizumu* (pp. 149–69). (Tokyo: Kenkyusha).

Maher, J. (1993) The language situation of Japan. *The Encyclopedia of Language & Linguistics* 4, 452–3.

Maher, J. (1994) Shigo to iu Shinwa: Ainugo no Renaissance (The Myth of Language Death: The Ainu Language Renaissance). In J. Maher and N. Honna (eds) *Atarashii Nihonkan, Sekaikan ni mukatte: Nihon ni okeru Gengo to Bunka no Tayosei* (pp. 116–131). Tokyo: Kokusaishoin.

Maher, J. (1996) North Kyushu Creole: A language-contact model for the origins of Japanese. In D. Denoon, M. Hudson, G. McCormack and T. Morris-Suzuki (eds) *Multicultural Japan: Palaeolithic to Postmodern* (pp. 31–45). Cambridge: Cambridge University Press.

Maher, J. (1997) Community languages in Japan. In Kokuritsu Kokugo Kenkyujo (ed.) *Proceedings of the Conference on Language Treatment*. Tokyo: Bonjinsha.

Maher, J. and Honna, N. (1994a) *Atarashii Nihonkan, Sekaikan ni mukatte: Nihon ni okeru Gengo to Bunka no Tayosei*. [Towards a New Order: Linguistic and Cultural Diversity in Japan]. Tokyo: Kokusai Shoin.

Maher, J. and Honna, N. (1994b) Hajime ni. In J. Maher and N. Honna (eds) *Atarashii*

Nihonkan, Sekaikan ni mukatte: Nihon ni okeru Gengo to Bunka no Tayosei (pp. 7–15). Tokyo, Kokusaishoin.

Maher, J. and Macdonald, G. (1995) _Diversity in Japanese Culture and Language_. London and Sydney: Kegan Paul International.

Maher, J. and Yashiro, K. (1991) _Nihon no Bairingarizumu_. [Bilingualism in Japan]. Tokyo: Kenkyuusha.

Maher, J. and Yashiro, K. (1995a) _Multilingual Japan_. Clevedon: Multilingual Matters.

Maher, J. and Yashiro, K. (1995b) Introduction. In J. Maher and K. Yashiro (eds) _Multilingual Japan_ (pp. 1–12). Clevedon: Multilingual Matters.

Mervio, M. (1995) Cultural representation of the Japanese in international relations and politics. _Acta Universitatis Tamperensis_, Ser. A, Vol. 448.

Nakagawa, H. (1995) _Ainugo Chitose Hogen Jiten_ (Ainu–Japanese Dictionary. Chitose Dialect). Tokyo: Sofukan.

Nakagawa. H. (1997) _Ekusupuresu Ainugo_ (Express Ainu). Tokyo: Heibonsha.

Nakagawa, H. (1999) Present and future. In W.W. Fitzhugh and C.O. Dubreuil (eds) _Ainu: Spirit of a Northern People_ (pp. 371–3). National Museum of Natural History, Smithsonian Institution.

Narita, T. and Hanazaki, K. (1975) _Kindaika no naka no Ainu Sabetsu Kozo_ (The Structure of Ainu Discrimination within Modernization). Tokyo: Akaishi Shobo.

Oda, K. (1984) Ikiru Ainu no sonzai to mirai. _Sekai_ 450, 283–7.

Okuda, O. (1998) On the objectives of linguistic research on the Ainu. In K. Matsumura (ed.) _Studies in Endangered Languages_ (pp. 143–148). Tokyo: Hituzi Syobo.

Peng, F.C.C. and Geiser, P. (1977) _The Ainu: The Past in the Present_. Hiroshima: Bunka Hyoron.

Pon, F. (1976) (revised 1986) _Ainugo wa ikite iru_ [Ainu is alive]. Tokyo: Shinsensha.

Sasamura, J. (1999) Beyond the Ainu Shinpo: An Ainu view In W.W. Fitzhugh and C.O. Dubreuil (eds) _Ainu: Spirit of a Northern People_ (pp. 369–70). National Museum of Natural History, Smithsonian Institution.

Sawai, H. (1998) The present situation of the Ainu language. In Matsumura Kazuto (ed.) _Studies in Endangered Languages_. Ichel Linguistic Studies, Vol. 1. Tokyo: Hituzi Syobo.

STV Radio (1988) _Ainugo Koza: 'Irankaratte'_. Text. Hokkaido: Sapporo Radio.

Siddle, R. (1996) _Race, Resistance and the Ainu_. London: Routledge.

Siddle, R. (1995) The Ainu: Construction of an image. In Maher and Macdonald (eds), (pp. 73–94).

Steele, W. (1995) Nationalim and cultural pluralism in modern Japan: Soetsu Yanagi and the Mingei Movement. In J. Maher and G. Macdonald (eds) _Diversity in Japanese Culture and Language_ (pp. 27–48). London and Sydney. Kegan Paul International.

Tamura, S. (1956) _Ainugo no doshi no kozo_ [The structure of Ainu verbs]. _Gengo Kenkyo_ 39, 21–38.

Tamura, S. (1960) Studies on the Ainu language. _Current Trends in Linguistics_ 2, 608–32.

Tamura, S. (1970) Personal affixes in the Saru dialect of Ainu. In R. Jakobson and S. Kawamoto (eds) _Studies in General and Oriental Linguistics, Presented to Shiro Hattori on the Occasion of his Sixtieth Birthday_. Tokyo: TEC.

Tamura, S. (S. Fukuda) (1974) Ainugo ni tsuite. _Gengo_ 3(1), 27–32.

Tamura, S. (1981) _Ainu-go no onsei shirio_, 3. Waseda Daigaku Gogaku Kyoiku Kenkyujo.

Tamura, S. (1985) Ikita Ainugo o manabu tame ni: daigaku nogogaku kyoiku no naka de. _Gengo_ 14(2), 42–5.

Tanimoto, K. (1999) To Live is To Sing. In W.W. Fitzhugh and C.O. Dubreuil (eds) *Ainu: Spirit of a Northern People* (pp. 282–6). National Nuseum of Natural History, Smithsonian Institution.

Toyoka, S. (1983) Ainu minzoku kara no Ainuron. *Chuo Koron* 98(2), 304–13.

Tsunemoto, T. (1999) The Ainu Shinpo. In W.W. Fitzhugh and C.O. Dubreuil (eds) *Ainu: Spirit of a Northern People* (pp. 366–8). National Nuseum of Natural History, Smithsonian Institution.

Yoshida, I. (1915–16) Ainu-go kaiwa hen. Nihon Jinruigaku, Vol. 30, Nos. 2, 5, 9, 10: 58–63,190–2, 219–2,387–92; Vol. 31, No. 6: 135–55.

Yokoyama, T. and Chiri, M. (1987) *Ainu Itak* (Ainugo Ilasto Jiten)Tokyo: Kagyusha.

Yokoyama, T. and Chiri, M. (1988) *Ainu Ukoyso-Itak* (Ainugo Kaiwa Ilasto Jiten). Tokyo: Kagyusha. Yoneda (Honda) Y. (1995) Comment on Maher's 'Community Languages in Japan'. *Language Management for Multicultural Communities: Individuals and Communities – Living the Differences.* Kokuritstu Kokugo Kenkyujo, Tokyo.

Chapter 15
Hebrew After a Century of RLS Efforts

B. SPOLSKY and E. SHOHAMY

The Revitalisation of Hebrew and the GIDS Model

In Fishman (1991), there is an admirable assessment of the revitalisation of Hebrew within terms of the GIDS (Graded Intergenerational Disruption Scale) model presented in that book. The antecedent to Fishman's book was his long career studying language shift. While many in the field of linguistics appeared not to notice what was happening to the objects of their study until Krauss (1991a,b) wrote about endangered languages, Fishman, from his earliest publications (Fishman, 1951), had been dealing with language loyalty and its reverse, language loss. He had spent his career working closely and sympathetically with members of groups which were concerned to stem language loss. From this rich and caring experience, he developed a sensitive and compassionate appreciation of the complexities and difficulties of the struggle to keep alive a language threatened by a larger and more powerful one. In Fishman (1991), he aims to translate this experience and his observations into a theory of what he calls 'RLS' or reversing language shift. This theory postulates seven steps or levels which define a state of language loss or determine the course of action that might best remedy it. Noble as the goal is, and valuable as the advice will hopefully turn out to be for groups resisting language loss, there are a number of problems left unsolved by the theory.

When the RLS and GIDS models are applied to Hebrew, some of the incertitude become clear. The facts about Hebrew presented in Fishman's book offer an excellent account of the process of Hebrew language 'revival' or 'revernacularisation' or 'revitalisation'. The three terms suggest the complexity of the process and select different views of it. *Revival*, perhaps the most popular, misses the frequently made point that Hebrew was in active if limited use during the hundreds of years that it was no longer a spoken language. Fishman's use of the term *revernacularisation* stresses the change from Hebrew as a classical literary sacred language to one with daily vernacular use (the term 'vernacular' is defined in this way in Stewart (1968) and in Fishman (1970)). My preference for the term *revitalisation*

(Spolsky, 1991, 1996a) highlights rather the critical importance of restoring 'vitality' or normal intergenerational transmission of the language as a mother tongue.

The question that we will ask in this paper is whether what has happened to Hebrew in the past century – the revival, revernacularisation and revitalisation – is best analysed as a case of reversing language shift, or whether it is sufficiently unique in both task, method and outcome to challenge the RLS model. Consider first the literal meaning of the term. The process of shifting from the use of Hebrew as a spoken vernacular may have started as early as the 6th century BCE, and certainly was well along for many living in ancient Israel by the beginning of the Common Era (Chomsky, 1957; Rabin 1973). How long Hebrew continued to be spoken among Jews is a matter of some debate but it is now generally believed that there were still monolingual speakers of Hebrew in villages of Judaea at the time of the Bar Kochba Revolt, in the second century of the Common Era, and native speakers even later.

It is during the latter part of this period of language loss that we should look for efforts to reverse Hebrew language shift. We find evidence in a number of statements in the Talmud calling for the use of Hebrew instead of Aramaic. When the battle to save the language is close to the end, a new strategy was proposed. Once it was clear that normal intergenerational transmission could no longer be counted on, a formal system of language preservation was mandated. When a boy reached the age of five, every father was required to start teaching him Hebrew. Fathers might delegate this responsibility to a school teacher. Every Jewish community was required to establish a school where this teaching could be done. Here we had the beginning of a policy of language preservation, of 'reversing language shift', through establishing institutions for formal educational transmission .

For a thousand and more years, this policy succeeded in keeping Hebrew alive as an active literary and sacred language, albeit in a special relationship with a functionally differentiated use of written Aramaic. The two closely related languages, Hebrew and Aramaic, have remained entwined ever since their first fateful meeting. Starting out as an imperial language of government and business (and it remains until this day the language in which a Jewish marriage contract (*ketuba)* and divorce papers (*get*) are written), Aramaic developed after the return from Babylon into a widespread vernacular, and thus into the first of a series of Jewish languages. Its use in the compilation of the Babylonian *Talmud* after the destruction of the Second Temple gave it a fixed place as a partner with

352 Africa and Asia

Hebrew in the *leshon hakodesh* that is still the language of Jewish sanctity. For most Jews, Hebrew-and-Aramaic remained the language of prayer, the language in which the sacred texts were written, the language most appropriate for writing. While there were Jewish communities with a low level of literacy, there were many others over the following centuries in which there were glorious examples of literary production in the language. One thinks of the religious poetry of the *payetanim* in the 7th century, or the magnificent Hebrew literature of the Arabic-Spanish period starting in the 10th century. This was again true of the *Haskalah*, the Enlightenment, at the end of the 18th century, a period marked also by the flourishing of Hebrew letters. This literary flame was still alight at the end of the 19th century, when it was pre-empted by a new concern for reviving Hebrew as a spoken language, in line with European nationalist movements of the time.

Treating the revitalisation of Hebrew at the end of the 19th century as a simple case of reversing language shift seems to call for one of two quite unlikely interpretations. First, we might consider it a new step, a thousand years later, to preserve the spoken language. But this is somewhat far-fetched – for a thousand years, Jews had been using a series of Jewish languages and co-territorial gentile languages for most vernacular purposes. Alternatively, we might consider it as an endeavour to reverse the loss of Hebrew literacy that was a consequence of the process of diminishing religious observance and education that occurred during the 19th century. This case too is hard to make, for it was an essential feature of Hebrew revival, as Fishman recognises, that it was to be a new revolutionary break with the past and so with the religiously motivated teaching of the sacred tongue to young boys. Both the territorial nationalism associated with Hebrew and the cultural nationalism that developed at the same time associated with the revival of Yiddish and its standardisation were secular movements, rejecting the religious beliefs that underlay the previous efforts to maintain Hebrew. The leaders of the Hebrew revival movement certainly did not wish to return to the old religiously controlled educational system that had preserved literacy for so long.

The drive for Hebrew revival in both Europe and Palestine, like the contemporaneous European-focused drive for changing the status of the Yiddish that was the communal vernacular of east European Jews, came not from within the religious community but from secularised and secularising ideologists, supporters of a new Jewish nationalism that in the case of Hebrew was largely territorialist and in the case of Yiddish, primarily cultural. In fact, the early opponents of the revernacularisation of Hebrew were those within the religious establishment who were most concerned with the continuation of the use of Hebrew for its restricted sacred, religious and literacy functions.

Except in a rhetorical sense, there was no aim to revive the variety or pattern of Hebrew that was being lost, but rather an ideological use of its associations with a Great Tradition to justify its inclusion among a set of other new slogans and symbols for nationhood. The rhetoric and images of the ancient language were recruited to the demands of the new Zionist movement. Look at the call for building the new city of Tel Aviv:

> We must urgently acquire a considerable chunk of land, on which we shall build our houses. Its place must be near Jaffa, and it will form the first Hebrew city, its inhabitants will be Hebrews a hundred percent; Hebrew will be spoken in this city, purity and cleanliness will be kept, and we shall not go in the ways of the *goyim*. (Cited and translated in Harshav (1993: 143) from the 1906 Prospectus for Tel Aviv.)

Hebrews, not Jews, speaking Hebrew only, pure and clean. The founders of Tel Aviv rejected at once the ways of the *goyim* (gentiles) and their languages and of the Jews (*yidn*) and their language Yiddish.

Returning to the terms of the GIDS model, there were at the time of this call for revival no 'socially isolated old folks' who were the vestigial users of Hebrew, but rather a well-developed classical sacred language, the focus of universal (more or less) male (mainly) elementary education, with developed home, school and community literacy, and with use of that literacy on the highest intra-community functions. The task undertaken by the Hebraisers then was quite unlike normal RLS activity (including the activities tried a little later for Yiddish). Some of the difficulties of attempting to fit both in the same model are illustrated in the effort to compare Hebrew language revitalisation with contemporary Maori RLS activities (Spolsky, 1996a). As a heuristic for checking structural similarities, the approach has some value, but the results are to show dissimilarity rather than shared features.

As the account in Fishman (1991) concedes, the process of revitalisation of Hebrew did not follow the model implied by GIDS, but it did include some of the specific steps included in that model. Fishman (1991: 291) accepts this uniqueness: the 'unprecedented goal' of 'revernacularising a language of sanctity and/or literacy'. It was a task to be accomplished, he also notes, with active opposition of the preservers of sacred literacy – the very people who would be expected to be involved in normal RLS.

Translating the complex multi-directional process that occurred into a simple model, Fishman acknowledges, is not easy, but he does summarise the Hebrew revernacularisation in these terms: 'The revernacularisation of

Hebrew started at stage 7 and then went onto stages 6, 5 (particularly for adults) and 4 in a fairly rapid but far from inevitable succession.' Now Stage 7 is defined as 'socially integrated and ethnolinguistically active' speakers 'beyond child-bearing age'. It is hard to see how this fits the Hebrew case, for the theorists like Ben-Yehuda and the practitioners like the Zionist pioneers were all social misfits, and of child-bearing age. They took little interest in the older generation, but, it is true, did hope to recruit others of their own age group to accept the ideology of the new language.

Stage 6 is more apt: the development of 'demographic concentrations' where 'intergenerational informal oracy' can be established. These concentrations – the older agricultural settlements like Petah Tikva, the revolutionary kibbutzim, and the spanking new city of Tel Aviv – played a key role in this crucial stage of revitalisation. There appear to have been two reinforcing stages. The first was the promulgation and acceptance of an ideological principle of using Hebrew in public, most effective in developing intergenerational transmission in the kibbutzim where most areas of life including the children's house were 'public'. The second was the acceptance of the need for intergenerational transmission and the willingness to allow or encourage children to speak the language.

Stage 5 (literacy at home, school and community) had in fact in the Hebrew case preceded Stages 7 and 6 (and by more than a 1000 years!), so that the next significant step was 4, the establishment of lower education in Hebrew. There were at this stage (under Turkish rule in Palestine) no compulsory education laws, so that again the GIDS model needs to be modified to fit the case. What happened was a process lasting about 20 years, as more and more Jewish schools started to teach in Hebrew. (Some orthodox schools, especially Hassidic ones, still continue to resist this step.)

Fishman does not analyse the remaining stages in GIDS terms, except to remark that Stage 3 was not a necessary step for Hebrew. This step of use in the 'lower work domain' has however played its role, as Hebrew has spread among Arabic speakers forced to learn it in the workplace. Nor does he discuss the critical importance of the political work in England that assured Hebrew of its official recognition by the British government from the very beginning of their rule over Palestine, moving it effectively into the 'lower governmental services and mass media' (Stage 2) and into the 'higher level educational, governmental and media efforts' even before independence.

We find it difficult, therefore, to fit the Hebrew case comfortably into the GIDS model, but clearly have benefited from it in identifying key factors to consider. The fact that the model did not prevent Fishman (1991) from giving such an accurate picture of Hebrew revival also suggests that he too sees the need for much greater flexibility. But if this 'unprecedented' case of success is not accounted for by the model, might one not start to wonder about whether it is too tight a straitjacket? Does the term 'stage' perhaps unduly constrain the model, by its implication of an ordered progression up (towards autonomy) as well as down?

The Costs of Hebrew RLS Success

To explore our concerns with the model further, we turn to the second part of our task, that of considering developments in the case of Hebrew since Fishman (1991) was written. When we try to do this, we are brought up by the realisation, adumbrated in the opening of this paper, that, in RLS studies, point of view is all important. For the last few years, we have been studying what has happened to the 'other' languages in Israel, and how they have fared under the impact of the strong Hebrew-focused ideology that appears to have been so important in establishing Hebrew vitality and vernacular use (Shohamy, 1995; Spolsky & Shohamy, 1999; Spolsky & Shohomy, in preparation). In this enterprise, we have become vividly aware of the many other languages that have succeeded or failed or not even tried to resist Hebrew. The fate of these languages is in fact the most obvious cost of the success of Hebrew RLS activities.

Here, again, it is not too clear that the GIDS model is going to be the most useful approach. Presumably, it has nothing much to say about the majority of languages brought to Israel by immigrants over the past century, who seem to have accepted without a murmur the established Hebrew-only (or, more recently, Hebrew-only-plus-English) ideology. Most have gone quietly through the normal language shift, arriving peace-fully at a resigned Stage 8, with vestigial individual use. Even a major world language like German, major competitor for functional control of higher education 85 years ago, accepted its defeat and was not generally passed on for more than half a generation; and another, French, depends on efforts from the metropolitan authorities and its ministry of *francophonie* to keep a grip of its impuissant status in the Israeli educational system. The vast majority of the Jewish languages, with or without a history of literacy, have generally failed to maintain status or use. But before we set out to analyse these cases and then reconsider the progress of Hebrew revival, we might ask whether there might not be a better framework for analysis than GIDS.

As we do this, it will become clear that we are not so much disagreeing with Fishman (1991) (we could probably write the rest of this paper simply using sentences from his book) as trying to work through our discomfort with some of his formulations. We use our own model (Spolsky & Shohamy, 1999), to suggest that RLS is a kind of language *policy*, which we define as an effort by someone claiming authority to alter the language *practice* or *ideology* of someone else.

We find the distinction between practice, ideology and policy to be useful. The language practice of a community – what Hymes (1974) called its ethnography of communication – comprises its language uses and implied rules for language use. Colouring but not necessarily changing language practice, a speech community also has a language ideology, or a set of beliefs about the reasons and values for those uses and rules for use. (This distinction comes from Fishman's reanalysis of Stewart's typology of languages, where Fishman showed the greater value of considering autonomy, historicity, etc. as beliefs or attitudes.) A language policy, on the other hand, is a formal attempt by someone who has or who claims authority to change the language use (or ideology) of members of a speech community. The critical element in the definition is that the sentence is active, with a definable agent. It excludes therefore hegemonies or unidentified conspirators, and requires that one says specifically who is doing the policy making. It also excludes (and this is more awkward), cases where a speaker makes a policy for himself only. Thus we distinguish between a family that has a *practice* of speaking Xish when grandfather is present from a family where the father has proclaimed a *policy* of speaking Xish at meals.

When applied to RLS, the definition we propose gives us a chance of defining the agent as small or weak or powerless or (at the very least) unofficial members of a small or weak or powerless or (at the very least) marginalised speech community. Putting things this way helps us understand the uneasiness we feel when the unofficial becomes official, when the powerless language's supporters become powerful, and when members of less powerful speech communities are forced to defend themselves against the newly empowered David, king and no longer shepherd boy. It helps us understand the reason that, while we sympathise with the start of the RLS activities in Québec on behalf of French, we do not sympathise with the RLS activities of France itself against its regional languages, Breton and Basque and Occitan (Ager, 1999), or even the Québec policy when it works against Hebrew signs in a kosher food store. Or why we do not consider Unz's activities in California to preserve English as deserving of the same regard as Estonian efforts to re-establish their language. It helps us understand too why we see Hebrew as a success story, up to the point that we realise its victory was not just over competing world languages like German and French, but also over small powerless ethnic languages like Yiddish and Judezmo and Hulaulá (Judeo-Aramaic) and Judeo-Yemenite and Juhuri (Judeo-Tat), to mention just a few, all with their own histories and cultures.

The problem is that RLS is not an isolated event affecting a single language but rather is interwoven with all the other languages in the speech community. Successful RLS for one language may be death or extermination for other languages. In the case of Hebrew, its success came at the cost of the indigenous language (the Arabic introduced into the region a thousand years earlier, which itself had displaced the Aramaic which had replaced Hebrew), and of the 40 or more languages brought in by Jewish immigrants. Its price was also the nurturing of a monolingual linguistic ideology that replaced the earlier general acceptance of the value of plurilingualism. Thus, if we were to write a book on RLS activities in Israel today (which is what we have done in our book called The Languages of Israel), it would (and does) start of by recounting the 'RLS success' of the revitalisation and revernacularisation of Hebrew, and then turns to the fate and RLS activities of Arabic and Yiddish and Ladino and Russian and Amharic and Circassian speakers. Keeping of course one eye open to the RLS efforts of Hebrew supporters who feel threatened by English.

A second point needs to be stressed (again it is already made in Fishman, 1991), and that is that the goal of RLS activities is seldom if ever purely a linguistic change. Most language policy is directed to non-linguistic goals, whether political unification or domination or independence, or cultural maintenance or reshaping, or economic efficiency or success, or educational enrichment or achievement. Even such a driven language policy maker as Eliezer Ben Yehuda started off, as Mandel (1993) has shown, as a nationalist before he saw the critical value of language as an instrument of achieving nationalism. The concentration on the language aspect in RLS is understandable from the point of view of the sociolinguist, but from the point of view of the language user, language is just one aspect of complex social and cultural and economic choices. As a Navajo student once remarked, she could make sure that her child grew up speaking Navajo, but only if she was prepared to live in a *hogan* and carry water a mile or more every day.

The Revitalisation of Hebrew in a Model of Language Practice, Ideology and Policy

Looking first at Hebrew RLS activities from the point of view of our model of practice, ideology and policy, then, the picture that emerges is something like this. In the period between 1890 and 1913, a number of Jews, mainly in eastern Europe and Turkish administered Palestine, but also in the United States, began to use Hebrew as a spoken language for daily use as well as for various written functions. These were in general not the same Jews who continued to use it for sacred and traditional Jewish educational functions. Starting with use in a few schools in agricultural settlements in Palestine and spreading to the newly established town of Tel Aviv and to some schools elsewhere, the practice of using Hebrew as a vernacular became common among children and a growing norm among committed adults in public. The practice was supported and spread by being part of the ideology of the new Zionist nationalist movement. It was promulgated as policy by some of the leaders of that movement, and won acceptance in some critical groups such as the Zionist Labour Party in Palestine. The supporters of the new policy were successful in 1911–13 in Palestine in a public struggle for a language policy for a planned tertiary technological institution.

The struggle in the early years was directed against two other languages in particular. The first 'enemy' was Yiddish, proclaimed in Tshernovits as 'a Jewish national language' by supporters of a non-territorial cultural nationalist movement (Fishman, 1980), and seen by supporters of Hebrew as a threat for ideological reasons as well as because of the fact that it was the normal vernacular of east European Jews, and of course of the very people who were now moving to Hebrew. The second 'enemy' in this early period was German, a generally accepted world language of culture and education, and the language naturally favoured by the major educational system, the *Hilfsverein* that was the founder of a number of schools at various levels in pre-war Palestine (Wahl, 1996). The battle against German was fought first in Palestine during the so-called Language War, and then again, in England, in the latter part of the First World War, where the German plan to replace Hebrew was decried in an active campaign conducted by supporters of Zionism and Hebrew (Cohen, 1918) in 1918. Bolstered by the results of a 'language census' conducted by the Zionist organisation that appeared to show that most Jews in Palestine spoke Hebrew (Bachi, 1956), the language was accepted by the British for inclusion in the official languages for the Military government and the subsequent Mandate.

Hebrew thus started in the 1920s ideologically supported within the Jewish community and officially recognised by the Mandatory government as the language for that community and its schools. The 'enemies' now changed. The active campaign for the diffusion of the language remained a central feature of Zionist and Israeli ideology. A Youth Legion formed in 1923 for the Protection of the Language continued its activities until 1936. During this critical period, strong campaigns were conducted against the two principal enemies, as they were identified by Ussishkin in his important speech at the 1923 third national conference of the Legion, English and Yiddish. He attacked those who used English in order to assert their elite status and closeness to the British rulers. His bitterest complaints however were against Yiddish, and one of the major victories of the Legion was to block the establishment of a chair of Yiddish at the Hebrew University.

By the late 1930s, however, Hebrew appears to have been so well enough established and institutionalised that there was no longer danger of loss. That is not to say that there have been no continuing pro-Hebrew or anti-Yiddish policies or arguments – just as French and English continue to take steps to protect themselves against suspected foes, so the supporters of Hebrew occasionally make efforts to strengthen the prospects for their language. The establishment of the State in 1948 provided an opportunity to reaffirm the place of Hebrew, but this was handled quite modestly, by dropping the Mandatory status of English as official and leaving Hebrew and Arabic. There is no constitutional requirement for Hebrew, and perhaps also no formal legal affirmation of its centrality. There were however numbers of localised decisions – maintenance of Arabic as language of instruction in Arab schools, establishment of the ulpan to teach Hebrew to professional immigrants, acceptance of use of other languages in limited areas – that worked together with the established ideology and that led in practice to the maintenance of Hebrew and its replacement of the multilingualism of earlier generations and of immigrants.

Resistance to Hebrew RLS by Other Languages

Changing sides, as it were, if we look at the 40 or so other languages that were themselves threatened by the shift to Hebrew, we find minimal evidence of RLS activities. There were some people, but very few, who followed the example of one head of family from Morocco and required Hebrew to be used and spoken before the family came to Israel, while he encouraged the use of Jewish Moroccan Arabic in the home after they were settled here. More general was the normal process of immigrant shift to the new language, with the second generation being passively bilingual and the third unable to speak the immigrant language. The ideological effects were to breed a locally nationalistic disparagement (Dorian, 1998) of all but the approved standard language, and a rejection of the seriousness or value of home or ethnic or community or traditional Jewish languages. Even

without formal policy, the monolingual Hebrew ideology came to dominate and have its inevitable effects on practice.

The main exceptions occurred in marginal or marginalised groups. As
already mentioned, the 1948 decisions maintained Arabic as language of
instruction in schools in the Arab sector. At the same time, Arab pupils
were expected to learn Hebrew. The result over half a century has been a
serious incursion of Hebrew into the Israeli Palestinian Arabic community:
Arabic remains the language of the home and village, but Hebrew is the
language of tertiary education and of activities outside the community.
Only lately have there been modest RLS efforts – complaints about the
loss of Arabic by children attending mixed kindergartens and schools in
towns like Jaffa and Haifa, legal cases seeking to have Arabic used on
public signs, moderate pressure to have it used in the Knesset, and even,
recently objection to use of Hebrew in a meeting of English teachers from
Arabic schools.

In another marginalised group, among the *haredi* (ultra-orthodox or
fundamentalist) opponents of political Zionism and Hebraisation, RLS
efforts have continued in favour of Yiddish, not of course for its secular and
cultural values but for its maintenance of an enclave within which
endorsed traditions can be continued. Here too, the evidence is of serious
erosion – most *haredi* children, including Hassidim, appear now to be
Hebrew-speaking or at best bilingual when their *heder* (elementary school)
teachers start a long process of bilingual education for boys in Hebrew and
Yiddish (Isaacs, 1998, 1999).

Of the immigrant groups, only the English-speakers, the recent Russian-
speakers and the Amharic-speakers among the Ethiopians, have been
successful in having the schools give a serious place to the teaching of their
language. In spite of the decision dropping English from the list of official
languages, it has continued to grow in status and use, bolstered by
economic prestige and by the status of English-speaking immigrants
(Spolsky, 1996b).

The success of Hebrew revitalisation (a success achieved half a century
ago) has left plenty of room for RLS activities for the other 40 languages. For
those who transfer their view of Hebrew as a language struggling for
revival to Hebrew as a language dominating others, there have been some
causes for moderate optimism in recent developments. There is for
instance the continued pressure for teaching of Arabic in Jewish schools,
recognised in the adding of one more compulsory year to the school curriculum and in renewed interest in teaching spoken Arabic in the elementary
schools mainly in the Tel Aviv region. There is the adoption by the Ministry
of Education in 1995–96 of a policy for language education in Israeli schools

that recognises multilingualism as a goal, and that accepts the value of maintaining immigrant languages (Ministry of Education, 1995, 1996). There is the subsequent approval of new curricula for Russian and Amharic.

There are also signs of affection for the now virtually extinct traditional Jewish languages, illustrated by the passing of a law establishing national authorities for Yiddish (not yet set up) and for Ladino (already in place). We do not have space or time to trace here these activities or to assess their prospects (see Spolsky & Shohamy, 1999). We mention them to stress the point that a study of current RLS activities in Israel would need to focus not just on efforts to defend Hebrew against real or imagined threats from English and other languages, but on attempts to defend other languages from now dominant Hebrew.

Nor do we have space to do more than allude to the continuing RLS activities for Hebrew outside of Israel. The Hebrew revival movement started in eastern Europe in the 19th century, and some of its energy moved to other Jewish communities, especially North America in the early years of the 20th century and in parts of Latin America and elsewhere later in the century. There were bursts of activity – in the US in the 1920s and again with the growth of the Jewish day school movement in the 1970s and 1980s. Bolstered by a number of Hebrew-speaking children of Israelis working or living in the Diaspora, there were hopes of serious RLS, but more recently the tone has become pessimistic, and most people involved believe that the chances for Hebrew revival in the Diaspora are now slight.

Colouring our arguments and analysis has been a reluctant (and hopefully erroneous) presentation of RLS as conflict, confrontation, forced binary choice between incompatible monolingualisms. One looks in vain for the kind of pluralism expressed in the Tshernovits resolution in favour of Yiddish as *a* (and not *the)* Jewish national language (Fishman, 1980). When we move outside the policy and ideological spheres into language practice, we do find in the perseverance of complex sociolinguistic repertoires in Israel some signs of a more pluralistic solution. This shows up in the complex code-switching, within as well as between languages, that marks actual language practice. Ideological acceptance of pluralism would permit a policy that treats RLS not as a struggle for existence but as the fine-tuning of complementary functional and social use of languages.

References

Ager, D. (1999) *Identity, Insecurity and Image: France and Language.* Clevedon: Multilingual Matters.

Bachi, R. (1956) A statistical analysis of the revival of Hebrew in Israel. *Scripta Hierosolymitana* 3, 179–247.

Chomsky, W. (1957) *Hebrew: The Eternal Language*. Philadelphia: The Jewish Publication Society of America.

Cohen, I. (1918) *The German Attack on the Hebrew Schools in Palestine*. London: Jewish Chronicle and Jewish World.

Dorian, N. (1998) Western language ideologies and small-language prospects. In L.A. Grenoble and L.J. Whaley (eds) *Endangered Languages: Current Issues and Future Prospects* (pp. 3–21). Cambridge: Cambridge University Press.

Fishman, J.A (1951) Zsveyshprakhikeyt in a yidisher shul. *Bleter far yidisher dertsiung* 4, 32–4.

Fishman, J.A. (1970) *Sociolinguistics: A Brief Introduction*. Rowley: Newbury House.

Fishman, J.A. (1980) Attracting a following to high-culture functions for a language of everyday life: The role of the Tshernovits Conference in the 'Rise of Yiddish'. *International Journal of the Sociology of Language* 24, 43–73.

Fishman, J.A. (1991) *Reversing Language Shift: Theoretical and Empirical Foundations of Assistance to Threatened Languages*. Clevedon: Multilingual Matters.

Harshav, B. (1993) *Language in Time of Revolution*. Berkeley: University of California Press.

Hymes, D. (1974) *Foundations in Sociolinguistics: An Ethnographic Approach*. Philadelphia: University of Pennsylvania Press.

Isaacs, M. (1998) Yiddish in the orthodox communities of Jerusalem. In Dov-Ber Kerler (ed.) *Politics of Yiddish: Studies in Language, Literature and Society* (pp. 85–96). Walnut Creek, CA: Altamira Press.

Isaacs, M. (1999) Contentious partners: Yiddish and Hebrew in Haredi Israel. *International Journal of the Sociology of Language* 138, 101–121.

Krauss, M. (1991a) Endangered languages. Paper read at Linguistic Society of America Annual meeting, January 1991.

Krauss, M. (1991b) The world's languages in crisis. *Language* 68 (1), 4–10.

Mandel, G. (1993) Why did Ben-Yehuda suggest the revival of spoken Hebrew? In L. Glinert (ed.) *Hebrew in Ashkenaz* (pp. 193–207). New York and Oxford: Oxford University Press.

Ministry of Education, Culture and Sport (1995) Policy for language education in Israel (in Hebrew). Jerusalem: Office of the Director-General.

Ministry of Education, Culture and Sport (1996) Policy for language education in Israel (in Hebrew). Jerusalem: Office of the Director-General.

Rabin, H. (1973) *A Short History of the Hebrew Language*. Jerusalem: Jewish Agency.

Shohamy, E. (1995) Problems in Israeli language policy: Language and ideology. In David Chen (ed.) *Education in the Twenty-first Century* (pp. 249–56). Ramat-Aviv: Ramot Publishing, Tel Aviv University.

Spolsky, B. (1991) Hebrew language revitalization within a general theory of second language learning. In R.L. Cooper and B. Spolsky (eds) *The Influence of Language on Culture and Thought: Essays in Honor of Joshua A. Fishman's Sixty-fifth birthday* (pp. 137–55). Berlin: Mouton.

Spolsky, B. (1996a) Conditions for language revitalization: A comparison of the cases of Hebrew and Maori. In S. Wright (ed.) *Language and the State: Revitalization and Revival in Israel and Eire* (pp. 5–50). Clevedon: Multilingual Matters.

Spolsky, B. (1996b) English in Israel after Independence. In J.A. Fishman, A. Rubal-Lopez and A.W. Conrad (eds) *Post-Imperial English*. Berlin: Mouton.
Spolsky, B. and Shohamy E. (1999a) Language in Israeli society and education. *International Journal of the Sociology of Language* 137, 93–114.
Spolsky, B. and E. Shohamy (1999b) *The Languages of Israel: Policy, Ideology and Practice*. Clevedon: Multilingual Matters.
Stewart, W. (1968) A sociolinguistic typology for describing national multilingualism. In J.A. Fishman (ed.) *Readings in the Sociology of Language* (pp. 531–45). The Hague: Mouton.
Wahl, R. (1996) German language policy in 19th century Palestine. MA thesis, English, Bar-Ilan University, Ramat-Gan.

Chapter 16

Can the Shift from Immigrant Languages be Reversed in Australia?[1]

M. CLYNE

In this chapter, I will use Joshua Fishman's model to consider how major changes in Australian society, government policies across the board, and the Australian and global economic situation are affecting language use and the prospects of the reversal of language shift of shift. I will first compare statistics from the 1986 and 1996 Australian censuses on language use and shift and other data on resources for the use of community (i.e. immigrant) languages. This will enable us to assess the extent to which the past decade has confirmed Fishman's (1991: 277) overall comment: 'Australian policies and processes constitute a positive but ineffective approach to RLS on behalf of recent immigrant languages . . . '

Although the general data will cover all community languages, specific points will be illustrated with information on particular languages. It should be stated that Australian census statistics on language use are limited to the home. In fact, many people speak a language other than English not in their own home but in those of their parents and other elderly relatives or in community groups. In general, the census statistics do not indicate evidence of large-scale reversal of language shift.

It is evident from Table 16.1 that all the groups for whom language shift data is available for both 1986 and 1996 have increased their shift to English in the first generation over the decade.

The number of groups for which comparable data at both the beginning and end of the decade are available, is smaller in the second generation than in the first. All groups on whom data was available in 1986 have increased their language shift, with the exception of Dutch-Australians whose shift was already extremely high in 1986.

Table 16.1 Language shift in the first generation: 1986 and 1996

Birthplace	Percent shift 1986	Percent shift 1996
Austria	39.5	48.3
Chile	NA[a]	9.8
France	27.5	37.2
Germany	40.8	48.2
Greece	4.4	6.4
Hong Kong	NA	9.0
Hungary	24.4	31.8
Italy	10.5	14.7
Japan	NA	15.4
Korea, Republic of	NA	11.6
Lebanon	5.2	5.5
Macedonia, Former Yugoslav Republic of	NA	3.0
Malta	26.0	36.5
Netherlands	48.4	61.9
Other Sth America	NA	17.2
Poland	16.0	19.6
PRC	NA	4.6
Spain	13.1	22.4
Taiwan	NA	3.4
Turkey	4.2	5.8

[a] Not available, but Spanish-speaking South America: 10.1%
Source: Clyne and Kipp (1997:459)

Table 16.2 Language shift in the second generation (aggregated), 1986 and 1996

Parents' birthplace	1986	1996
Germany	73.1	89.7
Greece	8.7	28
Hong Kong	NA	35.7
Italy	29.3	57.9
Malta	58.8	82.1
Netherlands	85.4	95
Poland	NA	75.7
PRC	NA	37.4

Source: Clyne and Kipp (1997: 464)

Stages 7 and 8

In terms of the stages on Fishman's Gradual Disruption Scale, Stage 8 is not relevant to community languages as Fishman himself indicates (1991: 255) because they are not in a complete state of disrepair and, in any case, their heartland lies outside Australia. Stage 7, where the use of the community language is confined to the elderly and not transmitted to younger people, already applied to some language communities at the time of Fishman's original study and has progressively reached other languages. For instance, the proportion of the 55 plus age group among Greek home users has almost doubled in the decade from 13.86% to 26%; among Dutch speakers it has risen from 38.66% to 53.8%; among German speakers from 33.6% to 47.8%, and among Latvian speakers from 63% to 66.7%. While there have been proportionate increases among Vietnamese (3.95% to 8%) and Arabic speakers (7.89% to 12.7%), the older language users still do not constitute a significant part of the population of these communities. A comparison between Tables 16.1 and 16.2 will indicate a high inter-generational language shift (e.g. German 48.2% to 89.7%; Greek 6.4% to 28%; Italian 14.7% to 57.9%). One of the reasons for the high inter-generational language shift is exogamy, which, while high for groups that are culturally similar to the dominant group or who share a religious denomination with them, increases for all groups with length of time in Australia. However, marriage between second and first generation Australians of similar ethnolinguistic background has revitalised community language use.

Unfortunately, Australian census data does not record information which might enable us to identify the third generation, thus we cannot ascertain third generation language maintenance or shift.

Stage 6: Intergenerational Community-Neighbourhood-Community Links on a Daily Basis

This is projected by Fishman (1991: 92) to be crucial to reversing language shift. It involves 'leav(ing) behind an already ongoing sociolinguistic modus vivendi and creat(ing) another that is demographically concentrated and intergenerationally continuous'. Fishman indicates that this has not occurred for immigrant languages in Australia, and we do not have much evidence that the situation has changed drastically since. On the contrary, many of the language communities have dispersed from their concentration areas in the past 10 years. This applies, for instance, to the Greek community which, in their 'stronghold', Melbourne, has moved from being one of the most concentrated communities to the second most dispersed one.

A recent study of Arabic, Chinese and Spanish language maintenance in Melbourne (Clyne & Kipp, 1999) indicates a sharp dividing line between over and under 35-year-olds and between the first and second generations in all the communities in language use and maintenance patterns. The lowest intergenerational shift is recorded in the community where the community-family-neighbourhood links are the strongest, the Arabic speakers.

In some of the older language communities, e.g. German (see Kipp *et al.*, 1995: 138–40), grandparents rather than parents are playing an increasing role in intergenerational language maintenance. There are three reasons for this: (1) a desire on the part of the parents to make their children bilingual, even if they themselves speak English at home; (2) the high degree of exogamy; and (3) upward mobility and socioeconomic conditions making it likely that both parents are in paid employment which often means that the grandparents or grandmother is/are the main caregiver(s) during the week, at last up to the time the children enter primary school. Many grandparents cherish this role, not only because of the grandchildren but also because it gives them the chance to pass on their language under societal conditions attitudinally far more favourable than when their own children were growing up. Even where the grandparents do not play this role, there is an increasing number of young people, notably middle class second generation Australians, who are using the one parent, one language principle (e.g. Saunders, 1982; Döpke 1993) to raise their children bilingually. However, I can only provide small-scale information in support of this statement. Of several hundred such parents participating in seminars conducted by the Language and Society Centre at Monash University over the past eight years, at least half are raising their children in German/English, and the other community languages represented have varied but include French, Italian, and to a lesser extent Greek, Polish, Spanish, Thai, Vietnamese and others. The motives for raising children bilingually are diverse. They include instrumental reasons such as the need to communicate with relatives in the family's country of origin, questions of identity (heritage), and particularly the perceived economic, cultural and cognitive advantages of bilingualism. Languages other than English are now considered a useful 'commodity' in educational and business circles in Australia. In many cases, simply the intrinsic value and enjoyment of being bilingual is considered something to pass on to the next generation and this is often done without community or extended family. This is an exception to the situation that Fishman (1991: 261) correctly detected, namely that his prerequisite of 'ethnoculturally intact communities that are self-regulating in cultural respects' is not being fulfilled in immigrant communities in

Australia because 'conceptual, residential and occupational modernity submerges them entirely in processes that they can neither control nor mitigate'. The situation unfavourable to RLS can be attributed to use ethnic separatism conflicting with the interactionist ideology of multiculturalism in Australia to which both the 'dominant' and most immigrant groups subscribe (Clyne & Kipp, in press: 331).

Demographically, there are some communities that are strongly concentrated in particular districts of a large city, such as Macedonian, Maltese, and Vietnamese in Melbourne and Macedonian, Vietnamese and Indonesian in Sydney. The areas of strong concentration are also those in which religious and secular community centres and ethnic shops are clustered. In the case of Macedonian and Vietnamese,. concentration has led to high community language use, but this cannot be said for Maltese, which has consistently registered a high language shift. This needs to be seen in the light of Maltese–English diglossia in pre-migration Malta and the influence of other languages and cultures over time in Malta. Maltese is a Semitic language, closely akin to Arabic. However, its vocabulary has been strongly influenced by English and Italian, and the language is written in Latin script. The Roman Catholic Church, to which almost all the population belongs, proximity to Italy, and a recent history of British colonialism, have greatly affected Maltese culture. In the late 1940s and early 1950s, when most Maltese immigrants to Australia left their homeland, English was the H language in Malta in a diglossic relationship with Maltese (in Fishman's (1967) sense of diglossia).

Another language for which community-language-neighbourhood links are available is Yiddish. Some 81% of the 2842 home users of Yiddish live in Melbourne, especially in two adjacent suburbs in which are located numerous synagogues and Jewish community centres, the majority of Melbourne's seven Jewish all-day schools, shops, and a Yiddish cultural centre and library. Generally, children and grandchildren live in close proximity to the (grand)parents. However, the vast majority of the Yiddish speakers are over 65. It is only in the most ultra-Orthodox of the Jewish communities, a Chassidic one, that Yiddish is surviving in the younger generation. This is probably related to the sharp boundary which the community has drawn around itself and the emphasis on Yiddish in the community's school. This is in turn necessitated by the reservation of Hebrew for the religious domain and the use of Yiddish as a medium of instruction for some secular subjects. In the less Orthodox and non-Orthodox communities/families of Yiddish background in the area, the strong concentration has little or no effect on the language maintenance. If anything, it has generated a Yiddish or Jewish ethnolect of Australian

English, which has taken over the symbolic function from Yiddish in in-group interaction. The ethnolect has lexical items and grammatical structures transferred from Yiddish (cf. Clyne *et al.*, in press). There is a primary day school run by a secular Yiddishist group operating from pre-school to Grade 6. This school has instruction in culture subjects (e.g. History, Literature, Music) through the medium of Yiddish. The children are generally from families in which either English or Russian is the main home language but many of the pupils have some access to the language through grandparents. Nine of 18 in Grade 6 in 1998 and 4 out of 20 in Grade 5 indicated to the school that they were speaking Yiddish to family members as a result of being in the Yiddish programme while 6 out of 18 and 4 out of 20 in Grade 5 have introduced some Yiddish (through words and songs) into non-Yiddish-speaking families (pers. comm., Renee Zufi). Due to the small numbers involved, the evidence for RLS of Yiddish is somewhat tentative.

Stage 5: Formal Linguistic Socialisation Through Agencies or Institutions under Xish Control that do not Need to Satisfy Yish Standards re Compulsory Education

As Fishman (1991: 262) points out, 'immigrant languages are served by impressively large numbers of part-time "community-supported ethnic group schools"'. There were, in 1997, nearly 90,000 pupils attending ethnic supplementary schools in a total of 73 languages, including 40,000 in New South Wales and 30,000 in Victoria. Chinese (22,026), Arabic (12,219), and Greek (12,139) are the languages with the largest numbers of students. This constitutes a substantial change from 1986, when Greek schools taught the majority of ethnic school students. Greek schools are usually conducted several afternoons a week after day school. Most of the other programmes are on Saturday or Sunday mornings and most of the part-time community language schools teach language and culture. Many, particularly Greek ones, also give religious instruction, and some impart history of the country of origin.

The schools are utilised in many communities, especially the longer established ones with high language shift rates, e.g. German, for RLS, e.g. German, often by parents who are themselves second generation Australians with rather limited German (Kipp *et al.*, 1995: 139–40). However, the expectations of parents from a programme of two or three hours per week are enormous considering that there is often virtually no backup at home. This applies particularly to exogamous families. There is a little more success in making oral bilinguals literate in the community language.

Although part-time ethnic schools are the responsibility of the community group running them, they are subsidised by the Australian government. At the primary level, they are fully in control of their syllabus. Some of these part-time schools, however, also prepare candidates for the examination at the end of secondary school which also serves as university entrance. In Victoria, this is less frequent than in other states because the Victorian School of Languages, a part of the Victorian Education Department operating on Saturdays from centres in 10 state schools (see Stage 4b) has taken over this task for most languages. (The exceptions are Latvian, where the ethnic school forms part of the Victorian School of Languages, and Chinese, where some ethnic schools prepare candidates for the Victorian Certificate of Languages, the matriculation examination, in Chinese).

There is no provision, in the RLS model, for the supportive role of public libraries with holdings (books, newspapers, magazines, videos) in the community languages of the district. Libraries could not be seen in terms of increased power sharing. Nevertheless, they provide major resources for literacy development in community languages as well as inout in formal registers of the languages. Such holdings are utilised by community groups, families, and individuals engaged in RLS or in the literacy development of children who have oral skills in the community language.

The comparison between 1986 and 1997 for Victoria shows only a 41.4% increase in the number of books in community languages with substantial increases in Chinese, Arabic, Greek, and Russian, holdings for the first time in Kurdish, Somali, and Ukrainian, and the small holdings in languages such as Armenian, Latvian, and the Scandinavian languages being written off. The latter means that the language maintenance of some low demand languages is no longer being supported by libraries. (See Table 16.3)

Stage 4

Stages 4 to 1 are, according to Fishman (1991: 401) that 'RLS is on the strong side', 'transcending diglossia in search of increased power-sharing'. However, as we shall see under 1 and 2, it is unlikely that the media are having an RLS effect in Australia.

Stage 4a: X-ish Sponsored and Controlled Schools that are Attended in Lieu of Meeting Compulsory Education Requirements

There is a tradition in Australia of non-government primary and secondary schools, which are attended by about a third of Australian

Table 16.3 Book holdings in community languages in Victorian public libraries

Language	1986 Total	1997 Total
Albanian	438	109
Arabic	8,344	15,254
Armenian	78	–
Bulgarian	4	–
Chinese	5,131	47,063
Croatian[a]	–	5,825
Czech	912	194
Danish	61	–
Dutch	6,381	3,139
Finnish	53	–
French	9,011	7,472
German	13,074	9,142
Greek	39,821	54,512
Hebrew	74	460
Hindi	325	1,255
Hungarian	4,134	979
Indonesian	115	705
Italian	57,152	54,752
Japanese	306	379
Khmer	106	529
Korean	91	1
Kurdish	–	133
Laotian	6	–
Latvian	260	–
Lithuanian	645	718
Macedonian	3,188	2,223
Maltese	3,369	2,174
Norwegian	4	–
Polish	6,748	9,573
Portuguese	1,800	95
Romanian	147	239
Russian	3,650	7,279
Serbian	–	1,885
Serbo-Croatian/Croatian/Serbian/Yugoslav[b]	9,602	–
Singhalese	–	3

Table 16.3 (cont.)

Language	1986 Total	1997 Total
Slovak	110	–
Slovenian	1,493	248
Somali	–	8
Spanish	15,283	19,201
Swedish	14	–
Tagalog	10	467
Thai	242	13
Turkish	1,222	12,512
Tuvalli/Kiribati	–	13
Ukrainian	–	264
Vietnamese	3,601	41,286
Yiddish	370	85
Total	212,274	300,179

[a] See 1986 Serbo-Croation/Croation, etc. figures
[b] See Croatian and Serbian

school pupils. Of these, about 80% are at Roman Catholic schools, either parish primary schools or secondary regional schools or secondary schools varying in their socioeconomic status, previously conducted by religious orders. As Fishman (1991: 264) points out, Catholic schools are generally multiethnic. The exceptions are three Maronite (Lebanese Eastern rite Catholic) primary schools, two in Sydney and one in Melbourne which teach for a number of hours of the day in Arabic. Not all the children speak Arabic at home. Almost all the Roman Catholic schools teach Italian as a second language, which is no longer identified with a local community and some of them also offer other languages, usually French or an Asian language. A small number of Catholic schools have maintenance programmes in languages of special importance in the local community, such as Arabic, Chinese, French, Maltese, Tagalog or Vietnamese.

Most of the other non-government schools are elitist, being modelled on the British 'public schools', charge high fees, and are affiliated with either the Anglican or Uniting Church.[2] Lutheran schools teach German but as a heritage rather than a community language. The 16 Jewish day schools, seven of which are in Melbourne, all teach Hebrew, although this varies from Classical Hebrew to Ivrit (Modern Israel Hebrew) depending on the ideology of the school (Klarberg, 1983). Hebrew is sometimes the medium of instruction in the Jewish Studies or Religious Studies programme. Two of the Jewish schools in Melbourne teach part of the secular curriculum in Hebrew, one at primary, the other at secondary level. The latter excludes from this elective programme the small minority of native speakers of Israeli Hebrew. In addition there are the Chassidic and Yiddishist schools using Yiddish as a medium of instruction (see Stage 6, above).

During the past decade, there has been an increase in the number of Greek Orthodox and Greek Community, Coptic Orthodox, Islamic, and other ethnic or non-'mainstream' religious day schools. Typically, the Greek Orthodox and Greek Community private schools teach Modern Greek for more hours per week than most state schools would but few of them have any component of bilingual education. The children in most of the schools are nearly all of Greek background but not all of those speak Greek at home. In one school in Melbourne, however, which describes itself as multicultural, non-denominational and with a low fees structure, about 64% of the children are non-Greek speaking. There are separate Greek classes for home background and non-background students. The school has a sizeable Greek library, and the general environment gives plenty of opportunity for the use of the Greek language (see Clyne *et al.*, 1995). Ecclesiastical Greek is introduced through the teaching of the Liturgy in Greek Orthodox Religious Instruction in both ethnic day schools and state schools. Passages from the Koran are committed to memory as part of Religious Instruction in Islamic day schools, in part-time ethnic schools (see Stage 5), and in those state schools where communities have provided Religious Education teachers.

About 90% of the pupils in the two Coptic schools in Melbourne are of Egyptian background and the others are from other Arabic-speaking families. Arabic is taught to all pupils but it is not a medium of instruction in other subjects although some written work can be submitted in Arabic in some other subjects. As parents were initially apprehensive about giving Arabic too central a role in the school, most teachers of secular subjects appointed are not Arabic speakers, and this has weakened the position of Arabic. The 22 Islamic schools in Australia are multicultural insofar as the children come from a range of ethnolinguistic backgrounds and for many, such as those of Pakistani, Malay and Bosnian backgrounds, Arabic is for them a sacred but not a spoken language. Arabic is taught as a second language in Islamic schools but not used as a medium of instruction.

Insofar as the language taught is the family's (former) community language, the above schools have been successful in some cases, in reversing language shift in two ways – both by giving the children a competence in the language sufficient to use with elderly relatives where the language is no longer spoken in their own homes, and by raising interest in the language, which has encouraged them to use it where possible and utilise stays in the country of origin to improve their competence. As there has been no detailed study of this, the above statements remain anecdotal. Certainly the numbers of second generation speakers of languages such as Greek marrying first generation speakers either by bringing them home from study periods in the country of origin or after meeting them here encouraged by their own competence in and enthusiasm for the language has provided opportunities for home language transmission to the third generation.

Stage 4b: Xish Programmes in Yish Schools

In the 1970s and 1980s, the number of languages taught in Australian schools and assessed at the end-of-school examinations increased dramatically as a result of multiculturalism policy. Also, languages other than English (LOTEs) are now widely taught at primary level in many states. Constitutionally, education is a responsibility of the states, so prioritisation of languages and provision for their delivery varies vastly between states. Also, the quality of programmes differs very much between schools. At one end there are partial immersion-type programmes, at the other end satellite television language programmes supervised by teachers with a very limited knowledge of the language. States have usually prioritised eight languages, which include some of the major community languages, such as Italian, Greek, and sometimes Vietnamese and/or Arabic, and several of the languages prioritised for other reasons, such as Mandarin and German, are also among the more widely used community languages. Some states also emphasise other languages of community significance. Of the 43 languages assessed for examination purposes, not all are taught in mainstream day schools and of course no one school offers more than a few. The Education Departments in Victoria, New South Wales and South Australia have a section which runs language programmes in schools on Saturdays for those pupils who cannot take them in their regular school. So at one centre, courses may be offered in French, Japanese, Vietnamese, Spanish, Ukrainian, Hungarian, Macedonian, and Arabic, while at another, say, German, Italian, Russian, Mandarin, Farsi, Khmer, Croatian, Greek, Latvian, and Turkish. There are 20 such centres in Victoria.

It is difficult to generalise on whether Xish or Yish school institutions or part-time ethnic schools are likely to stimulate RLS the most. However, students from both mainstream day schools and the Education Department's Saturday schools have produced far better results at the 1997 Year

12 Arabic examination than their counterparts in Dish schools while 21.3% of the top students in Chinese were prepared by part-time ethnic schools and the rest by Yish schools (Clyne & Kipp, in press).

Some language subjects are taken mainly by people with a home background in the language, which in itself varies a lot but some (e.g. Spanish, Mandarin, Indonesian) are taken by pupils with different levels of home background as well as beginners. In some primary school immersion programmes this stimulates language development in both groups and a stronger motivation to speak the language among the home background students (Imberger, 1986). However, now that LOTEs are perceived as a commodity, they are accompanied by false assumptions about who the programmes are intended for and about students with a home background taking something away from those without a background. Standardisation procedures limit the number of very high scores and make them more uniform across subjects. So for instance in 'Asian' languages perceived to be more difficult languages there is a fear that the standard has risen out of reach of students from other ethnic backgrounds. Four state examination boards have devised LOTE forms to interrogate students on their home and other use of the language to classify them according to advantage in order to moderate the grades. In some languages there are now 'first language' examinations with constraints on admission to 'second language' examinations. While there are good reasons for examining recent arrivals with substantial experience of schooling in a country where the language is spoken in a different way from other students, this does not apply to, say, second or third generation Australians with a limited background in the language. For them, what they have achieved in the language due to determination deserves credit, and special treatment and the suspicion of an unfair advantage is a serious demotivation for maintenance of reversing language shift. It seems as if they are not even permitted to have a share in their own community language when it has a coveted market value. This is particularly so because the special needs of later generation limited bilinguals (and, for instance, of speakers of other fang yan (regional varieties) such as Cantonese or Hakka learning Mandarin) are hardly addressed. Fishman's scepticism that language programmes in Yish schools can contribute to long-term language maintenance or to RLS is justified, especially in an atmosphere of greed and self-interest as we have at present.

Stage 3: Xish Work Spheres

I cannot add anything to Fishman's perceptive account, indicating that any use of immigrant languages in the work sphere is unlikely to promote intergenerational transmission. The only thing that has happened since 1991 has been the large-scale immigration of East, South and South-East Asians who often run family businesses, and the development of the policy of Productive Diversity. The former has only had a temporary effect because of the large proportion of children of Asian immigrants entering university and the professions. However, there are certainly young people who work in businesses in areas of, say, Vietnamese concentration. The policy of Productive Diversity owed its origins to former Prime Minister Paul Keating (1992) and was soft pedalled by the subsequent Conservative federal government but further developed in Victoria under the conservative state government there under the title of The Multicultural Advantage. The aim is to utilise the cultural and linguistic resources of the nation or state to further the economic progress but at the same time celebrate cultural diversity. This gives motivation and input and output opportunities to bilinguals, especially younger ones.

Stage 2: Media and Government Services

Fishman differentiates between local and national media. In Australia, the community language press generally has a nationwide circulation regardless of where it is published. There is a government-run network of community language radio stations and a television station that transmits to the whole of Australia community language programmes with English subtitles, English programmes of a multicultural nature, and regular (in some cases, daily) satellite news broadcasts in 15 languages. The network has two stations in each of Sydney and Melbourne, one local and one national, and one (taking national broadcasts) in each of the other capital cities and regional areas. Other radio and TV stations are local. These include three Arabic-language, two Greek-language, one Turkish-language, one Italian-language and one Italian–English bilingual commercial stations in Melbourne, two Arabic, two Greek, two Spanish and one Italian in Sydney, one Macedonian in nearby Wollongong and one each in Greek and Italian in Adelaide.3 Whether a programme is local or national, has very little significance in terms of LM and RLS. What is more important is whether the broadcasts are produced by professionals or by community members. The government-run network and the commercial stations have professionals. The remaining multilingual stations (including one television station each in Melbourne, Sydney, Adelaide) are community stations 'where the people make the programmes'. This contributes to LM in that it encourages people to prepare material of a high standard in the community language. However, many listeners complain about non-standard regional varieties, regional accents or mixed language, and the broadcasts are not taken seriously as models. In Melbourne, in addition to the language-specific stations, government community language radio broadcasts outnumber those on community stations by about 2:1; in Adelaide and Brisbane they are about equal; and in Perth, the government run service offers about 25% more hours than the community station. The community-run programmes are less numerous in other centres. Most languages are represented on both types of stations but sometimes newer languages (Oromo, Somali), those of smaller communities not desiring government support (Romany) or languages or varieties equated with those of other communities (Flemish, Malay) are transmitted only on community stations. All in all, there are now 75 radio stations broadcasting in a total of 97 community languages for 1393 hours per week. The following comparison between 1986 and 1998 covers the 11 stations with the most community language broadcasting. (See Table 16.4)

It will be seen that the number of hours of community language broadcasts on these stations has doubled since 1986, that the allocation for nearly all languages has increased, and that many new language have been added.

Young people continue to show little interest in the radio programmes (see Clyne & Kipp, 1999, for the situation in Arabic, Chinese, and Spanish). There are a small number of exceptions where second generation bilinguals run targeted segments on some of the language programmes.

Public access multilingual television programmes run for 8½ hours per week in 28 languages in three capital cities: The national television details are given under Stage 1 below.

As Fishman (1991: 271), points out, the second generation disinterest in the ethnic press and community language radio makes them ineffective in RLS. However, I would like to stress the role of radio and especially TV as a resource for and an indirect contribution to RLS. The presence of community languages in the public domain gives a legitimacy to inter-generational transmission and parent–child interaction in a community language in the presence of non-speakers of the language. Such consistent community language use without apology or criticism, representing one of the major changes in Australia in the past two decades, is essential for the success of RLS. It is one of the issues that many families raising children bilingually are concerned about. Moreover, the electronic media do provide a resource towards reactivating the community language and activating passive skills, though, of course, they cannot instigate or even provide a context for such RLS.

Table 16.4 The 11 ethnic language community radio stations with the most broadcasts in community lanauges 1986 and 1998 [Transmission of LOTE per week (hrs)] 1:10 = 1 hr. 10 mins

Languages	Number of hours for 1986	Number of hours for 1998
Afghani	–	2:00
Albanian	1:00	6:45
Arabic	17:45	105:45
Armenian	5:00	10:00
Assyrian	2:30	7:00
Azerbaj	–	1:00
Baltic (Estonian/Latvian/Lithuanian)	11:30	–
Belarusan	–	1:30
Bengali	0:15	4:20
Bosnian[a]		10:00
Bulgarian	2:45	3:00
Burmese	–	6:00
Cantonese[b]		28:45
Catalan	0:45	1:00
Celtic[c]	–	1:00
Chinese	8:30	–
Cook Islander Maori	–	3:45
Croatian	16:20	34:30[d]
Czech	5:15	5:45
Cypriot	1:30	
Danish[e]		4:30
Dari	0:10	3:21
Dutch (incl. Flemish)	21:00	23:00
Esperanto	–	1:00
Estonian[f]	–	4:00
Ethiopian	–	1:30
Fijian	–	8:00
Finnish[g]	–	7:15
French	14:00	20:30
Gaelic (Irish)	–	9:30
Geetanjal[i]	–	0:30

Table 16.4 (*cont.*)

Languages	Number of hours for 1986	Number of hours for 1998
German (incl. Swiss and Austrian)	31:00	37:15
Greek	68:00	104:15[h]
Gujarati	0:15	1:00[i]
Hebrew[j]	–	10:30
Hindi	0:30	19:20[k]
Hindustani	1:30	–
Hmong	–	2:00
Hungarian	12:00	18:15
Indian	5:15	–
Indonesian	2:25	16:00
Islanders'	1:00	–
Italian	51:30	76:45
Japanese	0:30	5:00
Jewish (Hebrew/Yiddish)	8:00	–
Kannada	0:15	1:00
Khmer	3:00	11:00
Korean	2:00	14:00
Kurdish	0:38	5:30
Laotian	2:00	6:00
Latvian[l]	–	7:00
Lithuanian[m]	–	5:30
Macedonian	13:40	48:30
Malay	–	3:30
Maltese	20:30	25:00
Mandarin[n]	–	25:00
Maori	1:00	7:45
Marathi[o]	–	2:00
Mauritian[p]	–	2:00
Norwegian[q]	–	2:30
Oromo	–	1:00
Pakistani	0:45	–
Persian-Farsi	–	6:45
Polish	20:45	39:30

Table 16.4 (*cont.*)

Languages	Number of hours for 1986	Number of hours for 1998
Portuguese	9:15	22:00
Punjabi	1:00	8:20
Pushtu[r]	–	0:09
Romanian	2:00	9:00
Romany	–	0:30
Russian	10:45	20:00
Samoan	0:45	11:15
Scandinavian (Danish/Swedish/Icelandic/Finnish)	14:15	–
Scottish	2:45	3:00
Serbian	9:50	26:00
Serbo-Croatian	2:00	5:00[s]
Sinhalese	1:15	12:15[t]
Slovak	3:30	4:45
Slovenian	6:06	8:30
Somali	–	2:15
Spanish	33:00	50:30
Sri Lankan	2:00	–
Swedish	–	3:30[u]
Tagalog	3:45	9:15
Tamil	2:45	8:45[v]
Telegu[w]	–	1:30
Thai	0:30	7:45
Tibetan	–	1:00
Timorese	1:00	2:00
Tongan	2:15	9:15
Turkish	18:30	30:15[x]
Ukrainian	12:45	12:15
Urdu[y]	1:00	8:45[z]
Vietnamese	7:30	46:30
Vlach	–	1:00
Welsh	0:15	3:00
Yiddish[a1]	–	7:00

Table 16.4 (*cont.*)

Languages	Number of hours for 1986	Number of hours for 1998
Yugoslav	7:51	–
Zaza	–	0:30
Totals	506:15	1154:15

[a] See 1986 'Serbo-Croation' figures for comparison; [b] See 1986 'Chinese' figures for comparison; [c] See 1986 'Scottish' figures; [d] See also 1986 'Yugoslav' figures; [e] See 1986 'Scandinavian' figures; [f] See 1986 'Baltic' figures for comparison; [g] See 1986 'Scandinavian' figures; [h] See also 1986 'Cypriot' figures; [i] See also 1986 'Indian' figures; [j] See 1986 'Jewish' figures; [k] See also 1986 'Indian' figures; [l] See 1986 'Baltic' figures for comparison; [m] See 1986 'Baltic' figures; [n] See 1986 'Chinese' figures; [o] See 1986 'Indian' figures; [p] See 1986 'French' figures; [q] See 1986 'Scandinavian' figures; [r] See also 1986 'Afghani' figures; [s] See also 1986 'Yugoslav' figures; [t] See also 1986 'Sri Lankan' figures; [u] See 1986 'Scandinavian' figures for comparison; [v] See also 1986 'Sri Lankan' figures; [w] See 'Indian' figures; [x] See also 1986 'Cypriot' figures; [y] See also 1986 'Pakistani' figures; [z] See also 1986 ' Pakistani' figures; [a1] See 1986 'Jewish' figures.

Stage 1: National Media and Central and Regional Government Services

Public notices are now issued in a range of community languages. These include numerous announcements on elections and voting procedures, health, safety and social security matters (including child care and old age pensions), legal questions and rights, traffic code, the education system, and library facilities. The choice of languages depends largely on the specific needs of the language community, but most multilingual notices of a general nature are now in 20 languages. In local announcements it tends to depend on the ethnolinguistic composition of the population. The Department of Social Security has targeted Arabic, Bosnian, Cambodian, Chinese, Croatian, Farsi, Greek, Hungarian, Italian, Korean, Maltese, Macedonian, Filipino/Tagalog, Polish, Portuguese, Russian, Serbian, Spanish, Turkish, and Vietnamese. A telephone interpreter service operates in about 90 languages. However, this is to satisfy the needs of some first generation groups and not an incentive for reversing language shift although it probably does afford legitimacy to community languages. Although Australia does not have a *de jure* official language, most of the business of government and administration takes place in English. Government departments do employ bilinguals to offer services to people of non-English-speaking backgrounds. Such employees receive a special language loading. This provides an incentive to maintain and develop bilingual skills.

Table 16.5 Community language newspapers/periodicals

Language	1986	1996
Arabic	7	8
Armenian	1	–
Bulgarian	1	–
Chinese	2	24
Czech	1	1
Dutch	3	2
Fijian-Indian	–	1
Estonian	1	1
Finnish	2	1
French	1	1
German	3	2
Greek	15	10
Hungarian	4	1
'Indian'	–	6
Indonesian	–	1
Iranian (Farsi)	–	2
Italian	10	2
Japanese	–	4
Korean	3	7
Latvian	1	1
Lao	–	1
Macedonian	2	4
Maltese	2	1
Polish	5	4
Portuguese	2	2
Russian	2	4
Scandinavian	1	–
Slovenian	1	1
Spanish	6	4
Thai	–	1
Turkish	14	7
Ukrainian	5	1
Urdu	1	(See Indian)
Vietnamese	9	13
Serbian	3	2
Croatian	5	3
'Yugoslav'	2	–
Total	102	117

Since 1986, the number of community language newspapers has increased marginally from 102 to 117. There are now more newspapers in 'new' languages and some of the old ones have folded. Most of them are weeklies; there are also monthly, fortnightly and twice-weekly newspapers. For the first time there are now daily newspapers in an immigrant language – five in Chinese. (See Table 16.5)

Community language newspapers present material in varying proportions, according to the period of settlement in Australia, on homeland and international events and Australian news, especially from the multicultural scene and the relevant ethnic communities. This helps maintain vocabulary and structures, and sometimes introduces readers to neologisms from the heartland of the language. Newspapers sometimes provide readers with a model for expressing in the community language the exigencies of life in Australia. Fishman's (1991) contention that such newspapers have little appeal to the second generation because of their content. is confirmed in a recent study of Arabic, Chinese and Spanish language use and maintenance patterns, where not only the second generation but generally the under-35s rarely read ethnic newspapers (Clyne & Kipp, 1999).

The number of hours of programmes in community languages on the government station, SBS, has more than doubled since 1986. The distribution of the languages has altered a little in that period as Table 16.5 will indicate, with new languages added and some allocated more time. Substantial gains have been recorded not only for languages of newer migrants such as Cantonese, Mandarin, Russian, and Indonesian but also, for example, French, Italian, Greek, Spanish and German, largely due to regular news broadcasts in those languages. It will be noted that the annual transmission time for a number of languages is minimal, probably one film. Unlike radio, television does not allocate a specific slot to a particular language according to demographic statistics. Availability of suitable films is also a criterion. Unfortunately, regular children's TV series in community languages are no longer shown, as language-specific telecasts other than the news have to be sub-titled to ensure a wide group of viewers and it is considered that children are unable to process sub-titles sufficiently well. Young speakers of Arabic, Chinese (Cantonese or Mandarin) and Spanish are more likely to watch television and videos in their community languages (e.g. movies, game shows, series) than listen to radio in them (Clyne & Kipp, 1999). However, there is also discontent with the content of television programmes. (See Table 16.6)

The Internet could be a means of assisting RLS in that it could make age and interest appropriate input available, and force them into output in the community language in interaction with people in touch with a peer group

Table 16.6 Number of hours on national (SBS) television, 1986 and 1996

Language	1986	1996
Arabic	33.95	131.07
Armenian	3.94	–
Assamese	–	3.39
Bengali	1.47	7.52
Cantonese	19.48	133.26
Catalan	–	2.54
Czech	43.72	23.00
Danish	8.97	29.09
Estonian	–	2.37
Euskal	–	1.18
Farsi	–	10.56
French	136.81	561.28
Gaelic	–	1.07
German	197.09	325.49
Greek	123.53	264.15
Hebrew	6.07	17.59
Hindi	14.07	26.35
Hungarian	32.54	35.41
Icelandic	2.54	3.47
Italian	255.63	436.37
Japanese	77.16	155.12
Khmer	–	4.45
Korean	4.77	14.30
Kurdish	–	2.48
Letzebuergesch	–	1.36
Lithuanian	–	1.53
Macedonian	9.22	–
Malayalam	–	2.04
Maltese	–	1.59
Mandarin	15.29	202.28
Mongolian	–	1.20
More	–	1.25
Norwegian	2.83	14.30
Polish	42.43	90.02
Portuguese	36.08	44.10
Romanian	–	9.43

Table 16.6 (cont.)

Language	1986	1996
Romany	–	1.50
Russian	36.71	228.03
Serbian	10.97	5.05
Serbo-Croatian	33.54	–
Slovenian	10.16	3.36
Spanish	105.68	232.17
Swedish	25.25	26.38
Tagalog	–	6.42
Thai	–	3.51
Tok Pisin	–	1.51
Turkish	20.56	28.38
Ukrainian	1.50	20.08
Vietnamese	–	22.43
Welsh	4.32	6.23
Yiddish	–	2.05
Total	1415.10	3181.19

in the country of origin and in other immigrant communities, as well as promoting literacy skills. However, most young people use the Internet exclusively in English. (There are some exceptions in Taiwan–Mandarin community, a very recent group, and among Spanish speakers.)

General Context and Outlook

During the decade or so under review, substantial changes have occurred in the expectations of the role of government. The 'user principle' now presides in all areas. The partly social agenda of the 1970s and 1980s was replaced in the subsequent years by an anti-social one determined by short-term economic objectives. Governments have privatised many of their assets, ranging from hospitals to prisons, from public transport to gas, water supply to electricity. They have shed many of the responsibilities that go with these assets. One year after the first year of our statistical decade, Australia's *National Policy on Languages* (Lo Bianco, 1987) was released. Its guiding principles included the maintenance and development of community languages and the provision of services in community languages. It provided rationale for language maintenance on the basis of social equity, cultural enrichment, and economic strategies.

Under community pressure, the *Australian Language and Literacy Policy,* the brainchild of the then Minister for Employment, Education and Training, John Dawkins, retained the guiding principles rhetorically. But it marked the shift to an economic agenda, stressing English literacy and competence in languages of economic importance to Australia (especially those of the Asian region). Fourteen languages were declared priority languages, including some that are predominantly justified on the basis of being prominent community languages (e.g. Greek, Vietnamese) as well as some that are, among things, important community languages (e.g. Mandarin, Italian, Spanish, Arabic) This had the effect of relegating languages-in-education policy to the states, which have the constitutional responsibility for (primary and secondary) schools. It meant that vastly different policies were developed and different priority languages were chosen in the individual states.

A subsequent policy, *Asian languages and Australia's Economic Future* (Rudd, 1994) reinforced more explicitly the emphasis on Japanese, Indonesian, Mandarin, and Korean for economic motives. Nevertheless, the state Education Departments' Saturday schools continued to teach a wide range of languages, and the number of languages examined at the final secondary school-cum-university entrance examination was increased to 43, covering a large proportion of the community languages used in Australia. This includes a considerable number with very low enrolments. These have remained on the list despite occasional threats due to the cost of administrating examinations for such a small clientele.

On the other hand, savage cuts to the operating grants of universities and especially Arts faculties has led to the closure of many language programmes and to rationalisation in the case of others (offering most languages in only one university in a city and requiring the students to take them at another institution). This is frustrated by travel time and time table clashes. Sometimes arrangements are made by which staff from one university offer a language course on another campus. However, numerous language programmes that have been closed in recent years were unique in that state (e.g. Hindi in Victoria) or nationwide (e.g. Dutch and Khmer). This not only takes away the opportunity to study the language for language maintenance purposes; it also wipes out the chances of an ongoing supply of secondary and primary teachers of the language (or of other professionals with a high competence and credentials in the language trained in Australia). All this, together with the situation outlined under Stage 4b, underlines the need for ongoing involvement of Xians in the implementation of policies affecting Yian languages.

Financial cuts and the need to prioritise have reintroduced the distinction between maintaining an 'important' and an 'unimportant' language which had been soft-pedalled with the advent of the policy of Multiculturalism in the 1970s. Such a differentiation is not (as yet) influencing language maintenance/shift trends. With high shifts from German and French and quite substantial ones from Italian and Spanish Spanish and low shifts from Macedonian, Turkish, and probably Vietnamese, they suggest the reverse trend (see Tables 16.1 and 16.2).

Of the categories of immigrants entering Australia, business migration has gained most in significance over the past decade. Many of the families coming under this scheme are from Hong Kong and Taiwan. On the one hand, many of them (especially those from Hong Kong) already have a high level of English proficiency, on the other hand they tend to maintain close contacts with the countries of origin through business and families; it is likely that they will not need to reverse shift in the future.

A success story in RLS motivated by factors other than the above but utilising the family-community-neighbourhood links (Stage 6) is that of Macedonian. In 1994, in deliberations on the recognition of the newly independent Republic of Macedonia, the Australian government bowed to pressure from Greek diplomatic representatives and sections of the Greek community to refer to the new state as the Former Yugoslav Republic of Macedonia. In addition, the Macedonian community should now be officially called the Macedonian-Slav community to distinguish it from members of the Greek community from the Northern Greek region of Macedonia. The state government of Victoria, which has the strongest concentration of both Greek and Macedonian speakers, declared that the Macedonian language should in future be known as Macedonian (Slavonic). Both the official change of the name of a community language by a government in Australia and the affixation of the name of a language family to the name of a language are unprecedented. From a practical point of view, the same final school examination is termed Macedonian (Slavonic) in Victoria and Macedonian elsewhere in Australia. From a linguistic point of view, there is no other 'Macedonian language' from which this one needs to be distinguished. An appeal by the Macedonian community to the Human Rights and Equal Opportunity Commission (1997) was unsuccessful but was overturned by the Supreme Court following an appeal by the Macedonian community in 1998. The latter verdict was affirmed in 2000, following a further appeal by the Victorian Government. However, the community's outrage has translated into very strong determination to maintain and transmit the language. Macedonian is the only European language which has experienced an increase in the number of home users in Australian over the period 1991 to 1996 (10.7%

following a rise of 41.3% in the five years before – the numbers having increased from 45,610 in 1986 to 71,347 in 1996). This could not be due to new migration but should be attributed to a combination of underclaiming before, second generation maintenance, RLS, and perhaps even some overclaiming. While the activists and teachers tend to come from the Aegean region, and of earlier vintage, the highest maintenance rates are among families from former Yugoslavia. It would be interesting to see if similar RLS is prompted for other languages in immigrant settings due to grievances at home and abroad.

In the 1980s, a number of young couples of Latvian parentage who normally communicated in English at home shifted back to Latvian when their first child was born to ensure intergenerational transmission. However, the strong impetus to maintain the language declined when the political motivation subsided with the collapse of the Soviet Union and the independence of Latvia.

While the vast majority of Australians are opposed to racism4, some public opposition to non-discriminatory immigration policy in 1984, some hostility to Arabs and Muslims during the Gulf War (1990), and the emergence of a far right party (1997–98) seem to have affected the motivation to language maintenance of different groups in different ways. Chinese-Australians have been more reluctant to transmit their community language while in other groups, such as Arabic speakers, perceived racism has led to stronger language, maintenance efforts and successful representations to government and the teaching profession arguing for the importance of their language and culture for all Australians (Clyne & Kipp, 1999). This cultural variation could support intercultural differences in the 'coreness' of language in the value system (Smolicz, 1981) and the ambivalencce of host community attitudes as a factor in language maintenance and shift (Kloss, 1966).

Closing Remarks

From the above it will be evident that reversing language shift is not something that has occurred widely or successfully in Australia, although opportunities for language maintenance and delaying language shift are quite plentiful. Language shift can be reversed in Australia but it has not been reversed very much. Many of the measures discussed in Fishman's writings are not favoured by either ethnic communities and families or by wider Australian society because they detract from the interactionist aspects of multiculturalism and from desired socioeconomic mobility, at least by the second generation. The crucial Stage 6 is therefore difficult to achieve.

The Australian situation demonstrates clearly the usefulness and appropriateness of Fishman's model for the description, explanation and prediction of RLS. As all sociolinguistic situations vary, it is necessary to adapt the model to local conditions. In this case, a small number of adjustments of a general or particular nature have been canvassed:

(1) Deliberate efforts for intrinsic, instrumental or integrative motives to raise children bilingually either in the context of an extended family or community or simply through targeted communication with one parent (thus even without Stage 6).

(2) National and local media may not always be a useful basis for a distinction but there may be other differentiations in the nature of the media.

(3) Media, both print and electronic, may not be as far forward in the GiDS schema as suggested for intergenerational transmission of minority languages as they may not be used or desired by later generations for content reasons.

(4) Since Fishman (1991), new technologies have started playing a greater role in the lives of ordinary people, and they could facilitate or inhibit RLS. The place of new technologies such as the Internet are perhaps worth considering as they potentially link later generation users of a language with the heartland of the language community and with communities in other minority situations maintaining the language. They can also add motivation, input and output opportunities for literacy in the community language. This relies on the heartland ensuring that the language has and maintains a place on the Internet.

It is also suggested that the political context and position of the language in Australia and beyond could provide incentives for the various stages in RLS.

Notes

1. My thanks are due to Kylie Martin for help with the collection and analysis of data. I also thank the ethnic schools associations and media authorities in each state and territory, Irene Donohoue Clyne, Edina Eisikovits, Renee Zufi, Lee Hubber and various community language radio stations, and the Working Group on Multicultural Library Services (Victoria) for valuable information, and Joshua Fishman and Joseph Lo Bianco for helpful comments.

2. The Uniting Church is the product of the amalgamation of the Methodist, Congregational and most of the Presbyterian Churches.

3. In addition, there are some pay stations – two Chinese and one each in Arabic,

Croatian, Farsi, Greek, Korean, Portuguese, Turkish, and Indian languages in
Sydney, one each in Chinese, Greek, Macedonian, and Portuguese in Melbourne, and one in Greek in Adelaide.
4. This was clear during the 1998 election and in the results.

References

Clyne, M.E., Eisikovits, E. and Tollfree, L. (in press) Ethnic varieties of Australian
English. In P. Collins and D. Blair (eds) *English in Australia* Amsterdam:
Benjamins.
Clyne, M., Jenkins, C., Chen, I. and Wallner, T. (1995) *Developing Second Language
From Primary School*. Canberra: National Languages and Literacy Institute of
Australia.
Clyne, M. and Kipp, S. (1997) Trends and changes in home language use and shift in
Australia, 1986–1996. *Journal of Multilingual and Multicultural Development* 18,
451–73.
Clyne, M. and Kipp, S. (1999) *Pluricentric Languages in an Immigrant Context*. Berlin:
Mouton de Gruyter.
Dawkins, J. (1991) *Australia's Language: The Australian Language and Literacy Policy*.
Canberra: Australian Government Publishing Service.
Döpke, S. (1993) *One Parent One Language: An Interactional Approach*. Amsterdam:
Benjamin.
Fishman, J.A. (1967) Bilingualism with or without diglossia: Diglossia with or with-
out bilingualism. *Journal of Social Issues* 23(2), 29–38.
Fishman, J.A. (1991) *Reversing Language Shift*. Clevedon: Multilingual Matters.
Imberger, B. (1986) Children from German-speaking families. In M. Clyne (ed.) *An
Early Start*, (pp. 112–27). Melbourne: River Seine.
Kipp, S., Clyne, M. and Pauwels, A. (1995) *Immigration and Australia's Language Re-
sources*. Canberra: Australian Government Publishing Service.
Klarberg, M. (1983) *The Effect of Ideology on Language Teaching*. PhD thesis. Monash
University.
Kloss, H. (1966) German American language maintenance efforts. In J.A. Fishman
(ed.) *Language Loyalty in the United States* (pp. 206–52). The Hague: Mouton.
Lo Bianco, J. (1987) *National Policy on Languages*. Canberra: Australian Government
Publishing Service.
Ozolins, U. (1993) *The Politics of Language in Australia*. Cambridge: Cambridge Uni-
versity Press.
SBS (1997) *Annual Report 1996/97*. Canberra: Australian Government Publishing
Service.
Saunders, G. (1988) *Bilingual Children from Birth to Teens*. Clevedon: Multilingual
Matters.
Smolicz, J.J. (1981) Core values and cultural identity. *Ethnic and Racial Studies* 4,
75–90.

Chapter 17

Is the Extinction of Australia's Indigenous Languages Inevitable?[1]

J. LO BIANCO and M. RHYDWEN

Introduction

In *Reversing Language Shift* (1991) Joshua Fishman considered immigrant origin minority languages and Australian indigenous languages together. Fishman was well aware of the improbability of the co-location of such different categories of languages, stating that these: 'represent two very different sociolinguistic constellations and, also, two very different sets of experiences and expectations *vis-à-vis* the Australian anglo and anglified mainstream' (p. 252).

We are grateful that in *Can Threatened Languages be Saved?* Professor Fishman has decided to allocate separate chapters to these two categories of languages. This chapter of RLS Revisited does not contrast the status of a single language in 1988 with its status in 1998. The demography of indigenous languages in Australia is such that precise quantification is impossible. However, several instances of RLS effort (and instances of language revival) are reported. Many of these were obtained by direct contact with field workers and communities, and others from literature and research produced since RLS 1991. We also evidence the manner in which policy-making can marginalise minority languages when power structures do not represent the interests of their speakers.

The treatment of aggregated Australian RLS efforts contrasts with the single-language focus of other case studies: Irish, Basque, Frisian, Navajo, Spanish, Yiddish (secular and ultra-orthodox), Maori, Hebrew, Quebec French and Catalan. The specificity of these instances makes discussion of case studies straightforward and generalisations may be made depending on the representativeness and typicality of the cases.

However, for Australian indigenous languages we must either assume that all the settings (there are many hundreds) are among themselves consistent to allow extrapolations to be made or we need to discuss specific examples with a view to discerning what is particular about them in the context of the Graded Intergenerational Disruption Scale (GIDS).

The GIDS and Australian Indigenous Languages

The GIDS is a 'heuristic device' for ascertaining the extent of dislocation of intergenerational transmission of a language. The higher the stage at which the language is located (8 being higher than 1) the greater the degree of disruption of the 'normal' transmission pattern and characteristics. Stage 8, however, involves disruption not to the pattern of *transmission* of a language code, but of the code itself, i.e. of its integrity as a code for transmission.

The sociocultural setting and context of Australian languages is unique. The speaker populations reside only in Australia and for many of the languages the local relationship to land is a critical context for the use of the language. The transfer of the communicative practices of speakers to other forms of speech results in the death and extinction of these languages. This, in turn, means the disappearance of the sociocultural universe uniquely given life by the languages. It is our contention in this chapter that GIDS (a scale to calibrate an index of disruption) may require modification to accommodate such characteristics.

This is not just as a result of the sociolinguistically marked differences between indigenous and immigrant languages and their relationship to English. It has also to do with the complex language ecology of communication among indigenous communities, traditionally multilingual and multidialectal. The social structures of indigenous speech communities are dramatically unlike those of the wider society, nor are they similar to those of other minority speech communities that have entered westernised mainstream society.

There are three principal reasons for considering modifications to GIDS. Firstly, those minority languages that function in societal structures that resemble the state hierarchies of late modernity (with elaborate administration and authority processes, personalised notions of identity and individualism, and capitalist techno-economy rewards and patterns) could conceivably incorporate 'governmental functions, mass media and higher education' and other macro-functions anticipated in the GIDS. For many Australian indigenous languages, however, Stage 1 and Stage 2 comprehensiveness is neither possible nor ever traditionally encountered. Stage 6 would have represented the maximal level and may still be the maximally achievable objective.

Secondly, the functions for which intergenerational transmission of an

Australian indigenous language are critical are transmissive activities across age cohorts, significant culturally marked relationships, and the whole ensemble of traditional life (belief systems, practices, customary and law activity). A complete activity is conceivable with a Stage 6 character to the language but no stage beyond this seems to be indispensably important.

This last point, of course, raises a recurring tension about intergenerational language maintenance. Domain separation and diglossic patterns of communication have been identified as essential for some intergenerational language retention contexts, but this may not be possible, or needed, in all cases. Fishman (1991: 401) points out that at GIDS Stages 4 to 1 RLS efforts are strong and 'transcending diglossia in search of increased power sharing'. This aspiration seems beyond any Australian indigenous language, except perhaps for traditional ceremonial life where the power relations are dramatically reversed between indigenous languages and English.

It is here though that the 'changing the climate' approach of much of Australian RLS effort is centrally important. Without a dislodging of English from what McConvell (1992: 215) calls the principle of 'conveying of social meaning' (rather than domain) the power imbalance between these languages and English is too great. This is especially acute in relation to GIDS 4b (Xish programmes in Yish schools) where considerable RLS effort is directed in Australia, in the belief that the wider identification of Aborigines with their ancestral life (and languages) needs to be restored prior to any possibility of greater Xish use.

Thirdly, indigenous communities' communication repertoires involve Australian languages other than their own, other dialects of their language, and evolving linguae francae, as well as English (including indigenised Englishes). In such a communication complex the 'shifting' that occurs can be among a dynamic range of alternatives, in several directions, and continually.

A central premise of the GIDS thesis is that intergenerational language maintenance depends on community-family-neighbourhood control of institutional resources and processes that permit continuous and socially grounded 'natural' or at least convenient domains of use of the marked language. Boundary maintenance is critically important. The 'outside' language cannot be permitted to invade the boundaries of the 'inside' since it will erode its distinctive domain and undermine its transmission prospects.

Stable situations of bilingualism are thus predicated on domain separation and diglossic patterns of communication, except perhaps for languages which can marshal sufficient territorial and institutional resources (GIDS 1 languages) to 'power share' with languages of wider communication such as English.

Types of Language Loss

Two main types of language loss have taken place among indigenous languages in Australia, both of which result in extinction: an abrupt dislocative and extreme form and a slower, generational, attrition. The former often results in the total disruption of all transmission (and of any later re-learning prospects) of the language, while the second can, at best, retain within the living memory of speakers sufficient language resources on which to base a revival or renewal activity. The former may be called language loss by *rupture* and the latter language loss by *attrition*.

The initial contact period between white settlers and indigenous Australians produced many examples of the loss of language by rupture, via the extermination of all speakers, their total dispersal so that no transmission possibilities remained, or other forms of extreme denigration and damage to the speech community. The period since has involved a slow, seemingly inexorable attrition of all the domains of life traditionally functioning in Australian languages and their colonisation by other forms of speech, especially various forms of English.

Schmidt (1990/1993: 123–5; see also Dixon, 1989: 123) identified five stages of language loss by attrition. She points out that these are ' . . . abstract points on a sliding scale, with the healthy language at one pole and total adoption of the replacing language at the other' noting that it is not necessary for all languages to pass through all stages.

Stage 1 languages have strong vitality, being actively transmitted to children and being the 'primary language of the community'. The language is known fluently by most speakers who rely on it as their principal means of communication. A wide range of speech styles is in regular use and the language tends not to have wide internal morpho-syntactical or lexical variations.

Stage 2 languages involve contractions in speaker numbers and increasing use of an alternative language. However, the language is still transmitted intergenerationally, (and in a relatively complete form) although not all of its new learners acquire a fully functional range of competency in the speech styles of the language. There is evidence of the influence of the replacing language within the linguistic features of the threatened language.

Stage 3 languages are no longer transmitted to the younger generation.

Such languages remain fully functional only for some older users. Radical simplifications are occurring from the replacing language which younger members of the community are already using as their main means of communication. Intergenerational communication makes use of pervasive code-switching. The repertoire of speech styles activated in the threatened language for all speakers is much restricted.

Stage 4 languages have no fluent speakers left. Their use is only in piece-meal fashion (as markers and 'acts of identity') interspersed in speech that is principally conducted in the replacing language.

Stage 5 has seen the loss not only of fluent, but also of semi-speakers of the threatened language. The replacing language is used as the first language of all the community's members. Very occasional markers of 'dif-ference' remain in the speech of the community. The language is near-death and can be considered extinct when its last fluent speaker dies.

Schmidt's (and Dixon's) Stage 1 and Stage 2 (healthy) levels are built on rather different criteria from the GIDS levels 1 and 2, where societal macrofunctions are critically important criteria.

Schmidt's 'rough' calculation is that there are 20 Australian indigenous languages at Stages 1 and 2, 50–60 at Stage 3, between 170 and 180 at Stages 4 and 5. More than two thirds of Aboriginal languages are already extinct or are nearing extinction (i.e. at Stages 4 and 5). About 90% of Aboriginal Australians no longer speak their Aboriginal language.

Only Stage 1 and 2 languages can be considered to have 'vitality' and at present rates of attrition (at least one distinct language becomes extinct each year) the number of languages at Stages 1 and 2 will halve within the lifetime of the next generation.

The Status and Prospects for Australian Indigenous Languages

The grim conclusion in Fishman (1991) about the negligible long-term survival prospects of Australia's indigenous languages has been continu-ally reiterated for some time. Since 1991, however, several important public inquiries have been undertaken into the status of and issues surrounding Australia's indigenous language heritage (Schmidt, 1990/1993; House of Representatives, 1992; NLLIA, 1994; McKay, 1996).

Regrettably, none of these reports has yielded any coherent or committed policy response (for utterly different specific reasons, though for an overarchingly common factor): the relative political powerlessness of the speakers of endangered languages and the overwhelming power of a system of policy making that is oriented towards granting greater priority to English, and perhaps inadvertently but nevertheless powerfully, to marginalising language maintenance.

(In demonstration of the powerful effect of the ability of policy makers to constitute the primary focus of educational language policy towards dominant linguistic norms we discuss the discursive practice of making policy (if not quite 'on the run' at least policy 'in the making') with an extract of a recent and highly relevant Parliamentary debate (see Lo Bianco, 1999a).

The asymmetrical power to name the 'problems' experienced by indigenous people means that in Parliament questions about support for indigenous language and cultural education can be deflected into a discussion about the underperformance of Aboriginal children on English literacy tests.[2]

Many language workers and indigenous language advocates maintain strong activity and commitment toward RLS but not usually with the expectation of full restoration. In this regard Schmidt (1990/1993: 106) states: 'If successful language revival is taken to mean the full restoration of the language to a state of strong vitality (by re-establishing the broken language transmission link; regaining full conversational language knowledge and fluency; and active use of the language by all generations in wide range of social contexts), the chances of success for threatened Aboriginal languages are, in all probability, fairly remote. To my knowledge, there are no instances in Aboriginal Australia .. of language revival efforts achieving such goals.' Schmidt does however support language revival efforts with more modest (realistic?) goals.

Indigenous language speakers and language workers sometimes refer to the work of regional language centres as resembling language hospitals where a range of emergency procedures (corpus planning and status planning) are undertaken to restore languages to some semblance of health.

Working with Australian Aboriginal languages the signs apparently indicate that most of them are beyond saving. Yet despite the chances of survival being negligible, there is a vast community based effort to keep languages alive. Subsequent sections discuss the intervention of language workers in a variety of maintenance and revival initiatives.

Categorising Aboriginal Languages

On its release *Reversing Language Shift* was hailed in Australia as the 'the nearest thing that I know of to a user's manual for language maintenance intervention'. (McConvell, 1992: 210). Aboriginal language workers have expressed misgivings about the applicability of all levels of the GIDS framework for Aboriginal language maintenance. Some of these misgivings undoubtedly arose because it is depressing to read that most of the languages display symptoms that indicate they are not going to survive and that the kinds of strategies being used are unlikely to be successful. However, the reactions to RLS have not all been couched in these emotional terms. Rather, the message is that because of the particular nature of Aboriginal languages (and their sociocultural contexts) some of the theories on which RLS is based may need modification (McConvell, 1992; McKay, 1996). It may be that the apparent hopelessness of the situation of Aboriginal languages has contributed to the generation of critiques and alternative theories that allow at least a little optimism about the future.

A first reading of RLS as a user's manual might lead one to think that what is necessary is to work systematically through the stages from wherever one's particular Xish is on the GIDS scale, up to Stage 1. There is no doubt that the majority of Aboriginal languages are at Stage 8 on the GIDS. Although estimates about the number of extant languages and dialects vary considerably,[3] there is little doubt that most have few young speakers (only 20 according to Schmidt, 1990/1993). In view of the bleak outlook for most Aboriginal languages, the enthusiastic language maintenance worker might look at the languages which were high on GIDS (but not necessarily on Schmidt's Stages 1 and 2 where different criteria are applied) and then try to discover how this might be achieved in other contexts. Yet it soon becomes apparent that there are problems with categorising any Aboriginal languages.

Some languages are being transmitted intergenerationally and used extensively within particular speech communities, but whether they would be defined as GIDS 1 is debatable because of the incommensurability of emic and etic (insider and outsider) formulations of what constitutes 'the highest educational, occupational, governmental and media activities' (Fishman, 1991: 107).

For Aboriginal people prior to initial contact with whites (and for people in some areas first contact is still within living memory) the 'highest educational, occupational, governmental and media activities' always did take place in their own language/s (though what these terms actually mean in such contexts is difficult to decide). This language may now be used for those same activities; but what is widely judged, certainly by the wider community, to constitute, say, 'the highest educational activity' is no longer knowledge of traditional law which is embodied in the oral stories, rituals and songs, but nationally accredited qualifications such as university degrees.

Thus, from one perspective, the 'highest' activities, such as important ceremonies and discussion of community politics, take place in the local languages in some Aboriginal communities. From another perspective it is apparent that those people who exert institutionally sanctioned power in the community (teachers, medical staff, administrators and community leaders) must use English for some, if not all, their occupational activities.

It could be argued that the few communities in which intergenerational transmission is still strong (and many community activities take place in local languages) the languages are at 1 on the GIDS, at least for the purposes of serving as a model of what is possible in the Australian context. However, given the pervasive spread of incorporation of the entire national population of most countries into the web of economic and governmental information collection and technological invasion of previously secure social spaces, even the strongest languages remain extremely vulnerable.

In Europe, a language such as Breton with 500,000 speakers, is regarded as a minority language. Even Manx, spoken in the Isle of Man off the west coast of northern England, long regarded as extinct, has 200–300 speakers who learned it as adults. Such a result would be regarded as a major triumph in Australia and evidence of great vitality. Of course, stating the bald facts (that most Aboriginal languages have fewer that 500 speakers) disguises the fact that many languages have never had more than a comparatively small number of speakers.

Yet it would be dangerous to be lulled into thinking that because languages with small populations have survived in the past, they will continue to do so, particularly in the face of accelerating technological change. Each situation, where Aboriginal language maintenance is an issue, is unique and any attempt to generalise or typify is likely to run into problems.

A few situations will nevertheless be described below, because they exemplify some of the variety of issues that arise in working with Aboriginal languages and which impact on RLS prospects. Some of the complexities that arise in situations where the language is regarded as strong will be discussed first.

What is Shifting?

Among the languages always included on any list of strong Aboriginal languages is Yolngu Matha, a group of dialects spoken by around 6000 people in North East Arnhem Land. The Yolngu people are renowned for their independence and pride. Their land was not impinged upon by whites until the founding of a mission station at Yirrkala in 1934 followed by mineral exploration in the 1960s and they have been able to retain their languages. Indeed, as McConvell reports, the area is unusual in that, unlike most speakers of Aboriginal languages, the Yolngu people of NE Arnhem Land do not feel compelled to speak English when in the presence of whites (McConvell 1991: 50). However, even in those areas where there is no apparent or immediate threat to the survival of Aboriginal community languages, the nature of those languages and the extent to which shift is occurring within them, are issues of considerable concern.

The children in Yirrkala and the surrounding homelands who would, in the past, have spoken one of the Yolngu Matha clan languages, are now speaking Dhuwaya, a koine. This is a simplified version of one of the closely related local dialects, Gumatj, which was used initially for Bible translation and later in the school Bilingual Program (Amery, 1985).

Language shift within Aboriginal languages is occurring elsewhere in Arnhem Land. Increasingly linguae francae are replacing clan dialects. At Galiwin'ku and Milingimbi Djambarrpuyngu is generally spoken by both adults and children. This phenomenon is not confined to Arnhem Land. At Wadeye (formerly Port Keats) Murrinh-Patha has become the lingua franca.

This raises interesting questions. Although some of these shifts are partially attributable to white intervention, in the sense that the language used as a lingua franca is often that used by early Bible translators (and in school bilingual programmes) it is also the case that the languages were selected for those purposes because they were already dominant languages in the community. Certainly the changing patterns of settlement, with Aboriginal people living together in permanent housing in settlements much larger than in the past, has led to changes in language use that reflect the different situation. Traditionally in Arnhem Land, and many other areas, clans are exogamous so that people would have married someone who spoke a different dialect and everyone would be bilingual, if not multilingual.

According to Gale, the 'immediate threat to clan languages in NE Arnhem Land is not English' (1993: 30). As in several other communities where the use of ancestral Aboriginal languages is strong and the languages are being transmitted intergenerationally, other local languages are being lost in the process of language shift to a lingua franca.

That an Aboriginal language is healthy and being transmitted intergenerationally is a cause for celebration in the face of the dominance of English. Yet if the vitality of the language is at the expense of other local languages, the celebration is also a wake. Moreover the importance of clan dialects to Aboriginal systems of land tenure should be recognised.

Describing the Yolngu land tenure system, Williams asserts that 'Words, especially names, comprise a category of a land-owning group's most important non-corporeal property..the importance of names lies in their relation to land, the group's most important real property' (1986: 42).

Knowledge of the clan language is essential to maintaining evidence of land tenure, and the complex relations between social groups and a shift from clan languages to a single Aboriginal language impacts upon cultural maintenance just as a shift to English would.

At Roeborne, in Western Australia, Yindjibarndi is taught in the local primary school. The Western Australian education department is committed to offering a language other than English in every primary school by the year 2000. Yindjibarndi is not the language of the locality of Roeborne, which is Ngarlama country; it has become the lingua franca following the removal of people from a wider area to what was previously named the Roeborne Native Reserve. While the teaching of Yindjibarndi in the school is welcomed by the local Aboriginal community such a move reinforces the status of a language that is not in fact local.

It should be noted that the disruption of traditional patterns of language use can have profound legal and cultural implications. Land claims, in which Aboriginal people make legal bids to claim title to their traditional lands, are based upon Aboriginal people being able to show an ongoing and continuous relationship to the land being claimed. Linguistic knowledge can be evidence of such a relationship. If local people are no longer able to speak the local language because it has been superseded by a different language (albeit a traditional Aboriginal language that may be closely related) this can have far-reaching legal implications.

In some 'strong' languages, such as Warlpiri (with 3000 speakers) and Tiwi (1500 speakers) there is evidence that the varieties spoken by younger people are influenced by English. The Warlpiri spoken by children at Lajumanu is reported to be changing and has far more English borrowings than their parents' variety (Cataldi, 1990); and at Bathurst and Melville Islands, the 'Modern Tiwi' spoken by younger people shows the influence of English (Lee, 1983). Thus, although the languages are surviving, there is concern that the varieties spoken by the younger generation may signal the start of their gradual demise. Other Aboriginal languages are being replaced not by English but by one of the two widely spoken creoles.

Both Kriol (spoken across much of north Australia) and Torres Straits Creole (spoken in the Torres Straits Islands and parts of north Queensland) are English-based.[4] Kriol is used formally in a bilingual school programme in Barunga and informally in many other schools. Both creoles are Aboriginal and/or Islander languages and they retain many characteristics typical of such languages. For example, the pronominal system of Kriol, with its dual and plural inclusive and exclusive forms, is like that of the local ancestral languages rather than like English.

The use of Kriol as a lingua franca is often seen as the cause of the decline in ancestral language use, yet it is sometimes argued that in such cases, Aboriginal languages are being replaced by new Aboriginal languages. These languages, with around 20,000 speakers each, are evidently very healthy, yet the fact that they are replacing the use of ancestral languages in many communities means that language maintenance there is often complex and contentious.

It has been demonstrated that even in the situations where Aboriginal languages are relatively strong (and which might be regarded as GIDS 1 languages within the communities where they are used) there is no room for celebration or complacency. Languages are often strong only because others are weak, because they have become linguae francae.

In situations where this is not the case, there is often evidence of other kinds of change. Thus, it is clear that language shift is occurring every-where, and is not restricted to those situations where Aboriginal languages are apparently heading towards extinction; nor is it unidirectional towards English (though undoubtedly this is the most common type of language loss by attrition).

Languages on the Edge

However, the majority of languages are not strong but weak. Very many Aboriginal and Islander languages are extinct or have only a few elderly speakers and most are at GIDS 8, requiring extensive intervention by both community members and professionals. Given the endangered state of Aboriginal languages the term *revival* is sometimes used to refer to virtu-ally all language work. However, revival is more accurately applied when speaking about languages that are not in daily use by several generations. *Revival* includes *reclamation* (when there are no speakers of a language but only historical records), *renewal* (where there are a few older people who have some, usually incomplete, knowledge of the language) and *revitalisation* (when there are some older speakers but younger people do not use the language).

The terms language *maintenance* and language *revival* clearly refer to different phases of a cognate activity (revival in its various forms must precede maintenance for endangered languages). This is mainly due to the massive disruption to indigenous people caused by European colonisation, a disruption that has amounted to genocide in some instances.[5]

Much of the work by linguists at the language centres around Australia focuses on documenting and recording the few remaining speakers of such languages. However, despite a vast community based effort for revival and documentation, and a strong maintenance effort by communities and language professionals, the data and facts are elusive.

As a dramatic illustration of this an employee at the Yamaji Language Centre in Geraldton in Western Australia reported to Rhydwen in 1998 that she had recently found three speakers of Ngarlawankga, a language previously considered to be extinct! Ngarlawankga was spoken by people in a neighbouring region but the workers at the language centre in that region thought the last speakers had died. It transpired that three speakers of Ngarlawankga had relocated to an area near the boundaries between the two regions and had somehow been overlooked in previous language survey work. The same worker had also found two speakers of Malgana (another language previously reported to be extinct) and was able to document some of the language before the speakers passed away.

It is clear (from the frequency with which one hears such stories from those who work with languages at grassroots level) that this is not an unusual occurrence. For this reason it is not really possible to document with certainty the socio-demographics of the indigenous speech communities (though it is undoubtedly the case that the overwhelming trend is towards attrition).

The last decade of language policy has produced a network of funded Regional Language Centres which conduct a wide range of community based activities for documentation, surveying and describing languages, as well as for RLS activity of many kinds. Nevertheless work with such languages is still hampered by the financial constraints on language centres in remote areas where off-road vehicles are essential and fuel bills astronomical.

Case Studies of Revival Initiatives and Other RLS Activity

There are some remarkable instances of language initiatives, some of which are provisionally successful instances of the kinds of modest revival that are feasible in the Australian context. The following four case studies are taken from McKay (1996).

Borroloola and Barkly Tableland, Northern Territory

The white impact on the various Aboriginal groups who live in the Borroloola region has affected each group differently over time depending on the whites' economic interests in the areas where each group lived (i.e.

first cattle industry, then fishing and more recently mining and tourist industries).

Historically, the Yanyuwa and Garrawa people suffered less than any other group in the region from the white impact because white settlers had a lesser interest in their geographical areas. Interestingly, the Yanyuwa and Garrawa languages are the only two Aboriginal languages still spoken by a reasonable number of people in the region.

Currently, around 500 Aboriginal people live in the Borroloola region. Kriol or Aboriginal forms of English are the two main languages spoken in this community. The two main Aboriginal languages still spoken are: Garrwa and Yanyuwa. There remain a few speakers of two other Aboriginal languages: Marra and Kudanyji. About 14% of the Borroloola Aboriginal population are still full speakers of Garrwa, and 11% are full speakers of Yanyuwa. All fluent speakers in these two languages are middle-aged to older people. In each language group, the equivalent of twice the number of fluent speakers have partial competence in the language of the community. Out of the total Aboriginal population, 31% of the people speak no traditional Aboriginal language.

In 1916 the Marlandarri camp was set up. It included a strong Yanyuwa community. The camp served to enforce segregation of Aborigines from whites but it also provided Aborigines more control over their lives.

In 1963, the linguist Jean Kirton noted that parents spoke to their children in Kriol. There are two different possible explanations for this: (1) parents used Kriol to help their children learn English; or (2) parents used Kriol in response to their children's use of Kriol. They would do so out of traditional politeness that promotes understanding between speakers as the primary goal of verbal interaction over the protection of one's language. However, children heard Yanyuwa being spoken around them all the time and consequently they were still able to speak it themselves later on in their lives. The youngest people who can still speak Yanyuwa today spent their childhood at Marlandarri camp. Over time, the linguistic homogeneity of the Yanyuwa people was broken down by different circumstances and events. The most significant of these being work patterns and intermarriages. Kriol was the lingua franca used by the different linguistic groups working in the stations.

In the past, 'flu' epidemics which caused the death of older speakers or floods which forced people to move (and more recently the introduction of television and videos) are other events which impacted negatively on the Yanyuwa people's ability to retain their language. Still further factors contributing to language loss are governmental disregard for residence patterns in decisions affecting the rebuilding of Aboriginal dwellings.

Those decisions contribute to the breakdown of kin relationships so important for language maintenance. Finally, the increase of non-Aboriginal residents in the region make traditional languages and cultures harder to retain.

In the face of linguistic adversity, the response of Aboriginal people has been to switch to English (non-standard English) hoping to give their children a better chance in the non-traditional world. It is only recently that new generations are starting to see that it is possible for two languages and cultures, despite their differences in status, to coexist just as traditional languages have coexisted in the past.

Historically the first school established in the Borroloola region promoted the teaching of English (at the request of the Aboriginal community). Aboriginal languages were used by children in and outside the classroom. During the early 1970s indigenous languages were prohibited and denigrated in the school system. In 1994, a division of opinion was documented between the different groups involved in the school community as to whether and/or how indigenous languages should be taught. Aboriginal people themselves (like the small group of white parents and teachers) are divided on this issue.

Also in the past, the work of linguists such as Jean Kirton in Christian missions has helped the maintenance of Aboriginal languages. Notably these linguists translated songs of the Bible in the local Aboriginal languages. Those songs are today often the only form of traditional language Aboriginal children (and white children too) hear and use at school and also in churches. The Borroloola Project is an example of a language revival initiative.

The project started in 1987 as one of the activities of the Papulu Apparr-kari Language Centre in Tennant Creek. The aim of the project is to record material from elderly speakers of Garrwa and Yanyuwa (in writing or on video) to ensure that younger generations have access to local Aboriginal knowledge. The material collected ranges from lists of body parts, trees, plants, etc. as well as taped stories, oral history and ceremonial singing, videos of bush medicine and collection of dyes and pandanus for basket weaving. There are positive outcomes to the project despite the lack of appropriate funding which prevents the materials collected from being turned into usable teaching materials:

- Through the project, languages and cultures that are in decline are being documented.
- The children who take part in the bush trips to collect data interact with the old people in the indigenous languages.

- Finally the project helps the language project team to gain status as an official source of authority from which help can be sought regarding language matters in the community.

As an example of language 'renewal' and 'revitalisation' we can consider the Aboriginal Language and Culture Programmes in Barkly Region Schools (including Borroloola). A study carried out in 1990–91 in the Barkly and Sandover regions of the Northern Territory showed that a majority of Aboriginal people spoke Aboriginal English or a variety of Kriol as their first language. They expressed the need for better English and literacy programmes in schools. Most Aboriginal people also wanted the local Aboriginal languages and cultures to become part of the school curriculum.

The region does not have an official bilingual programme. However, local (and often short-lived) Aboriginal studies programmes are run in schools under, in most cases, the initiative of Aboriginal student teachers or graduate teachers who have gained the confidence to act within the Western education system. One of the main drawbacks of these programmes is that they often do not provide actual language teaching.

In the Barkly area, Aboriginal studies programmes either fall within the Northern Territory Department of Education's second languages policy or its Social and Cultural Education (SACE) Guidelines. The 'second languages' policy is only a recommendation to schools and this category also does not appropriately cover the specific language needs of Aborigines. The SACE Guidelines, on the other hand, do not cover the sort of programmes Aborigines wish to implement. Overall, the lack of strong policy support means that Aboriginal language and culture programmes have not attained a secure place in the school system.

Apart from policy issues, one of the main problems in the successful implementation of Aboriginal Studies programmes is the lack of appropriate teacher training. Firstly the school system needs to recognise and support Aboriginal people who are in the position to provide language and culture education (elders and younger people alike). This support must include training in indigenous language literacy and language matters at all levels, according to need and particularly on-site in remote communities.

The study referred to suggests that measures can be taken which have proved to encourage and motivate Aboriginal people to establish language and culture programmes in local communities. These measures include the provision of opportunities involving Aboriginal people in language work of various types and the provision of language education for teachers in

order to prepare them to find local solutions related to language maintenance which includes learning how to work with the appropriate community elders.

Gumbaynggir people and language near Kempsey, New South Wales

Generally speaking the Gumbaynggir people, the main Aboriginal
community from the mid-north coast of New South Wales, were less
affected by white contact than other Aboriginal groups in other regions.
However, in the 1860s when white settlers started to introduce European
agriculture in the area, the Gumbaynggir people started to suffer severe
discrimination and social isolation. Most Gumbaynggir people now live in
the main small towns in the area.

The Gumbaynggirr people started to lose their traditional language
during the 'Protection' era (1880s) when Aboriginal children where
removed from their families and institutionalised in order to be assimilated
into white society. Adults were also moved from their original areas to
work in stations in other regions where they mixed with Aboriginal groups
who spoke different traditional languages. Intra-group marriages became
more common and contributed to the decline in the use of traditional
languages. In the 1950s only pockets of older speakers still spoke
Gumbayngirr.

In 1994, only seven speakers of the language were identified in the
region. One of those speakers mentioned that it is only in 1986 that she
started to re-use her traditional language during meetings organised by the
newly established Gumbaynggir Language and Culture Group.
Gumbaynggirr people now mainly speak various forms of English.
However, the traditional social and cultural system is still alive and
apparent in, for example, the continuing importance given to kinship relationships and Aboriginal speech forms of English.

The use of Aboriginal Englishes, however, has not helped the
Gumbaynggir people to be more accepted by the dominant society. It is
only in recent years that Aborigines in the region are trying to reconnect
with their linguistic and cultural heritage mainly through the work of a
Language Centre.

Language revival initiatives work through the Muurrbay Aboriginal
Language and Culture Cooperative in Kempsey. As in the Borroloola case
it is mainly under the initiatives of elders (in this case encouraged by an
outsider, Brother Steve Morelli) that the Gumbaynggir Language and
Culture group was established and later became the Muurrbay Aboriginal
and Culture Cooperative. The Cooperative is now funded as a Regional

Language Centre. The Centre has undertaken initiatives in language revitalisation and revival including: writing Gumbaynggir in a simple way, collecting and recording excerpts of the language, memories and songs from living speakers. This groundwork for language renewal was then used to produce language teaching materials, writing of dreaming stories and plays and writing of a Gumbaynggir dictionary.

One of the Centre's concerns is to avoid superficiality in the materials it produces and the teaching it delivers. Language materials are based on research from various sources including the Centre's own data by also tapes and documents held by the Australian Institute of Aboriginal and Torres Strait Islander Studies and the University of New England.

In 1994, the Language and Culture Centre conducted a traineeship in language and culture maintenance as well as other language and culture programmes in primary and secondary schools. Among the outcomes of the centre's activities towards language renewal and language revitalisation are that the Language Centre believes that there are now more Aboriginal people who have basic knowledge of Gumbaynggir than five years before it started its language activities. A far greater number of members in the community (children and adults) have at least had some contact with their traditional language and culture. It was noted that most Gumbaynggir people want to learn Gumbaynggir names, phrases, place names, songs and stories.

The Centre's main successes have been to revive the language skills of the surviving speakers and to pass them on to younger people who now have the responsibility to keep the language and culture alive. It has also helped the Aboriginal community in the region to reconnect with its heritage.

Jaru at Yarunam (Ringers Soak), East Kimberley, Western Australia

One characteristic of the Jaru people's history with white contact is that as one of the latest groups to be dispossessed of their land they were able to use changes in political and social circumstances to successfully regain access to their land in 1983.

In the stations where Aborigines worked Jaru language was tolerated, unlike in other stations in other regions. This contributed to the maintenance of the local traditional language. The whole Jaru community was keen to enter the Catholic value system as long as it was not at the expense of their traditional culture. Most Aboriginal people in the Yarunam community speak Jaru, including all children and Aboriginal adults from non-Jaru descent such as the Warlpiri. Other languages (of limited use) in the community are Warlpiri, Kriol, Ngardi and Gurindji.

The local school has run a bilingual English-Jaru programme since its establishment. Since 1990, a teacher linguist visits regularly to assist in the ongoing running and development of the programme. Local women are heavily involved in the programme. In 1990, some of these women enrolled in a language worker training course. The two nuns involved in the running of the school provide evening classes for adults (religious instruction, literacy classes, etc.).

Some of the problems regarding the teaching of Jaru at the school are that the programme seems to employ well-used materials, thereby preventing older children from expanding their language skills. Language games seem to dominate the approach to teaching the Jaru language leaving doubts as to whether any effective language learning is really taking place.

In 1994 some initiatives were taken to start teaching English as a second language in the school. Some of the issues which have prevented successful learning of the Jaru language have been when non-Aboriginal linguists or teachers become the experts on spelling and grammar in the local language leaving the Aboriginal population of the school feeling disempowered. The sometimes heavy-handed criticism of the older Aboriginal speakers towards the younger generation's language also accounts for some of the young Jaru people turning to English or a Creole to avoid negative feedback.

The local Catholic Church use of the Jaru language and culture in liturgy plays a role in language maintenance. Both a local priest and a linguist developed Jaru writing which was introduced at the school in the mid-1980s. An extensive grammar of Jaru was published in 1981. In 1992 the Kimberley Language Resource Centre also produced a draft Jaru Dictionary.

There are several factors that contribute to language maintenance prospects in the Yarunam community. Jaru is the dominant language of use in daily life. The history of the region has allowed the language to live on (through tolerance of Jaru in the stations). There has been a close and non-oppressive relationship between the Jaru community of the local Catholic Church. The Jaru programme in the school has fostered the learning of the language and its status. The women's involvement in the school has provided a bridge between the school and the community. The support provided by the teacher-linguist has also been important. There is a positive sense that Jaru people are in control of their community and that their relative isolation from the town lifestyle has been a positive contributory factor.

However, there are several factors that threaten Jaru language maintenance. The gradual increase of the use of Aboriginal English is an indicator of future problems. This is compounded by the number of intermarriages and the increase in interaction with non-Jaru people, mainly through council meetings, school and church. There is also concern that the language programme at the school is not developing as a 'proper' language programme.

Saibai Island and Torres Strait, Far North Queensland

Traditionally two distinct Aboriginal languages were spoken in the Islands of Torres Strait along with many dialects; most people, however, were monolingual. Torres Strait Islanders had much contact with the inhabitants of the Papuan Coast.

In the 1840s, indigenous languages entered into competition with other languages (European and Melanesian) with the discovery and exploitation of commercial quantities of Beche-de-mer, pearl shell and trochus. Pacific Pidgin English soon became the lingua franca among marine workers. The arrival of the London Missionary Society further activated the progressive loss of the traditional languages in the region. In the late 19th century as Pacific Pidgin English started to be used by children as their first language it soon became a Creole.

The widespread use of Torres Strait Creole came about out of necessity for a lingua franca among the diverse ethnic groups brought together by the development of the marine industries, but also because the local indigenous population perceived this Creole as being English itself. This erroneous belief started to be eroded only when Torres Strait Islanders meet with native English-speaking soldiers in the Australian Army during the Second World War.

The association of English and Creoles in local administration churches and schools contributed to the prestige of Creoles. It is also through the use of Creoles that the different groups of Torres Strait Islanders were able to develop a pan-Islander consciousness in between the two world wars. After the Second World War (and by 1980) half of the population of Islanders had migrated to the Australian mainland. This group of islanders realised then that the Creole they spoke did not give them equal status to whites in Australian society. There are, however, different attitudes towards the use of Creole among older and younger generations of Torres Strait Islanders.

The Native Title decision in the High Court of Australia (1993) affects the Murray Islands and has prompted new interest in the revival of traditional languages. (Under the terms of the Native Title decision one demonstration of continuing association with claimed land as a criterion for a gaining land ownership is language retention).

Overall, despite the various language maintenance projects in the Torres

Strait and some isolated instances of individual initiatives, the indigenous
language movement in the region tends to be relatively inactive.
Compared with Torres Strait, Sabai was less affected by white impact
because the island had less to offer economically. The biggest white impact
was felt mainly after the arrival of missionaries in 1871. The white impact as
well as new diseases and abnormal floods after the Second World War
contributed to the dispersal and dislocation of the Sabai population. In the
1990s only 300 Sabai people still lived on the island. The Anglican Church
has had a significant role over the past 100 in years in providing strength
and unity among the local population.

The main language used by the majority of the population on the island
is Kalaw Kawaw Ya. Most people use the Torres Strait Creole as a second
language. Children can speak some Creole before they start school. Both
English and Creole are widely reinforced among children when they start
secondary school on Thursday Island.

In Sabai Island State School the official language of instruction is
English. There is no formal Kalaw Kawaw Ya language programme in the
school but the language is used widely in the lower grade classrooms. Sabai
people are divided between their interest in maintaining their language
(although this interest is not always strong among children) and their
recognition of English as a language of necessity to have access to the wider
white Australian society. There is a perception in the Sabai community that
language matters should be left to elders and people with linguistic
training. This does not always permit language revival initiatives.

The language used in the local church is usually Kalaw Kawaw Ya with
some uses of English and Creole. Written Kalaw Kawaw Ya has existed for
a long time. There is a tendency now to rely on the spread of Kalaw Kawaw
Ya literacy for language maintenance to the potential detriment of the use
of spoken language.

Interest in language issues is relatively high among the Sabai community. However, many Sabai people who have received linguistic training
are often not employed in positions where they make use of this training or
they no longer live on the island. Two major initiatives have contributed
(and still contribute) to the maintenance of Kalaw Kawaw Ya: the introduction of a Kalaw Kawaw Ya Language Programme in Thursday Island State
High School and the use of Kalaw Kawaw Ya in Indigenous Language
Broadcasting.

Language maintenance on Sabai Island has not been attributed to particular programmes or activities but to a complex of attitudes and circumstances which combine to facilitate the transmission of the traditional
language across generations. The relative homogeneity of the local

community together with the unifying influence of the Church (combined with the generally experienced feeling among Sabai people that their identity is linked with the use of their language) are the main support factors for language maintenance. However, the factors that currently threaten language maintenance are the political and social status of English and of English speakers as well as the dual roles of Torres Strait Creoles (Creole as violating identity or as a marker of identity). The breakdown of intergenerational linkages (children spend less time with elders in the bush) is another disruptive factor. Insistence on the use of English as the language of instruction in education is also problematic since it reduces the style range that children have access to.

Apart from these cases in McKay (1996) direct contact with field workers indicates other interesting language maintenance initiatives across the continent. Kaurna, a language spoken in the region of South Australia where Adelaide is situated, lost its last fluent speaker in 1929. Kaurna had been well documented in the middle of the 19th century but written records did not provide a good indication of the sound system. This was reconstructed by comparing the written records with recordings of a neighbouring and related language, made earlier this century. Recently, Nungas (Aboriginal people of the Adelaide area) have renewed their interest in tracing their Kaurna ancestry.

In 1986, Kaurna Plains School (a Nunga school) started a Kaurna language programme and in 1994 a senior secondary programme started and Kaurna has since been recognised as an accredited secondary school subject (Nathan, 1996). Kaurna is certainly worthy of inclusion as a revival initiative and immensely commendable in its scope and ambition. However, it is still an 'acquired' language and its intergenerational transmission status and chances must rank as problematical.

The case of Noongar is also encouraging. As previously mentioned, in Western Australia all primary schools will have a 'Languages other than English' programme by the year 2000. In Langford Primary School in suburban Perth, all the children learn Noongar as their second language. Almost half the children at the school are Aboriginal. About 3% are from a variety of other non-English-speaking (immigrant) backgrounds. Noongar is the language that incorporates the dialects of the Noongar people, the Aborigines of the south-west of the state, including Perth. When the first edition of Wilfred Douglas' book documenting Noongar was written in 1968, many of the remaining speakers were very elderly. Douglas describes the difficulty of eliciting evidence that people had any knowledge of the language at all. Now, however, there has been a resurgence of interest and pride. The people who teach Noongar at the school have themselves had to learn the language, reclaim it for themselves, and now are teaching it to both Aboriginal and non-Aboriginal children, none of whom are familiar with it. By having the language taught as a core mainstream subject, it is hoped that the stigmatisation of Aboriginal languages will be reversed.

Such programmes acknowledge the fact that generations of banning the use of Aboriginal languages by those children for whom it is a first language is why Aboriginal people have grown up ashamed to speak or transmit their languages. This is a problem in most areas, even away from major urban centres, where there has been extensive contact with whites. The Noongar example is also positive but its capacity to become the first language of a self-regulating cultural community, and the language transmitted to a new generation, however small numerically, of Xmen is highly problematical. Such revival programmes have value as cultural maintenance and awareness even if they do not succeed, or cannot succeed, in totally restoring a language.

The stigma attached to the speaking of Aboriginal languages is widespread. McConvell has documented how children at Turkey Creek, in the north of Western Australia (whose ancestral language is Kija) laughed uproariously at a film of children in another community speaking Pitjantjatjara (1986: 116). The Kija children's mother tongue is Kriol, although their parents are bilingual in Kija and Kriol.

Thus, in a few situations where a language is a GIDS level 8, it is taught within a mainstream school programme in Aboriginal schools or schools with a high Aboriginal population. In Perth, the introduction of Noongar into schools has occurred as there has been development of Aboriginal Studies programmes in schools and universities.

Whilst ultimately languages cannot be maintained without intergenerational transmission, the climate in which such transmission can occur has to be created. Reversing Language Shift cannot mean 'fossilising' language. According to Mühlhausler (1992) it is 'language ecologies' that ought to be cultivated rather than languages in isolation (this notion is suggested in Fishman's call for boundary preservation) and social space for minority speech communities. All living languages are constantly shifting. Any attempt to stop that process is bound to be frustrated but there are tools that can be used to try to control the direction, speed and consequences of language shift.

Australian initiatives for language revival of indigenous languages have been fired by optimism and struggle rather than any widespread or systematic adoption of a planned revival approach. In any case the documentary basis for this is largely unavailable. It has been demonstrated that apparently 'strong' languages are extremely vulnerable. It has also been shown that, despite this, unexpected examples of revival in places where languages have been believed to be long dead can sometimes occur.

Chronology of Policy Moves for Indigenous Languages

The public policy interest in indigenous languages commenced seriously in 1973[6] with Commonwealth (Federal) government intervention in Northern Territory schools (then under Commonwealth jurisdiction) to commence bilingual education.[7] However, in policy terms it was not until 1987 and the adoption of a comprehensive approach to national language planning that explicit attention was paid to language maintenance and intergenerational retention of indigenous languages.

> For the first time since the European arrival about 200 years before, the Commonwealth Government formally recognised indigenous Aboriginal languages through a *National Policy on Languages* in 1987.... The *National Policy on Languages* is noteworthy as the first formal Commonwealth Government policy recognising the viability and worth of Aboriginal languages and their endangered state .... Although considerably less than the $6 million originally advocated in the Lo Bianco report, the NALP (National Aboriginal Languages Program) is significant, for this was the first time that the Commonwealth Government had allocated a sizeable portion of money specifically for the maintenance of Australian Aboriginal languages, as a means of implementing an official language policy statement. (Schmidt, 1993: 43–4)

Fishman (1991: 277–8) contrasts the critical need for efforts at RLS to be sequentially planned and to be 'RLS informed' against the 'superficial institutional flourishes' that government supports, and earlier remarks that many of the steps taken are 'either largely unrelated, non-productive or even counter-productive as far as intergenerational RLS-pay off is concerned'. He regards boundary setting and boundary preservation as crucially important (domain separation requires this) and notes that such needs contrast with the 'ethos of shared participationism that dominates both democratic and authoritarian regimes'. He advocates 'small scale self-regulation and self-help at the local level'.

These critiques of policy are of fundamental importance for any appreciation of what ought to be done. But what is policy? And whose policies count? And, as Fishman asks, can policy really make a difference? In considering these questions we will need to address what kinds of policy exist and notions of the linguistic culture within which these policies are enacted.

Ball (1993) makes a distinction between policy *as text* (referring to the legislative-administrative form that policies take) and policy *as discourse* (referring to the ongoing 'talk and writing' that precedes, accompanies and follows the text).

Schiffman (1996) introduces the idea of *linguistic culture* (a notion that folds all language policies into an overarching envelope of cultural framing attitudes, ideologies and histories). According to Schiffman linguistic culture impacts seriously on the prospects of achieving the stated goals of language policy. We cannot understand overt language policy and its chances of success without reference to the 'covert' realm of underlying linguistic culture, the '..belief system, collection of ideas and decisions and attitudes about language' (Schiffman, 1997: 59).

Goals of RLS in Australian indigenous languages must be understood within frames of the complex relation between policy and context, between ideological and societal framing and the actual realisation of RLS, what Fishman refers to as *RLS payoff*.

There have been constant shifts in public policy for languages in Australia. The main official positions of government policy, as well as influential documents or other developments, can be dated from the 1973 introduction of bilingual education in areas of Commonwealth jurisdiction (essentially the Northern Territory, which subsequently attained 'self-rule').

The formation in 1981 of the Aboriginal Languages Association (by community activists, academics, teachers and others) to lobby, support, research and coordinate national effort on behalf of Aboriginal languages coincided with vigorous lobbying by ethnic community organisations for a national language policy which would have language maintenance as one of its key goals. A national coalition involving both ethnic and Aboriginal activists came into operation in that year (Ozolins, 1993).

Some 10 significant policy-influencing documents succeeded each other until a policy breakthrough under the National Policy on Languages, adopted by Federal Cabinet on 4 June 1987, the first official explicit language policy. This incorporated principles of Aboriginal self-determi-nation and language maintenance rights. Under the NPL the first programme for Aboriginal language support, the National Aboriginal Languages Programme, was established.

Also at this time the Australian Advisory Committee of Languages and Multicultural Education was established to oversee the implementation of the NPL; with a Standing Committee comprised mainly of (and chaired by) indigenous people, to advise on Aboriginal languages and to disburse NPL funding to community language maintenance projects. NALP was subsequently incorporated into the Aboriginal Education Strategic Initiatives Programme (AESIP) under the Education (Supplementary Assistance) Act 1989 as part of AEP and then later subsumed by a new national language policy: *Australia's Language: The Australian Language and Literacy Policy*. Finally, the National Languages and Literacy Strategy (NALLS), nominated by the Minister for Aboriginal and Torres Strait Islander Affairs in the Joint Policy Statement for the AEP National Priorities for 1993–95, took over responsibility for indigenous languages funding.

This pattern of progressive assertion in policy of language maintenance rights has, however, been interrupted with the expansion of public concern, fanned by political intervention, over English literacy achievement standards. In 1997 this concern took the form of several key documents:

- Mapping Literacy Achievement, Masters, G. and Foster, M., DEETYA
- Literacy Standards in Australia, Minister for Employment, Education, Training and Youth Affairs
- Aspects of Literacy, Assessed Skill Levels, 1996, Australian Bureau of Statistics.

The cumulating effect of these early developments had been a widespread acceptance of the benefits and desirability of 'two way' education: Aboriginal and wider society, English and ancestral language (where applicable) within a culturally appropriate pedagogy. However, these effects have recently come starkly up against a countervailing force with the concern for English literacy attainments generally (and specifically for Aboriginal children) making vulnerable the case for bilingual education and language maintenance initiatives.

Policy and Power: Defining Problems and Shaping Prospects

The latest (and bleakest) chapter in public policy concerns the 1998–99 abandonment of public funding support for indigenous language bilingual education. The Northern Territory's education approach is exemplified in its 1995 report on its bilingual education (Northern Territory Department of Education 1997a and 1997b). In 1995 there were 21 accredited bilingual programmes (using 34 languages and dialects) distributed across 16 Department of Education schools, 3 Catholic and 1 independent school. The stated 'main aims' of these programmes are:

- to support and promote Aboriginal languages and culture;
- to foster proficiency in school work through the use of the Aboriginal languages;
- to develop competency in Literacy in English and Aboriginal languages;
- to develop competency in Mathematics (Northern Territory Department of Education, 1997a: v).

It is interesting that these programmes are seen to respond to key policy developments referred to above such as the National Aboriginal and Torres Strait Islander Education Policy, the goals of the National Aboriginal Languages and Literacy Strategy and recommendations of the Royal Commission into Aboriginal Deaths in Custody.

Appendix One is an extract from the Official Hansard record of the stormy debate that took place in the House of Representatives on 10 December 1998. The extract serves to highlight a critically important aspect of public policy (policy here understood as *discourse*). The fracas is about the decision of the NT government to remove funding from Aboriginal bilingual education programmes, originally established by the Commonwealth government when education in the NT was jurisdictionally Commonwealth responsibility (Lo Bianco, 1999a).

The Commonwealth government has been accused of backing the NT decision. Both governments are pushing English and are accused of using the low (English) literacy achievement standards of Aboriginal children as a ruse for getting rid of bilingual education. The extract points out how language policy (i.e. language policy *as discourse*) is made in debate by who has the power to define what the problem is and points up that in the RLS versus English dichotomy how without any capacity for 'self-regulation' minority community languages maintenance is vulnerable.

Several scholars of public policy processes have noted the crucial importance of what is sometimes referred to as 'problem definition' (Edelman, 1988; Majone, 1989; Drey, 1984). In this process there is a contest to name (and constitute by such naming) a field or area as 'the problem' to which public resources will be devoted.

One of the deficiencies of formal language planning theory is precisely its inability (see Lo Bianco, 1999b) to deal with policy as discourse, and with the discourse as shaping the policy (Yeatman, 1990).

In the extract we note a contest (made sharp and angry by the time constraint and the overtly politicised character of the debate) about what precisely is lost and gained by the Northern Territory's decision in relation to bilingual education. For the Minister the issue and problem is the overrepresentation of Aboriginal children among those performing least well in English literacy assessments. For the opposition questioners the issue with bilingual education is bilingualism and issues of cultural maintenance. Which construction of 'the problem' prevails (and which is silenced) makes a significant difference to how complex multifaceted issues become the object of policy makers' attention.

Constructing *literacy* as the main problem of Aborigines (and of *literacy* as being effectively synonymous with English) is the culmination of a process commenced in the 1992 *Australian Language and Literacy Policy* which aimed to reverse the multiculturalist orientation of the National Policy on Languages (Moore, 1996).

The dominant rationalisation for language policy at the Commonwealth has been progressively changed from one concerned with efforts to bolster multilingualism in community contexts and in the public sphere, to one where economic and trade (and general 'efficiency' criteria) dominate. Such rationalisations while they avoid the overt language and nomenclature of assimilation may often lead to the same effect.

Literacy in English is named and constituted as the principal focus of language policy. As far as languages other than English are concerned the facilitation of external trading relations with newly powerful northern trade partners occupy the most persuasive parts of the policy discourse.

Community-oriented language maintenance is relegated to a subordinate standing with neither vigour nor resources to sustain those few token acclamations which remain in the policy documentation. The policy texts often remain very positive. The policy discourse, how the powerful have talked about why the state should concern itself with language issues, has side-lined and made vulnerable multicultural oriented language policy.

At the same time the wider community focused approach of the *National Policy on Languages* has been narrowed to an education focus. Despite the commendable efforts of education based interventions, the narrow education framework within which language maintenance, retrieval and revival activities have been grounded is doomed to failure.

Linguistic culture has been captured by an ideology of economism, in which rationales of trade, efficiency, consumerism and globalised economic pressures dominate. Intergenerational transfer and maintenance of minority languages (as the GIDS stipulates) depends on coherence of community-family-neighbourhood institutions and their authenticity. These in turn depend on some capacity of speaker populations to autonomously create, govern and reform their communal institutional environments and settings.

But all this runs up against the long reach of consumer economy and the kind of society consumption economics generates. All community controlled social space is eroded by the long reach of administration, economy and wider societal values. The net of public-bureaucratic monitoring (with the establishment of standards for measurement of normalised achievement in education, certification and accreditation of virtually all fields of endeavour) is incorporating more and more of previously private life within the surveillance systems of government, public authorities and corporations.

Whereas literacy issues were once a primary concern of developing nations (based on its presumed universal achievement in developed nations) for reasons of national consolidation and the creation of national cultures in often post-colonial settings the 'knowledge economy' and cut-throat globalisation has stimulated developed nations to embrace policies for literacy enhancement.

These trends were anticipated in the 1991 Australian Language and Literacy Policy (prefiguring a monolingual orientation it was ominously titled: The Language of Australia). 1997 is probably the culmination of that trend. It can be called the year of literacy. Virtually all other considerations of language policy are sublimated to literacy, which is becoming the Australian variant of English-only. Moore (1996) shows some of the origins of this in the adoption by both major political forces in Australian public life of the economistic logic previously associated with the 'new right'.

International global competitiveness has also made a belief in the achievement of improvements in average education levels (symbolised by literacy in national languages) a commitment of all governments (OECD, 1996, 1998) within a paradigm of human capital theorisations. Investing in humans (as capital assets) is conceived as one of the main roles of the state. All else is left to the competitive market place. Normalising measurements are given encouragement by the need for comparison which reduces cultural differences and contextual settings. In such a climate the policy discourse is so utterly dominated by what in Australia has come to be called 'economic rationalism' (user pays, small government, privatisation of public resources, etc.) that public policy around sustaining community efforts to reverse language shift have no place.

If this were to result in a shrinking of the state away from its involvement in community and family life, Aboriginal Australia may be permitted the space for self-determination and self-regulation sufficient to allow ancestral languages legitimate control of GIDS 1-like activity and resources. Regrettably, this does not appear to be the case.

Observations about GIDS and RLS for Australian Indigenous Languages

To summarise then, it is clear that the principles of the GIDS and RLS (1991) describe the parlous state of Australia's indigenous language ecologies and document their meagre prospects for longer-term survival. Despite occasional instances of revival efforts that attain short-term, unexpected and spiritually uplifting gains for communities of speakers of traditional languages the pattern of attrition and extinction appears inexorable. Indeed it has probably accelerated in the decade since RLS was published. We have also argued that the state, motivated by economistic logic of social incorporation, and even benevolently intended discourses of 'equality' continues to find ways to invade the social spaces and 'social meanings' whose conservation is critical to the retention and intergenerational transmission of indigenous languages. Finally we have argued that language policy is discursive as much as it is textual. In its manifestation as discourse asymmetrical power relations mean that the interests of monolingual ideologies and practices of nation making are destructive of diversity and multilingualism.

Specifically about the Graded Intergenerational Disruption Scale we argue that:

(1) It is unclear how the levels one and two of the GIDS apply to indigenous situations or to languages whose terminological range and discourse patterns (and present power structures in the wider society) make it unlikely that these languages would ever fulfil all of the functions envisaged (e.g. higher education). Conversely, the principles of diglossia and domain separation make it unlikely that such functional extension would be needed for intergenerational language maintenance if the 'social meanings' that the indigenous languages uniquely carry were able to be assured even within social spaces and practices unprotected from the invasive pattern of English.

(2) There is a major need to theorise policy in ways that permits a nuanced consideration of the discursive power of 'monolingualising' institutions and forces. 'Policy' can only lead to real change for RLS if control of resources and means for decision making and the institutional domains where language socialisation occurs is in the hands of those affected. The effects of competitive globalisation are powerfully counteracting any such capacity.

(3) Although the National Aboriginal Languages Programme was community based and did not just operate within the formal (Yish) education sphere later appropriations of language maintenance policy, although they were better funded, did overly emphasise the Yish education domain.

(4) These developments and the general orientation of formal policies beginning with the 1991 Australian Language and Literacy Policy have commenced a policy conversation in which the relative claims of first language maintenance have been ranked against the demands of a national standardising claim for English literacy. This has had the deleterious effect of judging bilingual education in terms of Yish norms and specifically elevating English literacy to superordinate importance. The planned removal of funding for bilingual education, and the policy makers reconstrual of 'the problem' of indigenous bilingual education as a matter of English literacy to approximate national rigidly normalised benchmarks are direct consequences of this 'strategic naming' of language issues.

(5) The notion of domain only applies in a most general sense, and McConvell's suggested replacement of the principle of 'social meaning' for 'macro-domain' and diglossia is promising in that indigenous languages communicative practices may better be able to be accommodated within GIDS.

Notes

1. The assistance of Chantal Crozet is gratefully acknowledged.
2. Official Hansard Commonwealth of Australia Parliamentary Debates, House of Representatives Thursday 10 December 1998. Topic: Northern Territory, Bilingual Education, pp. 1872–1875. See Appendix One.
3. According to a draft report by FATSIL (p.c. Lester Coyne, president FATSIL) there are 328 indigenous languages and dialects which are 'either in current use or are being researched for the purpose of revival'. Ethnologue lists 151, of which 67 are described as 'nearly extinct' or 'extinct' and 33 that have fewer than 50 speakers. Dixon (1980: 1) reports '200 distinct languages'; while the House of Representatives (1992: 1) comments: ' Before European settlement of Australia there were approximately 250 Aboriginal and Torres Strait Islander languages. These were quite distinct languages which between them included about 600 dialects.'
4. For descriptions of Australian creoles see Sandefur (1979) and Shnukal (1991).
5. See, for example, *Bringing them Home*, Report of the National Inquiry into the Separation of Aboriginal and Torres Strait Islander Children from their Families, Sydney: Human Rights and Equal Opportunity Commission (1997), (AGPS).
6. Watts, B., McGrath, W. and Tandy, J. (1973) *Bilingual Education in Schools in Ab-*

original Communities in the Northern Territory. Canberra: Department of Education.

7. These programmes have recently come into the public spotlight with the release of an NT government report announcing the progressive removal of funding for bilingual education in public schools. Interestingly in this context the former Minister for Education responsible for establishing these programmes wrote on 15 December 1998 in a letter published in *The Australian Newspaper* (p. 12) (Kim Beazley Snr, Minister for Education 1972–75) that while '(preserving) an aspect of Aboriginal culture' might have been an effect of such programs it was certainly not the intention. The main aim was enhancing the learning of English literacy'. This claim has been much contested in the subsequent debate.

References

Ball, S.J. (1993) What is policy? Texts, trajectories and toolboxes. *Discourse* 13(2), 10–17.

Cataldi, L. (1990) Language maintenance and bilingual education at Lajamanu School. In C.Walton and W. Eggington (eds) *Language: Maintenance, Power and Education in Australian Aboriginal Contexts.* Darwin: Northern Territory University.

Dixon, R.M.W. (1980) *The Languages of Australia.* Cambridge: Cambridge University Press.

Dixon, R.M.W. (1989) The original languages of Australia, 3, 26–34.

Douglas, W.H. (1976) *The Aboriginal Languages of the South-West of Australia.* Canberra: Australian Institute of Aboriginal Studies.

Drey, D. (1984) *Problem Definition in the Policy Analysis.* Lawrence: The University of Kansas Press.

Edelman, M.J. (1988) *Constructing the Political Spectacle.* Chicago: The University of Chicago Press.

House of Representatives Standing Committee of Aboriginal and Torres Strait Islander Affairs (1992) *Language and Culture – A Matter of Surivival: Report of the Inquiry into Aboriginal and Torres Strait Islander Language Maintenance.* Canberra: Australian Government Publishing Service.

HREOC (1997) *Bringing them Home, Report of the National Inquiry into the Separation of Aboriginal and Torres Strait Islander Children from their Families.* Sydney: Human Rights and Equal Opportunity Commission, Australian Government Publishing Service.

Gale, M.A. (1993) *Code-Switching, Manymak or Yaka Manymak? A Discussion Paper on Language Use, Language Change and Language Loss.* Occasional Papers in Applied Linguistics. Darwin: Center for Studies of Language in Education, NTU.

Lee, J. (1983) *Tiwi Today.* PhD thesis. Australian National University.

Lo Bianco, J. (1987) *National Policy on Languages.* Canberra: Australian Government Publishing Service.

Lo Bianco, J. (1999a) Policy words: Talking bilingual education and ESL into English literacy. *Prospect* 14(20) 40–52.

Lo Bianco, J. (1999b) The language of policy, What sort of policy making is the officialization of English in the United States? In T. Huebner and K. Davis (eds) *Socio-political Perspectives on Language Policy & Planning in the USA* (pp. 39–62). Amsterdam: John Benjamins.

Majone, G. (1989) *Evidence, Argument and Persuasion in the Policy Process*. New Haven: Yale University Press.

McConvell, P. (1992) Review of Fishman 1991. *Australian Journal of Linguistics* 12 (1), 209–20.

McConvell, P. (1991) Understanding language shift: A step towards language maintenance. In S. Romaine (ed.) *Language in Australia*. Cambridge: Cambridge University Press.

McConvell, P. (1986) Aboriginal language programmes and language maintenance in the Kimberley. *Australian Review of Applied Linguistics*, 108–22.

McKay, G. (1996) *The Land Still Speaks: Review of Aboriginal and Torres Strait Islander Language Maintenance and Development Needs and Activities*. Commissioned Report No. 44. Canberra: Australian Government Publishing Service.

Moore, H. (1996) Language policies as virtual reality: Two Australian examples. *TESOL Quarterly* 30(3), 473–99.

Mühlhausler, P. (1992) Preserving language or language ecologies? A top-down approach to language survival. *Oceanic Linguistics* 31(2), 163–180.

Nathan, D. (ed.) (1996) *Australia's Indigenous Languages*. Adelaide: Senior Secondary Assessment Board of South Australia.

NLLIA (1994) *Backing Australian Languages, Review of the Aboriginal and Torres Strait Islander Languages Initiative Program* (Confidential Report). Canberra: Aboriginal and Torres Strait Islander Commission.

Northern Territory Department of Education (1997a) *1995 Annual Reports from Specialist Staff in Bilingual Programs in Northern Territory Schools*. Darwin: Government Printery Office of the Northern Territory.

Northern Territory Department of Education (1997b) *Aboriginal Education News, Issue 8, Aboriginal Languages in Schools*. Aboriginal Education Policy Support Unit on Northern Territory Indigenous Education Issues. Darwin: Northern Territory of Education.

OECD (1996) *Measuring What People Know, Human Capital Accounting for the Knowledge Economy*. Paris: Organization for Economic Co-Operation and Development.

OECD (1998) *Human Capital Investment, An International Comparison*. Paris: Organization for Economic Co-Operation and Development.

Ozolins, U. (1993) *The Politics of Language in Australia*. Cambridge: Cambridge University Press.

Sandefur, J. (1979) *An Australian Creole in the Northern Territory: A Description of Ngukurr-Bamyili Dialects (Part 1)*. SIL-AAB Series B, Volume 3. Darwin: Summer Institute of Linguistics.

Shnukal, A. (1991) *Broken: An Introduction to the Creole Language of Torres Strait*. Canberra: ANU. (Pacific Linguistics C107).

Schmidt, A. (1990/1993) *The Loss of Australia's Aboriginal Language Heritage*. Canberra: Aboriginal Studies Press.

Schiffman, H.F. (1996) *Linguistic Culture and Language Planning*. Routledge: London and New York.

Williams, N. (1986) *The Yolngu and their Land: A System of Land Tenure and the Fight for its Recognition*. Canberra: Australian Institute of Aboriginal Studies.

Yeatman, A. (1990) *Bureaucrats, Technocrats, Femocrats: Essays on the Contemporary Australian State*. Sydney: Allen & Unwin.

Chapter 18
RLS in Aotearoa/New Zealand
1989–1999

R. BENTON and N. BENTON

When I say there is not, this does not necessarily mean a negation; when I say there is, this also does not signify an affirmation. Turn East-ward and look at the Western Land; face the south and the North Star is pointed out there! (Yung-chia, 'Song of Enlightenment', quoted in Suzuki, 1959, 65)

The 1996 Census of Population and Dwellings in New Zealand included at least one amazing revelation: almost 22% of the population of Māori ancestry could 'have a conversation about a lot of everyday things' in Māori, and about half of these were under the age of 25 (Statistics NZ, 1997b: 79–80). Only a year before, a survey undertaken by Statistics New Zealand (who also conducted the census) for the Māori Language Commis-sion and the Ministry of Māori Development, indicated that less than 14% of the Māori population over 16 years of age had 'medium', 'high', or 'very high' fluency in Māori, and that the median age of these speakers was closer to 50 than to 25 (Te Puni Kōkiri, 1998: 34–5). These latter figures corresponded quite closely to what might have been expected based on projections from a more extensive sociolinguistic survey of Māori language use undertaken in the 1970s (Benton, 1997).

On the surface, the census figures indicated a spectacular reversal of language shift in the space of a year, and one for which formal institutions could presumably take much of the credit, since the official summary of the 1995 survey results noted that the marae [community gathering place for ceremonies and important meetings], school and church were the places where Māori was most commonly heard or spoken, and that although 'educational institutions ... have become very strong Māori language zones', 'for many children at kōhanga [Māori-language pre-schools] and kura [Māori-medium primary schools] these are the only places they ever hear or speak Māori.' (Te Taura Whiri, 1995). They are thus at once an affir-mation of the durability of the 'quasi-miraculous mystique' of the upturn in

Māori language knowledge and use noted six or seven years before, in *Reversing Language Shift* (RLS), while calling in to question the central thesis of that work, that such transformations can only be sustained when they are anchored solidly in home and neighbourhood intergenerational language transmission.

The account which will be presented here must lie somewhere within the mystic triangle which has the 1995 survey, the 1996 census, and the potentially observable but still well-hidden objective reality of what people really know and do, as its defining points. It is based on personal observations, discussions with parents, kaumātua [respected elders], teachers, children, scholars and people-in-the-street, along with the perusal of literally hundreds of reports and documents (one of the authors has, for example, looked at every report on a Māori-medium educational institution produced by the Education Review Office from 1997 to the middle of 1999). But in the end, although we hope that it is located closer to the point where the triangle touches the situation as it was (more or less!) at the beginning of 1999, this exposition remains the personal view of two people who have been involved in supporting and researching the resurgence and fortunes of the Māori language in New Zealand over the last four decades of the 20th century.

Then and Now

The overview of the situation of the Māori language in Chapter 8 of RLS is a good starting point for a discussion of what has happened in the intervening decade, which in turn can form the basis for reflecting on the validity of the 'Graded Intergenerational Disruption Scale' (GIDS) as a representation of the stages through which the process of reversing language shift must pass on the way to complete and comprehensive revitalisation.

We will first look at what the situation was then, and how it appears now, in relation to each of the 'stages' on the GIDS.

Stage 8

Stage 8 is that at which 'most vestigial users of Xish are socially isolated old folks and Xish needs to be reassembled from their mouths and memories' (RLS: 88). Although it would be an exaggeration to assert without qualification that Māori as a living language had been disrupted to this extent by 1989, in many parts of New Zealand, including many communities where most people regarded themselves as Māori, this was in fact the case, and quite probably still is. For example, in 222 of the 275 North Island geographical areas listed in Appendix 1 of the overview of the 1973–79 survey of Māori language use (Benton, 1991), fluency in Māori was limited mainly to adults over the age of 45, and in 29 of these areas, understanding of the language was similarly restricted, although there were only four localities where the language had virtually disappeared. It is likely that a survey of the South Island would have yielded an even bleaker picture, and almost certainly the South Island dialect of Māori was without native speakers at that time.

The kōhanga reo (Māori-medium pre-school) movement was designed to help remedy this situation, by reassembling the language from the 'mouths and memories' of the grandparental generation, for transmission to the very young – while enabling the parental generation to learn alongside their children if they had the time and inclination. Since the number of pre-school children who could speak Māori fluently in 1979 was very small indeed, almost certainly less than a hundred, this situation has changed dramatically, even if the census figures of 10,263 Māori children under 5 capable of holding a conversation in the language (compared with 45,202 who could speak only English) are wildly exaggerated. Furthermore, kōhanga supervisors, parents, and teachers in Maori-medium classes have put considerable effort into discovering ways of speaking Māori naturally in everyday situations. Even taking Māori from the status of a language to be taught to a language to be *used* in school, let alone at home, has required these language activists to discover and reconstruct the ways in which the 'language-in-culture' might be transmitted naturally to a new generation of speakers.

At the end of the 1980s, Māori was, at the macro-level, still teetering on the brink of Stage 8; the pretence that it was far more secure, while justifiable as a fiction of the kind one of New Zealand's most eminent jurists characterised approvingly as a device 'not to establish the truth, but to subvert it in the interests of justice' (Salmond 1893: 85), was an expression of faith and hope, rather than a dispassionate reading of the facts. By 1999, it is a few centimetres further from the edge of the abyss, with an impressive array of ropes and safety gear to help ensure that this distance is increased. At the micro-level, there are undoubtedly many communities where the Stage 8 scenario is still a lived reality, with rescue and reconstruction yet to be accomplished.

Stage 7

At Stage 7, most active users of the language are 'socially integrated and ethnolinguistically active' adults whose own children are grown up. This was the general situation in many of the 222 worst-affected areas surveyed in the 1970s. It was the widespread presence of older Māori-speakers in rural communities and urban neighbourhoods which made possible the spectacular growth of both the kōhanga reo, and the Ataarangi movement[1] (oriented towards the Māori language needs of whole families, and working through homes rather than educational institutions), which pre-dated the kōhanga and continues to flourish. These two movements often act in partnership at the local level, but the Ataarangi receives no govern-ment funding and is therefore not subject to government control. The revitalisation of Māori is still heavily dependent on the ethnolinguistically active members of the grandparental generation to sustain it. However, their ranks must be filled increasingly by second-language learners, that is, by members of the generation raised as English-speakers, for many of whom Māori was a language occasionally heard in childhood, but seldom understood. Their own parents (or, for quite a number, their grandparents) cooperate in this enterprise, helping to enhance and extend the Māori language competence of a new parental generation.

Leaving the census figures to one side, casual observation would lead one to conclude that, especially in localities served by strong Māori-medium educational institutions, and among Māori teachers, tertiary level students, and professionals, there are considerably more younger adults who are actively using Māori in everyday situations, and especially in bringing up their own children. But whether these people number hundreds or thousands is very difficult to say. The official report on the 1995 National Māori Language Survey found that only 10% of Māori-speakers under 45 spoke Māori at home to some extent every day, compared with 56% who said that they never spoke Māori at home. An impressive 11% of all 'Māori speakers', that is about 6.5% of Māori over the age of 16 (which would have amounted to about 20,000 people if the survey results were extrapolated to the entire Māori population) said that they spoke Māori at home all the time (TPK [1998]: 33). Most of these were 'highly fluent', and therefore older, speakers, but the potential of this trend for moving the disruption of the language situation away from levels 7 and 8 would, if confirmed and sustained, be considerable.

Stage 6

This is the critical stage in the RLS scheme of things, the stage which must be consolidated and secured if the later stages are to be achieved on a sustainable basis. It has three components: (1) the establishment of informal communicative links between generations through the revital-ised language; (2) the 'demographic concentration' of this activity – that is, anchoring it within a community or neighbourhood; and (3) institutional

reinforcement of this natural use of the language. The 6.5% of the population surveyed in 1995 who spoke Māori most of the time could be the
vanguard for the intergenerational transmission of the language. Of
course, one might speak Māori consistently without securing the cooperation of the rest of the household. In the 1970s survey, 10.5% of fluent
speakers used Māori as the main language for talking with their children,
which mirrors the 1995 results. However, in only about 8% of homes was
Māori the main language used when the family was gathered for a meal.
(Benton, 1991: 10, 28) We do not know what the situation is in 1999, but it
would probably be safe to say that while the number of Māori-speaking
households may not have increased, there would be many more children
spoken to and speaking Māori regularly at home than there were in 1989.
However, it is clear that even on the most liberal reading of the census
figures, which indicate that while 17% of Māori children under the age of 15
can speak Māori, almost 70% speak only English (Statistics NZ, 1997b: 79),
that this is not yet the norm, and therefore, for the overwhelming majority
of Māori people, even the first component of Stage 6 has yet to be secured.

The second aspect, the 'demographic concentration' of Māori-speakers,
so that they could form a geographic as well as an affective community, is
still far from being realised, and may be very difficult to achieve even in the
long term, unless 'language-in-culture' can be meaningfully and accept-
ably separated from 'language-in-biologically-mediated-ethnicity'. The
reason for this is that in very many important respects, while Māori descent
may not always be a sufficient condition for claiming Māori ethnicity in
Māori eyes, it is still in many important respects a necessary one. The condition is genealogically rather than racially based, but it nevertheless acts as a
very formidable barrier to the extension of group membership. It is one
which for some tribal groupings at least is applied with equal force to Māori
and non-Māori alike; for example, legally adopted children who do not
have a biological parent of appropriate ancestry cannot be registered as
beneficiaries of the Tainui Confederation's Settlement with the Crown,
even if they are of (non-Tainui) Māori ancestry and were adopted at birth
by qualified foster-parents (personal communication from Tainui Beneficiary Roll Officer, 1998).

Since the 1980s the Māori population has been overwhelmingly located
in urban areas, with more than 60% in the larger cities, and only 13–14% in
small rural localities (Statistics NZ, 1997b: 24). Although in some of the
minor urban areas, and indeed in some suburbs of the cities, Māori may be
either in a majority, or at least living close enough to each other to constitute
a community which could influence the linguistic norms of the area, there
is no reason at the moment to imagine that such a radical move away from

English would happen on a significant scale. Even where there are institutions to support such a development, there may be a notable lack of consensus on the extent to which Māori should be used. For example, in a section of a small town just south of Auckland, which includes an important traditional Māori settlement and tribal centre, there are two state-funded primary schools, located very close to each other. Each is attended by over 300 children, mostly Māori, from similar socio-economic and tribal backgrounds. One has taught entirely through the medium of Māori for more than 10 years, and the other through the medium of English with a little Māori language taught on the side (although in May 1999 plans were announced for possibly one bilingual class in 1999 or 2000). Both are regarded as excellent schools with very well-qualified and highly committed staff (many teachers at the English-medium school have qualifications for Māori immersion teaching). This situation underlines the fact that when Māori parents are given a choice, an education through Māori, in order to enhance and reinforce the opportunity for their children to use the language in other settings, is just one factor among others which influence a decision.

Within such communities, some families will actively encourage the use of Māori at home and in the neighbourhood, but others will remain basically English-speaking. There will be clusters of Māori-speaking households forming mini-neighbourhoods, but their members will also be socialising regularly in English with other people living very close by. The use of Māori may spread gradually out from these clusters, but there are powerful counter-forces not just outside the gates, but within the home. Meanwhile, the communities which do form (apart from a few isolated rural areas where the language survived as the lingua franca through the 1980s), are likely to be networks of non-contiguous households whose members have strong ideological commitments to revitalising the language – and who may indeed adopt compensatory measures like those outlined in RLS (p. 94) and used already by the Friulians and others. In New Zealand, the Māori Language Commission has taken this point to heart, and has started publishing a special bilingual newsletter to encourage and assist families in this respect (Taura Whiri, 1998).

The third element which must be present for Stage 6 to be completed is 'institutional reinforcement'. Joshua Fishman is right in emphasising the family, despite the erosion of its effectiveness in Euro-American society, as a potential bulwark of resistance to the forces of homogenisation. RLS is not politically neutral; it can be, and undoubtedly often is, when part of a community or ethnically-based movement, an antidote to the effectiveness of the 'propaganda of conformity' (Ellul, 1973: 74). As Jacques Ellul points out, it is primary groups such as the family which protect the individual sociologically from becoming a mere cipher within a highly manipulable mass society:

In individualist *theory* the individual has eminent value, man himself is the master of his life; in individual *reality*, each human being is subject to innumerable forces and influences, and is not at all master of his own life. As long as solidly constituted groups exist, those who are integrated into them are subject to them. But at the same time they are protected by them against such external influences as propaganda. (Ellul, 1973: 91)

Fishman sees the 'home-family-neighbourhood-community institutions and processes' as 'the heart and soul of stage 6' (RLS: 95). He states categorically that *'one cannot jump across or dispense with'* this stage (emphasis in original), and adds that 'without an intimate and sheltered harbor at stage 6, an RLS movement tends towards peripheralisation ... and faces the danger of prematurely tilting at dragons (the schools, the media, the economy)'. Yet New Zealand schools, despite the ultimately external regulation to which they are subjected, are in fact often key community and neighbourhood institutions, subject to a fair degree of community influence and control.

Furthermore, from our observations, so many people, and especially children, spend a significant portion of their day watching television within their own homes, that this institution cannot be written out of the Stage 6 equation. Although (and because) family members have control of this institution only to the extent that they can refuse to watch its effusions, the television set undoubtedly constitutes a powerful force for the socialisation of all family members, and particularly the young. It occupies a central place in the lives of many families, occupying often a number of key locations within the home – a central place within the family room, and often individual bedrooms as well. It is still almost entirely English-medium, and constitutes a powerful counter-force within the home to the efficacy of Māori language revitalisation efforts. This medium unremittingly whispers, shouts, and displays its message – 'get with it; only English really counts'. Although its comparatively poor relations, radio and the print media, may have less immediate influence, there is a case also for noting their effects at Stage 6, rather than at Stage 2 (where we will rejoin them).

Another neighbourhood institution is the local shop. Perhaps in the long run we will see the emergence of small shopkeepers as a subset of the Māori petty bourgeoisie. At present this role is undertaken mostly by immigrants from the Indian subcontinent and Fiji, who are more likely to speak Bengali, Gujarati, Hindi or Urdu than Māori. Like their predecessors of various ethnicities in many rural areas in the days when everyone spoke Māori, they would undoubtedly learn that language if knowing it would bring them more and better business. For the moment, there are few neighbourhood institutions and processes, apart from the kōhanga reo and, in some cases, schools, which most Māori-speaking families can rely on to support their efforts effectively and consistently.

The Māori-medium elementary schools belong to Stage 4 of the GIDS scale, and will be discussed in relation to this. However, in the discussion of the New Zealand situation in RLS, the kōhanga reo were seen as a supporting institution in the context of Stage 6. Throughout the 1990s, just under half the Māori children enrolled in pre-school facilities attended kōhanga reo, although the proportion had dropped from 49.2% (14,027 children) in 1993 to 43.5% (13,353 children) in 1997. However, Māori attendance at pre-school institutions of any kind is much lower than for the general population (around 45%, compared with nearly 70% for non-Māori), so less than a quarter of the total number of pre-school children of Māori ancestry will have experienced Māori-medium care of this kind during the 1990s. Although kōhanga reo are in theory entirely Māori-medium, in practice the amount of Māori used depends on the capabilities, skill, and support received by the kaiako (teachers). Increasingly, these are second-language learners of Māori, whose fluency in the language ranges from excellent to minimal. It is possible therefore that some Māori children catered for at other pre-school institutions (increasing, although still small, numbers of which are also bilingual or Māori-medium) will have received better exposure to everyday Māori than those at some kōhanga. According to the Ministry of Education (1998), by 1997 83.5% of Māori children and 61.5% of non-Māori received at least some Māori-language tuition at a pre-school centre.

Most if not all of the caveats concerning the likely effectiveness of kōhanga reo expressed in Chapter 8 of RLS (see pp. 238–9) remain valid in 1999. The potential of these institutions is still powerful, and many operate effectively, achieving their goals of transmitting the language-in-culture from one generation to another in a way that approximates the ideal. Others (as might be expected within a federation of 700–800 disparate local groups) fall far short of expectations. The centres no longer depend on the Department of Māori Affairs (which was replaced by a much smaller Ministry of Māori Development in the restructuring of government agencies launched at the end of the 1980s). They are now governed by a separate Trust, which receives substantial government funding through the

Ministry of Education, and each kōhanga operates under a charter from the Minister of Education. While nominally free, community-based initiatives, the kōhanga are in fact bound by a multitude of regulations enforced by the Trust and various government agencies, and very closely monitored by the Education Review Office.

In some rural areas, as noted in RLS (p. 239), kōhanga (and other educational agencies) have become markedly antiquarian, emphasising or even reassembling a local or regional dialect (in a way reminiscent of Stage 8), and seeking out distinctively local traditions and ways of doing things. This does complicate the task of encouraging literacy in Māori, but not to as great a degree as might be imagined. Most teachers and parents are now quite happy to have and used printed materials written in other dialects, provided they can also get materials in their own as well. Many teachers, even those using a *de facto* standard in urban, multi-dialectal settings, and whether at kōhanga or elementary school, make a lot of their own reading materials anyway, pasting Māori text over English, or writing and illustrating their own books. Furthermore, the differences between the major North Island dialects are very slight when compared with, say, English dialects in England. It is the political corollary of the strong resurgence of tribal chauvinism outside the metropolitan areas which is more serious than the linguistic, as the State is the main beneficiary of such divisions within Māoridom.

The flow-on effects from the kōhanga to the families of the children enrolled are varied. However, although it would be easy to find cases to illustrate the lack of influence on language policy and practice (in regard to a shift from English) in the home, let alone the neighbourhood, the best kōhanga have been able to involve families in language learning and play their intended role in revitalising both the language and the culture (cf. Royal Tangaere, 1997a; Douglas, 1991). An excellent description and analysis of one family's experiences in this regard has been completed recently by Margie Hohepa (1998), and another useful study has been published by the NZ Council for Educational Research (Royal Tangaere, 1997b). It is very unlikely that the degree of 'parental involvement and "relinguification"' suggested by Fishman (RLS: 239) as a prerequisite for entry to the kōhanga reo could be enforced without decimating the institutions. In the past, the Māori Language Commissioner had advocated this kind of drastic action, preferring 80 properly organised kōhanga to 800 disorganised ones. But there are now too many vested interests at stake and furthermore the danger of throwing the babies out with the bath water is too great to contemplate such draconian measures now. 'Relinguification' remains a goal, but one which may be only a little less difficult to achieve within the kōhanga than outside it.

We will return to the significance of Stage 6 later in the chapter, in relation to Stage 2, and when we consider official policy pronouncements and how some of these have been implemented, along with the role of the language in symbolising and maintaining inter-group boundaries.

Stage 5

The fifth stage in the RLS exposition of the GIDS is characterised by the extension of the oral communication which is the main focus of level 6, to literacy activities within the home, school and community. The social and political constraints mentioned in connection with this stage in RLS are real and well-attested in many societies. The most important factors for the New Zealand situation relate to Fishman's caution that this stage 'deals with only part of the total education domain, a part that is entirely Xish, primarily literacy focused, socialisation-related and entirely under intra-communal control' (RLS: 98). This stage constitutes, in the RLS scheme of things, 'the roof ... to the first and most difficult phase of RLS'. If and when achieved, it will give speakers of the revitalised language independence from the print media of the dominant one where 'informational, attitudinal, ideological/philosophical and recreational communications are concerned', enhancing the psychological bonds and cultural integration of the revitalising community. Very clearly then, the literacy we are dealing with here is not simply initial literacy development for children, but a Freirean critical literacy for the empowerment of the entire community. It is in this latter aspect of Stage 5, vernacular literacy for adult empowerment, that New Zealand may be weighed in the balance and found wanting.

The achievement of Stage 5 in relation to Māori language revitalisation is complicated by the fact that most Māori adults are able to read and write (in English), although the *level* of adult literacy in general causes some concern; the government's Literacy Task Force (1999: 10–11) noted claims the '20 per cent of children are failing in their literacy learning in New Zealand schools', and that 'levels of performance' among adults are lower among Māori than for the general population. While some Māori nationalists and RLS advocates have rejected literacy in Māori as an unwanted intrusion of pākehā technology into the sacred core of Māori culture, in general Māori-medium educators have vigorously promoted the acquisition of literacy through Māori. The pioneers among them established their elementary schools quite independently of the government, and some continue to work through informal 'home-schooling' networks in preference to government-financed institutions. Furthermore, as is noted in RLS, historically literacy was acquired by Māori very soon after the first contact with print, and for more than half a century there was a vigorous Māori-language press with a wide readership, covering all the topical issues of the day, local and international.

However the availability of wide-ranging and topical printed matter in Māori has been minimal since the 1920s, for a variety of reasons, not least of which has been compulsory education largely or entirely through the medium of English, with the accompanying propaganda relegating Māori language to the status of an archaic survival of little consequence in modern life (cf. Benton 1981). For adults, the problem is now fundamentally not a lack of ability to read in Māori, but that there is an inadequate quantity and variety of material to read. Throughout the 1990s a very strong emphasis has been placed on the provision of reading materials for younger children, and substantial progress have been made. However, adults still have little to choose from. A succession of Māori-oriented magazines which have been produced since the 1960s, published alternatively by the former Department of Māori Affairs (*Te Ao Hou, Te Kaea, Tu Tangata*), NZ Māori Council (*Te Kaunihera Māori*), and private interests (most notably *Mana*), have all been predominantly English-medium, with Māori-language content declining rather than increasing in volume over the years. The Māori local newspapers, which are far more modest in their appearance, also cater most comprehensively for their primarily English-speaking readers.

In 1998, *Mana* published an issue highlighting the current state of Māori language revitalisation – the set of articles was titled 'A dying language – or are the kids the cure?'. The Māori language content was confined to the odd sentence and heading, mostly in advertisements. The magazine is a very high quality, full-colour production, and therefore expensive to print and unable to devote costly space to material that would be inaccessible to most readers. It highlights the dilemma of the Māori press. Although there is limited government financial support for Māori radio, print media have to take their chance in the open market. To remain financially viable, they have to cater to a largely English-speaking readership, even if most of their readers are Māori. This applies also to creative writing and non-fiction, except when it is targeted towards the school market and likely to succeed there. Thus, except when writing for school children, Māori authors, including Māori-speaking authors, are likely to write in English. There is a much larger, often international, readership for these writers, along with the possibility of gaining major recognition and prestigious awards (Keri Hulme's *The Bone People*, which gained the Booker Prize, may never have been noticed if it had been written in Māori). The very small domestic Māori-language market (the English-language market is small enough!) could not sustain an unsubsidised publishing programme. Authors also have to compete with television, and possibly too the negative side-effects of the notion that, in any case, Māori is not a language for reading. What is available is not designed to stimulate the growth of a mass market for Māori-language print – mostly serious biographies, historical and traditional accounts, and pamphlets conscientiously produced by government agencies warning of the dangers of smoking, or advising one how to enrol as an elector. There is also a growing stack of Education Review Office reports, curriculum statements and other official documents, frequently written in a language loaded with technical neologisms which render them unintelligible to many otherwise highly literate native speakers.

Stage 4

Stage 4 sees the incorporation of the revitalising language into formal education at the elementary level, either in a partial way under outside control (type 4b schools), or as the major or sole medium in schools which also are controlled by the language community rather than by outside, 'Y-ish', authorities (type 4a). Although this dichotomy is convenient, it is hard to apply in New Zealand, where all schools, official disclaimers notwithstanding, are very firmly under state control, and where several generations of primary socialisation through the *form* of the English language (the semantic content hiding behind the form may often have been Māori) have made it possible for Māori to transform an institution, retaining English as its working language while operating within palpably Māori framework in almost every other respect. Many people do this at home every day, and they can do it equally effectively and naturally at school (given the official constraints that affect everyone).

There has been a very substantial growth in type 4a schools in the 1990s. According to the Ministry of Education's Statistical Profile for 1998, there were 27,181 Māori children and 4,886 non-Māori receiving Māori-medium education in 1997. The comparable figures for 1992 were 16,501 and 1375 respectively. These programmes were spread over a total of 472 schools, up from 318 in 1992. By 1997 there were 54 Kura Kaupapa Māori (state schools teaching almost solely through Māori and run according to Māori cultural norms), 11 other immersion schools, 86 bilingual schools, 115 immersion classes, and 220 bilingual classes. The points of growth had been in the 'bilingual' schools and kura kaupapa Māori – which had numbered 20 and 8 (mostly private) schools respectively in 1989. However, while the definition of 'immersion' education was fairly strict (at least 20 hours a week, i.e.

80% of the school's teaching hours), 'bilingual' education included everything between 3 and 19 hours instruction through Māori. By 1997, 9654 children were receiving immersion education (as defined above), just over
twice as many as in 1992, and 10,405 were receiving between 12 and 30%,
more than treble the 1992 figure. The middle group (just over 12,000 children) receiving 30–80% of their education through Māori had grown more
slowly (from just under 10,000 five years before). Overall, this meant that
about 19% of Māori children were receiving a part (sometimes quite a small
part) of their education through Māori by 1997, as were just under 1% of
non-Māori. In addition, over 55,000 children (25,528 Māori and 29,871 non-
Māori) were studying Māori language as a subject in elementary school for
a minimum of three hours a week. This meant that just over a third of Māori
children were spending three hours or more a week learning in or about the
Māori language by 1997. It should be noted that there were more children
engaged in learning through Māori in 1996, and the 1998 figures had not
been released when this chapter was written, so although there is a strong
overall upward movement between 1992 and 1997, a plateau could also
have been reached. The Ministry of Education's report (1998) makes this
comment:

> There was a 2% decrease in the numbers of schools offering Māori
> medium education, and a 4% decrease in the number of student
> enrolments between 1996 and 1997. However, there was an 11%
> increase in the numbers of students enrolled in schools with a total or
> near total immersion in Māori over the same period. The more favor-
> able funding policy for high levels of immersion was likely to have
> been a causal factor here.

Mention has been made of Kura Kaupapa Māori, the 'Māori agenda'
schools referred to also in RLS. The founders of the original Kura Kaupapa
Māori formed themselves into a very powerful lobby group in 1989, the
year when a major restructuring of the education system took place, and
secured statutory recognition for their then private or unofficial schools as
a special category of state school. The government shortly afterwards
agreed to allow five new Kura to be established each year, either as new
schools, or through the re-designation of existing schools. One of the tenets
of the movement was adherence to a philosophical statement known as *Te
Aho Matua* (literally 'the first thread', i.e. the statement of fundamental
principles underlying Māori thought and action). By the mid-1990s, the
Ministry of Education had agreed to consult the Rūnanga (council) to
which the majority of the Kura belonged before approving new ones, and
also included acceptance of Te Aho Matua as a pre-condition for being

given state recognition. This move was disputed by some schools and communities, and indeed one of the first and largest of the Kura refused to formally subscribe to the statement and left the Rūnanga. In 1998, at the request of the Rūnanga, a Bill to amend the Education Act was presented to the House of Representatives seeking among other things to amend the principal Act by inserting a requirement that to be designated a Kura Kaupapa Māori a school must be one that 'operates in accordance with Te Aho Matua (as defined in section 155A)', and specifying that:

> Te Aho Matua is a statement that sets out an approach to teaching and learning that applies to Kura Kaupapa Māori … (s. 155A (1))
> Te Kaitiaki o Te Aho Matua ['the Guardian of Te Aho Matua'] is the body identified by the Minister of Māori Affairs as being the most suitable to be responsible for determining the content of Te Aho Matua, and for ensuring that it is not changed to the detriment of Māori. (s.155B (1))

The Bill received enthusiastic endorsement from many politicians, convinced that this regulation was 'what Māori wanted', but at the Select Committee stage they learned that it was not what all Māori wanted. It remains to be seen whether what were originally independent schools will come under the ideological control of an organising group chosen by the state to represent and enforce a legislatively defined 'Māori' world view.

Disputes about Te Aho Matua aside, type 4a education is much better established than it was in 1989, although very far from universal and with as yet unknown effects on supporting or being a catalyst for the consolidation of Stage 6. Again, as with so much in Māori education and language policy in New Zealand, form is one thing, content may be something else. Many Kura Kaupapa Māori are small (under 50, sometimes less than 20 students), ill-equipped, lacking stable staffing, unable to recruit trained teachers, adversely affected by internal disputes, and sometimes without teachers who have sufficient knowledge of Māori to teach effectively through the language. Even when the staff are competent and the curriculum is well-handled, there is always the possibility that the strain of having to receive all their schooling through a second language which is not well-supported outside the school will eventually produce a negative reaction among children. Parents sometimes report that their children have become 'fed up' with Māori after a few years of immersion education and have had to be transferred to an English-medium school; teachers at one Kura Kaupapa Māori reported to us that they had noticed Māori was used much less in the playground once the school changed from a bilingual to a 'total immersion' programme. They put this down to the fact that the children had to have a release once they got out of the classroom because not being allowed to use English was so stressful and difficult for many of them.

There has been a rapid expansion in the number of type 4b schools and programmes, some of which are substantial enough to constitute genuine dual medium approaches, mid-way between types 4a and 4b, but others would be token programmes linguistically, although some of the latter would be palpably Māori in most other respects. In RLS, it was noted that all too often this 'taha Māori' approach lacks 'real life, real results, real societal input when measured from the point of view of the urgent RLS needs of a severely weakened language and culture' (p. 243). Grin and Vaillancourt in their report to the NZ Treasury on language revitalisation policy suggested that the apparent waste of resources on type 4b schooling might be addressed by:

> *in the short run,* giving preference for enrolment in Māori-medium education to Māori and increasing their supply by shifting teachers to these schools. This may require temporarily reducing the teaching of Māori to Pakeha to zero. (1998: 215, emphasis in original)

However, teachers cannot be moved around like pawns on a chess board in a democratic country, and even if they could, simply having a Māori teacher, even a Māori-speaking teacher in front of a class is not going to guarantee either excellence in Māori-medium education, nor acceptance by the community (the Boards of Trustees of some community schools would still prefer an unqualified teacher from their own tribal group to a better-qualified outsider). Furthermore, despite their short-term uselessness in terms of ensuring a language shift of the kind necessary for Stage 6 success, many of these programmes have had a real and lasting effect on getting Māori language accepted as something normal, interesting, and even learning well when the opportunity arises. Of course, they may also lull people into a sense of complacency, and are very useful to the Ministry of Education as an easy way of boosting the Māori language learning statistics. The real impact in support of RLS has undoubtedly been made by the best Kura Kaupapa Māori (official and otherwise) and dual medium programmes. But in relation to immersion programmes generally, it is asking too much of many parents to choose small, ill-equipped schools staffed by untrained and / or a succession of short-term teachers, even if it is type 4b, when a type 4a or even a well-run English-medium school is just around the corner. That many parents still do choose an immersion programme in such circumstances is a tribute to their stubborn resolve, and an indication of the desperate state of the revitalisation process.

Joshua Fishman commented that 'as long as Māori parents themselves are neither Māori-speaking nor RLS-conscious … there is no certainty that they will prefer type 4a schools to the type 4b schools which are much more plentiful and much less Māori-focused' (RLS: 241). In fact, Māori parents when asked to choose in the abstract often prefer Māori-focused dual-medium schools. Very many parents are RLS conscious, but, with an eye on their children's future, and knowing what has happened to them as a result of an inadequate education, would still opt for English-medium education if monolingual schooling in Māori were the only alternative. Furthermore, there is at present no guarantee that even type 4a schools can escape sufficiently from the 'Y-controlled' regulatory framework to transmit the 'language-in-culture' to the satisfaction of those who have been raised in more traditional backgrounds. One member of the Māori Education Commission notes that 'Most people learning the Māori language in the schools … speak the same type of language, no matter whether they are non-Māori or Māori. … The ethos of the culture is being lost' (Pere, 1999: 9).

Māori focus within an English linguistic milieu, in the formation of 'Xmen through Y-ish', is the life experience of many Māori. In the 1995 Māori language survey, only 13% overall agreed with the statement that 'you have to speak Māori to be a real Māori' (with practically none in the under–25 age group, and little difference between speakers and non-speakers), while 82% disagreed (TPK, 1998: 57–9). Something more even than the 'language-in-culture' will be needed to convince the mass of people that the effort to become fluent in Māori is worth making – by sending their children to Māori-medium schools, many are hoping that for the next generation making such a decision will be easier.

Stage 3

For Māori, the discussion of Stages 3, 2 and 1 in RLS was combined, 'because they generally constitute no more than gleams in the eyes of a few stubborn idealists rather than any substantial reality or genuine RLS opportunity' (p. 243). We will separate them in this account because the gleams are stronger and the RLS opportunities vary in potentiality from one stage to another.

Stage 3 covers the 'lower work sphere' involving inter-communal trans-actions, and is still almost entirely an English domain. This is almost as true of the intra-Māori work sphere (which is part of Stage 6 and will be alluded to again below) as it is of the mixed one (in which most employed Māori are located). The 1995 survey indicated that while the majority (59%) of the 44% of Māori-speakers who were in paid employment spoke Māori occasionally in that domain, only 11% spoke Māori 'most or all of the time', with another 11% speaking Māori 'about half the time' (TPK, 1998: 51). Opportunities to use Māori at work thus appear to be very similar overall now to the situation in the 1970s, when 57% of fluent speakers reported using Māori at least occasionally to fellow-workers, and 62% when talking with clients. This 'holding the line' probably represents a net gain since the publication of RLS, but the toehold remains precarious.

It remains the case that the Māori Trust Boards and land incorporations have done little or nothing to create *Māori-speaking* employment opportunities for the Māori *masses*. The mass employment opportunities which have been created have been mainly in areas such as hotels and other tourism-related businesses, and, on a smaller scale, in fisheries, forestry and farming. Since a majority of the beneficiaries of these trusts do not speak Māori, it would be difficult for them to discriminate in favour of Māori-speakers where this is not clearly justified by the work involved. In any case, the investment policy of the wealthier trusts generally follows that enunciated by the Waikato Raupatu Lands Trust:

> The subsidiary companies were set up to separate the governance functions from commercial activities. *The subsidiaries' role is to make money.*
>
> Funds made available by the corporates to date are coming back to tribal members through marae, education, sports and cultural grants. (TMTB, 1998: 8, emphasis added)

The grants do include support for kōhanga reo, but RLS is not a top priority for this or any other Māori corporate giant. Interventions at the compulsory education level are not generally supported financially by these tribal agencies, however, because it is felt very strongly that this is a state responsibility, which under the Treaty of Waitangi includes nurturing the Māori language, and tribal resources should not be used to subsidise state functions. If it could be shown that RLS would increase the tribes' *monetary* wealth, the attitude would be different. So far, the evidence for this is lacking.

We have not heard of anyone being sacked in recent years for speaking Māori at work, and there are locations (e.g. for service workers in some universities, or road gangs) where speaking Māori at work would be normal, or even encouraged, so this aspect of 'safety at work' is not particularly problematic. However, as only a minority even of *Māori* workers and customers are capable of sustaining a conversation in Māori, the balance is still tilted towards English in the lower work sphere as much in 1999 as it was in 1989.

Stage 2

Stage 2 embraces language in the lower governmental services and mass media – 'local, community based, influenced and influencing' – but excludes the higher spheres of either. Māori was supported better at this stage than at Stage 3 in 1989, and further advances appear to have been made in the decade following. By the end of 1998, for example, the Cabinet had approved in principle a set of guidelines to assist public service depart- ments to implement the government's Māori language policies, plans and practices. These included an admonition to departments to ensure that all staff had a 'basic knowledge' of Māori. An example of what might be regarded as basic would, however, allay the anxiety of anyone worried about the possibility of a massive shift to Māori as the lingua franca of the public service: 'all staff will be able to pronounce Māori place names and other words correctly, will know the sound values for the alphabet used in Māori and will know and be able to use as appropriate simple greetings'. There is a lot of attention directed towards form (bilingual signage and stationery and so on, but there are also provisions for creating special posi- tions which require communicative abilities in Māori, and for additional remuneration for appointees with this skill. Furthermore, many govern- ment offices have made Māori language tuition above the 'basic' level available to their employees, and, possibly better focused towards RLS at Stage 6, Māori is taught and often enthusiastically learned by inmates in many prisons.

In fact, in the public sector, job opportunities for Māori-speakers at this level are good, and have increased rapidly throughout the decade. Ability to speak Māori to a high level is often listed as a desirable quality for government employees, even when it is not essential. However, there is no guarantee that holders of such positions will have the opportunity to use the language regularly for ordinary communicative purposes. Exceptions would be some social workers, and Education Review Office officials who are responsible for auditing kōhanga reo and immersion programmes – not only do they have to deal with Māori-speaking school staff members, but their official reports are written in Māori, with only a brief summary appended in English. However, the continued closure, sale, downsizing or corporatisation of state agencies means that the scope of directives of this kind is increasingly limited in range, and the overall impact on RLS has yet to be ascertained.

In broadcasting, the potential to make a positive impact on RLS has been greater, both in relation to the broadcasters themselves (who, if broad- casting through Māori, have enhanced opportunities both for interaction with other speakers and for developing their personal communicative competence and confidence), and to their audience of mature and developing speakers. The area of consolidation has been radio broadcasting, where government funding has enabled 22 local (mostly tribally based) radio stations to eke out a fairly miserable existence. The amount of state funding is dependent on the number of hours devoted to Māori-language broadcasting per week, but it is insufficient to meet the costs involved – most stations rely on volunteer staff and fund-raising in order to survive. This latter feature does make them more like neighbourhood associations of the Stage 6 type. They do support RLS in a tangible manner, by communicating with their grassroots listeners in local talk shows, broadcasting world and local news in a manner reminiscent of the Māori newspapers of the turn of the previous century. They also supply a Māori-speaking work environment straddling Stages 3 and 2. Furthermore, they contribute to the natural development of a communicative standard Māori, by providing opportunities through networking for speakers of various dialects to communicate regularly and meaningfully with each other.

Apart from a disastrous experiment with a channel in Auckland in 1996–97, which produced some very good programmes for a very small fraction of the possible audience (it was allocated a frequency outside the range of most television sets), Māori is seldom heard on local, let alone national, television. We have argued here and elsewhere (see above, also Benton, 1991) that Māori-language television is essential to the survival of the language *while television retains such a significant place in family life*. If people would turn off their television sets, the channel would not be needed. Be that as it may, television in New Zealand promotes language shift away from Māori, rather than helping to reverse it. In the print media at the local level, there is also little to promote RLS. Some local papers have a paragraph or two of editorial in Māori, and a few locally-based Māori papers have more, but nothing remotely comparable to what is available through English for the same potential readership.

On balance, one could say that the changes at Stage 2 appearing to support RLS have been largely cosmetic, although local Māori radio stations have almost certainly fed back positively into what RLS developments there may have been at Stage 6.

Stage 1

Stage 1 in RLS, the prelude to success if built on solid foundations at each of the lower levels, is characterised by some use of the language in the higher educational level, and higher government, occupational and media efforts. Māori has made some inroads at this level. For example, at the

University of Waikato it is possible to obtain a Bachelors degree entirely through the medium of Māori (several dozen students have graduated through this programme over the last few years), and to write a Masters or Doctoral thesis in Māori (again, these options have been and are being exercised). Furthermore, students in any course are permitted to write essays and examination answers in Māori (which the university translates into English if a suitably qualified Māori-speaking examiner is not available). Many subjects in the Māori Department are available only through the medium of Māori. However, in an effort to attract more students to bolster a falling roll, this department has recently decided to offer English-medium versions of some of these courses.

In the higher levels of government, Māori has ceremonial functions, but this does not keep large numbers of Māori-speakers employed or speaking Māori. At least one influential Māori organisation (the Waikato Raupatu Lands Trust) plans to require all its employees to be fluent Māori-speakers, and has instituted compulsory Māori-language classes to achieve this goal. However, such a policy, like that of government agencies employing Māori-speakers, may not necessarily be followed by RLS at home. National television has miniscule amounts of Māori-medium transmission on only one channel. National public radio has been broadcasting news and commentaries in Māori since World War II, in recent years several times a day at peak listening periods. However, in May 1999 the government funding agency decided that these broadcasts were 'not cost-effective', and that they should cease from 1 July. The Chief Executive of the funding agency, commenting on the decision, commented that 'There are probably better ways by which RNZ can contribute to the revitalisation of the Māori language, such as programmes in English that create positive and accurate beliefs about the Māori language, and profiling Māori language events and music' (*The Dominion* 12 May 1999, p. 9). The 'normalisation' function which they fulfilled seems to have been discounted completely.

All in all, with the partial exceptions noted above, the situation in 1999 is still marked mostly by 'symbolic flourishes' (RLS: 245) – with one of the most effective of these, the daily Māori language current affairs bulletins on national radio, about to disappear.

Stage 6 Revisited

The importance of this Stage 6 is well recognised by people working for the revitalisation of the Māori language in New Zealand, and the ideas expressed by Joshua Fishman in RLS, and especially on the importance of home and neighbourhood language use, have been studied and quoted extensively by scholars, students, activists, politicians and government officials. Studying and quoting is one thing, however, and putting ideas into practice quite another. When asked in November 1998 by an opposition member:

> ... given that the home and community are arguably the essential domains for Māori language revitalisation and maintenance, what are his current specific educational plans to address the development of Māori language within the home and community? (Hansard, 1998: 3282)

the Minister of Māori Affairs initially replied that the home and community were only one 'vital element' in revitalisation, the other being 'teaching of Māori language in all our Primary Schools'. Pushed further on this issue with additional questions in February 1999, the Minister finally announced that:

> Through the Māori Language strategy, and its Māori Language Education Plan, Government will be seeking to encourage Māori adults to learn Māori and to use it with their children of all ages. In addition, it is anticipated that Māori will develop their own Māori language learning and Māori language use schemes. (Hansard, 1999: 51)

Although the 'Māori Language Education Plan' has yet to be revealed, the government does have defined policy objectives (Te Puni Kōkiri, 1998: 65), and a strategy which only obliquely or inferentially touches on supporting the use of the language in the home and neighbourhood. The official Māori language objectives, paraphrased, are:

(1) to increase opportunities to learn Māori;
(2) to improve proficiency of people in speaking, reading, writing, and listening to Māori;
(3) increasing the number of situations where Māori can be used;
(4) increase the rate at which the language is modernised;
(5) to raise the prestige and appreciation of Māori language and Māori–English bilingualism among all New Zealanders.

The strategy through which they are to be implemented also has five points:

(1) the development and implementation of a Māori language plan;
(2) the fostering of Māori language radio and television;
(3) the supply of Māori language guidelines to government departments;

(4)   the development and implementation of Māori language corpus
      activities;
(5)   coordinated monitoring and evaluation of Māori language activities.

This strategy once more seems to concentrate on the frills, which look good
and are easily counted, than on the substance which can only be achieved
through hard work with and by communities. Séan de Fréine, in his
perceptive analysis of the Irish situation, stresses that the channels of
communication which sustain the life of a language and culture within a
community 'need to be embodied in permanent institutions and customs
whose role is thus *primarily functional*' (1965: 87, emphasis added). In this
context, the remarks in RLS about the lack of neighbourhood economic
bases for Māori (p. 237) are very important. Some attention does seem to be
given to the extra-linguistic goals of this aspect of community development
by at least one of the very large tribal confederations (Ngai Tahu), which
has also sponsored concentrated language-immersion courses for adults.
Even more work along these lines has been done by the much smaller Ngāti
Raukawa tribe at Otaki, near Wellington, which has also set up its own
higher educational institution, and supported grass-roots radio stations
and other ventures which have had language and cultural objectives linked
to the economic ones. The general trend, however, has been to join the
global economy and put financial dividends and the development of
managerial and entrepreneurial skills first (while assuming that necessary
or desirable linguistic and cultural investments can be supported through
these later).

   The Basques are *Euskaldunak* – 'speakers of the Basque language'
(Saizarbitoria, 1985: 18); Māori on the other hand are *Tāngata whenua*,
'people of the land'; the ideology of language has come to the fore after the
loss of both, but it is perhaps the land which is more important in defining
identity. Thus, to succeed, a strategy aimed at restoring 'language in
culture' may also have to include 'language with the land'. This taking
account of fundamentals, which does not need to degenerate into fundamentalism or atavism, becomes even more important with the government's plan to emphasise corpus planning to modernise the language.
Such a policy could well lead to Māori's becoming a calque of English, if the
puristic policy followed since its inception by the Māori Language
Commission is continued. This already has had a potentially disruptive
effect on Stage 6 efforts by unnecessarily widening the gap between the
official language taught through the schools and the language familiar to
older native speakers. The general approach taken by Māori since the first
contact with other languages is to appropriate the foreign word (with suit-

able phonological modifications) along with the new object or concept (thus *miere*, from French *miel*, 'honey', and so on). This has enabled the semantic integrity of indigenous Māori vocabulary to be maintained. However, the Commission has brought a Trojan horse into the semantic citadel, and in the name of protecting the purity of the language in effect hastened its colonisation. This point is well illustrated in the concluding sentences of one of the contributions to the *Mana* feature on the state of Māori:

> I still tend to use words like Hanuere for January rather than Kohitatea when I write letters, because it's more familiar to me …
> I'm not denying the place of these new words, but it's a form of Māori that I'm not comfortable with. I suppose I'll get used to it and start saying them.
> When we lose our old people who are native speakers, this form of Māori language will eventually be used more widely. This is the Māori language of the days ahead. (Kingi 1998: 36)

His discomfort is well-founded. Kohitātea is the eighth month in the Māori lunar calendar (which begins the yearly cycle with the riding of the Pleiades around the end of June), and thus (traditionally) partly coincides with January. Until the Māori Language Commission decided to replace the 'borrowed' words used to denote the Greco-Roman solar months for the previous 150 years, there was a clear conceptual difference embedded in the different lexical representations for these notions. A new generation of Māori will have to learn when Kohitātea is not Kohitātea, something their elders did not need to worry about at all.

Assessing GID

The developments in New Zealand relating to the various levels of the GIDS for Māori illustrate, we believe, both the general usefulness of the scale as a framework for assessing the degree of disruption, along with the multiple interconnectedness of the stages through both overlapping and feedback loops.

The analogy with the Richter Scale (RLS: 87) is interesting and could be developed further. The most violent earthquake at Stage 8 could have an amplitude 400,000,000 times greater than the smallest recordable tremor; the logarithmic progression of the stages, not at all inappropriately applied to the disruption that affects language transmission in cases like those discussed in RLS, is something which may easily be overlooked by readers with an arithmetical frame of mind. Thus the disruption which has

occurred when Stage 8 has been reached is almost infinitely worse than that which obtains generally when Stages 1 and 2 are all that need attention. However, just as the damage done by earthquakes varies according to distance from the epicentre and the nature of the terrain, the GIDS to be really useful must be able to take into account measurements of damage across the countryside, so to speak, rather than be linked too closely to either the least or worst-affected regions.

In the computation of the 'Total GIDS Scores' in RLS (405, table 14.4) a weighting has been allocated according to the stage at which intervention is necessary and proceeding, with Stage 6 and stages higher than those receiving attention seemingly ignored, giving, in the Māori case, a much gentler estimate of the extent of the damage to be repaired. There will, of course, be a large element of arbitrariness in any measurement of this kind, with much depending on the viewpoint, perceptiveness, and priorities of the observer. It is axiomatic in RLS, and indeed well supported by empirical evidence, that Stage 6 is the critical one; that the process of RLS (or enabling language *regeneration*, of which we will say a little more below) cannot proceed with the hope of ultimate success until this stage has been achieved. Indeed, in the economic analysis completed for the New Zealand government by Grin and Vaillancourt, seven 'status of success' conditions were identified. Of these, Avant-garde (political agitation and consciousness), and Technical effectiveness were, in their judgement, well met; Redistribution (availability of government funding) and Normalcy (public acceptance) partly met; Shadow price (the comparative cost of using Māori rather than English) and Strict preference (the degree of commitment to use the language whenever possible) mostly not met; and Individual preference hardly even attempted. This analysis both supports the contention that Stage 6 factors are the most critical, and confirms the negative rating for Māori language revitalisation at this stage in RLS. On almost any reading of the scale, Māori would still be in the zone of maximum disruption.[2]

The Vitality of Hope

Any reading of the situation in New Zealand, at the beginning or the end of the decade that saw the publication of RLS, is gloomy, but the fact that a few survivors seem to have been pulled from the rubble should at least give cause for hope. The overall assessment of one of New Zealand's pioneer Māori-speaking broadcasters, writing in the issue of *Mana* devoted to the language situation, confirms our reading of the GIDS. He offers scant comfort for the complacent, or for those who think that the icing can substitute for the cake:

... And now [the Minister of Broadcasting has] come up with his cunning plan. A government-appointed trust to run a television UHF channel that will broadcast a few hours a day of Māori language programs.

....

Māori ought to think twice on this one, though. If they go along with [the Minister's] plan, and it turns out not to be so cunning after all, they're putting more nails in the coffin of the Māori language. As our cover story indicates, it's on its death bed. (Fox, 1998)

One Māori scholar, writing about the struggles of a group of Māori parents to meet the economists' 'strict preference' and 'individual preference' conditions, while striving to build a 'Stage 6' environment for their families, points out that all living languages, whether endangered or not, are constantly re-created by those who speak them. She suggests that rather than working to 'reverse language shift', with the implication that we are travelling back to something old and by-passed, or even of 'revitalisation', with its implication of emulating the work of Dr Frankenstein (our metaphor, not hers!), we talk instead of facilitating language *regeneration* (Hohepa, 1998: 46). Such a renewal is constant and forward-looking. It is deeply rooted in the past through cultural and historical bonds which go far beyond mere sentimental attachment, providing both a secure anchorage in the present, and the sustenance and impetus for growth and development in the future. Māori-speaking families are thus heirs of the past, but not its prisoners.

The road towards RLS/revitalisation/regeneration for Māori winds its way through poorly signposted and almost certainly dangerous territory. The reasons why some may try to continue to travel this road are well rehearsed in RLS and need not be repeated here. But these reasons are ill-understood, and may not convince the 'average citizen'. The views expressed in a letter to the editor of the *Waikato Times* (in response of an attempt by a local High School principal to compel all students claiming Māori ethnicity to study Māori language) are probably representative of a significant portion of the New Zealand 'mainstream'. It was published under the heading 'Where's the link?'

Responsibility of education is to prepare children for what they will experience in a real modern world. For the life of me, I cannot see where a Māori language fits into that arena. However I have no problem with children once they have grown up, or anyone choosing to learn a Māori means of verbal communication. However the user and not the taxpayer should pay.

There is nothing about Māori culture which can't be explained adequately in any other language. To suggest, as Mr Elliott of Fraser High School does, that Māori language is the key to Māori culture, is arrogant nonsense and a typical example of the brain washing tactics, some would call subversion, being used to dupe the taxpayers of this country and to milk us to the tune of billions of dollars each year to implement and support an abhorrent apartheid regime.

Feelings, thoughts, actions, events and material things, all relate to 'culture'. Language (a completely separate issue) does nothing else but communicates the different perceptions of culture. Language certainly doesn't create or even influence culture. I challenge Mr Elliott or anyone to prove and give examples of a clear link between any culture and any language. (Gordge, 1998)

Given what we know, and the comparatively small gains for Māori, despite the hard work and sacrifice of many people in the closing decades of the 20th century, is it reasonable to continue to strive towards the regeneration of the language? George Lakoff has given us a definition of reason:

Reason is the mechanical manipulation of abstract symbols which are meaningless in themselves, but can be given meaning by virtue of their capacity to refer to things either in the actual world or in possible states of the world. (1987: 7)

And Miguel de Unamuno long before provided a response:

For living is one thing, and knowing is another; and … perhaps there is such an opposition between the two that we may say that everything vital is anti-rational, not merely irrational, and that everything rational is anti-vital. And this is the basis of the tragic sense of life. (Unamuno, 1954: 34)

It is also the hope for the future, the difference between being human and being a machine. RLS has to transcend mere rationality, lest rationality itself be transformed into an oppressive instrument for ensuring predictability and conformity.

Notes

1. The Ataarangi movement grew out of an initiative taken by a Māori writer, Katerina Mataira, and the late Ngoi Pewhairangi, supported by the NZ Council for Adult Education, to train volunteers in an approach to language teaching influenced by the work of Caleb Gaetano. The volunteers worked with families to bring the Māori language competence of the group up to a level from which it

could be used communicatively within the family and further developed independently. The movement was well-established by the end of the 1970s, and continues to support language revitalization initiatives through volunteer work and through courses organized in partnership with some educational institutions. Apart from a small seeding grant in the early stages of its operation, Te Ataarangi has received no funding from NZ government agencies and has remained a purely grassroots organization.

2. The overall placement of a language on the GID Scale could well be calculated by assessing on a percentage basis at each level the degree to which the status applied to the (potential) linguistic community as a whole, with a weighting then applied to calculate the significance of this disruption. The weighting could follow that implied in the RLS computations (i.e. level 8 counts as 8 points, level 1 as 1), and then the overall disruption summarized by the match between the assessed score and the range of scores obtained by adding the maxima for each level. So a total score of 31 on the revised 1989 scale (which is about where Māori would have been) becomes equivalent overall to Stage 8, in other words, very serious disruption indeed, despite a few ticks in some of the higher-level boxes. Such an exercise might do much to jolt out of their complacency those who think they are working for RLS, but assume a top-down approach is sufficient. To underline this still further, the weightings could be determined through the accumulation of Fibonacci numbers, which would give the complete achievement of Stages 8, 7 and 6 a possible 78% influence on the total score, as against 58% on the current RLS scale. Under such a system, Māori, alas, would still be located at Stage 8 in 1999 (as against possibly scraping in to Stage 7 on the alternative suggested), although a movement towards a higher level of security between 1989 and 1999 would be discernible.

References

Benton, R.A. (1981) *The Flight of the Amokura: Oceanic Languages and Formal Education in the South Pacific*. Wellington: NZCER.

Benton, R.A. (1991) Notes on the case for Māori language television. *New Language Planning Newsletter* 5(4), 1–4.

Benton, R.A. (1997) *The Māori Language: Dying or Reviving?* Wellington: New Zealand Council for Educational Research.

De Fréine, S. (1965) *The Great Silence*. Dublin: Foilseacháin Náisiúnta Teoranta.

Douglas, E.Te.K. (1991) Māori language nests (Kōhanga Reo) – Their impact on New Zealand communities. *Journal of Indigenous Studies* 3(1), 13–31.

Ellul, J. (1973) *Propaganda: The Formation of Men's Attitudes*. New York: Vintage Books.

Fox, D.T. (1998) A cunning plan. *Mana* 22(4).

Grin, F. and Vaillancourt, F. (1998) Language revitalisation policy: An analytical survey – theoretical framework, policy experience and application to Te Reo Māori. (Report to The Treasury, Wellington, New Zealand / Aotearoa; released under the Official Education Act).

Gordge, M. (1998) Where's the link? (Letter to the Editor). *Waikato Times*, 24 February 1998, p. 6.

Hansard (1998) *Parliamentary Debates (Hansard) House of Representatives First Session*,

Fortyfifth Parliament, 1998, Hansard Supplement 10. Wellington: New Zealand Government.

Hansard (1999) *Parliamentary Debates (Hansard) House of Representatives First Session, Fortyfifth Parliament, 1999. Hansard Supplement 11.* Wellington: New Zealand Government.

Hohepa, M.K. (1998) 'Hei Tautoko i te Reo': Māori language regeneration and whānau bookreading practices. Unpublished PhD. Thesis (Education), University of Auckland.

House of Representatives (1998) Education (Te Aho Matua) Amendment Bill. Wellington: New Zealand Government.

Kingi, M. (1998) Be strong – and let others hear. *Mana* 22(36).

Lakoff, G. (1987) *Women, Fire, and Dangerous Things: What Categories Reveal about the Mind.* Chicago: University of Chicago Press.

Literacy Task Force (1999) *Report of the Literacy Task Force.* Wellington: Ministry of Education.

Ministry of Education (1998) *Ngā Haeata Mātauranga: Annual Report 1997/8 and Strategic Direction for Māori Education 1998/99.* Wellington: Ministry of Education.

Pere, R.T.R. (1999) Te reo rangatira me ōna tikanga. *Māori Education Commission* [Newsletter] Issue 2, May 1999, 7–10.

Royal Tangaere, Arapera (1997a) Te kōhanga reo: More than just a language nest, in *Māori Keynote Addresses to the NZARE Annual Conference, 1996.* Palmerston North: NZ Association for Research in Education.

Royal Tangaere, Arapera (1997b) *Te Puawaitanga o te reo Māori: Ka hua te hä o te pōtiki I roto i te whānau: Ko tēnei te tāhuhu o te Kōhanga Reo.* Wellington: New Zealand Council for Educational Research.

Saizarbitoria, R. (1985) Author's Foreword to *100 Meter.* [Bilbao]: Basque American Foundation – Spain.

Salmond, J. (1893) *The First Principles of Jurisprudence.* London: Steven & Haynes.

Statistics New Zealand (1997a) *Census 96: National Summary.* Wellington: Statistics New Zealand.

Statistics New Zealand (1997b) *Census 96: Māori.* Wellington: Statistics New Zealand.

Suzuki, D. (1959) *An Introduction to Zen Buddhism.* London: Arrow Books.

Tainui Maaori Trust Board and Waikato Raupatu Lands Trust (1998) *He Riipoata-A-Tau 1998.* [Hopuhopu: TMTB & WRLT].

Te Puni Kōkiri/Ministry of Māori Development (TPK) [1998]. *The National Māori Language Survey/Te Mahi Rangahau Reo Māori.* (Wellington: Te Puni Kōkiri/Ministry of Māori Development).

Te Taura Whiri i te Reo/Māori Language Commission (1995) *Āe Rānei, he Taonga Tuku Iho? National Māori Language Survey 1995,* Provisional Findings. Wellington: Te Taura Whiri i te Reo & Te Puni Kōkiri.

Te Taura Whiri i te Reo/Māori Language Commission (1998) *Ko te Whānau:* Wellington: Māori Language Commission.

Unamuno, M. de (1954) *The Tragic Sense of Life.* New York: Dover Publications.

Chapter 19

From Theory to Practice (and Vice Versa): Review, Reconsideration and Reiteration

J.A. FISHMAN

Having 'read around the world', visiting both old and new cases of RLS efforts (a dozen and a half in all), the time has come both to attempt a summary of what has been learned and to consider how well RLS appears to be formulated and implemented a decade after its launching (Fishman, 1991). All of my comments below take as their points of departure the views and opinions reported by my colleagues in this volume, to whom I am most grateful for their cooperation, no matter how much I may agree or disagree with one or another of them, whether theoretically or empirically. Although I will use and explain much of the theoretical schemata initially employed in 1991, it is nevertheless the case that as a result of working on this volume 'there have been some changes made', both in detail and in general approach.[1]

Ideological Clarification

My initial stance that it was not terribly crucial for the practice of RLS to spell out its ideological foundations (the 'why?' of RLS), since those involved in RLS obviously knew why they were doing so, seems to me, in retrospect, to have assumed greater unanimity and clarity of purpose than RLSers themselves frequently evince. It still amazes me that individuals who have spent their entire adult lives (and often good chunks of their adolescent years as well) engaged in RLS efforts are, nevertheless, often uncomfortable and somewhat tongue-tied about explaining why they are involved in this way, whether to themselves or to the doubting Thomases that surround them, among Xians and among Yians alike. It is as if there were some contra-intuitive, contra-normative or irrational aspects of their own beliefs, values and behaviours that are so generally questioned by others that RLSers themselves often can't really totally free themselves of some nagging doubts about their preoccupation with their own threatened language.

Five Ideological Challenges to RLS

Monetary values, ethnocultural values and cultural democracy

RLS is concerned with the recovery, recreation and retention of *a complete way of life*, including non-linguistic as well as linguistic features. Some of the features of both kinds are solidly documented in memories, texts and realia of the near and distant past. Others are innovative extensions and inventions required in order to cope with the differences between now and then, between an interrupted past and the partly unprecedented present. All cultures and the social identities that they foster – even those of well-established and seemingly unthreatened Yian societies – are partially continuations and partially innovations relative to their own pasts. When both continuations and innovations are under local self-regulation they fuse together into a seemingly seamless authentic whole. RLS is the linguistic part of the pursuit of ethnocultural self-regulation which democracies and international bodies are increasingly recognising as a basic right for indigenous (and often also for immigrant) populations. Entry into the European Union and several other European and North Atlantic organisations for 'cooperation and security' has repeatedly been postponed for post-Soviet eastern European countries because these countries still have not worked out amicable, accepting and supportive policies with respect to their own indigenous minorities. The absence of such mutually agreed upon policies in Slovakia, Roumania and Belorus, for example, has been taken as contravening the standards that members of these organisations must attain and abide by. RLSers must realise that such organisations and their declarations, treaties and conventions are pursuing goals that are consonant with the building blocks of modern democratic societies. Rather than being in any way questionable or retrogressive, these are goals that should be pursued with heads held high.

But are these goals realistic with respect to maximising success *vis-à-vis* the material dimensions of individual and societal success? The European Union seems to think so, pointing to ultimate higher productivity (overall and in minority regions) of countries with more progressive minority policies. But the opponents of RLS efforts never tire of pointing out that most major reward systems are linked to Yish use and, indeed, Yish mastery. They claim that it is more rewarding to link local populations linguistically with the widest economic and social system to which they can gain access.

They stress that those languages are most 'useful' that yield the greatest 'social advancement' and that Xish is hardly in the running in those terms. They claim that language policies succeed when and only when they correspond to labour-market considerations. In short, Yians and Xians- via-Yish frequently persuade those advocating and using Xish that such efforts are pernicious *vis-à-vis* the economic success of their own co-ethnics. Such claims are often devastating for Xish parents who need to establish a 'Xish home-language policy' in which to raise their own children. Parents are seldom familiar with the objective economic findings on which the policies and declarations of the most modern inter-polity organisations are based and they need to be reassured that they will not be handicapping their own children by socialising them and educating them in Xish (see, e.g. Grin, 1997, 1999).

It is in such grass-roots discussions – particularly when the immediate economic potential of Xish is low – that the true complexity of Xish values and identity need to be stressed. Xians are invariably bilingual (much more so than Yians) and, therefore, in no way cut off from the economic rewards that are presumably inherent in Yish. Yish will long (and perhaps even always) be part of the education of Xish children. If only knowledge of Yish stood between Xish workers and Yish-controlled rewards, the economic well-being of the former would be much better off than it usually is. Furthermore, the economic reward dimension is not the only one that defines Xish individual and social identity (nor, for that matter, that defines Yish individual and social identity either). Societally weaker languages always need more than mere economic rationales. It is not labour-market access but economic power which is disproportionately in Yish hands and that is a problem that will rarely be overcome on linguistic grounds alone. As a result, even Xian bilingualism usually does not lead to any redistribution of economic power and, that being the case, the maintenance of Xish identity and cultural intactness becomes all the more important for community problem solving, health, education and cultural creativity. Vulgar materialism (whether Marxist or capitalist) does not begin to do justice to the nuanced and complexly interrelated human values, behaviours and identities that are essentially non-materialistic or even anti-materialistic in nature (among them being family loyalty, friendship ties, spirituality, affection and intimacy, aesthetics and the corpus of ethics that each culture expresses and continually develops). Isn't it the mark of higher cultures to have other than material values, the latter being merely the most elementary expression of individual and group needs? Do not Yians too pride themselves precisely on the non-material attainments of Yish ethnocultural life?

The 'normality' of minority language death

Another frequent ideological trap faced by RLSers is the claim that language shift is only a normal consequence of minority–majority relations and that previous generations of Xians not only accepted such shift without a murmur, but even did so gladly 'as the price of admission'. Ostensibly, then, current RLSers are just trouble-makers, disturbers of civility, by 'arousing the natives', in addition to standing in the way of the latter's material progress. On the other hand, however, Yians would probably agree that (insofar as they themselves are concerned) 'dying without a murmur' is hardly a great virtue and that those in danger of death ought, at least, to be read their 'Miranda rights', i.e. informed of the probable consequences of their actions and allowed to request the aid of a lawyer or advocate. Wouldn't at least some of those Xians, who presumably accepted language shift without a murmur, have been more reluctant to do so if they had been made aware of the fact that *there were other viable options* (X + Y bilingualism, for example), on the one hand, and that the promised rewards for language shift were by no means guaranteed? Shouldn't Xians be suspicious of a point of view that assumes that it is natural for their culture and identity to die, whereas it is not at all natural for the same to happen to Yians? Isn't 'natural' merely used to disguise a power play and to discourage resistance to it? And, finally, aren't those few who did 'murmur' (protest and attempt RLS), who denied that it was more noble and civilised for their culture to die than to live, being overlooked or even besmirched for resisting? Isn't history being rewritten *ex post facto* to favour the winners *ab initio*?

Yish is peaceful; RLS is inherently conflictual

A third Yian mainstream ploy is to bemoan the purported 'conflictual nature' of RLS. It is not the majority Yians who are conflictual (even though they punitively control and implement by far the major reins of power and of the purse) but the unequal efforts of Xians that are responsible for all trouble-making. Even the much vaunted 'no language policy' of many democracies is, in reality, an anti-minority-languages policy, because it delegitimises such languages by studiously ignoring them and, thereby, not allowing them to be placed on the agenda of supportable general values. Certainly most RLS efforts (those referred to throughout this volume as constituting Stages 8–5) are quite the opposite of confrontational in any real sense; they are inherently based upon efforts to win over public opinion by seeking support, approval and recognition, both in the Yian camp and in the Xian camp as well. Many would argue that even Stage 4 is non-confrontational since compulsory education, of whatever kind, must still meet all of the requirements of the Yian authorities. Stages 3–1 are equally non-confrontational if pursued via the normal democratic political processes of compromise, bargaining and coalition building. Isn't the accusation against RLSers of 'fostering conflict and confrontation' a case of 'the pot calling the kettle black'? In almost all cases the power at the disposition of RLSers is puny indeed in comparison with the power directed against them that they must overcome. Isn't the confounding of political and physical struggle a Yian demagogic rather than a democratic tactic? Isn't even the expression 'political struggle' merely a metaphor which includes the entire political process, including compromise, coalition building, bargaining, the right to petition and organise, etc., etc.? And isn't a political struggle the best guarantee that no physical struggle will obtain? Is it really wise to leave RLSers with only a 'damned if you do, damned if you don't' Hobson's choice?

Your nationalism is worse than mine!

The relationship between RLS-efforts and other types of organised minority ethnonational efforts is a fourth phenomenon that troubles some Yian ideological critics. It is undoubtedly true that such a relationship often obtains. Just as nationalism is ethnicity rendered conscious and mobilised, so RLS is language maintenance rendered conscious and mobilised. RLS depends on eliciting and activating the ethnocultural sympathies, conscious identities and overt loyalties of a threatened language's traditionally associated ethnocultural population. Local/regional ethnocultural movements exist peacefully within most (if not actually all) democratic polities of the world. If not permitted to function peacefully, they have no option but to function clandestinely, but function they must, because they are an expression of an important part of the identity and of the problem solving potential of their supporters. Do they constitute a potential for 'trouble' for Yians and their authorities? Only if oppressed. In an increasingly global society such oppression makes even less sense than heretofore, since even the already recognised political boundaries are increasingly meaningless for the purposes of directing or conducting the major econotechnical, commercial and communicational processes that are at the very heart of globalisation. However, the coming of globalisation in certain aspects of human functioning makes 'localisation' even more important in modern part-identity, equally so for state-nation, nation-state and sub-state populations (RLS being of particular relevance for the latter).

One language per country is enough (particularly if it is my language in my country)

The disingenuous nature of the Yian attack on 'RLS-efforts as an expression of Xish ethnicity' is evident in a fifth Yian ideological position that 'one language per country is enough' (Myhill, 1999; Edwards, 1994). Cynically claiming that Yians have as much right to 'a place of their own' as do Xians, they champion territoriality as the basis of Yian language policy, returning the moral level of the discussion to the level of 19th century imperialisms. There are only c. 200 polities in the world today and some 4000 to 6000 languages. Carrying the above outlandish view to its logical conclusion would be tantamount to consigning thousands of languages to extinction or suicide, on the one hand, or to that very same endless territorial subdivision of the world of which Yians frequently and falsely accuse minority ethnocultural activists. There is no need for such either/or scenarios, just as there is no need to choose between the territorial and the ethno-identity (or personality) principle of human aggregation. These are both false Cartesian dichotomies imposed upon phenomena that are in reality hierarchical co-occurrences. Just as there is no mind–body dichotomy, so minorities are well accustomed to both an ethnic and a civil (territorial) identity and it is high time that Yians accepted the true complexity of their own identificational potential, particularly as the world of globalisation engulfs them just as surely as it will engulf the Xians. To expect Xians to give up Xish merely because they are living in Yland, is tantamount to expecting Yians to give up Yish just because they are living in a world increasingly dominated by Anglophone technological-economic-military power.

It is ludicrous for Yians to appeal for sympathy with their 'agony' on being faced by ethnolinguistic minorities in their midst. Are Yians, therefore, unable to socialise their own children into their traditional ethnolinguistic cultures? Are they unable, therefore, to manage their own ethnocultural affairs, to support their own educational, governmental and mass-media institutions as well as foster their own economic viability? To equate the dangers to Yish exclusive territorial and institutional *domination* to the dangers to Xish cultural *existence* is to evince a moral blindspot of disconcerting proportions. It is but one more example of the truism that ethnolinguistic democracy is denied downward in the power hierarchy but appealed for (and struggled for) upward in the power hierarchy. It is yet another example of Yians wanting to have it both ways, i.e. to dominate those hierarchically below them, without being dominated by those hierarchically above them, in a world in which they themselves have much more power than do Xians.

The above five ideological criticisms of RLS activities require constant orientational efforts, both within Xian circles as well as in explaining Xian aspirations for ethnocultural self-perpetuation to Yians. RLSers need feel no embarrassment in opposing the above charges because they are not only baseless and self-serving, but they are also fed by impoverished and impoverishing views of the true richness of the human personality, of human identificational processes and of the growing search for meaningfulness in post-modern global society. The struggle for RLS is a struggle for a more humane humanity all over the world and, yes, it is ultimately a struggle on behalf of Yians too! In today's world, with its growing multicultural emphases, with its march toward civil nationalism in state-nations and in nation-states alike, with its growing 'terralingual' environmentalism (in which the protection of ethnolinguistic diversity is viewed as literally part and parcel of environmental protection of all other natural resources), there should be less and less need for RLSers to explain themselves, let alone defend themselves, in their efforts which can ultimately benefit us all.

Ideological Supports for RLS

We are the only ones on whom Xish can count for support

Hungary and Finland are two European polities with a joint myth: that they are 'orphans' in Europe and that the very future of their language, culture and people, therefore, rests entirely on their own shoulders. No one else will come to their assistance because they have no 'family' relationship with any others. Quebec too has made much of this line of support. It is 'the only possible champion of French on the entire American continent' (setting aside French Guiana, the francophone Caribbean islands and St Pierre and Miquelon as too insignificant to count in the struggle with such giants as English and Spanish). But this moving argument, a justification for special efforts because of special responsibilities, is one that many can utilise. Not only is Spain the only possible defender of Spanish in Europe, but so is Galicia the only possible defender of Gallego. Not only is Israel the only possible political entity in the entire world that might defend Hebrew, but so is Malta with respect to Maltese. Indeed, this argument lays bare the constantly surprising fact that even apparently mighty nations and languages often are self-declared weaklings in need of urgent self-protective measures. French in France is deathly afraid of the worldwide (and particularly the European and most particularly the entertainment-media and econotechnical) power of English and does not blush to claim the right of self-protection at every turn. But this is obviously an argument of special relationship, affection and responsibility which applies many-fold more – or at least equally – to most 'really' threatened languages the world over.

Coupled with the admonition that modern polities cannot really be monolingual anyway, and that in a multicultural stance they can better attract and hold the loyalties of all of their citizens of varying ethnicities, the special responsibility of Xians for Xish seems eminently reasonable and even more urgent. If the defenders of English in the USA feel threatened by Spanish, what should the defenders of Navaho feel *vis-à-vis* English? Sweden is a perfect example of the balance between Yish recognition of Xish minorities and the self-defence that Yish advocates are also entitled to. Having recognised five minority languages as co-official languages of Sweden (among them Finnish, a regional variety of Finnish, Eskimo, Romani and Yiddish) by virtue of their having been used there continuously for several centuries, Sweden has also adopted special measures for the 'overarching goal' of cultivation and support of Swedish (Jernudd, 1999). Indeed, no one (neither Xians nor Yians) feels safe when not in control of their own cultural boundaries and cultural functions. This is a feeling that Xians and Yians can both recognise and on behalf of which that they can hopefully work together via the democratic processes of compromise and mutual accommodation. The European Union's 'Bureau of Lesser Used Languages' and various of its treaties, charters and conventions have established the significance of such languages for the unity and the progress of Europe, in addition to the numerous state languages (potentially 30 to 50 in number) and the 11 official languages of the Union itself. Certainly this is an ideological precedent that RLSers can and should broadcast, both within Europe and elsewhere as well.

Community and 'virtual community' are not the same thing at all as far as intergenerational mother tongue transmission are concerned

The alacrity with which some RLSers have turned to bringing out their own language-encoded versions of Windows 2000, lends a special urgency to the realisation that intergenerational mother tongue transmission depends on the existence of *real community* rather than its 'virtual' pale shadow. Indeed, although cyber-space can be put to use for RLS purposes, neither computer programmes, e-mail, search engines, the web as a whole, chat boxes nor anything directly related to any or all of them can substitute for face-to-face interaction with *real family imbedded in real community*. Ultimately, nothing is as crucial for basic RLS success as intergenerational mother-tongue transmission. *Gemeinschaft* (the intimate community whose members are related to one another via bonds of kinship, affection and communality of interest and purpose) is *the real secret weapon of RLS*. This may seem like a puny and archaic weapon in competition with globalisation, which threatens not only minority languages but even much of worldwide Yish capacity to maintain resources, decision making and even many of the institutions of socialisation (such as the school) in the hands of local languages and cultures. Globalisation itself is built around controls and connections that make it possible for the major players to shift jobs, cultures, environmental problems and labor standards back and forth. The basic problem of RLS is the problem of how Xish can possibly eke out a safe-harbour for itself in the face of such unprecedented competition.

The answer is that RLS need not be in opposition to globalisation *per se*; it can function as an addition to and as a welcome alternative to complete globalisation and can be orthogonal to it. Modern humanity desperately needs to restrict or compartmentalise-off certain of its most human processes from contamination by globalisation. The family is not a business and is not 'operated efficiently' so as to show a 'bottom line' profit. Neither is friendship, childhood socialisation and enculturation, neighbourliness or community mindedness and community participation in religious, educational, entertainment, 'hobbying' activities or acts of comforting and assisting the sick, poor and bereaved. These go on wherever communities insist upon and contribute to retaining a realm of existence which is not governed by office and business affairs. They are powerful shields against alienation and their power resides exactly in the fact that they can be kept unrelated to and uncompetitive with the massive *Gesselschaft* with which they co-exist. Their weakness is their strength, their unimportance from a purely dollars and cents perspective is their importance for our sanity and privacy in the midst of myriad urban, modern, global intrusions into our lives.

Although most RLS movements are urban in location and in the economic processes in which their supporters are engaged, they are rural and religious in metaphor and in myth and, therefore, they strike a bargain with urban hyperconnectedness, compartmentalising it off from the realms of intimacy and ethnocultural identity. RLS movements seek linkages to histories, cultures and identities that predate globalisation and that smack of eternal verities that are substantially outside the orbit of globalisation. The hunger for ethnocultural roots and for more traditional religious affiliation, unrelated as the two may be, are notable precisely in the populations most impacted by the pace of globalisation. RLS promises greater self-regulation of one's home, family, neighbourhood and community, on the one hand, and of one's own history and culture, on the other hand. It is a promise that appeals to all those who realise that notwithstanding all of the much-touted benefits of globalisation, the world is all too much with us and in us. Many also long for a corner in which they can be their intergenerational selves and be with others of that same longing too, and that is the RLS corner in which their own traditionally interpreted language, customs, beliefs, holidays, stories, foods and sanctities can continue to prevail. Many Yians long for this too and that longing should be tapped in soliciting Yian sympathy, understanding and even assistance in conjunction with the far greater Xian plight.

On Remaking, Rethinking and Generalising from Local History

Like the post-60s ethnic revival as a whole, RLS was not supposed to happen. However, not only has it happened, but some of the very processes of globalisation and post-modernism that were supposed to be most dele- terious to purportedly 'parochial' identities have actually contributed most to their re-emergence as 'part-identities'. The increasing ubiquity of the civil state, of civil nationalism and, therefore, of a shared supra-ethnic civil nationalism as part of the identity constellation of all citizens, has resulted in more rather than less recognition of multiculturalism at the institutional level and a more widespread implementation of local ethnicity as a coun- terbalance to civil nationalism at the level of organised part-identity. The result is a growing recognition of the need to rethink the history of the Yish- controlled state in terms of 'one country, many cultures'.

The Latvian government recently revised its originally anti-Russian 'Lat- vian Only' language policy (Ozolins, 1999) not so much to curry favour with Russia as to curry favour with the Council of Europe, the European Union, the Organisation for Security and Cooperation in Europe and Nato, all of which require 'conformity with international norms *vis-à-vis* minorities' in their member states (as well as in states that seek to be considered for membership). The Israeli premier Ehud Barak, in his 1999 post-election victory speech, extended 'a warm and firm hand to the secular, religious, ultra-Orthodox settlers, Sephardim and Ashkenazim, Ethiopian and Rus- sian immigrants, Arabs, Druze, Circassians and the Bedouins [because] all are part of the Israeli people'. What a revision of history, when an ethnonational state (a state that originally viewed itself as created by and for one people) comes to view itself as a civil state which belongs to all its citi- zens, of whatever ethnicity, all of them entitled to retain their respective ethnicities as part of their total identities! Indeed, Yians too are merely another local minority when viewed in global perspective, particularly if they seek to be recognised by the international community of nations. To attain such recognition and acceptance 'from above', they need to implement justice for those whom they rule. Thus does globalisation itself foster 'localisation' in its wake. The removal of trade-walls makes bilingualism an asset rather than a debit and a more rather than a less valuable individual and collective attribute. How can all of this be explained, and how does RLS fit into any explanation that is parsimoniously satisfying and predictively useful?

Of course, both vulgar Marxism and vulgar historicism immediately come to the fore. If even Cicero realised that local identities tend to be reinterpreted in the direction of the greatest possible rewards (Roman roads, Roman commerce, Roman peace), then it should come as no surprise that some latter-day thinkers have also concluded that economics may be the strongest force influencing the fate of endangered communities. But it is too late for a fruitful replay of the 19th century Marx/Weber debate, in which the latter held that culture helped fashion economic reality every bit as much as the latter contributed to the former. The exact borders separating the two (culture and economics) are not that clear at any rate, given that there are no cultures without their own economic processes and that there are no economic processes that are not culturally imbedded. One thing we can be sure of, however, is that RLS becomes necessary because of extra-economic considerations as well and that an effective programme of RLS involves a plan as to how to focus resources rather than merely the extent of the programme's economic wherewithal *per se*. Vulgar Marxism and economic determinism merely leave RLSers empty and hopeless, for, under most foreseeable circumstances they will possess markedly fewer resources than will their opponents. The basic RLS question is, therefore, how best to use the scarce resources at the command of RLSers, rather than to call a moratorium on RLS until such time as more 'nearly competitive' resources are at hand.

Another danger is to arrive at conclusions with respect to RLS desiderata by overemphasising a particular (but limited) pool of historical experience. Most RLS theories and efforts are byproducts of European indigenous minority problems. Certainly, however, such problems cannot be the only ones from which a general (and all-inclusive) RLS theory should be derived. On the other hand, only the local circumstances of any particular case can fully account for that case (but for no other case). Both of these risks are well illustrated in the papers that constitute the bulk of this volume. The indigenous minority cases do not, however, speak to the immigrant cases and the latter rarely speak to the former. The fortunes of immigrant languages are substantially influenced by 'home country' events, most prominent among them the relationships between the 'home country' and the 'host country'. The ease (cost and frequency) with which immigrants can revisit the home country, economic cycles in both places and the extent to which they are in tandem or unrelated, the degree or similarity between 'old' and 'new' immigrant cohorts (enabling or disabling them insofar as united ethnocultural efforts are concerned), the presence or absence of co-linguals from different countries of origin, are other important considerations that are particularly relevant to immigrant languages but far less so, if at all, for indigenous ethnolinguistic groups.

Obviously, all of the above considerations, pertinent though they may be for the future of Spanish in the USA (currently a touchy topic for many adherents and opponents of RLS among American linguistic minorities), are not relevant – unless reconceptualised in much more general terms – for indigenous (aboriginal) minorities in the USA or elsewhere of the very kinds that Terralingua (Note 2, Preface) is most concerned about. Obviously, the outcome of RLS efforts in any particular case are overdetermined by that case's own particular historical dynamics; but to convert that history into a general theory (or into a substitute for general theory) is to engage in vulgar historicism. Certainly, the specifics of any case must be taken into consideration in all local action, but general theory must rise above such specifics, just as the specifics themselves, important though they may be, must be seen as merely exceptional addenda and refinements for the general theory. Examples of such specifics are the mobilising impact of 'language insult' suffered by Xish in Yland, the 'adrenalin-like' impact of the annual speaking-singing-listening convention of Xish-speakers in Zland, and the certainty that a single Yian living for many months with one of the last, aging speakers of Xish will then give the language a new lease on societal life among Xians-via-Yish; these are other examples of 'good things to do' that can only naively be recommended as sufficient for general theory or for general application elsewhere. Local description is a very delicate and indispensable intellectual tool, but it is not the same as, nor does it necessarily even contribute to general theory or general practice, any more than clinical practice necessarily leads to a generalised understanding of health and disease (although it is essential for arriving at such).

Desiderata for a Value-based General Theory of RLS

I have sometimes been asked why RLS is so little related to the general theory of social change. My first answer has been that RLS recognises democratic responsibility for cultural self-determination by minorities, whereas social change theory has ignored any moral responsibility toward those who suffer as a result of social change. My second answer has been that social change theory views modernisation as an inevitable universal and ubiquitous process that pertains to all of culture, whereas RLS attempts to differentiate between faster and slower moving sectors of change and to foster greater self-regulation of the latter for the purposes of language-and-identity retention. Both of these differences are important for a general theory of RLS. RLS is applied to individual cases of threatened languages on the basis of a general theory derived from an examination of many diversified individual cases (immigration, conquest, exile, genocide, commercial domination, spread of innovation and superior knowledge, etc.). Individual cases, like clinical medicine, often require adjustments and modifications of the general theory so that it can apply to all cases rather than just to one or more specific individual ones.

A Value-based General Theory

Although RLS is firmly grounded in democratic processes, it neverthe-less recognises that simple 'majority rule' does not in and of itself satisfy important requirements for the existence of a just and good society. It utilises and espouses advocacy and self-reliance on behalf of neglected, overlooked or even demeaned minorities as its two chief means of bringing about needed changes to which the majority is generally oblivious or outright unsympathetic. Rank and file minority members too, taking their cue from the majority, may also be silent with respect to their cultural misfortunes. RLS-efforts seek to make both Xians and Yians more conscious and more knowledgeable about all that is lost, individually and collectively, when a culture's traditionally associated language is lost. On the one hand, it criticises the implicit Yish view that Xish is of little value. On the other hand, it offers leadership and advice *vis-à-vis* fostering Xish. The RLS movement realises that ideological clarification with respect to the importance of RLS and cultural self-management is also not enough and that cultural democracy must be actively promoted and implemented as well. Justice, cooperation, compassion, self-reliance and cultural democ-racy are espoused as interrelated avenues toward cultural empowerment of the powerless who may have come to take Yish control as natural and inevitable. Many of the above-mentioned features of RLS are similar to other modern movements on behalf of greater distributive justice, e.g. unionism, feminism and cooperativism. Like them, RLS also aspires to acti-vate educators, the helping professions and researchers, not to mention ordinary members of the Xish community, on behalf of transforming those segments and institutions of their society whose contributions are essential if greater justice for all is finally to be attained and if biases, hopelessness and ignorance in connection with Xish are to be overcome.

A General Theory with Applied Implications

RLS theory seeks to be directive or implicational *vis-à-vis* social action, rather than merely descriptive or analytic of the sociocultural scene. It steers clear of shibboleths, such as leaving 'it' to the government, or to the schools, or to symbolic and formulaic insertions of Xish on web-sites, or e-mail in Xish as substitutes for home, family, neighbourhood, community based face-to-face language use *per se*. Prescribing more 'institutions, positive attitudes or prestige and active speakers' for a threatened language is no better than giving a patient a peptalk, urging him/her to 'get a good grip on yourself'. Stressing the importance of the 'social meaning' of Xish even in unprotected environments leaves activists totally at sea as to where in real life to start, given different degrees of erosion in different community settings and unprotected environments. Certainly, situational switching into Xish for the attainment of traditional 'social meaning' cannot long continue after massive language shift has galloped along for any appreciable number of years. Similarly, 'festivities of social meaning' are notoriously weak as effective social forces for engendering normal, daily language use.

Attitudinal advice is easy to give but hard to implement. Furthermore, starting as far back as the 1940s, Einar Haugen noted that attitudes toward threatened languages seem to improve quite noticeably toward the very end, when their imminent demise is already quite evident. The Irish case also is a good example of how attitudes and use can be quite unrelated to one another. and how a plethora of governmentally funded institutions can yield very little active language use either in the short run or in the long. Small and retentive languages in many parts of the globe are seemingly without formal institutions, large numbers of speakers or noticeably positive attitudes or prestige. On the other hand, Latin seems to have had all of the above highly touted desiderata and nevertheless lost its vernacular speakers, remaining only as a classical tongue for very limited functions among a very limited clientele. Additionally, if such *ad hoc* considerations are to have any utility as guides to action, we must know how they rank relative to each other. We must also know why they and only they have been selected for use (rather than, e.g. demographic concentration as distinct from simply the total number of speakers, or the proximity of a stronger economy associated with a rival language). Lastly, it would be very desirable to know what proportion of what criterion of language use they account for, either singly or *en toto*, and the degree of usefulness that RLSers can derive from them. Unfortunately, such data is unavailable for any of the proposed approaches, including those that I have proposed.

The stagewise nature of 1991 RLS-theory has been accused of having implications of evolutionary inevitability. Actually, these stages are intended only for purposes of diagnostic and programmatic location. ('where to start' and 'what to aim at when'). The movement from one stage to another is totally a result of self-directed activity, rather than of any natural process of a built-in developmental nature. The stages (which will be commented upon below) are nothing but a logical set of priorities or targets to guide RLS-efforts toward a desired goal. It places the responsibility for most RLS action on those who advocate an 'Xian-via-Xish' identity. It requires an enterprising and committed Xian community for its stability and does not take any comfort in the possible assistance of Yiansvia-Xish (Germans who have learned to speak Yiddish (as a means of penance for the Holocaust) or mainstream New Zealanders who have learned to speak Maori as an expression of sympathy for the Maori plight), who have a different community base and for whom pro-Xish efforts are normally situational, temporary, idiosyncratic and even reversible. RLS cannot be based on acts of charity by outsiders. Accordingly, RLS theory realises that multiculturalism, though welcome as an atmosphere effect, is not enough. It is overly diffuse in its ideological and practical focus and usually ignorant as to the consequences of the far greater compartmentalisation, minimalisation and subsequent evanescence of Xish than of Yish. None of the foregoing substitutes for genuine RLS-efforts by Xians, just as none lead anywhere near the establishment or the reinforcement of an intergenerational speech-community of Xians-via-Xish. Only such a community will successfully integrate Xish into a continuing and evolving Xian way of life. Without an *actual* ethnolinguistic community home, the greater prestige of a thousand computer specialists constituting a *virtual* interactive community, or a dozen Nobel prize laureates posting their works on the internet, will not augur nearly as well for the future of Xish as a thousand intergenerationally related ordinary 'rank and file' daily speakers living in proximity to one-another. RLS theory can explain why this is so, while others cannot do so, because they are not anchored in a theory that relates intergenerational Xish transmission to a theory of normal speech community functioning.

Stages of RLS: Priorities and the Linkages Between Them

RLS theory, being more than merely a descriptive tool, attempts to locate the functional disruption of X in social space and has suggested a widely (which is not yet to say 'universally') useful series of stages for doing so. Such *location helps establish both focus and priorities* for RLS efforts, rather

STAGES OF REVERSING LANGUAGE SHIFT:
SEVERITY OF INTERGENERATIONAL DISLOCATION
(read from the bottom up)

1. Education, work sphere, mass media and governmental operations at higher and nationwide levels.
2. Local/regional mass media and governmental services.
3. The local/regional (i.e. non-neighbourhood) work sphere, both among Xmen and among Ymen.
4b. Public schools for Xish children, offering some instruction via Xish, but substantially under Yish curricular and staffing control.
4a. Schools in lieu of compulsory education and substantially under Xish curricular and staffing control.

II. RLS to transcend diglossia, subsequent to its attainment

5. Schools for literacy acquisition, for the old and for the young, and not in lieu of compulsory education.
6. The intergenerational and demographically concentrated home-family-neighbourhood-community: the basis of mother-tongue transmission.
7. Cultural interaction in Xish primarily involving the community-based older generation.
8. Reconstructing Xish and adult acquisition of XSL.

I. RLS to attain diglossia (assuming prior ideological clarification)

Figure 19.1 GIDS scale

than merely presenting a redundant restatement of Xish's functional, institutional or attitudinal deficiencies. The fulcrum of the GIDS scale is commonly Stage 6 (the home-family, neighbourhood, community, i.e. the crucial nexus of intergenerational mother tongue transmission), but other stages may be considered the fulcrum for particular languages *vis-à-vis* particular functions that are being targeted in particular cases. Stages below 6 (i.e. with numbers larger than 6) are indicative of either the absence of native speakers (Stage 8) or the absence of speakers of child-bearing age or younger (Stage 7). These stages certainly represent serious circumstances for any RLS movement aiming at a return to vernacular functions. The further away from the selected fulcrum stage, the less direct and certain is the possibility of linkage to that fulcrum. This then is the second purpose of the GIDS scale: *to cause the viewer to consider the linkage factor* and its potential for strengthening the selected fulcrum.

The functions of threatened languages in particular tend toward self-compartmentalisation. They do not possess the power (in terms of undisputed association with dynamic functions) to spill over substantially and predictably into other functions, particularly not into functions at any distance from those in which they are acquired. Thus, RLS is not, as some have claimed, a step-by-step 'from the bottom upward' effort or theory, because linkages must be sought and instituted from above as well as from below, so that additional and attractive functions can propel RLS and motivate those attracted to it. Nor must RLS be worked on in a lock-step stage-by-stage progression. As long as the crux-stage is targeted consensually and with a clear understanding of what false priorities will 'cost', and as long as the linkages from that stage to those below and above it are constantly reinforced and reassessed, there is no harm in skipping over a stage that does not correspond to a desired functional sphere for Xish. Multistage efforts are definitely not contra-indicated if: (1) the priority stage is kept first and foremost, and (2) the linkages to it are really operational rather than merely assumed as self-evident. Not all stages are germane in all cases, because not all cases are equally or similarly in disarray. Stages 8 and 7 may well be immaterial for RLS efforts aimed at Stages 2 and 1. An RLS effort that has revernacularisation as its crux goal and that then mostly emphasises the 'secret language function' of Xish when travelling abroad, or Xish greetings by the president at international conferences taking place in Xland, or of Xish exhibits for touristic and commercial visitors, is clearly disregarding the question of linkages between its goals and its efforts. Obviously, the crux-stage for religious or learned Classicals must be different than that for lingering vernaculars that still possess some immediate everyday functional possibilities and safe harbours. While it is also true that many cases consist of separated or disparate stages (e.g. 6 + 2), the GIDS scale asks 'which of these is the crux-stage and how substantial and reliable is the linkage between the auxiliary stage(s) and the crux stage?'.

Some of my colleagues have granted that the GIDS scale has a 'heuristic' value. but caution that it is not to be taken literally or at face value. If by 'heuristic' they mean 'roughly orientational', I beg to differ. If by 'heuristic' they mean 'an aid to discovery and to trial and error solutions' I will not protest. It is not the last word that will ever be said in the difficult area of RLS. Certainly, no culturally neutral set of universal functions either exists or can exist. But it is not a minor matter to have one's priorities right and to be sure that they are supported by functions outside of themselves and, particularly, on either side of themselves. I do not remember these points having been made by others before GIDS-scale-based RLS theory appeared on the scene.

Comments on Particular Stages

The pre-intergenerational transmission stages

Stages 8 and 7 are neither unimportant nor hopeless insofar as Stage 6 is concerned. RLS movements have a great deal to gain from data collection from elderly and isolated native speakers (or 'once speakers, now semi-speakers') that are highlighted by Stage 8. The activists, linguists and teachers associated with the Xish movement can find, via tapping Stages 8 and 7) folklore (songs, proverbs, riddles, stories, jokes, prayers), vocabulary and grammatical forms that can subsequently be utilised in young-adult second language instruction groups, in infant-care and child-care groups, in Xish instruction to parenting and grandparenting groups, etc. Authentic linguistic paradigms, lexical items and texts enable RLS-efforts to attain the linkage with Xian history and tradition which Xish is presumable better able to express and convey than can Yish. Furthermore, such materials are more likely to be derived from a pre-Yian-hegemony stage and, therefore, foster autonomy motivated distancing (*Ausbau*) in those cases where Xish has been considerably altered over time due to growing Yian social and linguistic hegemony (whether or not it is a closely related language to begin with). Even RLS efforts that are well-focused at Stage 6 should seek to benefit from feedback linkages from Stage 8 and 7 efforts.

But there are yet other ways in which Stage 7 can be even more productive insofar as Stage 6 is concerned. Clubs and other neighbourhood groups consisting of 'Seniors' can be linked to Stage 6 as 'visitors', guides or demonstrators for story-telling, traditional arts and crafts instruction (and the attainment of personal competence for community events when such arts and crafts are particularly appropriate), camping and hiking guides, singing and cooking partners and, above all, as baby sitters and infant and child-care resources. An ongoing relationship between a group of children and a group of still active seniors can be extremely rewarding for all concerned, although it requires supervision and may not be entirely without monetary costs or associated legalities. The benefits are definitely 'two way' since the 'seniors' (who may be anywhere from mid-40s and up in age) may also need language maintenance reinforcement and their exposure to supervised interaction with school and nursery youngsters may foster such language maintenance among the seniors themselves. RLS-efforts need to include an active LM outreach component since a 'revolving door' inflow of young speakers and an outflow of old speakers is not in the best interests of RLS by any means, Seniors represent a clientele for all neighbourhood public use of Xish: lectures, choruses, dramatic circles, writing contests, speaking contests, folkloristic events (including folk-dances and folk concerts etc., etc.). Seniors and their events must be treasured and nurtured, rather than considered expendable merely because seniors are well beyond childbearing age. Particularly where their own children are the generation of 'returnees' to Xish, the parents of these returnees are also the grandparents of a hoped for 'new growth' for Xish. Given the mobility of modern generations, even adopted parents and adopted grandparents are extremely valuable kin-relationships for any RLS movement.

The Intergenerational Transmission Stages

Home, family, neighbourhood, community

Several colleagues who treat essentially non-urban and not yet fully modernised speech communities have commented that Stage 6 essentially encompasses their entire sociocultural space. I must grant that this points-up a deficiency in the original GIDS model. There must be intra-stage differentiations, so that not all such groups are necessarily lumped together and so that any language maintenance and RLS variation that exists among them can be more fully highlighted. As a sociologist primarily oriented towards the study of urban and national societies, I was insufficiently aware of *intra*-Stage 6 sociofunctional differentiation in connection with *inter*-generational mother tongue transmission. The more's the pity, then, that my anthropological colleagues who are more attuned to such intra-Stage 6 variation have not suggested some lines of analysis that could be followed. Is the nuclear family such a sub-dimension?, or the early childhood play-group?; or grandparents and child/ infant care arrangements?; or ceremonial occasions? etc., etc. It would certainly be highly desirable to study several cases where GIDS Stage 6 exhausts more than half of any local culture's total 'speech-interaction space', in order to refine our current general theory of RLS in accord with frequently occurring situational interactions. A 6a, 6b, 6c . . . 6n typology could then be worked out and examined for international compatibility. When Stage 6 is 'all there is', it becomes even more crucial to protect it in order that intergenerational mother tongue transmission not be disrupted or dissipated.

Colleagues have also presented (wittingly and unwittingly) at least two modern dislocations that undercut the effectiveness of Stage 6 when vernacular functions are considered the prime target of RLS. The first of these is concerned with major modernity related disruptions of family functioning (e.g. via divorce, intermarriage, frequent family dislocation) during early childhood. The second is the assumption that any long-term meaningful relationship in Xish is sufficient to establish an inter-generational mother tongue transition. Neither of the circumstances mentioned above need be fatal for RLS, but neither of them is in any way obviously conducive to RLS and, therefore, both can be considered extra-neous if not contra-indicated. Certainly post-Stage 6 interactions may be linked to Stage 6 in a mutually reinforcing way, but they cannot be substi-tuted for that stage due to their lesser affective, more time and place boundedness and more encapsulated or narrowly compartmentalised functional natures.

Perhaps it is in connection with Stage 4, the school that meets compul-sory education requirements, that the GIDS scale and its approach to RSL has received the most criticism among readers worldwide (although far less so from the colleagues participating in this volume). 'Teach it in the schools' has been such a popular nostrum for whatever ails Xish (or Xian culture as a whole, and, truth be told, for far too many things that ail Yish and Yian culture as well among their own adherents – which may be the original source from which this error spills over to Xish RLSers), that any questioning of the efficacy of the school for RLS purposes has smacked as rank heresy to many. But it is exactly here that the difference between language learning and other school subjects, on the one hand, and between language learning and RLS, on the other hand, appear most clearly. Languages are not 'subjects' *per se* and they cannot be successfully acquired unless they are used for the purposes of active communication.[2] The lack of appreciation for this truth underlies the failure of solely school-based language study worldwide. Language study for RLS purposes will fail even more drastically and painfully, unless Xish has a society in which it can function, *before* school begins, *outside* of school during the years of schooling and afterwards, when formal schooling is over and done with.[3] Untold hours and dollars have been spent for naught because of disregard or mere lip-service for this fundamental truth.[4] RLS is essentially a functional reversal *vis-à-vis* Xian society more generally, much more so than it is merely the pro-forma introduction of a subject in schools that meet compulsory education requirements.

Even school-based instruction in religious or secular classicals cannot be retained unless there is an after-school life for these venerable languages, either in churches or in vocations that require them. If these functions are neighbourhood based, they are part of Stage 6. If they are part of out-of-neighborhood reality, they are part of Stages 3 to 1. In all cases (with the possible exception of academic linguists), *languages are not their own rewards*. If they remain functionally locked away in the schools, they may be learned (youngsters have an amazing ability and capacity to learn 'useless' matters which they never need again, once their schooling is over), but they will not accomplish the wonderful goals of communication with neighbours far and near, improvement of commerce and diplomacy, attainment of social mobility, and familiarity with the brightest stars of world literature – and much, much less yet will they accomplish RLS – unless they are linked to 'real life' stages before, during and after school. The RLS school (whether of Stage 4a or 5, or even at the university level) must keep reality firmly in mind. Schools tend to be compartmentalising institutions. They have their own authority structure, personnel, reward system, budget and evaluation procedures. It is very easy for them to become sheltered workshops, a world apart and unto themselves. When that happens, they effectively cease to contribute to the RLS process. This realisation does not constitute a downgrading of the school's functions in conjunction with RLS. It merely stresses the fact that, with respect to languages, linkages are crucial for schools, regardless of whether another Stage (like Stage 6) is the crux-Stage or the school itself is the crux-Stage.

Literacy in Xish is frequently an important RLS goal. Yish advocates often play down the legitimacy or importance of Xish literacy, as part and parcel of denying Xish any serious intellectual claims as a whole. If schools are to help attain literacy in Xish there must be linkages between the school and an out-of-school literature, press, commercial institutions, organisational and governmental record keeping or other literacy-based occupations. On the whole, however, literacy in Xish will usually remain a weak competitor with literacy in Yish (most frequently acquired in the very same schools). It is Yish literacy that makes the greater contribution to social mobility and the Central Education Authorities that ultimately control both Stage 4a and 4b schools, constantly make sure that the Yish education domain is particularly stressed, evaluated and rewarded. Thus, the school's role in Xish literacy training is inevitably a two-edged sword. It often reveals a somewhat naive and inevitably self-serving view when over-eagerly pushed by educators. Furthermore, oral Xish education can more easily be out-of-school linked and may explain why some Third World groups (e.g. many Hopi, ultra-Orthodox Yiddish speakers and Quechua) have never fully opted for school-based literacy to begin with and basically trust in Stage 5 education, because it is almost completely free from the control of Yish authorities and can, therefore, more often be viewed as a form of indigenous enculturation and socialisation. This is something no Stage 4 school can do for them with so few compromises.

Students frequently bolster the numbers of speakers, readers and writers of Xish, but their RLS 'ability' (like anyone else's ability) is far from being the same as 'performance' and it is performance in social functions which is the 'litmus-test' of RLS attainment. As one of my colleagues in this volume has rightly observed, the capacity of schools to produce competent bilinguals is far greater than the capacity of the bilingual community to reproduce itself! The size of the hiatus between these two criteria is inversely proportional to the success of RLS and of the school's contribution to that success. The entire difference among the three types of schools included in the GIDS scale (recognition of three types of schooling – admittedly the trichotimisation of a continuum – is hardly a sign of downgrading the phenomenon under consideration!) is trivial if these differences are not related to functional linkages. Nevertheless, schools may serve RLS in additional ways, beyond the pursuit of literacy and of oral competence alone. Schools can serve to ideologise the young on behalf of RLS. Secondary and Tertiary School students and young adults as a whole are the ones that most need to be moved (and to be moved most quickly) from school to Xish life out of school, either by moving from Stage 5 to 6 or from Stage 4 to 6. It is relatively easy to found (and even to fund) a school; it is much harder to graduate a cohort of fluent and active Xish speakers; and it is hardest of all for this cohort to continue being fluent and active speakers of Xish until they find an equally committed life-partner and start nuclear families of their own. It is at this step that intergenerational transmission is achieved and that the required social linkages to the Xish school attain their RLS goal.

RLS-related schools are not at all the same as ordinary FLES or other second language education. RLS related schools must be cognizant of the special methods and materials that are required for a language that has only a limited out-of-school reality. These schools cannot afford to teach imaginary Xish conversations at airports, hotel check-ins, luxury-car sales-offices and other social mobility related and Yish dominated interactions. The programme of study that is required for RLS is an identity formation one, an Xian-via-Xish ideologising one, a community building one and a community membership one. The teachers, programmes and materials for such programmes are likely to be non-existent or in extremely short supply. Teachers may need to prepare their own materials for years – led by exemplary teacher trainers and curriculum/materials specialists – before there is a sufficient market for recognised publishers to enter into the prep-aration and sale of such items. However, the proximity of schools to homes and parents, the crucial links between schools and communities, on the one hand, and between schools and ideology on the other hand, constitute both the rewards and the challenges that RLS teachers can expect for their labours. If they work as hard on linkages to 'out of school' and 'after school' as they work on their 'in school' lesson plans, then they will really be an asset to RLS rather than a detour or a cul-de-sac.

The 'high power' stages

The further above Stage 6 (and particularly above Stage 4) the greater the contribution that GIDS stages make to fostering Xian social power and individual social mobility. As might be expected, these stages are particu-larly problematic for Xish, because of the Yish social control and superi-ority in resources that envelop them. An example of this can often be found even in the local work-sphere which is often ethnically mixed as a result of the demographic marginalisation of Xians even in their 'own' traditional region. Xish media are often very pale imitations of Yish media, both in quality and in quantity and the minor Xish media that do exist have never been evaluated from the point of view of their linkage realisation, particu-larly *vis-à-vis* Stage 6. The media can interfere with intergenerational Xish mother-tongue transmission more easily and more frequently than they can reinforce it, if only because there are ever so much more Yish media than Xish media. Higher education is another instance of the potential danger of higher stages for RLS. Not only is such education oriented toward life and success in the Yish world, but (unless radicalised for RLS purposes) it rarely links back to Xish mother tongue transmission and to the Stage 6 nexus in which such transmission transpires. Every Xish dollar devoted to Stage 1 consumes dollars that could have been devoted to Xish neighbourhood institutions and activities of all kinds. The media are less under Xian community control than are local nurseries, kindergartens, neighbourhood health services, scouting groups, sports clubs, choruses, dramatic groups, job training services, libraries, homework assistance groups, test-review groups, hobby clubs, charitable outreach organisations, summer camps, etc., etc.[5] The latter serve as the sinews of growing up Xian in an Xish-speaking community and can more evenly compete with their Yish counterparts, and at lesser expense when doing so, than can Xish media with Yian media (and international media under Yian auspicies) *en toto*. Neighbourhood and community events and activities are real neighborhood life and they feed back to one's real family immediately. Media, at best, only creates a 'virtual' community and, taking a leaf from Australian experience along these lines, much more of a Yish than of an Xish one at that.[6] Black English media programmes have not made Black English speakers out of 'White English' listeners, nor will they ever do so based on the few hours per week involved and the differential statuses of the two dialects. Indeed, if the truth be told, the comical and counterculture contexts in which Black English programmes are commonly situated may well 'turn off' more Black English speakers than they attract 'White English' speakers!

All or Nothing at all!

Rocking chair languages vs reaching too high and losing it all

There are three possible alternative strategies for RSL efforts. One is 'shoot for the moon!' Another is 'anything is better than nothing'. The third is 'the right step at the right time'. Tragically, the first approach mentioned above has attracted all too much attention, most of it of the lip-service variety. In reality, never being satisfied is much more of an RLS disease than being satisfied with minimal and purely symbolic accommodations by the Yish authorities. In the face of the truth that Yish is still the only truly indispensable language, one that every Xian must learn for certain vital functions, those who opt and counsel to 'shoot for the moon' actually advise that those who seek to defend a threatened language are obliged (or so some argue) to wage a total multi-front struggle. 'One cannot save the value of a competence unless one saves . . . the whole set of political and social conditions of production' of the producers/consumers (Bourdieu, 1991: 57). But surely this is a prophecy of doom disguised by whistling in the dark. Which Yish communities or even polities today can be said to control 'the whole set of political and social conditions of production'?

Similarly one-sided and misguided *vis-à-vis* the realities of RLS is the very similar view that real change can be attained only if full control of resources and means for decision making and the institutional domains where language socialisation occurs is in the hands of Xians. This merely restates the problem of Xish in more academic terms and still leaves the threatened language-in-society without a plan of action. Distributive justice may strike some as highly desirable, but the barriers in the way of its direct attainment are so formidable that postponing RLS until they are overcome essentially means postponing meaningful RLS until it may be too late for its more than ornamental attainment. Views such as the above are also impoverishing, socially and morally, because they imply that RLS can succeed only to the extent that it replaces Yish monism by Xish monism. This spells the death knell for pluralism and peaceful coexistence. In most cases, the best that RLS can hope for, as a starting point for its never ending road into the future, is to disengage from dependence upon and supervision by the Yish authorities. The most meaningful way in which this can be done from the very outset is to stress the role of Xish in family, intimacy, and ethnocultural authenticity in local identity. Rendering kith and kin into important allies (even on a cross-border basis) is more important initially (and for a long time thereafter) than conquering outer space. Pointing out the perfidy that may hide behind the use of Xish by Yish authorities (a use that can be halted at will and that does not feed back to the intergenerational transmission nexus) is more immediately and effectively instrumental than being co-opted by such gambits.

While it is undoubtedly true that 'a [person's] reach must exceed his/her grasp', the theory of linkages between higher order and lower order stages is a more instrumental truth. It helps differentiate between RLS for the current generations (by focusing on 7, 6 and 5) and RLS for the next generation (by focusing on 4, 3 and 2). Neighbourhood and community focus already provides a series of targets for RLS that go beyond the home and family into pre-school, extra-curricular and a host of parent alone, child alone and parent–child interactions. Home-family-neighbourhood-community undoubtedly benefit from higher level linkages (especially if such linkages have been built-in *ab initio*), but the outreach vs the compartmentalisation impact of these linkages is under RLS guidance rather than under Yish control. That's a big difference. Does this make Xish into a rocking chair language? How many languages of atomic physics are there really today anyway (even in the Yish sphere)? Is 'anything short of everything' a capitulation to obsolescence? Hardly! The vast majority of languages in the age of globalisation will, at most, reach as high as being languages of popular science for the majority of their speakers, of up to secondary education and lower tertiary education for a much smaller majority and of local humanistic specialisation only for a small minority. Dutch is not insulted thereby, nor Danish, exposed as they already are to English as Basque and Catalan are to Spanish (and English too). 'Reasonableness in all things' is a far better maxim for the pursuit of RLS in a focused linkage pattern than is 'the sky's the limit'.

Focus and priorities are not equivalent, by any means, to obsolescence, folklorisation, self-limitation to 'rocking chair' status or oblivion in the rocket age. Focus and priorities merely build the recognition that, whether with or without political boundaries, most languages will not have significant participatory functions in global power attainment nor in direct competition for functional superiority with those few languages that do have such power attainment. Weakened and threatened languages must certainly pursue their security and their future elsewhere. They must not exhaust themselves and diminish themselves in an impossible as well as an impoverished view of what they signify in the lives of their own speech communities. Their 'members' will forever be bi- or trilingual, with each of their languages – even the most powerful among them – 'enacting' only special and complementary functions. If they play their cards intelligently, there will always be functional space for smaller languages and RLS-advocates must be in the forefront of those who know what to aim at and how to reinforce their primary goals through subsidiary ones.

When is 'too high', too high? Certainly when it neglects the basic crucial stages for intergenerational transmission. Certainly when it neglects the linkages between higher stages and the crux stages that are required if Xish is to break out of a pattern that is both downward and dependent on Yish approval, sufferance or support. Any RLS theory must realise that many languages (not all, as some claim) function across several stages simultaneously. Some even stage-jump, and develop a pattern that ignores a particular stage (e.g. Stage 5 or 4a). Stages are linear and human lives and societal functioning are not. Nevertheless, not all language-communities have the same problems, resources, goals or aspirations and, therefore, they cannot all have the same tactical strategies. Xish must cut out of Yish control and do so without entering into competition with Yish on the very turf that Yish controls. There are 'haves' and 'have nots' on the language scene as there are on all other scenes. But there are functions that Xish has and can defend that Yish does not have. And these are the logical functions around which to build the RLS fortresses and to which all efforts must link back. They must also be the points of departure from which to attain functional expansion, doing so from a few positions of relative strength rather than from many positions of relative weakness.

Of course, it is also possible for RLS to aim too low (to see the telephone and the personal computer as the same kind of intrusive danger as television and cinema). But, as this volume amply illustrates, 'they don't hardly make that kind no more'. Certainly, my own views do not counsel a retiring and isolating self-enfeeblement. The highest power stage that one can safely and effectively productively regulate and make use of is the crux beyond which functional attempts must be made and back to which linkages must be secured. To do otherwise is simply to demonstrate that Xish is second best, rather than putting its best foot forward. The third mistaken RLS path is the 'anything is better than nothing' one. Fortunately, it has few principled defenders (although it does sometimes have exploitative practitioners) and is little more than aspirin for terminally diseased patients. RLS must be a plan of action and a plan must certainly have priorities rather than lack them.

Gains and losses during the final decade of the 20th century

A decade is usually very little time in which to either experience much change in RLS circumstances or to note much payoff from differential RLS efforts. However, the decade of the 90s *has* revealed a number of notable changes in this field. First of all, the field as such came into being, as an identifiable area of international interest, both among individual academics, organisational entities and, more and more often, among Yish authorities as well. Many of those who had laboured alone in this field for what must have seemed an eternity, have finally realised that they are not alone at all, that others share their concerns, realise the justice of their complaints and the significance of their goals, not only locally but at an international and pan-human level. This constitutes a tremendous change in general atmosphere and we must pause not only to acknowledge it, but to ponder why it occurred when it did and whether it will really make a difference in RLS (or merely amount to window-dressing disguising and hiding old wounds). Just as the ethnic revival of the 60s and 70s led to the unprecedented growth in multiculturalism advocates in the mainstream *per se* during the 80s and 90s, so the latter turn of events, in turn, has prompted calls for affirmative action and positive intervention on the language scene too. But will the sympathies of European Union affiliates, the advocacy of environmentalists sensitive to the linkage between terra-diversity and lingua-diversity, and the pious resolutions of well-meaning international bodies really make a difference either in the rates of intergenerational mother-tongue transmission or in the attainment of any other specific RLS goals (or will they merely become undertakings without any differences in outcome)?

Advanced technology and globalisation have redefined much of life. In the process of so doing they have impacted and changed such core relationships and experiences as family, neighbourhood and community. Yet each child is still born into a specific nuclear family and that family is situated in a particular community, however altered both family and community have become over the past century. Xian families now need RLS education (how to be parents – and even how to be grandparents – in Xish. 'How to *"do"* RLS in your home' is a course that one can and should be enrolled in repeatedly in every RLS setting and that should be sponsored by every RLS movement and team-taught by the most experienced, inventive and dedicated advocates that are available. Among the things that need to be taught are the joys and responsibilities of immediate community. The benefits of RLS in counteracting anomie should not be minimised. *Gemeinschaft* can be alive and well – in the very midst of galloping *Gesellschaft* – for those who realise that what it has to offer (above and beyond the ideological claims to authenticity and fidelity, neither of which should be dismissed in the slightest) is a balm to the spirit and a new and special kinship with those to whom one 'belongs' in a very special way and with very special links that only Xish can activate and maintain. An RLSer's life is not an easy one, but the struggle for Xish is a struggle for meaning in life and, therefore, that struggle is, in great part, also its own reward, a reward 'beyond rubies'.

So, can threatened languages be saved? It is really too early to answer the above basic question on empirical grounds, but it may be indicative of what the future portends that none of our cases has reported any substantial progress attributable by local observers to general atmospheric circumstances such as international treaties and conventions. Although a positive atmosphere for RLS may be preferable to a negative one (actually, even that is by no means certain, since the motivational intensification attributable to moderate opposition must not be entirely written off), the direct and 'evaluatable' linkage between such general positiveness and specific RLS goals may be lacking or insufficient. Certain litigious climates (e.g., the Frisian and the Maori scenes) should be watched with particular care in order to fathom the likelihood and the circumstances required for legal measures, legislation, treaties, agreements, court orders and monetary compensatory awards to be able to make a practical difference in connection with specific RLS priorities and linkages. Should such actions prove to be effective in specific cases, they must still be differentiated from the contributions of more general conventions and agreements arrived at by international agencies and organisations that lack concrete power to enforce their resolutions. Although conclusive evidence is lacking, there is no reason to be overly optimistic in either case, because a lack of priorities and linkages seems to characterise the entire legalistic approach.

None of the dozen individual cases that were studied in the late 80s, and early 90s and that have been re-examined in this volume at the very close of one century and the beginning of the next, have experienced dramatic successes during the decade separating one evaluation from the other. Although widespread attitudinal positiveness toward Xish and substantial self-reported language competence in Xish are given in many cases, the discrepancies between attitudes and performance are as noteworthy in conjunction with RLS as they are in conjunction with all areas of 'moral behavior' where 'the spirit is willing but the flesh is weak'. On the other hand, there are a few telling cases in which a palpable sense of exhaustion seems to hang heavily in the air. Somewhat more than a dozen years ago, at an international sociolinguistic conference held in the Basque Country, the local university students in the audience asked a representative of the Catalan Secretariat of Language Policy how Basque could best get to the initial 'take off' stage which Catalan had presumably already experienced a decade earlier. Today, the question might well be reversed, with Catalans asking the Basques where they get the energy 'to keep at it', in view of the post-nationalism that globalisation is fostering so widely. Catalan is still a success case by any reasonable criterion, but can RLS succeed in advancing and stabilising itself *vis-à-vis* Yish if only what is reasonable is pursued? The fatigue that is fostered by not being able to hold on (on a long-term basis) to reasonable success may be every bit as wearying as the fatigue that ultimately overcomes those who have never achieved any success at all.

The comfort that minority languages could take a decade ago from Australian language policy, in comparison to the policies regarding aboriginal languages there or immigrant languages in the USA, has largely vanished in the interim. Instead of Australia being the forerunner of a sea change in the valuation of aboriginal or immigrant languages on the part of English-dominant host-countries, the direction of influence has run in the opposite direction. The traditional American negativeness toward such languages (whether with or without an English Only stampede) has crossed the Pacific and invaded Australia. Immigrant languages, in particular, usually remain in the most unenviable position, but note the special circumstances, external in one case and internal in the other, that have made both Puerto Rican Spanish and ultra-Orthodox Yiddish into exceptions to that general rule.

Quebec has thus far twice not opted for independence (whether with or without association with Canada), and, were it to do so in the coming decade (it would only require a miniscule change in 'New Canadian' votes for this to happen), the impact on French RLS in its neighbouring provinces would almost certainly not be an immediately positive one. As for the remaining success case, Hebrew in Israel does show some movement (even if only in a cleverly ineffective way) toward regrets about the Zionist decimation of the other major Jewish languages there (particularly Yiddish,

Ladino/Judezmo, Judeo-Arabic and Judeo-Persian). Such regrets have multiplied sufficiently during the past decade (see, e.g. Shohamy, 1999) to lead at least to a tokenistic establishment of entertainment oriented governmentally funded 'authorities' for the first two language mentioned above. If there was ever any doubt that RLS should not be held captive by Yish governments, Israel seems destined to become the perfect proof of that point. On the other hand, political independence seems to have become an uncertain RLS attraction or proven value, and not in Quebec alone (where the overwhelmingly francophone population may soon have needed three chances in which to think it over, if, indeed, it is only three). Puerto Rico seems to be inching toward a plebiscite on statehood vs either independence or continued Commonwealth status during the next decade (Ramirez, 2000). There seems to be even less interest than usual in independence there. Instead, there is a growing realisation that Spanish can be as much endangered in Puerto Rico with independence as without it, given that Spanish–English bilingualism is inevitable, whether on the mainland or on the island, due to continuing individual and societal dependence on the USA in both locations.

We are left then with an ambiguous scenario: the general climate of opinion *vis-à-vis* threatened languages has improved in an amorphous and largely still ineffectual sense, whereas actual RLS prospects and attainments have improved very little, if at all, during the past decade, and seem even to have deteriorated somewhat in some surprising cases. Is this a harbinger of the growing and long-heralded triumph of globalisation over ethnonationalism? Probably no such complete triumph is in the offing, because, as we have noted before, globalisation itself also prompts (and even requires) a greater recognition of local co-identity and authenticity. We are, therefore, left with a human struggle which defies the complete victory of either the old or the new. The complexity of human motives and identities is rarely better illustrated than via the RLS scene, where neither total triumph nor total resignation, neither total reason nor total irrationality are in the offing and where particularism and globalisation cohabit in a sometime antagonistic as well as in a sometime cooperative marriage. Human societies will just have to make room for both and, indeed, will have to do so increasingly, as migration and globalisation ('the free movement of populations and goods') both continue to advance during the next century. Because RLS may well become somewhat more rational and practical in focus-selection and in linkage-attainment efforts, many more threatened languages may, as a result, be better off with it than without it. Yet these languages may not cease to be threatened as a result. Yish languages too may come to realise that RLS tactics also have much to offer them (as, e.g., in the Swedish case), rather than being totally devices of Xish languages alone.

So can threatened languages be saved? This question now has an informed though uncertain answer: Yes, more of them can be saved than has been the case in the past, but only by following careful strategies that focus on priorities and on strong linkages to them, and only if the true complexity of local human identity, linguistic competence and global inter-dependence are fully recognised. More languages are threatened than we think, and they are not necessarily only the smaller, more disadvantaged ones either. The languages of the world will either all help one another survive or they will succumb separately to the global dangers that must assuredly await us all (English included) in the century ahead.

Notes

1. The notational convention of designating the *threatened* language as X or Xish and its speakers as Xians (not as Xmen, as before, since it has been pointed out that the latter designation is not always regarded as gender neutral [even though 'German' may be so regarded]), while its *threatening* and stronger co-territorial competitor is referred to as Y or Yish, will be continued here. This convention too has been criticised, purportedly for reducing languages and human population to mere lifeless and morally equivalent symbols. Nevertheless, since the entire message and intent of RLS is to champion and foster the unique role of languages in their own traditionally related populations and functions, the handiness of the shorthand designations, coupled with the transparency of the contexts in which they are employed, seems to me to outweigh the objections to them.
2. It is here, at the level of communication with 'real speakers', that 'school language' can actually weaken RLS by fostering a variety which differs from that of the 'last Mohican' speakers. 'School language' differs from home and street language everywhere in the world, and it is a problem everywhere for children from communities in which school-discrepant speech dominates and literacy is slight. But for threatened languages there is a danger that the school variety will further weaken the vernacular and even eventually replace it, undercutting any claim for authenticity that Xish may have sought to stake out, and fostering instead a variety which is both overly puristic and stilted lexically, on the one hand, and rife with the usual learners' errors and foreign markedness, on the other.
3. The entire attempt to ideologically clarify the Xian-via-Xish authenticity Welt-anschauung – an attempt that must precede rather than come as an afterthought to the establishment of schools for RLS purposes – is rendered null and void when Xish becomes merely a subject (much like algebra) with no genuine societal roles or statuses to enact. The 'de-ethnicised ethnic school' is a phenomenon which results from the routinisation of Xish and its detachment from parental or communal reality.
4. Indeed, the school dedicated to Xish may have to become an active builder of after-school and out-of-school Xian society, in order that the school itself can then

make sense and make a difference in the lives of the generations that are associated with it. Such a school may well have to have a longer school day, a longer school week and a longer school year in order to involve parents, teachers and students in the joint and constant task of creating and fostering the community through which intergenerational mother tongue transmission takes place and is nourished. Obviously, the child-centred, permissive and progressive school, whatever its virtues, is not in tune with RLS needs and purposes.

5.   The mass-media 'fetish' of some minority language activists appears in its true unrealistic light when one but pauses to consider how few books and records get produced per annum (notwithstanding their much lower cost) in most Xish settings. If small-scale, thin market literacies require a topical or genre niche in order to hold their own in a Yish world, this is all the more so in connection with self-produced radio or TV, where Yish programmes are super-abundant. I do make an obvious exception for *self-regulated communication technologies* such as computers, e-mail and web sites which enable Xian youngsters, parents, teachers and activists of all kinds to network, stay in touch with one another, exchange pro-Xish materials and programmes, engage in desk-top publishing and arrange regular *actual* community functions. Indeed, these self-regulated communication technologies are content neutral. They are facilitators of any stage and can, therefore, constitute part of regular Stage 6 or Stage 4 functioning, just as does the telephone and the fax machine. They do not, however, constitute substitutes for the natural intergenerational mother tongue transmission process and, therefore, must be linked to it by RLSers themselves.

6.   There might be some promise in adding a 'language key' to TV programmes in largely Xian regions, much like the violence, sex, vulgarity keys that are already commonly available to parents who want to block certain types of programmes from their children's viewing. If a 'Yish key' is either practically or ethically contra-indicated, then it may be preferable to set certain days or hours for TV viewing by younger children. Sooner or later, however, they must be helped to face the pervasiveness of Yish and its functional role in their individual and societal role repertoire. This is a far more constructive educational goal for home and school, than to patronise tokenistic Xish programmes, produced by and for Yish authorities, that merely use a number of Xish lexical items in ways that prepare for Yish life, rather than fostering RLS at the home, family, neighbourhood and community levels.

References

Bourdieu, P. (1991 *Language and Symbolic Power*. Cambridge, MA: Harvard University Press (translation of Ce que parler veut dire. 1982. Paris: Fayard).

Edwards, J. (1994) Ethnolinguistic pluralism and its discontents: A Canadian study and some general observations. *International Journal of the Sociology of Language* 110, 5–82. (Also note a dozen comments by other specialists, immediately after the 'focus' article).

Fishman, J.A. (1997) *In Praise of the Beloved Language: A Comparative View of Positive Ethnolinguistic Consciousness*. Berlin: Mouton.

Fishman, J.A. (ed.) (1999) *Handbook of Language and Ethnic Identity*. New York: Oxford University Press.

Grin, F. (1977) Amanegement linguistique; de bon usage des concepts d'offre et de demande. In Norman Labie (ed.) *Etudes recentes en linguistique de contact*. Bonn: Bimmler, 117–34.

Grin, F. (1999) Market forces, language spread and linguistic diversity. In Kontra, Miklos, Robert Phillipson, Tove Skutnabb-Kangas and Tibor Varady (eds) *Language: A Right and a Resource: Approaches to Linguistic Human Rights* (pp. 169–86). Budapest: Central European University Press.

Jernudd, B. (1998) Proposal for an action plan to benefit the Swedish language (translation of the summary of the original document published in the Swedish Language Committee's Newsletter Sprakvard, 2, 1998). *New Language Planning Newsletter* 13(1), 4–5.

Haugen, E.I. (1953) *The Norwegian Language in America*. 2 vols. Philadelphia: University of Pennsylvania Press. (Reprinted in one volume. 1969. Bloomington: Indiana University Press.)

Myhill, J. (1999) Identity, territoriality and minority language survival. *Journal of Multilingual and Multicultural Development* 20(1), 34–50.

Ozalins, U. (1999) Between Russian and European hegemony: Current language policy in the Baltic Sates. *Current Issues in Language and Society* 6(1),6–47.

Prilleltensky, I. (1994) *The Morals and Politics of Psychology*. Albany: State University of New York Press.

Ramirez, C. (ed.) (2000) Spanish and English in Puerto Rico: Past, present and future. *International Journal of the Sociology of Language* 145 (entire issue).

Shohamy, E. (1999) Language and identity of Jews in Israel and in the diaspora. In D. Zisenwine and D. Shers (eds) *Present and Future: Jewish Culture, Identity and Language* (pp. 79–99). Tel Aviv: Tel Aviv University (School of Education).

Index

Note: Page references in italics indicate tables and figures.

492 Can Threatened Languages be Saved?

– and Australian indigenous languages
392-4, 396-7, 412, 419-20
– and Catalan 260, 268, 274-5
– and Euskara (Basque) 234, 248-56, 257-8
– and Frisian 223-30
– and group vitality framework 110-11
– and Hebrew 350-5
– and international context 216
– and Irish 195-6
– and Maori 424-46
– and Navajo 24, 29-40
– and Oko 291-5, 307
– and Otomí 154-7, 163
– priorities and linkages 465-8, 476, 481
– and Puerto Rican Spanish 51, 70
– and Quebec French 110-11, 112-13
– and Quechua 171-85
– and Yiddish 84-5, 96-7
grammar
– Ainu 332, 333
– Andamanese 314-15
– Catalan 277
– Jaru 408
– Otomí 155-6
Greek
– in Australia 366-7, 369-70, 373-4, 376, 381,
383, 386, 389-90 n.3
– in Quebec 116
Greenland, and Eskimo languages 187
Grenoble, L. & Whaley, L. 187, 188-9
Grimes, B.F. 170
Grin, F. & Vaillancourt, F. 437, 446
Grinevald, C. 182, 184
group vitality analysis
– and demography -5, 102-7, 110-12, 113,
120-1, 133
– and Euskara 236-8
– and Graded Intergenerational Disruption
Scale 110-13
– and institutional control 107-8, 110-12,
113, 117, 119, 241, 255-6
– and Quebec French 101-13, 103
– and status 108-10, 111-12, 119
– and subjective vitality questionnaire
111-12
Grupo Artístico Cultural Saraguro 174
Grupo Intiñan 174
Grupo Rumiñahui 174
Guatemala, and Mayan 187
Gudschinsky, S.C. 316
Gujarati, in New Zealand 430
Gumatj dialect 399
Gumbayngirr (Aboriginal language) 406-7
Gumperz, 187

Gurindji (Aboriginal language) 407
Guugu Yimidhirr (Aboriginal language)
188

Haboud, M.I. 166, 168, 176
Hadda, Janet 80, 88-9
Halpern, Moyshe Leyb 77
haredim
– and Hebrew 360
– and Yiddish 89-90
Harshav, B. 75, 353
Harwood, J. et al. 102, 112
Haugen, Einar 464
Hausa language (Nigeria) 286, 294, 302, 304
Haviland, 188
Hawaiian language, and university courses
190-1 n.14
hebraisms, in Yiddish 93
Hebrew 350-63, 457
– and Arabic 354, 357, 359-60
– and Aramaic 351-2, 357
– in Australia 372-3
– and GIDS 350-5
– and other languages 355-61, 479-80
– and practice, ideology and policy 355-9
– in Quebec 132, 356
– revitalisation 265-6, 350-5, 357, 361
– as sacred language 351-3, 358, 368
– and Yiddish 87, 93, 94, 356-7, 358-9
see also children; community
Hekking, E. 155
Herder, J. G. 8
'Heritage' languages, in Quebec 116-17,
120, 122-3, 134, 136
Hindi
– and Andamanese 314-20
– in Australia 386
– in New Zealand 430
Hirago, Sadamo 345-6
Hohepa, M.K. 431
Hokkaido, and Ainu 326-32, 337, 341, 344
Hokkaido Ainu Association 324, 335, 337
Hokoto, Iboshi 330
Holland see Dutch; Friesland; Frisian
Holm, W. & Holm, A. 34
Holm, Wayne 31
Honda, Yoneda 333, 344
Hopi language 472
Hornberger, N.H. 168, 172, 177, 189-90 n.1,
191 nn.15,16
Huarani language (Andes) 170
Hulaulá (Judeo-Aramaic), and Hebrew 356
Hulme, Keri 433
Hungarian, in Australia 374, 381